Fodor's

VIRGINIA AND MARYLAND

11th Edition

Where to Stay and Eat
for All Budgets

Must-See Sights
and Local Secrets

Ratings You Can Trust

Fodor's Travel Publications   New York, Toronto, London, Sydney, Auckland
www.fodors.com

FODOR'S VIRGINIA AND MARYLAND

Editor: Maria Teresa Hart

Writers: Nina Callaway, Mike Lillis, Amy McKeever, Donna Owens, Alice Powers, Evan Serpick, Ramona Settle, Ginger Warder

Editorial Contributors: Debbie Harmsen, Heidi Leigh Johansen, Mark Sullivan, Amanda Theunissen

Production Editor: Carrie Parker

Maps & Illustrations: David Lindroth, Mark Stroud, *cartographers;* Bob Blake, Rebecca Baer, *map editors;* William Wu, *information graphics*

Design: Fabrizio La Rocca, *creative director;* Guido Caroti, Siobhan O'Hare, *art directors;* Tina Malaney, Chie Ushio, Ann McBride, Jessica Walsh, Nora Rosansky, *designers;* Melanie Marin, *senior picture editor*

Cover Photo: (Red barn below the ridge line of the Shenandoah Mountains, Warren County, VA): Terry Donnelly

Production Manager: Angela L. McLean

COPYRIGHT

11th Edition

ISBN 978–0–307–48052–1

ISSN 1075–0711

SPECIAL SALES

This book is available at special discounts for bulk purchases for sales promotions or premiums. Special editions, including personalized covers, excerpts of existing books, and corporate imprints, can be created in large quantities for special needs. For more information, write to Special Markets/Premium Sales, 1745 Broadway, MD 6-2, New York, NY 10019, or e-mail specialmarkets@randomhouse.com.

AN IMPORTANT TIP & AN INVITATION

Although all prices, opening times, and other details in this book are based on information supplied to us at press time, changes occur all the time in the travel world, and Fodor's cannot accept responsibility for facts that become outdated or for inadvertent errors or omissions. So **always confirm information when it matters**, especially if you're making a detour to visit a specific place. Your experiences—positive and negative— matter to us. If we have missed or misstated something, **please write to us.** Share your opinion instantly through our online feedback center at fodors.com/contact-us.

PRINTED IN THE UNITED STATES OF AMERICA

10 9 8 7 6 5 4 3 2 1

Eugene Fodor:
The Spy Who Loved Travel

As Fodor's celebrates our 75th anniversary, we are honoring the colorful and adventurous life of Eugene Fodor, who revolutionized guidebook publishing in 1936 with his first book, *On the Continent, The Entertaining Travel Annual*.

Eugene Fodor's life seemed to leap off the pages of a great spy novel. Born in Hungary, he spoke six languages and graduated from the Sorbonne and the London School of Economics. During World War II he joined the Office of Strategic Services, the budding spy agency for the United States. He commanded the team that went behind enemy lines to liberate Prague, and recommended to Generals Eisenhower, Bradley, and Patton that Allied troops move to the capital city. After the war, Fodor worked as a spy in Austria, posing as a U.S. diplomat.

In 1949 Eugene Fodor—with the help of the CIA—established Fodor's Modern Guides. He was passionate about travel and wanted to bring his insider's knowledge of Europe to a new generation of sophisticated Americans who wanted to explore and seek out experiences beyond their borders. Among his innovations were annual updates, consulting local experts, and including cultural and historical perspectives and an emphasis on people—not just sites. As Fodor described it, "The main interest and enjoyment of foreign travel lies not only in 'the sites,' . . . but in contact with people whose customs, habits, and general outlook are different from your own."

Eugene Fodor died in 1991, but his legacy, Fodor's Travel, continues. It is now one of the world's largest and most trusted brands in travel information, covering more than 600 destinations worldwide in guidebooks, on Fodors.com, and in ebooks and iPhone apps. Technology and the accessibility of travel may be changing, but Eugene Fodor's unique storytelling skills and reporting style are behind every word of today's Fodor's guides.

Our editors and writers continue to embrace Eugene Fodor's vision of building personal relationships through travel. We invite you to join the Fodor's community at fodors.com/community and share your experiences with like-minded travelers. Tell us when we're right. Tell us when we're wrong. And share fantastic travel secrets that aren't yet in Fodor's. Together, we will continue to deepen our understanding of our world.

Happy 75th Anniversary, Fodor's! Here's to many more.

Tim Jarrell, Publisher

CONTENTS

About This Book. 6

1 EXPERIENCE VIRGINIA AND MARYLAND 7
What's Where. 8
Virginia and Maryland Planner. . . 10
Virginia and Maryland
Top Attractions 12
Virginia and Maryland
Top Experiences 14
If You Like. 16
Great Itineraries 18
Virginia and Maryland with Kids . . 22

2 WASHINGTON, D.C. 23
Orientation and Planning. 24
Where to Eat 55
Where to Stay. 65
Nightlife and the Arts. 70
Sports and the Outdoors 72
Shopping. 75

3 NORTHERN VIRGINIA. 79
Orientation and Planning. 80
Alexandria. 85
Arlington. 97
Mount Vernon, Woodlawn, and
Gunston Hall. 106
Fairfax County. 111
Loudoun County. 117

4 D.C.'S MARYLAND SUBURBS . 123
Orientation and Planning. 124
Montgomery County. 129
Prince George's County 141

5 CENTRAL AND WESTERN VIRGINIA 153
Orientation and Planning. 154
Charlottesville and the
Blue Ridge 158

Shenandoah Valley. 176
Southwest Virginia 192

6 RICHMOND, FREDERICKSBURG, AND THE NORTHERN NECK . . 203
Orientation and Planning. 204
Richmond 209
Petersburg 225
Fredericksburg 228
The Northern Neck. 238

7 WILLIAMSBURG AND HAMPTON ROADS 245
Orientation and Planning. 246
The Historic Triangle. 250
Hampton Roads Area 277
Virginia's Eastern Shore 296

8 BALTIMORE. 303
Orientation and Planning. 304
Exploring Baltimore 310
Where to Eat 328
Best Bets for Baltimore
Dining 332
Where to Stay. 340
Best Bets for Baltimore
Lodging. 341
Nightlife and the Arts. 347
Sports and the Outdoors 350
Shopping. 352
Side Trips from Baltimore. 355

9 FREDERICK AND WESTERN MARYLAND 359
Orientation and Planning. 361
Frederick. 365
Side Trips from Frederick 373
Western Maryland 378

10 ANNAPOLIS AND SOUTHERN MARYLAND 393

    Orientation and Planning. 394

    Annapolis 397

    Calvert County 412

    St. Mary's County 419

    Charles County. 423

11 MARYLAND'S EASTERN SHORE 425

    Orientation and Planning. 426

    Queen Anne's County. 430

    Kent County 436

    Cecil County. 441

    Talbot County 443

    Dorchester County 453

    The Lower Eastern Shore 456

TRAVEL SMART VIRGINIA AND MARYLAND 469

    Getting Here and Around. 470

    Essentials 474

INDEX. 481

ABOUT OUR WRITERS 496

MAPS

    Exploring Washington, D.C. . . 32–33

    The Mall 35

    The Monuments 37

    The White House Area. 42

    Capitol Hill 46

    Downtown 51

    Where to Eat and Stay in Washington, D.C.. 58–59

    Northern Virginia 84

    Old Town Alexandria, Virginia . . . 90

    Arlington National Cemetery, Virginia 100

    Mount Vernon, Woodlawn, and Gunston Hall, Virginia. 107

    D.C.'s Maryland Suburbs 127

    Montgomery County, Maryland. 130

    Prince George's County, Maryland. 143

    Central & Western Virginia. 159

    Richmond, Petersburg, and the Northern Neck 207

    Richmond, Virginia 213

    Fredericksburg, Virginia 231

    The Northern Neck. 240

    The Historic Triangle. 252

    Colonial Williamsburg 259

    Hampton Roads Area 278

    Virginia's Eastern Shore 298

    Baltimore, Maryland 312–313

    Where to Eat and Stay in Baltimore 330–331

    Side Trips from Baltimore. 355

    Frederick and Western Maryland. 363

    Frederick, Maryland 366

    Side Trips from Frederick 374

    Southern Maryland. 398

    Annapolis, Maryland. 401

    Maryland's Eastern Shore. . 432–433

ABOUT
THIS BOOK

Our Ratings

Sometimes you find terrific travel experiences and sometimes they just find you. But usually the burden is on you to select the right combination of experiences. That's where our ratings come in.

As travelers we've all discovered a place so wonderful that its worthiness is obvious. And sometimes that place is so experiential that superlatives don't do it justice: you just have to be there to know. These sights, properties, and experiences get our highest rating, **Fodor's Choice**, indicated by orange stars throughout this book.

Black stars highlight sights and properties we deem **Highly Recommended**, places that our writers, editors, and readers praise again and again for consistency and excellence.

By default, there's another category: any place we include in this book is by definition worth your time, unless we say otherwise. And we will.

Disagree with any of our choices? Care to nominate a place or suggest that we rate one more highly? Visit our feedback center at www.fodors.com/feedback.

Budget Well

Hotel and restaurant price categories from ¢ to $$$$ are defined in the opening pages of each chapter. For attractions, we always give standard adult admission fees; reductions are usually available for children, students, and senior citizens. Want to pay with plastic? **AE, D, DC, MC, V** following restaurant and hotel listings indicate if American Express, Discover, Diners Club, MasterCard, and Visa are accepted.

Restaurants

Unless we state otherwise, restaurants are open for lunch and dinner daily. We mention dress only when there's a specific requirement and reservations only when they're essential or not accepted—it's always best to book ahead.

Hotels

Hotels have private bath, phone, TV, and air-conditioning and operate on the European Plan (aka EP, meaning without meals), unless we specify that they use the Continental Plan (CP, with a Continental breakfast), Breakfast Plan (BP, with a full breakfast), or Modified American Plan (MAP, with breakfast and dinner), or are all-inclusive (AI, including all meals and most activities). We

always list facilities but not whether you'll be charged an extra fee to use them, so when pricing accommodations, find out what's included.

Many Listings	
★	Fodor's Choice
★	Highly recommended
⊠	Physical address
↔	Directions or Map coordinates
⌂	Mailing address
☎	Telephone
🖷	Fax
⊕	On the Web
✉	E-mail
🖅	Admission fee
☉	Open/closed times
Ⓜ	Metro stations
🖃	Credit cards
Hotels & Restaurants	
🏨	Hotel
🛏	Number of rooms
♿	Facilities
⛾	Meal plans
✕	Restaurant
✍	Reservations
🜨	Dress code
⚲	Smoking
🕮	BYOB
Outdoors	
🏌	Golf
⛺	Camping
Other	
☾	Family-friendly
⇒	See also
⊠	Branch address
☞	Take note

Experience Virginia and Maryland

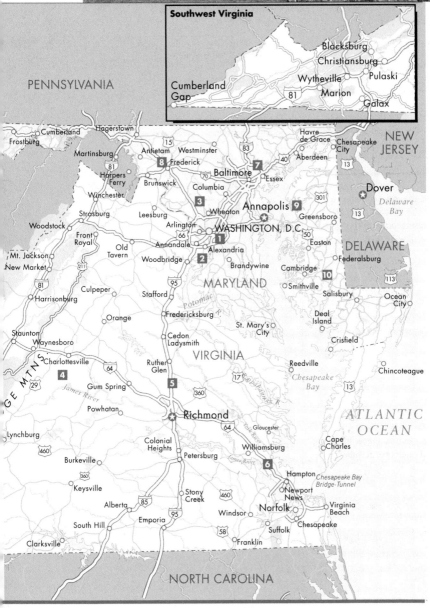

Southwest Virginia

Cumberland Gap

Blacksburg
Christiansburg
Wytheville
Marion
Pulaski
Galax
81

PENNSYLVANIA

NEW JERSEY

Cumberland
Frostburg
Hagerstown
Martinsburg
81
Harpers Ferry
Winchester
Antietam
Westminster
8 Frederick
Brunswick
Columbia
Baltimore
7
Essex
Havre de Grace
Chesapeake City
Aberdeen
40
13
Dover
Delaware Bay

Strasburg
Woodstock
Front Royal
Old Tavern
Leesburg
Arlington
66
3
Wheaton
Annapolis **9**
WASHINGTON, D.C.
Greensboro
301
13

Mt. Jackson
New Market
211
81
Harrisonburg
Culpeper
1
Annandale
2 Alexandria
Woodbridge
Brandywine
50
Easton
DELAWARE
Federalsburg
113

Staunton
Waynesboro
Charlottesville
Orange
Stafford
Fredericksburg
Potomac R.
MARYLAND
Cambridge
Smithville
Salisbury
Deal Island
Ocean City

4
64
29
James River
Gum Spring
Powhatan
Cedon
Ladysmith
Ruther Glen
5
VIRGINIA
St. Mary's City
Crisfield
Reedville
Chesapeake Bay
Chincoteague
13

Lynchburg
460
Burkeville
360
Keysville
Alberta
85
South Hill
Clarksville
Colonial Heights
Petersburg
95
Stony Creek
Emporia
Richmond
360
64
Williamsburg
James River
Windsor
58
Franklin
Gloucester
6
Hampton
Newport News
Norfolk
Suffolk
Chesapeake
Cape Charles
Virginia Beach
Chesapeake Bay Bridge-Tunnel
ATLANTIC OCEAN

BLUE RIDGE MTNS.

NORTH CAROLINA

Dining: The Basics

Haute cuisine and down-home diners. Regional specialties and global ethnic fare. Whether it's produce hailing from family farms or seafood from the Chesapeake Bay, deliciously diverse fare awaits you in Maryland and Virginia.

A favorite in both states is the sweet, delectable meat of the famed blue crab. In the Tidewater area of Virginia, peanuts are king; Smithfield is renowned for ham; and Central Virginia is the birthplace of savory Brunswick stew. In southern Maryland, stuffed ham and beaten biscuits are much beloved, while on Maryland's Eastern Shore crispy fried chicken remains a staple.

In cities like Richmond and Charlottesville—as well as historic Frederick, Norfolk, and metropolitan Baltimore—innovative chefs are emphasizing fresh, local ingredients and serving up everything from trendy bistro fare to exquisite nouveau cuisine.

But restaurants aren't the only places to find good food in these parts. Maryland's roadside stands and farmers' markets are crammed with fresh produce such as sweet Silver Queen corn, heirloom tomatoes, and ripe melons. In Virginia, the country markets in the mountains are a great source for things like freshly baked bread and homemade apple pie.

Lodging: The Basics

Maryland and Virginia have plenty of options for a good night's sleep, from sprawling luxury resorts to budget motels.

Throughout the region, cozy Colonial-era inns offer a plethora of amenities: full-service spas, world-class golf, cooking schools, sailing classes, and tours of wineries, to name a few. In Virginia, grand historic hotels that conjure the golden age are enjoying a glorious renaissance and a new generation of guests. In small picturesque towns across Maryland, charming B&Bs offer a relaxed setting, many with water views. In Baltimore, a new wave of upscale and boutique chain hotels (with on-site restaurants, lounges, and modern conveniences) offer easy access to museums, sporting facilities, and copious shopping and dining options.

Getting Here and Around

Three major airports act as hubs for visitors to the region: **Baltimore/Washington International Airport** (BWI ⊕ www.bwiairport.com), **Dulles International Airport** (IAD), and **Ronald Reagan Washington National Airport** (DCA ⊕ www.metwashairports.com).

Although it's not a hard-and-fast rule, it's true that the most convenient way to get around is by car. To give you an idea of distances: in Maryland it takes about 2½ hours to go from downtown Baltimore to the beaches of Ocean City; or three hours to get to Deep Creek Lake from the D.C. suburbs.

As for rush-hour warnings, both of the beltways (Baltimore or D.C.) get clogged during morning and evening rush hours, and arteries leading to same (I–95, I–83, I–270) can also get backed up under certain conditions. You may also want to avoid Maryland's busy Bay Bridge during peak travel times: on summer Friday nights and Saturday mornings, check current conditions (☎ 877/229–7726 ⊕ www.baybridge.com).

Outside of Washington, D.C., with its reliable **Metro** subway (⊕ www.wmata.com), public transportation options are limited but include: **Amtrak** (⊕ www.amtrak.com) and, in Maryland, the **MARC** (⊕ www.commuterpage.com) commuter trains. Baltimore also has its own subway and buses.

VIRGINIA AND MARYLAND TOP ATTRACTIONS

Antietam National Battlefield

(A) Antietam was the site of the deadliest one-day battle in American history. Today the battlefield in Sharpsburg, Maryland, is maintained to look as it did on that fateful day of September 17, 1862. For additional perspective, the new Heart of the Civil War Heritage Area Exhibit and Visitor Center is located in the historic Newcomer House on the battlefield.

Shenandoah National Park

(B) Imagine a postcard snapped by Mother Nature and you have Shenandoah. Perhaps the best-known element of this treasured historic park is the picturesque 105-mi-long Skyline Drive, but the park also features more than 500 mi of hiking trails, and access to Virginia's Blue Ridge Mountains and the Appalachian Trail.

Virginia Beach and Ocean City

(C) Of the myriad things to do in Virginia Beach and Ocean City, Maryland—from kayaking to surfing—it's the well-maintained beaches and lively oceanfront boardwalks that bring folks back year after year. Watch trained dolphins at the Virginia Aquarium & Marine Science Center or hike the trails through the wetlands at First Landing State Park. Ocean City's amusement parks, golf, and fishing tournaments are popular, and the town presents numerous free events, including movies on the beach.

Colonial Williamsburg

(D) Part of Virginia's "Historic Triangle," this restored 18th-century Colonial city features some 300 acres that include 88 original structures and hundreds of other homes, shops, and public buildings where patriots laid the groundwork for the nation's founding. Colonial Williamsburg operates several museums, and visitors can enjoy period dining at several dining taverns and even stay at historic Williamsburg Inn. New offerings have incorporated the Native American

presence and diplomacy during the Colonial period.

Baltimore's Inner Harbor

(E) The waterside promenade is home to a constellation of museums, specialty shops, restaurants, and hotels, with attractions geared to both families and adults. The National Aquarium, Baltimore Maryland Science Center, American Visionary Art Museum, and the Reginald F. Lewis Museum of Maryland African-American History and Culture are all within walking distance. So is posh Harbor East, the city's newest waterfront community.

City of Annapolis

(F) Maryland's state capital represents the many sides of this state: watch the noon formation of midshipmen at the U.S. Naval Academy, or tour its newly renovated Naval Academy Chapel and expanded Naval Academy Museum. Sail or even race aboard a 74-foot schooner; or meander the cobblestone streets of downtown to see numerous landmarks that illuminate American history.

Washington, D.C.

(G) There's a world to explore in D.C.—from cultural landmarks such as the Smithsonian Institution and its museums to the monuments of the sweeping National Mall. America's full history comes alive in this diverse and cosmopolitan world capital, where many attractions are free and open to the public. Locals and visitors from every corner of the globe enjoy the District's interesting, eclectic, and historic neighborhoods filled with shopping and dining options. There's also a vibrant nightlife and arts scene, ranging from the famed Kennedy Center to regional theater.

VIRGINIA AND MARYLAND TOP EXPERIENCES

Chow Down on Crabs

To Marylanders and Virginians alike, the humble crustacean known as the blue crab is king. Watermen in both states harvest the crabs from Chesapeake Bay (typically from April to November, though you'll find them on menus year-round). First, decide how you want to eat this delectable edible. Choose from jumbo lump or back-fin crab cakes (fried or broiled); steamed crabs (in water or beer) liberally sprinkled with spicy Old Bay seasoning; soft-shell style (lightly floured or breaded then fried, and served on a sandwich bun with lettuce and tomato); deviled; or fluffed. Unless you're having some type of gourmet crab dish, it's practically heresy to use drawn butter or elaborate sauces. Concerns about overfishing have led to stricter regulations by lawmakers, with the hope that the blue crab will survive for future generations.

Race Aboard a Schooner

Evening sailing races take place in Annapolis every Wednesday night from mid-April through September. About 130 boats compete, and organizers have created a special class so that two 74-foot Woodwind Schooners compete in a match race against one another. Guests who take the Wednesday night Woodwind cruise can experience the heady thrill of being aboard and participating in the race. Afterwards, many locals and tourists head to the Boatyard Bar and Grill in nearby Eastport—also accessible by water taxi. *Sail Magazine* has ranked the lively spot one of the top 12 Sailing Bars in the World.

Explore the Happy Trails

The sylvan scenery of Virginia and Maryland lends itself to all types of nature exploration. Along the eastern shores of both states, animal lovers can spy wild "ponies" (technically they're small horses) on Chincoteague and Assateague islands, in Virginia and Maryland respectively. The mountainous west delights ardent outdoors enthusiasts: Green Ridge State forest in Maryland has 46,000 acres of oak and hickory forests and mountain bike trails; you can hike through Shenandoah National Park in Virginia or Catoctin Mountain Park in Maryland, and nearly 600 mi of the famed Appalachian Trail passes through both states.

Breathe in Real History

Virginia and Maryland, along with Washington, D.C., have always played a seminal role in American history. In Virginia you can tour the homes of U.S. presidents ranging from George Washington and Thomas Jefferson to Harrison, Madison, Monroe, and Wilson. Richmond is home to St. John's Church where Patrick Henry gave his famous "Give me Liberty" speech. In Maryland, sites range from the venerable U.S. Naval Academy to the sweeping views of Fort McHenry in Baltimore, where patriot Francis Scott Key was inspired to pen "The Star-Spangled Banner." Last but not least, D.C. was the center of activity for the United States government throughout the Civil War, and many attractions—from Lincoln's Cottage (the President's summer home during the war) to the chairs that Grant and Lee sat in during the surrender at Appomattox (on display at the National Museum of American History), all pay homage.

Sip Some Vintage Virginia

Virginia boasts more than 130 wineries that produce hundreds of thousands of cases annually. But the real joy of Virginia wine comes from exploring the scenic vineyards and farms, sampling vintages in tasting rooms, and soaking up the spirit of the viticulture at hundreds of annual wine events and festivals. Maryland also has its share of skilled winemakers, and the state boasts six official wine trails. Westminster is home to the state's oldest and largest wine festival, held every September.

Explore an Island

Depart by ferry from Crisfield over the Chesapeake Bay to Smith Island, Maryland, a tiny, secluded community accessible only by boat, and home for generations to watermen and their families. Enjoy a family-style meal featuring crabs or oysters, and for dessert, don't skip the island's delicious cakes—stacked eight to 10 layers high and frosted, they have been designated Maryland's state cake by lawmakers. Tangier Island in Virginia is similarly quaint and known for its delectable seafood, while the northern Chesapeake Bay has more developed options like Kent Island.

Hear Heritage Music

Sample the musical soul of Virginia's country connections, by traveling "The Crooked Road," otherwise known as Virginia's Heritage Music Trail. Country music traces its beginnings to this region's mountains and deep valleys, and the area remains a hotbed of bluegrass and toe-tapping Old Time music. Plan ahead to attend two annual August events: the Carter Family Traditional Music Festival in Hiltons; and the Old Fiddlers Convention in Galax, held since 1935.

Experience Life along the Waterfront

Discover the region's newest waterfront communities. National Harbor, just outside D.C., is an enclave of upscale residences, retail stores, restaurants, offices, and nightspots situated on 300 acres that was once swampland along the historic Potomac River. About an hour north, Harbor East, one of Baltimore's newest neighborhoods, extends the city's scenic waterfront and world-renowned Inner Harbor. With yacht slips in full view, it boasts chic boutiques, an upscale movie theater, office high-rises, and gourmet dining.

Play Ball

Take yourself out to a ball game at Oriole Park at Camden Yards in downtown Baltimore. With its steel trusses and arched brick facade, the home of the Baltimore Orioles is considered one of America's most beautiful ballparks. The 48,000 seats provide fine views of the asymmetrical field; the natural grass turf (a vibrant green Kentucky bluegrass blend) is impeccably manicured; and, besides traditional ballpark fare, food offerings include pit beef and Maryland's famed crab cakes.

IF YOU LIKE

Great Battlefields

Some of the fiercest and most pivotal battles ever staged on American soil took place in Maryland and Virginia, including campaigns during the American Revolution, the War of 1812, and, of course, the Civil War. The National Park Service operates many of these battlefield sites as living-history museums, with carefully preserved or reconstructed fortifications; interpretive centers that show dramatic films and exhibits; and a wide range of narrated walking and driving tours. You don't have to be a history buff to appreciate the significance of these seminal venues; in ways large and small, they helped determine the very course of U.S. history.

•At Maryland's Antietam National Battlefield, the bloodiest single day of battle of the Civil War occurred on September 17, 1862. When it was over, more than 23,000 Union and Confederate soldiers had been killed or wounded.

•During the War of 1812, Baltimore's star-shaped Fort McHenry was where Francis Scott Key penned "The Star-Spangled Banner" while the British bombarded the beleaguered city.

•No tour of Civil War sites is complete without a stop at Manassas National Battlefield Park (aka "Bull Run") in Northern Virginia, where Union and Confederate troops met twice on the battlefield; the battles yielded two important victories for the Confederacy.

•When French and American troops led by General George Washington forced the British to surrender at Yorktown Battlefield, the Revolutionary War drew to a dramatic close.

Swank Country Inns

Small, tranquil, and increasingly sophisticated, the mountain towns and bay-side villages of Virginia and Maryland are home to some of the most sumptuous country inns in America.

•Antrim 1844 appeals to those who relish history and romance. The supremely elegant antebellum mansion, which is on the National Register of Historic Places, has 40 plush rooms and suites, and is just a short drive (about 15 mi south) from historic Gettysburg.

•Since 1766 the Homestead has been one of the most distinguished resorts in the Mid-Atlantic. Thanks to a recent multimillion-dollar renovation, the lavish resort in Hot Springs, Virginia, with a view of the Allegheny Mountains, is now even better.

•The Inn at Little Washington in central Virginia is a favorite of top celebs and politicos. The legendary inn has become a must-do experience for those who appreciate fabulous gourmet dinners, beautiful English country-house decor, and a peaceful setting.

•Set on 220 manicured acres on Maryland's Eastern Shore, the Kent Manor Inn earns praise for its 24 elegant rooms, panoramic water views, and sumptuous Sunday brunch and seafood, all served in a charming restaurant.

•The Clifton Inn in Charlottesville, Virginia, overlooks Monticello Mountain and consists of 100 acres of rolling Virginia countryside deeded to Thomas Jefferson's daughter Martha upon her marriage. Befitting its Federal heritage, the stately columned main house and the buildings that now comprise the inn are furnished in comfortable elegance.

Taking to the Water

Maryland and Virginia are not only traversed by countless rivers, they fringe the Atlantic Ocean and both are home to Chesapeake Bay. So it's no wonder that there's great appreciation for maritime pursuits. Companies around the region rent all types of boats and offer a wide range of tours and excursions. In the mountains of both states, you'll find exhilarating white-water rafting. Even taking a ride on a tour boat in Baltimore's Inner Harbor or along the Potomac River in Washington, D.C., offers plenty of interesting scenery. Last but not least, mammoth cruise ships depart from Baltimore year-round, heading to the Caribbean, Canada, and exotic locales.

•In Maryland you can spend a full day exploring the Chesapeake Bay on a boat excursion. From Annapolis, Watermark Journeys schooner tours go as far as St. Michaels on the Eastern Shore.

•Fans of deep-sea fishing need look no farther than Maryland's Ocean City Fishing Center, which has more than 30 vessels providing charter sport fishing trips to catch blue marlin, wahoo, and big-eye tuna.

•For an unusual view of Washington, D.C.'s monuments and prominent buildings, take one of the kayaking tours on the Potomac offered by the Thompson Boat Center in Georgetown. You can also take a sightseeing tour with Capitol River Cruises from the Georgetown Waterfront, or try the pedal boats in the Tidal Basin.

•In Virginia, Richmond has Class IV rapids running right through its downtown, and statewide rafting and kayaking are popular options.

National Parks and Forests

From the mountains to the seashore, a number of stunning—sometimes historic—national parks are part of Virginia and Maryland's landscapes. The parks provide wonderful opportunities for scenic country drives and bike rides, camping, or stays in rustic park-service lodges. Prepare for sometimes up-close encounters with myriad wildlife, from bald eagles to wild horses. The famous Appalachian Trail cuts a rugged path through both states, and virtually every major park and forest has rigorous hikes and shorter nature walks.

•A 37-mi-long barrier island that borders both Virginia and Maryland's shores, Assateague Island National Seashore is full of pristine beaches, wild horses, deer, and some 300 species of birds.

•Blackwater National Wildlife Refuge, southeast of Annapolis, is one of the East Coast's premier spots for viewing thousands of migratory geese and ducks in season, and birds ranging from bald eagles to ospreys. Visitors can explore the area by car, bike, or kayak.

•Catoctin Mountain Park in Western Maryland is home to the Camp David presidential retreat, but its other claim to fame is its beauty. The area boasts some 20 mi of scenic hikes and the highest cascading waterfall in the state.

•The Potomac River, the waterway that divides Maryland and Virginia, is the route of the 185-mi linear park, the C&O Canal National Historical Park. It's a favorite with hikers and bicyclists.

•In Virginia's Shenandoah Mountains lies the breathtaking Skyline Drive, a celebrated 105-mi route through Shenandoah National Park.

GREAT ITINERARIES

THE BEST OF VA, MD, AND D.C.

Days 1 and 2: Washington, D.C.

To make the most of your two days in D.C., start at the National Mall where you can marvel at the monuments and check out a handful of the Smithsonian's wildly diverse museums. A tour of the White House is a highlight, but be forewarned: you must reserve months in advance, and it's one of the toughest tickets in town. A visit to the Capitol is a good alternative; you can reserve online in advance, and they seldom turn anyone away who shows up.

On your second day, venture into some of the city's diverse residential neighborhoods, such as DuPont Circle, U Street, Adams-Morgan, or Georgetown. Each abounds with chic shops, restaurants, galleries, and handsome Victorian town houses. Culture-vultures shouldn't miss the Phillips Collection modern-art museum in DuPont Circle, and nature-lovers should enjoy sweeping Rock Creek Park, easily accessible from either the Georgetown or DuPont Circle neighborhoods.

Day 3 and 4: Baltimore

On days 3 and 4 drive up I–95 or Route 295 to Baltimore, the largest and best-known city in Maryland; it's a must-see for first-time visitors. Although quite different in look and feel from neighboring Washington, D.C., B'more, as locals call it, is historically and culturally interesting in its own right. After you arrive, take in some of the major sights clustered around the colorful Inner Harbor, such as the National Aquarium of Baltimore and the American Visionary Art Museum.

Consider staying overnight at the city's new convention center hotel, which adjoins Oriole Park at Camden Yards and has views of the ball field. On your second day in the city, visit the Walters Art Museum and Baltimore Museum of Art, both must-sees, and check out the new arts and entertainment district, Station North, which has innovative store-front theaters and galleries, an art-house cinema, hip clubs, coffee shops, and eateries. Other neighborhoods worth exploring include artsy Mount Vernon, historic Fells Point, yuppie Canton, kitschy Hampden, and posh Harbor East.

Day 5: Annapolis and Solomons

On the morning of Day 5, head southeast from Baltimore via I–97 to experience Maryland's Colonial past in Annapolis. The state capital, Annapolis is also home to the impressive grounds of the U.S. Naval Academy. On the bustling waterfront, aka City Dock, a statue of *Roots* author Alex Haley stands. His ancestors helped comprise the port city's significant early free and enslaved black population. Nearby, dozens of cute shops offer clothing, ice cream, and souvenirs, while restaurants offer Maryland's famous crab cakes or crab soup. Be sure to stop into Chick and Ruth's Delly on Main Street where they recite the Pledge of Allegiance every morning, and serve sandwiches named after Maryland politicians. Mid-afternoon, follow Route 2 into rural and scenic southern Maryland, eventually winding your way to the lovely town of Solomons, a cherished getaway for Chesapeake Bay boaters. The Back Creek Inn gets high marks as a lovely place to spend the night.

Day 6: Alexandria

The morning of Day 6 head south to the historic village of St. Mary's City, where archaeologists and other experts have been doing reconstruction work related to the area's early English settlement in the 1600s. Then head north up Route 5 and west on I–495 to reach Alexandria, an excellent base for exploring northern Virginia's top sites, such as Arlington Cemetery, Mount Vernon (George Washington's home), and Manassas National Battlefield Park. Alexandria has a little bit of everything: critically-acclaimed gourmet restaurants, a charming Old Town shopping district; a variety of hotels; renowned arts centers and festivals; and 18th- and 19th-century architecture. History buffs may want to visit the Georgian-inspired Christ Church—where both George Washington and Robert E. Lee were pew holders, or the African-American museum, which unveils little-known facts about Alexandria's role and black leadership in early Civil Rights actions.

Days 7: Charlottesville

From Alexandria head west on I–495 and then I–66; exit at Front Royal and then drive along Skyline Drive through beautiful Shenandoah National Park. Keep in mind that it can take a while (about two to three hours) to drive along this meandering scenic road. At U.S. 33, travel east to U.S. 29, and then south to the lively and inviting university town of Charlottesville. Here you can find a number of fine restaurants and galleries, as well as appealing hotels. Use "C-ville" as a base for exploring Thomas Jefferson's life—be it his plantation home, Monticello, or the regal campus of the University of Virginia. Another presidential stop is James Madison's estate, Montpelier. If you have time, definitely consider checking out one of the many fine wineries in the general vicinity, such as Barboursville, which offers tastings and excellent tours. There's also a Monticello wine trail with about two dozen stops.

Day 8: Richmond

Drive east on I–64 from Charlottesville to reach Virginia's capital, Richmond, which is home to several fine museums, Civil War sites, and historic neighborhoods. An especially appealing section for a stroll is the Victorian Fan District, home to the excellent Virginia Museum of Fine Arts and close to the grand Jefferson Hotel. Richmond is a short drive from Petersburg and Pamplin Historical Park, where the historical interpretations are cutting-edge; they also incorporate African American history. In the evening, stroll downtown to the revitalized Shockoe Bottom and Shockoe Slip areas, where the cobblestone streets are lined with cool restaurants and lively bars and lounges. Also check out Carytown, a hip district known as Richmond's "Mile of Style," with funky little shops (many independently owned), nightlife, and restaurants.

Days 9 and 10: Williamsburg

Continue east from Richmond along I–64 to Williamsburg, your base for exploring such historic sites as the early English settlements of Jamestown and the Revolutionary battlefield at Yorktown. You'll want to spend a full day touring the museums and living history of Colonial Williamsburg, with its many house-museums staffed by costumed interpreters. Plan to spend the night in the Colonial Houses of Williamsburg, which offer the most authentically historic lodging experience. On your final day, if you still have energy and time, you might want to continue along I–64 east to the Hampton Roads area to spend a little time at the Mariners' Museum and the USS *Monitor* Center or the Chrysler Museum of Art in the maritime city of Norfolk. You could also continue directly to the resorts of Virginia Beach, or drive up U.S. 13, which affords you access to both Virginia's and Maryland's Eastern Shore regions.

A CIVIL WAR TOUR

Day 1: Hampton

Start your tour at Hampton, on the Virginia Peninsula, where the Union general George McClellan launched his drive toward Richmond. The Hampton History Museum contains excellent exhibits on Civil War ironclad ships. Nearby is Fort Monroe—the Union stronghold in which the president of the Confederacy, Jefferson Davis, was imprisoned.

Days 2 and 3: Richmond

On Day 2 drive northwest on I–64 up the peninsula to Richmond's Museum and White House of the Confederacy and the National Battlefield Park Visitor Center. Also see the Virginia Historical Society Museum of Virginia History, which has some 800 pieces of Confederate weaponry (although only a few are on display), and the American Civil War Center at Historic Tredegar, the only museum of its kind to explore the war through three interwoven perspectives: Union, Confederate, and African-American. On Day 3, proceed 20 mi south on I–95 to Petersburg, the city that was under an extended siege by Grant's army. Visit 1,500-acre Petersburg National Battlefield, the Siege Museum, and Pamplin Historical Park—which commemorates an important Union attack on Lee's supposedly impenetrable defense line—before returning to spend the night in Richmond.

Day 4: Fredericksburg

For Day 4, proceed north from Richmond up I–95 to Fredericksburg, which has blocks of historic Civil War–era homes and a Confederate Cemetery with the remains of more than 2,000 soldiers. Detour to see the four battlefields at Fredericksburg/Spotsylvania National Military Park, then venture an hour outside of town to see Stratford Hall plantation, where Robert E. Lee was born.

Days 5 and 6: Northern Virginia

For days 5 and 6, base yourself around Arlington or Fairfax, which puts you close to the key attractions in this area—from Fredericksburg, you reach the area by heading north up I–95. Spend one day touring Manassas National Battlefield

Park (aka "Bull Run"), site of two important Confederate victories—it's here that General Thomas Jonathan Jackson earned the nickname "Stonewall" when he and his brigade "stood like a stone wall." On your second day, head to Arlington National Cemetery and Arlington House (Lee's home for 30 years before the Union army confiscated it and turned the grounds into the cemetery).

Day 7: Frederick and Western Maryland

From northern Virginia, head north on I–270 into Maryland. Take U.S. 70 west toward Boonsboro and follow it to Maryland's Heart of the Civil War Heritage Area Exhibit and Visitor Center. It's housed inside the historic Newcomer House at Antietam National Battlefield. The nearby town of Frederick is a perfect base for additional Civil War exploration. See Frederick's National Museum of Civil War Medicine with its 3,000 artifacts. Nearby is Monocacy National Battlefield, where Union troops thwarted a Confederate invasion of Washington, D.C.

Days 8 and 9: Lexington

From western Maryland follow I–81 south back into Virginia and through the Shenandoah Valley to reach Lexington, a quaint and scenic college town (home to

Washington and Lee University) where many buildings date back to the 1700s. Visit the Lee Chapel and Museum, where Lee is buried, and the Virginia Military Institute Museum, which has displays on Stonewall Jackson. Jackson is buried here as well; and you can see the only house he ever owned, which is now a museum.

Day 10: Richmond

On your final day return to Richmond via Appomattox to spend some additional time exploring any of the city's Civil War–related attractions. Stop at Appomattox Court House, where Lee formally surrendered to Grant, thus officially ending the Civil War. The park here consists of some 27 original structures, and the self-guided tour is exceptionally good. From here it's a leisurely and scenic drive east on U.S. 460 and then northeast on U.S. 360 back to the state capital.

VIRGINIA AND MARYLAND WITH KIDS

From quirky museums to pastoral outings, Maryland and Virginia have much to offer families with kids. Top activities include:

•The 100-year-old **Virginia Zoological Park** in Norfolk spans 53 acres along the Lafayette River and is home to nearly 400 animals. Special features include an underwater viewing deck, tree-dwelling bear species, and an orangutan exhibit with a 60-foot viewing window.

•Show the texting generation what life was like on a 19th-century farm at the **Carroll County Farm Museum.** Built in 1852, the 140-acre site in Westminster, Maryland includes barns, a smokehouse, springhouse, blacksmith shop, and early farm memorabilia.

•Imagine a 15,000-square-foot winter wonderland crafted of ice (2 million pounds worth). That's what you'll find at the annual **Christmas on the Potomac** celebration, at Gaylord National Resort, a glass-encased mega-resort on the Potomac River, just outside Washington, D.C. Kids will marvel at the 60-foot glass Christmas tree, an indoor snowfall, and 2 million dazzling lights. The exhibit is kept at a brrr-inspiring 9 degrees. November through January.

•Raucous hayrides and tea parties, a nature center with a 20-foot waterfall, vast gardens and a children's farm are all part of the grand, 100-acre estate in Richmond called **Maymont Park.** Kids can get around by open-air tram or horse-drawn carriage. Boy Scouts and Girl Scouts can earn service badges here, too.

•Baltimore's Inner Harbor has the kiddie set covered. At the **Port Discovery Children's Museum** children—ages two to 10—can bang drums, sing karaoke in a recording studio, or take a time capsule to Egypt to find a Pharaoh's lost tomb. The Maryland Science Center features hands-on exhibits like a bed of nails and a human digestion exhibit complete with, er, body noises. IMAX films, planetarium shows, and a rooftop observatory complete the fun. At the National Aquarium, kids can view massive tanks with 11,000 aquatic animals, travel to Australia, and immerse themselves in an exhibit that goes beyond 3-D—it's actually 4-D!

•The **Brunswick Railroad Museum** in Brunswick, Maryland, features a huge model railroad built to scale that depicts the B&O passenger line. Kids can view rail equipment and memorabilia, photos, Victorian costumes, furnishings, and toys.

•**South Mountain Creamery,** a commercial farm in Middletown, Maryland, offers kids a mooo-ving experience and a taste of daily farm life—for free. Youngsters can watch cows being milked in the milking parlor, and then help feed baby calves with a bottle.

•At the **Children's Museum of Virginia** in Portsmouth, children can shop at a pint-size grocery store or work in a miniature bank. Displays range from ceramic arts and sculpture to magic with science, and kid-friendly lessons on sound dynamics.

Washington, D.C.

WORD OF MOUTH

"I wish all Americans could go [to D.C.] at least once. It really makes you feel such a sense of pride and patriotism as you visit these wonderful symbols of our history and liberty. Take in as much as you can and enjoy it and don't worry about the things you don't have time to see—all of it is special. Have a great time!"

—texasjo

Updated by
Mark Sullivan

The Byzantine workings of the federal government, the sound bite–ready oratory of the well-groomed politicians, and the murky foreign policy pronouncements issued from Foggy Bottom cause many Americans to cast a skeptical eye on anything that happens "inside the Beltway." Washingtonians take it in stride—all in a day's work. Besides, such ribbing is a small price to pay for living in a city with charms that extend far beyond the bureaucratic.

World-class museums and art galleries (nearly all of them free), tree-shaded and flower-filled parks and gardens, bars and restaurants that benefit from a large immigrant community and droves of young people, and nightlife that seems to get better with every passing year are as much a part of Washington as floor debates or filibusters.

The city that calls to mind politicking, back-scratching, and delicate diplomatic maneuvering is itself the result of a compromise. The deal was struck when Virginia's Thomas Jefferson agreed that the federal government would assume the war debts of the colonies if Alexander Hamilton and other Northern legislators would agree to locate the capital on the banks of the Potomac, near George Washington's estate at Mount Vernon. Soon after, in 1791, Pierre-Charles L'Enfant, a French engineer who had fought in the Revolution, designed a city with a "vast esplanade" now known as the "Mall," wide diagonal boulevards crossing a grid of streets, and a focal triangle formed by the Capitol, the president's house, and a statue where the Washington monument now sits. Although L'Enfant's plans seem grand now, for almost a century this city was little more than a sparsely populated swamp with empty dirt avenues. Cattle grazed on the Mall and America's famous early leaders worked in and inhabited dank, dilapidated buildings.

ORIENTATION AND PLANNING

GETTING ORIENTED

The city is divided into the four quadrants of a compass (NW, NE, SE, SW), with the U.S. Capitol at the center. Because the Capitol doesn't sit in the exact center of the city (the Washington Monument does), Northwest is the largest quadrant.

If someone tells you to meet them at 6th and G, ask them to specify the quadrant, because there are actually four different 6th and G intersections (one per quadrant). Within each quadrant, numbered streets run north–south, and lettered streets run east–west (the letter J was omitted to avoid confusion with the letter I). The streets form a fairly simple grid—for instance, 900 G Street NW is the intersection of 9th and G streets in the NW quadrant of the city. Likewise, if you count the letters of the alphabet, skipping J, you can get a good approximation of an address for a numbered street. For instance, 1600 16th Street NW is close to Q Street, Q being the 16th letter of the alphabet if you skip J.

As if all this weren't confusing enough, Major Pierre L'Enfant, the Frenchman who originally designed the city, threw in diagonal avenues recalling those of Paris. Most of D.C.'s avenues are named after U.S. states. You can find addresses on avenues the same way you find those on numbered streets, so 1200 Connecticut Avenue NW is close to M Street, because M is the 12th letter of the alphabet when you skip J.

PLANNING

WHEN TO GO

Washington has two delightful seasons: spring and autumn. In spring the city's ornamental fruit trees are budding, and its many gardens are in bloom. By autumn most of the summer crowds have left and you can enjoy the sights in peace. Summer can be uncomfortably hot and humid. Winter weather is mild by East Coast standards, but a handful of modest snowstorms each year bring this southern city to a standstill.

GETTING HERE AND AROUND
AIR TRAVEL

The major gateways to D.C. are Ronald Reagan Washington National Airport in Virginia, 4 mi south of downtown Washington; Dulles International Airport, 26 mi west of Washington, D.C.; and Baltimore/Washington International-Thurgood Marshall (BWI) Airport in Maryland, about 30 mi to the northeast. By Taxi, expect to pay $10–$15 to get from National to downtown, $50–$60 from Dulles, and $90 from BWI.

The Metro subway ride downtown from Ronald Reagan Washington National Airport takes about 20 minutes and costs about $1.85, depending on the time of day and your final destination.

Washington Flyer links Dulles International Airport and the West Falls Church Metro station. The 20-minute ride is $10 one-way and $18 round-trip for adults, free for children under six. Buses run every half hour from 5:45 am to 10:15 pm. Fares may be paid with cash or credit card. The Washington Metropolitan Area Transit Authority (WMATA) operates express bus service between Dulles and several stops in Downtown D.C., including the L'Enfant Plaza Metro station. Bus 5A, which costs $3.10, runs every hour between 5:30 am and 11:30 pm. Exact fare is required.

Amtrak and Maryland Rail Commuter Service (MARC) trains run between BWI and Washington, D.C.'s Union Station from around 6 am to 10 pm. The cost of the 30-minute ride is $9–$44 on Amtrak and $6 on MARC, which runs only on weekdays. A free shuttle bus transports passengers between airline terminals and the train station. Washington Metropolitan Area Transit Authority (WMATA) operates express bus service (Bus B30) between BWI and the Greenbelt Metro station. Buses run between 6 am and 10 pm. The fare is $3.10.

National, Dulles, and BWI airports are served by SuperShuttle. The approximately 20-minute ride from Reagan National to downtown averages $14; the roughly 45-minute ride from Dulles runs $29; the ride from BWI, which takes about 60 minutes, averages $37.

BUS TRAVEL

Several inexpensive bus lines run between New York City and Washington, D.C., including BoltBus, Megabus, Today's Bus, and Vamoose. All the buses are clean, the service satisfactory, and the price can't be beat. Believe it or not, with advance planning, you might be able to get a round-trip ticket for just $2. Several of the bus lines offer power outlets, Wi-Fi, and a frequent-rider loyalty program. GotoBus is an online booking agent that sells bus tickets and tours offered by several bus lines. It's a fast and easy way to compare prices.

The red, white, and blue WMATA buses ($1.35, $3.10 on express buses) crisscross the city and the nearby suburbs. Buses require exact change in bills, coins, or both. You can eliminate the exact-change hassle by purchasing a seven-day bus Metrobus pass for $11, or better yet, the rechargeable SmarTrip card at the Metro Center sales office, open weekdays from 7:30 am to 6:30 pm.

The DC Circulator offers $1 rides to cultural and entertainment destinations along three routes within the city's central core. The north–south route runs from the DC Convention Center at 6th Street and Massachusetts NW, to the Southwest Waterfront, at 6th Street and Maine Avenue. The east–west route runs from Union Station at Columbus Plaza NW, to Georgetown, at M Street and Wisconsin Avenue NW. A third loop, operating on weekends only from 10 am to 6 pm, circles the National Mall and includes stops at the National Gallery of Art and the Smithsonian. Passengers can pay cash when boarding (exact change only) or use Metro Farecards, SmarTrip cards, all-day passes, and Metro bus transfers. Tickets also may be purchased at fare meters or multispace parking meters on the sidewalk near Circulator stops. Machines accept change or credit cards and make change. Buses run every 5–10 minutes from 7 am to 9 pm, seven days a week.

CAR TRAVEL

A car is often a drawback in Washington, D.C. Traffic is horrendous, especially at rush hour, and driving is often confusing, with many lanes and some entire streets changing direction suddenly during rush hour. Interstate 95 skirts D.C. as part of the Beltway (also known as I–495 in parts), the six- to eight-lane highway that encircles the city.

Parking here is an adventure; the police are quick to tow away or immobilize with a boot any vehicle parked illegally. Private parking lots downtown often charge around $5 an hour and $25 a day. There's free three-hour parking around the Mall on Jefferson and Madison drives, though these spots are almost always filled. The closest free parking is in three lots in East Potomac Park, south of the 14th Street Bridge. Note that it's illegal to use a handheld phone while driving in Washington, D.C., and that radar detectors are illegal in D.C. and Virginia.

METRO TRAVEL

The Metro, which opened in 1976, is one of the country's cleanest, most efficient, and safest subway systems. It begins operation at 5 am on weekdays and 7 am on weekends. The Metro closes on weekdays at midnight and weekends at 3 am. Lighted displays at the platforms show estimated arrival and departure times of trains, as well as the number of cars available. Eating, drinking, smoking, and littering in stations and on the trains are strictly prohibited.

The Metro's base fare is $1.65; the actual price you pay depends on the time of day and the distance traveled. Up to two children under age five ride free with a paying passenger. Buy your ticket at the Farecard machines, some of which accept credit cards. You can buy one-day passes for $7.80 and seven-day passes for $39. Locals use the SmarTrip card, a plastic card that can hold any fare amount and can be used throughout the Metro, bus, and parking system. The cost of each ride is deducted as you enter the subway. Buy passes or SmarTrip cards at the Metro Center sales office or online.

TAXI TRAVEL

You can hail a taxi on the street just about anywhere in the city, though they tend to congregate around major hotels. There are a number of different cab companies in the city, and as a result D.C. cabs do not have a uniform appearance (unlike New York's yellow cabs, for example). And you may find yourself in a taxi that's older and a bit run-down. Drivers are allowed to pick up more than one fare at a time. Diamond, Mayflower, and Yellow are three reputable cab companies used by locals and visitors alike.

After 70 years of a zone system, taxis in the District are now on time and distance meters. The base rate for the first one-sixth mi is $3. Each additional one-sixth mi and each minute stopped or traveling at less than 10 mph is 25¢. There is a $2 surcharge per piece of large luggage in the trunk and a 50¢ per bag handling charge. There is a $2 surcharge for radio dispatch and $1.50 for each additional person.

TRAIN TRAVEL

More than 80 trains a day arrive at Washington, D.C.'s Union Station. Amtrak's regular service runs from D.C. to New York in 3¼–3¾ hours and from D.C. to Boston in 7¾–8 hours. Acela, Amtrak's high-speed service, travels from D.C. to New York in 2¾–3 hours and from D.C. to Boston in 6½ hours. Two commuter lines—Maryland Rail Commuter Service and Virginia Railway Express—run to the nearby suburbs. They're cheaper than Amtrak, but they don't run on weekends.

TOURS

Old Town Trolley Tours ($32), orange-and-green motorized trolleys, take in the main downtown sights and also head into Georgetown and the upper Northwest in a speedy two hours if you ride straight through. However, you can hop on and off as many times as you like. Tourmobile buses, authorized by the National Park Service, operate in a similar fashion, making 25 stops at historic sites between the Capitol and Arlington National Cemetery. Tickets, available at kiosks at Union Station and Arlington National Cemetery, are $25 for adults.

Special tours of government buildings with heavy security, including the White House and the Capitol, can be arranged through your representative's or senator's office. ■ TIP→ Plan up to six months in advance of your trip as limited numbers of these so-called VIP tickets are available. Governmental buildings close to visitors when the Department of Homeland Security issues a high alert, so call ahead. The United States Capitol Visitor Center leads free tours of the historic Capitol. Register in advance for tickets online or get them directly from the Center.

Guided walks around Washington, D.C., and nearby communities are routinely offered by the Smithsonian Associates Program; advance tickets are required. Tour DC specializes in walking tours of Georgetown and Dupont Circle, covering topics such as the Civil War, the Underground Railroad, and Kennedy's Georgetown. Anecdotal History Tours leads tours in Georgetown, Adams-Morgan, and Capitol Hill, as well as tours of where Lincoln was shot and the homes of former presidents. Washington Walks has a wide range of tours, including "I've Got a Secret" featuring Washington, D.C., lore. The nonprofit group Cultural Tourism DC leads guided walking tours that cover the history and architecture of neighborhoods from the southwest waterfront to points much farther north.

ESSENTIALS

Air Contacts Baltimore/Washington International-Thurgood Marshall Airport (*BWI* ☎ *410/859–7100* ⊕ *www.bwiairport.com*). **Dulles International Airport** (*IAD* ☎ *703/572–2700* ⊕ *www.metwashairports.com/Dulles*). **Ronald Reagan Washington National Airport** (*DCA* ☎ *703/417–8000* ⊕ *www. metwashairports.com/National*).

Bus Contacts BoltBus (☎ *877/265–8287* ⊕ *www.boltbus.com*). **GotoBus. com** (☎ *202/408–8200* ⊕ *wwwgotobus.com*). **Megabus** (☎ *877/462–6342* ⊕ *www.megabus.com*). **Today's Bus** (☎ *202/408–8200* ⊕ *www.todaysbus.com*). **Vamoose** (☎ *877/393–2828* ⊕ *www.vamoosebus.com*).

Metro Contacts Washington Metropolitan Area Transit Authority (*WMATA* ☎ *202/637–7000, 202/638–3780 TTY, 202/962–1195 lost and found* ⊕ *www. wmata.com*).

Taxis and Shuttle Contacts DC Taxicab Commission (☎ *202/645–6018* ⊕ *www.dctaxi.dc.gov*). **Diamond** (☎ *202/387–6200*). **Mayflower** (☎ *202/783–1111*). **SuperShuttle** (☎ *800/258–3826 or 202/296–6662* ⊕ *www.supershuttle. com*). **Washington Flyer** (☎ *888/927–4359* ⊕ *www.washfly.com*). **Yellow** (☎ *202/544–1212*).

Tour Contacts Anecdotal History Tours (☎ *301/294–9514* ⊕ *www. dcsightseeing.com*). **Cultural Tourism DC** (☎ *202/661–7581* ⊕ *www. culturaltourismdc.org*). **Department of State** (☎ *202/647–3241, 202/736–4474 TDD* ⊕ *www.state.gov/m/drr*). **Old Town Trolley Tours** (☎ *202/832–9800* ⊕ *www.historictours.com*). **Smithsonian Associates Program** (☎ *202/357–3030* ⊕ *www.smithsonianassociates.org*). **Tour D.C** (☎ *301/588–8999* ⊕ *www. tourdc.com*). **Tourmobile** (☎ *202/554–5100 or 888/868–7707* ⊕ *www. tourmobile.com*). **United States Capitol Guide Service** (☎ *202/252–6827* ⊕ *www.visitthecapital.gov*). **Washington Walks** (☎ *202/484–1865* ⊕ *www. washingtonwalks.com*).

TOP REASONS TO GO

■ **Shop in Georgetown:** Stroll the cobblestone streets and dip into shops offering cutting-edge fashion and priceless antiques.

■ **Explore the Smithsonian:** Spend days savoring a variety of brilliant exhibits in the Smithsonian's 13 museums, all free.

■ **Walk the Halls of Power:** At the White House, the Capitol, and the Supreme Court, take a peek behind the curtain.

■ **Taste the Emerging Theater Scene:** Feast your eyes on brilliantly staged productions at the Kennedy Center, Shakespeare Theatre, Arena Stage, and Woolly Mammoth.

■ **Get a Bird's-Eye View:** At the Washington Monument, enjoy a full view of this marble- and monument-laden city.

2

Train Contacts Amtrak (☎ *800/872–7245* ⊕ *www.amtrak.com*). **Maryland Rail Commuter Service** (*MARC* ☎ *800/325–7245* ⊕ *www.mtamaryland.com*). **Union Station** (✉ *50 Massachusetts Ave. NE* ☎ *202/371–9441* ⊕ *www.unionstationdc.com*). **Virginia Railway Express** (*VRE* ☎ *703/684–1001* ⊕ *www.vre.org*).

Visitor Information DC Visitor Information Center (✉ *1300 Pennsylvania Ave. NW, White House Area* ☎ *866/324–7386 or 202/289–8317* ⊕ *www.dcchamber.org*). **National Park Service** (☎ *202/619–7275 "Dial-a-Park" park information* ⊕ *www.nps.gov*). **Smithsonian** (☎ *202/633–1000 or 202/633–5285* ⊕ *www.si.edu*).

DISCOUNTS AND DEALS

It's actually hard to spend money on activities in D.C. All the Smithsonian museums and national memorials are free, as are many other museums and attractions. Summertime is heaven for budget travelers, when free outdoor concerts and festivals occur every week.

PLANNING YOUR TIME

If you have a day or less in D.C., your sightseeing strategy is simple: take the Metro to the Smithsonian stop and explore the area around the Mall. Allow four or five hours to tour the monuments. This includes time to relax on a park bench and to grab a snack from a vendor or one of the snack bars east of the Washington Monument and near the Lincoln Memorial. If you're visiting during the first two weeks in April, take extra time around the Tidal Basin and the Washington Monument to marvel at the cherry blossoms. With more time at your disposal, you have a chance both to see the sights and to get to know the city.

EXPLORING WASHINGTON, D.C.

There's no denying that Washington, the world's first planned capital, is also one of its most beautiful. And although the federal government dominates many of the city's activities and buildings, there are always places where you can leave politics behind. Washington is a city of vistas—pleasant views that shift and change from block to block, a marriage of geometry and art. Unlike other large cities, Washington isn't dominated by skyscrapers, largely because, in 1899, Congress passed a height-restrictions act to prevent federal monuments from being over-shadowed by commercial construction. Its buildings stretch out grace-fully and are never far from expanses of green. Like its main industry, politics, Washington's design is a constantly changing kaleidoscope that invites inspection from all angles.

Washington's centerpiece is the National Mall, a mile-long stretch of grass that reaches from the Capitol past the bulk of the Smithsonian's grand museums to the Washington Monument. The White House, due north of the Washington Monument, and the other major monuments, to the southwest, are not far away. In recent years Downtown, north of Pennsylvania from the Capitol to the White House, has become the city's nerve center, quickly gentrifying with new bars, restaurants, world-class theaters, and a renovated Smithsonian Museum of American Art and National Portrait Gallery. The tree-shaded streets of Georgetown, up Pennsylvania Avenue from the White House, are lined with million-dollar row houses and the city's best upscale shopping. U Street, once Washington's Harlem, has regained its status as D.C.'s hippest neighbor-hood. The neighborhoods along the Metro's red line—Dupont Circle, Woodley Park, and Cleveland Park—offer a pleasant respite from the federal bustle and some top-notch shops and art galleries.

THE MALL

The Mall is the heart of almost every visitor's trip to Washington. The front yard for nearly a dozen free museums, a picnicking park, a jogging path, and an outdoor stage for festivals, movies, musical performances, and fireworks, America's town green is the closest thing the capital has to a theme park.

TOP ATTRACTIONS

C **National Air and Space Museum.** This is the country's second most visited Fodor's Choice museum, attracting 9 million people annually to the world's largest col-★ lection of historic aircraft and spacecraft. Its 23 galleries tell the story of aviation from the earliest human attempts at flight to supersonic jets and spacecraft. Look up to see the world's most famous aircraft: hov-ering above are the *Wright 1903 Flyer,* which Wilbur Wright piloted over the sands of Kitty Hawk, North Carolina; Charles Lindbergh's *Spirit of St. Louis*; the X-1 rocket plane in which Chuck Yeager broke the sound barrier; and the Lockheed Vega that Amelia Earhart piloted in 1932. You can touch the displayed 4-billion-year-old slice of moon rock collected by *Apollo 17* astronauts.

Immerse yourself in space by taking in an IMAX film or a planetar-ium presentation. The movies—some in 3-D—employ swooping aerial scenes that make you feel as if you've left the ground and fascinat-ing high-definition footage taken in deep space. ■ TIP➔ **To make sure you get in, buy IMAX theater and planetarium tickets up to two weeks in advance.** ⊠ *Independence Ave. and 6th St. SW, The Mall* ☎ *202/357–1729; 202/357–1686 movie information; 202/357–1729 TDD* ⊕ *www.*

nasm.si.edu ⧉ *Free, IMAX $10, planetarium $8.50* ⊙ *Daily 10–5:30* Ⓜ *Smithsonian.*

National Gallery of Art, East Building. Architect I.M. Pei designed this dramatic structure, incorporating two interlocking spaces shaped like triangles. Despite its severe angularity, Pei's building is inviting. Inside, the sunlit atrium is dominated by a colorful 76-foot-long Alexander Calder mobile. Masterpieces from every famous name in 20th-century art—Pablo Picasso, Jackson Pollock, Piet Mondrian, Roy Lichtenstein, Joan Miró, Georgia O'Keeffe, and dozens of others—fill the galleries. The bold shapes and brilliant teals and fuschias of Henri Matisse's giant paper cutouts (on view only between 10 and 2 Monday through Saturday and 11 to 3 on Sunday) make them among the most innovative, important, and purely enjoyable works of modern art. ■ TIP➡ **The cheat sheet "What to See in An Hour" pinpoints 15 highlights of the East Building.** An underground concourse lined with gift shops, a café, and a cafeteria links to the West Building. ⊠ *Constitution Ave. between 3rd and 4th Sts. NW, The Mall* ☎ *202/737–4215; 202/842–6176 TDD* ⊕ *www.nga. gov* ⧉ *Free* ⊙ *Mon.–Sat. 10–5, Sun. 11–6* Ⓜ *Archives/Navy Memorial.*

National Gallery of Art, West Building. The two buildings of the National Gallery hold one of the world's foremost collections of paintings, sculptures, and graphics. The rotunda, with 24 marble columns surrounding a fountain topped with a statue of Mercury, sets the stage for the masterpieces on display in more than 100 galleries. ■ TIP➡ **There are many free docent-led tours every day, and a recorded tour of highlights is available for a $5 rental fee on the main floor adjacent to the rotunda.** The permanent collection includes *Ginevra de' Benci*, the only painting by Leonardo da Vinci on display in the Western Hemisphere; *The Adoration of the Magi* by Fra Angelico and Filippo Lippi; *Daniel in the Lions' Den* by Peter Paul Rubens; a self-portrait by Rembrandt; Salvador Dalí's *Last Supper*, and works by impressionists such as Edgar Degas, Claude Monet, Auguste Renoir, and Mary Cassatt. ⊠ *4th St. and Constitution Ave. NW, The Mall* ☎ *202/737–4215; 202/842–6176 TDD* ⊕ *www.nga. gov* ⧉ *Free* ⊙ *Mon.–Sat. 10–5, Sun. 11–6* Ⓜ *Archives/Navy Memorial.*

National Museum of Natural History. This is one of the world's great natural history museums, filled with the largest African bull elephant ever found, whale bones, fossils, and other natural delights—124 million specimens in all. A *Tyrannosaurus rex* and his dinner, a feisty *Triceratops*, are poised for action in the popular **Dinosaur Hall.** The IMAX theater shows two- and three-dimensional natural history films throughout the day. Buy advance tickets when you arrive, then tour the museum. The Discovery Room has hands-on research activities and workshops for kids. ⊠ *Constitution Ave. and 10th St. NW, The Mall* ☎ *202/633–1000; 202/357–1729 TDD* ⊕ *www.mnh.si.edu* ⧉ *Free, IMAX $8.50, Butterfly Pavilion $6, but free Tuesday* ⊙ *Museum daily 10–5:30* Ⓜ *Smithsonian or Federal Triangle.*

★ **National Museum of American History.** The 3 million artifacts in the country's largest history museum explore America's cultural, political, and scientific past, with holdings as diverse and iconic as Abraham Lincoln's top hat, Thomas Edison's lightbulbs, and Judy Garland's ruby slippers

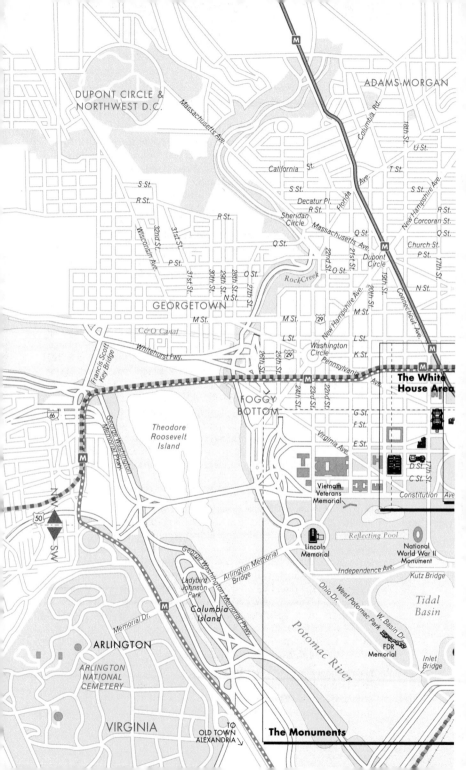

The Monuments

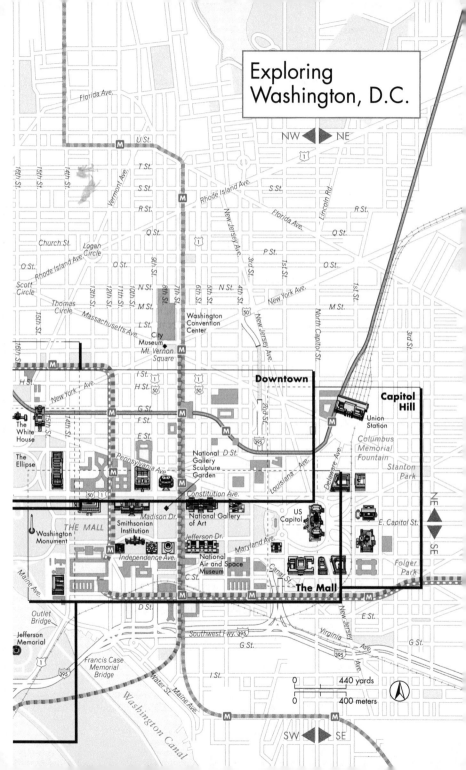

Exploring Washington, D.C.

NW ◄► NE

Florida Ave.

U St.

T St.

S St.

R St.

Rhode Island Ave.

S St.

Lincoln Rd.

R St.

Q St.

Church St.

Logan Circle

Q St.

New Jersey Ave.

P St.

3rd St.

1st St.

Florida Ave.

O St.

Rhode Island Ave.

O St.

9th St.

N St.

New York Ave.

M St.

Scott Circle

13th St.

12th St.

11th St.

10th St.

8th St.

7th St.

6th St.

5th St.

4th St.

N St.

M St.

North Capitol St.

3rd St.

Thomas Circle

Massachusetts Ave.

L St.

City Museum

Mt. Vernon Square

Washington Convention Center

50

2nd St.

Downtown

Capitol Hill

15th St.

I St.

H St.

H St.

50

50

Union Station

Columbus Memorial Fountain

New York Ave.

G St.

F St.

G St.

395

Stanton Park

The White House

14th St.

E St.

Pennsylvania Ave.

National Gallery Sculpture Garden

D St.

Louisiana Ave.

Delaware Ave.

NE

SE

The Ellipse

15th St.

Constitution Ave.

E. Capitol St.

Madison Dr.

National Gallery of Art

US Capitol

Folger Park

THE MALL

Smithsonian Institution

Jefferson Dr.

Maryland Ave.

Washington Monument

Independence Ave.

National Air and Space Museum

Canal St.

The Mall

16th St.

Maine Ave.

C St.

D St.

New Jersey Ave.

E St.

G St.

Outlet Bridge

Southwest Fwy. 395

Virginia Ave.

395

Jefferson Memorial

1

395

Francis Case Memorial Bridge

G St.

1 St.

0 ___ 440 yards

0 ___ 400 meters

Water St.

Maine Ave.

Washington Canal

SW ◄► SE

from *The Wizard of Oz*. The museum's nickname, "America's attic," is apt: its 20 exhibition galleries are crammed with unexpected items and stories from every nook and cranny of American history. ⊠ *Constitution Ave. and 14th St. NW, The Mall* ☎ *202/633–1000; 202/633–5285 TDD* ⊕ *www.americanhistory.si.edu* ▭ *Free* ⊙ *Daily 10–5:30* Ⓜ *Smithsonian or Federal Triangle.*

★ **United States Holocaust Memorial Museum.** A permanent exhibition tells the stories of the millions killed by the Nazis between 1933 and 1945, and it doesn't pull any punches. Upon arrival, you are issued an "identity card" that details the life of a holocaust victim. The museum recounts the Holocaust through documentary films, video- and audio-taped oral histories, and a collection that includes items such as a freight car like those used to transport Jews from Warsaw to the Treblinka death camp and the Star of David patches that Jews were made to wear. The museum is not recommended for children under 11, although Daniel's Story, a ground-floor exhibit not requiring tickets, is designed for children ages 8 and up. Timed-entry passes (distributed on a first-come, first-served basis at the 14th Street entrance starting at 10 or available in advance through the museum's Web site) are necessary for the permanent exhibition. ∎ **TIP**➜ **Allow extra time to enter the building in spring and summer, when long lines can form.** ⊠ *100 Raoul Wallenberg Pl. SW, enter from Raoul Wallenberg Pl. or 14th St. SW, The Mall* ☎ *202/488–0400; 800/400–9373 for tickets* ⊕ *www.ushmm.org* ▭ *Free* ⊙ *Daily 10–5:30* Ⓜ *Smithsonian.*

WORTH NOTING

Bureau of Engraving and Printing. Paper money has been printed here since 1914, when the bureau relocated from the redbrick-towered Auditors Building at the corner of 14th Street and Independence Avenue. You can only enter the bureau on the tours, which last about 35 minutes. From March through August, free same-day timed-entry tour passes are issued starting at 8 am at the Raoul Wallenberg Place SW ticket booth. ⊠ *14th and C Sts. SW, The Mall* ☎ *202/874–2330; 866/874–2330 tour information* ⊕ *www.moneyfactory.gov* ▭ *Free* ⊙ *Sept.–Mar., tours weekdays 9–2, visitor center weekdays 8:30–3:30; Apr.–Aug., tours weekdays 9–7, visitor center 8:30–7:30* Ⓜ *Smithsonian.*

The Freer and Sackler Galleries. Home to one of the world's finest collections of Asian art, the Smithsonian's **Freer Gallery of Art** was made possible by an endowment from Detroit industrialist Charles Lang Freer. Opened in 1923, the collection includes more than 27,000 works of art from the Far and Near East. Freer's friend James McNeill Whistler is represented in the vast collection. The Peacock Room, a blue-and-gold dining room decorated with painted leather, wood, and canvas, was designed by Whistler for a British shipping magnate. Nearby, the **Arthur M. Sackler Gallery** houses works from the Middle East and Southeast Asia. A lower-level exhibition gallery connects the two museums. ⊠ *1050 Independence Ave. SW, The Mall* ☎ *202/633–1000, 202/357–1729 TDD* ⊕ *www.asia.si.edu* ▭ *Free* ⊙ *Daily 10–5:30* Ⓜ *Smithsonian.*

Hirshhorn Museum and Sculpture Garden. Sculpture on the National Mall runs mostly to marble columns and dead presidents, but the Hirshhorn

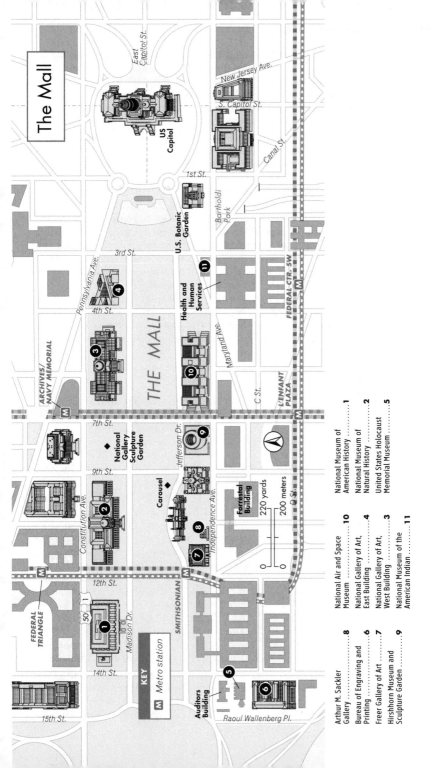

The Mall

US Capitol

East Capitol St.

New Jersey Ave.

S. Capitol St.

Canal St.

1st St.

Bartholdi Park

U.S. Botanic Garden

3rd St.

Pennsylvania Ave.

4th St.

ARCHIVES/ NAVY MEMORIAL

Health and Human Services

11

4

3

THE MALL

10

Maryland Ave.

FEDERAL CTR. SW

C St.

L'ENFANT PLAZA

7th St.

National Gallery Sculpture Garden

9th St.

Jefferson Dr.

9

Carousel

Constitution Ave.

2

Independence Ave.

Forrestal Building

Q St.

8

7

0   220 yards
0   200 meters

12th St.

SMITHSONIAN

FEDERAL TRIANGLE

Madison Dr.

1

50
1

14th St.

15th St.

Auditors Building

Raoul Wallenberg Pl.

5

6

KEY

M *Metro station*

Arthur M. Sackler Gallery **8**

Bureau of Engraving and Printing **6**

Freer Gallery of Art **7**

Hirshhorn Museum and Sculpture Garden **9**

National Air and Space Museum **10**

National Gallery of Art, East Building **4**

National Gallery of Art, West Building **3**

National Museum of the American Indian **11**

National Museum of American History **1**

National Museum of Natural History **2**

United States Holocaust Memorial Museum **5**

presents a bold alternative: a 32-foot-tall yellow cartoon brush-stroke sculpture by pop-art iconographer Roy Lichtenstein. Conceived as the nation's museum of modern and contemporary art, the Hirshhorn holds more than 11,500 works by masters like Pablo Picasso, Joan Miró, Piet Mondrian, Willem de Kooning, and Andy Warhol. These are displayed in a round 1974 poured-concrete building designed by Gordon Bunshaft. Dubbed the "Doughnut on the Mall" when it was built, it's now seen as a fitting home for contemporary art. ⊠ *Independence Ave. and 7th St. SW, The Mall* ☎ *202/633–1000; 202/633–8043 TDD* ⊕ *www. hirshorn.si.edu* ✉ *Free* ⊙ *Museum daily 10–5:30, sculpture garden daily 7:30–dusk* Ⓜ *Smithsonian or L'Enfant Plaza (Maryland Ave. exit).*

National Museum of the American Indian. The Smithsonian's newest museum is the first national museum devoted to Native American artifacts, presented from a Native American perspective. The undulating exterior, clad in pinkish-gold limestone from Minnesota, evokes natural rock formations shaped by wind and water. Inside, four floors of galleries cover 10,000 years of history of the thousands of native tribes of the western hemisphere. The exhibits are arranged to showcase specific tribes and themes, rather than a chronological history. Some visitors find this approach confusing, but touring with a guide can help bring the history and legends to life. ⊠ *4th St. and Independence Ave. SW, The Mall* ☎ *202/633–1000* ⊕ *www.americanindian.si.edu* ✉ *Free* ⊙ *Daily 10–5:30* Ⓜ *L'Enfant Plaza.*

THE MONUMENTS

Washington is a city of monuments. In the middle of traffic circles, on tiny slivers of park, and at street corners and intersections, statues, plaques, and simple blocks of marble honor the generals, politicians, poets, and statesmen who helped shape the nation. The monuments dedicated to the most famous Americans are west of the Mall on ground reclaimed from the marshy flats of the Potomac. This is also the location of Washington's greatest single display of cherry trees, gifts from Japan.

Franklin Delano Roosevelt Memorial. This 7½-acre memorial to the 32nd president employs waterfalls and reflection pools, four outdoor gallery rooms—one for each of Roosevelt's terms as president—and 10 bronze sculptures. The granite megaliths that connect the galleries are engraved with some of Roosevelt's most famous quotes. Although today the memorial is one of the most popular in the District, it's had its share of controversy. When unveiled, the monument did not depict Roosevelt with a wheelchair, which he used for the last 24 years of his life, including those in which he led the nation through World War II. However, this was the first D.C. memorial purposely designed to be wheelchair accessible, and the first to honor a First Lady, Eleanor Roosevelt. ⊠ *West side of Tidal Basin* ☎ *202/426–6841* ⊕ *www.nps.gov/ fdrm* ✉ *Free* ⊙ *24 hrs; staffed daily 8 am–midnight* Ⓜ *Smithsonian.*

Fodor's Choice ★ **Jefferson Memorial.** The monument honoring the third president of the United States was modeled by John Russell Pope after a style that Jefferson had used himself when he designed the University of Virginia. In the 1930s Congress decided that Jefferson deserved a monument positioned

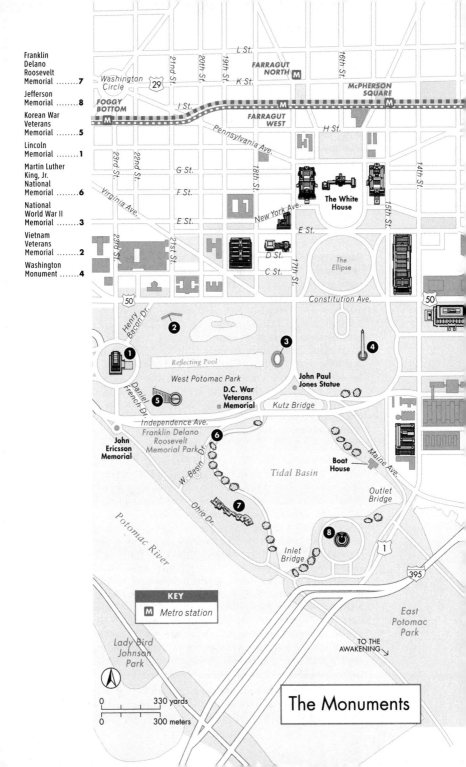

Franklin Delano Roosevelt Memorial 7

Jefferson Memorial 8

Korean War Veterans Memorial 5

Lincoln Memorial 1

Martin Luther King, Jr. National Memorial 6

National World War II Memorial 3

Vietnam Veterans Memorial 2

Washington Monument 4

The Monuments

KEY

🅼 Metro station

0   330 yards
0   300 meters

as prominently as those in honor of Washington and Lincoln, so workers scooped and moved tons of river bottom to create dry land on this spot directly south of the White House. Dedicated in 1943, it houses a statue of Jefferson, and its walls are lined with inscriptions based on the Declaration of Independence and his other writings. One of the best views of the White House can be seen from its steps. ⊠ *Tidal Basin, south bank* ☎ *202/426–6841* ⊕ *www.nps.gov/thje* ✉ *Free* ⊙ *Daily 8 am–midnight* Ⓜ *Smithsonian.*

> **CAPITAL FACTS**
>
> In 2001, after protest by disability advocate groups, Congress approved adding a bronze statue to the FDR memorial showing the president in his wheelchair. When it was added to the entrance of the memorial in 2001, it became the first statue to show a world leader in a wheelchair.

Korean War Veterans Memorial. This memorial to the 1.5 million United States men and women who served in the Korean War (1950–53) highlights the high cost of freedom. Nearly 37,000 Americans were killed on the Korean peninsula, 8,000 were missing in action, and more than 103,000 were wounded. Nineteen oversize stainless-steel soldiers toil through a rugged triangular terrain toward an American flag; look beneath the helmets to see their weary faces. The reflection in the polished black granite wall to their right doubles their number to 38, symbolic of the 38th parallel, the latitude established as the border between North and South Korea in 1953, as well as the 38 months of the war. Etched with the faces of 2,400 unnamed servicemen and servicewomen, the wall says simply, "Freedom is not free." ⊠ *West end of Mall at Daniel French Dr. and Independence Ave.* ☎ *202/426–6841* ⊕ *www.nps.gov/kwvm* ✉ *Free* ⊙ *24 hrs; staffed daily 8 am–midnight* Ⓜ *Foggy Bottom.*

Fodor'sChoice
★
Lincoln Memorial. Henry Bacon chose a Greek Doric style for this white Colorado-marble temple to Lincoln because he felt that a great defender of democracy should be memorialized in the style found in the birthplace of democracy. Although detractors thought it inappropriate that the humble president be honored with what amounts to a modified but grandiose Greek temple, this memorial has become one of the nation's most recognizable icons. Its powerful symbolism makes it a popular gathering place: In its shadow, Americans marched for integrated schools in 1958, rallied for an end to the Vietnam War in 1967, and laid wreaths in a ceremony honoring the Iranian hostages in 1979. It may be best known, though, as the site of Martin Luther King Jr.'s "I Have a Dream" speech. Daniel Chester French's 19-foot-high somber statue of the seated president, in the center of the memorial, is composed of 28 interlocking pieces of Georgia marble. ■TIP➔ **The best time to see the memorial itself is at night, when spotlights illuminate the facade.** ⊠ *West end of Mall* ☎ *202/426–6841* ⊕ *www.nps.gov/linc* ✉ *Free* ⊙ *24 hrs; staffed daily 8 am–midnight* Ⓜ *Foggy Bottom.*

Martin Luther King Jr. National Memorial. Located strategically between the Lincoln and Jefferson memorials and adjacent to the FDR Memorial, the crescent-shaped King Memorial sits on a 4-acre site on the curved

D.C.'s Statues and Stories

Washington, D.C., has more equestrian statues than any other city in the nation; stone-and-metal men atop steeds are everywhere, watching the city from traffic circles, squares, and parks. The statues proliferated in the 19th century, when Civil War generals who went into politics seemed virtually assured of this legacy—regardless of their success in either endeavor.

Standing in Lafayette Square across from the White House, the statue of President Andrew Jackson is by sculptor Clark Mills, who had never seen an equestrian statue, much less created one. To get the proportions of the rearing horse correct, Mills had a horse trained to remain in an upright position so he could study the anatomy of its muscles.

Directly up 16th Street from Lafayette Square at Massachusetts and Rhode Island avenues is a statue of Lt. Gen. Winfield Scott, in the circle bearing his name. He was to be shown atop his favorite mount, a lightweight mare, but right before the statue was cast, some of Scott's descendants decided that a stallion would be a more-appropriate horse for him to ride into battle upon (regardless of historical accuracy). The sculptor, H. K. Brown, was forced to give the horse a last-minute sex change.

Farther up Massachusetts Avenue, at 23rd Street, is a statue of Civil War Gen. Philip Henry Sheridan, also in a circle bearing his name. The piece is by Gutzon Borglum, who completed more than 170 public statues, including the head of Abraham Lincoln in the Capitol Rotunda, and whose final work was Mount Rushmore's presidential faces. The statue of the leader riding Rienzi (who was later renamed Winchester for Sheridan's victory there) stands in the type of circle Pierre-Charles L'Enfant envisioned in his plan for Washington—a small, formal park where avenues come together surrounded by isolated houses and buildings.

The statue of Gen. William Tecumseh Sherman at 15th Street and Treasury Place is often overlooked—in summer, the general's head is obscured by trees, and all year long he presents his back and his mount's hindquarters to pedestrians. He's positioned where he is thought to have stood while reviewing the Union troops on their victorious return from Georgia. The bar at the Hotel Washington, which affords some of the best views of the city, is also the place for a good look at Sherman.

A long-held theory says that the number of raised legs on the mount of an equestrian statue reveals how the rider died: one leg raised means the rider died of wounds sustained in battle, two legs raised means the rider died in battle, and four feet on the ground means the rider died of natural causes. None of this is true, though, and of the more than 30 equestrian statues in Washington, only about a third (including Scott, Sheridan, and Sherman, but not Jackson) follow this "code."

—Lisa Greaves

bank of the Tidal Basin. Visitors enter through a center walkway cut out of a huge boulder, the Mountain of Despair. From the Mountain, the Stone of Hope is visible. The symbolism of the mountain and stone are explained by King's words: "With this faith, we will be able to hew out of the mountain of

> **CAPITAL FACTS**
>
> The Jefferson Memorial was dubbed "Jefferson's muffin"; critics lambasted the design as outdated and too similar to that of the Lincoln Memorial.

despair a stone of hope." The centerpiece was carved by Chinese sculptor Lei Yixin, whose design was chosen from more than 900 entries in an international competition. Fittingly, Yixin first read about King's "I Have a Dream" speech at age 10 while visiting the Lincoln Memorial. The 28-foot tall granite boulder includes Lei's rendering of King, whose eyes meet Jefferson's gaze. The themes of democracy, justice, hope, and love are reflected through more than a dozen quotes from King's speeches, sermons, and writings. At press time the memorial was set to open in summer of 2011, but there may be delays. ⊠ *401 F St. NW* ☎ *202/737–5420 or 888/484–3373* ⊕ *www.mlkmemorial.org* ☞ *Free* ☼ *24 hrs; staffed daily 8 am–midnight* Ⓜ *Smithsonian.*

National World War II Memorial. This somber monument honors the 16 million Americans who served in the armed forces, the more than 400,000 who died, and all who supported the war effort at home. An imposing circle of 56 granite pillars, each bearing a bronze wreath, represents the U.S. states and territories of 1941–45. Four bronze eagles, a bronze garland, and two 43-foot-tall arches inscribed with "Atlantic" and "Pacific" surround the large circular plaza. The roar of the water comes from the Rainbow Pool, here since the 1920s but recently renovated as the centerpiece of the memorial. The Field of Stars, a wall of 4,000 gold stars, commemorates the more than 400,000 Americans who lost their lives in the war. ⊠ *17th St. at east side of Washington Monument* ☎ *202/426–6841* ⊕ *www.wwiimemorial.com* ☞ *Free* ☼ *24 hrs* Ⓜ *Smithsonian.*

Fodor's Choice ★   **Vietnam Veterans Memorial.** "The Wall," as it's commonly called, is one of the most visited sites in Washington. The names of more than 58,000 Americans who died in the Vietnam War are etched in its black granite panels, creating a somber, dignified, and powerful memorial. It was conceived by Jan Scruggs, a former infantry corporal who served in Vietnam, and designed by Maya Lin, then a 21-year-old architecture student at Yale. The names of more than 58,000 Americans are etched on the memorial's black granite panels, which reflect the sky, the trees, and the faces of those looking for the names of friends or relatives who died in the war. For help in finding a name, ask a ranger at the blue-and-white hut near the entrance. Thousands of offerings are left at the wall each year: letters, flowers, medals, uniforms, snapshots. ⊠ *Constitution Gardens, 23rd St. and Constitution Ave. NW* ☎ *202/426–6841* ⊕ *www.nps. gov/vive* ☞ *Free* ☼ *24 hrs; staffed daily 8 am–midnight* Ⓜ *Foggy Bottom.*

☺ Fodor's Choice ★   **Washington Monument.** At the western end of the Mall, the 555-foot, 5-inch Washington Monument, the world's tallest masonry structure, punctuates the capital like a huge exclamation point. The cornerstone was laid in 1848, but building stopped in 1854 for 20 years, in part due to members of the anti-Catholic Know-Nothing party stealing and destroying a block donated by Pope Pius IX. During this period, herds of cattle grazed on the grounds of the half-finished monument. A clearly visible ring about a third of the way up the

> **CAPITAL FACTS**
>
> The White House wasn't ready for its first occupant, John Adams, the second U.S. president, until 1800; George Washington, who seems to have slept everywhere else, never stayed here.

obelisk testifies to this unfortunate stage of the monument's history: the stone used for the second phase of construction came from a different stratum. The view from the top takes in most of the District and parts of Maryland and Virginia. ■**TIP→** A limited number of timed-entrance tickets are available each morning at the kiosk on 15th Street. Tickets are also available online. ⊠ *Constitution Ave. and 15th St. NW* ☎ *202/426–6841; 877/444–6777 for advance tickets* ⊕ *www.nps.gov/ wamo; www.recreation.gov for advance tickets* ⊠ *Free; $1.50 service fee per advance ticket* ⊙ *Daily 9–5* Ⓜ *Smithsonian.*

THE WHITE HOUSE AREA

In a world full of recognizable images, few are better known than the whitewashed, 132-room mansion at 1600 Pennsylvania Avenue. The residence of perhaps the single most powerful person on the planet, the White House has an awesome majesty, having been the home of every U.S. president but George Washington. The president's neighborhood includes some of the city's oldest houses.

TOP ATTRACTIONS

Fodor'sChoice **White House.** Irishman James Hoban's plan, based on the Georgian
★ design of Leinster Hall in Dublin and of other Irish country houses, was selected in a 1792 contest. The building has undergone many structural changes since then. Major renovations occurred after the British burned the House in 1814 and a piano almost broke through the second-story floor during President Truman's Administration because of the House's deteriorating condition. Truman had the entire structure gutted and restored, adding a second-story porch to the south portico.

■**TIP→ To see the White House you need to contact your representative or senator. To visit in spring or summer, you should make your request about six months in advance.** The self-guided tour includes several rooms on the ground floor and, on the State Floor, the large white-and-gold **East Room,** the site of presidential social events. In 1814 Dolley Madison saved the room's full-length portrait of George Washington from torch-carrying British soldiers by cutting it from its frame, rolling it up, and spiriting it out of the White House. The **State Dining Room,** second in size only to the East Room, is dominated by G. P. A. Healy's portrait of Abraham Lincoln, painted after the president's death.

Since White House tours are self-guided, it's a good idea to come to the **White House Visitor Center** (⊠ *Entrance: Department of Commerce's Baldrige Hall, E St. between 14th and 15th Sts.* ☎ *202/208–1631,*

Corcoran
Gallery of Art **6**

Decatur
House **4**

Lafayette
Square **3**

Renwick
Gallery **5**

White House **2**

White House
Visitor Center **1**

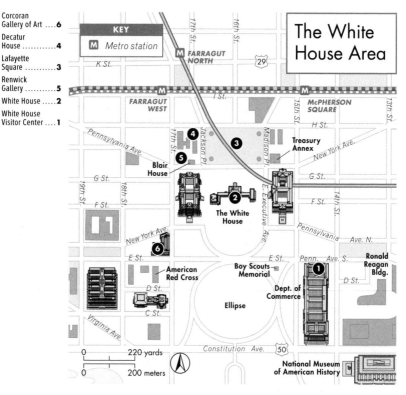

202/456–7041 24-hr information line ⊕ www.nps.gov ☉ Daily 7:30–4), first to catch the photographs, artifacts, and videos that relate to the White House's construction, decor, and residents. ✉ *1600 Pennsylvania Ave. NW ☏ 202/208–1631; 202/456–7041 24-hr info line ⊕ www.whitehouse.gov 🎫 Free; reservations required ☉ Tours Tues.–Sat. 7:30–12:30 Ⓜ Federal Triangle, Metro Center, or McPherson Sq.*

WORTH NOTING

Corcoran Gallery of Art. The Corcoran looks like a museum and acts like a gallery, blending classic elegance and experimental edge. Washington's first art museum, housed in a Beaux-Arts marble mansion, has an important collection of 18th-, 19th-, and 20th-century European and American art. Masterworks by the great earlier American artists, including John Copley, Gilbert Stuart, Rembrandt Peale, Mary Cassatt, and John Singer Sargent, are in constant rotation. As the parent of the Corcoran School of Art, the museum is also devoted to showcasing cutting-edge contemporary art, from established superstars to undiscovered talents. You're sure to see something contemporary and fun: mixed-media, sound, and video art transforming a room, or even live performance art. Purchase advance tickets for special exhibitions, as they tend to be popular. ✉ *500 17th St. NW, White House area ☏ 202/639–1700 ⊕ www.corcoran.org 🎫 $10; admission for special* *exhibitions, $12–$35* ⊙ *Mon., Wed., Fri., and weekends 10–5; Thurs. 10–9* Ⓜ *Farragut W or Farragut N.*

Decatur House. This redbrick Federal-style building designed by Benjamin Latrobe for naval hero Stephen Decatur was the first private residence on Lafayette Square. Occupants of the house have included Henry Clay, Martin Van Buren, and the Beales, a prominent western family. The house, now operated by the National Trust for Historic Preservation, has a first floor furnished as it was in Decatur's time and a second floor done in the Victorian style favored by the Beales. Many of the row houses along Jackson Place date from the pre–Civil War or Victorian periods; even the more-modern additions, though—such as those at 718 and 726—are designed to blend in with their more historic neighbors. ⊠ *748 Jackson Pl. NW, White House area,* ☎ *202/842–0920* ⊕ *www.decaturhouse.org* 🎫 *$5* ⊙ *Mon.–Sat. 10–5, Sun. noon–4; tours every hr at quarter past the hr* Ⓜ *Farragut W.*

Lafayette Square. With such an important resident across the street, the National Capital Region's National Park Service gardeners lavish extra attention on this square's trees and flower beds. During the construction of the White House, workers' huts and a brick kiln were set up, and soon residences began popping up around the square, including the Blair House, which is now used by heads of state visiting Washington. Soldiers camped in the square during the War of 1812 and the Civil War, turning it both times into a muddy pit. Today protesters set their placards up in Lafayette Square.

In the center of the park is a large **statue of Andrew Jackson.** Erected in 1853 and cast from bronze cannons that Jackson captured during the War of 1812, this was the second equestrian statue made in America. The other statues in the park are of foreign-born soldiers who helped in America's fight for independence. In the southeast corner is the park's namesake, the **Marquis de Lafayette,** the young French nobleman who came to America to fight in the Revolution. ⊠ *Bounded by Pennsylvania Ave., Madison Pl., H St., and Jackson Pl., White House area* Ⓜ *McPherson Sq.*

QUICK BITES One block north of Pershing Park is the **W Hotel** (⊠ *515 15th St. NW, White House area* ☎ *202/661–2400* ⊕ *www.wwashingtondc.com* Ⓜ *Metro Center*), where the view from the POV Roof Terrace is one of the best in the city. Tapas are served, as are all manner of libations.

Renwick Gallery. The Renwick Gallery is a luscious French Second Empire–style mansion across the street from the White House. Designed by James Renwick in 1859 to hold the art collection of Washington merchant and banker William Wilson Corcoran, the building today is a branch of Smithsonian American Art Museum, housing the museum's collection of decorative art and crafts. Check out Kim Schahman's 1955 *Bureau of Bureaucracy*: a beautifully crafted wooden cabinet full of cupboards to nowhere, bottomless drawers, drawers within drawers, hidden compartments, and more. This wonderful metaphor for the labyrinthine workings of government is appropriately set in a room with a view to the Eisenhower Executive Office Building. ⊠ *Pennsylvania Ave. at 17th St.*

NW, White House area ☎ *202/633–2850; 202/633–5285 TDD* ⊕ *www.americanart.si.edu* ✉ *Free* ☉ *Daily 10–5:30* Ⓜ *Farragut W.*

CAPITOL HILL

The people who live and work on "the Hill" do so in the shadow of the edifice that lends the neighborhood its name: the gleaming white Capitol. More than just the center of government, however, the Hill also includes charming residential blocks lined with Victorian row houses and a fine assortment of restaurants, bars, and shops.

TOP ATTRACTIONS

🕙 **Capitol.** The Capitol's cornerstone was laid by George Washington in a Masonic ceremony on September 18, 1793. The "Congress House" grew slowly and suffered a grave setback on August 24, 1814, when British troops marched on Washington and set fire to the Capitol, the White House, and numerous other government buildings. In 1855, to keep the scale correct after the edifice was elongated to accommodate a growing government, work began on a taller, cast-iron dome. President Lincoln was criticized for continuing this expensive project while the country was in the throes of the Civil War, but he called the construction "a sign we intend the Union shall go on." This twin-shell dome, a marvel of 19th-century engineering, rises 285 feet above the ground and weighs 4,500 tons. It expands and contracts up to 4 inches a day, depending on the outside temperature.

Fodor's Choice ★

Tours start under the center of the **Rotunda's** dome, at the center of which is Constantino Brumidi's 1865 fresco, *Apotheosis of Washington.* South of the Rotunda is **Statuary Hall,** once the legislative chamber of the House of Representatives. The room has an architectural quirk that maddened early legislators: a slight whisper uttered on one side of the hall can be heard on the other. To the north, on the Senate side, is the chamber once used by the Supreme Court, and, above it, the splendid Old Senate Chamber, both of which have been restored.

The **Capitol Visitor Center,** a $600-million subterranean education and information area beneath the east lawn of the Capitol, opened in December 2008. You can now register for tickets online or get them directly from the Center where tours will start. Free gallery passes to watch the House or Senate in session can be obtained only from your representative's or senator's office. Expect at least a 30-minute wait going through security when you enter the Capitol. Bags can be no larger than 14 inches wide, 13 inches tall, and 4 inches deep, and other possessions you can bring into the building are strictly limited. (The full list of prohibited items is posted online.) There are no facilities for checking personal belongings. ■ TIP➔ **Security measures may change, so call before your visit.** ✉ *East end of Mall, Capitol Hill* ☎ *202/226–8000* ⊕ *www.visitthecapitol.gov* ✉ *Free* ☉ *Tours 8:30–4:30* Ⓜ *Capitol S or Union Station.*

Supreme Court Building. It wasn't until 1935 that the Supreme Court got its own building: a white-marble temple with twin rows of Corinthian columns designed by Cass Gilbert. Before then, the justices had been moved around to various rooms in the Capitol; for a while they even met in a tavern. The Supreme Court convenes on the first Monday in October and remains in session until it has heard all of its cases and handed down all of its decisions (usually the end of June). On Monday through Wednesday of two weeks in each month, the justices hear oral arguments in the velvet-swathed court chamber. Visitors who want to listen can choose to wait in either of two lines. One, the "three- to five-minute" line, shuttles you through, giving you a quick impression of the court at work. If you choose the other, and you'd like to stay for the whole show, it's best to be in line by 8:30 am. The *Washington Post* carries a daily listing of what cases the court will hear. ⊠ *One 1st St. NE, Capitol Hill* ☎ *202/479–3000* ⊕ *www.supremecourtus.gov* ☜ *Free* ☉ *Weekdays 9–4:30; court in session Oct.–June* Ⓜ *Union Station or Capitol S.*

WORTH NOTING

Library of Congress. Provisions for a library to serve members of Congress were originally made in 1800, when the government set aside $5,000 to purchase books that legislators might need to consult. This small collection was housed in the Capitol but was destroyed in 1814, when the British burned the city. Thomas Jefferson, then in retirement at Monticello, offered his personal library as a replacement, noting that "there is, in fact, no subject to which a Member of Congress may not have occasion to refer." Jefferson's collection of 6,487 books laid the foundation for the great national library. The largest library in the world now has almost 130 million items—2.7 million recordings, 12 million photographs, 4.8 million maps, and 58 million manuscripts—on approximately 530 mi of bookshelves.

Built in 1897, the copper-dome **Thomas Jefferson Building**, based on the Paris Opera House, is the oldest of the three that make up the library. The building's octagonal Main Reading Room contains a grand central desk surrounded by mahogany readers' tables under a 160-foot-high domed ceiling. Computer terminals have replaced card catalogs, but books are still retrieved and dispensed the same way: readers (18 years or older) hand request slips to librarians and wait patiently for their materials to be delivered. Items from the library's collection—which includes one of only three perfect Gutenberg Bibles in the world—are on display in the Jefferson Building's second-floor Southwest Gallery and Pavilion. ■ TIP→ To even begin to come to grips with the scope and grandeur of the library, taking one of the free hourly tours is highly recommended. Well-informed docents can bring you into spaces—such as the glassed-in observation deck over the Main Reading Room—that are closed to solo visitors. ⊠ *Jefferson Bldg., 1st St. and Independence Ave. SE, Capitol Hill* ☎ *202/707–9779* ⊕ *www.loc.gov* ☜ *Free* ☉ *Mon.–Sat. 8:30–4:30; reading room hrs may extend later. Free tours Mon.–Sat. at 10:30, 11:30, 1:30, and 2:30, and weekdays at 3:30* Ⓜ *Capitol S.*

QUICK BITES

True to its name, **The Hawk 'n' Dove** (⊠ *329 Pennsylvania Ave. SE, Capitol Hill,* ☎ *202/543–3300* Ⓜ *Capitol South*) may well be the best place in town to overhear aides talk partisan politics over pints. The menu is long on the likes of pastrami sandwiches and old-fashioned chipped beef on toast.

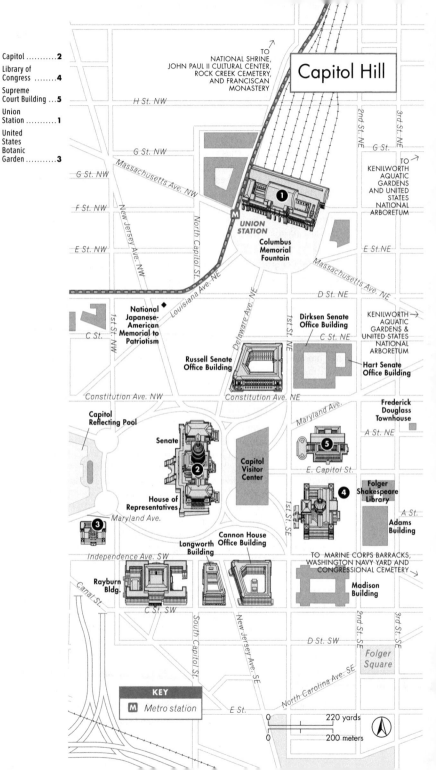

Capitol Hill

Capitol **2**

Library of
Congress **4**

Supreme
Court Building ...**5**

Union
Station **1**

United
States
Botanic
Garden **3**

TO
NATIONAL SHRINE,
JOHN PAUL II CULTURAL CENTER,
ROCK CREEK CEMETERY,
AND FRANCISCAN
MONASTERY

H St. NW

G St. NW

G St. NW

Massachusetts Ave. NW

F St. NW

E St. NW

M UNION
STATION

Columbus
Memorial
Fountain

New Jersey Ave. NW

North Capitol St.

❶

2nd St. NE

3rd St. NE

G St.

TO
KENILWORTH
AQUATIC
GARDENS
AND UNITED
STATES
NATIONAL
ARBORETUM

E St. NE

Massachusetts Ave. NE

D St. NE

National
Japanese-
American
Memorial to
Patriotism

1st St.

C St.

Louisiana Ave. NE

Delaware Ave. NE

Russell Senate
Office Building

1st St. NE

Dirksen Senate
Office Building

C St. NE

KENILWORTH →
AQUATIC
GARDENS &
UNITED STATES
NATIONAL
ARBORETUM

Hart Senate
Office Building

Constitution Ave. NW

Constitution Ave. NE

Frederick
Douglass
Townhouse

Capitol
Reflecting Pool

Senate

❷

House of
Representatives

Capitol
Visitor
Center

Maryland Ave.

❸

Maryland Ave.

1st St. SE

❺

E. Capitol St.

A St. NE

❹

Folger
Shakespeare
Library

A St.

Adams
Building

Independence Ave. SW

Longworth
Building

Cannon House
Office Building

TO MARINE CORPS BARRACKS,
WASHINGTON NAVY YARD AND
CONGRESSIONAL CEMETERY →

Rayburn
Bldg.

Canal St.

C St. SW

South Capitol St.

New Jersey Ave. SE

Madison
Building

2nd St. SE

3rd St. SE

D St. SW

Folger
Square

North Carolina Ave. SE

E St.

0   220 yards

0   200 meters

CLOSE UP

L'Enfant, D.C.'s Architect

The life of Pierre-Charles L'Enfant, architect of the city of Washington, has all the elements of a television miniseries: a handsome and idealistic 22-year-old Parisian volunteers in the American war for independence; he rises to the rank of major of engineers and is popular with fellow officers (and their wives); he becomes the toast-of-the-town architect in New York City and is selected by President George Washington to plan the new Federal City; he is fired amid controversy and dies bitter and broke; he is vindicated posthumously.

L'Enfant was educated as an architect and engineer in France, and at least one of his teachers profoundly influenced his career and, ultimately, his plan for Washington: he studied landscape architecture with André LeNotre, who designed the gardens at Versailles. Congress voted in 1785 to create a permanent Federal City, and in 1789 L'Enfant wrote to George Washington with an offer to create a capital "magnificent enough to grace a great nation." He got the job, and arrived in Washington in 1791 to survey the land.

L'Enfant's 1791 plan borrowed much from Versailles, including ceremonial circles and squares, a grid pattern of streets, and broad, diagonal avenues. He described Jenkins Hill, the gentle rise on which he intended to erect the "Congress House," as "a pedestal waiting for a monument." He envisioned the area west of the Congress House (what we now know as the Mall) as a "Grand Avenue, 400 feet in breadth, and about a mile in length, bordered with gardens, ending in a slope from the houses on each side."

Pennsylvania Avenue was to be a broad, uninterrupted line running from the Capitol to the site chosen for the Executive Mansion, but the construction of the Treasury Building in 1836 ruined this straight sight line. The area just north of the White House (basically the president's front yard) was to be part of "President's Park," but Thomas Jefferson, concerned that large, landscaped White House grounds weren't befitting a democratic country, ordered that the area be turned into a public park (now Lafayette Park).

Though skilled at city planning, headstrong L'Enfant had trouble with the game of politics. Things went slightly awry early on when L'Enfant had difficulty with the engravers of the city plan, they got worse when he expressed his resentment at dealing with Secretary of State Thomas Jefferson rather than the president, and they hit rock bottom when he enraged the city commissioners by tearing down a manor house being constructed where he had planned a street. The house belonged to Daniel Carroll—one of the commissioners. Only 11 months after his hire, L'Enfant was let go. He continued to work as an architect, but when he died in 1825 he was poor and bitter, feeling he hadn't been recognized for his genius. His contributions to the city were finally recognized, though, when in 1909, amid much ceremony, his body was moved from his original burial site in Maryland to Arlington Cemetery at the request of the Washington, D.C., board of commissioners.

Union Station. Chicago architect and commission member Daniel H. Burnham patterned Washington's train depot after the Roman Baths of Diocletian (AD 305). In its heyday, during World War II, more than 200,000 people passed through the building daily. By the 1960s, however, the decline in train travel had turned the station into an expensive white-marble elephant, and by 1981 rain was pouring in through its neglected roof. The Union Station you see today is the result of a restoration, completed in 1988, intended to begin a revival of Washington's east end. Between train travelers and visitors to the shops and restaurants, 70,000 people a day pass through the Beaux-Arts building. The jewel of the structure is the main waiting room, with a 96-foot-high coffered ceiling inlaid with 8 pounds of gold leaf. Forty-six statues of Roman legionnaires, one for each state in the Union when the station was completed, ring the grand room. ⊠ *50 Massachusetts Ave. NE, Capitol Hill* ☎ *202/289–1908* ⊕ *www.unionstationdc.com* Ⓜ *Union Station.*

QUICK BITES

On Union Station's lower level are more than 20 food stalls with everything from pizza to sushi.

United States Botanic Garden. Established by Congress in 1820, this is the oldest botanic garden in North America. The recently renovated glass building, a Victorian design, sits at the foot of Capitol Hill, in the shadow of the Capitol building. It offers an escape from the stone and marble federal office buildings that surround it; inside are exotic rain-forest species, desert flora, and trees from all parts of the world. A special treat is the extensive collection of rare and unusual orchids. Walkways suspended 24 feet above the ground provide a fascinating view of the plants. A relatively new addition is the National Garden, which emphasizes educational exhibits. ⊠ *1st St. and Maryland Ave. SW, Capitol Hill* ☎ *202/225–8333* ⊕ *www.usbg.gov* 🎫 *Free* ☉ *Daily 10–5; National Garden closes at 7* Ⓜ *Federal Center SW.*

DOWNTOWN

In recent years developers have rediscovered the "East End," which had been a hole in the city since riots rocked the capital in 1968 after the assassination of Martin Luther King Jr. Buildings are now being torn down, built up, and remodeled at an amazing pace. **Penn Quarter,** the neighborhood immediately surrounding the once down-at-the-heels stretch of Pennsylvania Avenue, has blossomed into one of the hottest addresses in town for nightlife and culture. With its proximity to the venerable Ford's Theatre and the National Theater, as well as the acclaimed progressive Woolly Mammoth Theatre and the prestigious Shakespeare Theatre, the neighborhood can rightfully claim to be Washington's own theater district. Meanwhile, new galleries, restaurants, and other cultural hot spots are constantly appearing.

TOP ATTRACTIONS

International Spy Museum. It's believed that there are more spies in Washington than in any other city in the world, making it a fitting home for this museum, which displays the world's largest collection of spy

artifacts. There's a mix of flash and fun, with toys used by actual opera-
tives as well as James Bond's Aston Martin and tales of celebrity spies
like singer Josephine Baker, chef Julia Child, and actress Marlene Diet-
rich. "Operation Spy," a one-hour "immersive experience" works like
a live-action game, dropping you in the middle of a high-stakes foreign
intelligence mission. Advance tickets are recommended, particularly
in spring and summer. ⊠ *800 F St. NW, East End* ☎ *202/393–7798*
⊕ *www.spymuseum.org* ⌨ *$18; Operation Spy, $14; combination
admission $30* ⊙ *Apr.–Oct., daily 9–8; Nov.–Mar., daily 10–6* Ⓜ *Gal-
lery Pl./Chinatown.*

National Archives. The National Archives are at once monument,
museum, and the nation's memory. Headquartered in a grand marble
edifice on Constitution Avenue, the agency is charged with preserving
and archiving the most historically important U.S. government records.
Its 8 billion paper records and 4 billion electronic records date back to
1775. The star attractions are the Declaration of Independence, Constitution, and Bill of Rights. These are housed in the Archives' cathedral-
like rotunda, each on a marble platform, encased in bulletproof glass,
and floating in pressurized helium, which protects the irreplaceable
documents. In the permanent exhibit you can find anything from the
Emancipation Proclamation to the first issue of *Mad* magazine. Reservations are recommended. ⊠ *Constitution Ave. between 7th and 9th
Sts., The Mall* ☎ *202/501–5000; 202/501–5205 tours* ⊕ *www.nara.
gov* ⌨ *Free* ⊙ *Mar. 15–Labor Day, daily 10–7, Labor Day–Mar. 14,
daily 10–5:30; tours weekdays at 10:15 and 1:15* Ⓜ *Archives/Navy
Memorial.*

National Portrait Gallery. Devoted to the intersection of art, biography,
and history, this collection houses nearly 20,000 images of men and
women who have shaped U.S. history. The gallery has the only complete
collection of presidential portraits outside the White House, starting
with Gilbert Stuart's iconic "Lansdowne" portrait of George Washington. Interesting perspectives include the plaster cast of Abraham Lincoln's head and hands; political cartoonist Pat Oliphant's sculpture of
George H.W. Bush bowling; and Shepard Fairey's red, white, and blue
portrait of President Barack Obama. From a moving bronze sculpture
of Martin Luther King Jr. to Andy Warhol's Marilyn Monroe prints, to
Madonna's 1985 *Time* magazine cover, the third-floor gallery offers a
vibrant and colorful tour of the people who shaped the today's culture.
The building itself, built between 1836 and 1863, is considered one of
the country's finest examples of Greek Revival architecture. ⊠ *8th and
F Sts. NW, East End* ☎ *202/633–8300; 202/357–1729 TDD* ⊕ *www.
npg.si.edu* ⌨ *Free* ⊙ *Daily 11:30–7* Ⓜ *Gallery Pl./Chinatown.*

★ **Newseum.** This landmark $450 million glass-and-silver structure is on
Pennsylvania Avenue, set smack between the White House and the
Capitol: a fitting location for a museum devoted to the First Amendment and the essential role of a free press in maintaining democracy. The
90-foot-high media-saturated atrium is overlooked by a giant breaking-
news screen and a news helicopter suspended overhead. From there,
14 galleries display 500 years of the history of news, including exhibits
on the First Amendment, global news, and the way radio, television,

and especially the Internet have transformed how we find out about the world. Live news programs—from presidential debates to town hall meetings—are regularly filmed in the museum's central live news studio, and audiences are often welcome to watch. ■ TIP→ The best way to tour the museum is by viewing the orientation films on the ground floor, then taking the elevator up to the top floor and working your way down. ⊠ 555 Pennsylvania Ave. NW, East End ☎ 888/639–7386 ⊕ www.newseum. org ⌨ $20 ⊙ Daily 9–5 Ⓜ Archives/Navy Memorial.

WORTH NOTING

Ford's Theatre. On the night of April 14, 1865, during a performance of Our American Cousin, John Wilkes Booth entered the state box at this successful music hall and shot Abraham Lincoln in the back of the head. The stricken president was carried across the street to the house of tailor William Petersen and died the next morning. The Ford's Theatre Society launched a two-year, $40-million campaign to transform the theater and its basement museum of Lincoln artifacts into a block-long, Lincoln-centered cultural campus commemorating the president. Opened in early 2009, it includes the renovated theater, the expanded museum, and the historically restored home of William Peterson, where Lincoln died. ■ TIP→ Visits require a free, timed-entry ticket, available at the box office or online. ⊠ Ford's Theatre, 511 10th St. NW Petersen House, 516 10th St. NW, East End ☎ 202/426–6924 ⊕ www.fordstheatre.org ⌨ Free ⊙ Daily 9–5 Ⓜ Metro Center or Gallery Pl.

National Building Museum. The open interior of this mammoth redbrick edifice is one of the city's great spaces, and has been the site of many inaugural balls. The eight central Corinthian columns, each made of brick covered with plaster, are among the largest in the world, rising to a height of 75 feet. The museum is devoted to architecture, design, landscaping, and urban planning. The permanent exhibit "Washington: Symbol and City" tells the story of the backwater that eventually became the nation's capital (beginning by debunking the myth that Washington was built on a swamp!). Among the most popular permanent exhibits is the Building Zone, where kids ages two to six can get a hands-on introduction to building by constructing a tower, exploring a kid-size playhouse, or playing with bulldozers and construction trucks. Tours are offered daily at 11:30, 12:30, and 1:30. ⊠ 401 F St. NW, between 4th and 5th Sts., East End ☎ 202/272–2448 ⊕ www.nbm.org ⌨ Free ⊙ Mon.–Sat. 10–5, Sun. 11–5 Ⓜ Judiciary Sq.

Smithsonian American Art Museum. Home to the United States' first federal art collection, the Smithsonian American Art Museum is considered the world's biggest and most diverse collection of American art. Its more than 41,000 works span three centuries, from colonial portraits to 21st-century abstractionists. Among the thousands of American artists represented are John Singleton Copley, Winslow Homer, Mary Cassatt, Georgia O'Keeffe, Edward Hopper, David Hockney, and Robert Rauschenberg. There are free docent-led tours every day at noon and 2. ⊠ 8th and G Sts. NW, East End ☎ 202/633–7970; 202/633–5285 TDD ⊕ www.americanart.si.edu ⌨ Free ⊙ Daily 11:30–7:30 Ⓜ Gallery Pl./Chinatown.

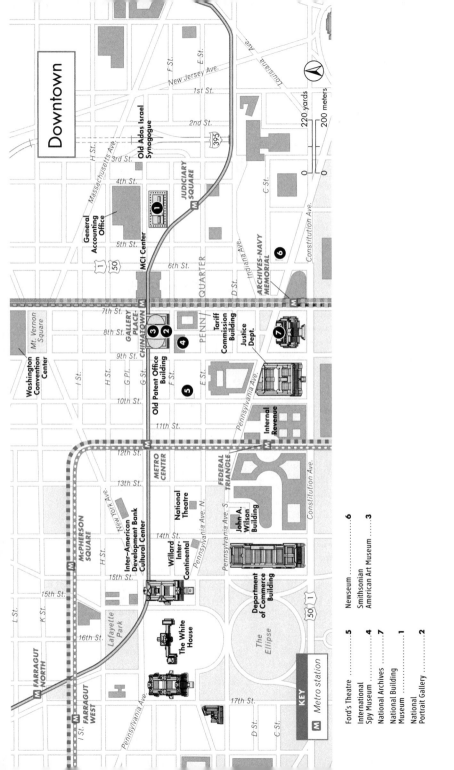

Downtown

Old Adas Israel Synagogue

New Jersey Ave.
1st St.
2nd St.
3rd St.
4th St.
5th St.
6th St.

General Accounting Office

MCI Center

JUDICIARY SQUARE

395

ARCHIVES-NAVY MEMORIAL

Constitution Ave.

C St.

D St.

Indiana Ave.

QUARTER

PENN

7th St.
8th St.
9th St.
10th St.
11th St.

GALLERY PLACE-CHINATOWN

Old Patent Office Building

F St.
E St.

Tariff Commission Building

Justice Dept.

Internal Revenue

Pennsylvania Ave.

Washington Convention Center

Mt. Vernon Square

I St.
H St.
G Pl.
G St.

METRO CENTER

12th St.
13th St.

McPHERSON SQUARE

New York Ave.

Inter-American Development Bank Cultural Center

National Theatre

Willard Inter-Continental

FEDERAL TRIANGLE

John A. Wilson Building

Pennsylvania Ave. N.
Pennsylvania Ave. S.

Constitution Ave.

14th St.
15th St.
16th St.
17th St.

FARRAGUT NORTH
FARRAGUT WEST

L St.
K St.

Lafayette Park

The White House

Department of Commerce Building

The Ellipse

50 1

D St.
C St.

Massachusetts Ave.
H St.

220 yards
200 meters
0

KEY

M Metro station

Ford's Theatre **5**

International
Spy Museum **4**

National Archives **7**

National Building
Museum **1**

National
Portrait Gallery **2**

Newseum **6**

Smithsonian
American Art Museum **3**

GEORGETOWN AND FOGGY BOTTOM

Long before the District of Columbia was formed, Washington's oldest and wealthiest neighborhood was a separate city with a harbor full of ships and warehouses filled with tobacco. Washington has filled in around Georgetown over the years, but the former tobacco port retains an air of aloofness. Today some of Washington's most famous residents call Georgetown home, including former *Washington Post* executive editor Ben Bradlee, political pundit George Stephanopoulos, Senator (and 2004 presidential nominee) John Kerry, and *New York Times* op-ed doyenne Maureen Dowd. This is one of Washington's main areas for restaurants, bars, nightclubs, and boutiques.

Foggy Bottom, across the Potomac from Georgetown, has three main claims to fame: the State Department, the Kennedy Center, and George Washington University. Its name is derived from the wharves, breweries, lime kilns, and glassworks that were near the water. Smoke from these factories combined with the swampy air of the low-lying ground to produce a permanent fog along the waterfront.

TOP ATTRACTIONS

C&O Canal. When it opened in 1850, this waterway's 74 locks linked Georgetown with Cumberland, Maryland, 184 mi to the northwest, and kept Georgetown open to shipping after its harbor had filled with silt. Lumber, coal, iron, wheat, and flour moved up and down the canal, but it was never as successful as its planners had hoped. Today the canal is part of the National Park System; walkers follow the towpath once used by mules while canoeists paddle the canal's calm waters. You can glide into history aboard a mule-drawn canal boat ride. The National Park service provides the hour-long rides from about mid-April through late October; tickets cost $7 and are available across the canal, next to the Foundry Building. The schedule varies by season, with limited rides in spring and fall. In summer the boats run at least twice a day from Wednesday through Sunday. Call the visitor center for the exact schedule on the day of your visit. Canal-boat rides also depart from the Great Falls Tavern visitor center in Maryland. ⊠ *Canal Visitor Center, 1057 Thomas Jefferson St. NW, Georgetown* ☎ *202/653–5190* ⊕ *www. nps.gov/choh*

★ **Dumbarton Oaks.** One of the loveliest places for a stroll in Washington is Dumbarton Oaks, the acres of enchanting gardens adjoining Dumbarton House in Georgetown. Planned by noted landscape architect Beatrix Farrand, the gardens incorporate elements of traditional English, Italian, and French styles such as a formal rose garden, an English country garden, and an orangery (circa 1810). You enter the gardens at 31st and R streets. In 1944 one of the most important events of the 20th century took place at **Dumbarton House,** when representatives of the United States, Great Britain, China, and the Soviet Union met in the music room to lay the groundwork for the United Nations. Career diplomat Robert Woods Bliss and his wife Mildred bought the property in 1920 and tamed the sprawling grounds, and removed later 19th-century additions that had obscured the Federal lines of the 1801 mansion. In 1940 the Blisses gave the estate to Harvard University, which maintains world-renowned collections of Byzantine and pre-Columbian art here. Both collections are small but choice. The Byzantine collection includes beautiful examples of both religious and secular items executed in mosaic, metal, enamel, and ivory. Pre-Columbian works—artifacts and textiles from Mexico

and Central and South America by peoples such as the Aztec, Maya, and Olmec—are arranged in an enclosed glass pavilion designed by Philip Johnson. Normally on view to the public are the lavishly decorated music room and selections from Mrs. Bliss's collection of rare illustrated garden books. ☒ *1703 32nd St. NW, Georgetown* ☎ *202/339–6401 or 202/339–6400* ⊕ *www.doaks.org* ☐ *Museum: free; Gardens: $8, free Nov.–Mar.* ☽ *Museum: Tues.–Sun. 2–5; gardens: Apr.–Oct., Tues.–Sun. 2–6, Nov.–Mar., Tues.–Sun. 2–5.*

WORTH NOTING

Old Stone House. What was early American life like? Here's the capital's oldest window into the past. Work on this fieldstone house, thought to be Washington's oldest surviving building, was begun in 1764 by a cabinetmaker named Christopher Layman. Now a museum, it was used as both a residence and a place of business by a succession of occupants. Five of the house's rooms are furnished with the simple, sturdy artifacts—plain tables, spinning wheels, and so forth—of 18th-century middle-class life. The National Park Service maintains the house and its lovely gardens, which are planted with fruit trees and perennials. ☒ *3051 M St. NW, Georgetown* ☎ *202/426–6851* ⊕ *www.nps.gov/olst* ☐ *Free* ☽ *Daily 10–5.*

DUPONT CIRCLE AND NORTHWEST D.C.

The main thoroughfares of Connecticut, New Hampshire, and Massachusetts avenues all intersect at Dupont Circle, with a small, handsome park and a splashing fountain in the center. Upscale restaurants, offbeat shops, coffeehouses, art galleries, and specialty bookstores give the neighborhood a distinctive, cosmopolitan air. Stores and clubs catering to the neighborhood's large gay community are abundant. Most of the sights in other sections of Northwest D.C. are immediately adjacent to Red Line Metro stops, but all can be easily reached by serious walkers, who will appreciate the leafy thoroughfares of these neighborhoods.

TOP ATTRACTIONS

Fodor's Choice ★ **National Zoo.** While recent attention has focused on giant pandas Tian Tian and Mei Xiang, the Smithsonian's free zoological park is full of red pandas, clouded leopards, and Japanese giant salamanders, as well as the traditional lions, tigers, and bears. The zoo makes for a picturesque stroll on warm days, but be prepared for crowds on sunny weekends. Carved out of Rock Creek Park, the zoo is a series of rolling, wooded hills that complement the many innovative compounds showing animals in their native settings. Elephant Trails is one of the newest additions

to the park. This sprawling habitat gives the Asian elephants plenty
of room to spread out. The zoo is
known for its successful breeding
programs, and everything from
massive gorillas to tiny kiwis has
been born on the premises. Locals
often participate in naming them.
⊠ *3001 Connecticut Ave. NW,
Woodley Park* ☎ *202/673–4800 or
202/673–4717* ⊕ *www.si.edu/natzoo* ✉ *Free, parking $10* ☉ *Apr–Oct.,
daily 10 am–6 pm; Nov.–Mar., daily 10–4:30* Ⓜ *Cleveland Park or
Woodley Park/Zoo.*

WORD OF MOUTH

"One of our very favorite museums that just reopened is the
Phillips collection. It is right in
Dupont, so would make a nice
afternoon activity followed by dinner." —CherylP

President Lincoln's Cottage. In June 1862 President Lincoln moved from
the White House to this Gothic Revival cottage on the grounds of the
Soldiers' Home to escape the oppressive heat of wartime Washington
and to grieve for the loss of his son Willie. Lincoln and his wife lived
in the cottage from June to November of 1862, 1863, and 1864—a
quarter of his presidency—and it was here that he became consumed
with the idea of emancipation and wrote the Emancipation Proclamation. Considered the most significant historic site of Lincoln's presidency
outside the White House, Lincoln's Cottage opened for public tours in
2008. The tours attempt to re-create a visit to the cottage similar to
what Lincoln's many visitors in the 1860s experienced. ■ TIP➔ **Advance
reservations, available online, are highly recommended.** ⊠ *Armed Forces
Retirement Home at Rock Creek Church Rd. and Upshur St. NW,
Upper Northwest* ☎ *202/829–0436* ⊕ *www.lincolncottage.org* ✉ *$12*
☉ *Mon.–Sat. 9:30–4:30, Sun. 11:30–5:30* Ⓜ *Georgia Ave./Petworth.*

WORTH NOTING

Phillips Collection. The first museum of modern art in the country, the
masterpiece-filled Phillips Collection is unique in origin and content. It
opened in 1921 in the Georgian Revival mansion of collector Duncan
Phillips, who wanted to showcase his art in a museum that would stand
as a memorial to his father and brother. Having no interest in a painting's market value or its faddishness, Phillips searched for pieces that
impressed him as outstanding products of a particular artist's unique
vision. At the heart of the collections are impressionist and modern masterpieces by Pierre-Auguste Renoir, Vincent van Gogh, Paul Cézanne,
Edgar Degas, Pablo Picasso, Paul Klee, and Henri Matisse. The collection's most famous piece is Renoir's magnificent work of impressionism,
Luncheon of the Boating Party. ⊠ *1600 21st St. NW, Dupont Circle*
☎ *202/387–2151* ⊕ *www.phillipscollection.org* ✉ *Free for permanent
collection weekdays; admission varies weekends and for special exhibitions* ☉ *Tues., Wed., Fri., and Sat. 10–5; Thurs. 10–8:30; Sun. 11–6*
Ⓜ *Dupont Circle.*

Washington National Cathedral. Construction of Washington National
Cathedral—the sixth-largest cathedral in the world—started in 1907;
it was finished and consecrated more than 70 years later. Like its 14th-
century Gothic counterparts, the stunning cathedral (officially the
Cathedral Church of St. Peter and St. Paul) has a nave, flying buttresses,

transepts, and vaults that were built stone by stone. ■ **TIP**→ **The expan-sive view of the city from the Pilgrim Gallery is exceptional.** The cathedral is Episcopalian, but it's the site of frequent ecumenical and interfaith services. On the grounds of the cathedral is the compact, English-style **Bishop's Garden.** Boxwoods, ivy, tea roses, yew trees, and an assortment of arches, bas-reliefs, and stonework from European ruins provide a counterpoint to the cathedral's towers. ⊠ *Wisconsin and Massachu-setts Aves. NW, Upper Northwest* ☎ *202/537–6200; 202/537–6207 tour information* ⊕ *www.nationalcathedral.org* ✉ *Suggested tour dona-tion $5* ☉ *Weekdays 10–5:30, Sat. 10–4:30, Sun. 1–4. Tours: week-days 10–11:30 and 1–4, Sat. 10–11:30 and 12:45–3:30, Sun. 1–2:30* Ⓜ *Cleveland Park or Tenleytown. Take any 30 series bus.*

WHERE TO EAT

Dupont Circle is dense with restaurants and cafés, many with out-door seating. On Georgetown's main drags, Wisconsin Avenue and M Street, white-tablecloth establishments coexist easily with hole-in-the-wall joints. Chinatown, centered on G and H streets NW between 6th and 8th, hosts Chinese, Burmese, Thai, and other Asian restaurants. In the East End, restaurants of all stripes (some casual and moderately priced, others upscale and trendy) have sprung up to serve the crowds that attend games at the MCI Center and that enjoy the increasingly chic bar scene. Capitol Hill has a number of bars that cater to congres-sional types who need to fortify themselves with food and drink after a day spent running the country, and Union Station houses a large food court offering quick bites that range from barbecue to sushi.

One way to keep prices down at more-upscale places is to go for pre-theater menus, where choices may be limited and the tab lower. Many high-end restaurants have separate bar menus that showcase the cre-ativity of the chef at gentler prices. Going to a heavy hitter for lunch rather than dinner is another option. All restaurants are open daily for lunch and dinner unless stated otherwise.

WHAT IT COSTS					
	¢	$	$$	$$$	$$$$
At dinner	under $10	$10–$17	$18–$25	$26–$35	over $35

Prices are per person for a main course at dinner.

CAPITOL HILL

$$$

NEW AMERICAN

✕ **Art and Soul.** Best known as Oprah's longtime personal chef, Art Smith is now serving the Washingtonian crowd at this funky new Southern-fried spot, located in the Liaison Capitol Hill. The signature dish here is the hoecake, a once modest slab of fried cornmeal scarfed down by overworked and cash-strapped field workers during the 19th century. Smith and executive chef Ryan Morgan gussy up their hoecakes with three sets of toppings: blue cheese and arugula, blue crab and braised beef, and a truly decadent mélange of caviar, crème fraiche, and cured salmon. Low Country classics such as shrimp with grits, and pork chops served with vinegar-spiked redeye gravy are also on hand. ⊠ *415 New Jersey Ave. NW, Capitol Hill* ☎ *202/393–7777* ⊕ *www.artandsouldc. com* ⊟ *AE, MC, V* Ⓜ *Union Station* ✛ *5G.*

¢ ✗ **Jimmy T's Place.** This D.C. institution is tucked in the first floor of an
AMERICAN old row house only five blocks from the Capitol. Sassy waiters, talk-
☺ ative regulars, and this small diner's two boisterous owners, who run the grill, pack the place daily. Soak in the local culture or read the paper as you enjoy favorites such as grits, bacon, omelets, or the homey eggs Benedict, made with a toasted English muffin, a huge piece of ham, and lots of hollandaise sauce. The anything-goes atmosphere makes it a great place for kids. Breakfast is served all day. ⊠ *501 E. Capitol St. SE, Capitol Hill* ☎ *202/546–3646* ⊟ *No credit cards* ⊘ *Closed Mon. and Tues. No dinner* Ⓜ *Eastern Market* ✛ *5H.*

$$ ✗ **Johnny's Half Shell.** The Southern-tinged mid-Atlantic fare—pristine
SEAFOOD Kumamoto oysters, flavorful seafood stews, fried oyster po'boys, and a stellar pickled-onion-and-blue-cheese-topped hot dog—is as good as it gets. And a new pastry chef is turning out a worthy coconut cake. Not surprisingly, the crowd is heavy on politicos drawn as much by the buzz and big-band tunes. Members of Congress can also be found downing a quick Gruyère-cheese omelet during breakfast on weekdays. ⊠ *400 N. Capitol St. NW, Capitol Hill* ☎ *202/737–0400* ⊕ *www.johnnyshalfshell. net* ⊟ *AE, MC, V* ⊘ *Closed Sun.* Ⓜ *Union Station* ✛ *5H.*

$$ ✗ **Montmartre.** With its sidewalk café, cheerful yellow walls, fresh flow-
FRENCH ers, and lusty yet chic fare, Montmartre evokes the Left Bank of Paris. Here's an unpretentious bistro that straddles classic and modern effort-lessly with dishes like cream of chestnut soup, braised rabbit with olives and shiitake mushrooms, hanger steak with caramelized shallots, and cod with homemade spaetzle. It's a politicians' hangout, but you'd never know it by the cozy, rustic feel of the place. ⊠ *327 7th St. SE, Capi-tol Hill* ☎ *202/544–1244* ⚃ *Reservations essential* ⊟ *AE, DC, MC, V* ⊘ *Closed Mon.* Ⓜ *Eastern Market* ✛ *5H.*

$$ ✗ **Sonoma.** This chic multilevel wine bar has pours aplenty (in both tast-
AMERICAN ing portions and full glasses) along with well-thought-out charcuterie boards piled with prosciutto, bresaola with house-made condiments like pickled ramps, and figs braised in wine. There's more-conventional fare, too, like a juicy Wagyu burger with Taleggio cheese and grilled onions. By day the crowd skews to Senate staffers, by night the place becomes a hipster scene in the bar on the second level—think low tables and sofas—while a youngish crowd shares cheese plates in the crowded street-level dining room. ⊠ *223 Pennsylvania Ave. SE, Capitol Hill* ☎ *202/544–8088* ⊕ *www.sonomadc.com* ⚃ *Reservations essential* ⊟ *AE, D, DC, MC, V* ⊘ *No lunch weekends* Ⓜ *Capitol* ✛ *6G.*

CHINATOWN

$$ ✗ **Café Atlántico.** The menu is always exciting at this *nuevo Latino* restau-
LATIN AMERICAN rant with friendly service. Conch fritters come with tiny avocado ravioli, and scallops are served with coconut rice, ginger, squid, and squid-ink oil. On weekends Atlántico offers "Latino dim sum," tapas-size

portions of dishes such as duck confit with passion-fruit oil, pineapple shavings, and plantain powder. À la carte, the plates are $3 to $9, but for $35 you can get a deluxe tasting menu ($25 for a vegetarian tasting menu). The bar makes mean cocktails with *cachaça*, a liquor distilled from sugarcane juice. You are unlikely to find a more extensive

selection of South American wines anywhere in the city. At Minibar, a six-stool bar on the second floor, you can explore a $95 tasting menu of about 30 creative morsels, such as a foie-gras "lollipop" coated with cotton candy, conjured up before your eyes. The space generally closes from mid-August to mid-September. ✉ *405 8th St. NW, Chinatown* ☎ *202/393–0812* ⊕ *www.cafeatlantico.com* 🍴 *Reservations essential* ▤ *AE, DC, MC, V* Ⓜ *Archives/Navy Memorial* ✛ *5E.*

$–$$

SPANISH

✕ **Jaleo.** You are encouraged to make a meal of the long list of tapas at this lively Spanish bistro, although entrées such as paella are just as tasty. Tapas highlights include the *gambas al ajillo* (sautéed garlic shrimp), fried potatoes with spicy tomato sauce, and the grilled chorizo. Adventurers are encouraged to sample the octopus with paprika; those with a sweet tooth should save room for the crisp apple charlotte and the chocolate hazelnut torte. ✉ *480 7th St. NW, Chinatown* ☎ *202/628–7949* ⊕ *www.jaleo.com* ▤ *AE, D, DC, MC, V* Ⓜ *Gallery Pl./Chinatown* ✛ *5E.*

$–$$

AMERICAN

☺

✕ **Matchbox.** The miniburgers, served on toasted brioche buns with a huge mound of fried onion strings, get the most press, but the main clue to what to order at this convivial triple-decker bar-restaurant is the glowing wood-burning pizza oven. The personal pizzas are "New York–style," with a thin, crisp crust. You probably won't mistake them for the very best of New York, but the pizza margherita comes close. Homey plates such as grilled filet mignon with horseradish potatoes and spicy pecan-crusted chicken add substance to the menu. There's a great lineup of draft beers and oddball martinis, and the kitchen stays open until 1 am on weekends. ✉ *713 H St. NW, Chinatown* ☎ *202/289–4441* ⊕ *www.matchboxdc.com* ▤ *AE, MC, V* Ⓜ *Gallery Pl./Chinatown* ✛ *4E.*

¢–$

MEXICAN

✕ **Oyamel.** The specialty at this Mexican stunner is *antojitos*, literally translated as "little dishes from the street." But the high ceilings, gracious service, and gorgeous Frida Kahlo–inspired decor are anything but street, and even the smallest of dishes is bigger than life when doused with chocolatey mole poblano sauce or piquant lime-cilantro dressing. Standouts include house-made margaritas topped with a clever salt foam, the Veracruz red snapper in a hearty olive-tomato confit, and grasshopper tacos. Yes, those are bugs basted in tequila and pepper sauce—and they're delightful. ✉ *401 7th St. NW, Chinatown* ☎ *202/628–1005* ⊕ *www.oyamel.com* ▤ *AE, D, MC, V* Ⓜ *Archives/ Navy Memorial* ✛ *5F.*

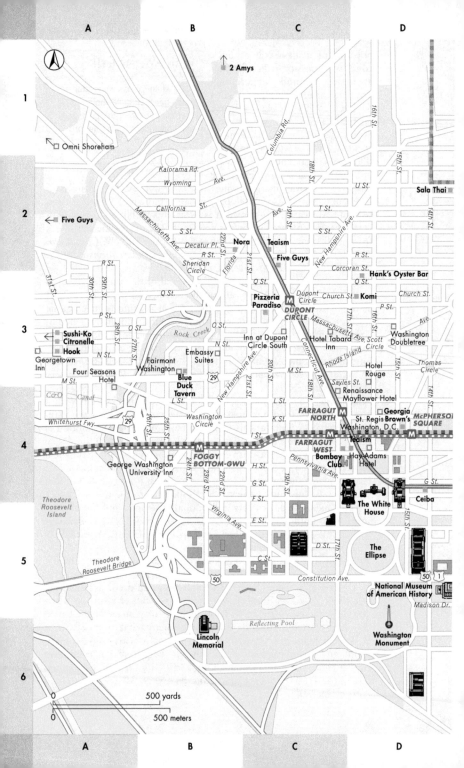

2 Amys

Omni Shoreham

Kalorama Rd.

Wyoming

California St.

← Five Guys

Massachusetts Ave.

Decatur Pl.

S St.

Florida

Sheridan Circle

R St.

Q St.

Nora **Teaism**

Five Guys

Corcoran St.

Hank's Oyster Bar

O St.

Pizzeria Paradiso

Dupont Circle

Church St. **Komi**

P St.

DUPONT CIRCLE

Church St.

31st St.

30th St.

29th St.

28th St.

27th St.

R St.

P St.

Rock Creek

Massachusetts Ave.

Washington Doubletree

Sushi-Ko
Citronelle
Hook

N St.

O St.

N St.

Inn at Dupont Circle South

Hotel Tabard Inn

Scott Circle

Thomas Circle

Georgetown Inn

Fairmont Washington

Embassy Suites

New Hampshire Ave.

20th St.

Rhode Island Ave.

Hotel Rouge

15th St.

14th St.

Four Seasons Hotel

M St.

Blue Duck Tavern

21st St.

M St.

Sayles St.

Renaissance Mayflower Hotel

C&O Canal

L St.

L St.

K St.

FARRAGUT NORTH

Georgia
St. Regis **Brown's**
Washington, D.C.

McPHERSON SQUARE

Whitehurst Fwy.

26th St.

25th St.

Washington Circle

I St.

FARRAGUT WEST

Teaism

George Washington University Inn

FOGGY BOTTOM-GWU

H St.

Pennsylvania Ave.

Bombay Club

Hay-Adams Hotel

Theodore Roosevelt Island

24th St.

23rd St.

22nd St.

19th St.

G St.

Ceiba

G St.

F St.

The White House

17th St.

15th St.

E St.

Virginia Ave.

D St.

The Ellipse

Theodore Roosevelt Bridge

C St.

50

Constitution Ave.

National Museum of American History

Madison Dr.

Reflecting Pool

Lincoln Memorial

Washington Monument

0   500 yards

0   500 meters

Sala Thai

16th St.

15th St.

18th St.

Columbia Rd.

19th St.

U St.

T St.

S St.

R St.

22nd St.

21st St.

New Hampshire Ave.

Connecticut Ave.

18th St.

17th St.

16th St.

29

29

50

1

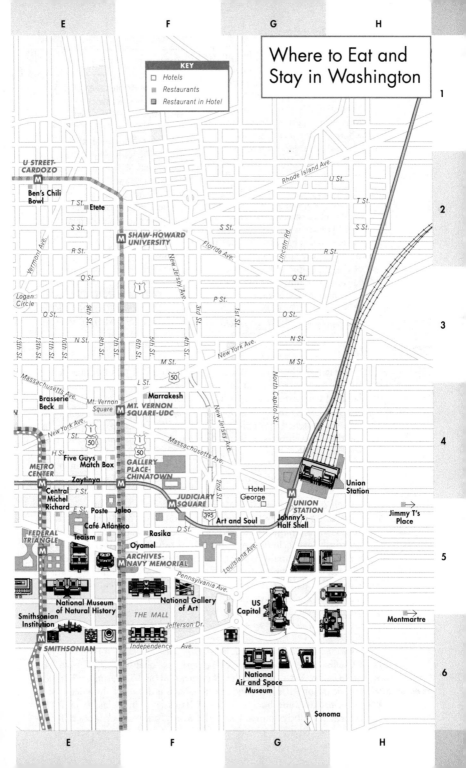

Where to Eat and Stay in Washington

KEY
- □ Hotels
- ■ Restaurants
- ■ Restaurant in Hotel

U STREET-CARDOZO
Ⓜ

Ben's Chili Bowl

Etete

T St.

S St.

R St.

Q St.

SHAW-HOWARD
UNIVERSITY
Ⓜ

Florida Ave.

Rhode Island Ave.

U St.

T St.

S St.

R St.

Q St.

Lincoln Rd.

Vermont Ave.

Logan
Circle

O St.

N St.

13th St.
12th St.
11th St.
10th St.
9th St.
8th St.
7th St.
6th St.
5th St.
4th St.
3rd St.

New Jersey Ave.

P St.

New York Ave.

M St.

L St.

50

Massachusetts Ave.

Brasserie
Beck

Marrakesh

Mt. Vernon
Square

MT. VERNON
SQUARE-UDC
Ⓜ

Massachusetts Ave.

New Jersey Ave.

2nd St.

1st St.

O St.

N St.

M St.

North Capitol St.

New York Ave.
50
I St.

H St.

Five Guys
Match Box

GALLERY
PLACE-
CHINATOWN
Ⓜ

Louisiana Ave.

Union
Station

METRO
CENTER
Ⓜ

Zaytinya

Central
Michel
Richard

F St.

E St.

Poste

Jaleo

JUDICIARY
SQUARE
Ⓜ

395

Art and Soul

Hotel
George

UNION
STATION
Ⓜ

Johnny's
Half Shell

Jimmy T's
Place

Café Atlántico

Rasika

D St.

FEDERAL
TRIANGLE
Ⓜ

Teaism

Oyamel

ARCHIVES-
NAVY MEMORIAL
Ⓜ

Pennsylvania Ave.

National Museum
of Natural History

National Gallery
of Art

THE MALL

Jefferson Dr.

US
Capitol

Montmartre

Smithsonian
Institution

SMITHSONIAN
Ⓜ

Independence Ave.

National
Air and Space
Museum

Sonoma

$$ ✕ **Rasika.** This trendy Indian restaurant pairs an adventurous wine list with spicy fare in a supersleek setting. The chef, London export Vikram Sunderam (from Bombay Brasserie), comes from a town where curries never get short shrift. He has prepared a menu of traditional delights, like a fiery chicken green masala, alongside newer, more inspired ones, like lamb miniburgers, tiny crab cakes with Indian spices, and fried spinach leaves with sweet yogurt sauce. Libations at the bar are concocted with as much creativity as the food. Muted shades of cream, apple-green, and cinnabar and dangling crystals evoke the

INDIAN

Fodor's Choice

★

subcontinent but in a stylish, modern way. ⊠ *633 D St. NW, Chinatown* ☎ *202/637–1222* ⊕ *www.rasikarestaurant.com* ▭ *AE, D, DC, MC, V* ☉ *Closed Sun. No lunch weekends* Ⓜ *Archives/Navy Memorial* ✛ *5F.*

DOWNTOWN

$$$ ✕ **Brasserie Beck.** Give in to sensory overload at this homage to the railway dining rooms that catered to the prewar European elite. Every detail of Beck's decor exudes luxury, from the vintage-accented clocks that stand above mahogany booths to the exposed stainless-steel kitchen (now rechristened the "epicurean solarium"). The food is just as rich as you'd expect: entrée-size salads with bacon and egg, *fruits de mer* platters laden with enough shellfish for a small army, and a dizzying lineup of artisanal beers. The production is impressive, and you'll remember the food fondly after returning home—but you might long for a simple sandwich afterwards. ⊠ *1101 K St. NW, Downtown,* ☎ *202/408–1717* ⊕ *www.beckdc.com* ▭ *AE, MC, V* Ⓜ *McPherson Sq.* ✛ *4E.*

FRENCH

$$ ✕ **Ceiba.** At this very popular Latin restaurant you'll probably want to start with a mojito or a pisco sour cocktail, then taste the smoked-swordfish carpaccio or Jamaican crab fritters. This is a menu meant for grazing, but the main courses, like rib eye with chimichurri sauce and *feijoada* (stew of beans and meat) made from pork shanks, still satisfy. Also stellar are desserts such as Mexican vanilla-bean cheesecake with guava jelly, and cinnamon-dusted churros to dip in Mexican hot chocolate. Island-theme murals, angular cream banquettes, an open kitchen, and vaulted ceilings set the scene. ⊠ *701 14th St. NW, Downtown* ☎ *202/393–3983* ⊕ *www.ceibarestaurant.com* ▭ *AE, D, DC, MC, V* ☉ *Closed Sun. No lunch Sat.* Ⓜ *Metro Center* ✛ *4D.*

AMERICAN

$$–$$$ ✕ **Central Michel Richard.** French powerhouse chef Michel Richard has set up camp Downtown with this semicasual bistro offering up Franco-American spin-offs like fried chicken, leek-and-mussel chowder, and a ginger-flecked tuna burger. Rows of hams hang in a glass case. Light fixtures are subtly stamped with the word "Central." A jazzy portrait

FRENCH

Fodor's Choice

★

of Richard (think Andy Warhol) stares down from one wall. The mood is playful and low-key; cocktails and champagne flow. And there are even a few carry-overs from Richard's more formal Citronelle in Georgetown like "Le Kit Kat," the chef's take on a Kit Kat bar. ⊠ *1001 Pennsylvania Ave. NW, Downtown* ☎ *202/626–0015* ⊕ *www.centralmichelrichard.com* ⌂ *Reservations essential* ⊟ *AE, D, MC, V* ⊘ *No lunch weekends* Ⓜ *Metro Center* ✛ *5E.*

$$

SOUTHERN

✕ **Georgia Brown's.** An elegant New South eatery and a favorite hangout of local politicians, Georgia Brown's serves shrimp Carolina-style (head intact, with steaming grits on the side); thick, rich crab soup; and such specials as grilled salmon and slow-cooked green beans with bacon. Fried green tomatoes are filled with herb cream cheese, and a pecan pie is made with bourbon and imported Belgian dark chocolate. ■ TIP→ **The Sunday "jazz brunch" adds live music and a decadent chocolate fondue fountain to the mix.** The airy, curving dining room has white honeycomb windows and unusual ceiling ornaments of bronze ribbons. ⊠ *950 15th St. NW, Downtown* ☎ *202/393–4499* ⊕ *www.gbrowns. com* ⌂ *Reservations essential* ⊟ *AE, D, DC, MC, V* ⊘ *No lunch Sat.* Ⓜ *McPherson Sq.* ✛ *4D*

¢

JAPANESE

Fodor's Choice
★

✕ **Teaism.** This informal teahouse stocks more than 50 teas (black, white, and green) imported from India, Japan, and Africa, but it also serves healthful and delicious Japanese, Indian, and Thai food as well as tea-friendly sweets like ginger scones, plum muffins, and salty oat cookies. You can mix small dishes—tandoori kebabs, tea-cured salmon, Indian flat breads—to create meals or snacks. There's also a juicy ostrich burger or *ochazuke,* green tea poured over seasoned rice. The smaller Connecticut Avenue branch (enter around the corner, on H Street; closed on weekends), tucked neatly on a corner adjacent to Lafayette Park and the White House, is a perfect spot to grab lunch after touring the nation's power center. Breakfast is served daily. ⊠ *400 8th St. NW, Downtown* ☎ *202/638–7740* ⊕ *www.teaism.com* ⊟ *D, MC, V* Ⓜ *Archives/Navy Memorial* ✛ *4D* ⊠ *800 Connecticut Ave. NW, Downtown* ☎ *202/835–2233* Ⓜ *Farragut W* ✛ *2C.*

¢–$

MIDDLE EASTERN

Fodor's Choice
★

✕ **Zaytinya.** This sophisticated urban dining room with soaring ceilings is a local favorite for meeting friends or dining with a group. Zaytinya, which means "olive oil" in Turkish, devotes practically its entire menu to Turkish, Greek, and Lebanese small plates, known as mezes. To get the full experience, make a meal of three or four of these, such as the popular braised lamb with eggplant puree and cheese, or the locally made goat cheese wrapped in grape leaves with tomato marmalade. ■ TIP→ **So many options make this a great choice for vegetarians and meat lovers alike.** Reservations for times after 6:30 are not accepted; come prepared to wait on Friday and Saturday nights. Belly dancers perform on Wednesday nights. ⊠ *701 9th St. NW, Downtown*

☎ *202/638–0800* ⊕ *www.zaytinya.com* ▤ *AE, DC, MC, V* Ⓜ *Gallery Pl./Chinatown* ✛ *4E.*

DUPONT CIRCLE

$–$$
SEAFOOD

✕ **Hank's Oyster Bar.** The watchword is simplicity at this popular and chic take on the shellfish shacks of New England. A half-dozen oyster varieties are available daily on the half shell, both from the West Coast and local Virginia waters, alongside another half-dozen daily fish specials. An amuse-bouche of cheddar Goldfish crackers adds a touch of whimsy. Don't be shy about asking for seconds on the complimentary baking chocolate presented along with your check—the kitchen doesn't serve sweets, but it doesn't need to. ✉ *1624 Q St. NW, Dupont Circle* ☎ *202/462–4265* ⊕ *www.hanksdc.com* ▤ *AE, MC, V* Ⓜ *Dupont Circle* ✛ *3D.*

$$$$
NEW AMERICAN
Fodor's Choice
★

✕ **Komi.** Johnny Monis, the young, energetic chef-owner of this small, personal restaurant, offers one of the most adventurous dining experiences in the city. The five-course prix-fixe is $74 and showcases contemporary fare with a distinct Mediterranean influence. ▰ TIP➔ **Reservations open 30 days in advance—and the longer you wait, the smaller your chance at a coveted table.** Star plates include fresh sardines with pickled lemons, suckling pig over apples and bacon with polenta, and mascarpone-filled dates with sea salt. ✉ *1509 17th St. NW, Dupont Circle* ☎ *202/332–9200* ⊕ *www.komirestaurant.com* ☖ *Reservations essential* ▤ *AE, D, MC, V* ☾ *Closed Sun. and Mon. No lunch* Ⓜ *Dupont Circle* ✛ *3D.*

$$$
AMERICAN
Fodor's Choice
★

✕ **Nora.** Chef and founder Nora Pouillon helped pioneer the sustainable-food revolution with the first certified organic restaurant in the country, and her seasonal, sustainable ingredients are out of this world. Settle into the sophisticated and attractive quilt-decorated dining room and start with the mushroom, leek, and Brie tart or a locally grown salad. Entrées such as pepper-crusted steak and roasted salmon with parsnips emphasize the well-balanced, earthy ingredients. ✉ *2132 Florida Ave. NW, Dupont Circle* ☎ *202/462–5143* ⊕ *www.noras.com* ☖ *Reservations essential* ▤ *AE, D, MC, V* ☾ *Closed Sun. No lunch* Ⓜ *Dupont Circle* ✛ *2B.*

$
ITALIAN
☺

✕ **Pizzeria Paradiso.** A trompe-l'oeil ceiling adds space and light to a simple interior at the ever-popular Dupont Circle Pizzeria Paradiso. The restaurant sticks to crowd-pleasing basics: pizzas, panini, salads, and desserts. Although the standard pizza is satisfying, you can enliven it with fresh buffalo mozzarella or unusual toppings such as potatoes, capers, and mussels. Wines are well chosen and well priced. The intensely flavored gelato is a house specialty. ✉ *2003 P St. NW, Dupont Circle* ☎ *202/223–1245* ⊕ *www.eatyourpizza.com* ▤ *DC, MC, V* Ⓜ *Dupont Circle* ✛ *3C.*

GEORGETOWN AND FOGGY BOTTOM

$$–$$$
NEW AMERICAN
Fodor'sChoice
★

✕ **Blue Duck Tavern.** Many chefs are fond of artisanal and local ingredients. Chef Brian McBride is so committed to the cause that fixings are often strewn across marble counters in the restaurant's show kitchen. By now diners have gotten used to watching pastry chefs churn ice cream to be served minutes later in glass ice buckets, but sweets— and watching for the town's biggest political names to claim their favorite tables—aren't the only pleasures. The kitchen wows with Modern American riffs like a double-cut pork chop with bourbon-glazed peaches, a marrowbone with creamy insides, and a meaty hanger steak. The dining room is stylish, done up with Shaker furniture and quilts. ✉ *1201 24th St. NW, Foggy Bottom* ☎ *202/419–6755* ⊕ *www.blueducktavern.com* ⚞ *Reservations essential* ▭ *AE, D, DC, MC, V* Ⓜ *Foggy Bottom/GWU* ✛ *3B.*

$$$$
FRENCH
Fodor'sChoice
★

✕ **Citronelle.** See all the action in the glass-front kitchen at chef Michel Richard's flagship California-French restaurant. Appetizers might include foie gras with lentils prepared three ways, and main courses run to lobster medallions with lemongrass, saddle of lamb crusted with herbs, and breast of squab. Desserts are luscious: a crunchy napoleon with filament-like pastry and the very special "chocolate bar," Richard's dense, rich take on a Snickers candy bar. A chef's table in the kitchen gives you a ringside seat (reserve at least a month ahead). The fixed-price menu costs $155, or $230 with wine pairings. The bar menu has morsels such as mushroom "cigars" and Serrano ham. ✉ *Latham Hotel, 3000 M St. NW, Georgetown* ☎ *202/625–2150* ⊕ *www.citronelledc. com* ⚞ *Reservations essential* 🎩 *Jacket required* ▭ *AE, D, DC, MC, V* ☉ *No lunch* ✛ *3A*

¢
AMERICAN
☺

✕ **Five Guys.** One of the quirky traditions of this homegrown fast-food burger house is to note on the menu board where the potatoes for that day's fries come from, be it Maine, Idaho, or elsewhere. The place gets just about everything right: from the grilled hot dogs and hand-patted burger patties—most folks get a double—to the fresh hand-cut fries with the skin on and the high-quality toppings such as sautéed onions and mushrooms. Add an eclectic jukebox to all of the above and you've got a great burger experience. There are a number of different locations around D.C. including Dupont Circle and Chinatown. ✉ *1335 Wisconsin Ave. NW, Georgetown* ☎ *202/337–0400* ⊕ *www.fiveguys. com* ▭ *MC, V* ✛ *A2* ✉ *1645 Connecticut Ave. NW, Dupont Circle* ☎ *202/328–3483* Ⓜ *Dupont Circle* ✛ *C2* ✉ *808 H St NW, Chinatown* ☎ *202/393–2900* Ⓜ *Gallery Pl./Chinatown* ✛ *4E.*

$$–$$$
SEAFOOD

✕ **Hook.** Barton Seaver, the young chef who stunned Georgetown's old guard of gourmands with this ode to the "sustainable seafood" movement, is no longer cooking here—but his kitchen remains in capable hands. From weakfish to yahoo, all of the uncommon fish on the menu are caught using environmentally friendly methods that preserve overfished seafood populations like swordfish and salmon. Conscious-ness aside, your palate is in for a treat for lunch, brunch, or dinner. The wood-grilled calamari with basil pesto is an unforgettable appetizer. Pastry chef Heather Chittum's fresh basil ice cream and homemade donuts stuffed with Nutella are also not to be missed. ⊠ *3241 M St. NW, Georgetown* ☎ *202/625–4488* ⊕ *www.hookdc.com* ⚑ *Reserva-tions essential* ▭ *AE, MC, V* ⊘ *No lunch Mon* ✢ *3A.*

$–$$ ✗ **Sushi-Ko**. At one of the city's best Japanese restaurants, daily specials
JAPANESE   are always innovative: sesame oil–seasoned trout layered with crisp wonton crackers, and a sushi special might be salmon topped with a touch of mango sauce and a sprig of dill. You won't find the restaurant's delicious ginger, mango, or green-tea ice cream at the local Baskin-Robbins. ⊠ *2309 Wisconsin Ave. NW, Georgetown* ☎ *202/333–4187* ⚑ *Reservations essential* ▭ *AE, D, MC, V* ⊘ *No lunch Sat.–Mon.* ✢ *3A.*

GLOVER PARK

$ ✗ **2 Amys**. Judging from the long lines here, the best pizza in D.C. is
PIZZA   uptown. Simple recipes allow the ingredients to shine through at this
☾   Neapolitan pizzeria. You may be tempted to go for the D.O.C. pizza (it has *Denominazione di Origine Controllata* approval for Neapoli-tan authenticity), but don't hesitate to try the daily specials. Roasted peppers with anchovies and deviled eggs with parsley-caper sauce have by now become classics. At busy times the wait for a table can exceed an hour, and the noisy din of a packed house may discourage some diners. ⊠ *3715 Macomb St. NW, Glover Park* ☎ *202/885–5700* ⊕ *www.2amyspizza.com* ⚑ *Reservations not accepted* ▭ *MC, V* ⊘ *No lunch Mon.* ✢ *1B.*

U STREET

¢ ✗ **Ben's Chili Bowl**. Long before U Street became hip, Ben's was serving
AMERICAN   chili. Chili on hot dogs, chili on Polish-style sausages, chili on burgers,
☾   and just plain chili. Add cheese fries if you dare. The faux-marble bar and shiny red-vinyl stools give the impression that little has changed since the 1950s, but turkey and vegetarian burgers and meatless chili are a nod to modern times. Ben's closes at 2 am Monday through Thurs-day, at 4 am on Friday and Saturday. It opens late, at 11 am and closes early, at 8 pm on Sunday. Southern-style breakfast is served from 6 am weekdays and from 7 am on Saturday. ⊠ *1213 U St. NW, U Street Cor-ridor* ☎ *202/667–0909* ⊕ *www.benschilibowl.com* ▭ *No credit cards* Ⓜ *U St./Cardozo* ✢ *E2.*

¢–$ ✗ **Etete**. The best of the city's Ethiopian restaurants, Etete doesn't hold
AFRICAN   back on the spices. Savory pastries known as *sambusas* are filled with
☾   fiery lentils, and ginger brightens a stew of vegetables. The sharing of dishes and the mode of eating—rather than using utensils diners tear off pieces of *injera*, a spongy pancake-like bread to scoop up stews and sautées—make for exotic and adventurous dining at this style-conscious eatery. ⊠ *1942 9th St. NW, U Street Corridor* ☎ *202/232–7600* ▭ *AE, D, DC, MC, V* Ⓜ *U St./African-American Civil War Memorial/Car-dozo* ✢ *2E.*

¢–$ ✕ **Sala Thai.** Who says Thai food has to be sweat-inducing? Sala Thai
THAI makes the food as spicy as you wish, because this chef is interested in
flavor, not fire. Among the subtly seasoned dishes are *panang goong*
(shrimp in curry-peanut sauce), chicken sautéed with ginger and pineapple, and flounder with a choice of four sauces. Mirrored walls and
warm lights soften this small dining room, as do the friendly service
and largely local clientele. The Dupont and U Street locations are most
popular. ✉ *1301 U St. NW, U Street corridor* ☎ *202/462–1333* ⊕ *www.
salathaidc.com* Ⓜ *U St./Cardozo* ✉ *2016 P St. NW, Dupont Circle*
☎ *202/872–1144* ⊟ *AE, D, DC, MC, V* Ⓜ *Dupont Circle.* ✢ *2D.*

WHERE TO STAY

Forced to cater to all stripes, from lobbyists with expense accounts to
those in town for the free museums, from bigwigs seeking attention to
those flying under the radar, Washington's rooms suit everyone. The
high-end and business-class hotels are located mainly near the halls of
power, whether in Georgetown row houses, near the White House, or
on Capitol Hill. Downtown, quickly becoming the city's nerve center,
also has its fair share. There's a good chance that if you stay in one of
the pricier digs in these areas you can sign a guest register touched by
diplomats and then sleep in beds where royalty rested. The District's
boutique hotels and cool guesthouses tend to congregate in the shadier
areas of northwest D.C.

WHAT IT COSTS				
	¢	$	$$	$$$	$$$$
For two people	under $125	$125–$210	$211–$295	$296–$400	over $400

Prices are for a standard double room in high season, excluding 14.5%
room tax.

CAPITOL HILL

$$$$ 🏨 **Hotel George.** This hotel burst onto the scene in 1998, introducing
Fodor'sChoice the city to the concept of contemporary boutique lodging. More than
★ a decade later, it still excels at providing a fun and funky alternative to
the cookie-cutter chains. Portraits of America's first president by Andy
Warhol protégé Steve Kaufman adorn public areas and add a pop of
bright color to the mostly white public spaces. Guest rooms, done in
cream and beige with cobalt-blue accents, have 300-count Egyptian cot-
ton linens, marble-topped ergonomic desks, and expansive flat-screen
TVs. **Pros:** close to Union Station; popular restaurant; updated fitness
center. **Cons:** small closets; some reports of street noise; ultra-modern
feel not everyone's cup of tea. ✉ *15 E St. NW, Capitol Hill* ☎ *202/347–
4200 or 800/576–8331* ⊕ *www.hotelgeorge.com* ⇥ *139 rooms, 1 suite*
⌂ *In-room: safe, DVD, Internet, Wi-Fi. In-hotel: restaurant, room service, bar, gym, laundry service, Wi-Fi hotspot, parking (paid) some pets
allowed* ⊟ *AE, D, DC, MC, V* Ⓜ *Union Station* ✢ *5G.*

DC HOTEL TIPS

If you can stand semitropical weather, come in August, during the congressional recess, when Washington is calm and less expensive. Rates also drop in late December and January, except around an inauguration.

Reservations: With more than 63,000 guest rooms, Washington can almost always provide a place to stay—though it's always prudent to reserve. Hotels often fill up with conventioneers, politicians in transit, families, and, in spring, school groups. Hotel rooms in D.C. can be hard to come by during the Cherry Blossom Festival in late

March or early April, and also in May, when so many graduate from college. Late October's Marine Corps Marathon also increases demand for rooms. The **Washington, DC Convention and Tourism Corporation** (☎ 800/422–8644 ⊕ www. washington.org) runs a reservation service.

Parking: Nightly hotel parking fees range from free (often in the suburbs) to $30 (downtown). This sometimes involves valet parking, with its implied additional gratuities. Street parking is free, but sparse, on Sunday and usually after 6:30 pm weekdays.

DOWNTOWN

$$$$ 🏨 **Renaissance Mayflower Hotel.** The magnificent block-long lobby with its series of antique crystal chandeliers and gilded columns is a destination in itself. Guest rooms at this grande dame hotel, which opened its doors in 1925 for Calvin Coolidge's inauguration, are done in soothing yellows, green, tans, and blues. Town and Country, the hotel's inside-the-Beltway power bar, has been a place for political wheeling and dealing for nearly as long as the hotel. Sam the bartender mixes up 101 martinis to keep guests happily in the drink. Work off the booze and the crab cakes, a favorite on the menu at the hotel's elegant Café Promenade, in the spa-like fitness center. **Pros:** historic building; near dozens of restaurants; a few steps from Metro. **Cons:** rooms vary greatly in size; no pool. ⊠ 1127 Connecticut Ave. NW, Downtown ☎ 202/347–3000 or 800/228–7697 ⊕ www.marriott.com ➳ 657 rooms, 74 suites ⌂ In-room: Internet. In-hotel: restaurant, room service, bar, gym, laundry service, Wi-Fi hotspot, parking (paid) ⊟ AE, D, DC, MC, V Ⓜ Farragut N ✛ 4C.

$$$$ 🏨 **St. Regis Washington, D.C.** Don't forget to admire the hand-painted
Fodor's Choice ceiling in the newly restored lobby of the St. Regis, a 1926 landmark
★ hotel that reopened in January 2008 after an extensive 16-month restoration. Pratesi linens line the beds, a 15-inch LCD TV is recessed behind the bathroom mirror in every guest room, and personal butlers now carry BlackBerrys, so while you're out you can e-mail requests like "Please pack my bags." Just two blocks from the White House, this Italian Renaissance–style hotel attracts a formal business crowd. If you check in with children, hotel staff will give them F.A.O. Schwarz teddy bears and bring kid-size robes to your room. **Pros:** close to White House; historic property; exceptional service. **Cons:** no pool; most rooms don't have great views; very expensive. ⊠ 923 16th St. NW,

2

Downtown ☎ *202/638–2626* ⊕ *www.stregis.com/washington* ⇲ *175 rooms, 25 suites* ⛵ *In-room: safe, refrigerator (some), DVD, Internet, Wi-Fi. In-hotel: restaurant, room service, bar, gym, laundry service, spa, Wi-Fi hotspot, parking (paid), some pets allowed* ▭ *AE, D, DC, MC, V* Ⓜ *Farragut North* ✚ *4D.*

$ 🏨 **Washington Doubletree Hotel.** Just off Scott Circle, the Doubletree offers ☺ spacious, recently renovated guest rooms that have comfortable beds, well-equipped workstations, clock radios with MP3 players, and cof-feemakers. An American bistro, 15 Ria, brings a New York sensibility to the hotel, which is only six blocks from the White House. **Pros:** child-friendly; good location; new fitness center. **Cons:** no pool; limited street parking. ✉ *1515 Rhode Island Ave. NW, Downtown* ☎ *202/232–7000 or 800/222–8733* ⊕ *www.washington.doubletree.com* ⇲ *181 rooms, 39 suites* ⛵ *In-room: safe, refrigerator, Internet. In-hotel: restaurant, gym, Wi-Fi hotspot, parking (paid)* ▭ *AE, D, DC, MC, V* Ⓜ *Dupont Circle* ✚ *3D.*

DUPONT CIRCLE

$$$ 🏨 **Hotel Rouge.** This postmodern hotel bathed in red succeeds at bring-
Fodor's Choice ing Florida's South Beach club scene to D.C. guest rooms. With spe-
★ cialty themes such as "chill or chow," the rooms are decorated with swanky eye-catching furniture. In the hip lobby lounge the bartenders are always busy concocting sweet new drinks. Bar Rouge, the cocktail lounge, attracts club-going denizens at all hours. **Pros:** great lounge scene; gay-friendly vibe; good location. **Cons:** no pool; the scene is not for everybody. ✉ *1315 16th St. NW, Dupont Circle* ☎ *202/232–8000 or 800/738–1202* ⊕ *www.rougehotel.com* ⇲ *137 rooms* ⛵ *In-room: safe, kitchen (some), refrigerator (some), DVD. In-hotel: room service, bar, gym, Wi-Fi hotspot, parking (paid), some pets allowed* ▭ *AE, D, DC, MC, V* Ⓜ *Dupont Circle* ✚ *3D.*

¢–$ 🏨 **Hotel Tabard Inn.** Three Victorian town houses were consolidated to form the Tabard, one of the oldest hotels in D.C. Although the wooden floorboards creak and room sizes vary considerably (some share bath-rooms), the dimly lighted hotel feels like an Old World inn, with alluring nooks and crannies inside and a brick-walled garden outside. The Tab-ard Inn's fireside bar may be one of the city's coziest winter retreats, and the restaurant remains a favorite among locals. Free passes are provided to the nearby YMCA, which has extensive fitness facilities. **Pros:** afford-able choice; lots of character; Sunday-night jazz in the hotel lounge. **Cons:** some shared bathrooms; limited privacy, steps to climb. ✉ *1739 N St. NW, Dupont Circle* ☎ *202/785–1277* ⊕ *www.tabardinn.com* ⇲ *40 rooms, 25 with bath* ⛵ *In-room: no TV (some), Wi-Fi. In-hotel: restaurant, bar, laundry facilities, Wi-Fi hotspot, some pets allowed* ▭ *AE, D, DC, MC, V* ⊖ *Continental breakfast* Ⓜ *Dupont Circle* ✚ *3C.*

$–$$ 🏨 **The Inn at Dupont Circle South.** This is the inn where everybody knows your name. Innkeeper Carolyn Torralba jokes that her guests are "her babies," and the personal attention shows: there are many repeat cus-tomers here. Most rooms have private baths; all have featherbeds and typical inn decor complete with doilies, bric-a-brac, and impressionist posters. Carolyn serves a hot breakfast in the parlor or on the sun porch.

Pros: personable innkeeper; across from Metro; children welcome; airport shuttle. **Cons:** creaking floors; steps to climb; not all rooms have private baths. ⊠ *1312 19th St. NW, Dupont Circle* ☎ *202/467–6777 or 866/467–2100* ⊕ *thedupontcollection.com* ⇨ *8 rooms, 3 with shared bath* ⚷ *In-room: safe, refrigerator, Wi-Fi. In-hotel: laundry facilities, Wi-Fi hotspot, parking (paid)* ▤ *AE, MC, V* ⦿ *Full breakfast* Ⓜ *Dupont Circle* ⊹ *3C.*

GEORGETOWN AND FOGGY BOTTOM

$$–$$$ 🏨 **Embassy Suites Washington, D.C.** Plants cascade over balconies beneath
⟳ a skylight in this modern hotel's atrium, which is filled with classical columns, plaster lions, wrought-iron lanterns, waterfalls, and tall palms. Within walking distance of Georgetown and Dupont Circle, the suites here are suitable for both business travelers and families. Beverages are complimentary at the nightly manager's reception, and the rate includes cooked-to-order breakfast. There's a kids' corner with movies and games, and the Italian restaurant, Trattoria Nicola's, serves lunch and dinner. **Pros:** family-friendly; all suites; pool to keep the little ones—and sweaty tourists—happy. **Cons:** not a lot of character; museums not in walking distance. ⊠ *1250 22nd St. NW, West End* ☎ *202/857–3388 or 800/362–2779* ⊕ *www.embassysuites.com* ⇨ *318 suites* ⚷ *In-room: refrigerator, Wi-Fi. In-hotel: restaurant, room service, bar, pool, gym, laundry service, parking (paid)* ▤ *AE, D, DC, MC, V* ⦿ *Full breakfast* Ⓜ *Foggy Bottom/GWU or Dupont Circle* ⊹ *3B.*

$$$$ 🏨 **Fairmont Washington.** The large glassed-in lobby and about a third of
⟳ the bright, spacious rooms overlook a central courtyard and gardens. Rooms are comfortable, if not the city's most modern. The informal Juniper restaurant serves mid-Atlantic fare and has courtyard dining; there's a champagne brunch on Sunday in the Colonnade Room. ■ TIP➔ **The health club is one of the best in the city.** Families have access to the pool, kids' menus and crayons in the restaurant, and a babysitting referral service. Family packages include things like a trip to visit the pandas at the National Zoo. **Pros:** fitness fanatics will love the health club; lots of kid-friendly features. **Cons:** pricey; far from most attractions. ⊠ *2401 M St. NW, Foggy Bottom* ☎ *202/429–2400 or 866/540–4505* ⊕ *www.fairmont.com* ⇨ *406 rooms, 9 suites* ⚷ *In-room: safe, Internet. In-hotel: restaurant, room service, bar, pool, gym, parking (paid), some pets allowed* ▤ *AE, D, DC, MC, V* Ⓜ *Foggy Bottom/GWU* ⊹ *3B.*

$$$$ 🏨 **Four Seasons Hotel.** After a whopping $40 million renovation, the Four
⟳ Seasons has reasserted its role as Washington's leading hotel. Impec-
Fodor's Choice cable service and a wealth of amenities have long made this a favorite
★ with celebrities, hotel connoisseurs, and families. Luxurious, ultramodern rooms offer heavenly beds, flat-screen digital TVs with DVD players, and French limestone or marble baths with separate showers and sunken tubs. A 2,000-piece original art collection graces the walls, and a walk through the corridors seems like a visit to a wing of the National Gallery. The formal Seasons restaurant offers traditional dishes with an elegant twist, as well as a popular Sunday brunch. **Pros:** edge of Georgetown makes for a fabulous location; lap-of-luxury feel;

impeccable service. **Cons:** expensive; challenging street parking; far from Metro. ✉ *2800 Pennsylvania Ave. NW, Georgetown* ☎ *202/342–0444 or 800/332–3442* ⊕ *www.fourseasons.com/washington* ↩ *160 rooms, 51 suites ☍ In-room: safe, Internet, Wi-Fi. In-hotel: restaurant, room service, bar, children's programs (ages 5–6), pool, gym, parking (paid), some pets allowed* ⊟ *AE, D, DC, MC, V* Ⓜ *Foggy Bottom* ⊕ *4A.*

$ ⛉ **Georgetown Inn.** Reminiscent of a gentleman's club, this Federal-style hotel seems like something from the 1700s. The quiet, spacious guest rooms are decorated in a colonial style. The redbrick hotel, in the heart of historic Georgetown, lies near shopping, dining, galleries, and theaters. The publike Daily Grill restaurant serves American cuisine. **Pros:** shoppers love the location; good price for the neighborhood; some nice views. **Cons:** a hike to Metro; congested area. ✉ *1310 Wisconsin Ave. NW, Georgetown* ☎ *202/333–8900 or 888/587–2388* ⊕ *www.georgetowncollection.com* ↩ *86 rooms, 10 suites ☍ In-room: Wi-Fi. In-hotel: restaurant, room service, bar, gym, Wi-Fi hotspot, parking (paid)* ⊟ *AE, D, DC, MC, V* Ⓜ *Foggy Bottom* ⊕ *3A.*

$ ⛉ **George Washington University Inn.** This boutique hotel is in a quiet neighborhood a few blocks from the Kennedy Center, the State Department, and George Washington University. Wrought-iron gates lead through a courtyard to the hotel's front entrance, where beveled-glass doors open onto a small lobby with a gray marble floor. Rooms, which vary in size and configuration, have colonial-style furniture and complimentary high-speed Internet access. Guests also receive free entry to the nearby Bally Total Fitness club. **Pros:** good price; close to Metro. **Cons:** not many amenities; far from museums. ✉ *824 New Hampshire Ave. NW, Foggy Bottom* ☎ *202/337–6620 or 800/426–4455* ⊕ *www.gwuinn.com* ↩ *64 rooms, 31 suites ☍ In-room: safe, kitchen (some), refrigerator, Wi-Fi. In-hotel: restaurant, bar, laundry facilities, laundry service, parking (paid)* ⊟ *AE, DC, MC, V* Ⓜ *Foggy Bottom/GWU* ⊕ *4B.*

WOODLEY PARK AND UPPER NORTHWEST

$$$–$$$$ ⛉ **Omni Shoreham Hotel.** This elegant hotel overlooking Rock Creek
🌣 Park has been lovingly tended and is aging gracefully. The light-filled
Fodor's Choice guest rooms have a soothing garden palette and feature flat-screen TVs
★ and marble bathrooms. The vast art deco-and-Renaissance–style lobby welcomes visitors, who in the past have ranged from the Beatles to heads of state (the hotel has played host to inaugural balls since its 1930 opening). There is even a resident ghost said to haunt Suite 870. Families will love the larger-than-typical guest rooms, kiddie pool, bird-watching, bike rentals, and movie nights. ■TIP➡ **Parents: Ask the concierge about story time and cuddles with the guide dog for the blind who trains at the hotel.** **Pros:** historic property; great pool and sundeck; good views from many rooms. **Cons:** not Downtown; big. ✉ *2500 Calvert St., NW, Woodley Park* ☎ *202/234–0700 or 800/834–6664* ⊕ *www.omnihotels.com* ↩ *818 rooms, 16 suites ☍ In-room: safe, refrigerator (some), DVD (some), Internet, Wi-Fi. In-hotel: restaurant, room service, bar, children's programs (ages 3–13), pool, gym, laundry service, spa, Wi-Fi hotspot, bicycles, parking (paid), some pets allowed* ⊟ *AE, D, DC, MC, V* Ⓜ *Woodley Park/Zoo* ⊕ *1A.*

NIGHTLIFE AND THE ARTS

From buttoned-down political appointees to laid-back folks who were born here, Washingtonians have plenty of options when they head out for the night. Most bars are clustered in several key areas. Penn Quarter, near the Verizon Center and U Street NW between 12th and 15th streets, is quickly becoming one of the hottest spots in town. Georgetown has dozens of bars, nightclubs, and restaurants at the intersection of Wisconsin and M streets. A host of small live-music venues and popular bars line the 18th Street strip in Adams-Morgan between Columbia Road and Kalorama Avenue. The stretch of Pennsylvania Avenue between 2nd and 4th streets SE has a half-dozen Capitol Hill bars. Hill staffers also hang out on Barrack's Row, 8th Street SE south of D Street. For a high-powered happy hour, head to the intersection of 19th and M streets NW, near lawyer- and lobbyist-filled downtown.

> ## WORD OF MOUTH
>
> "The Dupont Circle area is a great area at night for all kinds of restaurants and activities. It feels like a neighborhood when you're out at night. The Metro stop is an easy walk from here. If you want to have more choices at night and if you are in town for longer than a day or so, I would pick the Dupont Circle area." —EmilyC

D.C. has also gone from being a cultural desert to a thriving arts center in the past 40 years. To satiate the educated young professionals who flock here for opportunities in government, the arts scene has exploded. To sift through the flurry of events, check out the daily "Guide to the Lively Arts," in the *Washington Post,* and the "Weekend" section on Friday. On Thursday, look for the free weekly *Washington CityPaper* (⊕ *www.washingtoncitypaper.com*). The *Washington Post* (⊕ *www.washingtonpost.com/cityguide*) also publishes an Internet-based entertainment guide.

TICKETplace sells half-price, day-of-performance tickets for select shows. ⊠ *Old Post Office Pavilion, 406 7th St. NW, Downtown* ☏ *202/842–5387* ⊕ *www.ticketplace.org* Ⓜ *Archives/Navy Memorial.*

LIVE MUSIC

Fodor'sChoice
★
The Birchmere. A legend in the D.C. area, the Birchmere is one of the best places outside the Blue Ridge Mountains to hear acoustic folk, country, and bluegrass. Enthusiastic crowds have enjoyed performances by artists such as Mary Chapin Carpenter, Lyle Lovett, Leon Redbone, and Emmylou Harris. More recently, the club has expanded its offerings to include jazz performers such as Diane Schuur and Al Jarreau, and blues artists like Robert Cray and Buddy Guy. ⊠ *3701 Mt. Vernon Ave., Alexandria, VA* ☏ *703/549–7500* ⊕ *www.birchmere.com.*

Fodor'sChoice
★
Black Cat. Come here to see the latest local bands as well as indie stars such as Neko Case, Modest Mouse, and Clinic. Dave Grohl, lead singer of the Foo Fighters and formerly of Nirvana, owns a stake in the club. The post-punk crowd whiles away the time in the Red Room, a side

bar with pool tables, an eclectic jukebox, and no cover charge. The club also is home to Food for Thought, a vegetarian café. ⊠ *1811 14th St. NW, U Street corridor* ☎ *202/667–7960* ⊕ *www.blackcatdc.com* Ⓜ *U Street/Cardozo.*

Blues Alley. Head here for a classy evening in an intimate setting, complete with great music and outstanding New Orleans–style grub. The cover charge is typically $25 for well-known performers such as Mose Allison, and more for top acts like Wynton Marsalis. There is also a $10 food or drink minimum. ■ TIP➜ You can come for just the show, but those who enjoy a meal get better seats. ⊠ *1073 Wisconsin Ave. NW, near M St., Georgetown* ☎ *202/337–4141* ⊕ *www.bluesalley.com* Ⓜ *Foggy Bottom.*

PERFORMANCE VENUES

Fodor'sChoice
★

John F. Kennedy Center for the Performing Arts. On the bank of the Potomac River, the gem of the D.C. arts scene is home to the National Symphony Orchestra, the Washington Ballet, and the Washington National Opera. The best out-of-town acts perform at one of three performance spaces— the Concert Hall, the Opera House, or the Eisenhower Theater. Eclectic performers can be found at the Center's smaller venues, including the Terrace Theater, showcasing chamber groups and experimental works; the Theater Lab, home to cabaret-style performances like the audience-participation hit Sheer Madness; the KC Jazz Club; and a 320-seat family theater. But that's not all. On the Millennium Stage in the center's Grand Foyer you can catch free performances almost any day at 6 pm. ■ TIP➜ On performance days, a free shuttle bus runs between the Center and the Foggy Bottom/GWU Metro stop. ⊠ *New Hampshire Ave. at Rock Creek Pkwy. NW, Foggy Bottom* ☎ *202/467–4600 or 800/444–1324* ⊕ *www.kennedy-center.org* Ⓜ *Foggy Bottom/GWU.*

THEATER

Arena Stage. The first regional theater company to win a Tony Award, Arena Stage performs innovative American theater, reviving some classic plays and showcasing the country's best new writers. It's newly expanded space features three different stages: a theater in the round seating 650, a modified thrust stage theater seating 514, and "Cradle," a new 200-seat black-box theater for experimental productions. ⊠ *1101 6th St. SW, Waterfront* ☎ *202/488–3300* ⊕ *www.arenastage. org* Ⓜ *Waterfront.*

Gala Hispanic Theatre. This company attracts outstanding Hispanic actors from around the world. Plays are presented in English or in Spanish with instant English translations supplied through earphones. The company performs in the newly renovated Tivoli Theatre in Columbia Heights, a hot spot for Latino culture and cuisine. ⊠ *Tivoli Sq., 3333 14th St. NW, 14th and Park Rd., Columbia Heights* ☎ *202/234–7174* ⊕ *www.galatheatre.org* Ⓜ *Columbia Heights.*

Shakespeare Theatre. This acclaimed troupe, known as one of the world's three great Shakespearean companies, crafts fantastically staged and acted performances of works by Shakespeare and his contemporaries.

The theater has undergone an amazing transformation. Complementing the existing stage in the Lansburgh Theatre is the Sidney Harman Hall, which opened in October 2007. The new stage provides a 21st-century, state-of-the-art, mid-size venue for an outstanding variety of performances, from Shakespeare's *Julius Caesar* to the hilarious *Abridged History of America*. ⊠ *450 7th St. NW, Downtown* ☎ *202/547–1122* ⊕ *www.shakespearedc.org* Ⓜ *Gallery Pl./Chinatown or Archives/Navy Memorial.*

Studio Theatre. One of the busiest groups in the city, this independent company produces an eclectic season of classic and offbeat plays in four spaces: the original Mead and Milton theaters, the newer 200-seat Metheny Theatre, and the experimental Stage 4. The theater is part of the revitalized 14th Street Corridor. ⊠ *1333 P St. NW, Dupont Circle* ☎ *202/332–3300* ⊕ *www.studiotheatre.org* Ⓜ *Dupont Circle.*

Fodor'sChoice **Woolly Mammoth.** Unusual avant-garde shows with edgy staging and solid
★ acting have earned Woolly Mammoth top reviews and favorable comparisons to Chicago's Steppenwolf. The troupe's talent is accentuated by its modern 265-seat theater in Penn Quarter near the Verizon Center. ⊠ *641 D St. NW, Downtown* ☎ *202/393–3939* ⊕ *www.woollymammoth.net* Ⓜ *Gallery Pl./Chinatown or Archives/Navy Memorial.*

SPORTS AND THE OUTDOORS

Washington's 69 square miles are in part a fantastic recreational backyard, with dozens of beautiful open spaces. Rock Creek Park has miles of wooded trails and paths for bikers, runners, and walkers that extend to almost every part of the city. The National Mall connects the Lincoln Memorial and the Capitol building. With the monuments as a backdrop, you can spike a volleyball, ride a bike, or take a jog. Into watching more than doing? Washington's myriad professional sports teams will sate your hunger for top-level competition no matter what your favorite game.

BICYCLING

The numerous trails in the District and its surrounding areas are well maintained and clearly marked.

For scenery, you can't beat the **C&O Canal Towpath** (⊕ *www.nps.gov/choh*), which starts in Georgetown and runs along the C&O Canal into Maryland. You could pedal to the end of the canal, nearly 200 mi away in Cumberland, Maryland, but most cyclists stop at Great Falls, 13 mi from where the canal starts. The occasionally bumpy towpath, made of gravel and packed earth, passes through wooded areas of the C&O Canal National Historical Park. You can see 19th-century locks from the canal's working days, and if you're particularly lucky, you may catch a glimpse of mules pulling a canal barge. The barges now take passengers, not cargo.

Cyclists interested in serious training might try the 3-mi loop around the golf course in **East Potomac Park** (☎ *202/485–9874 National Park*

Service) at Hains Point, the southern area of the park (entry is near the Jefferson Memorial). It's a favorite training course for dedicated local racers and would-be triathletes.

Rock Creek Park covers an area from the edge of Georgetown to Montgomery County, Maryland. The bike path there is asphalt and has a few challenging hills, but it's mostly flat. You can bike several miles without having to stop for cars (the roadway is closed entirely to cars on weekends). The two separate northern parts of the trail, which begin in Bethesda and Silver Spring, merge around the Washington, D.C., line. Many bikers gather at this point and follow the trail on a path that goes past the Washington Zoo and eventually runs toward the Lincoln Memorial and Kennedy Center. Fifteen miles of dirt trails are also in the park; these are best for hiking.

RENTALS

Better Bikes (✉ *1902 16th St. NW at New Hampshire Ave., Adams Morgan* ☎ *202/293–2080* ⊕ *www.betterbikesinc.com*) offers free delivery of rental bikes—mountain, hybrid, kids', and bikes with baby buggies from $38 to $48 per day—to most local hotels. Rentals include helmets, backpacks, locks, and tips on where to bike. Reservations are required.

Big Wheel Bikes (✉ *1034 33rd St. NW, Georgetown* ☎ *202/337–0254* ⊕ *www.bigwheelbikes.com*), near the C&O Canal Towpath, rents multispeed bikes for $25 per day and $15 for three hours. Tandem bikes, kids' bikes, and bikes with baby carriers are also available.

BOATING AND SAILING

Surrounded by the beloved cherry trees and overlooked by the Jefferson Memorial, the **Tidal Basin** is a scenic spot for paddleboating. Canoeing, sailing, and powerboating are all popular on the **Potomac River** north and south of the city. You can dip your oars just about anywhere along the river—go canoeing in the C&O Canal, sailing in the widening river south of Alexandria, or even kayaking in the raging rapids at Great Falls, a 30-minute drive from the capital.

RENTALS

The Boathouse at Fletcher's Cove (✉ *4940 Canal Rd., at Reservoir Rd., Foxhall* ☎ *202/244–0461* ⊕ *www.fletcherscove.com*), just north of Georgetown, rents 17-foot rowboats for $11 per hour and $20 per day. Canoes are available for rent at $11 per hour and $22 per day. Single kayaks are $8 per hour and $24 per day, while double kayaks are $15 per hour and $35 per day.

Thompson's Boat Center (✉ *2900 Virginia Ave. NW, Foggy Bottom* ☎ *202/ 333–4861 or 202/333–9543* ⊕ *www.thompsonboatcenter.com* Ⓜ *Foggy Bottom/GWU*) is near Georgetown and Theodore Roosevelt Island. The center rents canoes for $8 per hour and $22 per day. Single kayaks are $8 per hour and $24 per day, and double kayaks are $10 per hour and $30 per day. Rowing sculls are also available, but you must demonstrate prior experience and a suitably high skill level.

Tidal Basin (✉ *Bordered by Independence Ave. and Maine Ave., The Mall* ☎ *202/479–2426* ⊕ *www.tidalbasinpeddleboats.com* Ⓜ *Farragut W*), in front of the Jefferson Memorial, rents paddleboats beginning in mid-March and usually ending in October. The entrance is at 1501 Maine Avenue SW, on the east side of the Tidal Basin. You can rent two-passenger boats at $10 per hour and four-passenger boats at $18 per hour.

ICE-SKATING

Fodor's Choice ★ The **National Gallery of Art Ice Rink** (⊠ *Constitution Ave. NW, between 7th and 9th Sts., Downtown* ☎ *202/289–3361* Ⓜ *Archives/Navy Memorial*) is surrounded by the gallery's Sculpture Garden. The art deco design of the rink makes it one of the most popular outdoor winter sites in Washington. In spring the rink becomes a fountain.

The prime location of the **Pershing Park Ice Rink** (⊠ *Pennsylvania Ave. and 14th St. NW, Downtown* ☎ *202/737–6938* ⊕ *www.pershingparkicerink.com* Ⓜ *Metro Center*), a few blocks from the White House, major hotels, and a Metro station, makes this rink one of the most convenient spots in Washington for outdoor skating.

PROFESSIONAL SPORTS

Fodor's Choice ★ **D.C. United** (⊠ *Robert F. Kennedy Stadium, 2400 E. Capitol St. SE, Capitol Hill* ☎ *202/547–3134* ⊕ *www.dcunited.com* Ⓜ *Stadium*) is one of the best Major League soccer (U.S. pro soccer) teams. International matches, including some World Cup preliminaries, are often played on RFK Stadium's grass field, dedicated exclusively to soccer play. Games are April through September. You can buy tickets, which generally cost $25–$65, online or at the RFK Stadium ticket office.

★ One of pro hockey's top teams, the **Washington Capitals** (⊠ *6th and F Sts., Downtown* ☎ *202/432–7328* ⊕ *www.washingtoncaps.com* Ⓜ *Gallery Pl./Chinatown*), plays home games October through April at the Verizon Center and features hockey superstar Alex Ovechkin. Seats on the main level range from $75 to $300, and those in the upper deck range from $35 to $60. Tickets can be purchased online or at the Verizon Center box office.

The WNBA's **Washington Mystics** (⊠ *6th and F Sts., Downtown* ☎ *202/432–7328* ⊕ *www.wnba.com/mystics* Ⓜ *Gallery Pl./Chinatown*) play at the Verizon Center in Downtown Washington. The Mystics perennially lead the WNBA in attendance, despite a losing record. The games are loud, boisterous events. Ticket prices range from $17 to $70, with courtside tickets for $125.

Baseball has returned to D.C., where the **Washington Nationals** (⊠ *1500 S. Capitol St. SE* ☎ *202/675–6287* ⊕ *washingtonnationals.mlb.com* Ⓜ *Navy Yard*) of the National League play in their new spectacular home, Nationals Park. Tickets range from $5 to $325. The $5 tickets are only available on game day at the park box office. Individual game tickets may be purchased at the park or online. ∎ TIP→ **The Metro is a hassle-free and inexpensive way to get to the ballpark. Parking is very scarce.**

The **Washington Redskins** (☎ *301/276–6000 FedEx Field stadium* ⊕ *www.redskins.com*) have the largest football stadium in the NFL, but all 80,000 seats are held by season-ticket holders. Occasionally you can find tickets advertised in the classifieds of the *Washington Post* or buy them from online ticket vendors and auction sites—at top dollar, of course. ■ TIP→ **Fans can see the players up close and for free at training camp, held in August.**

The NBA's **Washington Wizards** (✉ *6th and F Sts., Downtown* ☎ *202/432–7328* ⊕ *www.nba.com/wizards* Ⓜ *Gallery Pl./Chinatown*) play from October to April at the Verizon Center and feature superstar Gilbert Arenas. Tickets for individual games cost $40 to $850. The team also offers $10 seats in the upper level and courtside seats for a whopping $2,500. Buy tickets online or from the Verizon Center box office.

RUNNING

Running is one of the best ways to see the city, and several scenic trails wend through Downtown Washington and nearby northern Virginia. It can be dangerous to run at night on the trails, although the streets are fairly well lighted. Even in daylight, it's best to run in pairs when venturing beyond public areas or heavily used sections of trails.

Fodor'sChoice
★

The most popular running route in Washington is the 4.5-mi loop on the **Mall** around the Capitol and past the Smithsonian museums, the Washington Monument, the Reflecting Pool, and the Lincoln Memorial. At any time of day hundreds of runners, speed walkers, bicyclists, and tourists make their way along the gravel pathways. For a longer run, veer south of the Mall on either side of the Tidal Basin and head for the Jefferson Memorial and East Potomac Park, the site of many races.

SHOPPING

African masks; kitchenware as objets d'art; bargains on Christian Dior, Hugo Boss, and Burberry; paisley scarves from India; American and European antiques; books of every description; handicrafts from almost two dozen Native American tribes; busts of U.S. presidents; textiles by the armful; fine leather goods—all this and more can be found in the nation's capital. **Georgetown** is not on a subway line and parking is difficult at best, but people still flock here for tony antiques, elegant crafts, and high-style shoe and clothing boutiques, along with national chains. **Dupont Circle,** a younger, less staid version of Georgetown, has many art galleries, offbeat shops, and specialty book and record stores that give it a cosmopolitan air. Northeast of Dupont, **U Street,** once known for its classy theaters and jazz clubs and then its decline, has been revitalized with a string of chic clothing stores and home-wares shops. As the **Capitol Hill** area has become gentrified, unique shops and boutiques have sprung up, many clustered around the redbrick **Eastern Market,** where a weekend flea market presents nostalgia and local crafts by the crateful.

CAPITOL HILL/EASTERN MARKET

MARKET

Eastern Market. Vibrantly colored produce and flowers; freshly caught fish; fragrant cheeses; and tempting sweets are sold by independent vendors at Eastern Market, which first opened its doors in 1873. On weekends a flea market and an arts-and-crafts market add to the fun. The redbrick building was gutted by fire in April 2007. A $22 million reconstruction has not only made the market more structurally sound, but has restored it to its original Victorian grandeur. Now it is a vibrant and lively gathering place complete with entertainment, art showings, and a pottery studio. ⊠ *7th St. and North Carolina Ave. SE, Capitol Hill* ⊕ *www.easternmarketdc.com* ⊗ *Closed Mon* Ⓜ *Eastern Market.*

DUPONT CIRCLE

ART GALLERIES

Fodor's Choice **Hemphill Fine Arts.** This spacious gem of a contemporary gallery shows
★ established artists in all mediums such as Jacob Kainen and William Christenberry as well as emerging ones like Colby Caldwell. ⊠ *1515 14th St. NW, 3rd fl., Logan Circle* ☎ *202/234–5601* ⊕ *www. hemphillfinearts.com* ⊗ *Closed Sun. and Mon.* Ⓜ *Dupont Circle.*

BOOKS

★ **Kramerbooks & Afterwords.** One of Washington's best-loved independents, this cozy shop has a choice selection of fiction and nonfiction. Open 24 hours on Friday and Saturday, it's a convenient meeting place. Kramerbooks shares space with a café that has late-night dining and live music from Wednesday to Saturday. ■ **TIP→** **There's a computer with free Internet access available in the bar.** ⊠ *1517 Connecticut Ave. NW, Dupont Circle* ☎ *202/387–1400* ⊕ *www.kramers.com* Ⓜ *Dupont Circle.*

Second Story Books. A used-books and -records emporium that stays open late, Second Story may lead bibliophiles to browse for hours. ⊠ *2000 P St. NW, Dupont Circle* ☎ *202/659–8884* ⊕ *www.secondstorybooks. com* Ⓜ *Dupont Circle.*

WOMEN'S CLOTHING

★ **Kid's Closet.** If filling a little one's closet is on your list, stop here for high-quality contemporary infant and children's clothing and toys. Open since 1982, the shop carries sizes 0–7 for boys and 0–16 for girls. ⊠ *1226 Connecticut Ave. NW, Dupont Circle* ☎ *202/429–9247* ⊕ *www.kidsclosetdc.com* ⊗ *Closed Sun.* Ⓜ *Dupont Circle.*

Betsy Fisher. Catering to women of all ages and sizes in search of contemporary and trendy styles, this store stocks one-of-a-kind accessories, clothes, shoes, and jewelry by well-known designers like Diane Von Furstenberg. A small selection of up-and-coming designs is also available. ⊠ *1224 Connecticut Ave. NW, Dupont Circle* ☎ *202/785–1975* ⊕ *www.betsyfisher.com* Ⓜ *Dupont Circle.*

GEORGETOWN

ANTIQUES AND COLLECTIBLES

Jean Pierre Antiques. Very Georgetown, this gorgeous shop sells antique furniture from France, Germany, and Italy. ✉ *2601 and 2603 P St. NW, Georgetown* ☎ *202/337–1731* ⊕ *www.jeanpierreantiques. com* Ⓜ *Dupont Circle.*

WORD OF MOUTH

"Breakfast. Wander. Shop. I think Georgetown would fit the bill nicely." —obxgirl

Marston Luce. House and garden accessories are in the mix here, but the emphasis is on 18th- and 19th-century French country furniture discovered by the owner on yearly buying trips in Europe. They also carry Scandinavian painted furniture. ✉ *1651 Wisconsin Ave. NW, Georgetown* ☎ *202/333–6800* ⊕ *www.marstonluce.com* ☉ *Closed Sun.* Ⓜ *Foggy Bottom/GWU.*

CLOTHING

Commander Salamander. Open since 1979, this funky outpost sells clothes for punks, goths, and ravers. Retro aficionados will also find clothing and accessories for their wardrobes. Sifting through the assortment of leather, chains, toys, and candy-color makeup is as much entertainment as it is shopping. ✉ *1420 Wisconsin Ave. NW, Georgetown* ☎ *202/337–2265* Ⓜ *Foggy Bottom/GWU.*

Sassanova. There are high-end shoes in this girly shop for every occasion—be it a walk on the beach or through a boardroom. Brands carried include Lulu Guinness, Emma Hope, and Sigerson Morrison. Jewelry, bags, and shoes for kids round out the selection. ✉ *1641 Wisconsin Ave. NW, Georgetown* ☎ *202/471–4400* ⊕ *www.sassanova.com.*

Urban Chic. It's hard to imagine a fashionista who wouldn't find something here—whether she could afford it might be another story. Gorgeous suits, jeans, cocktail dresses, and accessories from Catherine Malandrino, Ella Moss, Rebecca Taylor, and Susana Monaco are to be had. The handbags are a highlight. ✉ *1626 Wisconsin Ave. NW, Georgetown* ☎ *202/338–5398* ⊕ *www.urbanchiconline.com.*

HOME FURNISHINGS

A Mano. The store's name is Italian for "by hand," and it lives up to its name, stocking colorful hand-painted ceramics, hand-dyed tablecloths, blown-glass stemware, and other home and garden accessories by Italian and French artisans. There are even adorable kids' gifts. Items are now also available in their online catalog. ✉ *1677 Wisconsin Ave. NW, Georgetown* ☎ *202/298–7200* ⊕ *www.amano.bz.*

SPAS AND BEAUTY SALONS

Blue Mercury. Hard-to-find skin-care lines—Laura Mercier, Trish McEvoy, are just two—are what set this homegrown, now national, chain apart. The retail space up front sells soaps, lotions, perfumes, cosmetics, and skin- and hair-care products. Behind the glass door is the "skin gym," where you can treat yourself to facials, waxing, massage, and oxygen treatments. ✉ *3059 M St. NW, Georgetown* ☎ *202/965–1300* ⊕ *www.*

bluemercury.com Ⓜ *Foggy Bottom/GWU* ✉ *1619 Connecticut Ave. NW, Dupont Circle* ☎ *202/462–1300* Ⓜ *Dupont Circle.*

U STREET

ANTIQUES AND COLLECTIBLES

GoodWood. This friendly shop sells vintage and antique wood furniture, including wonderful 19th-century American pieces, along with stained glass, mirrors, and other decorative items—even a small but gorgeous collection of estate jewelry. ✉ *1428 U St. NW, U Street Corridor* ☎ *202/986–3640* ⊕ *www.goodwooddc.com* ☯ *Closed Mon.–Wed.* Ⓜ *U St./Cardozo.*

CLOTHING

Nana. A hip and friendly staff is one of the reasons why D.C. women love this store. Another is the stock of both new and vintage women's clothes at affordable prices, plus handmade jewelry and cool handbags. ✉ *1528 U St. NW, upstairs, U Street Corridor* ☎ *202/667–6955* ⊕ *www.nanadc.com* Ⓜ *U St./Cardozo.*

HOME FURNISHINGS

Muléh. Exquisite contemporary Indonesian and Filipino home furnishings and trendy clothes from L.A. and New York fill this expansive showroom. The furniture pieces, which are the primary focus of the store, are made from fine organic materials. It's sort of like wandering through a luxury resort in Southeast Asia and finding a fabulous clothing boutique tucked in the back. ✉ *1831 14th St. NW, U Street Corridor* ☎ *202/667–3440* ⊕ *www.muleh.com* ☯ *Closed Mon.* Ⓜ *U St./Cardozo.*

Northern Virginia

WORD OF MOUTH

"I agree that just a morning at Mt. Vernon does not do justice for the visit . . . there is a LOT to see, especially if the young ones are interested in Washington's life as a farmer, his real passion."
—rb_travelerxATyahoo

Updated by Amy McKeever

Although D.C. gets all the recognition for its place in the nation's history, visitors to the region might be surprised by the richness of Northern Virginia. This border region—which originally contributed some of the land to create D.C.—is chockablock with historical references and diverse cultural experiences. Some of the greatest presidents used D.C.'s southern neighbor for their own plantation homes. (George Washington's grand home Mount Vernon is a star attraction.) An influx of immigration has also brought an exciting variety of cuisines to satisfy anyone's palate.

Traffic between the District and Northern Virginia goes both ways (each way slowly). Nearby areas have grown significantly in the recent past and have modern housing, government, and office buildings. Tysons Corner in Fairfax County has major retail outlets clustered close to the I–495 Beltway and has office buildings sprawling across 25.8 million square feet. The area employs about 128,000 people, many of them commuters. Expansion toward Dulles International Airport has been particularly massive, especially along the toll road to the airport. Because of their proximity to D.C., many residents consider themselves Washingtonians, though some Washingtonians think otherwise.

ORIENTATION AND PLANNING

GETTING ORIENTED

Just across the Potomac River from the nation's capital is a region equally steeped in early American history. Although Northern Virginia is now home to mainly federal employees, past residents have included George Washington and Robert E. Lee. These are ideal regions in which to learn about colonial and Civil War–era America and enjoy the diversity of a region that continues to attract immigrants from around the world.

Alexandria. Among the northernmost cities in Virginia, Alexandria was once part of the District of Columbia and now shares its border. Buildings in Alexandria's old downtown, referred to as "Old Town," retain a unified style from the Federal period (1780–1830). Alexandria was a thriving Colonial port, and these days Old Town is also a bustling nightspot with a variety of ethnic restaurants and dozens of pubs.

Arlington. Slightly to the west of Alexandria and also along the D.C. border lies Arlington. Home to Arlington National Cemetery, the Pentagon, and the Marine and Air Force memorials, Arlington is to military history what Alexandria is to Colonial history.

TOP REASONS TO GO

Take a Moment to Reflect at Arlington National Cemetery: See Arlington House and its Washington view; learn about prominent early Virginia families: Washington, Custis, Randolph, and Lee. Visit the Tomb of the Unknowns, the Kennedy graves, and those of other famous Americans, all within these sacred grounds.

Get to Know the First President at Mount Vernon: Visit the historic plantation and learn about George Washington's many contributions as a farmer, patriot, general, and president. See his threshing barn, gristmill, distillery, and personal artifacts,

and experience the new interactive displays.

Return to the First Shot of the Civil War: Explore the site of the first Civil War battle at Manassas National Battlefield Park in the peaceful Virginia countryside. A second Battle of Manassas lasted three days and resulted in 3,300 killed. (The Confederacy won both battles.)

Wonder at the Views in Great Falls: Visit the scenic fall line of the Potomac River, a barrier to upriver navigation that necessitated settlements at Georgetown and Alexandria and the Patowmack Canal, remnants of which are in the park, and later the C&O Canal.

Mount Vernon, Woodlawn, and Gunston Hall. These three estates on the shores of the Potomac were home to some of the most important figures in Colonial America. George Washington resided at Mount Vernon plantation. He gave his step-granddaughter a portion of the land, upon which she and her husband constructed Woodlawn. Another Revolutionary figure, George Mason, lived at Gunston Hall, where he developed a strong philosophy that heavily influenced the Bill of Rights.

Fairfax County. Moving even farther south and into the heart of Northern Virginia, Fairfax County is one of the most rapidly developing counties in the region, with office buildings and upscale shopping overtaking the Tysons Corner area. However, Northern Virginia's rural roots have been preserved in Manassas, where the Manassas National Battlefield Park honors the soldiers of two major Civil War battles, and at Great Falls Park, an ideal site for hiking and boating.

Loudoun County. Farthest away and to the west of D.C., visitors can find the capital of Virginia's horse country. Loudoun County plays host to various fox hunts and steeplechases each year. It is also the home of a burgeoning Virginia wine industry.

PLANNING

WHEN TO GO

Washington, D.C., was built on a swamp, so expect muggy weather if visiting in the summer months. Winter on rare occasions gets extremely cold, but also beautifully snowy. Still, spring and fall are the best bets for a trip. Expect large crowds at Arlington Cemetery around holidays such as Veterans Day and Memorial Day. Major events in D.C. such as the Cherry Blossom Festival in March and April do affect hotel prices and crowds in these areas.

In December the **Historic Alexandria Candlelight Tour** (☎ *703/838–4242* ⊕ *oha.alexandriava.gov*) is a one-night visit to historic houses for light refreshment and performances of period music of the holiday season. Over Presidents Weekend in February, **George Washington's Birthday** (☎ *703/549–7662* ⊕ *www.washingtonbirthday.net*) is celebrated in Alexandria, Virginia, with a parade—175 floats and marching units— and a reenactment of a Revolutionary War skirmish at Fort Ward nearby. The **Virginia Gold Cup** (☎ *540/347–2612* ⊕ *www.vagoldcup. com*), steeplechase horse races held in May near Middleburg in Northern Virginia, has been among the most prominent social and sporting events of the state since the 1920s.

GETTING HERE AND AROUND
AIR TRAVEL
Three major airports serve both suburban Maryland and the Washington, D.C., area. Baltimore-Washington International (BWI) Airport, 10 mi south of Baltimore off I–95 and Route 295, is closer to Montgomery and Prince George's counties than Ronald Reagan National Airport or Washington Dulles International Airport. Alexandria is only a few miles from Ronald Reagan Washington National Airport.

CAR TRAVEL
A car is a must to travel throughout the counties, but avoid the Capital Beltway (I–495) during morning and afternoon rush hours. At those times the congestion is second only to that of Los Angeles.

The Capital Beltway, I–495, circles the District of Columbia through Virginia and Maryland (and enters the District very briefly, as it crosses the Wilson Bridge), providing a circular bypass for I–95 around Washington. During commute hours it becomes congested—toward Tysons Corner in the morning, and away in the evening—so if you plan to spend most of your time in downtown Washington or within the Beltway, it would be prudent to select lodging north of the I–95/I–495 interchange. Note that HOV restrictions prohibit single-person vehicles on I–66 inside the Beltway eastbound during morning rush hour and westbound during evening rush hour.

Roads that run through the region and into downtown Washington include Wisconsin, Connecticut, Georgia, New Hampshire, and Pennsylvania avenues; routes 1 and 50 (the latter turns into New York Avenue upon entering the District); Baltimore Washington Parkway; and I–295, all of which get busy 7:30–9 am and 5–6:30 pm. Giving parking tickets is one of the things capital-area jurisdictions do best, so if you park at meters, be careful and keep the meter fed. Also read parking signs carefully. There are many variations, and they are often quite confusing.

The outer loop in Maryland around the intersection with I–270 is congested in the morning rush, as is the inner loop in the evening rush. Interstate 270, which intersects with I–495 in Montgomery County, reaches destinations north of Rockville in Montgomery County. The Custis Memorial Parkway, I–66, runs east–west between Washington,

D.C., and I–81 near Front Royal, which takes you south through the Shenandoah or north to West Virginia.

METRO TRAVEL

Washington Metropolitan Area Transit Authority (WMATA) provides subway service (Metrorail) in the District and in the Maryland and Virginia suburbs. The Orange, Blue, and Yellow lines serve Northern Virginia. It begins operation at 5 am on weekdays and 7 am on weekends and closes on weekdays at midnight and weekends at 3 am. During the weekday peak periods (5–9:30 am and 3–7 pm), trains come along every three to six minutes. At other times trains run about every 12–15 minutes.

The Metro's base fare is $1.60; the actual price you pay depends on the time of day and the distance traveled. Up to two children under age five ride free with a paying passenger. Buy your ticket at the Farecard machines, some of which accept credit cards. One-day passes are $9 and seven-day passes are $47. ■TIP→ **Make sure you hang on to your Farecard—you need it to exit at your destination.** Locals use the SmarTrip card, a plastic card that can hold any fare amount and can be used throughout the subway system. SmarTrip fares are also cheaper than paying with cash. Buy passes or SmarTrip cards at the Metro Center sales office.

TAXI TRAVEL

Taxicabs are free to operate in adjoining jurisdictions and this is vital, considering that there are two states plus the District and several counties and cities in a small area. Virginia taxis are metered with rates set by the jurisdiction (about a $2.75 flag fare with 34¢ for every sixth of a mile in Alexandria and 40¢ for every fifth of a mile in Arlington). Taxis are usually waiting near the busier Metrorail stations like Ballston, King Street, and Rosslyn, and the bigger hotels.

Taxis at the Virginia airports are very tightly regulated. Washington Flyer cabs serve Dulles International Airport exclusively from the airport but any taxi can deliver there. A starter outside the arrivals area at Reagan National loads taxicabs from a regulated line of incoming taxis and will provide a fare sheet if desired. An airport fee of $2.50 is added to your fare to pay for this service. Some taxi drivers accept credit cards, but ask first.

TRAIN TRAVEL

Amtrak serves the region with six trains to Alexandria and two to Manassas in each direction daily. Amtrak's Autotrain terminal is in Lorton, between Springfield and Woodbridge and just off I–95. The Alexandria station is colocated with a major bus hub and a Metrorail station. Virginia Railway Express (VRE) provides cheap workday service between Union Station in Washington, D.C., and Fredericksburg and Manassas, with 18 stops, including all Amtrak stations along the route. VRE offers discounted multiride, five-day, monthly, and senior ticket fares. Free parking is available at most suburban VRE stations.

Amtrak has scheduled stops in New Carrollton and at BWI Airport as part of its East Coast service.

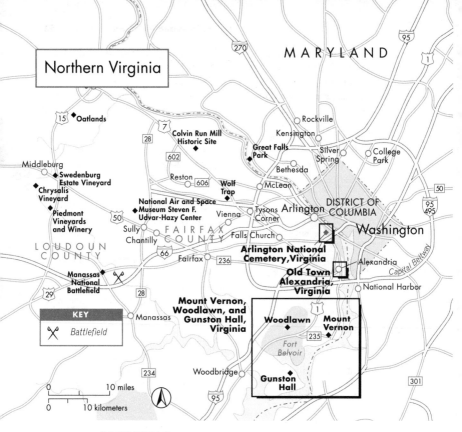

Northern Virginia

MARYLAND

Oatlands
Colvin Run Mill Historic Site
Rockville
Kensington
Great Falls Park
Silver Spring
College Park
Middleburg
Swedenburg Estate Vineyard
Chrysalis Vineyard
Reston
Bethesda
McLean
Wolf Trap
National Air and Space Museum Steven F. Udvar-Hazy Center
Vienna
Tysons Corner
Arlington
DISTRICT OF COLUMBIA
Piedmont Vineyards and Winery
Sully
Chantilly
FAIRFAX COUNTY
Falls Church
Washington
LOUDOUN COUNTY
Fairfax
Arlington National Cemetery, Virginia
Alexandria
Capital Beltway
Manassas National Battlefield
Old Town Alexandria, Virginia
National Harbor
KEY
Battlefield
Manassas
Mount Vernon, Woodlawn, and Gunston Hall, Virginia
Woodlawn
Mount Vernon
Fort Belvoir
Woodbridge
Gunston Hall
0   10 miles
0   10 kilometers

ESSENTIALS

Air Contacts SuperShuttle (☎ 800/258–3826 or 202/296–6662 ⊕ www.supershuttle.com). **Washington Flyer** (☎ 888/927–4359 ⊕ www.washfly.com).

Metro Information Metrorail (☎ 202/637–7000 ⊕ www.wmata.com).

Train Contacts Virginia Railway Express (VRE ☎ 800/743–3873 ⊕ www.vre.org).

DISCOUNTS AND DEALS

Purchase the Key to the City from the Alexandria Visitors Center for discounted admission to nine museums in the historic Old Town ($12). The pass includes admission to Carlyle House Historic Park, Gadsby's Tavern Museum, the Stabler-Leadbeater Apothecary Museum, the Lee-Fendall House Museum & Garden and more. It also includes special offers and discounts from local shops and restaurants.

RESTAURANTS

There is no need to go into the District to find a decent restaurant. Alexandria and Arlington have a wide variety of ethnic and American restaurants at reasonable prices. Alexandria has several good restaurants near the river on and around King Street, but parking is tough and the Metrorail station is far away. In Arlington there is a good variety of dining between the neighborhoods of Ballston and Rosslyn around five closely spaced Metrorail stations. The Shirlington area, just off

Shirley Highway south of the Pentagon and with loads of free parking, has become a convenient and reasonable dining destination for both Arlington and Alexandria.

HOTELS

It's best to book your hotel room in advance. Occupancy rates are high, and you're likely to pay only a little less than you would in Washington. Tourists coming to see Washington's cherry blossoms make spring the busiest season. December and January tend to be the slowest and least expensive months, except around a presidential inauguration.

Lodging choices range from familiar hotel chains to homes with 18th-century architecture blended with modern amenities. **Alexandria & Arlington Bed and Breakfast Network** (✉ *4938 Hampden La., Suite 164, Bethesda* ☎ *703/549–3415 or 888/549–3415* ⊕ *www.aabbn.com*) can arrange accommodations in Northern Virginia.

WHAT IT COSTS					
	¢	$	$$	$$$	$$$$
Restaurants	under $10	$10–$16	$17–$23	$24–$30	over $30
Hotels	under $100	$100–$160	$161–$230	$231–$300	over $300

Restaurant prices are per person for a main course at dinner. Hotel prices are for a standard double room, excluding state and local taxes.

PLANNING YOUR TIME

You'll want to devote most of your time to the areas closest to Washington, D.C., such as Arlington and Alexandria. These are easily connected to one another via Metrorail and Metrobus. It wouldn't be unusual to spend the day visiting Arlington's monuments to the military, yet end the day with a seafood dinner in Old Town Alexandria. Allow about an hour for travel through the District of Columbia via Metrorail, however, especially on weekends or during non–rush hours. Another quick trip from Virginia is to ride the ferry across the Potomac River from either Mount Vernon or Alexandria to stroll the National Harbor in Maryland or the streets of Georgetown. For all other vehicular crossings, the Capital Beltway traverses the Potomac as well, via the American Legion and Woodrow Wilson bridges.

If you have more time, drive away from the capital toward Manassas, Middleburg, and Occoquan. Plan to spend at least half a day or more in each outlying town. Enjoy the slower pace of life and go wine tasting, antiques shopping, or picnicking in the many parks.

ALEXANDRIA

A lively mix of historic homes, taverns, restaurants, and shops, Alexandria seems to exist in two or three centuries at once. Founded in 1749 by Scottish merchants eager to capitalize on the booming tobacco trade, Alexandria first emerged as one of the most important ports in Colonial America. The city dwarfed Georgetown—Washington's oldest neighborhood—in the days before the Revolution, and through the

Civil War had one of the country's largest slave markets. Alexandria is linked to many significant events and personages of the Colonial, Revolutionary, and Civil War periods. Members of the Lee family of Revolutionary and Civil War fame lived here, and George Washington had a town house and attended church here, though he lived a few miles south in Mount Vernon.

For many African-Americans fleeing slavery, part of their journey on the Underground Railroad included a stop in Alexandria. This was true of one of the largest and most celebrated slave escapes, in which 77 individuals, many of whom labored in homes in Alexandria, took refuge on the *Pearl,* a ship bound for New Jersey, which left from Washington's 7th Street Wharf in April 1848. Unfortunately the ship was captured in Maryland and most of its passengers were returned to Bruin's Slave Jail. Harriett Beecher Stowe modeled her account of the slave trade in *Uncle Tom's Cabin* on this establishment.

This vibrant past remains alive in the historic district of **Old Town Alexandria**—an area of cobbled streets, restored 18th- and 19th-century homes, churches, and taverns close to the water. The main arteries of this district are Washington Street (the G.W. Parkway as it passes through town) and King Street. Most points of interest are on the east (Potomac) side of Washington Street.

GETTING HERE AND AROUND
Alexandria is only a few miles from Ronald Reagan Washington National Airport. It's easy to get there by Metrorail, taxi, water taxi, or Metrobus. Visit the Old Town sights on foot if you're prepared to walk 20 blocks or so; parking is usually scarce, especially close to the river, and the parking police seem to catch every violation (especially in alleys). ■ TIP→ The visitor center at Ramsay House will give you a 24-hour permit for free parking at any two-hour metered spot.

TOURS Old Town Experience runs walking tours that leave from the Ramsay House Visitors Center 10:30 am Monday through Saturday and 2 pm Sunday; tickets are $15. Another tour operator, Footsteps to the Past, also leads tours from the visitor center at 1:30 pm Monday through Saturday; tickets are $15. Alexandria Colonial Tours leads guided walking tours of historic Alexandria by reservation. Ghost-and-graveyard tours (reservations not required) are conducted Friday, Saturday, and Sunday nights, although in summer you can also take a tour on Wednesday and Thursday nights. Tours are nightly in October.

TIMING AND PRECAUTIONS
As with anywhere in the D.C. area, beware main roads at rush hour, from 7:30 am to 9 am and 5 pm to 6:30 pm. King and Duke streets in Alexandria will be tough to navigate in those hours, and the Metro will be crowded. The Woodrow Wilson Bridge is also notorious for delays at this hour.

ESSENTIALS
Taxi **Alexandria Yellow Cab** (☎ 703/548–7505)

Tours **Alexandria Colonial Tours** (☎ 703/519–1749). **The Old Town Experience** (☎ 703/836–0694). **Footsteps to the Past** (☎ 703/683–3451).

Train Contacts **Alexandria Amtrak station** (✉ *110 Callahan Dr.*
☎ *703/836–4339).*

Visitor Information **Alexandria Convention and Visitors Association**
(✉ *Ramsay House, 221 King St., Alexandria* ☎ *703/746–3301 or 800/388–9119*
⊕ *www.visitalexandria.com).*

EXPLORING

TOP ATTRACTIONS

Appomattox Confederate Statue. In 1861, when Alexandria was occupied
by Union forces, the 800 soldiers of the city's garrison marched out of
town to join the Confederate Army. In the middle of Washington and
Prince streets stands a statue marking the point where they assembled.
In 1885 Confederate veterans proposed a memorial to honor their fallen
comrades. This statue, based on John A. Elder's painting *Appomattox,*
is of a lone soldier glumly surveying the battlefields after General Robert
E. Lee's surrender. The names of 99 Alexandria Confederate dead are
carved on the base. ✉ *Washington and Prince Sts., Old Town.*

Boyhood Home of Robert E. Lee. The childhood home in Alexandria of the
commander of the Confederate forces of Virginia is a fine example of
a 19th-century Federal town house. The house is privately owned and
not open to visitors. ✉ *607 Oronoco St., Old Town.*

Carlyle House. Alexandria forefather and Scottish merchant John Carlyle
built a grand house here, completed in 1753 and modeled on a country manor house in the old country. Students of the French and Indian
War will want to know that the dwelling served as General Braddock's
headquarters. The house retains its original 18th-century woodwork
and is furnished with Chippendale furniture and Chinese porcelain. An
architectural exhibit on the second floor explains how the house was
built; outside there's an attractive garden of Colonial-era plants. ✉ *121
N. Fairfax St., Old Town* ☎ *703/549–2997* ⊕ *www.carlylehouse.org*
🌐 *$5* ◷ *Tues.–Sat. 10–4, Sun. noon–4, guided tour every ½ hr.*

Christ Church. Both Washington and Robert E. Lee were pewholders in
this Episcopal church, which remains in nearly original condition. (Washington paid quite a lot of money for pews 59 and 60.) Built in 1773, this
fine example of an English Georgian country-style church has a Palladian
window, an interior balcony, and an English wrought-brass-and-crystal
chandelier. Docents give tours during visiting hours. ✉ *118 N. Washington St., Old Town* ☎ *703/549–1450* ⊕ *www.historicchristchurch.org*
🌐 *$5 donation suggested* ◷ *Mon.–Sat. 9–4, Sun. 2–4.*

☪ **Gadsby's Tavern Museum.** The two buildings that now comprise this
★ museum—a circa-1785 tavern and the 1792 City Hotel—were centers
of political and social life. George Washington celebrated his birth-
days in the ballroom. Other noted patrons included Thomas Jefferson, John Adams, and the Marquis de Lafayette. The taproom, dining
room, assembly room, ballroom, and communal bedrooms have been
restored to their original appearance. The tours on Friday evenings are
led by a costumed guide carrying a lantern. ✉ *134 N. Royal St., Old
Town* ☎ *703/838–4242* ⊕ *www.gadsbystavern.org* 🌐 *$5, lantern tour*

*$5 ⊘ Nov.–Mar., Wed.–Sat. 11–4, Sun. 1–4, last tour at 3:45; Apr.–
Oct., Tues.–Sat. 10–5, Sun. and Mon. 1–5, last tour at 4:45; tours 15
mins before and after the hour. Half-hour lantern tours Mar.–Nov.,
Fri. 7–9:30.*

★ **George Washington Masonic National Memorial.** Because Alexandria, like
Washington, D.C., has no really tall buildings, the spire of this memorial dominates the surroundings and is visible for miles. The building
overlooks King and Duke streets, Alexandria's major east–west arteries. It's a respectable uphill climb from the King St. Metrorail and bus
stations. From the ninth-floor observation deck (reached by elevator)
you get a spectacular view of Alexandria and Washington, D.C., but
access above the first and mezzanine floors is by guided tour only. The
building contains furnishings from the first Masonic lodge in Alexandria. George Washington became a Mason in 1752 in Fredericksburg,
and became Charter Master of the Alexandria lodge when it was chartered in 1788, remaining active in Masonic affairs during his tenure as
president, 1789–97. ⊠ *101 Callahan Dr., Old Town* ☎ *703/683–2007*
⊕ *www.gwmemorial.org* ▭ *Free* ⊘ *Daily 9–4; 1-hr guided tour of
building and observation deck daily at 10, 11:30, 1:30, and 3.*

Lee-Fendall House. At historic Lee Corner at North Washington and
Oronoco streets, the Lee-Fendall House was built in 1785; over the
course of the next 118 years it was home to 37 members of the Lee
family and served as a Union hospital. The house and its furnishings,
of the 1850–70 period, present an intimate study of 19th-century
family life. Highlights include a splendid collection of Lee heirlooms,
period pieces produced by Alexandria manufacturers, and the beautifully restored, award-winning garden. ⊠ *614 Oronoco St., Old Town*
☎ *703/548–1789* ▭ *$5* ⊘ *Wed.–Sat. 10–4; Sun. 1–4; sometimes closed
for private events.*

Lyceum. Built in 1839 and one of Alexandria's best examples of Greek
Revival design, the Lyceum is also the city's official history museum.
Over the years the building has served as the Alexandria Library, a
Civil War hospital, a residence, and offices. Restored in the 1970s for
the Bicentennial, it has an impressive collection including examples of
18th- and 19th-century silver, tools, stoneware, and Civil War photographs taken by Mathew Brady. ⊠ *201 S. Washington St., Old Town*
☎ *703/838–4994* ⊕ *www.alexandriahistory.org* ▭ *$2 donation sug-
gested* ⊘ *Mon.–Sat. 10–5, Sun. 1–5.*

Ramsay House. The best place to start a tour of Alexandria's Old Town
is at the **Alexandria Convention and Visitors Association,** in Ramsay
House, the home of the town's first postmaster and lord mayor, William Ramsay. The structure is the site of the first house in Alexandria.
The unusually helpful staff hands out brochures, maps for self-guided
walking tours, and 24-hour permits for free parking at any two-hour
metered spot. You can also use a free computer station to plan your
travels. ⊠ *221 King St., Old Town* ☎ *703/838–4200; 800/388–9119*
⊕ *www.funside.com* ▭ *Guided tours $10–$15* ⊘ *Daily 10–8; tours
Mon.–Sat. 10:30, Sun. 2.*

3

♻ **Torpedo Factory Art Center**. Torpedoes were manufactured here by the U.S.
★ Navy during World War II. Now the building, housing the studios and
workshops of about 160 artists and artisans, has become one of Alexandria's most popular attractions. You can observe printmakers, jewelry
makers, sculptors, painters, and potters as they create original work in
their studios. The Torpedo Factory also houses the Alexandria Archaeology Museum, which displays artifacts such as plates, cups, pipes, and
coins from an early tavern, and Civil War soldiers' equipment. If digging
interests you, call to sign up for the well-attended public digs (offered
once a month from June to October: ☎ 703/838–4399 ⌦ $5 ⌦ Reservations essential). ⊠ 105 N. Union St., Old Town ☎ 703/838–4565
⊕ www.torpedofactory.org ⌦ Free ☉ Fri.–Wed. 10–6, Thurs. 10–9.

**QUICK
BITES**
The Dairy Godmother (⊠ 2310 Mount Vernon Ave., Del Ray ☎ 703/683–
7767 ⊕ www.thedairygodmother.com ☉ Closed Tues.). Out in Del Ray, this
Wisconsin-style frozen custard shop was a local family favorite long before
President Obama came in with his daughters for a Father's Day treat. The
Dairy Godmother features daily flavors of custard and sorbet like maple
walnut or strawberry balsamico, as well as sundaes like the Dusty Road
(made with hot fudge and malt powder).

WORTH NOTING

Alexandria Black History Museum. This museum, devoted to the history
of African-Americans in Alexandria and Virginia, is at the site of the
Robert H. Robinson Library, a building constructed in the wake of a
landmark 1939 sit-in protesting the segregation of Alexandria libraries.
The federal census of 1790 recorded 52 free African-Americans living in
the city. The port town was one of the largest slave exporting points in
the South, with at least two highly active slave markets. ⊠ 902 Wythe
St., Old Town ☎ 703/838–4356 ⊕ oha.alexandriava.gov/bhrc ⌦ $2
☉ Tues.–Sat. 10–4.

Athenaeum. One of the most noteworthy structures in Alexandria, this
striking, reddish-brown Greek Revival edifice at the corner of Prince
and Lee streets stands out from its many redbrick Federal neighbors.
Built in 1851 as a bank (Robert E. Lee had an account here) and later
used as a Union Army hospital, then as a talcum powder factory for
the Stabler-Leadbeater Apothecary, the Athenaeum now houses the gallery of the Northern Virginia Fine Arts Association. They also offer
ballet classes through the Washington School of Ballet. This block of
Prince Street between Fairfax and Lee streets is known as **Gentry Row,**
after the 18th- and 19th-century inhabitants of its imposing three-story
houses. ⊠ 201 Prince St., Old Town ☎ 703/548–0035 ⊕ www.nvfaa.org
⌦ Free ☉ Thurs., Fri., Sun. noon–4; Sat. 1–4. Times subject to change
so call to confirm.

Captain's Row. Many of Alexandria's sea captains once lived on this
block. The ships sailing to America during the Revolution weren't fully
loaded with cargo, and they used stones to balance the ship during
the passage. These stones were then used to pave the streets, as can be
witnessed best on Prince and Princess streets. ⊠ Prince St. between Lee
and Union Sts., Old Town.

Appomattox
Confederate
Statue **17**

Alexandria
Black History
Museum **11**

Athenaeum **4**

Boyhood
Home of
Robert E. Lee ... **10**

Captain's Row ...**5**

Carlyle House ...**7**

Christ Church .. **13**

Friendship Fire
House **15**

Gadsby's
Tavern
Museum **8**

George
Washington
Masonic Nat'l.
Memorial **16**

Lee-Fendall
House **9**

Lloyd House ... **12**

Lyceum **14**

Old
Presbyterian
Meeting House ..**3**

Ramsay House ...**1**

Stabler-
Leadbeater
Apothecary **2**

Torpedo Factory
Art Center........**6**

Old Town
Alexandria,
Virginia

♻ **Friendship Fire House.** Alexandria's showcase firehouse dates from 1855 and has the appearance and implements of a typical 19th-century firehouse. The Friendship Fire Company, however, was established in 1774 and bought its first engine in 1775. Among early fire engines on display is a hand pumper built in Philadelphia in 1851. Most everything can be seen through the windows even when the firehouse is closed. ⊠ *107 S. Alfred St., Old Town* ☎ *703/838–3891* ⊕ *oha.alexandriava. gov/friendship* ☞ *Free* ⊙ *Sat. and Sun. 1–4.*

Lloyd House. A fine example of Georgian architecture, Lloyd House was built in 1797 and is owned by the City of Alexandria and used for offices for the Office of Historic Alexandria. The interior has nothing on display so it is best admired from outside. ⊠ *220 N. Washington St., Old Town.*

Old Presbyterian Meeting House. Except from 1899 through 1949, the Old Presbyterian Meeting House has been the site of an active Presbyterian congregation since 1775. Scottish pioneers founded the church, and Scottish patriots used it as a gathering place during the Revolution. Four memorial services were held for George Washington here. The tomb of an unknown soldier of the American Revolution lies in a corner of the small churchyard, where many prominent Alexandrians— including Dr. James Craik, physician and best friend to Washington and

John Carlyle—are interred. The original sanctuary was rebuilt after a lightning strike and fire in 1835. The interior is appropriately plain; if you'd like to visit the sanctuary you can borrow a key in the church office, or just peek through the many wide windows along both sides. ⊠ *321 S. Fairfax St., Old Town* ☎ *703/549–6670* ⊕ *www.opmh.org* 🎫 *Free* ☉ *Weekdays 9–4:30.*

Stabler-Leadbeater Apothecary. Once patronized by George Washington and the Lee family, the Stabler-Leadbeater Apothecary is among the oldest apothecaries in the country (the reputed oldest is in Bethlehem, Pennsylvania). Some believe that it was here, on October 17, 1859, that Lt. Col. Robert E. Lee received orders to lead Marines sent from the Washington Barracks to help suppress John Brown's insurrection at Harpers Ferry (then part of Virginia). The shop now houses a museum of 18th- and 19th-century apothecary memorabilia, including one of the finest collections of apothecary bottles in the country. In fact, they have so many that curators are still processing them all. ■ TIP➜ **Tours include discussions of Alexandria life, as well as the history of the family that owned and ran the shop for 141 years.** Tours designed especially for children are available. ⊠ *105–107 S. Fairfax St., Old Town* ☎ *703/838–3852* ⊕ *www.apothecarymuseum.org* 🎫 *$5* ☉ *Apr.–Oct., Tues.–Sat. 10–5, Sun. and Mon. 1–5; Nov.–Mar., Wed.–Sat. 11–4, Sun. 1–4.*

QUICK BITES

Afterdeck Cafe at Washington Sailing Marina. Grab a seat on this restaurant's deck beside the Potomac River (⊠ 1 Marina Dr. ☎ 703/548–0001), where you can watch sailboats and airport operations and enjoy salads, sandwiches, flatbread pizzas, several reasonable draft beers, soft drinks, and coffee. It's ½-mi south of Ronald Reagan National Airport just off the George Washington Memorial Parkway.

WHERE TO EAT

¢   ✕**Eamonn's A Dublin Chipper.** A nod to his native Ireland, this fish-and-chips joint is Chef Cathal Armstrong's latest addition to his growing Old Town Alexandria empire—he also runs the acclaimed Restaurant Eve and Majestic Café. This 20-seat, counter-service, chipper-with-attitude serves up crispy cod and fries with your choice of seven different sauces from classic tartar to curry. Down it with a pint of Guinness or an Irish soda and finish with a piping hot fried Mars bar, a weird-but-wonderful dessert treat that's the perfect end to a battered meal. ■ TIP➜ **When the pirate flag is flying and a blue light glows at an unmarked door, head upstairs to the PX, a 21st-century speakeasy operated by Armstrong and his wife.** ⊠ *728 King St., Arlington* ☎ *703/299–8384* ⊕ *www. eamonnsdublinchipper* ▤ *AE, MC, V.*

$$$–$$$$
AMERICAN

✕**The Grille at the Morrison House.** On a quiet street in central Alexandria, this hotel dining room serves breakfast and dinner only. The cuisine is French and American with Southern influences and an emphasis on local ingredients. Entrées on the tasting menu rotate seasonally but include popular dishes such as a progression of scallops and also pork cheeks. Or try the oysters Rockefeller or burger topped with Virginia ham and Mountaineer cheese on toasted brioche. A pianist entertains in the intimate dining room on some nights. The Grille hosts an afternoon tea every third Saturday of the month for $38. ⊠ *Morrison House, 116 S. Alfred St.* ☏ *703/838–8000 or 866/834–6628* ⊕ *www. thegrillealexandria.com* ⊟ *AE, DC, MC, V* ⊘ *No lunch.*

$
ITALIAN

✕ **Il Porto.** Inside an old building just one block from the Potomac, Il Porto's interior is reminiscent of Italy, with plaster walls, exposed wooden beams, and checkered tablecloths. The menu includes traditional Italian versions of veal, seafood, pasta, and chicken, and creative interpretations such as *Paradiso Terra e Mare* (chicken, shrimp, scallops, and chopped clams in white-wine-and-lemon sauce). Healthful touches include whole-wheat pasta and organic wines. ⊠ *121 King St.* ☏ *703/836–8833* ⊕ *www.ilportoristorante.com* ⊟ *AE, D, MC, V.*

$$–$$$
AMERICAN

✕ **La Porta's.** At the west end of Old Town and about two blocks from the King St. Metrorail station, La Porta's combines food with a variety of gentle, good music nightly in an intimate setting. Fresh seafood is the strong suit here, especially the crab cakes. Monday and Tuesday you can choose two entrée specials plus a bottle of wine for $29 per couple—a great deal. Park free in their enclosed lot beside the restaurant. Brunch is served Sunday 11–3. ⊠ *1600 Duke St.* ☏ *703/837–9117* ⊕ *www.laportas.net* ⊟ *AE, D, DC, MC, V* ⊘ *No lunch Sat.* Ⓜ *King St.*

$$
SPANISH

✕ **Las Tapas.** A big, bright, authentic Spanish restaurant, Las Tapas specializes in, what else? There are 62 tapas on the menu, such as tortilla espanola, plus substantial entrées, including five kinds of paella. Indeed, Paella Valenciana is the signature dish in this friendly restaurant. Order a jug of the red, white, or specialty sangrias to accompany your meal. Then sit back and watch the flamenco dancers, who perform Tuesday and Thursday nights; Wednesday, Friday, and Saturday nights bring Spanish guitar music. ⊠ *710 King St.* ☏ *703/836–4000* ⊕ *www.lastapas. us* ⊟ *AE, D, DC, MC, V.*

$$$
FRENCH

✕ **Le Refuge.** This petite French restaurant one block from Alexandria's busiest intersection has been a local favorite for more than 25 years. It is Alexandria's oldest French restaurant with its original owners, Jean Francois and his wife Francoise. Enjoy lovingly prepared, authentic French country fare with beaucoup flavor; popular selections include trout, bouillabaisse, garlicky rack of lamb, frogs' legs, and beef Wellington. Polish it all off with an order of profiteroles or crème brûlée. Personal service (they don't like to keep you waiting between courses) makes this cozy restaurant popular. ⊠ *127 N. Washington St.* ☏ *703/548–4661* ⊕ *www.lerefugealexandria.com* ⊟ *AE, DC, MC, V* ⊘ *Closed Sun.*

$$–$$$
AMERICAN

✕ **Majestic Café.** A 1930s-era landmark that had been closed since 1978, the Majestic Café reopened in 2002 and Chef Cathal Armstrong took over in May of 2007, bringing local chef Shannon Overmiller with him. An art deco facade remains; inside, the café brings a modern sensibility to its 1930s origins. The cooking style is rustic American, with an emphasis on simplicity and seasonal products. Some of the comfort food on the menu includes home-style meat loaf and mashed potatoes, while other dishes include Amish chicken two ways and fried green tomatoes with burrata cheese and basil puree. On Sunday, in addition to the regular menu, Majestic Café offers a special family-style dinner for $22 per person, including dessert. Themes for these dinners include "Summer Lovin'" and "The Harvest." The restaurant is about eight blocks from the Metrorail. ⊠ *911 King St.* ☎ *703/837–9117* ⊕ *www.majesticcafe.com* ⊟ *AE, D, DC, MC, V* Ⓜ *King St.*

¢–$ ✕ **Rocklands.** This homegrown barbecue stop is known for its flavor-
BARBECUE ful pork ribs smoked over hickory and red oak. Sides like silky corn
Ⓒ pudding, rich mac 'n' cheese, and crunchy slaw are as good as the meats, which cover everything from beef brisket and chopped pork barbecue to chicken and fish. The family crowd comes for dinner, but they also do popular take-out. There is another branch in Arlington at 3471 Washington Boulevard. ⊠ *25 S. Quaker La., Alexandria, VA* ☎ *703/778–9663* ⊕ *www.rocklands.com* ⊟ *AE, MC, V.*

$$ ✕ **Rustico.** Located in the north end of Old Town, Rustico is known as
AMERICAN much for its substantial beer menu as its hearth-fired pizzas and sea-sonal ingredients. This upscale pub carries about 300 beers, including 25 on draught. The food is as rustic as the brick-and-plaster walls, with modern flair like a truffled couscous carbonara topped with a poached egg, or homemade thick-cut fries tossed in Caesar or ranch dressing. Rustico's even got you covered on carryout with six packs that you can take home along with your barbecue pork pizza. ⊠ *827 Slaters La., Alexandria* ☎ *703/224–5051* ⊕ *www.rusticorestaurant.com* ⊟ *AE, D, DC, MC, V* ⊙ *Closed Mon.* Ⓜ *Braddock Rd.*

$$ ✕ **Taverna Cretekou.** Whitewashed stucco walls and colorful macramé
GREEK tapestries bring a bit of the Mediterranean to the center of Old Town. On the menu are *exohikon* (lamb baked in a pastry shell) and a fish sauteed with artichokes, and the extensive wine list includes only Greek choices, such as the special Taverna Cretekou wine made in the south of Kalamata. In warm weather you can dine in the canopied garden. ■ TIP→ **Thursday evenings bring live music, and if you are so moved, plates for breaking are $2 each—*opa*!** A buffet brunch is served on Sunday. ⊠ *818 King St.* ☎ *703/548–8688* ⊕ *www.tavernacretekou.com* ⊟ *AE, MC, V* ⊙ *Closed Mon.*

$$$ ✕ **Vermilion.** Be sure to make reservations because foodies flock from
AMERICAN DC for a taste of Chef Anthony Chittum's award-winning modern American menu at Vermilion. This upscale casual establishment puts an emphasis on the casual with its exposed brick walls, ceiling beams, and gas lamps. Chittum favors locally sourced, sustainable ingredients, though quality trumps local here so you may find an Alaskan halibut on this Mid-Atlantic menu alongside a braised shortrib and caramelized onion *crespelle*. Vermilion is also one of the area's favorite weekend brunch spots. Tuesday and Wednesday evenings bring live music to the first-floor lounge, as well as the first Sunday of each month. ⊠ *1120 King St., Alexandria* ☎ *703/684–9669* ⊕ *www.vermilionrestaurant.com* ⊟ *AE, MC, V.*

WHERE TO STAY

$–$$ 🏨 **Best Western Old Colony Inn.** Just north of Old Town in a peaceful location within walking distance of most local attractions, this redbrick two-story hotel offers free shuttle service to the Braddock Road Metrorail stop, Old Town, and Washington Reagan National Airport. Rooms have Federal-style cherry furnishings with a work desk and upholstered lounge chair. If the munchies hit in the middle of the night, raid the 24-hour snack bar. **Pros:** rates include a hot breakfast buffet, free local calls, and a newspaper; children under 18 stay free. **Cons:** rooms are a bit drab, with quilted floral bedspreads; location is a bit of a hike from most of Old Town's sights. ⊠ *1101 N. Washington St.* ☎ *703/739–2222 or 800/937–8376* ⊕ *www.bestwestern.com* ⪻ *49 rooms* ⅋ *In-room: a/c, refrigerator, DVD, Internet. In-hotel: restaurant, gym, laundry facilities, laundry service, parking (free)* ⊟ *AE, D, DC, MC, V* ⑩ *BP.*

$$–$$$ ⛢ **Embassy Suites Old Town Alexandria.** The relaxing sound of rushing
☾ water from the atrium fountain adjacent to the restaurant greets you inside this modern all-suites hotel three blocks from Alexandria's landmark George Washington Masonic Temple. Train buffs should request a suite facing the Amtrak and Metrorail stations across the street. Each suite has a living room with overstuffed sofa and chairs and a work desk; beds have an abundance of fluffy pillows. A free shuttle is available to transport you to the scenic Alexandria riverfront, which has shops and restaurants. **Pros:** the cooked-to-order breakfast is complimentary; kids can romp in the playroom. **Cons:** train station across the street can be noisy; Wi-Fi use costs $12.95 a day. ⊠ *1900 Diagonal Rd.* ☎ *703/684–5900 or 800/362–2779* ⊕ *www.embassysuites.com* ⪻ *268 suites* ⅋ *In-room: a/c, kitchen, refrigerator, Internet. In-hotel: restaurant, pool, gym, laundry facilities, laundry service, Wi-Fi hotspot, parking (paid)* ⊟ *AE, D, DC, MC, V* ⑩ *BP* Ⓜ *King St.*

$$$ ⛢ **Hotel Monaco Alexandria.** There's just a fine line between history and modernity in Old Town Alexandria, home to not only George Washington's old haunts but also award-winning restaurants and funky shops. Hotel Monaco reflects that spirit clearly through its luxurious guestrooms where the crimson and silver of a Civil War soldier's uniform inspire the decor and mix harmoniously with 21st-century amenities like 37-inch flat-screens and plush animal print robes. Teal woodwork and overstuffed couches make the lobby an inviting place for a complimentary cup of coffee or glass of wine. **Pros:** central location to Old Town sights; guests enjoy a complimentary wine happy hour in the lobby between 5 pm and 6 pm daily. **Cons:** thin walls mean you might hear conversations in adjoining rooms or barking dogs in the hallway. ⊠ *480 King St.* ☎ *703/549–6080* ⊕ *www.monaco-alexandria. com* ⪻ *241 rooms, 10 suites* ⅋ *In-room: a/c, safe, Wi-Fi. In-hotel: restaurant, room service, bar, pool, gym, spa, laundry facilities, laundry service, Wi-Fi hotspot, parking (paid), some pets allowed* ⊟ *AE, D, DC, MC, V.*

$$–$$$ ⛢ **Morrison House.** The architecture, parquet floors, crystal chandeliers,
★ decorative fireplaces, and furnishings here are so faithful to the Federal period (1790–1820) that it's often mistaken for a renovation rather than what it is: a structure built from scratch in 1985. The hotel blends Early American charm with modern conveniences. Some rooms have fireplaces and four-poster beds, but all have hair dryers, bathrobes and a pack of fresh-baked cookies on your pillow. The highly regarded Grille restaurant serves American contemporary cuisine. **Pros:** in the heart of Old Town, about a 15-minute walk from the train and Metrorail

stations; modern building with historic charm. **Cons:** can be a little pricey; fireplaces are decorative only. ⊠ *116 S. Alfred St.* ☎ *703/838–8000 or 800/367–0800* ⊕ *www.morrisonhouse.com* ⤴ *42 rooms, 3 suites* ⑂ *In-room: a/c, DVD. In-hotel: 2 restaurants, room service, bars, Wi-Fi hotspot, parking (paid)* ⊟ *AE, DC, MC, V* Ⓜ *King St.*

NIGHTLIFE AND THE ARTS

BARS AND PUBS

Murphy's Irish Pub (⊠ *713 King St., Old Town* ☎ *703/548–1717)* has authentic Irish entertainment nightly and a blazing fire when winter comes. Aficionados praise Alexandria's **Shenandoah Brewing Company** (⊠ *652 S. Pickett St.* ☎ *703/823–9508)* for its stouts and ales, especially the Bourbon Stoney Stout, aged in oak casks previously used to make premium bourbon. Inside, the atmosphere is slightly industrial and the menu is limited to foods grown or made in Virginia: peanuts, potato chips, chili, and a delicious beer-queso dip. **Union Street Public House** (⊠ *121 S. Union St., Old Town* ☎ *703/548–1785* ⊕ *www.unionstreetpublichouse.com)* has three dining rooms and two bars that twist through this 200-year-old building. Although it's also a restaurant, come late for a beer in the busy main bar or chat with friends in the cozy OysterBar area.

LIVE MUSIC

The **Birchmere** (⊠ *3701 Mt. Vernon Ave.* ☎ *703/549–7500* ⊕ *www.birchmere.com)* is one of the best places outside the Blue Ridge Mountains to hear acoustic folk and bluegrass. It also gets more than its share of headliners, including frequent visitors Mary Chapin Carpenter, Lyle Lovett, and Dave Matthews. Tickets are on the expensive side, with big names fetching up to $95. **La Porta's** (⊠ *1600 Duke St.* ☎ *703/683–6313* Ⓜ *King St.)* has jazz combos nightly. **Las Tapas** (⊠ *710 King St., Old Town* ☎ *703/836–4000)* has flamenco dancing Tuesday and Thursday nights and Spanish guitar music Wednesday, Friday, and Saturday nights, without cover charge.

SPORTS AND THE OUTDOORS

BOATING

If you can't snag one of the boats at the Washington Sailing Marina, try **Belle Haven Marina** (⊠ *George Washington Pkwy.* ☎ *703/768–0018)*, south of Wilson Bridge just off George Washington Memorial Parkway. This rustic outfit rents Sunfish ($30 for two hours weekdays, $35 weekends), Flying Scots ($46 for two hours weekdays, $54 weekends), and canoes and kayaks ($20 for two hours), from April to October. All-day rates are available. The **Washington Sailing Marina** (⊠ *1 Marina Dr.* ☎ *703/548–9027* ⊕ *www.washingtonsailingmarina.com)*, on the George Washington Memorial Parkway just south of the airport, rents sailboats from around mid-May to mid-October. Aqua Fins are $15 per hour, the larger Flying Scots are $19 per hour. There's a two-hour minimum, and reservations are required (along with certification from a sailing school or passing a written test). Phone early; boats are limited.

HIKING

Huntley Meadows Park (✉ 3701 Lockheed Blvd. ☎ 703/768–2525 🖙 Free ☉ Park daily dawn–dusk; call for visitor center hrs), a 1,425-acre refuge, is made for birders. You can spot more than 200 species—from ospreys to owls, egrets, and ibis. Much of the park is wetlands, home to a variety of aquatic species. A boardwalk circles through a marsh, enabling you to spot beaver lodges, and 4 mi of trails wind through the park, making it possible that you'll see deer, muskrats, and river otters as well.

> **RENT A BIKE**
>
> Rent a bike at the idyllic **Washington Sailing Marina**, on the Mount Vernon Bike Trail. A 12-mi ride south will take you to the front doors of Mount Vernon, and a 6-mi ride north across the Memorial Bridge will put you at the foot of the Washington Monument. Cruisers cost $8 per hour or $25 per day. The marina is open 9–5 daily.

The **Mount Vernon Trail** is a favorite with Washington runners and bikers. You can access it from the north just short of Key Bridge in Rosslyn, beside the I–66 off-ramp. The path crosses the George Washington Parkway, going to Theodore Roosevelt Island (directly across the river from the Kennedy Center), past Ronald Reagan Washington National Airport, and on to the Alexandria waterfront. This stretch is approximately 9½ mi one-way. South of National Airport, the trail runs beside the Washington Sailing Marina. The southern section of the trail (approximately 9 mi) takes you along the banks of the Potomac from Alexandria all the way to Mount Vernon. It passes Jones Point (under the Wilson Bridge), the southern apex of the original District of Columbia, just before entering protected wetlands for about 2 mi beginning at Hunting Creek.

SHOPPING

Old Town Alexandria is dense with antiques shops—many of them quite expensive—that are particularly strong in the Federal and Victorian periods. The Alexandria Convention and Visitors Association has maps and lists of the dozens of stores (available at Ramsay House).

The **Antique Guild** (✉ 113 N. Fairfax St., Old Town ☎ 703/836–1048 or 800/518–7322 ⊕ www.theantiqueguild.net) is where silver flatware and estate jewelry goes when it's ready for a new home. Alexandrian pet owners come to **The Dog Park** (✉ 705 King St., Old Town ☎ 703/888–2818) to spoil their four-legged friends. The friendly owner greets visitors as they enter the shop and helps them find the toys and treats (including special doggie cookies) that their pets will love, whatever the breed. Located just off King Street, **Hysteria** (✉ 125 S. Fairfax St., Old Town ☎ 703/548–1615) is Old Town's best bet for women's designer duds. Friendly shopkeepers are at the ready to help you find the right party dress, knit sweater, or chunky necklace from brands like Badgley Mischka and Trina Turk. Chefs and foodies alike hit **La Cuisine** (✉ 323 Cameron St. ☎ 703/836-4435 ⊕ www.lacuisineus.com ☉ Closed Sun.) for their gourmet goods. For more than 30 years, this independently owned shop has sold professional equipment from Mauviel copper to Sabatier knives, along with a large selection of spices and other imports. Dating to 1753, the **Saturday Morning Market at Market Square** (✉ *City Hall, 301 King St.*) may be the country's oldest operating farmers' market. Vendors sell baked goods, fresh produce, plants, flowers, and high-quality crafts. Come early; the market opens at 5 am, and by 11 am it's all over. **Sumpter Priddy III, Inc.** (✉ *323 S. Washington St., Old Town* ☎ *703/299–0800* ⊕ *www.sumpterpriddy.com*) specializes in American furniture from the early 19th century and folk art in different mediums.

ARLINGTON

★ Arlington has evolved since the end of World War I from a farming community into one of sprawling homes, large-scale retailing, and office buildings small to colossal. Connected to Washington by four bridges and three subway lines, the county is vital to the capital, providing office space to the federal government and housing to its employees. First the War Department, then Department of Defense and all military service headquarters were moved to the Pentagon, then numerous other government offices and bureaus moved to Arlington and nearby Virginia communities like Langley (home of the CIA) as they required larger quarters than were available in Washington. This trend continues. For the visitor, Arlington offers somber reflection at the nation's cemetery, a plethora of dining and lodging options, and easy access to the attractions of Washington.

Carved out of Fairfax County when the District of Columbia was created, Arlington was returned to Virginia along with the rest of the state's contribution in 1846, and until 1920 was the County of Alexandria. In the 19th century, members of the Custis family, including Martha Washington's first husband, had extensive land holdings in the area. Arlington was the name of the Custis family home that became the home of Robert E. Lee, now the Custis-Lee Mansion in Arlington Cemetery.

GETTING HERE AND AROUND
If you arrive at Reagan National Airport, Arlington is an easy drive west along the George Washington Parkway. Many parts of Arlington are easily accessible via Metrorail, as both the Orange and Blue lines run through parts of the county. The Orange Line heads through Clarendon and Ballson, while the Blue Line takes riders through Rosslyn and Pentagon City. The Yellow Line also meets up with the Blue Line for a portion of its trip through Arlington. Taxis are also readily available throughout the area.

TIMING AND PRECAUTIONS
Rush hour, which lasts from 7:30 am to 9 am and 5 pm to 6:30 pm on weekdays, slows down traffic through Arlington, especially on the heavily trafficked I–66, Route 50, and George Washington Parkway. Also be careful driving at these times through urban centers such as Rosslyn.

ESSENTIALS
Bus Contacts **Arlington Transit** (☎ *703/228–7433* ⊕ *www.arlingtontransit.com*).

Taxi **Arlington Blue Top Cab** (☎ *703/243–8294*).

Visitor Information Arlington County Convention and Visitors Services
(✉ *1100 N. Glebe Rd., Arlington* ☎ *800/296–7996* ⊕ *www.stayarlington.com*).

EXPLORING

TOP ATTRACTIONS

Arlington House. It was in Arlington that the two most famous names in Virginia history—Washington and Lee—became intertwined. George Washington Parke Custis, raised by Martha and George Washington, his grandmother and step-grandfather, built Arlington House (also known as the Custis-Lee Mansion) between 1802 and 1818 on his 1,100-acre estate overlooking the Potomac. After Custis's death, the property went to his daughter, Mary Anna Randolph Custis. In 1831 Mary married Robert E. Lee, a graduate of West Point. For the next 30 years she lived at Arlington House while Lee went wherever the Army sent him, including the superintendency of West Point.

In 1861 Lee was offered command of the Union forces in Washington. It was understood that the first order of business would be a troop movement into nearby Virginia. He declined and resigned from the U.S. Army, deciding that he could never take up arms against his native Virginia. The Lees left Arlington House that spring, never to return. Federal troops crossed the Potomac not long after that, fortified the estate's ridges, and turned the home into the Army of the Potomac's headquarters. Arlington House and the estate were confiscated in May 1864 when the Lees failed to pay $92 and change in property taxes in person. (General Lee's eldest son sued the U.S. government, and after a 5–4 decision by the U.S. Supreme Court, was eventually compensated for the land.) Two hundred nearby acres were set aside as a national cemetery in 1864. One thousand soldiers were buried there by the end of that year. Soldiers from the Revolutionary War and the War of 1812 were reinterred at Arlington as their bodies were discovered in other resting places.

The building's heavy Doric columns and severe pediment make Arlington House one of the area's best examples of Greek Revival architecture. The plantation home was designed by George Hadfield, a young English architect who, for a while, supervised construction of the Capitol. The view of Washington from the front of the house is superb. In 1933 the National Park Service acquired Arlington House and continued the restoration that the War Department had begun, and in 1972 Congress designated the Custis-Lee Mansion as Arlington House, the Robert E. Lee Memorial. It looks much as it did in the 19th century, and a quick tour takes you past objects once owned by the Custises and the Lees.

In front of Arlington House, next to a flag that flies at half staff whenever there's a funeral in the cemetery, is the flat-top **grave of Pierre Charles L'Enfant,** designer of Washington, DC. ✉ *Between Lee and Sherman Drs.* ☎ *703/235–1530* 🎟 *Free* ⊙ *Daily 9:30–4:30.*

Fodor's Choice **Arlington National Cemetery**. More than 250,000 American war dead, ★ as well as many notable Americans (among them presidents William Howard Taft and John F. Kennedy, General John Pershing, and Admiral

Robert E. Peary), are interred in these 624 acres across the Potomac River from Washington, established as the nation's cemetery in 1864. While you're at Arlington there's a good chance you'll hear a bugler playing taps, or the sharp reports of a gun salute. Approximately 28 funerals are held daily (it's projected that the cemetery will be filled in 2060). To get here, you can take the Metrorail to either the Rosslyn or Arlington Cemetery station and then walk about 0.5 mi, arrive by Tourmobile tour bus, walk across Arlington Memorial Bridge (southwest of the Lincoln Memorial), or drive to the large paid parking lot at the skylighted visitor center on Memorial Drive ($1.75 per hour for the first three hours, then $3.50 per hour). Stop at the **Visitor Center** for a free brochure with a detailed map of the cemetery. If you're looking for a specific grave, the staff can consult microfilm records and give you directions to it. You should know the deceased's full name and, if possible, his or her branch of service and year of death.

Tourmobiles leave daily 8:30–6:30 (in fall and winter, daily 8:30–4:30) from just outside the visitor center, where you can buy tickets ($7.50) good all day for unlimited reboarding in the cemetery. The Tourmobile stops at the Kennedy grave sites, the Tomb of the Unknowns, and Arlington House. Arlington Cemetery is included in the Washington Tourmobile ticket ($27), which includes transportation across the Potomac from the Lincoln Memorial to the visitor center. ■ TIP→ **Touring the cemetery on foot means a fair bit of hiking, but it can give you a closer look at some of the thousands of graves spread over these rolling Virginia hills.** If you decide to walk, from the visitor center head to the ornate Memorial Gate, then west on Roosevelt Drive, and turn right on Weeks Drive. ⊠ *West end of Memorial Bridge* ☎ *703/607–8000 to locate a grave* ⊕ *www.arlingtoncemetery.mil* ⊠ *Free* ☾ *Apr.–Sept., daily 8–7; Oct.–Mar., daily 8–5.*

★   **Kennedy graves.** A moving part of any visit to Arlington National Cemetery is a visit to the graves of John F. Kennedy and other members of his family. President Kennedy is buried under an eternal flame near two of his children, who died in infancy, and his wife, Jacqueline Bouvier Kennedy Onassis; his is the most-visited grave site in the country. The graves are a moderate walk west of the visitor center. Across from them is a low wall engraved with quotations from Kennedy's inaugural address. Nearby, marked by a simple white cross, is the grave of his brother Robert Kennedy. ⊠ *Sheridan and Weeks Drs.*

Section 7A. Many distinguished veterans are buried in this area of Arlington National Cemetery near the Tomb of the Unknowns, including boxing champ Joe Louis, ABC newsman Frank Reynolds, actor Lee Marvin, and World War II fighter pilot Colonel "Pappy" Boyington. ⊠ *Crook Walk near Roosevelt Dr.*

Tomb of the Unknowns. Many countries established a memorial to their war dead after World War I. In the United States, the first burial at the Tomb of the Unknowns took place at Arlington National Cemetery on November 11, 1921, when the unknown soldier from the "Great War" was interred under the large white-marble sarcophagus. Unknown servicemen killed in World War II and Korea were buried in 1958. The

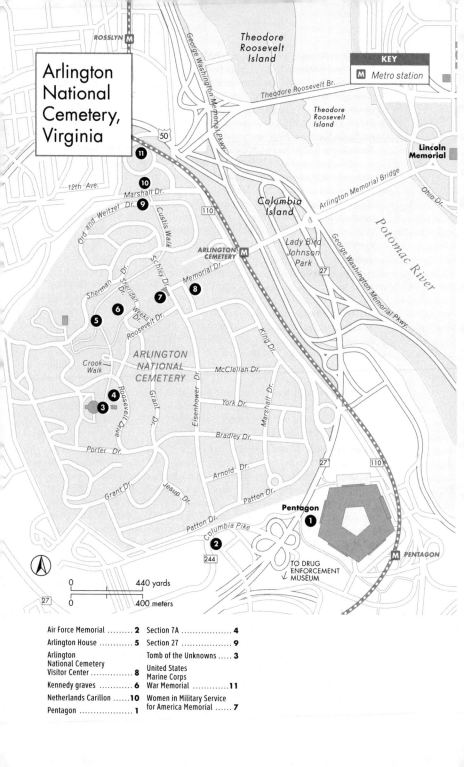

Arlington National Cemetery, Virginia

KEY

Ⓜ Metro station

Theodore Roosevelt Island

Theodore Roosevelt Br.

Theodore Roosevelt Island

Lincoln Memorial

ROSSLYN Ⓜ

George Washington Memorial Pkwy.

50

⓫

12th Ave.

⓵⓪

⑨

Marshall Dr.

Ord and Weitzel Dr.

Custis Walk

110

Columbia Island

Lady Bird Johnson Park

Arlington Memorial Bridge

Ohio Dr.

ARLINGTON CEMETERY Ⓜ

Potomac River

Sherman Dr.

Schley Dr.

Sheridan Dr.

Weeks Dr.

Memorial Dr.

⑦

⑧

⑤

⑥

Roosevelt Dr.

27

George Washington Memorial Pkwy.

Crook Walk

ARLINGTON NATIONAL CEMETERY

King Dr.

McClellan Dr.

④

③

Roosevelt Drive

Grant Dr.

Eisenhower Dr.

York Dr.

Marshall Dr.

Porter Dr.

Bradley Dr.

Grant Dr.

Jesup Dr.

Arnold Dr.

Patton Dr.

27

110

Pentagon

①

Patton Dr.

Columbia Pike

②

244

TO DRUG ENFORCEMENT MUSEUM

Ⓜ PENTAGON

0 ———— 440 yards
0 ———— 400 meters

27

Air Force Memorial	.... **2**	Section 7A	.... **4**
Arlington House	.... **5**	Section 27	.... **9**
Arlington National Cemetery Visitor Center	.... **8**	Tomb of the Unknowns	..... **3**
Kennedy graves	.... **6**	United States Marine Corps War Memorial	.... **11**
Netherlands Carillon	......**10**	Women in Military Service for America Memorial	...... **7**
Pentagon	.... **1**		

unknown serviceman killed in Vietnam was laid to rest on the plaza on Memorial Day 1984, but was disinterred and identified in 1998. Officials then decided to leave the Vietnam War unknown crypt vacant. Soldiers from the Army's 3rd Infantry ("The Old Guard") keep watch over the tomb 24 hours a day, regardless of weather conditions. Each sentinel marches exactly 21 steps, then faces the tomb for 21 seconds, symbolizing the 21-gun salute, America's highest military honor. The guard is changed with a precise ceremony during the day—every half hour from April through September and every hour the rest of the year. At night the guard is changed every hour.

The Memorial Amphitheater west of the tomb is the scene of special ceremonies on Veterans Day, Memorial Day, and Easter. Mementos from foreign governments are displayed in an indoor trophy room. Across from the amphitheater are memorials to the astronauts killed in the 1986 *Challenger* space shuttle explosion and to the servicemen killed in 1980 trying to rescue American hostages in Iran. Rising beyond that is the main mast of the USS *Maine,* the American ship sunk in Havana Harbor in 1898, killing 299 men and sparking the Spanish-American War. ⊠ *End of Crook Walk.*

WORTH NOTING

Air Force Memorial. Dedicated in 2006, this memorial honors the service and sacrifices of the men and women of the U.S. Air Force and its predecessor organizations of the U.S. Army. Three curved spires—up to 270 feet tall—represent the bomb burst maneuver famously performed by the USAF Thunderbird Demonstration Team. The memorial is just uphill from the Pentagon, beside the Navy Annex on Columbia Pike, and easy to see from a distance. ⊠ *Columbia Pike at Joyce St.*

OFF THE BEATEN PATH

Drug Enforcement Administration Museum. The very compact DEA Museum, inside one entrance to DEA headquarters, is across the street from the Fashion Centre at Pentagon City. It displays the methods and effects of dangerous drugs on America, starting with quaint 19th-century ads for opium-laced patent medicines and cocaine tooth drops (opiates, cannabis, and cocaine were unregulated then). Displays show current methods of illegal drug production, international drug smuggling, and the means of intercepting illegal drug shipments. Some displays are too stark for children. ⊠ *700 Army Navy Dr., at Hayes St.* ☎ *202/307–3463* ⊕ *www.deamuseum.org* ⌨ *Free* ⊗ *Tues.–Fri. 10–4* Ⓜ *Pentagon City.*

Netherlands Carillon. Outside the Arlington National Cemetery is the lovely and unusual 49-bell musical carillon presented to the United States by the Dutch people in 1960 in gratitude for aid received during World War II. For a good view of Washington, look to the east across the Potomac. From this vantage point the Lincoln Memorial, the Washington Monument, and the Capitol appear side by side. The bells are programmed to play patriotic music including the "Star-Spangled Banner" and "America the Beautiful" and even the Dutch national anthem. Call the National Park Service for times. ⊠ *Meade and Marshall Drs.* ☎ *202/289–2500.*

Pentagon. This office building, the headquarters of the U.S. Department of Defense, is one of the largest in the world. The Capitol could fit into any one of its five wedge-shaped sections. Approximately 23,000 military and civilian people work here. Astonishingly, construction on this mammoth office building began on Sept. 11, 1941, and was completed in less than two years. Construction was overseen by General Leslie Grove, then a colonel, who later led the Manhattan Project to develop the atom bomb.

Parts of the structure were rebuilt following the September 2001 crash of hijacked American Airlines Flight 77 into the northwest side of the building. The damaged area was removed in just more than a month, and rebuilding proceeded rapidly (in keeping with the speed of the original construction). Renovations on all areas damaged by the terrorist attack were completed by spring 2003.

Tours of the building are given on a limited basis to educational groups by advance reservation. ■ TIP→ **Tours for the general public can be arranged through your congressional office or online with two weeks advance notice.** You can also drive right by, fairly close, with unobstructed views of all sides, or visit the 9/11 Memorial, open to the public without reservations. ✉ *I–395 at Columbia Pike and Rte. 27* ☎ *703/695–1776* ⊕ *pentagon.afis.osd.mil.*

Section 27. Nearly 3,800 former slaves are buried in this part of Arlington National Cemetery. They're all former residents of Freedman's Village, which operated at the Custis-Lee estate for more than 30 years beginning in 1863 to provide housing, education, and employment training for ex-slaves who had traveled to the capital. In the cemetery the headstones are marked with their names and the word "Civilian" or "Citizen." Buried at Grave 19 in the first row of Section 27 is William Christman, a Union private who died of peritonitis in Washington on May 12, 1864. He was the first soldier (but not the first person) interred at Arlington. ✉ *Ord and Weitzel Dr. near Custis Walk.*

■ OFF THE
BEATEN
PATH

Theodore Roosevelt Island. The island wilderness preserve in the Potomac River has 2½ mi of nature trails through marsh, swampland, and upland forest. It's an 88-acre tribute to the conservation-minded 26th president. Cattails, arrowarum, pickerelweed, willow, ash, maple, and oak grow on the island, which is also a habitat for frogs, raccoons, birds, lizards, and the occasional red or gray fox. The 17-foot bronze statue of Roosevelt, toward the center of the woods, was done by Paul Manship. A pedestrian bridge connects the island to a parking lot on the Virginia shore, which is accessible by car only from the northbound lanes of the George Washington Memorial Parkway. ✉ *From downtown DC, take Constitution Ave. west across Theodore Roosevelt Bridge to George Washington Memorial Pkwy. north; follow signs or walk or bike across bridge beginning at Kennedy Center* ☎ *703/289–2500 for park information* ⊠ *Free* ☉ *Island daily 6–10* Ⓜ *Rosslyn.*

United States Marine Corps War Memorial. Better known simply as "the Iwo Jima," this memorial, despite its familiarity, has lost none of its power to stir the emotions. Honoring Marines who gave their lives since the Corps was formed in 1775, the statue, sculpted by Felix W. de Weldon, is based on Joe Rosenthal's Pulitzer Prize–winning photograph of five Marines and a Navy corpsman raising a flag atop Mt. Suribachi on the

Japanese island of Iwo Jima on February 19, 1945. By executive order the U.S. flag flies day and night from the 78-foot-high memorial. On Tuesday evenings from early June to mid-August there's a Marine Corps sunset parade on the grounds of the memorial. Call ☎ *703/289–2500* for start times. On parade nights a free shuttle bus runs from the Arlington Cemetery visitors parking lot.

Women in Military Service for America Memorial. What is now this memorial next to the visitor center was once the Hemicycle, a huge carved retaining wall faced with granite at the entrance to Arlington National Cemetery. Built in 1932, the wall was restored, with stairways added leading to a rooftop terrace. Inside are 16 exhibit alcoves showing the contributions that women have made to the military—from the Revolutionary War to the present—as well as the history of the memorial itself. A 196-seat theater shows films and is used for lectures and conferences. A computer database has pictures, military histories, and stories of thousands of women veterans. A fountain and reflecting pool front the classical-style Hemicycle and entry gates.

WHERE TO EAT

$–$$ ✕ **Carlyle.** Whether you eat at the bustling bar or in the dining room
AMERICAN   upstairs, you'll find an imaginative, generous interpretation of modern American cooking. Start with the blue crab fritters, then move on to entrées such as pecan-crusted trout. The warm, flourless, chocolate-macadamia nut waffle with vanilla ice cream is classic. Carlyle is especially known for its fantastic weekend brunch, where you can pair brioche French toast with a glass of Virginia sparkling cider. You can even buy a loaf of bread at the restaurant's own bakery, the Best Buns Bread Company, next door. ⊠ *4000 Campbell Ave., Shirlington* ☎ *703/931–0777* ⊕ *www.greatamericanrestaurants.com/carlyle* ⊟ *AE, MC, V.*

¢–$ ✕ **Nam Viet.** Autographed photos of U.S. military and political leaders
VIETNAMESE   gaze down from the walls at this Vietnamese restaurant just a block off Wilson Boulevard. The sweet-and-spicy salmon soup has many fans, as do the *cha gio* (spring rolls) and the green-papaya salad (with shrimp or beef jerky). Dine outside in good weather. Try to arrive early in the evening to find a parking space, as residents tend to fill up the street parking later on. ⊠ *1127 Hudson St., Clarendon* ☎ *703/522–7110* ⊕ *www. namviet1.com* ⊟ *AE, D, DC, MC, V* Ⓜ *Clarendon.*

¢   ✕ **Pho 75.** Drab walls and communal tables may seem cafeteria-style,
VIETNAMESE   but that's part of what makes Pho 75 one of the most authentic Vietnamese restaurants in the D.C. area. Customers come from across the region to line up at this no-frills joint for the high-quality traditional noodle soup. Choose your bowl size and then what kind of meat (and how many kinds of meat) you want to cook in the soup, including flank steak, brisket, tendon, tripe, and eye-of-round steak. Pay at the counter as you leave—and don't forget to bring cash as Pho 75 doesn't take credit cards. ⊠ *1721 Wilson Blvd., Arlington* ☎ *703/525–7355* ⊟ *No credit cards.*

¢–$ ✕ **Ray's Hell Burger.** The rise of this Arlington burger joint—owned by the
AMERICAN   same pun-loving proprietor of Ray's the Steaks—heralded the beginning

of D.C.'s gourmet burger craze. Garnish your own 10-ounce burger with traditional condiments like American cheese, applewood smoked bacon, pickles, onions and Ray's own sauce, or go for a more unusual combination like the Burger of Seville, which comes with seared foie gras, sauteed mushrooms, bordelaise sauce, and truffle oil between toasted brioche buns. ⊠ *1713 Wilson Blvd., Arlington* ☎ *703/841–0001* ▭ *AE, MC, V.*

$$–$$$ ✕**Willow Restaurant.** This handsome restaurant and bar in mahogany
CONTINENTAL and jewel tones with 1930s-style photographs has a jazz-era feel. Its elegance can be felt in the polished wooden floors and the spacious dining rooms outfitted with white tablecloths. The cuisine combines the freshest ingredients with classic French and Italian influences. Featured are grilled flat breads with innovative toppings, bacon-wrapped monkfish, and a spicy coconut and lime fish stew. Park free in the building's garage to avoid the conscientious parking enforcement. ⊠ *4301 N. Fairfax Dr., Ballston* ☎ *703/465–8800* ⊕ *www.willowva.com* ▭ *AE, D, DC, MC, V* Ⓜ *Ballston.*

WHERE TO STAY

$$ ⌷**Hilton Arlington and Towers.** Traveling to Arlington Cemetery, Washington, and Alexandria sights is easy from this hotel, just above the Ballston Metrorail stop. Rooms make use of neutral colors and traditional mahogany furniture. The hotel has direct access via a skywalk to an adjacent shopping mall. **Pros:** renovated fitness center; all suites have hot tubs; you can't get any closer to the Metro and shopping. **Cons:** fee for Internet use in rooms; parking fee of $17 a day; the busy neighborhood can get noisy. ⊠ *950 N. Stafford St., Ballston* ☎ *703/528–6000 or 800/445–8667* ⊕ *www.hilton.com* ➷ *204 rooms, 5 suites* ⌂ *In-room: a/c, Internet. In-hotel: restaurant, room service, bar, gym, laundry service, parking (paid)* ▭ *AE, D, DC, MC, V* Ⓜ *Ballston.*

¢–$ ⌷**Holiday Inn Arlington at Ballston.** You can get to the major sights of
Ⓒ Northern Virginia and D.C. quickly from this hotel, two blocks (or a free shuttle ride) from the Ballston Metrorail station. It is also across the street from the Custis jogging trail. Guest rooms have a navy and burgundy color scheme with duvet comforters, an overstuffed chair with ottoman, and a mahogany dresser and work desk. Kids love the suspended model railroad at Lacey Station Dining Car Restaurant (named for the railroad station that was once 200 feet away); hotel guests 12 and under eat free from the kids' menu. Parking is free Friday and Saturday nights. **Pros:** perks for kids; free shuttle to the Metro; free parking on weekends. **Cons:** service sometimes suffers with a busy staff; fee for parking during the week. ⊠ *4610 N. Fairfax Dr., Ballston* ☎ *703/243–9800* ⊕ *www.hiarlington.com* ➷ *221 rooms, 2 suites* ⌂ *In-room: a/c, Internet. In-hotel: restaurant, room service, bar, pool, gym, laundry facilities, laundry service, parking (paid)* ▭ *AE, D, DC, MC, V* Ⓜ *Ballston.*

$$$$ ⌷**Hotel Palomar Arlington.** Ideally situated on the banks of the Potomac, with the Rosslyn Metrorail station across the street and walkable across the Key Bridge from Georgetown, the Hotel Palomar Arlington is a trendy boutique hotel. Rooms are decorated in neutral hues with splashes of teal and orange. The headboards of the soft beds are uphol-stered in a chocolate and cream houndstooth pattern. The hotel's Mind. Body.Spa program allows guests to order in-room spa services, or they can ask for a complimentary yoga bag of accessories to use with televi-sion fitness programming. **Pros:** nice extra touches like the yoga acces-sories; small feel for a larger hotel; close to Georgetown's restaurants, shopping, and nightlife. **Cons:** parking is tough to find in downtown Rosslyn; hotel provides only valet parking. ✉ *1121 N. 19th St., Rosslyn* ☎ *703/351–9170* ⊕ *www.hotelpalomar-arlington.com* ⤴ *154 rooms, 25 suites* ⚒ *In-room: a/c, safe, DVD, Internet. In-hotel: restaurant, room service, bar, gym, spa, laundry service, parking (paid), some pets allowed* ⊟ *AE, D, DC, MC, V.*

$$$$ ⊡ **Marriott Crystal Gateway.** This elegant, modern Marriott caters to the business traveler and those who want to be pampered. Its two towers rise 17 stories above the highway; inside is mahogany, marble, and lots of greenery. Rooms have contemporary styling with fabrics in hues of gold and red blended with cherry furniture. Concierge Lounge serves refreshments weekdays from 6 am to 11 pm. Although the hotel does offer unlimited in-room high-speed Internet access and long-distance phone calls in the 48 contiguous states as part of its "Wired for Busi-ness" package, there is a cost of $14.95 per day. **Pros:** rooms come with flat-screen HD TVs that allow you to connect your iPod, laptop, video camera, or camcorder; great for business travelers; connects under-ground to Metro station. **Cons:** fee for Internet access; area has a corpo-rate feel. ✉ *1700 Jefferson Davis Hwy., Crystal City* ☎ *703/920–3230 or 800/228–9290* ⊕ *www.marriott.com/wasgw* ⤴ *615 rooms, 82 suites* ⚒ *In-room: a/c, Internet. In-hotel: 2 restaurants, room service, bars, pool, gym, laundry facilities, laundry service, Wi-Fi hotspot, parking (paid)* ⊟ *AE, D, DC, MC, V* Ⓜ *Crystal City.*

NIGHTLIFE AND THE ARTS

BARS

Originally a D.C. institution, **Capitol City Brewing Company** (✉ *4001 Campbell Ave. Shirlington* ☎ *703/578–3888* ⊕ *www.capcitybrew.com*) made its first move out of the District with this prime spot on the Shir-lington promenade. Sip on a signature brew from Amber Waves Ale to Prohibition Porter while noshing on beer-friendly appetizers like black-and-tan onion rings or southwest keg rolls. The Colorado-based **Rock Bottom Brewery** (✉ *4238 Wilson Blvd., No. 1256, Ballston* ☎ *703/516–7688* ⊕ *www.rockbottom.com* Ⓜ *Ballston-MU*) pours ales, lagers, and porters alongside fixings such as fried chicken, barbecued ribs, pizza, and cheesecake made with the house stout.

MUSIC

IOTA. The bands at IOTA play alt-country or rock to unpretentious, attentive crowds. Expect to fight your way to the bar—it gets crowded quickly. There's music for a cover charge of $10 to $15 almost every night, except in the café, which serves food and charges no cover. ✉ *2832 Wilson Blvd., Clarendon* ☎ *703/522–8340* ⊕ *www.iotaclubandcafe. com* Ⓜ *Clarendon.*

SPORTS AND THE OUTDOORS

Arlington's 36 mi of multiuse trails and 50 mi of connecting bicycle lanes and routes take you along the Virginia side of the Potomac from Key Bridge to Mount Vernon with connections at Key Bridge to the Chesapeake and Ohio Canal tow path and from it to the Washington Crescent trail, and to the Custis trail that joins the Four Mile Run and farther west, the Washington & Old Dominion Trail that goes all the way to Purcellville, west of Leesburg.

SHOPPING

Crystal City Shops (☎ *703/922–4636* ⊕ *www.thecrystalcityshops.com*) comprises more than 200 street-level and underground stores and restaurants connected to the Crystal City Metrorail station and near a Virginia Railway Express (VRE) station. **Fashion Centre at Pentagon City** (✉ *1100 S. Hayes St., Pentagon City* ☎ *703/415–2400* ⊕ *www. fashioncentrepentagon.com* Ⓜ *Pentagon City*) is anchored by Macy's and Nordstrom. This four-story mall includes such shops as the Coach Store, Swatch, babyGap, Sephora, Williams-Sonoma, and an Armani Exchange. In addition to a skylighted food court, there are two full-service restaurants to choose from, including the popular Arlington chain Harry's Tap Room.

MOUNT VERNON, WOODLAWN, AND GUNSTON HALL

Long before Washington was planned, the shores of the Potomac had been divided into plantations by wealthy traders and gentlemen farmers. Most traces of the Colonial era were obliterated as the capital grew in the 19th century, but several splendid examples of plantation architecture remain on the Virginia side of the Potomac, 15 mi or so south of D.C. In one day you can easily visit three such mansions: Mount Vernon, the home of George Washington and one of the most popular sites in the area; Woodlawn, the estate of Washington's step-granddaughter; and Gunston Hall, the home of George Mason, author of the document on which the Bill of Rights was based. (Expect the longest wait times at Mount Vernon, particularly in spring and summer.) Set on hillsides overlooking the river, these estates offer magnificent vistas and bring back to vivid life the more palatable aspects of the 18th century. They are all accessible from I–95, south of Alexandria.

MOUNT VERNON

16 mi south of Washington, D.C., 8 mi south of Alexandria, VA.

GETTING HERE AND AROUND

The best way to get to Mount Vernon is by car, although it's also possible to take a cruise ship here from spots in Maryland, D.C., and Virginia. Various tour buses also stop at Mount Vernon, including the Tourmobile that departs from Arlington National Cemetery.

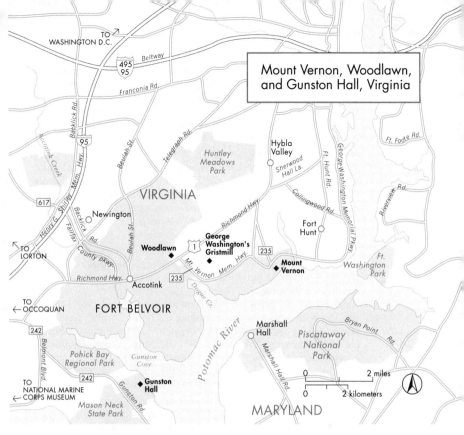

Mount Vernon, Woodlawn, and Gunston Hall, Virginia

TIMING AND PRECAUTIONS

Rush hour, which lasts from 7:30 am to 9 am and 5 pm to 6:30 pm on weekdays, slows down traffic on I–95 and the George Washington Memorial Parkway.

ESSENTIALS

Potomac Riverboat Company (☎ 703/684–0580 or 877/511–2628 ⊕ www. potomacriverboatco.com).

Spirit Cruises (☎ 866/835–8851 ⊕ www.entertainmentcruises.com).

EXPLORING

☾ **Mount Vernon.** This plantation and the surrounding lands had been in the
Fodor's Choice Washington family for nearly 70 years by the time George inherited it all
★ in 1743. Before taking over command of the Continental Army, Washington was an accomplished farmer managing the 8,000-acre plantation, operating five farms on the land. He oversaw the transformation of the main house from an ordinary farm dwelling into what was, for the time, a grand mansion. The inheritance of his widowed bride, Martha, is partly what made that transformation possible.

The red-roof main house is elegant though understated, with a yellow pine exterior that's been painted and coated with layers of sand to resemble white-stone blocks. The first-floor rooms are quite ornate, especially the formal large dining room, with a molded ceiling decorated with agricultural motifs. The bright colors of the walls, which match the original paint, may surprise those who associate the period with pastels. Throughout the house are smaller symbols of the owner's eminence, such as a key to the main portal of the Bastille—presented to Washington by the Marquis de Lafayette—and Washington's presidential chair. As you tour the mansion, guides are stationed throughout the house to describe the furnishings and answer questions.

The real treasure of Mount Vernon is the view from around back: beneath a 1,400-foot piazza, the home's dramatic riverside porch overlooks an expanse of lawn that slopes down to the Potomac. In springtime the view of the river (a mile wide where it passes the plantation) is framed by dogwood blossoms. In the 19th century, steamboats rendered honors when passing the house during daylight hours.

You can stroll around the estate's 500 acres and three gardens, visiting the workshops, kitchen, carriage house, greenhouse, slave quarters, and—down the hill toward the boat landing—the tomb of George and Martha Washington. There's also a pioneer farmer site: a 4-acre hands-on exhibit with a reconstruction of George Washington's 16-side treading barn as its centerpiece. Among the souvenirs sold at the plantation are stripling boxwoods that began life as clippings from bushes planted in 1798, the year before Washington died. A tour of house and grounds takes about 4½ hours. A limited number of wheelchairs are available at the main gate. Evening candlelight tours are offered weekend evenings in late November and early December.

Just inside the main entrance, the orientation and education centers on either side illustrate George Washington's life and contributions with interactive displays, movies, life-size models, and objects such as furnishings, Revolutionary War artifacts, books, and personal effects.

Also, a National Treasure tour explores behind the scenes of the movie filming, including a chance to see the basement of the house. These tours sell out quickly so reserve ahead of time.

George Washington's Gristmill—a reproduction—operates on the site of his original mill and distillery. Records kept by Washington helped archaeologists excavate the distillery in the late 1990s, and it was reconstructed and reopened to the public in 2007. During the guided tours, led by costumed interpreters, you meet an 18th-century miller and watch the water-powered wheel grind grain into cornmeal just as it did 200 years ago. The mill is 3 mi from Mount Vernon on Route 235 between Mount Vernon and U.S. Route 1, almost to Woodlawn. Tickets can be purchased either at the gristmill itself or at Mount Vernon's Ford Orientation Center. ⊠ *Southern end of George Washington Pkwy., Mount Vernon* ☎ *703/780–2000* ⊕ *www.mountvernon.org* ☜ *$15, gristmill $4, combination ticket $17* ☼ *Mar., Sept., and Oct., daily 9–5; Apr.–Aug., daily 8–5; Nov.–Feb., daily 9–4.*

WOODLAWN

3 mi west of Mount Vernon, 15 mi south of Washington, DC.

GETTING HERE AND AROUND

Just a few miles down the highway from Mount Vernon, the best way to reach Woodlawn is by car.

EXPLORING

Woodlawn. This plantation home was once part of the Mount Vernon estate. From here you can still see the five trees of the bowling green that fronted Washington's home. The house was built for Washington's step-granddaughter, Nelly Custis, who married his favorite nephew, Lawrence Lewis. (Lewis had come to Mount Vernon from Fredericksburg to be his Uncle George's social secretary so that the statesman could have more time to manage his five farms.)

The Lewises' home, completed in 1805, was designed by William Thornton, a physician and amateur architect from the West Indies who drew up the original plans for the U.S. Capitol. Like Mount Vernon, the Woodlawn house is constructed wholly of native materials, including the clay for its bricks and the yellow pine used throughout its interior. Built on a site selected by George Washington, the house has commanding views of the surrounding countryside and the Potomac River beyond. In the tradition of Southern riverfront mansions, Woodlawn has a central hallway that provides a cool refuge in summer. Inside the house is a bust of George Washington set on a pedestal so the crown of the head is at 6 feet, 4 inches. Washington's actual height is believed to have been 6 feet, 2 inches, however, the pedestal was built two inches taller to accommodate for the inches lost when it was placed outside and sunk into the garden.

Woodlawn was once a plantation where more than 100 people, most of them slaves, lived and worked. As plantation owners, the Lewises lived in luxury. Docents talk about how the family entertained and how the slaves prepared these lavish meals as well as their own. As intimates of the Washingtons' household, the Lewises displayed a collection of objects in honor of their illustrious benefactor. Many Washington family items are on display today. Woodlawn opened its doors to the public as a National Trust for Historic Preservation site in 1952.

Also on the grounds of Woodlawn is the **Pope-Leighey House.** One of Frank Lloyd Wright's "Usonian" homes, the structure was built in 1941 as part of the architect's mission to create affordable housing. It was moved here from Falls Church, Virginia, in 1964, to save it from destruction during the building of Route 66. By design a very small, sparsely furnished home, it features many of Wright's trademark elements, including the use of local materials. Visitors are mostly students of architecture or of Wright. An in-depth tour is given on the first Sunday of the month. ⊠ *9000 Richmond Hwy., Alexandria* ☎ *703/780–4000* ⊕ *www.woodlawn1805.org* ▧ *$8.50 each for Woodlawn and Pope-Leighey House, combination ticket $15* ☽ *Mar.–Dec., Thurs.–Mon. 10–5; limited guided tours in Mar.; tours leave every hr for Woodlawn and every half hr for Pope-Leighey; last tour at 4.*

In between visits to others sites off I–95 like Gunston Hall and Wood-lawn, pop over to Occoquan for a relaxing afternoon. This tiny village on the shores of the Occoquan River was founded in 1734 as a trading post. It was the main delivery point for mail between the North and South during the Civil War. Occoquan today is an ideal getaway for antiques and art shopping, or fishing and boating along the river.

The **Artists' Undertaking Gallery** (✉ *309 Mill St.* ☎ *703/494–0584* ⊕ *www. theartistsundertaking.com* ⊘ *Daily 11–5*) displays the work of local artisans, including basket weavers, painters, and potters. Family-run **Occoquan Antiques** (✉ *405 Mill St.* ☎ *703/499–9312* ⊘ *Closed Mon., Wed.*) specializes in mahogany furniture from the 1920s and 1930s. **Three Story Tellers** (✉ *304 Mill St.* ☎ *703/494–1994* ⊕ *www.3storytellers. com* ⊘ *Closed Tues.–Thurs.*) is dedicated entirely to children and spe-cializes in multicultural and award-winning books.

After working up an appetite browsing, be sure to stop by **Mom's Apple Pie Company** (✉ *126A Commerce St.* ☎ *703/497–7437* ⊕ *www. momsapplepieco.com*) to indulge in a forkful of the mind-blowing black raspberry pie (or whatever is seasonal). **The Garden Kitchen** (✉ *404 Mill St.* ☎ *703/494–2848* ⊕ *www.gardenkitchen.com*) has a homey atmo-sphere that perfectly matches its low-key lunch menu, which includes peanut-butter-and-jelly sandwiches and quiche lorraine.

GUNSTON HALL

9 mi south of Woodlawn, 24 mi south of Washington, DC.

GETTING HERE AND AROUND
Located about 20 minutes south of Woodlawn via Richmond Highway, the best way to reach Gunston Hall is by car.

EXPLORING

Gunston Hall Plantation. Down the Potomac from Mount Vernon, was the home of another important George. Gentleman farmer George Mason was a colonel of the Virginia militia and author of the Virginia Dec-laration of Rights, the model for the U.S. Bill of Rights, which called for freedom of the press, tolerance of religion, and other fundamental democratic principles. Mason was a framer of the Constitution but refused to sign the final document because it didn't stop the importation of slaves, adequately restrain the powers of the federal government, or include a bill of rights. Mason's objections spurred the movement for the inclusion of the Bill of Rights into the Constitution.

Mason's home was begun about 1755. The Georgian-style mansion has some of the finest hand-carved ornamented interiors in the country. It's the handiwork of the 18th century's foremost architect, William Buck-land, who also designed the Hammond-Harwood and Chase-Lloyd houses in Annapolis, but was at the time an indentured servant car-penter/joiner. Gunston Hall is built of native brick, black walnut, and yellow pine. The style of the time demanded absolute symmetry in all structures, which explains the false door set into one side of the center hallway and the "robber" window on a second-floor storage room. The house's interior, with carved woodwork in styles from Chinese

Fodor's Choice
★

to Greek, has been meticulously restored, with paints made from the original formulas and carefully carved replacements for the intricate mahogany medallions in the moldings. Restored outbuildings include a kitchen, dairy, laundry, and smokehouse, and a schoolhouse has also been reconstructed.

The formal gardens, recently under excavation by a team of archaeologists, are famous for their boxwoods—some were planted during George Mason's time, making them among the oldest in the country. The Potomac is visible past the expansive deer park, and Mason's landing road to the river was recently found and cleared. Also on the grounds is an active farmyard with livestock like those of Mason's era. Special programs, such as archaeology tutelege and a plantation Christmas celebration, are available. A tour of Gunston Hall takes at least 45 minutes; tours begin on the front porch of the house. Buy tickets at the visitor center, which includes a museum and gift shop. ⊠ *10709 Gunston Rd., Mason Neck* ☎ *703/550–9220* ⊕ *www.gunstonhall.org* ▨ *$9* ⊙ *Daily 9:30–5; last tour at 4:30, tours every ½ hr on the hr.*

OFF THE BEATEN PATH
♻
Fodor's Choice
★

National Museum of the Marine Corps. Eighteen miles south on I–95, next to the Marine Corps Base Quantico, the glassy atrium of the National Museum of the Marine Corps soars into the sky. The design for this 118,000-square-foot homage to the military's finest was inspired by the iconic photograph of Marines lifting the American flag on Iwo Jima. Inside the museum, visitors are able to see the flag itself, as well as experience the life of a Marine. The museum is completely interactive, from the entrance where drill instructors yell at new "recruits" in surround-sound, to the Korean War exhibit, where visitors walk through a snowy mountain pass and shiver from the cold while listening to the 2nd Platoon fight on the other side of the mountain. The museum also has a staggering collection of tanks, aircraft, rocket launchers, and other weapons. There is even a rifle range simulator ($5) where guests of all ages can learn how to hold a rifle and practice hitting targets. Ooh-rah! ⊠ *18900 Jefferson Davis Hwy., Triangle* ☎ *877/635–1775* ⊕ *www.usmcmuseum.org* ▨ *Free* ⊙ *Daily 9–5.*

SHOPPING
Nine miles from Gunston Hall, **Potomac Mills** (⊠ *2700 Potomac Mills Circle, Woodbridge* ☎ *703/496–9301* ⊕ *www.potomacmills.com*) bills itself as Virginia's most popular attraction. There are about 220 discount and outlet stores here, including Nordstrom Rack, T. J. Maxx, OFF 5TH Saks Fifth Ave. Outlet, and Bloomingdale's. Swedish furniture giant IKEA is also next to the complex.

FAIRFAX COUNTY

In 1649 King Charles II of England gave the land that would become Fairfax County to seven English noblemen. It became a county in 1742 and was named after Thomas, sixth Lord Fairfax. Widespread tobacco farming, the dominant industry in the 18th century, eventually depleted the land. After tobacco, dairy farming became the major agricultural activity, and by 1925 Fairfax was first among all Virginia counties in dairy production. Today the economy depends upon business and government, and Fairfax County has one of the highest per capita incomes in the country. Wolf Trap, the only national park dedicated to the performing arts, is here, and throughout the year it draws concertgoers from miles around.

ESSENTIALS

Fairfax County Visitors Center (✉ *7927 Jones Branch Dr., South Wing 100, McLean* ☎ *703/752–9500* ⊕ *www.fxva.com*).

CHANTILLY

8 mi northwest of Fairfax.

Located in western Fairfax County, Chantilly is home to Dulles International Airport as well as the Smithsonian's National Air and Space Museum Steven F. Udvar-Hazy Center. During the Civil War, Union and Confederate troops clashed here in the Battle of Chantilly.

GETTING HERE AND AROUND

The best way to reach Chantilly is by car. For those looking to beat a long layover, Virginia Regional Transit provides a bus service to the National Air and Space Museum from Washington Dulles International Airport.

EXPLORING

★ **National Air and Space Museum Steven F. Udvar-Hazy Center.** This Washington Dulles International Airport satellite of the National Mall's Air and Space Museum opened in 2003 to commemorate the 100th anniversary of the Wright brothers' flight. The gargantuan facility displays 123 aircraft and 141 large space artifacts, including rockets, satellites, experimental flying machines, a Concorde, the Space Shuttle *Enterprise,* the *Enola Gay,* and a Lockheed SR-71 Blackbird, which in 1990 flew from Los Angeles to Washington, D.C., in just over an hour. An IMAX theater here shows films about flight. Parking is free after 4 pm. ✉ *14390 Air and Space Museum Pkwy.* ☎ *202/633–1000* ⊕ *www.nasm. si.edu/udvarhazy* 💳 *Free, IMAX $9, parking $15* ⊙ *Daily 10–5:30.*

Sully. The main attraction for those who come to Chantilly, this Federal-period home has changed hands many times since it was built in 1794 by Richard Bland Lee, Northern Virginia's first representative to Congress. Citizen action in the 20th century saved it from destruction during construction of nearby Dulles Airport. In the 1970s the house and its outbuildings were restored to their original appearance, with a representative kitchen and flower gardens. A 45-minute tour is offered every hour on the hour, and tours of the outbuildings and slave quarters are available daily at 2 pm. Educational programs, special events, and living-history programs are held here throughout the year. ✉ *Rte. 28, 3601 Sully Rd.* ☎ *703/437–1794* ⊕ *www.fairfaxcounty.gov/parks/sully* 💳 *$6* ⊙ *Wed.–Mon. 11–4.*

MANASSAS

16 mi southwest of Fairfax.

South of Chantilly in western Fairfax County, Manassas was considered a strategic crossroads during the Civil War, which is why two key Confederate-won battles were fought on these grounds. Now the battlefield remains the top reason to visit.

GETTING HERE AND AROUND

From Dulles International Airport, take VA–28 south to Manassas. Interstate 66 also goes out to Manassas, right past the battlefield. Local bus system OmniRide runs during rush hour between Manassas Mall and various points in D.C., while OmniLink connects Manassas to nearby towns and Metro Direct travels to West Falls Church Metro station.

TIMING AND PRECAUTIONS

Traffic in Manassas is not as bad as elsewhere in Northern Virginia. However, it's never a bad idea to stay away from main roads from 7:30 to 9 am and 5 to 6:30 pm, rush hour, as many Manassas residents commute to the District of Columbia.

EXPLORING

Manassas National Battlefield Park. The Confederacy won two important victories—in July 1861 and August 1862—at this battlefield, also known as Bull Run. General Thomas Jonathan Jackson earned his nickname Stonewall here, when he and his brigade stood "like a stone wall." When the second battle ended, the Confederacy was at the zenith of its power. Originally farmland, the battlefield bore witness to casualties of nearly 30,000 troops. The Stone House, used as an aid station during the war, still stands. President Taft led a peaceful reunion of thousands of veterans here in 1911—50 years after the first battle. The "Peace Jubilee" continues to be celebrated at the Manassas courthouse every summer. A self-guided walking or driving tour of the park begins at the visitor center, whose exhibits and audiovisual presentations greatly enhance a visit. Bull Run is a 26-mi drive from Washington; from Arlington and Fairfax take I–66 west (use I–495 to get to I–66 from Alexandria) to Exit 47B (Sudley Road/Route 234 North). Don't be fooled by the earlier Manassas exit for Route 28. The visitor center is ½ mi north on the right. ✉ *6511 Sudley Rd.* ☏ *703/361–1339* ⊕ *www.nps.gov/mana* ⌨ *$3 for 3 days* ☉ *Park daily dawn–dusk, visitor center daily 8:30–5.*

WHERE TO STAY

$ 📺 **Courtyard Manassas Battlefield Park.** You can't get much closer to the Manassas Battlefield than this—it's down the block from the main entrance. Business travelers appreciate the hostelry's location near the Dulles High Tech Corridor, with plenty of dining and shopping nearby. This beautifully landscaped, three-story hotel has comfy guest rooms that feature luxurious linens, down comforters, thick mattresses, and fluffy pillows. **Pros:** close to the Manassas Battlefield; complimentary newspaper available in the lobby. **Cons:** no shuttle bus offered; area is light on public transportation. ✉ *10701 Battleview Pkwy.*

☎ *703/335–1300* ⊕ *www.marriott.com* ⇆ *137 rooms, 12 suites* ⬙ *In-room: a/c, refrigerator, Internet. In-hotel: restaurant, pool, gym, laundry facilities, Wi-Fi hotspot, parking (free)* ⊟ *AE, D, DC, MC, V.*

TYSONS CORNER

11 mi northwest of Alexandria.

A highly developed commercial area of office buildings, hotels, restaurants, and two major shopping centers, Tysons Corner is a fashionable address in the Washington, D.C., area.

GETTING HERE AND AROUND

Beware of the grating traffic jam on every road, side street, and parking lot at rush hour. The main routes, 123 and 7 and International Drive, are the worst; I–495, the Beltway, is less affected. Weekends can also bring bumper-to-bumper traffic on these roads, as residents from throughout Fairfax County and beyond like to shop at the malls in Tysons.

ESSENTIALS

Tysons Westpark Transit Station (⊠ *Tyco Rd. and International Dr., off the Dulles Toll Rd.*).

WHERE TO EAT

$$$–$$$$ ✕ **Capital Grille.** A small group of urban restaurants are tucked in a

AMERICAN   pocket of high-end stores in the suburb of Tysons Corner. Among them is the Capital Grille, where meat and potatoes means fine dry-aged porterhouse cuts and delicious cream-based traditional mashed potatoes. Pair it with a selection off the list of more than 30 premium wines. Another don't-miss is the panfried calamari with hot cherry peppers. Dine in elegance, as Oriental carpets meet dark mahogany wood and plush leather seating, and gold-framed portraits hang on the walls. ⊠ *1861 International Dr., at Rte. 7, McLean* ☎ *703/448–3900* ⊕ *www.thecapitalgrille.com* ⊟ *AE, D, DC, MC, V* ⊘ *No lunch weekends.*

$–$$ ✕ **Clyde's of Tysons Corner.** A branch of a popular Georgetown pub,

ECLECTIC   Clyde's has four art deco dining rooms, one or more of which may be devoted to private parties. The Palm Terrace has high ceilings and lots of faux greenery; less formal dining rooms adjoin each other and a couple of bars. Clyde's mostly attracts workers from the nearby corporate buildings, who appreciate the attentive service and high-quality fare. The lengthy, eclectic menu always includes fresh fish dishes, such as trout Parmesan. The wine list is equally long. ⊠ *8332 Leesburg Pike, Tysons Corner* ☎ *703/734–1900* ⊕ *www.clydes.com* ⊟ *AE, D, DC, MC, V.*

WHERE TO STAY

$$$$ ▭ **Ritz-Carlton, Tysons Corner.** One of the most elegant hotels in the DC area has large guest rooms with modern furniture and flat-screen TVs. Booking a concierge room gives you access to an exclusive club with five complimentary mini-meals, drinks throughout the day, and sweeping views of the Virginia countryside. On the third floor is the expansive European Day Spa. The lobby lounge's dark-panel walls and safari animal bronzes make it feel like a 19th-century club room. The hotel adjoins the exclusive Tysons Galleria mall. **Pros:** true luxury experience; the location adjoining the Tysons Galleria mall is ideal for browsing Saks Fifth Avenue or Neiman Marcus; there's also a multitude of dining options, from Legal Sea Foods to P.F. Chang's China Bistro. **Cons:** like any hotel in the Tysons Corner area, it's burdened with heavy shopper and commuter traffic; a stay here is a hit to the wallet. ✉ *1700 Tysons Blvd., McLean* ☎ *703/506–4300* ⊕ *www.ritzcarlton.com* ↝ *348 rooms, 50 suites* ♿ *In-room: a/c, safe, Internet. In-hotel: restaurant, bar, pool, gym, spa, laundry service, Wi-Fi hotspot, parking (paid)* ▭ *AE, D, DC, MC, V.*

SHOPPING

The **Galleria at Tysons II**. Across a busy highway from Tysons Corner Center, the Galleria has about 100 generally upscale retailers, including Saks Fifth Avenue, Versace, and Neiman Marcus, and a variety of average-to-good restaurants (like Maggiano's) and fast-food outlets. ✉ *2001 International Dr., McLean* ☎ *703/827–7730* ⊕ *www.tysonsgalleria.com.*

Tysons Corner Center. Anchored by Bloomingdale's and Nordstrom, Tysons Corner Center houses more than 300 stores and restaurants and a 16-screen AMC Theatre. Traffic is extremely heavy around the evening rush. ✉ *1961 Chain Bridge Rd., McLean* ☎ *703/893–9400* ⊕ *www.shoptysons.com.*

WOLF TRAP

13 mi west of Alexandria.

This tiny community, just northwest of Tysons Corner, is best known as home to the Wolf Trap National Park for the Performing Arts.

GETTING HERE AND AROUND

Beware of the traffic in nearby Tysons Corner where routes 123 and 7 and I–495, the Beltway, can be bumper-to-bumper. Those heading to Wolf Trap National Park for a concert can take Metrorail to the West Falls Church station where a Fairfax Connector bus provides round-trip service to the park.

EXPLORING

★ **Wolf Trap National Park for the Performing Arts.** A major venue in the greater DC area, Wolf Trap National Park for the Performing Arts hosts a wide variety of performances throughout the year in a beautiful outdoor setting. In warmer months popular and classical music, opera, dance, and comedy performances are given in a partially covered pavilion, the Filene Center, and in the Barns at Wolf Trap—two 18th-century barns transported from upstate New York—the rest of the year. Many food concessions are available; picnicking is permitted on the lawn, but not in the fixed seating under the pavilion.

Children's programs are emphasized at the outdoor Theatre in the Woods, including mime, puppetry, animal shows, music, drama, and storytelling. (No food or drink other than water is allowed in the theater.) A major event in September is the International Children's Festival. At any event, allow extra time for parking, and expect a traffic jam after the performance. The 100-plus acres of hills, meadows, and forests here are closed to general use from 90 minutes before to one hour after performances. Parking is free, and on performance nights Metrorail operates a $5 round-trip shuttle bus between the West Falls Church Metrorail station and the Filene Center. The fare is exact change only, and the bus leaves 20 minutes after the show, or no later than 11 pm—but it's almost unheard-of for any show to last longer than that. ✉ *1551 Trap Rd., Vienna* ☎ *703/255–1900; 703/938–2404 (fall–spring); 703/255–1868 (summer) Barns at Wolf Trap* ⊕ *www.wolftrap. org* ☉ *Daily dawn–dusk* Ⓜ *West Falls Church, then bus to Filene Center.*

☾ **Colvin Run Mill Historic Site.** Located about 3 mi southeast of Wolf Trap, this operating gristmill dates from the first decade of the 19th century, although the country store was added in the early 20th century. In addition to the restored gristmill, there are two exhibit rooms inside the miller's home. It offers tours every hour on the hour, with the last tour leaving at 3; educational programs; special events; and occasional outdoor concerts. You can picnic on the grounds, feed the ducks, and learn about America's technological roots. The Colvin Run Mill General Store originally served the local community and today offers penny candy, freshly ground cornmeal and wheat flour, and various old-fashioned goods. The mill itself usually operates Sunday afternoons from April to October. Call ahead to see if conditions permit grinding. ✉ *Rte. 7 at 10017 Colvin Run Rd., Great Falls* ☎ *703/759–2771* ⊕ *www.co.fairfax.va.us/parks/crm* ☒ *$6* ☉ *Wed.–Mon. 11–4.*

GREAT FALLS PARK

20 mi northwest of Alexandria.

Great Falls, a favorite getaway spot for Virginians and DC residents alike, is where the Potomac River builds up speed and crashes over steep rocks into the Mather Gorge.

GETTING HERE AND AROUND

From I–495 take the exit for Georgetown Pike and head west. But keep in mind that traffic here, as everywhere in the area, can be brutal during rush hour.

EXPLORING

★ **Great Falls Park.** Facing the C&O Canal National Historical Park across the Potomac River on the Maryland side is Great Falls Park, where the steep, jagged falls of the Potomac roar into the narrow Mather Gorge, the rocky narrows that make the Potomac churn.

The 800-acre park is a favorite for outings; here you can follow trails past the old Patowmack Canal and among the boulders and forests lining the edge of the falls. There are three overlooks in the park, two of which are handicap accessible. Horseback riding is permitted—maps are available at the visitor center—but you can't rent horses in the park. Swimming, wading, overnight camping, and alcoholic beverages are not allowed, but you can fish (a Virginia or Maryland license is required for anglers 16 and older), climb rocks (climbers must register at the visitor center or lower parking lot beforehand), or—if you're an experienced boater with your own equipment—go white-water kayaking (*below* the falls only). As is true all along this stretch of the river, the currents are deadly. Despite frequent signs and warnings, there are those who occasionally dare the water and drown.

A tour of the visitor center and museum takes 45 minutes. Staff members conduct special tours and walks year-round. ⊠ *9200 Old Dominion Dr.* ☎ *703/285–2966* ⊕ *www.nps.gov/grfa* ⊠ *$5 per vehicle; $3 for entry on foot, horse, or bicycle; admission good for 3 days* ☉ *Year-round, daily 7–dusk. Visitor center Apr.–Oct., daily 10–5; Nov.–Mar., daily 10–4.*

Chain Bridge. Downriver about 8 mi from Great Falls Park, the Chain Bridge links the District of Columbia with Virginia. It is named for the chains that held up the original structure. The Virginia side of the river in the area around Chain Bridge is known for its good fishing and narrow, treacherous channel.

WHERE TO EAT

$$$$ ✕ **L'Auberge Chez François.** Set in the Virginia countryside, this sprawling
FRENCH restaurant serves the German-influenced cuisine of Alsace. The decor
★ is romantic—a fireplace dominates the main dining room, and red-jacketed waiters courteously guide you through the all-inclusive six-course meal. *Choucroute* (sausage, duck, smoked pork, and foie gras served atop sauerkraut), and *Le Chateaubriand de L'Auberge*—served with fresh vegetables, béarnaise, and truffle sauce—are just two of the generously portioned entrées. You are asked in advance whether you'd like a soufflé. Say yes, unless the Alsatian plum tart is calling you instead. Make dinner reservations up to a month in advance. ⊠ *332 Springvale Rd., Great Falls* ☎ *703/759–3800* ⊕ *www.laubergechezfrancois.com* ⌟ *Reservations essential. Jacket and tie* ▭ *AE, D, DC, MC, V* ☉ *Closed Mon. No lunch.*

LOUDOUN COUNTY

Loudoun County, capital of Virginia's horse country and an hour away from D.C., abounds with historic villages and towns, antiques shops, wineries, farms, and heritage sites; the countryside is littered with stables, barns, and stacked-stone fences. The Potomac River borders the county on the north. In the major towns in Loudoun, such as Leesburg, Middleburg, and Waterford, residents keep alive traditional rural Virginia pursuits like fox hunts, steeplechases, and high-profile entertaining.

ESSENTIALS

Loudoun Tourism Council (⊠ *112-G South St. SE, Leesburg* ☎ *703/771–2617 ext. 11 or 800/752–6118* ⊕ *www.visitloudoun.org*).

MIDDLEBURG

40 mi west of Alexandria.

The area around here was surveyed by George Washington in 1763, when it was known as Chinn's Crossroads. It was considered strategic because of its location midway on the Winchester–Alexandria route (roughly what is now U.S. 50). Loudoun County also had the largest militia in the state of Virginia during the Revolutionary War. Many of Middleburg's homes include horse farms, and the town is known for its steeplechases and fox hunts in spring and fall. Attractive boutiques and stores line U.S. 50 (the main street). Roads out to the vineyards are often unpaved and narrow.

GETTING HERE AND AROUND

Travel to Middleburg requires a car. From farther north in Virginia and the DC area, take U.S. 50 south directly to Middleburg.

TIMING AND PRECAUTIONS

U.S. 50 gets busy during rush hour, from 7:30 to 9 am and 5 to 6:30 pm.

EXPLORING

Chrysalis Vineyard. Two miles east of town is the Chrysalis Vineyard, a 412-acre-and-growing vineyard dedicated to producing both old- and new-world varieties of wine and hoping to revive interest in the fabled Norton, a grape native to Virginia. The owner maintains she'd rather grow the world's best Norton than the 400th best cabernet. Wine tastings here emphasize the educational experience, as volunteers present each wine in detail to tasters. The entire experience takes about 45 minutes. Afterward, buy a bottle of wine and snag a picnic table near the tasting tents. Grills are available on a first come, first served basis. Chrysalis is also host to a number of music festivals throughout the year, including a jazz festival in May and the Norton Wine & Bluegrass Festival the first weekend in October. ⊠ *23876 Champe Ford Rd.* ☎ *540/687–8222* ⊕ *www.chrysaliswine.com* ☼ *Daily 10–5:30.*

Piedmont Vineyards and Winery. The vineyards in the Middleburg area often have tastings and tours. Three miles south of Middleburg, Piedmont Vineyards and Winery has 10 acres of vines, as well as an early-18th-century manor house. Piedmont specializes in white wines such as chardonnay and Seyval Blanc, but also makes some reds. ⊠ *2546D Halfway Rd.* ☎ *540/687–5528* ⊕ *www.piedmontwines.com* ☼ *Tasting room daily 11–5.*

Swedenburg Estate Vineyard. One mile east of Middleburg is the Swedenburg Estate Vineyard. The winery's modern building sits on a working farm, which raises Angus beef cattle. The Bull Run mountains form a backdrop for the vineyards. Swedenburg vineyard grows chardonnay, cabernet sauvignon, pinot noir, and Riesling. ⊠ *Valley View Farm, Rte. 50/23595 Winery La.* ☎ *540/687–5219* ⊕ *www.swedenburgwines.com* ☼ *Weekends 11–5, weekdays by appointment.*

WHERE TO STAY

$$ 🏠 **Middleburg Country Inn.** This three-story structure, built in 1820 and enlarged thereafter, was the rectory of St. John's Parish Emmanuel Episcopal Church until 1987. Its medium-size rooms are furnished with antiques and period reproductions. Unusual for a small inn, each guest room has its own phone and free Internet. A full country breakfast includes your choice of three entrées, and, when weather permits, you can eat your meal alfresco. The inn is within walking distance of the historic downtown. **Pros:** historic inn with free Internet; rooms include film library and complimentary ice cream. **Cons:** there's a $70 surcharge

if you book a room for Saturday night only; cancellations must be made 10 days in advance of stay to avoid one-night's lodging charge. ⊠ *209 E. Washington St., Box 2065* ☎ *540/687–6082 or 800/262–6082* ⊕ *www. middleburgcountryinn.com* ⟿ *4 rooms, 3 suites* ⟊ *In-room: a/c, Internet, Wi-Fi. In-hotel: restaurant, public Wi-Fi* ☰ *AE, D, MC, V* ⟊ *BP.*

$$ ⌸ **The Red Fox Inn and Tavern.** Built in 1728 of local fieldstone, Mr. Chinn's Ordinary (tavern) was sited on the vast estate of Thomas, sixth Lord Fairfax. George Washington visited the popular tavern in 1748. During the Civil War the inn served as a headquarters and hospital for Confederates. Today it is on the National Register of Historic Places. Bedside sweets, bathrobes, and the *Washington Post* delivered to your four-poster bedroom are extras that make for a special stay. **Pros:** romantic inn; in the center of town. **Cons:** the limited number of rooms can make this a difficult reservation to secure; pricey lodging option. ⊠ *2 E. Washington St., Box 385* ☎ *540/687–6301 or 800/223–1728* ⊕ *www.redfox.com* ⟿ *14 rooms* ⟊ *In-room: a/c, Internet. In-hotel: restaurant, Wi-Fi hotspot* ☰ *AE, D, MC, V* ⟊ *BP.*

EN
ROUTE

Fodor's Choice
★

Oatlands. Five miles south of Leesburg on Route 15, Oatlands is a former 3,408-acre plantation built by a great-grandson of Robert "King" Carter, one of the wealthiest pre-Revolution planters in Virginia. The Greek Revival manor house was begun in 1804 in the Federal style; a stately portico and half-octagonal stair wings were added in the 1820s. The house, a National Trust Historic Site, has been meticulously restored, and the manicured fields remain host to equestrian events from spring to fall. Among these is the Loudoun Hunt Point-to-Point in April, a race that brings out the entire community for tailgates and picnics on blankets. The terraced walls here border a restored English garden of 4½ acres. ⊠ *20850 Oatlands Plantation La. (Rte. 15)* ☎ *703/777–3174* ⊕ *www.oatlands.org* ⊠ *$10; additional fee for special events* ⊗ *Mar. 30–Dec. 30, Mon.–Sat. 10–5, Sun. 1–5; tours on the hr.*

LEESBURG

36 mi northwest of Alexandria.

Leesburg is one of the oldest towns in Northern Virginia. Its numerous fine Georgian and Federal buildings now house offices, shops, restaurants, and homes. In an early sign of changing allegiances, "George Town" changed its name to Leesburg in 1758 to honor Virginia's illustrious Lee family. When the British burned Washington during the War of 1812, many government records, including originals of the Declaration of Independence and the U.S. Constitution, went to Leesburg for safekeeping at the homes of Sheriff John Littlejohn and Clerk of Court Charles Binns.

GETTING HERE AND AROUND
Reach Leesburg via Route 7 or 267, which can both fill up with traffic during rush hour. Virginia Regional Transit also offers bus routes.

EXPLORING
Morven Park. Within the 1,200 acres that make up Morven Park are the Morven Park International Equestrian Institute (a private riding school) and two museums: Winmill Carriage Museum and the Museum of

Virginia's Winemaking Roots

In 1609 English settlers in Jamestown, Virginia, produced the first wine—however humble—in America. In the nearly 400 years since, it has been sink or swim for the state's wine industry—mostly sink. But after numerous tries, Virginia can claim some 135 wineries.

In 1611 the Virginia Company, eager to establish wine making in the Colonies, brought over French winegrowers along with slips and seeds of European vine stocks. For the next two centuries, French viticulturists attempted but failed to transplant European rootstock to the New World. In 1769 the Virginia Assembly appointed the Frenchman Andrew Estave as winemaker and viticulturist. He couldn't get the European stock to take either, but realized that the problem lay with Virginia's harsher climate of cold winters and hot, humid summers. Estave believed that growers should therefore use native American grapes, which were more likely to flourish.

Thomas Jefferson was anxious to promote grape growing, to encourage wine drinking for itself, and to create a cash-crop alternative to tobacco. Although he appreciated European wines, Jefferson believed that successful wine making in America would depend on native varietals. By 1800 he and other Virginians had begun developing hybrids of American and European varieties, resulting in grapes that combined American hardiness with European finesse and complexity. The most popular are still grown today.

A strong wine-making industry developed in Virginia between 1800 and the Civil War. The war's fierce battles destroyed many vineyards, but as recently as 1950 only 15 acres of grapes were being grown. In the 1960s the Virginia grape industry began a revival that has made it the sixth-largest wine-producing state. The revival began with American hybrids but has shifted to French hybrids.

Today Virginia's wines are winning national and international acclaim. The state sells more than 357,000 cases of wine yearly from close to 3,000 acres of wine grapes. The most popular variety, chardonnay, comes as a medium- to full-bodied dry white. It may be fruity, with a hint of apples or citrus. Other whites include vidal blanc, viognier, Riesling, Gewürztraminer, sauvignon blanc, and a Seyval blanc. Virginia's reds include cabernet franc, petit verdot, cabernet sauvignon, merlot, pinot noir, and Chambourcin.

Virginia's wineries are spread around the state in six American Viticultural Areas. The wine industry begun by Jefferson is in the Monticello region in central Virginia. Other areas are the Shenandoah, Northern Neck George Washington Birthplace, North Fork of Roanoke, Rocky Knob, and Virginia's Eastern Shore. Each area has been designated for its unique wine-growing conditions.

The "Virginia Winery Guide" lists each of the state's wineries (many offer tours and tastings). It's free and can be picked up at visitor information centers throughout the state or by contacting the **Virginia Wine Board** (☎ 804/344–8200, 800/828–4637 ⊕ www.virginiawine.org). From there you can also find descriptions of more than 500 wine events and festivals that take place each year, attracting half a million visitors.

Hounds and Hunting. The elegant mansion was originally a fieldstone farmhouse built in 1781. It evolved into a Greek Revival building that bears a striking resemblance to the White House (completed in 1800). Scenes from the Civil War film *Gods and Generals* and other movies were filmed here. In fact, the land was once a Confederate camp, remnants of which they are still finding today. Two governors have also lived here. The mansion and the Museum of Hounds and Hunting have been closed for an extensive renovation since 2003, although some rooms in the mansion have reopened; call to check. The Winmill Carriage Museum, housing more than 50 historic vehicles including one belonging to Grace Kelly and another belonging to Tom Thumb, is open to those taking the tours. ■**TIP**➔**Morven Park hosts Civil War reenactments the third Saturday of each month from April to mid-November.** Call for the latest info. ⊠ *Old Waterford Rd., 1 mi north of Leesburg* ☎ *703/777–2414* ⊕ *www.morvenpark.org* ✆ *$5* ⊙ *Tours Apr.–Nov., Fri.–Mon. 1–4; tours on the hr.*

WHERE TO EAT AND STAY

$$

AMERICAN

✕**Lightfoot Restaurant.** Housed in a Romanesque-Revival building (1888), this restaurant was the Peoples National Bank for more than half a century. Restored to its original grandeur, the restaurant was named in honor of Francis Lightfoot Lee, a signer of the Declaration of Independence. One of the wine "cellars" is actually the bank's vault. The seasonal American cuisine, based on local ingredients, includes Blue Ridge spinach salad, a variation on oysters Rockefeller, seared salmon topped with artichoke gratin and crab over orange couscous, slow-braised pork shank with a brandy glaze, and many kinds of seafood. ⊠ *11 N. King St.* ☎ *703/771–2233* ⊕ *www.lightfootrestaurant. com* ⊟ *AE, MC, V.*

$$$$

▣**Lansdowne Resort.** With 312 acres of hills and tall trees bordered by the Potomac River, Lansdowne specializes in outdoor activities and has miles of hiking and jogging trails. Polished wood furniture, handsome wall decorations, and marble-accented bathrooms help make the property elegant. On the Potomac restaurant serves a seasonal menu with fresh fish options. The Riverside Hearth, an upscale café overlooking an 18-hole golf course and driving range, is best known for its decadent Sunday brunch buffet. **Pros:** there's always something to do here between its tennis courts, pools, and 45 holes of championship golf courses; some areas of the hotel have beautiful views. **Cons:** the resort gets mixed reviews when it comes to service and friendliness of front desk staff; prices are high. ⊠ *44050 Woodridge Pkwy., off Rte. 7* ☎ *703/729–8400 or 800/541–4801* ⊕ *www.lansdowneresort. com* ⇆ *296 rooms, 14 suites* ⌂ *In-room: a/c, Wi-Fi. In-hotel: 3 restaurants, bars, golf courses, tennis courts, pools, gym, spa, bicycles, laundry service, parking (free)* ⊟ *AE, D, DC, MC, V.*

■ OFF THE BEATEN PATH

Waterford. The historic community of Waterford, 5 mi northwest of Leesburg, was founded by a Quaker miller and for many decades has been synonymous with fine crafts; its annual Homes Tour and Crafts Exhibit, held the first weekend of October with a Friday attached, includes visits to 18th- and 19th-century buildings. Waterford and more than 1,400 acres around it were declared a National Historic Landmark in 1970 in recognition of its authenticity as an almost-original, ordinary 19th-century village. Then in 2003 they bought a 144-acre farm that preserves the town's sightlines, protecting it from nearby development. Waterford also has an interesting Civil War history as a pro-Union town surrounded by the Confederacy. In fact, this community was home to the only organized Virginia cavalry unit to fight for the Union. Civil War and Revolutionary War reenactments still take place sometimes here. Visit the **Waterford Foundation** (✉ *40183 Main St.* ☎ *540/882–3018* ⊕ *www.waterfordva.org* ☉ *Tues.–Fri. 9–5 or by appt.*) to pick up booklets for your self-guided walking tour of the town. Walking tour is also available online.

D.C.'s Maryland Suburbs

WORD OF MOUTH

"Glen Echo has always been an enchanting place for children. Activities for kids include puppet shows, children's theater, exploring nature, making crafts, romping in the playground, and of course riding the famous Dentzel Carousel."

—Alicia

"Downtown Bethesda has some nice shops and a few galleries. Lots of restaurants. There is a nice movie theater, Landmark, that shows some offbeat movies."

—yestravel

Updated
by Amy
McKeever

Although D.C. has the monuments and Northern Virginia has a bevvy of colonial history, the Maryland suburbs hold a significant swath of the region's Civil War and agricultural history. This region was caught between the Union and the Confederacy—even though it was technically a northern state, suburban Maryland's land-based economy relied on slavery as much as its neighbors to the south. Civil War–era anecdotes crop up across the state, as do well-preserved wetlands and wildlife sanctuaries. Modern-day immigration has brought a variety of restaurants to the neighborhoods bordering D.C. that rival the city itself in authenticity.

Similar to the rest of the region, traffic in the Maryland suburbs can be a bear. Nearby areas have seen significant recent growth with an influx of both modern housing and government and office buildings. Federal agencies that maintain offices in Maryland include the National Institutes of Health, the Internal Revenue Service, and the National Aeronautics and Space Administration. A new development, National Harbor, built along the Maryland banks of the Potomac River has brought an influx of tourism and a brand new method of commuting—by water ferry—to Old Town Alexandria or Georgetown.

ORIENTATION AND PLANNING

GETTING ORIENTED

Suburban Maryland is an important stop for anyone looking to get a full picture of the history of the nation's capital. Its two counties fuse the region's Civil War history and agricultural past with the diversity of a modern metropolis.

Montgomery County. The large swath of land across the northwest border of D.C. is Maryland's Montgomery County. Bethesda and Silver Spring, two of D.C.'s most popular suburban cities, are in Montgomery County. There's also plenty for those who love the outdoors, including Glen Echo Park and the C&O Canal National Historical Park.

Prince George's County. East of Montgomery County, also bordering the District, is Prince George's County, best known for being home to the University of Maryland Terrapins. But the county also holds an important place in America's aviation history, as it boasts the nation's oldest continuously operating airfield. Fort Washington Park provides a shady relief from the urban sprawl.

TOP REASONS TO GO

Taste Bethesda's Best: This suburban town is loved for its diverse dining options in the Woodmont Triangle—from tender lamb dishes at Bacchus of Lebanon to quick and messy burritos at California Tortilla.

Get in Tune with Nature: Experience suburban Maryland's agricultural past at Piscataway Park, the Patuxent Research Refuge, or the Beltsville Agricultural Research Center. For outdoor adventure, try biking the Capital Crescent Trail.

Be Inspired by Clara Barton: Explore the history of the American Red Cross and its famous founder at the Clara Barton National Historic Site. Afterwards, take the path leading into Glen Echo Park to ride the antique carousel.

Go for the Views: Visit the C&O Canal National Historical Park for stunning views of the scenic fall line of the Potomac River, a barrier to upriver navigation that necessitated settlements at Georgetown and Alexandria.

4

PLANNING

WHEN TO GO

Summer months in suburban Maryland are humid just like the rest of the region. Although the winter is generally mild, the area doesn't handle snow very well so spring and fall are the best bets for a trip. Major events in D.C. such as the Cherry Blossom Festival in March and April do affect hotel prices and crowds in these areas.

Every May, Andrews Air Force Base plays host to the **Joint Services Open House & Air Show** (☎ 301/981–4424 ⊕ www.jsoh.org). It's the largest military open house in the United States, complete with demonstrations and an impressive air show. The first Saturday of October, Bethesda restaurants sell samples of their fare at the food festival, **Taste of Bethesda** (☎ 301/215–6660 ⊕ www.bethesda.org). Each June, the American Film Institute's Silver Theatre hosts **SILVERDOCS**, a star-studded documentary film festival (☎ 301/495–6700 ⊕ www.afi.com/silver).

GETTING HERE AND AROUND

AIR TRAVEL

Three major airports serve both suburban Maryland and the Washington, D.C., area. Baltimore-Washington International (BWI) Airport, 10 mi south of Baltimore off I–95 and Route 295, is closer to Montgomery and Prince George's counties than Ronald Reagan National Airport or Washington Dulles International Airport.

A taxi to Dulles or BWI airport is expensive, but BWI is well served by reasonable ground transportation. Washington Metropolitan Transit Authority (WMATA) has an express bus to the airport from its Greenbelt, Maryland, Metrorail station. All northbound Amtrak and Maryland State Penn Line trains from Washington's Union Station make a BWI stop, from which a free shuttle bus takes you to the terminal. Dulles is served by Washington Flyer bus every 30 minutes from the West Falls Church Metrorail station ($10), by Metrobus Route 5A express service ($6), and by van services like SuperShuttle ($35). The

Washington Metropolitan Area Transit Authority (WMATA) operates express bus service between BWI and the Greenbelt Metro station. Buses run between 6 am and 11 pm weekdays, and 8:45 am and 11 pm weekends. Exact fare ($6) is required. BWI is also served by SuperShuttle. By taxi, expect to pay around $40 to Laurel, $65 to Silver Spring, and $73 to Bethesda. Free shuttle buses carry passengers between airline terminals and the train station at BWI. Amtrak and Maryland Rail Commuter Service (MARC) trains run between BWI and Washington, DC's Union Station and Prince George's County from around 4:30 am to 10:30 pm. The cost of the 30-minute ride to Union Station is $13 to $34 on Amtrak and $6 on MARC, which runs only on weekdays.

CAR TRAVEL

An automobile is a must to travel throughout the counties, but avoid the Capital Beltway (I–495) during morning and afternoon rush hours. At those times the congestion is in the top five of America's worst commutes.

The Capital Beltway, I–495, circles the District of Columbia through Virginia and Maryland (and enters the District very briefly, as it crosses the Wilson Bridge), providing a circular bypass for I–95 around Washington. During commute hours it becomes congested—toward Silver Spring in the morning, and away in the evening—so if you plan to spend most of your time in downtown Washington or within the Beltway, it would be prudent to select lodging south of the I–95/I–495 interchange. Note that HOV restrictions prohibit single-person vehicles on I–66 inside the Beltway eastbound during morning rush hour and westbound during evening rush hour.

Roads that run through the region and into downtown Washington include Wisconsin, Connecticut, Georgia, New Hampshire, and Pennsylvania avenues; routes 1 and 50 (the latter turns into New York Avenue upon entering the District); Baltimore Washington Parkway; and I–295, all of which get busy 7:30 am to 9 am and 5 pm to 6:30 pm. Giving parking tickets is one of the things capital-area jurisdictions do best, so if you park at meters, be careful and keep the meter fed. Also read parking signs carefully. There are many variations, and they are often quite confusing. Traffic cameras in the Maryland portion of Connecticut Avenue are ever-ready to catch speedy drivers.

The outer loop in Maryland around the intersection with I–270 is congested in the morning rush, as is the inner loop in the evening rush. Interstate 270, which intersects with I–495 in Montgomery County, reaches destinations north of Rockville in Montgomery County.

METRO TRAVEL

Washington Metropolitan Area Transit Authority (WMATA) provides subway service (Metrorail) in the District and in the Maryland suburbs. Maryland's Montgomery County is served by the system's busiest route, the Red Line, and Prince George's County is served by the Blue, Orange, and Green lines. It begins operation at 5 am on weekdays and 7 am on weekends and closes on weekdays at midnight and weekends at 3 am. During the weekday peak periods (5–9:30 am and 3–7 pm), trains come along every three to six minutes. At other times trains run about every 12 to 15 minutes.

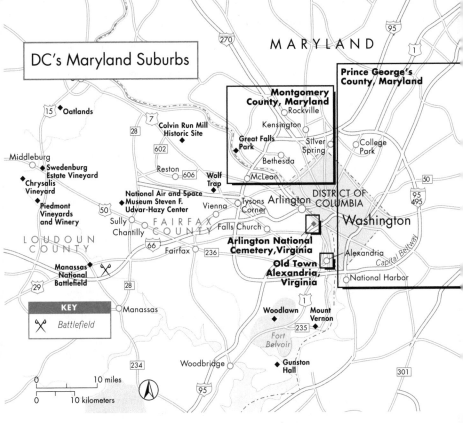

The Metro's base fare is $1.60; the actual price rises depending on the time of day and the distance traveled. Up to two children under age five ride free with a paying passenger. Buy your ticket at the Farecard machines, some of which accept credit cards. One-day passes are $9 and seven-day passes are $47. ■ TIP→ **Make sure you hang on to your Farecard—you need it to exit at your destination.** Locals use the SmarTrip card, a plastic card that can hold any fare amount and can be used throughout the subway system. SmarTrip fares are 25¢ cheaper than using cash. Buy passes or SmarTrip cards at the Metro Center sales office.

TAXI TRAVEL

Taxicabs are free to operate in adjoining jurisdictions and this is vital, considering that there are two states plus the District and several counties and cities in a small area. Maryland taxis are metered with rates set by the jurisdiction (about $4 to board and plus 50¢ for each quarter mile in Montgomery County and a $3 flag fare with 25¢ for every seventh of a mile in Prince George's County). Taxis are usually waiting near the busier Metrorail stations like Bethesda, Silver Spring, and Greenbelt, and the bigger hotels.

Taxis at the Virginia airports are very tightly regulated. Washington Flyer cabs serve Dulles International Airport exclusively from the airport but any taxi can deliver there. A starter outside the arrivals area at Reagan National loads taxicabs from a regulated line of incoming taxis and will provide a fare sheet if desired. An airport fee of $2.50 is added to your fare to pay for this service. Some taxi drivers accept credit cards, but ask first.

TRAIN TRAVEL

Amtrak serves the region with scheduled stops in New Carrollton and at BWI Airport as part of its East Coast service. The MARC commuter train has two lines that go through Montgomery and Prince George's counties, and it also goes into Washington's Union Station.

ESSENTIALS

Air Contacts SuperShuttle (☎ 800/258–3826 or 202/296–6662 ⊕ www. supershuttle.com). **Washington Flyer** (☎ 888/927–4359 ⊕ www.washfly.com).

Metro Information Metrorail (☎ 202/637–7000 ⊕ www.wmata.com).

Train Contacts Maryland Transit Administration (☎ 410/539–5000 ⊕ www. mta.maryland.gov).

DISCOUNTS AND DEALS

Order a free Destination Maryland Travel Guide from the Maryland Office of Tourism and receive a Maryland Welcome! Passport card for discounts at hotels, restaurants, and attractions throughout the state. Get two adult tickets for the price of one at Montpelier Mansion or the Surratt House Museum or enjoy 10% tickets to certain concert series at Strathmore. **Maryland Office of Tourism** (☎ 866/639–3526 ⊕ www. visitmaryland.org).

RESTAURANTS

Bethesda is one of the Washington area's culinary hotspots. Many Washington restaurants and celebrity chefs have opened Bethesda branches, and alfresco dining is available during good weather at most places. Bethesda's largest concentration of restaurants (about 75) is within the Woodmont Triangle, bounded by Old Georgetown Road, Wisconsin Avenue, and Rugby Avenue. Downtown Silver Spring and the new National Harbor also have their fair share of quality restaurants.

HOTELS

It's best to book your hotel room in advance. Occupancy rates are high, and you're likely to pay only a little less than you would in Washington. Tourists coming to see Washington's cherry blossoms make spring the busiest season. December and January tend to be the slowest and least expensive months, except around a presidential inauguration.

WHAT IT COSTS					
	¢	$	$$	$$$	$$$$
Restaurants	under $10	$10–$16	$17–$23	$24–$30	over $30
Hotels	under $100	$100–$160	$161–$230	$231–$300	over $300

Restaurant prices are per person for a main course at dinner. Hotel prices are for a standard double room, excluding state and local taxes.

PLANNING YOUR TIME

You'll want to devote most of your time to the areas closest to Washington, D.C., such as Bethesda and Silver Spring. These are easily connected to one another via Metrorail and Metrobus, though note that a ride between the two on Metrorail will take awhile as the train weaves into the heart of downtown D.C. and back out. Allow about an hour for travel across the District of Columbia via Metrorail, especially on weekends or during non–rush hours. Another quick way to get from Maryland to Virginia or D.C. is to ride the ferry across the Potomac River, from the National Harbor in Maryland to Alexandria, Mount Vernon, or Georgetown (via Alexandria). On the other side of the District, there is also an automobile ferry—White's Ferry—that connects Loudoun and Montgomery counties. For all other vehicular crossings the Capital Beltway traverses the Potomac via the American Legion and Woodrow Wilson bridges. The former connects Virginia's Fairfax County to Maryland's Montgomery County, while the Woodrow Wilson Bridge connects Alexandria to Prince George's County, Maryland.

If you have more time, drive away from the capital toward Kensington or Glen Echo. Plan to spend at least half a day or more in each outlying town. Enjoy the slower pace of life and go antiques shopping, dancing, or picnicking in the many parks.

MONTGOMERY COUNTY

In 1776 Montgomery County, named after Revolutionary War hero General Richard Montgomery, became the first Maryland county to drop the custom of naming jurisdictions after royalty. In between housing developments, strip malls, and office parks, the northern portion of the county retains traces of the area's agrarian beginnings.

ESSENTIALS

Montgomery County Conference & Visitors Bureau (✉ *111 Rockville Pike, Suite 800, Rockville* ☎ *240/777–2060 or 877/789–6904* ⊕ *www.cvbmontco. com*).

BETHESDA

2 mi north of Washington, D.C.

Bethesda was named in 1871 after the Bethesda Meeting House, which was built by the Presbyterians. The name alludes to a biblical pool that had great healing power. Today people seek healing in Bethesda at the National Institutes of Health and the soothing aqua vitae available in the suburb's acclaimed restaurants and bars. Bethesda has changed from a small community into an urban destination, but in certain ways time has stood still east of Bethesda in Chevy Chase, a tony town of country clubs, stately houses, and huge trees.

GETTING HERE AND AROUND

You can hail a taxi on the street just about anywhere in Bethesda or Silver Spring. Bright blue signs identify parking; on weekends you can park free in public garages.

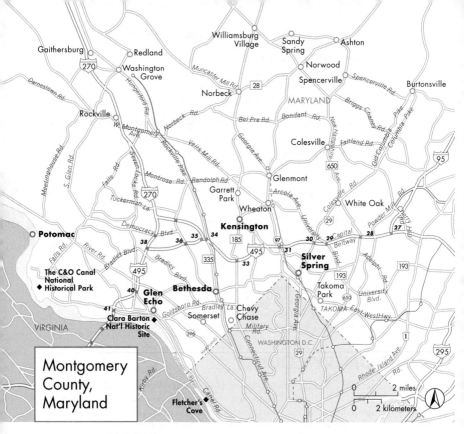

Montgomery
County,
Maryland

ESSENTIALS

Taxi Contact Montgomery Airport Sedan (☎ 301/926–9300). **Barwood Taxi-cabs** (☎ 301/984–1900).

EXPLORING

Audubon Naturalist Society. A self-guided nature trail winds through a verdant 40-acre estate and around the headquarters of the Audubon Naturalist Society. The estate is known as Woodend, as is the mansion, which was designed in 1927 by Jefferson Memorial architect John Russell Pope. The society leads wildlife identification walks, environmental education programs, and—September through June—a weekly Saturday bird walk at its headquarters. The bookstore stocks titles on conservation, ecology, and birding, as well as nature-related gifts such as jewelry and toys. ⊠ *8940 Jones Mill Rd., Chevy Chase* ☎ *301/652–9188; 301/652–1088 for naturalist tape* ⊕ *www.audubonnaturalist.org* ☞ *Free* ☉ *Grounds daily dawn–dusk; bookstore weekdays 10–5, Sat. 9–5, Sun. noon–5.*

National Institutes of Health (NIH). One of the world's foremost biomedical research centers, with a sprawling 322-acre campus, the NIH offers tours for the public, including an orientation tour at the NIH Visitor Information Center and one at the National Library of Medicine, that will likely be quite interesting to those interested in medicine and a little

4

dry to everyone else. The visitor center tour discusses how health and medicine has been transformed through discovery—discoveries that have kept the blood supply safe from disease and begun mapping the human genome. There are about 1,500 ongoing clinical trials at this facility at any given time, and tours will take you through the pediatric day unit, which offers a playroom for children and a program for them to connect with pediatric patients across the country via Internet. Then the tour continues to the pediatric oncology lab, where researchers are working to improve methods to help these very children. Although best known for its books and journals—there are about 14 mi worth of them—the National Library of Medicine also houses historical medical references dating from the 11th century. A library tour includes a look at historical documents, the library's databases, and "visible human" anatomical simulator. The library was built during the Cold War, and as guides will explain, the building's roof was designed to collapse in the event of an attack from the Soviet Union, protecting the books kept below ground. ⊠ *Visitor Information Center, 45 Center Dr., Bldg. 45* ☎ *301/496–1776* ⊠ *National Library of Medicine, 8600 Rockville Pike, Bldg. 38A* ☎ *301/496–7771* ⊕ *www.nih.gov* ⊠ *Free* ☉ *Call for tour times, library hrs, and information on forms of ID to bring, plus other security measures* Ⓜ *Medical Center.*

WHERE TO EAT

$$
MIDDLE EASTERN

✕ **Bacchus of Lebanon.** The lamb dishes and appetizers ("mezze") are excellent at this Lebanese restaurant. Try the *fatte bel lahm* (lamb cooked in sizzling butter on a bed of pita chips and smothered in yogurt sauce, garlic, and pine nuts). The lamb is so tender the meat comes apart at the slightest touch of your fork. Outdoor seating is available in a pretty courtyard with a stone fountain in the corner. Both vegetarians and meat eaters will find good options on the creative menu. ⊠ *7945 Norfolk Ave.* ☎ *301/657–1722* ⊕ *www.bacchusoflebanon.com* ⊟ *AE, D, MC, V.*

¢
SOUTHWESTERN

✕ **California Tortilla.** Friendly, quick service helps make this counter-service restaurant—which describes itself as "darned spunky"—a local favorite. The blackened chicken Caesar burrito is one of the top three sellers in the joint. Add spice to your meal with a dash or two from 75 hot sauces lined up on the wall, and grab a seat inside or out. On Monday nights, spin the Mystery Prize Burrito Wheel for discounts and freebies. Patrons can also subscribe to the restaurant's "Taco Talk" newsletter, which is read worldwide. ⊠ *4862 Cordell Ave.* ☎ *301/654–8226* ⊕ *www.californiatortilla.com* ⊠ *7727 Tuckerman La., Potomac* ☎ *301/765–3600* ⊟ *MC, V.*

$
INDIAN

✕ **Passage to India.** Although the delivery is sometimes stiff, the regional Indian dishes in this stately, quiet dining room are delicious and made with local ingredients. Anything tandoori is not to be missed and the goat curry and *kamal-kakri masala*, a lotus-stem-and-pea stew, are excellent. Pictures of rajas adorn the walls and the windows are fitted with wooden lattice screens creating a dramatic and romantic ambience. Sitar music plays softly in the background, rounding out your experience. ⊠ *4931 Cordell Ave.* ☎ *301/656–3373* ⊟ *AE, D, MC, V.*

$-$$ ✕ **Tara Thai.** Blue walls and paintings of sea life reflect the owner's child-
THAI   hood home in Thailand; so does the extensive menu at this branch of
a busy chain, whose many seafood dishes include fresh flounder and
rockfish. Favorites include the mild and traditional pad thai, the spicy
goong phuket (grilled black tiger shrimp topped with crabmeat and
chicken sauce), and chicken satay. Service is quick and friendly, making
Tara Thai an excellent place to stop and rest while shopping in nearby
stores. ✉ *4828 Bethesda Ave.* ☎ *301/657–0488* ✉ *12071 Rockville
Pike, Rockville* ☎ *301/231–9899* ▤ *AE, D, DC, MC, V.*

¢–$ ✕ **Tastee Diner.** The Tastees are part of the culinary past in the Washing-
AMERICAN   ton area, with a handful still left in Silver Spring, Laurel, and Bethesda,
the flagship location. These 24-hour diners are sentimental favorites
among many area residents, who value them for their hand-formed
hamburgers, the tastiness of which is subjective. Students and others
on low budgets (or little sleep) ignore the dust and relish the coffee,
which flows endlessly. Breakfast is served around the clock. ✉ *7731
Woodmont Ave.* ☎ *301/652–3970* ⊕ *www.tasteediner.com* ⌫ *Reservations not accepted* ▤ *MC, V.*

WHERE TO STAY

$$$ ▥ **Courtyard Marriott Chevy Chase.** A $30-million renovation has turned
this hotel, located inside one of the area's most upscale shopping dis-
tricts, into the first LEED Gold certified building in Montgomery
County, with the amenities to show for it. From a recycling center and
preferred parking for low-emission vehicles to complimentary bicycle
rentals, this hotel is as friendly to the environment as it is to its guests.
A high-tech lobby is outfitted with a boarding pass station where guests
can print their boarding passes before heading to the airport, and a large
touch-screen board that helps guests find nearby restaurants and shops.
Pros: just blocks from the Friendship Heights Metro on the DC border;
great for business travelers. **Cons:** hotel only has one suite. ✉ *5520
Wisconsin Ave., Chevy Chase* ☎ *301/656–1500* ⊕ *www.marriott.com*
⤳ *226 rooms, 1 suite* ⌫ *In-room: a/c, refrigerator, Internet, Wi-Fi. In-
hotel: restaurant, room service, bar, pool, gym, bicycles, laundry facili-
ties, laundry service, Wi-Fi hotspot, parking (paid)* ▤ *AE, D, DC, MC,
V* Ⓜ *Friendship Heights* ⦿ *CP.*

$$–$$$ ▥ **Embassy Suites.** Shopping and sightseeing couldn't be more convenient
★   at this all-suites hotel, which adjoins the upscale Chevy Chase Pavilion
and is an elevator ride up from the Friendship Heights Metro station.
Each suite includes a bedroom and separate living room with a sleeper
sofa, a kitchen space with a fridge and microwave, and a table suitable
for dining and working. The fitness center has more than 20 exercise
stations and a personal trainer for a fee. A dozen restaurants and no
fewer than three large shopping malls are within walking distance.
Pros: complimentary breakfast and evening cocktails in the sun-filled
atrium; great location adjacent to shopping and Metro. **Cons:** although
rooms come outfitted with noise-strip sealers and triple-pane windows,
you can still hear the street sounds from busy Wisconsin below; street
parking is scarce, and the garage is available only for a fee. ✉ *4300
Military Rd., Washington, DC* ☎ *202/362–9300 or 800/362–2779*
⊕ *www.embassysuites.com* ⤳ *198 suites* ⌫ *In-room: a/c, Internet,*

Wi-Fi. In-hotel: restaurant, room service, pool, gym, laundry service, Wi-Fi hotspot, parking (paid) ⊟ *AE, D, DC, MC, V* �‖⦿ *BP* Ⓜ *Friendship Heights.*

$$$–$$$$ ⊞ **Hyatt Regency Bethesda.** Part of a busy nexus of restaurants, world-class shops, and movie theaters, this hotel, next to the Metro entrance, is a convenient refuge for weary travelers. Rooms are classically under-stated, with spacious mahogany desks and iPod docks. The rooftop cov-ered pool shares space with a large gym that even has a hot towel bar. If you're staying over on a Saturday night, shell out the $10 to watch local comics perform at the Laugh Riot at the Hyatt—you can get on stage after the show and tell your own joke for a cash prize. **Pros:** entertain-ing amenities; great for business travelers; discounts for weekend stays. **Cons:** rooms are small compared to the price you pay for them; parking available only for a fee. ⊠ *1 Bethesda Metro Center, on 7400 block of Wisconsin Ave.* ☎ *301/657–1234 or 800/233–1234* ⊕ *www.hyatt.com* ⇨ *390 rooms, 7 suites* ⅏ *In-room: a/c, Internet, Wi-Fi. In-hotel: 2 res-taurants, room service, bar, pool, gym, laundry service, Wi-Fi hotspot, parking (paid)* ⊟ *AE, D, DC, MC, V* Ⓜ *Bethesda.*

NIGHTLIFE AND THE ARTS

Free concerts are held on Wednesday afternoons in summer at Bethesda Place Plaza, and Thursday evenings at Veterans Park. Catch anything from rock, reggae, and Hawaiian swing to jazz, funk, and blues.

THE ARTS

★ **Round House Theatre.** A sharp, state-of-the-art facility, this 400-seat theater is nationally known for its work in producing stage versions of literary works and other contemporary plays. Each season, which always includes at least one world premiere, consists of about 200 per-formances. ⊠ *4545 East-West Hwy.* ☎ *240/644–1100* ⊕ *www.round-house.org* Ⓜ *Bethesda.*

Strathmore. Local and national artists exhibit in the galleries and jazz, chamber, folk, and popular musicians perform year-round at this man-sion built around 1900. Whimsical pieces, part of the permanent col-lection, are on display in the sculpture garden. A Wednesday evening concert series features local musicians for $12. The 1,976-seat Music Centre, home to the Baltimore Symphony Orchestra in Montgomery County, opened in 2005. Strathmore's Tea is served in a well-lighted wood-panel salon Tuesday and Wednesday at 1 (reservations essen-tial). On Wednesday evenings in summer, concertgoers spread out on the expansive lawn to listen to free concerts—everything from Ukelele to Afrofunk. ⊠ *10701 Rockville Pike* ☎ *301/530–0540* ⊕ *www.strathmore.org* ⊠ *Free, Backyard Theater $7, tea $21* ◷ *Mon., Tues., Thurs., and Fri. 10–4; Wed. 10–9; Sat. 10–3* Ⓜ *Grosvenor/Strathmore.*

NIGHTLIFE

Juste Lounge. With a space large enough to accommodate loungers and dancers, karaoke (on Thursday), DJs spinning hip-hop and reggae, live music, and dance lessons, this swanky lounge draws an eclectic crowd. Smoke a hookah on the patio on weekends. ⊠ *6821 Reed St.* ☎ *202/393–0939* ⊕ *www.justelounge.com.*

SPORTS AND THE OUTDOORS

Ⓒ ★ **Cabin John Regional Park.** One of the best playgrounds in the Washington area, this park has plastic slides, swings, and mazes to delight both toddlers and preteens. On the park grounds there also an ice rink, indoor and outdoor tennis courts, a nature center, hiking trails, and a train that operates seasonally. An outdoor amphitheater brings the occasional concert or theater production. ✉ *7400 Tuckerman La.* ☎ *301/299–0024.*

Capital Crescent Trail. This paved trail runs along the old Georgetown Branch, a B&O Railroad line completed in 1910 that saw its last train in 1985. Bicyclists, walkers, in-line skaters, and strollers take the 7.5-mi route from near Key Bridge in Washington's Georgetown to Bethesda and Woodmont avenues in central Bethesda. The trail picks up again at a well-lighted tunnel at the Elm Street Park (4600 Elm Street) and continues into Silver Spring. From Bethesda to the outskirts of Silver Spring, the 3.5-mi trail is gravel. The Georgetown Branch Trail, as this section is officially named, connects with the Rock Creek Trail, which goes to Rockville in the north and Memorial Bridge past the Washington Monument in the south. For more information, contact the **Coalition for the Capital Crescent Trail** (☎ *202/234–4874* ⊕ *www.cctrail. org*). You can rent bikes at **Big Wheel Bikes** (✉ *6917 Arlington Rd., Bethesda* ☎ *301/652–0192*).

SHOPPING

Bethesda isn't known for bargains, although one of its best-known malls contains a Filene's Basement. Shoppers who love discounts should head north on Wisconsin Avenue to Rockville Pike (Route 355). Four of the area's seven regional malls are in Bethesda and the Chevy Chase section of Washington, D.C. Downtown Bethesda has no fewer than eight bookstores, including a huge Barnes & Noble.

CLOTHING

Lemon Twist. Inside this boutique are classic women's wear and children's clothes, gifts, and more from designers such as Lilly Pulitzer, Vera Bradley, and Vineyard Vines. But most of all Lemon Twist has been known for its customer service since 1977. ✉ *8530 Connecticut Ave., Chevy Chase* ☎ *301/986–0044.*

Wear It Well. From funky jackets and slacks to tailored business suits, this local shop specializes in items that wear and travel well. ✉ *4816 Bethesda Ave., Bethesda* ☎ *301/652–3713.*

DEPARTMENT STORES

Filene's Basement. The Boston-based upscale fashion discounter attracts bargain hunters looking for steep discounts on designer clothing—if you find something that suits you, it'll be the best deal in town by far. Off-price shoes, children's clothing, household goods, perfume, and accessories are sold as well. ✉ *5300 Wisconsin Ave. NW, Washington, DC* ☎ *202/966–0208* Ⓜ *Friendship Heights.*

Saks Fifth Avenue. Despite its New York origin and name, Saks is a Washington institution. It has a wide selection of European and American couture clothing; other attractions include the shoe, jewelry, fur, and lingerie departments. ⊠ *5555 Wisconsin Ave., Chevy Chase* ☎ *301/657–9000* Ⓜ *Friendship Heights.*

MALLS

Chevy Chase Pavilion. Across from Mazza Gallerie is the newer, similarly upmarket Chevy Chase Pavilion. Its women's clothing stores range from Alpaca International to JCrew and Stein Mart. ⊠ *5335 Wisconsin Ave. NW, Washington, DC* ☎ *202/686–5335* ⊕ *www.ccpavilion.com* Ⓜ *Friendship Heights.*

The Collection at Chevy Chase. This mall is the latest addition to the luxurification of Friendship Heights, which now can claim Bulgari, Dior, Ralph Lauren, Louis Vuitton, Jimmy Choo, and Barney's Co-op as residents. ⊠ *5471–5481 Wisconsin Ave. NW, Washington, DC* ☎ *No phone* ⊕ *www.thecollectionatchevychase.com* Ⓜ *Friendship Heights.*

Mazza Gallerie. This four-level mall is anchored by the ritzy Neiman Marcus department store and the discounter Filene's Basement. Other draws include Williams-Sonoma's kitchenware and a seven-screen movie theater. ⊠ *5300 Wisconsin Ave. NW, Washington, DC* ☎ *202/966–6114* ⊕ *www.mazzagallerie.com* Ⓜ *Friendship Heights.*

White Flint Mall. Bloomingdale's, Lord & Taylor, and Borders Books & Music, plus 125 other stores, pull in the serious shoppers. ⊠ *11301 Rockville Pike, North Bethesda* ☎ *301/231–7467* ⊕ *www. shopwhiteflint.com* Ⓜ *White Flint.*

GLEN ECHO

4 mi west of downtown Bethesda, 2.5 mi from the Capital Beltway.

Glen Echo, now a charming village of Victorian houses, was founded in 1891 by Edwin and Edward Baltzley, inventors of a type of mechanical eggbeater. The brothers fell under the spell of the Chautauqua movement, an organization that ran what can best be described as an educational summer camp with prominent lecturers and performers. To further their dream, the brothers sold land and houses, but the Glen Echo Chautauqua lasted only one season.

GETTING HERE AND AROUND

The Montgomery County Ride-On bus #29 operates daily between Glen Echo and the Friendship Heights and Bethesda Metro stations. By car, take I–495 to MD–190 (River Road).

TIMING AND PRECAUTIONS

Avoid I–495 during rush hour, which lasts from 7:30 am to 9 am and 5 pm to 6:30 pm on weekdays.

EXPLORING

Clara Barton National Historic Site. The Clara Barton National Historic Site is a monument to the founder of the American Red Cross. Known as the "angel of the battlefield" for nursing wounded soldiers during the Civil War, Barton used the striking Victorian structure at first to store Red Cross supplies (it was built for her by the town's founders). It later became both her home and the organization's headquarters. Today the building is furnished with many of her possessions and period artifacts. Access is by guided tour, which lasts approximately 35 minutes. ✉ *5801 Oxford Rd., next to Glen Echo Park parking lot, Glen Echo* ☎ *301/320–1410* ⊕ *www.nps.gov/clba* ✈ *Free* ☉ *Daily 10–5; tours on the hr 10–4, last tour leaves at 4.*

♻ **Glen Echo Park.** The Baltzley brothers' 10-acre compound, Glen Echo
Fodor's Choice Park, was once known for its whimsical architecture, including a stone
★ tower, from the Chautauqua period. The area was later the site of an amusement park, and you can still see the skeletons of the once-thriving rides. Only the splendid 1921 Dentzel **carousel** still runs (May–August, Wednesday and Thursday 10–2, weekends noon–6; September; weekends noon–6), with musical accompaniment from a rare Wurlitzer military band organ. The National Park Service now administers the property, which is the site of a puppet company and a children's theater. Social dances and classes from jazz to swing to salsa are held in the 1933 Spanish Ballroom. Art galleries have ongoing exhibits and demonstrations. ✉ *7300 MacArthur Blvd.* ☎ *301/634–2222* ⊕ *www. glenechopark.org* ✈ *Carousel rides $1.25, puppet shows $8, plays $15, cost of dances vary* ☉ *Daily dawn–dusk.*

WHERE TO EAT

$$$ ✕ **Irish Inn at Glen Echo.** This turn-of-the-20th-century inn used to be a
IRISH   biker bar and a brothel. Now it's a cozy, popular destination with a
★ pub and a restaurant, each serving excellent Irish comfort food. Try the bangers and mash, shepherd's pie, or the mustard-encrusted rack of lamb. The pub, which has an attractive selection of Irish whiskey and a relatively affordable menu, stays open until midnight, with live music on Sunday and Monday evenings. Closed Monday lunch. ✉ *6119 Tulane Ave.* ☎ *301/229–6600* ⊕ *www.irishinnglenecho.com* ▭ *AE, D, DC, MC, V.*

POTOMAC

8 mi north of Glen Echo, 7 mi northwest of Bethesda.

The popular translation of the Native American name "Patawomeck" is "they are coming by water." Although today's visitors are likely to drive, it is still possible to view the mighty Potomac River by hiking along the towpath of the C&O Canal and climbing the rocks at Great Falls, which Maryland and Virginia share a view of from opposite banks. Potomac is also known for its elegant estates and houses, as it is one of the wealthiest communities in the United States.

GETTING HERE AND AROUND
Potomac, and especially the C&O Canal National Historical Park, is best accessible by car given its location near the nexus of I–495 and I–270.

TIMING AND PRECAUTIONS
Rush hour, which lasts from 7:30 am to 9 am and 5 pm to 6:30 pm on weekdays, makes travel difficult on I–495 and I–270.

EXPLORING

The C&O Canal National Historical Park. This park extends along the Potomac River 184½ mi from Washington, DC, to Cumberland, Maryland. Three miles south of the town of Potomac, the **Great Falls Tavern,** a museum and visitor center, serves as the park's local anchor. Barge trips and a vista on the powerful Great Falls are the draws here. A ½-mi, wheelchair-accessible walkway to the platform on Olmsted Island provides a spectacular view of the churning waters. Swimming and wading are prohibited, but you can fish (a Maryland license is required for anglers 16 and older) or climb the rocky Billy Goat Trail; only experienced boaters can go white-water kayaking below the falls—all along this stretch of the river, the currents are deadly. ■ TIP→ The tavern ceased food service long ago, so if you're hungry, head for the seasonal snack bar a few paces north or bring your own picnic. ⊠ *11710 MacArthur Blvd.* ☎ *301/767–3714* ⊕ *www.nps.gov/choh* ⊠ *$5 per vehicle, $3 per person without vehicle, good for 3 days on MD and VA sides of park* ☉ *Park, daily sunrise–sunset; tavern and museum, daily 9–4:30; barge trips, May–Oct., Wed.–Sun. 11, 1:30, and 3.*

WHERE TO EAT

$$
FRENCH

✕ **Normandie Farm.** Built on top of a half-finished country club that was foreclosed on during the Great Depression, Normandie Farm maintains the French-American provincial cuisine and romantic, rustic surroundings that the original 1930s owners (sisters) grew to love during their time at cooking school in Normandy, France. The classic menu has likewise remained nearly unchanged; the most popular dishes are beef Wellington, poached salmon, and lamb chops accompanied by fabulous popovers. Although French flavor imbues the farm, famous locals—like Maryland crab—also have a starring role. ⊠ *10710 Falls Rd.* ☎ *301/983–8838* ⊟ *AE, D, MC, V* ☉ *Closed Mon.*

$$$$
AMERICAN
★

✕ **Old Angler's Inn.** The inn, where Civil War soldiers from the North and South found respite and Teddy Roosevelt stopped after hunting and fishing, was restored in 1957 when it began its foray into fine dining. It was then updated in 2008. Diners like the cozy fireplace and menu favorites like the Maryland crab cake appetizer with sesame seaweed salad. Everything is made fresh seasonally—the inn even makes its own ice cream and sorbet. For a more laid-back vibe, head to the beer garden for hot dogs and shrimp kabobs with live music (in good weather). ⊠ *10801 MacArthur Blvd.* ☎ *301/299–9097* ⊕ *www.oldanglersinn.com* ⊟ *AE, MC, V* ☉ *Closed Mon.*

KENSINGTON

4 mi northeast of Bethesda.

Established in 1890 as Knowles Station, Kensington was one of Montgomery County's first villages. Borrowing both its name and architecture from the tony London neighborhood, Kensington was a planned Victorian community from the start. Its neighbor Garrett Park even has a few "Chevy houses." Built in the 1920s, these smallish houses came with a mortgage that financed a Chevrolet in the driveway and an RCA radio inside. Start on Armory Avenue and wander through the historic district to see the entire spectrum of domestic architecture here.

GETTING HERE AND AROUND

Located just north of the Beltway, Kensington is best reached by car via I–495 to MD–185 (Connecticut Avenue). MARC's Brunswick Line also runs through Kensington as it travels from Washington, D.C., through Maryland to West Virginia. The MARC train, however, only runs on weekdays during commuter hours.

TIMING AND PRECAUTIONS

Avoid I–495 during rush hour, which lasts from 7:30 am to 9 am and 5 pm to 6:30 pm on weekdays.

ESSENTIALS

Maryland Transit Administration (☎ 410/539–5000 or 866/743–3682 TTY ⊕ www.mta.maryland.gov).

EXPLORING

Temple of the Church of Jesus Christ of Latter-day Saints. The Temple of the Church of Jesus Christ of Latter-day Saints is impossible to miss from the Beltway near Silver Spring. One of its white towers is topped with a golden statue of the Mormon angel Moroni. It's closed to non-Mormons, but a visitor center provides a lovely view of the mammoth white-marble temple and runs a film about prophet Joseph Smith and an interactive exhibit hall. Tulips, dogwoods, and azaleas bloom in the 56-acre grounds each spring. In December locals of all faiths enjoy the Festival of Lights—650,000 of them—and Nativity scenes. ⊠ 9900 Stoneybrook Dr. ☎ 301/587–0144 ⊗ Grounds and visitor center daily 10–9.

WHERE TO EAT

¢ ✕ **Café 1894.** This little counter-service café, named in honor of Kensing-
CAFÉ ton's christening, is also a full-service 70-seat restaurant with a charming courtyard linking the two. The egg soufflés, quiches, and pancakes are popular for breakfast, while a variety of wraps and salads are on the lunch menu. Café 1894's signature dish is turkey meat loaf with homemade mashed potatoes and fresh steamed vegetables. An ice-cream counter offers fresh berry toppings, homemade whipped topping, and specialty cones. The chef's emphasis is on organic and fair-trade products. ⊠ 10417 Armory Ave. ☎ 301/962–1894 ⊕ www.cafe1894.com ⊟ AE, D, MC, V ⊗ Closed Mon. No dinner Sun.–Wed.

SHOPPING

Fodor's Choice **Antique Row** (⊠ Howard Ave. ☎ 301/949–5333 ⊕ www.kensingtonan-
★ tiquerow.com), east of bustling Connecticut Avenue, consists of more than 80 shops selling jewelry, china, art, toys, silver, and furniture in buildings as old as some of the items. On the west side of Connecticut Avenue, Howard Avenue alternates auto-body repair shops with 100,000 square feet of antiques warehouses that specialize in furniture from Belgium, England, Italy, France, and the United States. For a full listing of the **Antique Dealers of West Howard Avenue**, visit ⊕ www. westhowardantiques.com. At **Antiques & Uniques** (⊠ 3762B Howard Ave. ☎ 301/942–3324) you can find porcelain dolls, Tiffany lamps,

and china. The **Prevention of Blindness Antiques Shop** (⊠ *3716 Howard Ave.* ☎ *301/942–4707*) sells furniture, linens, and vintage clothing.

SILVER SPRING

5 mi southeast of Kensington via Rte. 97.

With a population of more than 220,000, the greater Silver Spring area is one of Washington, D.C.'s largest suburbs and is currently undergoing something of a rebirth, with businesses and entertainment venues staking their claims in the original downtown area. Silver Spring was named when Francis Preston Blair, editor of the *Washington Globe,* friend to President Andrew Jackson, and owner of the Blair House (now the nation's official guest quarters for foreign dignitaries), was riding his horse through the countryside, looking for a pastoral retreat from Washington. His horse threw him, and, as he looked for his mount, he noticed a spring in which sand and mica shone like silver. Wheaton, a more-suburban locale 4 mi to the north, is home to the popular National Capitol Trolley Museum.

GETTING HERE AND AROUND

Silver Spring is easily accessible and one of suburban Maryland's main transportation hubs. Both Metrobus and Montgomery County's Ride On buses run several lines each through Silver Spring to D.C. and other points in Maryland. Silver Spring Metrorail station is a major stop on the Red line. Maryland Transit Administration's MARC Brunswick line commuter trains also run through Silver Spring. South of I–495, Silver Spring is only a 20-minute car trip to Washington, D.C., using main arteries like 16th Street or Georgia Avenue.

TIMING AND PRECAUTIONS

Silver Spring is hectic during rush hour, which lasts from 7:30 am to 9 am and 5 pm to 6:30 pm on weekdays, thanks to its prime location as a residence for D.C. commuters as well as its status as a business hub that brings even more commuters in. Avoid the roads and take the Metrorail when possible.

ESSENTIALS

Metro Information **Washington Metropolitan Area Transit Authority** (☎ *202/637–7000* ⊕ *www.wmata.com*).

Train Contacts **Maryland Transit Administration** (☎ *410/539–5000 or 866/743–3682 TTY* ⊕ *www.mta.maryland.gov*).

EXPLORING

Fodor'sChoice **American Film Institute Silver Theatre & Cultural Center.** This three-screen, ★ state-of-the-art center for film is a restoration of architect John Eberson's art deco Silver Theatre, built in 1938. The AFI hosts film retrospectives, new releases, on-stage appearances, and tributes to stars that have included Jeanne Moreau and Russell Crowe. Each June, in partnership with the Discovery Channel, the AFI hosts the glitzy SILVERDOCS. This documentary film festival is one of the world's best, supporting independent storytellers and honoring artistic excellence of the caliber of Spike Lee and Martin Scorcese through the Charles Guggenheim

Symposium. ⊠ *8633 Colesville Rd.* ☎ *301/495–6700* ⊕ *www.afi.com/
silver* Ⓜ *Silver Spring.*

Brookside Gardens. At the rolling 50-acre Brookside Gardens, the series
of theme areas highlight roses, azaleas, flowers with particularly potent
fragrance, and plants that attract butterflies, among many others. Two
conservatories house seasonal displays and exotic tropicals throughout
the year. The visitor center has an auditorium, classrooms for adults
and children, a 5,000-volume horticulture library, a gift shop, an information booth, and horticulture-related works by local artists on display. ⊠ *1800 Glenallan Ave., Wheaton, MD* ☎ *301/962–1400* ⊕ *www.
brooksidegardens.org* 🎟 *Free, class fees $11–$50* ⊙ *Conservatories
daily 10–5, visitor center daily 9–5, gift shop Mon.–Sat. 10–4 and Sun.
noon–4, horticulture library weekdays 10–3.*

National Capital Trolley Museum. A selection of historic trolleys have been
rescued, restored, and put on display at the National Capital Trolley
Museum, along with streetcars from Europe, Canada, the District of
Columbia, and elsewhere in America. The museum is run by volunteers
whose childhood fascination with trains never left them at the station.
Take a short ride through the countryside or play with an interactive
model trolley display. ⊠ *1313 Bonifant Rd., Wheaton, MD* ☎ *301/384–
6088* ⊕ *www.dctrolley.org* 🎟 *$4* ⊙ *Hrs vary seasonally; call to check
latest information. Last train leaves station ½ hr before closing time.*

ⓒ **National Museum of Health and Medicine.** Opened in 1862 to research
military medicine during the Civil War, this museum on the Walter Reed
Army Medical Center campus now features displays on the Lincoln
assassination and a trauma bay where the most severe cases in the Iraq
War were treated. The museum also boasts one of the world's largest
collections of microscopes. Because some exhibits are fairly graphic
(the wax surgical models and the preserved organs in particular), the
museum may not be suitable for young children or the squeamish.
Adult visitors must present a photo ID to enter. ⊠ *6900 Georgia Ave.
NW* ☎ *202/782–2200* ⊕ *nmhm.washingtondc.museum* 🎟 *Free* ⊙ *Daily
10–5:30; tours 2nd and 4th Sat. at 1* Ⓜ *Silver Spring.*

WHERE TO EAT

$$$$ ✕ **Mrs. K's Toll House.** In one of the last tollhouses in Montgomery
AMERICAN County, Mrs. K's has welcomed diners since 1930 and continues to
please both those in search of comfort food and those with adventurous palates. Designed to resemble a country inn, the restaurant is filled
with antique furniture, "Historic Old Blue" Staffordshire plates, and
Nicholas Lutz glass. Try the New Zealand lamb chops, marinated in
juniper berries, garlic, and rosemary. Both the menu and the decorations
change seasonally. The restaurant serves a popular brunch on Sunday.
⊠ *9201 Colesville Rd.* ☎ *301/589–3500* ⊕ *www.mrsks.com* ⊟ *AE, D,
DC, MC, V* ⊙ *Closed Mon.*

$$ ✕ **The Original Crisfield Seafood Restaurant.** With not much more elegance
SEAFOOD than a neighborhood barbershop, the prices here might seem absurd.
But you get your money's worth: no-nonsense seafood and an eyeful of
Old Maryland arrested in time. Crab cakes don't get any more authen-
tic than these, presented with just enough structural imperfection to

guarantee they're made by hand; the clam chowder—creamy, chunky, and served with a bottomless bowl of oyster crackers—is rendered with similar, down-home care. ✉ *8012 Georgia Ave.* ☎ *301/589–1306* ⊕ *www.crisfieldseafoodrestaurant.com* 🖃 *AE, MC, V* ⊗ *Closed Mon.*

WHERE TO STAY

$–$$ 🖥 **Comfort Inn.** This unpretentious chain hotel is close to Silver Spring's growing entertainment and dining hub on Colesville Road, as well as to the Silver Spring Metro. Rooms are decorated in green and burgundy, with flat-screen TVs, ergonomic desk chairs, and mahogany headboards. There isn't any room service, but many local restaurants will deliver. Silver Spring also offers a free Metro station shuttle that stops one block away from the hotel. **Pros:** a free Continental breakfast in the lobby includes cereals and even waffles; hotel was completely renovated in 2008. **Cons:** although it is only a few blocks from downtown Silver Spring, the location is in a more run-down and developing section of the neighborhood; fairly basic amenities. ✉ *7990 Georgia Ave.* ☎ *301/565–3444* ⊕ *www.comfortinn.com* ⤳ *130 rooms* ♿ *In-room: a/c, Internet. In-hotel: gym, laundry facilities, laundry service, Wi-Fi hotspot, parking (free)* 🖃 *AE, D, MC, V* ⏍ *CP* Ⓜ *Silver Spring.*

PRINCE GEORGE'S COUNTY

Named in 1696 for Denmark and Norway's prince (the husband of the heir to the throne of England, Princess Anne), the county was once famous for its tobacco auctions, which are still held in its southern end. Tobacco created a wealthy leisure class that enjoyed cricket, fox hunting, and horse racing, a sport still popular in the area. Much of the county today remains affluent.

Nature lovers should try to make a visit to the National Wildlife Visitor Center. Flight fans can check out the world's oldest continuously operating airport in College Park. For those who prefer 60-second thrills, Six Flags is full of roller coasters, waterslides, and kiddie rides. Sports fans may not be able to see the Redskins, but they can get a fix at a Maryland Terrapins game or at a Bowie Baysox minor-league baseball game. Historic sites, including the Surratt House Museum, are scattered throughout the county.

To tour the county, start in College Park and work your way up to Laurel. Then head south to the heart of the county before visiting sites along the Patuxent and Potomac rivers.

ESSENTIALS

Prince George's County Conference & Visitors Bureau (✉ *9200 Basil Ct., Suite 101, Largo* ☎ *301/925–8300 or 888/925–8300* ⊕ *www.visitprincegeorges.com*).

COLLEGE PARK

6 mi east of Silver Spring via I–495, 9 mi north of Washington, D.C.

As its name implies, College Park is primarily a university town on gently rolling terrain.

GETTING HERE AND AROUND

College Park is easily reached by Metrorail's Green line or Maryland Transit Authority's MARC Camden line, as well as by various buses, including WMATA's J4 and 80s lines or Prince George's County Route 14 bus. Driving is also a convenient transportation option as the town is just south of where I–495 and I–95 meet in Maryland.

TIMING AND PRECAUTIONS

Avoid driving near the I–495/I–95 exchange from 7:30 am to 9 am and 5 pm to 6:30 pm on weekdays when rush hour is at its worst.

EXPLORING

University of Maryland at College Park. One of the largest campuses in the country, the University of Maryland at College Park has an enrollment of about 37,000. The College Park campus began as an agricultural college in 1856, and became part of the University of Maryland in 1920. The university's athletic teams (the Terrapins) participate in the highly competitive Atlantic Coast Conference and draw large crowds to Byrd Stadium and the 17,950-seat Comcast Center. In Turner Hall, visitor-center staff provide information about the university and maps for getting around the sprawling campus of 1,200 acres and 270 build-ings. At the dairy, ice cream made from campus cows' milk is available by the cone or carton. ⊠ *Turner Hall, U.S. Rte. 1 at Rossborough La.* ☎ *301/314–7777* ⊕ *www.umd.edu* ⊗ *Turner Hall weekdays 9–5, Sat. 9–3. Dairy Oct.–Sept., weekdays 10–4.*

☾ **College Park Aviation Museum.** The Wright Brothers once trained military officers to fly at College Park Airport, the world's oldest continuously operating airport, which is now affiliated with the Smithsonian Insti-tution. The College Park Aviation Museum is a tribute to the Wright Brothers and early aviation. Children can spin propellers and dress up like aviators. In fall, the museum hosts the Hollywood Flyers film series, showing blockbusters and documentaries about flight. Screenings take place at 1 pm on Saturday, and are free with museum admission. At the Peter Pan program, preschoolers make airplanes and hear stories on the second and fourth Thursday of the month (10:30 to noon). On their Web site, the museum offers podcast audio tours in English, Spanish, and French. ⊠ *College Park Airport, 1985 Corporal Frank Scott Dr.* ☎ *301/864–6029* ⊕ *www.collegeparkaviationmuseum.com* ⊠ *$4* ⊗ *Daily 10–5.*

WHERE TO EAT AND STAY

$–$$ ✕ **Ledo's.** Students, alumni, and locals have made Ledo's pizza popular
PIZZA throughout the state. There are dozens of Ledo's franchises in Mary-land, but many insist that the best pizza—with smoked provolone so gooey you need a knife and fork—comes from the original restaurant, which opened in Adelphi in 1955 and moved to College Park in 2010. This location is still family run (the other franchises are under separate management) and serves up homemade lasagna and other dishes made with fresh ingredients. ⊠ *4509 Knox Rd., College Park* ☎ *301/422–8622* ⊕ *www.ledopizza.com* ▭ *MC, V.*

$–$$ ▥ **The Inn and Conference Center/University of Maryland and University Col-lege.** Renovated in 2004, the center is a certified green building, with an

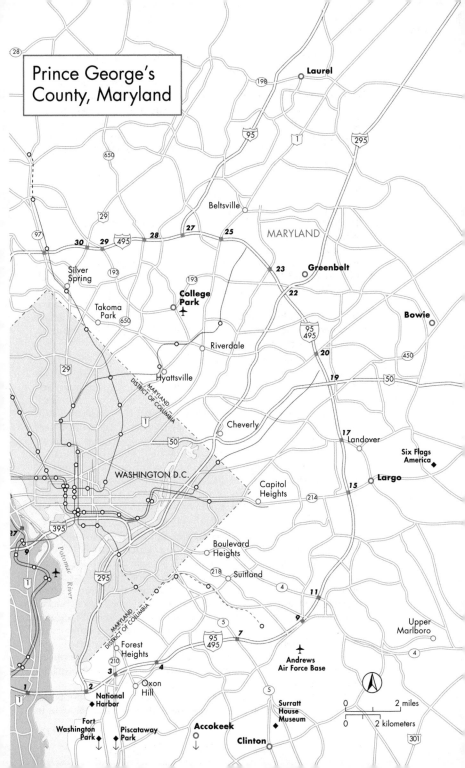

Prince George's County, Maryland

Laurel

MARYLAND

Silver Spring

Beltsville

Takoma Park

College Park

Greenbelt

Bowie

Riverdale

Hyattsville

Cheverly

Landover

Six Flags America

WASHINGTON D.C.

Capitol Heights

Largo

MARYLAND
DISTRICT OF COLUMBIA

Boulevard Heights

Suitland

Potomac River

Upper Marlboro

Forest Heights

MARYLAND
DISTRICT OF COLUMBIA

Andrews Air Force Base

National Harbor

Oxon Hill

Fort Washington Park

Piscataway Park

Accokeek

Surratt House Museum

Clinton

0   2 miles

0   2 kilometers

air-conditioning system that is chlorofluorocarbon free. Its location near the University of Maryland makes it a natural place to stay for visiting parents, complete with warmly appointed and spacious guest rooms. **Pros:** guests in need of their daily coffee fix can visit the Starbucks in the hotel lobby; two restaurants provide plenty of food options. **Cons:** it's tough to get a reservation in late May and early June due to nearby graduation ceremonies. ✉ *3501 University Blvd. E, at Adelphi Rd.* ☎ *301/985–7300 or 800/727–8622* ⊕ *marriott.com* ⬚ *237 rooms, 11 suites* ⚭ *In-room: a/c, refrigerator, Internet. In-hotel: 2 restaurants, bar, pool, gym, laundry facilities, laundry service, Wi-Fi hotspot, parking (paid)* ⊟ *AE, D, MC, V.*

NIGHTLIFE

R. J. Bentley's. While the food is decent, this restaurant is better known as the favorite watering hole of University of Maryland Terrapins fans. The walls are covered with license plates and gas-pump memorabilia, except the "wall of fame," hung with jerseys from the university's past athletes. Signed floorboards from the 2002 NCAA Men's basketball Final Four hang in the terrace area, where diners and drinkers can watch games on mounted television sets. Students and alumni head to this hangout for beer, chili, wings, and sandwiches; the bar packs in fans after home games. ✉ *7323 Baltimore Ave.* ☎ *301/277–8898* ⊕ *www. rjbentleys.net* ⊟ *AE, MC, V.*

OFF THE BEATEN PATH

Greenbelt. Planned as part of a New Deal program during the Great Depression, this city was one of three cooperative communities built for low- and middle-income families (the others are outside Milwaukee and in Ohio). These quasi-utopian "greenbelt" communities, constructed and planned by the U.S. Department of Agriculture, were meant to be self-sufficient areas, with the side benefit that they would relieve some of the housing pressure in nearby metropolitan areas. The town is now a National Historic Landmark. Walk down Crescent Road to the Greenbelt Community Center (15 Crescent Road) for a glimpse at some representative houses, including one International Style house (10b Crescent Road) filled with artifacts from the 1930s such as Fiestaware and children's toys. Inside the community center you'll find a small museum with displays explaining the history of the area.

Beltsville Agricultural Research Center. Three miles northeast of Greenbelt, the Agricultural Research Service's (ARS) research center in Beltsville has developed everyday innovations such as backyard fly traps, orange juice from concentrate, and seedless grapes. Today BARC's research priorities are climate change, food safety, nutrition and obesity, international food security, and bioenergy. When several offices were attacked by anthrax mailings in 2001, it was scientists at this Beltsville location who helped determine where the anthrax came from. The visitor center is inside a log lodge built in 1937 by the Civilian Conservation Corps, and tours take at least two hours. Because of their length and technical nature, tours are not recommended for children below middle-school age. There are neither free food samples nor cafeterias on-site, but ARS sponsors a farmers' market down the road from the visitor center on Thursdays. Reservations are essential; call at least three weeks in advance. ■ TIP→ The visitor center, building 302, is located on Powder Mill Road, about a half mile away from the main building on Baltimore Avenue. It may not show up on a GPS, so call ahead for directions. ⊠ *Bldg. 302, 10300 Baltimore Ave., Beltsville* ☎ *301/504–9403* ⊕ *www.ars.usda.gov* ⬚ *Free* ⊙ *Weekdays 8:30–4.*

LAUREL

11 mi north of College Park.

Three other Maryland counties claim a section of this town (Anne Arundel, Howard, and Montgomery) but most of the suburb is in Prince George's.

GETTING HERE AND AROUND

Located northeast of Washington, D.C., Laurel is sandwiched between I–95 and the Baltimore-Washington Parkway. The Maryland Transit Administration MARC train's Camden line makes two stops in Laurel, on Main Street and at the racetrack.

TIMING AND PRECAUTIONS

Avoid I–95 and the Baltimore-Washington Parkway during rush hour, which lasts from 7:30 am to 9 am and 5 pm to 6:30 pm on weekdays.

ESSENTIALS

Maryland Transit Administration (☎ *410/539–5000 or 866/743–3682 TTY* ⊕ *www.mta.maryland.gov*).

EXPLORING

Montpelier Mansion. On 70 acres of parkland, Montpelier Mansion is a masterpiece of Georgian architecture that George Washington used as a guesthouse on the way to and from the Constitutional Convention. It was built and owned by the Snowdens, who earned their wealth through farming and an iron foundry. Interesting features include a 35- by 16-foot reproduction of a hand-painted canvas floor cloth and an offset central hall staircase. Also on the property is an 18th-century summerhouse where ladies took their tea, boxwood gardens, an herb-and-flower garden with plants grown in the 1800s, and a cultural arts center with three galleries and artists' studios. ⊠ *Rte. 197 and Muirkirk Rd.* ☎ *301/953–1376; 301/953–1993 arts center* ⬚ *$3* ⊙ *Dec.–Feb., Mon.–Thurs. 11–3 self-guided tours, Sun. tours at 1 and 2; Mar.–Nov., Mon.–Thurs. 11–3 self-guided tours, Sun. noon–3 guided tours on the hr. Art center weekdays 8:30–5, weekends 10–5.*

Patuxent National Wildlife Visitor Center. One of the Department of the Interior's largest science and environmental education centers, the Patuxent National Wildlife Visitor Center, between Laurel and Bowie, showcases interactive exhibits on global environmental issues, migratory bird routes, wildlife habitats, and endangered species. A viewing station overlooks a lake area that beavers, bald eagles, and Canada geese use as a habitat. Weather permitting, you can take a 30-minute tram tour through meadows, forests, and wetlands and then explore the trails on your own. The paved Loop Trail runs -mi; another 3½ mi of trails crisscross the property. ⊠ *10901 Scarlet Tanager Loop, off Powder Mill Rd.* ☎ *301/497–5763* ⊕ *patuxent.fws.gov* ⬚ *Free, tram* *ride $3* ☉ *Daily 9–4:30; tram mid-Mar.–mid-Nov., weekends 11:30, 1, 2, and 3, summer weekdays 11:30; late June–Aug., weekdays 11:30; trails daily sunrise–4:30.*

SPORTS AND THE OUTDOORS
FISHING AND HUNTING
Patuxent Research Refuge. The mission of the refuge is to conserve and protect wildlife through research and habitat management, and to educate the public. The North Tract of the refuge is available for fishing. Educational programs are also available here. To enter, every visitor must check in and receive an access pass. A Maryland nontidal fishing license is also required for anglers. ⊠ *230 Bald Eagle Dr.* ☎ *410/674–3304; 410/674–4625 TDD* ⊕ *patuxent.fws.gov* ☜ *Free* ☉ *Daily 8–4.*

HORSE RACING
Laurel Park. Maryland has a long-standing love for the ponies. You can watch and wager on Thoroughbreds at this racetrack from January to April, a 10-day period in August, and September to December. Call to see when horses will be running, though races are simulcast seven days a week. ⊠ *Rte. 198 and Race Track Rd.* ☎ *301/725–0400.*

BOWIE

13 mi southeast of Laurel, 15 mi east of College Park.

Bowie started as a few buildings around a railroad junction in 1870, but has grown into the largest municipality in Prince George's County and the home of Bowie State University, a historically black college within the University of Maryland system.

GETTING HERE AND AROUND
Located about halfway between Washington, DC, and Baltimore, Bowie is best reached by car via the Baltimore-Washington Parkway or U.S. 50. However, the Maryland Transit Administration MARC train's Penn line also makes a stop at Bowie State University.

TIMING AND PRECAUTIONS
The Baltimore-Washington Parkway and U.S. 50 can get congested during rush hour, which lasts from 7:30 am to 9 am and 5 pm to 6:30 pm on weekdays.

ESSENTIALS
Maryland Transit Administration (☎ *410/539–5000 or 866/743–3682 TTY* ⊕ *www.mta.maryland.gov*).

EXPLORING
Belair Mansion. Built in the mid-1700s as a country retreat for provincial Maryland governor Samuel Ogle, the Georgian-style Belair Mansion was subsequently owned in the early 1900s by James Woodward. Ogle was instrumental during Colonial times in importing horses that improved the American Thoroughbred. The house displays British and Early American paintings, silver, and furniture. In 1908 Woodward built additions to the house, including the **Belair Stable,** which began the modern legacy of the Belair Stud, the line responsible for Omaha and his sire Gallant Fox, each of whom won the Triple Crown in the

1930s. One-hour self-guided tours of the mansion and stable emphasize the contributions of the families and their horses to racing history.
✉ *12207 Tulip Grove Dr.* ☎ *301/809–3089* 🖃 *Free, donations accepted*
🕑 *Tues.–Sun. noon–4.*

SPORTS AND THE OUTDOORS

🕓 **Bowie Baysox** (✉ *4101 N.E. Crain Hwy.* ☎ *301/805–6000* ⊕ *www.*
baysox.com), the AA affiliate of the Baltimore Orioles, play at the
10,000-seat Prince George's Stadium. Children have major-league
fun off the field at a carousel, moonbounce, child-oriented concession
stands, and a playground. Fireworks light up the sky at every home
game held on Friday and Saturday evenings between April and Labor
Day. Tickets cost $9.

LARGO

9 mi south of Bowie

Largo is an entertainment hub of suburban Maryland, boasting both Six
Flags America and FedEx Field, where D.C.'s popular Redskins play.

GETTING HERE AND AROUND

Largo sits directly east of Washington, D.C., just outside of the Beltway.
Metrorail's Largo Town Center station serves the area, though a car
may be necessary to get to some attractions.

TIMING AND PRECAUTIONS

Area roads can get congested during rush hour, which lasts from 7:30
am to 9 am and 5 pm to 6:30 pm on weekdays.

ESSENTIALS

Washington Metropolitan Area Transit Authority (☎ *202/637–7000* ⊕ *www.*
wmata.com).

EXPLORING

🕓 **Six Flags America.** Maryland's only amusement park, Six Flags America
combines a theme park with Hurricane Harbor, a water park. On the
"dry" side, high-speed revelers enjoy eight old-fashioned wood or modern steel coasters. "Batwing" puts riders headfirst, face and belly down,
with nothing between them and the ground but a safety strap. Children
under 48 inches can coast on a minimodel train, "drive" an 18-wheeler,
and earn their wings flying minijets. On the "wet" side, children of all
ages beat the heat whizzing down waterslides and swimming in pools.
The five-story Crocodile Cal's (named for Cal Ripkin, legendary star of
the Baltimore Orioles) Caribbean Beach House dumps 1,000 gallons of
water on unsuspecting passersby every few minutes. When your body
has been through enough, sit back for the stage and musical entertain-
ments. ✉ *13710 Central Ave., Largo* ☎ *301/249–1500* ⊕ *www.sixflags.*
com/america 🖃 *$50, kids under 48" $30, kids 2 and under free; parking*
$15 🕑 *Late Apr.–Labor Day, call ahead or check Web site calendar for*
hrs; Fright Fest, Oct., check hours online.

WHERE TO EAT AND STAY

$-$$ ✕ **Jasper's.** Locals come here as much to be seen as to eat. The Largo
AMERICAN location is one of four in the state. On the American menu, lobster
bisque, baked stuffed shrimp, and the grilled-chicken Caesar salad are
among the favorites; all desserts, including the peanut butter pie are
made in-house. Food is served well into the night, as late as 1 am on
Friday and Saturday nights. A giant television screen plays Redskins
games throughout the football season. ⊠ *9640 Lottsford Ct., near
FedEx Field, Largo* ☎ *301/883–2199* ⊕ *www.jaspersrestaurants.com*
🖃 *AE, D, DC, MC, V.*

$$ 🛏 **New Carrollton Landover Courtyard by Marriott.** This business-district
hotel caters to a corporate crowd, but it's also a convenient roosting
spot for visitors to Six Flags and other sights in suburban Maryland.
Recently renovated rooms come with Marriott's standard decor and
include a couch and large desk. Black-and-white photos add a touch
of personality. Guests can indulge in a hot breakfast every morning
or take a daily dip in the on-site pool. Prices for the basic rooms drop
below $100 on weekends. **Pros:** free shuttle service runs to the DC
Metro, Amtrak's New Carrollton station, and the IRS building; no fee
for parking. **Cons:** Wi-Fi available only in lobby; room service is lim-
ited to dinner between 5 and 10 pm. ⊠ *8330 Corporate Dr., Landover*
☎ *301/577–3373* ⊕ *marriott.com* ⥈ *136 rooms, 14 suites* ⚒ *In-room:
a/c, refrigerator, Internet. In-hotel: restaurant, room service, pool, gym,
Wi-Fi hotspot, parking (free)* 🖃 *AE, D, DC, MC, V.*

CLINTON

10 mi southwest of Upper Marlboro.

The origin of the name Clinton is unclear—the town used to be called
Surrattsville for Mary Surratt's husband, the postmaster John Surratt.

GETTING HERE AND AROUND
Clinton's location southeast of Washington, D.C., is near Andrews Air
Force Base—otherwise known as the President of the United States'
personal airport. MD-5 (Branch Avenue) runs through it and is the
best way to get there.

TIMING AND PRECAUTIONS
Area roads can get congested during rush hour, which lasts from 7:30
am to 9 am and 5 pm to 6:30 pm on weekdays.

EXPLORING

☾ **Oxon Cove Park.** This park preserves 20th-century farm life on a site
where the Piscataway Native Americans once lived and was also once
part of the Underground Railroad. Children can feed chickens, milk
cows, and take a wagon ride. There's a fine view of Washington over the
Potomac River. Throughout the year, the National Park Service offers
programs such as sheep shearing in May, cider making in September,
and "Talking Turkey," when kids can learn about and feed domestic and
wild turkeys in November. ⊠ *6411 Oxon Hill Rd., 5 mi northwest of
Clinton* ☎ *301/763–1062* ⊕ *www.nps.gov/oxhi* ⤢ *Free* ☉ *Daily 8–4:30;
reservations required for children's activities.*

★ **Surratt House Museum.** The Surratt House Museum, once a house and tavern, is where John Wilkes Booth sought refuge after assassinating President Lincoln. For her role in the conspiracy, Mary Surratt became the first woman to be executed by the federal government. She was said to have told one of her tenants to get the "shooting irons ready" for Booth as he was fleeing after the assassination. You can trace Booth's escape route on an electronic map at the visitor center. Costumed docents give tours of the house, talk about 19th-century life in Prince George's County, and discuss the Civil War, but they won't get into debates about Surratt's innocence or guilt. The Surratt Society sponsors a 12-hour John Wilkes Booth escape route tour in April and September that covers the 12 days Booth spent on the run in Maryland, Virginia, and Washington, DC. ⊠ *9118 Brandywine Rd.* ☎ *301/868–1121* ⊕ *www.surratt. org* ✉ *$3* ⊙ *Wed. tours by appointment; Thurs.–Fri. 11–3, weekends noon–4; tours every ½ hr.*

FORT WASHINGTON PARK

5 mi southwest of Clinton, 7 mi south of Oxon Hill.

GETTING HERE AND AROUND
You can reach Fort Washington by car via MD–210 (Indian Head Highway) or by Metrobus.

ESSENTIALS
Washington Metropolitan Area Transit Authority (☎ *202/637–7000* ⊕ *www. wmata.com*).

EXPLORING
Fort Washington Park. George Washington chose this site on a narrow portion of the Potomac River for the first fort to protect the nation's capital. It was destroyed during the War of 1812, only five years after its completion; the current fort was completed in 1824. Half-hour tours of the fort are given on request. On the first Sunday of each month from April through October, costumed volunteers fire the fort's cannons. If you cross the drawbridge over the moat, you can see the 7-foot-thick stone and masonry walls, gun positions, and other defenses. Although the fort is impressive, most people visit the park to picnic along the river. ⊠ *13551 Fort Washington Rd.* ☎ *301/763–4600* ✉ *$5 per car; $3 pedestrian, bike, or bus* ⊙ *Early Apr.–Oct., daily 9–5; Nov.–early Apr., daily 9–4:30.*

ACCOKEEK

10 mi south of Fort Washington.

By fighting off developers in the 1950s, the Accokeek Foundation helped keep the view from Mount Vernon as George Washington would have seen it. Today the once-rural area is being developed into a suburban community. Locals call Piscataway Park, tucked away at the end of the road by the river, a hidden treasure.

GETTING HERE AND AROUND

You can reach Accokeek by car via MD–210 (Indian Head Highway) or by Metrobus.

ESSENTIALS

Washington Metropolitan Area Transit Authority (*☎ 202/637–7000 ⊕ www. wmata.com*).

EXPLORING

Piscataway Park. On 4,000 acres of land bought to protect the view from Mount Vernon across the river, Piscataway Park attracts history buffs, horticulturists, naturalists, hikers, and families. At **National Colonial Farm** you can walk through a middle-class 18th-century farm dwelling and tobacco barn, as well as reproductions of a meat house and out-kitchen used by farmers not quite as prosperous as the Washingtons on the other side of the Potomac. Guides point out the farmhouse's most valuable materials: the glass in the windows and the ropes supporting the bed. Old-time animal breeds and heirloom crop varieties are both raised here. Also on hand is an herb garden as well as bluebirds, great blue herons, and bald eagles. *⊠ 3400 Bryan Point Rd., 5 mi south of Fort Washington Park ☎ 301/283–2113 Accokeek Foundation; 301/283–0112 National Park Service ⊕ www.nps.gov/pisc ⊗ Park daily dawn–dusk; National Colonial Farm mid-Mar.–mid-Dec., Tues.–Sun. 10–4; tours weekends at 1; mid-Dec.–mid.-Mar., weekends 10–4.*

NATIONAL HARBOR

12 mi south of downtown Washington, D.C., 2 mi west of Oxon Hill.

The National Harbor sprawls across 300 acres of previously abandoned banks of the Potomac River, across from Old Town Alexandria. Although it is still in development and construction is to be expected, the location already offers world-class accommodations, dining, and water taxi tours to other hot spots on the Potomac.

GETTING HERE AND AROUND

The easiest way to reach National Harbor is by car via I–295, I–95, or I–495. Water taxis from Old Town Alexandria or Georgetown are also convenient. Once in National Harbor, all you need to get around is a good pair of shoes.

ESSENTIALS

Visitor Information National Harbor Marina Office (*⊠ 168 National Plaza, National Harbor ☎ 301/749–1582 ⊕ www.nationalharbor.com*).

EXPLORING

American Market. Shop for local produce at this upscale outdoor market, which also features crafts such as hand-sewn dolls, hot glass jewelry, and folk-art prints. Pick up pecan butter tarts or applesauce sweetbreads to appease your sweet tooth. *⊠ 137 National Plaza, across from the Gaylord National Resort ⊕ www.americanmarketnh.com ⊗ May–Oct., Sat. 10–2.*

Art Whino. This exhibition showcases a collection of 133 artists specializing in pop-surrealism, low-brow, and urban contemporary art. *⊠ 173*

Waterfront St. ☎ *301/567–8210* ⊕ *www.artwhino.com* ☉ *Sun.–Mon. noon–6, Tues.–Sat. 10–10.*

Fodor's Choice ★ **The Awakening.** This sculpture depicts a 100-foot giant struggling to free himself from the earth. The display is actually five separate pieces buried in the ground, and was created by J. Seward Johnson. Its original location was at Hains Point in Alexandria, but it was moved to National Harbor in 2008. ✉ *National Plaza* ⊠ *Free.*

Potomac Riverboat Company. Jump aboard a cruise ship from National Harbor's dock for a water tour of Mount Vernon, Alexandria, Georgetown, or the monuments of Washington. The ferry to Mount Vernon includes admission to the grounds. The company also operates hourly water taxis across the Potomac to the dock in Alexandria, where National Harbor's visitors can find even more shopping and dining options. On Thursday evenings, dogs can join their owners for a tour of Alexandria's seaport. ✉ *Commercial Pier* ☎ *703/548–9000 or 877/511–2628* ⊕ *www.potomacriverboatco.com* ✉ *Taxis and tours $9–$38* ☉ *Call ahead for hrs.*

WHERE TO EAT AND STAY

$ AMERICAN ✕ **Elevation Burger.** One of the few restaurants in National Harbor without waiter service, this burger joint is known for its grass-fed organic beef and heaping servings of skinny fries. The original Elevation Burger comes with two patties and double the cheese, while a Half-the-Guilt burger consists of one beef patty and one veggie patty. Thick shakes, like chocolate mixed with black cherry, make the perfect accompaniment. ✉ *108 Waterfront St., National Harbor* ☎ *301/749–4014* ⊕ *www. elevationburger.com* ⊟ *AE, MC, V.*

$$–$$$ SEAFOOD ✕ **Moon Bay Coastal Cuisine.** Walk through the Gaylord National's 18-story atrium and across a small wooden bridge to find this historic Chesapeake fish market with bare wooden walls and a high ceiling exposing vents. Although it may look drab at first sight, Moon Bay Coastal Cuisine serves upscale seafood dishes and boasts a top-flight wine cave. Start off with the chopped salad or the laughing bird shrimp tempura. Entrée options include roasted grouper with yellow corn fondue and Hawaiian escolar with creamed black rice. Moon Bay also offers a few non-seafood options, such as fried herb-crusted chicken. ✉ *201 Waterfront St.* ☎ *301/965–2000* ⊟ *AE, D, DC, MC, V.*

$$$$ AMERICAN Fodor's Choice ★ ✕ **Old Hickory Steakhouse.** The signature restaurant of the Gaylord National Resort, Old Hickory serves prime cuts of meat in an elegant setting. It's perfect for a romantic evening with the sun setting over the harbor or for an expense-account evening of cocktails and fine cigars out on the terrace. Order the grass-fed beef tenderloin or a 24-ounce porterhouse with four sauce choices: béarnaise, bordelaise, green peppercorn, and blue cheese. And don't miss the slightly crispy truffle fries on the side; you won't be disappointed. Old Hickory also has its own full-time Maître d'Fromage who presents guests with artisanal cheese from around the world. Fish and chicken options are available, but the real draw is the expensive steak. ✉ *201 Waterfront St.* ☎ *301/965–4000* ⊟ *AE, D, DC, MC, V.*

4

$$ ⊡ **Aloft Washington National Harbor.** The second-floor lobby of this modern hotel becomes one of National Harbor's hippest hot spots on Friday nights when a DJ sets up across from the w xyz bar. Lofted ceilings and lounge seating make it feel as much like a nightclub as a hotel, while a fire pit on the lobby's patio burns year-round. Rooms are simple in shades of gray, purple, and indigo with platform beds, a small chair, and a bench underneath the 42-inch flat-screen. Complimentary copies of *National Geographic Traveler* and *Spin* magazines are available in each room. **Pros:** more affordable than many of the other accommodations at the ritzy National Harbor; flight board in lobby lists flight times for all three regional airports. **Cons:** small closets; not convenient to downtown D.C. ⊠ *156 Waterfront St., National Harbor* ☎ *301/749–9000* ⊕ *www.starwoodhotels.com* ⇆ *190 rooms, 6 suites* ⊘ *In-room: a/c, safe, refrigerator, Internet, Wi-Fi. In-hotel: bar, pool, gym, laundry facilities, laundry service, Internet terminal, Wi-Fi hotspot, parking (paid)* ⊟ *AE, D, DC, MC, V.*

$$$$ ⊡ **Gaylord National Resort & Convention Center.** The $800 million Gaylord
◔   National Resort & Convention Center is larger than life (and everything else around it). Guests at the 2,000-room resort can dine, shop, get pampered, and even go clubbing without ever leaving the property, which anchors the newly developed National Harbor waterfront. About a 25-minute ride to the National Mall, the Gaylord is shaping up to be a fun alternative for the D.C.-bound who don't mind commuting to museums and monuments. Room balconies opening onto the 230-foot-high glass atrium are a good place to watch the nightly dancing fountain show in the massive lobby below. **Pros:** upon check-in, kids get a free activity set and access to a family arcade; waterfront location. **Cons:** downtown D.C. is difficult to reach, though a hotel shuttle leaves every half hour for $13 per person; resort might be a bit too big for some. ⊠ *201 Waterfront Street, National Harbor* ☎ *301/965–2000* ⊕ *www.gaylordnational.com* ⇆ *2,000 rooms* ⊘ *In-room: a/c, safe, kitchen (some), refrigerator, DVD (some), Internet. In-hotel: 4 restaurants, bars, pool, gym, spa, children's programs, laundry service, Wi-Fi hotspot, parking (paid)* ⊟ *AE, D, DC, MC, V.*

NIGHTLIFE AND THE ARTS

Bobby McKey's Dueling Piano Bar. One of the busiest bars in the nightlife-friendly National Harbor, Bobby McKey's is the place to visit when you're in the mood to sing along to all your favorite bar songs from Journey to Billy Joel. A cavernous two-level restaurant wraps around a stage where two pianists vie for your affections through their musical prowess. ⊠ *172 Fleet St., National Harbor* ☎ *301/567–1488* ⊕ *www. bobbymckeys.com* ⊟ *$5 cover* ☉ *Wed.–Sat. 7–2.*

Central and Western Virginia

WORD OF MOUTH

"My husband and I would prefer staying in towns right off Blue Ridge Parkway and Skyline Drive (or within a few miles) that would be fun to walk around in at night."
— TravelinVic

"[Try] the Hotel Roanoke . . . I grew up in Roanoke and I think you will love being at this grand old hotel. From the hotel, you can walk over a covered foot bridge to the Taubman Art Museum, visit Center in the Square, and eat at lots of great restaurants. Check it out—you might find a great deal and I know you will love downtown Roanoke!"
— Elizabeth37

Updated
by Ginger
Warder

Eastern Virginia's coastal plains start rolling into the gently undulating Piedmont west of I–95. Charlottesville, 71 mi northwest of Richmond, epitomizes the refined elegance of this region, a center of culture amid the vineyards and homes of early-American presidents.

Jefferson, our nation's third president and a principal writer of the Declaration of Independence, left an indelible imprint on the region through his neoclassical Monticello home, the University of Virginia, and his summer retreat, Poplar Forest, farther south near Lynchburg. In fact, Jefferson's design aesthetic is evident in public buildings, monuments, and private homes throughout Virginia. But what few visitors know is that Jefferson was also the father of American viticulture, planting some of our nation's first vineyards around Monticello. Today, Virginia has over 160 wineries and is the fifth-largest wine producer in the U.S., and many of the stellar growers are found along the Monticello Wine Trail. The central and western regions of the state were also home to some of the bloodiest and most significant battles of the Civil War, including the surrender of the Confederate Army at Appomattox.

ORIENTATION AND PLANNING

GETTING ORIENTED

West of Richmond, Virginia stretches toward boardering West Virginia and Kentucky, with its most southwestern point more than a 400-mi drive from the state's capital city. Rolling countryside is broken up by the dramatic Blue Ridge and Appalachian mountains. One of the largest of the South Atlantic states, Virginia stretches 470 mi from the Eastern Shore to its western extremities.

Charlottesville and the Blue Ridge. Charlottesville, just east of the Blue Ridge, centers around Thomas Jefferson's architectural genius—Monticello and the University of Virginia. To the south, the restored Civil War–era village of Appomattox Court House is a peek back in time. Farther west the Blue Ridge juts suddenly out of the landscape. Skyline Drive in Shenandoah National Park and the Blue Ridge Parkway ride the spine of the Blue Ridge Mountains.

Shenandoah Valley. Beyond the Blue Ridge is the famed Shenandoah Valley, a 150-mi stretch of picturesque meadows and farms framed by mountains on either side. Along the western rim of Virginia is Winchester, which changed hands no fewer than 72 times during the Civil War. Farther south is Lexington, known for its ties to Confederate generals Robert E. Lee and Stonewall Jackson.

Southwest Virginia. In Roanoke, Virginia's largest city west of Richmond, the 81,000-square-foot Taubman Museum of Art has established the city's reputation as a cultural center. In this area you can hike and camp

TOP REASONS TO GO

Witness the Thomas Jefferson Triumvirate: Explore this renaissance leader's passion for architecture and agriculture at Monticello, the University of Virginia, and Poplar Forest.

Tour Presidential Homes: Get up close and personal not only with Jefferson, but also James Madison, James Monroe, and Woodrow Wilson at their restored homes.

Stand on the Frontlines: Relive the final days of the Civil War at Appomattox or explore the many battlefields of the Shenandoah region.

See Mountain Sights: Ride the Appalachian crests along the Blue Ridge Parkway and Skyline Drive. See a city beneath your feet from Roanoke's Mill Mountain, and soak in history at the Homestead Resort's Jefferson Pools, originally designed by that great statesman.

Hear Mountain Sounds: Dance to the twang of fiddles and banjoes outside the Floyd Country Store and all along the Crooked Road.

5

in the George Washington and Jefferson national forests, float along on the New River, and photograph wild ponies near the state's highest mountain. West of these valleys, the country becomes its most rugged, in the Allegheny Mountains along the Virginia–West Virginia border, and the deeply gorged Appalachian Plateau coal country in the state's far southwest tip. Known as the Allegheny Highlands, this region is undergoing a renaissance after years of neglect.

PLANNING

WHEN TO GO

The climate is temperate in this region from April through October, although summers tend to be very humid. Spring and fall are beautiful, filled with flowers and colorful foliage, but winter driving through this mountainous part of the state can be hazardous. Crowds are largest at major attractions during the summer months, and peak vacation weeks like Easter and Christmas, and visitors flock to Skyline Drive and Shenandoah National Park in the fall.

Summer festivals include the two-week-long **Virginia Highlands Festival** (☎ 276/623–5266 ⊕ www.vahighlandsfestival.org) in Abingdon, during late July–early August, which celebrates Appalachia with juried displays and demonstrations of arts and crafts, exhibitions of animals, sales of antiques, and performances of country music. During the first three weekends of August, "Shakespeare at the Ruins" at **Barboursville Vineyards** (☎ 540/832–3824 ⊕ www.barboursvillewine.com) brings outdoor performances of the Bard's classics to these beautiful vineyards, between Charlottesville and Orange. The **October Homes Tour and Crafts Exhibit** (☎ 540/882–3018 ⊕ www.waterfordfoundation.org/fair) in Waterford draws tens of thousands to this historic community. Also in October, the **Virginia Film Festival** (☎ 800/882–3378 ⊕ www.vafilm.com), in Charlottesville, is becoming a major event in the motion-picture industry, with screenings of important new movies and appearances by their stars.

10 BEST CIVIL WAR SITES

American Civil War Center at Historic Tredegar (⊕ *www.tredegar.org*)

Appomattox Court House National Historical Park (⊕ *www.nps.gov/apco*)

Fredericksburg-Spotsylvania National Military Park (⊕ *www.nps.gov/frsp*)

Manassas National Battlefield (⊕ *www.nps.gov/mana*)

Museum of the Confederacy (⊕ *www.moc.org*)

New Market Battlefield State Historical Park (⊕ *www.4.vmi.edu/museum/nm/*)

Pamplin Historical Park & The National Museum of the Civil War Soldier (⊕ *www.pamplinpark.org*)

Petersburg National Battlefield (⊕ *www.nps.gov/pete*)

Richmond National Battlefield (⊕ *www.nps.gov/rich*)

Virginia Civil War Trails (⊕ *www.civilwartraveler.com/EAST/VA/index.html*)

GETTING HERE AND AROUND
AIR TRAVEL

Many travelers to western Virginia prefer to fly into international airports in the Washington-Baltimore area (Dulles, Reagan National, Baltimore-Washington International), Richmond, or Greensboro, North Carolina, then commute by rental car; all three areas are within two hours' drive of western Virginia destinations.

The region's three largest airports—Charlottesville-Albermarle, Lynchburg, and Roanoke—are small and relatively hassle-free. Regional carriers using small jets and turboprops are the norm, though larger jets sometimes serve Roanoke. Tri-Cities Regional Airport is just across the state line in Blountville, Tennessee, for easy access to the Abingdon area.

CAR TRAVEL

The many pleasant highways and routes that snake through western Virginia's rolling countryside make driving a particularly good way to travel. The region's interstates (I–64, I–81, and I–77) are remarkably scenic, but the same mountainous terrain that contributes to their beauty can also make them treacherous. Dense valley fog banks, mountain-shrouding clouds, and gusty ridge-top winds are concerns at any time of the year, and winter brings ice and snow conditions that can change dramatically in a few miles when the elevation changes.

Interstate 81 and U.S. 11 run north–south the length of the Shenandoah Valley and continue south into Tennessee. Interstate 66 west from Washington, D.C., which is 90 mi to the east, passes through Front Royal to meet I–81 and U.S. 11 at the northern end of the valley. Interstate 64 connects the same highways with Charlottesville, 30 mi to the east. Route 39 into Bath County connects with I–81 just north of Lexington. Interstate 77 cuts off the southwest tip of the state, running north–south and crossing I–81 at Wytheville. Interstate 77 crosses two major ridges and passes through two mountain tunnels in Virginia.

Travelers will rarely find bumper-to-bumper traffic jams in Charlottesville or any other city in the region. The major exception: autumn Saturdays when the University of Virginia has a home football game. Virginia Tech games can similarly snarl traffic in the Roanoke–New River valley area, including on I–81.

TAXI TRAVEL

Taxis are generally ordered instead of hailed. If travel in the region takes you outside the city, a rental car is a better way to go.

TRAIN TRAVEL

Amtrak has service to Charlottesville and Staunton, en route from New York and Chicago. The same train stops at Clifton Forge for the Homestead Resort in Bath County, also home to the C & O Railway Heritage Center. A complimentary shuttle bus on Sunday, Wednesday, and Friday connects Roanoke (Campbell Court and Roanoke Airport Sheraton) and Clifton Forge Rail Station. Amtrak's *Crescent* runs between New York City and New Orleans and stops daily in Lynchburg and Charlottesville.

ESSENTIALS

Air Contacts Charlottesville-Albemarle Airport (✉ *8 mi north of Charlottesville at intersection of Rtes. 606 and 649 off Rte. 29, 100 Bowen Loop* ☎ *434/973–8342* ⊕ *www.gocho.com*). **Lynchburg Regional Airport** (✉ *Rte. 29 S, 350 Terminal Dr* ☎ *434/455–6090*). **Roanoke Regional Airport** (✉ *Off I–58, 5202 Aviation Dr NW1* ☎ *540/362–1999* ⊕ *www.roanokeairport.com*). **Tri-Cities Regional Airport** (✉ *2525 Hway 75Blountville, TN* ☎ *423/325–6000* ⊕ *www. triflight.com*).

DISCOUNTS AND DEALS

A Presidential Pass, purchased for $31 at Monticello, Ash Lawn-Highland, or Michie Tavern, grants access to these three sites with a $5 combined savings.

RESTAURANTS

Since Charlottesville is a college town, most restaurants are very casual. You will need reservations for popular fine-dining options like the C&O, and business casual is more appropriate for these upscale venues.

HOTELS

Both locally owned and major chain motels and hotels are plentiful along the interstate highways (I–81, I–64, I–77, I–66), with a particularly heavy concentration in the Charlottesville and Roanoke areas. Accommodations in private homes and converted inns are available through the **Bed and Breakfast Association of Virginia** (✉ *Box 1077, Standardsville 22973* ☎ *888/660–2228* ⊕ *www.innvirginia.org*). Various accommodations in and near Charlottesville can be found through **Guesthouses** (✉ *Box 5737, Charlottesville 22905* ☎ *434/979–7264* ⊕ *www.va-guesthouses.com*).

WHAT IT COSTS					
	¢	$	$$	$$$	$$$$
Restaurants	under $10	$10–$16	$17–$23	$24–$30	over $30
Hotels	under $100	$100–$160	$161–$230	$231–$300	over $300

Restaurant prices are per person for a main course at dinner. Hotel prices are for a standard double room, excluding state and local taxes.

PLANNING YOUR TIME

You'll need at least half a day for each of the president's homes, and you should allow a day for a scenic drive to some of the region's well-known wineries: there are 130 in or near Charlottesville. Plan to spend two to three days exploring Jefferson's hometown and the surrounding areas.

CHARLOTTESVILLE AND THE BLUE RIDGE

Surrounded by a lush countryside, Charlottesville is the most prominent city in the foothills of the Blue Ridge Mountains. Thomas Jefferson's hilltop home and the University of Virginia, the enterprise of his last years, draw appreciators of architecture. Twenty-five miles northeast, Orange County is where you'll find the estate of Jefferson's friend and compatriot James Madison. The tiny town of Washington, 30 mi beyond Orange, bears the stamp of another president: George Washington surveyed and plotted out this slice of wilderness in 1749. Lynchburg, to Charlottesville's south, is near the site of Jefferson's retreat home, the octagonal Poplar Forest, and the ending battle of the Civil War, Appomattox. On the Blue Ridge itself are popular Shenandoah National Park, the park's spectacular but often-crowded Skyline Drive, and Wintergreen Resort, a haven for outdoor sports.

CHARLOTTESVILLE

Charlottesville is 71 mi northwest of Richmond via I–64.

Charlottesville is still Jefferson's city, focused on Monticello and the University of Virginia. The downtown pedestrian mall, a brick-paved street of restored buildings that stretches along six blocks of Main Street, is the central hub for humans and canines alike. Outdoor restaurants and cafés, concerts, street vendors, and impromptu theatrical events keep things lively.

GETTING HERE AND AROUND

Charlottesville is off of I–64, just an hour from Richmond or two hours from Washington, D.C. Although the pedestrian mall in downtown Charlottesville is walkable, you'll need a car to see the historic presidential homes, wineries, and attractions in the region.

Charlottesville Area Transit (CAT) offers a free trolley service daily between downtown and the university. The University Transit Service at the University of Virginia has service to and from university buildings and parking lots, the hospital, on- and off-campus student housing, and the Barracks Road shopping center.

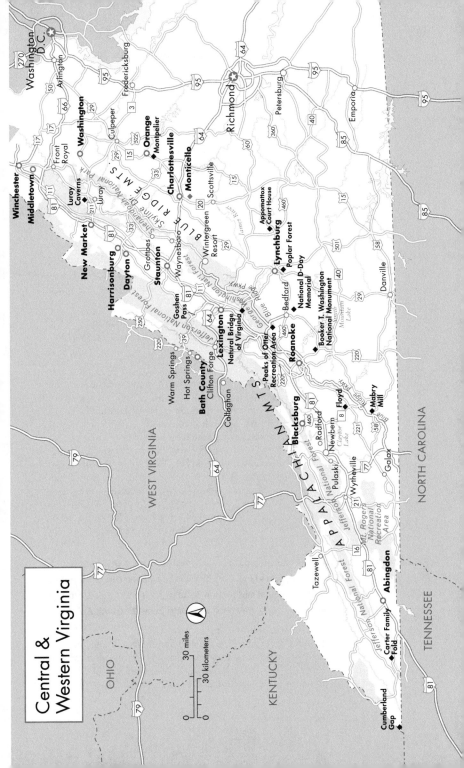

Central & Western Virginia

OHIO

KENTUCKY

WEST VIRGINIA

TENNESSEE

NORTH CAROLINA

Washington D.C.

Arlington

Front Royal

Winchester

Middletown

Washington

Culpeper

Fredericksburg

Richmond

Petersburg

Emporia

New Market

Luray Caverns

Luray

Harrisonburg

Dayton

Grottoes

Staunton

Waynesboro

Orange

Montpelier

Charlottesville

Monticello

Scottsville

SHENANDOAH NATIONAL PARK

BLUE RIDGE MTS

SKYLINE DRIVE

Wintergreen Resort

Appomattox Court House

Lynchburg

Poplar Forest

National D-Day Memorial

Bedford

Booker T. Washington National Monument

Danville

Warm Springs

Hot Springs

Bath County

Clifton Forge

Callaghan

Goshen Pass

Lexington

Natural Bridge of Virginia

Peaks of Otter Recreation Area

Roanoke

Blacksburg

Radford

Newbern

Claytor Lake

Pulaski

Wytheville

Galax

Floyd

Mabry Mill

Tazewell

Mt. Rogers National Recreation Area

Abingdon

Carter Family Fold

Cumberland Gap

George Washington Natl. Forest

Jefferson National Forest

Blue Ridge Pkwy.

James River

Smith Mountain Lake

APPALACHIAN MTS

N

30 miles

30 kilometers

Van on the Go shuttles is a car service that shuttles guests from the Charlottesville airport to hotels, downtown, and area tourist attractions, but it's more expensive ($59–$99) than a local taxi. Average taxi fare to the UVA area is around $25 and local fares are about $3.00 per mile.

TIMING AND PRECAUTIONS

Charlottesville is full of energy during the school year and can be very crowded on fall football weekends. If you want to avoid crowds in town or long waits at restaurants and attractions, visit on a weekday.

ESSENTIALS

Taxi Companies **AC Airport Cab & Wahoo Cab** (☎ 434/981–0585). **Quicksilver Taxi** (☎ 434/825–3499). **Taxinet** (☎ 434/245–8294). **Van on the Go** (✉ 201 Bowen Loop, Charlottesville-Albermarle Airport ☎ 434/975–8267 ⊕ www. vanonthego.com).

Train Station **Union Station** (✉ 810 W. Main St. ☎ 434/296–4559).

Transportation Information **Charlottesville Area Transit** (CAT ✉ 605 E. Main St. ☎ 434/970–3649). **University Transit Service at the University of Virginia** (✉ 1101 Millmont St. ☎ 434/924–7231).

Visitor Information **Charlottesville/Albemarle Convention and Visitors Bureau** (610 E. Main St, Charlottesville ☎ 434/293–6789 or 877/386–1103 ⊕ www.visitcharlottesville.org).

EXPLORING

Ash Lawn–Highland. Standing in contrast to the grandiose Monticello is the modest home of James Monroe, who held more major political offices than any other U.S. president. He intentionally kept it a simple farmhouse, building the home in 1799, 2 mi from his friend Jefferson's estate. A later owner added on a more prominent two-story section where two original Monroe rooms burned down. Though it definitely has a more common feel than Monticello, the small rooms in Ash Lawn–Highland are similarly crowded with gifts from notables and souvenirs from Monroe's time as envoy to France. Allow a couple of hours to visit Monroe's estate, a perfect way to complete a day that begins at Monticello. ✉ 1000 James Monroe Pkwy., Rte. 795 southwest of Monticello ☎ 434/293–45009 ⊕ www.ashlawnhighland.org 🎟 $10 ⏱ Apr.–Oct., daily 9–6; Nov.–Mar., daily 11–5.

QUICK BITES While you're strolling the downtown pedestrian mall, pick up a gourmet nosh from **Hamdingers Food Cart** (⊕ www.hamdingerscart.com). This one-man show makes global cuisine from local ingredients. Try the Moroccan chicken or masala curry. He's open weekdays from 11:30 until 2.

McGuffey Art Center. Housed in a converted 1916 school building, McGuffey Art Center contains the 2nd Street Gallery and the studios of painters, printmakers, metalworkers, and sculptors, all of which are open to the public. ✉ 201 2nd St. NW, Downtown ☎ 434/295–7973 ⊕ www.mcguffeyartcenter.com 🎟 Free ⏱ Tues.–Sat. 10–5, Sun. 1–5.

Monticello. Thomas Jefferson's home, long featured on the back of the U.S. nickel, is well worth the admission and the almost inevitable wait. Arrive early, ideally on a weekday, and allow at least three hours to explore the nuances of Jefferson's life as exemplified by the architecture, inventions, and layout throughout his grand, hilltop estate. Monticello (which means "little mountain") is the most famous of Jefferson's homes, constructed from 1769 to 1809. Note the narrow staircases—hidden because he considered them unsightly and a waste of space—and his inventions, such as a seven-day clock and a two-pen contraption that allowed him to make a copy of his correspondence as he wrote it without having to show it to a copyist. On-site are re-created gardens, the plantation street where his slaves lived, and a gift shop. ⊠ *Rte. 53* ☎ *434/984–9822* ⊕ *www.monticello.org* ⊠ *Mar.–Oct. $22; Nov.–Feb. $17* ⊗ *Mar.–Nov., daily 9–5; Dec.–Feb., daily 10–4.*

★ **University of Virginia.** The University of Virginia is simply called "The University" by many associated with it, annoying its rivals. Unquestionably, though, it is one of the nation's most notable public universities, founded and designed by 76-year-old Thomas Jefferson, who called himself its "father" in his own epitaph. Even if you're not an architecture or history buff, the green terraced expanse called the Lawn, surrounded by red-brick, columned buildings, is inviting. The Rotunda is a half-scale replica of Rome's Pantheon, suggesting Jefferson's Monticello and the U.S. Capitol. Behind the Pavilions, where senior faculty live, serpentine walls surround small, flowering gardens. Edgar Allan Poe's room—where he spent one year as a student until debt forced him to leave—is preserved on the West Range at No. 13. Campus tours (daily at 10, 11, 2, 3, and 4) begin indoors in the Rotunda, whose entrance is on the Lawn side, lower level. The **University of Virginia Art Museum** (⊠ *Bayly Bldg., 155 Rugby Rd.* ☎ *434/924–3592* ⊠ *Free* ⊗ *Tues.–Sun. noon–5*), one block north of the Rotunda, exhibits art from around the world from ancient times to the present day. ⊠ *University* ☎ *434/924–3239* ⊕ *www.virginia. edu* ⊠ *Free* ⊗ *Rotunda daily 9–4:45. University closed during winter break in Dec. and Jan. and spring exams 1st 3 wks of May.*

Virginia Discovery Museum. At the Virginia Discovery Museum children can step inside a giant kaleidoscope, explore a reconstructed log cabin, or watch bees in action in a working hive. The hands-on exhibits are meant to interest children (and their parents) in science, the arts, history, and the humanities. The museum is at the east end of the downtown mall. ⊠ *524 E. Main St., Downtown* ☎ *434/977–1025* ⊕ *www.vadm. org* ⊠ *$6* ⊗ *Tues.–Sat. 10–5, Sun. 1–5.*

WHERE TO EAT

Bodo's Bagels. You may have to wait in line at one the three locally owned locations, especially at breakfast, but locals swear these are the best bagels south of the Big Apple. In true New York style, bagels are boiled before being baked, and all 10 varieties are true water bagels made with no fats or preservatives. Lunchtime is also popular, and the low prices appeal to both students and visitors. There are also locations at 505 Preston Avenue and 1609 University Avenue. ⊠ *1418 Emmet St., Downtown* ☎ *434/293–6021* ⊕ *www.bodosbagels.com* ⌦ *Reservations not accepted* ⊟ *MC, V* ⊗ *No dinner Sunday.*

AMERICAN
★

Thomas Jefferson, a Brief Biography

One of the nation's foremost states-men, Jefferson is best known for his first contribution to the country: draft-ing the Declaration of Independence in 1776. The sum of the 33-year political career that followed is bet-ter remembered than its milestones, which do, however, bear repeating.

His first office of weight was that of governor of his beloved Virginia, beginning in 1779. In 1790 he served as secretary of state under his friend George Washington, and resigned in 1793. A Republican presidential can-didate in 1796, he lost by just three electoral votes to Federalist John Adams, and as rules then dictated, Jefferson became vice president. By the 1800 race, tensions between the Federalist and Republican parties were high and debilitating to a nation still finding its way. Jefferson won the nation's third presidency at this critical juncture and served two terms, after which he retired to Monticello.

The breadth of Jefferson's skills is astounding. He was a statesman, farmer and zealous gardener, writer, scientist, musician, and philosopher. One admiring contemporary described Jefferson as a man who could "calcu-late an eclipse, survey an estate, tie an artery, plan an edifice, try a cause, break a horse, dance a minuet, and play a violin." And as a lover of great wine, Jefferson introduced European vinifera grapes to Virginia. He has even been hailed as the father of the American gastronomic revolution, importing from France olive oil, Par-mesan cheese, raisins, and pistachios. The *Garden Book*, which he kept for upward of half a century, contains a wealth of minutiae, from plant-ing times to the preferred method of grafting peach trees.

It's often noted that this architect of democracy was also a slave owner. He owned about 200 slaves at any given time, and freed only 7 after his death, and one of the most enduring myster-ies surrounding Jefferson has been his relationship with Sally Hemings, one of his slaves. Jefferson went through an inquiry into his conduct during his last year as governor of Virginia, and while president, Federalists accused him of improper relations with a white woman and with Hemings.

Virginians love Jefferson because he loved Virginia. Monticello, his experi-ment in architecture that had him making changes until the day before he died, attracts 500,000 people every year. The University of Virginia, which Jefferson called "the hobby of my old age," is now one of the nation's elite public universities. Charlottesville honors its most famous resident in a number of ways. On April 13—Jeffer-son's birthday—the Thomas Jefferson Center for the Protection of Free Expression presents the Muzzle Award to those guilty of trying to quash free speech. On the anniversary of his death, Independence Day, Monticello is the site of a naturalization cer-emony for new Americans.

$$–$$$ ✕ **C&O Restaurant**. Don't let the exterior fool you: behind the boarded-
ECLECTIC up storefront hung with an illuminated Pepsi sign is an exemplary res-
★ taurant. The formal dining room upstairs, the lively bistro downstairs,
and the cozy mezzanine in between share a French-influenced menu
that has Pacific Rim and American Southwest touches. The heated
patio and urban terrace are also lovely dining spaces in fall and spring.
For a starter try the panfried sweetbread medallions; entrées include
steak *chinoise* with fresh ginger, tamari, and scallion cream sauce. The
chefs source their products from local markets and farms, so the menu
changes seasonally and the wine list is 300 labels strong. For night
owls, they offer a late night menu of appetizers, soups, salads, and
sandwiches. ✉ *515 E. Water St., Downtown* ☎ *434/971–7044* ⊕ *www.
candorestaurant.com* ▭ *AE, MC, V.*

¢–$ ✕ **Continental Divide**. Without a neon sign in the window of this locals'
SOUTHWESTERN favorite says "Get in here" you might miss this small storefront restaurant. The menu is Southwestern cuisine, with quesadillas, burritos, spicy pork tacos, enchiladas, and potent margaritas. Cactus plants
decorate the front window, and the booths have funky lights. It can get
crowded and convivial, but customers like it that way. ✉ *811 W. Main
St., Downtown* ☎ *434/984–0143* ⌦ *Reservations not accepted* ▭ *D,
DC, MC, V* ⊘ *No lunch.*

$–$$ ✕ **Crozet Pizza**. It may look like a shack, but this red clapboard restau-
PIZZA rant 12 mi west of Charlottesville has been serving up what is renowned
★ as some of Virginia's best pizza since 1977. You have about three dozen
toppings to choose from, including seasonal items such as snow peas
and asparagus spears. Like its outside, the interior is rustic, with portraits of the owners' forebears and one wall covered with business cards
from around the world. On weekends, takeout must be ordered hours
in advance. ✉ *5794 Three Notch'd Rd. at Rte. 240, Crozet* ☎ *434/823–
2132* ⊕ *www.crozetpizza.net* ▭ *No credit cards.*

$$$ ✕ **Duner's**. This former motel diner 5 mi west of Charlottesville fills up
AMERICAN early, and since they don't accept reservations, be prepared to wait up to
30 minutes. The fanciful menu, which changes daily, emphasizes fresh,
seasonal fare in its seafood and pasta dishes. Appetizers may include
lamb and green peppercorn pâté with grilled bread. Several fish selec-
tions appear daily on the menu, along with specialties like veal sweet-
breads or duck breast, Continental style. While there isn't a kids' menu,
the chef will make a burger or kid-friendly meal, and accommodate veg-
etarians or those with special diets. ✉ *4372 Ivy Road* ☎ *434/293–8352*
⊕ *www.dunersrestaurant.com* ⌦ *Reservations not accepted* ▭ *AE, MC,
V* ⊘ *No lunch.*

WHERE TO STAY

$$$–$$$$ ▦ **Boars Head Inn**. Set on 55 acres in west Charlottesville, this local land-
mark resembles an English country inn, with flower gardens, ponds,
and a gristmill from 1834. Rooms have king-size four-poster beds and
Italian linens and many are decked out with balconies or fireplaces.
There are lots of activities here, from cooking classes and wine tast-
ings to hot-air ballooning. The Old Mill Room restaurant, the Inn's
fine dining outlet, is open for a lunch buffet and dinner, while Bistro
1834 and the Birdwood Grill offer more casual fare. **Pros:** true luxury;

tons of amenities; sumptuous lunch buffet. **Cons:** add-on activities can make this a pricey stay; compared to other inns, this larger property can feel impersonal. ⊠ *200 Ednam Dr.* ☎ *434/296–2181* ⊕ *www. boarsheadinn.com* ⇥ *170 rooms, 11 suites* ⌂ *In-room: a/c, Internet, refrigerator (some), fireplace (some) In-hotel: 3 restaurants, golf course, tennis courts, pools, gym, spa* ⊟ *AE, D, DC, MC, V.*

$$$$ ⌂ **Clifton Inn**. This small inn is a member of the Relais & Chateaux
★ group, the ultimate in luxury. Top-shelf amenities include Mascioni linens and robes and Molton Brown toiletries in the 18 uniquely appointed rooms and suites, situated on 100 acres with spectacular views of the Blue Ridge Mountains. Many of the rooms are named to reflect the property's ties to the Jefferson family. About 350 acres passed to Thomas Jefferson's daughter and her husband, Thomas Mann Randolph, who established their home Edgehill on the property. The foundations of the main building are thought to be the original foundations of one of Mann's warehouses. **Pros:** great food; luxury in a small setting; free breakfast and tea; pet friendly; massive private lake. **Cons:** far from downtown Charlottesville; expensive. ⊠ *1296 Clifton Inn Dr.* ☎ *434/971–1800* ⊕ *www.cliftoninn.net* ⇥ *18 rooms* ⌂ *In-room: a/c, Internet. In-hotel: 2 restaurants, tennis court, pool* ⊟ *AE, D, MC, V.*

$$–$$$ ⌂ **High Meadows Vineyard Inn**. Federalist and Italianate architecture are joined by a hall in this bed-and-breakfast (and working vineyard), combining houses from 1832 and 1882. This 13-acre property is 15 mi south of Monticello and close to several top wineries, and their own vineyard is known for its pinot noir. All of the rooms have been recently renovated, with the addition of luxury linens and Arbonne toiletries. Dinner is served in the dining room by reservation Wednesday through Saturday, and a substantial breakfast is included in the room rate. The inn even keeps its own hens for true farm-to-table organic eggs. **Pros:** luxury amenities; winery on-site; historic property. **Cons:** farther from town; small size books up quickly. ⊠ *55 High Meadows La., Scottsville* ☎ *434/286–2218 or 800/232–1832* ⊕ *www.highmeadows.com* ⇥ *9 rooms, 2 cottages* ⌂ *In-room: a/c, no TV, Wi-Fi. In-hotel: restaurant* ⊟ *MC, V* ⧆ *BP.*

$$$$ ⌂ **Keswick Hall at Monticello**. If you've got the money for it, this 1912
Fodor's Choice Tuscan villa on 600 lush acres 5 mi east of Charlottesville is a luxuri-
★ ous, cosmopolitan retreat. Since it is now owned by the Orient-Express, you can expect the ultimate in top-drawer amenities and service. The 48 guest rooms and suites contain modern amenities like high-speed Internet and flat screen TVs, which exist in harmony with English and American antiques and claw-foot tubs. Some rooms have whirlpool baths and balconies. The 18-hole golf course, designed by Arnold Palmer, spreads across the rear of the estate. There's no check-in desk here; you are welcomed inside as if you are entering someone's home. The facilities of the private Keswick Club are open to those staying overnight. **Pros:** three restaurants and pub on-site; top-shelf toiletries. **Cons:** expensive for the area; lacking Colonial history of many inns. ⊠ *701 Club Dr., Keswick* ☎ *434/979–3440 or 888/778–2565* ⊕ *www. keswick.com* ⇥ *40 rooms, 8 suites* ⌂ *In-room: a/c, safe, Internet. In-hotel: 2 restaurants, golf course, tennis courts, pools, gym, spa, bicycles, some pets allowed* ⊟ *AE, D, DC, MC, V.*

$$$ 🏠 **Omni Charlottesville.** This attractive member of the luxury chain looms over the west end of the Downtown Mall. Triangular rooms at the point of the wedge-shaped building get light from two sides. Cherry-color furnishings and sage fabrics decorate the guest quarters, and potted plants soften the bright seven-story atrium lobby. **Pros:** steps from pedestrian mall; nice market and gift shop; modern hotel. **Cons:** some rooms are small due to the triangular shape of the building; no historical connection. ✉ *235 W. Main St., Downtown* ☎ *434/971–5500 or 800/843–6664* ⊕ *www.omnihotels.com* ⤴ *204 rooms, 7 suites* ♿ *In-room: a/c, Wi-Fi. In-hotel: restaurant, bar, pools, gym* ▤ *AE, D, DC, MC, V.*

$$ 🏠 **Silver Thatch Inn.** Four-poster beds and period antiques are just part of
★ the charm of this 1780 white-clapboard Colonial farmhouse 8 mi north of town. The friendly hosts help their guests arrange outdoor activities at nearby locations. The original structure was built to house Hessian soldiers captured during the Revolutionary War and still remains as the Hessian Room. **Pros:** fascinating Colonial history; romantic fireplaces; canopy beds; pub and restaurant on-site. **Cons:** small size means few amenities, particularly in the rooms. ✉ *3001 Hollymead Dr.* ☎ *434/978–4686 or 800/261–0720* ⊕ *www.silverthatch.com* ⤴ *7 rooms* ♿ *In-room: a/c, no phone, no TV, Wi-Fi. In-hotel: restaurant, pool, no kids under 14* ▤ *AE, D, DC, MC, V* ◉ *BP.*

$$$ 🏠 **200 South Street Inn.** Two Georgian houses, one of them a former brothel, have been combined and restored to create this old-fashioned inn in the historic district, two blocks from the Downtown Mall. Furnishings throughout are English and Belgian antiques, and several rooms come with a canopy bed, sitting room, fireplace, and whirlpool. **Pros:** central location; charming decor; historic inn. **Cons:** limited availability; two-night minimum on weekends. ✉ *200 South St., Downtown* ☎ *434/979–0200 or 800/964–7008* ⊕ *www.southstreetinn.com* ⤴ *16 rooms, 3 suites* ▤ *AE, DC, MC, V* ◉ *CP.*

$ 🏠 **Wintergreen Resort.** This is a great place to get away any time of year. 25 mi southwest of Charlottesville (via I–64, U.S. 250, and Route 151). With 6,700 acres of forest, six restaurants, and three golf courses, Wintergreen is more like a community in itself than just a resort. Skiing and snowboarding are the central attractions, with 20 downhill slopes and five chairlifts. One of the golf courses, Devils Knob at over 3,800 feet, is the highest in Virginia. Accommodations at the resort include everything from studio apartments to seven-bedroom houses. Most rooms have fireplaces and full kitchens; the housing units' wood exteriors blend into the surrounding forest. **Pros:** good skiing and summer outdoor activities; cozy rooms complete with fireplaces; many restaurants and other resort options. **Cons:** crowded in season; half-hour drive from Charlottesville. ✉ *Rte. 664, Wintergreen* ☎ *434/325–2200 or 800/266–2444* ⊕ *www.wintergreenresort.com* ⤴ *305 units* ♿ *In-room: a/c, kitchen (some), Wi-Fi. In-hotel: 6 restaurants, bar, golf courses, tennis courts, pools, gym, spa, bicycles, laundry facilities, laundry service* ▤ *AE, D, MC, V.*

EN
ROUTE
The Starr Hill Brewery (✉ *5391 Three Notched Rd., Crozet* ☎ *434/823–5671*) is one of the most well-respected breweries on the East Coast, featuring four house brews including Amber Ale, Pale Ale, Jomo Lager,

and Dark Starr Stout and open for tastings on Saturdays and Sundays from noon to 5. If apple cider is more to your taste, visit **Carter's Mountain Orchard** (✉ *1435 Carters Mountain Trail, Charlottesville* ☎ *434/977–1833*) for stunning views of Charlottesville and some of the best apples in the state.

NIGHTLIFE AND THE ARTS

For listings of cultural events, music, and movies, and a guide to restaurants, pick up a free copy of the *C-Ville Weekly* (⊕ *www.c-ville.com*), an arts-and-entertainment newspaper available in restaurants and hotels throughout the city. If you're near the University of Virginia campus, grab a free copy of the student newspaper, the *Cavalier Daily* (⊕ *www. cavalierdaily.com*), for the latest on college sports and events.

FESTIVALS

In March, **Virginia Festival of the Book** (☎ *434/924–6890* ⊕ *www.vabook. org*) draws authors that have included Garrison Keillor and Michael Ondaatje. Thousands attend the festival, which is open to the public and promotes literacy while celebrating the book. Every autumn, Charlottesville hosts the **Virginia Film Festival** (☎ *434/982–5277 or 800/882–3378* ⊕ *www.virginiafilmfestival.org*), with screenings of important new movies, panel discussions, and appearances by stars of the cinema. The movies are shown at four sites around the university and downtown.

SPORTS AND THE OUTDOORS

CANOEING AND KAYAKING

James River Runners Inc (✉ *10092 Hatton Ferry Rd., Scottsville* ☎ *434/ 286–2338*), about 35 minutes south of Charlottesville, offers canoe, kayak, tubing, and rafting trips down the James.

SPECTATOR SPORTS

The **University of Virginia** is part of the Atlantic Coast Conference. From November through February, the Cavaliers' perennially strong men's and women's basketball teams play against other NCAA Division I-A teams in University Hall. Fall brings football to Scott Stadium. For ticket prices, call the University of Virginia Athletic Ticket Office (☎ *804/924–8821 or 800/542–8821*). Check the *Cavalier Daily* for game times.

SHOPPING

Charlottesville, at heart an academic community, supports a large number of independent bookstores, especially specialists in used and antiquarian books. Whether it's a rare first edition you are seeking or just some rare bargains, try **Blue Whale Books** (✉ *115 W. Main St., Downtown* ☎ *434/296–4646*). Run by an antiquarian book dealer, the shop has thousands of books in all categories and price ranges, from one dollar to several hundred. **Daedalus Bookshop** (✉ *123 4th St. NE, Downtown* ☎ *434/293–7595*) has three floors of books crammed into every nook and cranny. **Heartwood Books** (✉ *5 Elliewood Ave., University* ☎ *434/295–7083*), close to the university campus, stocks scholarly works, including a good collection of theology and philosophy. Legal-thriller master John Grisham kicks off book tours at **New Dominion Bookshop** (✉ *404 E. Main St., Downtown* ☎ *434/295–2552*).

★ The **Downtown Mall** (✉ *Main St., Downtown* ⊕ *www.downtowncharlottes-ville.net*) is a six-block brick pedestrian mall with specialty stores, cinemas, art galleries, restaurants, and coffeehouses in restored 19th- and early-20th-century buildings.

ORANGE COUNTY

25 mi northeast of Charlottesville via Rte. 20, 60 mi northwest of Richmond.

Orange is a fertile agricultural area bearing reminders of the Civil War. Among the many estates dotting the countryside is the home of our nation's fourth president. A visit to Montpelier, the home of James Madison, is an easy side trip from the Charlottesville area, and a little over an hour's drive from Richmond. Orange is also home to one of Virginia's favorite wineries, Barboursville.

GETTING HERE AND AROUND

You'll need a car to explore this area in Virginia's north-central Piedmont region. With rural landscapes and views of the Blue Ridge Mountains, Orange County is about 90 mi southwest of Washington, D.C., about 75 mi northwest of Richmond, and about 25 mi from Charlottesville. From D.C., take I–66 West to Rt. 29 and head south to Rt. 3. From Richmond or Charlottesville, take I–64 West to Rt. 250 or Rt. 15. I–64 runs east–west and connects the two major north–south interstates, I–95 and I–81, while state routes 15 and 20 run through the heart of Orange.

EXPLORING

Exchange Hotel Civil War Museum. During the Civil War, a handsome Greek revival hotel was transformed into a Confederate receiving hospital for wounded and dying soldiers. In addition to weapons, uniforms, and the personal effects of Union and Confederate soldiers, the museum displays the often crude medical equipment used for amputations, tooth extractions, and bloodletting. One room re-creates a hospital ward; an estimated 70,000 soldiers were treated here between 1862 and 1865. The museum hosts an annual ghost walk every October. ✉ *400 S. Main St., Gordonsville* ☎ *540/832–2944* ⊕ *www.hgiexchange.org* 🏷 *$6* ⊙ *Apr.–mid-Nov., Mon.–Sat. 10–4, Sun. 1–4. Closed Wed.*

James Madison Museum. The James Madison Museum presents a comprehensive exhibition on the Founding Father most responsible for the Constitution (Madison became president in 1809). The collection includes some of the china and glassware recovered from the White House before the British torched it during the War of 1812.

WORD OF MOUTH

"Orange is a little less than 2 hours from D.C. in the direction of Charlottesville. Within a short drive you have historic homes—Monticello (Jefferson), Montpelier (Madison), and Ash Lawn (Monroe). You have lots of vineyards, including Barboursville, which lots of wine buffs have identified as an up-and-comer. You have fantastic B&Bs and antiques shops all over the place. Nice dinners are not hard to come by, either." —flo77

The fourth president's tiny Campeachy chair, an 18th-century piece made for him by his friend Thomas Jefferson, shows how short he was. ✉ *129 Caroline St.* ☎ *540/672–1776* ⊕ *www.jamesmadisonmus. org* ✑ *$5* ☉ *Mon.–Sat. 10–4, Sun. 1–4.*

Montpelier. Just outside Orange is the lifelong residence of James Madison (1751–1836), the fourth president of the United States. He grew up here, lived here with his wife, Dolley, and retired here after his presidency. A massive renovation was completed in 2008, removing parts of the mansion added by its 20th-century owners, the duPont family. In her will, Marion duPont Scott left the estate to the National Trust for Historic Preservation with the stipulation that it be returned to its original state. The mansion is now restored to its early-19th-century Madisonian state, a project that totaled $24 million. Some of the Madisons' possessions, as well as a tribute to the "Father of the Constitution," have been set up in an Education Center on the grounds. The walking tour includes a stop at the cemetery where James and his wife, Dolley, are buried. Exotic conifers planted by the duPonts dot the meadowlike grounds, and a walking path wanders amid an old-growth forest. The annual Montpelier Hunt Races, a steeplechase, have been held here since 1934 on the first Saturday in November. ✉ *Rte. 20, 4 mi southwest of Orange, 11395 Constitution Hwy., Montpelier Station* ☎ *540/672–2728* ⊕ *www.montpelier.org* ✑ *$16* ☉ *Apr.–Oct., daily 9–5; Nov.–Mar., daily 9–4.*

St. Thomas's Episcopal Church. The one surviving example of Jeffersonian church architecture, St. Thomas's Episcopal Church is a replica of Charlottesville's demolished Christ Church, originally designed by Virginia's preeminent architect and statesman. It's here that Robert E. Lee worshipped during the winter of 1863–64. The church's biggest decorative asset is its Tiffany window. Sunday services are at 8 am and 11 am. ✉ *119 Caroline St.* ☎ *540/672–3761* ⊕ *www.ndearing.com/stthomas. html* ✑ *Donations accepted* ☉ *Tours by appointment.*

WHERE TO STAY

$$–$$$ ⊡ **Mayhurst Inn.** An architectural rarity in the South, this Italianate Victorian mansion was built in 1859 by a grandnephew of James Madison, and generals Stonewall Jackson and Robert E. Lee were early guests. Now Mayhurst is a cozy and comfortable B&B surrounded by 37 acres of woods with hiking trails. Its rooms have floor-to-ceiling windows, marble fireplaces, and antique furnishings; some have whirlpool baths. Included with the room rate is a sumptuous three-course breakfast, evening wine and cheese, and soft drinks and snacks. **Pros:** antiques; historic; complimentary snacks; no age restriction for children. **Cons:** limited availability; nothing within walking distance. ✉ *12460 Mayhurst La.* ☎ *540/672–5597 or 888/672–5597* ⊕ *www.mayhurstinn.com* ➷ *8 rooms, 2 suites* ⚴ *In-room: a/c, Wi-Fi, no TV (some)* ▭ *AE, D, MC, V* ⦿*BP.*

Virginia's Wineries

Jamestown's Colonial settlers are believed to have made the first wine in Virginia, and Thomas Jefferson is touted as the father of American viniculture, but only in the past 30 years has the Commonwealth's wine industry truly come into its own. The number of wineries here has grown from fewer than 10 in the 1970s to more than 130 wineries in the Charlottesville area alone. As you drive through the state, keep an eye out for grape-cluster signs on the highway, which identify nearby wineries, or visit the Virginia Tourism Web site for free "wine trail" maps. The Monticello Wine Trail connects 22 area vineyards, including the **Jefferson Vineyards** (⊕ www.jeffersonvineyards.com), located on land where Thomas Jefferson himself grew grapes. Virginia is becoming well known on the national oenophile radar for its viogniers, and for vintages from vintners like Kluge.

For more information on Virginia vineyards and wineries, contact the **Virginia Wineries Association** (☎ 800/828–4637 ⊕ www.virginiawine.org) or the **Jeffersonian Wine Grape Growers Society** (☎ 434/296–4188 ⊕ www.monticellowinetrail.org), sponsor of the Monticello Wine Trail.

Among central and western Virginia's more popular wineries are Barboursville Vineyards, near Charlottesville, and Château Morrisette Winery, on the Blue Ridge Parkway in the southern part of the state.

Barboursville Vineyards. This vineyard between Charlottesville and Orange was the first in the state to grow only vinifera (old-world) grapes. The grapes were planted in 1976 on the former plantation of James

Barbour, governor from 1812 to 1814. His house, designed by Thomas Jefferson, was gutted by fire in 1884; the ruins remain are open to visitors for self-guided tours. ⊠ 17655 Winery Rd., near intersection of Rtes. 20 and 23, Barboursville ☎ 540/832–3824 ⊕ www.barboursvillewine.com 🖅 Tours free; tastings $5 ⊙ Tastings Mon.–Sat. 10–5, Sun. 11–5.

Château Morrisette Winery. With the Rock Castle Gorge nearby, this winery has spectacular surroundings. Tastings allow you to sample the 10 different wines produced here. ⊠ 287 Winery Rd. SW off Rte. 726, west of Blue Ridge Pkwy. at milepost 171.5, Meadows of Dan ☎ 540/593–2865 ⊕ www.chateaumorrisette.com 🖅 Tour and tasting $5 ⊙ Mon.–Thurs. 10–5, Fri. and Sat. 10–6, Sun. 11–5.

Kluge Estate. Established in 1999 on the same ridgeline as the birthplace of Virginia viticulture at Monticello, Kluge is making world-class whites, reds, and rosé in its 2,000-acre vineyard on Carter's Mountain. Grapes are harvested by hand and most of the wines are made in méthode traditionelle. Taste one of the chardonnays, a blanc de blanc, or a Bordeaux blend at the estate's Farm Shop, which also offers food and wine pairings. ⊠ 100 Grand Cru Dr., Charlottesville ☎ 434/977–3895 or 434/984–4855 ⊕ www.klugeestateonline.com ⊙ June–Oct., Sun.–Tues. 11–6; Wed.–Sat. 11–8.

5

WASHINGTON

63 mi north of Charlottesville.

Known as Little Washington to differentiate it from its big sister about 60 mi away, this tiny town packs in antiques shops, galleries, custom jewelry shops, and two theaters in roughly five blocks—perfect for an afternoon stroll. In 1749 young surveyor George Washington laid out the five-block-by-two-block grid; the town claims to be the very first Washington of all.

GETTING HERE AND AROUND

Little Washington is an easy drive from its big sister on 66 West from D.C. Take 29 South to Warrenton and head west on Route 211. From Charlottesville, head north on 29 to Route 231 toward Sperryville and then east on 211

TIMING AND PRECAUTIONS

Because the accommodations in this area are small inns and B&B's, space is limited. If you're planning to stay overnight, book in advance as weekends sell out quickly to Washingtonians looking for a nearby getaway. In the fall, you'll need to book up to a year in advance.

WHERE TO STAY

$ 🏠 **The Gay Street Inn.** Prepare to be pampered upon arrival with complimentary port and chocolates in the cozy library at this welcoming inn that will make you feel like a local. Located on the quiet end of town, this 1850's farmhouse furnished with antiques and period pieces is within walking distance of restaurants and shopping. Curl up in front of the fireplace on a chilly fall day or enjoy the scenery during warm weather from the spacious front porch. A full home-cooked breakfast in the serene sunroom is included. **Pros:** Wi-Fi, good location. **Cons:** limited number of rooms. ✉ *160 Gay St., Washington* ☎ *540/675–3288* ⊕ *www.gaystreetinn.com* 🛏 *4 rooms, 1 suite* ⚹ *In-room: a/c, Wi-Fi. In-hotel: Wi-Fi hotspot, parking (free), some pets allowed, no kids under 12* ▤ *AE, D, DC, MC, V.*

$$$$ 🏠 **The Inn at Little Washington.** What began as a small-town eatery in
Fodor's Choice 1978 has grown into a legend. The rich interior of the three-story white-
★ frame inn is the work of Joyce Conway-Evans, who has designed theatrical sets and rooms in English royal houses. Plush canopy beds, marble bathrooms, and fresh flowers make the rooms sumptuous. If you need more space, the Inn also has two luxurious cottages: the 3,200-square-foot Claiborne House and the smaller but equally charming Gamekeeper's Cottage, both steps from the main inn. Chef Patrick O'Connell's much-loved New American food is served in a slate-floor dining room with William Morris wallpaper, and his restaurant consistently wins respect

> **TALLY HO!**
>
> Virginians have thrilled to the chase (not kill) of foxhunting since the days of George Washington hunted with his own pack of hounds. There are 19 hunt clubs in the state recognized or registered with the Master of Foxhounds Association (MHFA) and many of those are in the Central and Western regions of the state. Check out ⊕ *www.foxhuntva.com.*

from international critics. For $350–$450 per person, gourmands can reserve a seat at the Chef's Table to watch the kitchen in action. The seven-course prix-fixe dinner is $148–$178 per person (depending on the day of the week and not including wine and drinks); rooms are equally pricey, with the Claiborne House topping out at $2,570 per night. There are also additional rate surcharges on weekends and during peak seasons. **Pros:** ultimate luxury; amazing in-house restaurant. **Cons:** must reserve months in advance; limited number of rooms. ✉ *309 Middle St., at Main. St.* ☎ *540/675–3800* ⊕ *www.theinnatlittlewashington. com* ⤴ *18 rooms, 3 suites, 2 cottages* ⚲ *In-room: a/c, Wi-Fi, safe. In-hotel: restaurant, bicycles* ▭ *MC, V* ☯ *Hotel and restaurant closed Tues. except in May and Oct.* ⭐ *CP.*

LYNCHBURG

66 mi southeast of Charlottesville via Rte. 29, 110 mi west of Richmond.

Lynchburg was founded by John Lynch, a Quaker pacifist, and Thomas Jefferson visited often when he was vacationing at his nearby retreat, Poplar Forest. The revitalization of the riverfront area and downtown is centered around the Bluffwalk Center, a complex of historic warehouses that are now home to trendy restaurants, a boutique hotel, and the Jefferson Brewery. In 2006, the National Trust for Historic Places awarded Lynchburg a "Great American Main Street Award." Lynchburg is also home to Liberty University, whose Snowflex Centre has become the region's top recreational attraction. Snowflex offers year-round skiing and snowboarding to students, locals, and visitors, but there are plenty of other outdoor activities as well, including the Blackwater Creek bike trails. Appomattox Courthouse National Historical Park is a must-see for Civil War buffs, and Jefferson fans will enjoy his octagonal Poplar Forest home.

GETTING HERE AND AROUND

Route 29, one of the major north–south highways in the state, runs directly through the heart of Lynchburg and can be accessed from most major interstates. From D.C., head west on I–66 to 29 south. Your exit sign will most likely say "Rt. 29/501 to Lynchburg." In many areas, Route 29 has bypasses around major cities: for example, it intersects I–64 at Charlottesville with a by-pass around the town. If you're not in a hurry, you can also take Route 60 from Richmond to Route 29, rather than I–64.

ESSENTIALS

Train Station Kemper Street Station (✉ *825 Kemper St.* ☎ *434/847–8247*).

Visitor Information Lynchburg Regional Convention and Visitors Bureau (✉ *216 12th St.* ☎ *434/847–1811 or 800/732–5821* ⊕ *www.discoverlynchburg. org*).

EXPLORING

Anne Spencer House and Gardens. Step into "Edankraal," the studio of this late poet of the Harlem Renaissance, and the place where Anne Spencer wrote her most significant poems. Hers is the only work of a Virginian to appear in the *Norton Anthology of Modern American and*

English Poetry. A librarian at one of Lynchburg's segregated black schools, Spencer (1882–1975) penned most of her work in this back-garden sanctuary, which has been left completely intact with her writing desk, bookcases, mementos, and walls tacked with photos and news clippings. ⊠ *1313 Pierce St.* ☎ *434/845–1313* ⊕ *www. annespencermuseum.com* ⊠ *$5* ⊙ *Tours by appointment.*

Legacy Museum of African-American History. This museum's rotating exhibits focus on such themes as health and medicine, education, business, the civil rights struggle, and the contributions African-Americans have made to society, the arts, and politics. ⊠ *403 Monroe St.* ☎ *434/845–3455* ⊕ *www.legacymuseum.org* ⊠ *$5* ⊙ *Wed.–Sat. noon–4, Sun. 2–4, and by appointment.*

Point of Honor. Built in 1815, the mansion on Daniel's Hill, Point of Honor, was named to commemorate the many duels fought on the site. Once part of a 900-acre estate, this redbrick house surrounded by lawns retains a commanding view of the James River. It was the home of Dr. George Cabell, a friend of Thomas Jefferson and the physician of Patrick Henry. The facade is elegantly symmetrical, with two octagonal bays joined by a balustrade on each of the building's two stories. Interiors have been restored and furnished with pieces authentic to the early-19th-century Federal period. ⊠ *112 Cabell St.* ☎ *434/847–1867* ⊕ *www.pointofhonor.org* ⊠ *$6* ⊙ *Mon.–Sat. 10–4, Sun. noon–4.*

★ **Poplar Forest.** A must-see on the Thomas Jefferson tour of Virginia is his "occasional retreat," Poplar Forest. The octagonal architecture, now standing in a residential neighborhood and surrounded by only a few remaining poplars, was conceived and built by Jefferson, and he sometimes stayed here between 1806 and 1813. This Palladian hermitage exemplifies the architect's sublime sense of order that is so evident at Monticello. Erected on a slope, the house has a front that's one story high, with a two-story rear elevation. The octagon's center is a square, skylighted dining room flanked by two smaller octagons. The restoration to its Jefferson-era state is ongoing, and likely to continue for years to come. Every July 4 there's a free celebration that includes a reading of the Declaration of Independence and living-history exhibits. ⊠ *1542 Bateman Bridge Rd., Rte. 661, Forest* ☎ *434/525–1806* ⊕ *www.poplarforest.org* ⊠ *$14 full tour, $4 grounds only* ⊙ *Apr.–Nov., Wed.–Mon. 10–4.*

OFF THE
BEATEN
PATH

Fodor'sChoice
★

Appomattox Court House. To many history buffs, the Civil War lives on, but the history books say it ended here, 25 mi east of Lynchburg, on April 9, 1865, when Confederate General Lee surrendered the Army of Northern Virginia to General Grant, leader of pursuing Union forces. There are 27 structures in the national historical park, restored to its 1865 appearance; most can be entered. A highlight is the reconstructed McLean House, in whose parlor the articles of surrender were signed.

✉ *3 mi northeast of Appomattox, on Rte. 24* ☎ *434/352–8987* ⊕ *www.
nps.gov/apco/* ⌨ *June–Aug. $4; Sept.–May $3* ⊙ *Daily 8:30–5.*

Red Hill–Patrick Henry National Memorial. In the town of Brookneal is the
final home of Revolutionary War patriot Patrick Henry, whose "Give
me liberty or give me death" speech inspired a generation. The 1770s
house has been reconstructed on its original site and contains numerous furnishings owned by the Henry family. Henry's grave is also on
the property. ✉ *1250 Red Hill Rd., 35 mi southeast of Lynchburg, off
Rte. 619, Brookneal* ☎ *434/376–2044* ⊕ *www.redhill.org* ⌨ *$6* ⊙ *Apr.–
Oct., daily 9–5; Nov.–Mar., daily 9–4.*

WHERE TO EAT

$$$ ✕ **Depot Grille.** Located on the historic riverfront, Depot Grille offers
AMERICAN classic American favorites including steaks, pasta, chicken, pork bar-
bequed ribs, and lump crab cakes. An extensive kid's menu and the
sound of passing trains make this a good choice for families. ✉ *10
Ninth St., Lynchburg* ☎ *434/846–4464* ⊕ *www.depotgrille.com* ▭ *AE,
MC, V, D.*

$$ ✕ **Shoemakers.** This elegant steak-and-seafood house is in the converted
AMERICAN tobacco warehouse district known as the Bluffwalk. With warm exposed
ⓒ brick walls and an urban sensibility, the restaurant offers a wide variety
of steaks, chops, and classic seafood dishes. Think traditional, with a
variety of cuts and preparations, in addition to seafood standards from
surf 'n turf to shrimp cocktail and lobster bisque. ✉ *1312 Commerce St.*
☎ *434/455–1510* ⊕ *www.shoemakersdining.com* ▭ *AE, MC, V.*

WHERE TO STAY

$ ⬚ **Craddock Terry Hotel.** This former shoe factory and tobacco warehouse
may now be a luxurious boutique hotel, but it still retains a whiff of its
footwear beginnings. In the 1800's, the Craddock-Terry Shoe Company
was the fifth largest in the world, so to pay homage to its roots, the hotel
serves a complimentary Continental breakfast delivered in a shoeshine
box. Located in the Bluffwalk Center, the Craddock Terry is within
walking distance of several restaurants and the Jefferson Brewery, in
addition to the two on-site restaurants. All rooms have scenic views
of the Blue Ridge Mountains or the James River. **Pros:** free breakfast,
parking, and Wi-Fi; historic building. **Cons:** upper price range; rooms
near train tracks can be noisy. ✉ *1312 Commerce St.* ☎ *434/455–1500*
⊕ *www.craddockterryhotel.com* ⤲ *44 rooms* ⌂ *In-room: a/c, refrigerator, Wi-Fi. In-hotel: restaurants, room service, bar, gym, laundry service,
Wi-Fi hotspot, parking (free)* ▭ *AE, D, DC, MC, V.*

SPORTS AND THE OUTDOORS

BIKING

Lynchburg's fine municipal "greenway" system of trails is open to
both bicyclists and hikers. The **Blackwater Creek Natural Area & Bikeway**
(☎ *434/847–1640 City of Lynchburg Parks and Recreation Dept.*) has
more than 12 mi of trails, most of them level and asphalt, which wind
through a pleasant tree-shaded natural area within the city limits. One
trail goes through a 500-foot tunnel. The **Percival's Island Trail**, three
blocks from one edge of the natural area and in the shadow of the

downtown skyline, extends for more than a mile along a narrow strip of land in the middle of the James River.

To rent a bike, contact **Blackwater Creek Bike Rental** (✉ *1611 Concord Tpke.* ☎ *434/845–0293*), which is open weekdays 1 to 5 and weekends from 9 to sunset.

SNOW SPORTS

Liberty Snowflex Centre (✉ *Liberty University* ☎ *434/582–3539* ⊕ *www. liberty.edu/snowflex*) at Liberty University offers both skiing and snow-boarding, a welcome addition for outdoor enthusiasts. Modeled after the European slopes that use this synthetic snow, the slopes on Candlers Mountain have built-in misting devices to keep them slick and enable year-round skiing. This is the first of its kind in the United States and is open to the general public as well as have reserved blocks of time for Liberty's students. Off-peak days are Monday–Thursday with rates of $5 per hour, and weekends are $7 per hour. Equipment rentals are available.

SHENANDOAH NATIONAL PARK

Southern entrance is 18 mi west of Charlottesville via I–81; northern entrance is at Front Royal.

GETTING HERE AND AROUND

There are four entrances to the park, with the northernmost at Front Royal off I–66 and Route 340 and the southernmost at Rockfish Gap, off I–64 and Route 250. Rockfish Gap is also the northernmost entrance to the Blue Ridge Parkway. In between, you can access the park at Thornton Gap via Route 211 and Swift Run Gap via Route 33. Be aware that the speed limit on Skyline Drive is 35 mph. Mileposts begin at 0.0 at the Front Royal entrance and continue to 105 at the southern end. If you're traveling with an RV, camping trailer, or horse trailer, you'll have to shift into low gear frequently and make sure you can clear Mary's Rock Tunnel, south of Thornton Gap, which measures 12'8".

TIMING AND PRECAUTIONS

Skyline Drive and the rest of Shenandoah National Park can get crowded on weekends and holidays, so avoid these times if possible. Winter is a wonderful time to experience the park's rugged beauty with few crowds, but most facilities are closed and bouts of ice and snow bring out barricades on parts of the drive.

ESSENTIALS

Visitor Information (ℹ *Park Superintendent, 3655 US Hwy. 211 E, Luray 22835* ☎ *540/999–3500* ⊕ *www.nps.gov/shen* 🎟 *Park and Skyline Dr. $15 car [$10 car Dec.–Feb.], $10 motorcycle, $8 bicycle or pedestrian [$5 Dec.–Feb.]; tickets are valid 7 days*).

EXPLORING

Shenandoah National Park. Though Shenandoah National Park is only a narrow ribbon on the map, stretching 70 mi along the Blue Ridge but rarely more than 5 mi wide, it is easy to imagine being much deeper in the wilderness as you travel through it or spend a night camping here. Steep, wooded ridges with rocky slopes stand out in the foreground of vistas taking in the Shenandoah Valley to the west and the Piedmont to the east. Skyline Drive traverses the park end to end, from Waynesboro to Front Royal, and is the most common way to see the park. But hikers can find beautiful terrain just yards from the drive on some of the park's 500 mi of trails, trout fishers may wade into more than 25

streams, and riders can rent horses for wilderness trail rides. Those who want to know more about the area's flora and fauna may want to take a guided hike, which naturalists lead daily throughout the season. The seasonal activities of the park are outlined in the *Shenandoah Overlook,* a free newspaper you can pick up on entering the park or on the park's Web site *(see Visitor Information above).*

Fodor's Choice ★ **Skyline Drive.** Alternating between open vistas and forest-hemmed stretches, Skyline Drive offers 105 mi of easily accessible wilderness. Designated as a National Historic Landmark, the two-lane highway runs from Rockfish Gap at Afton, Virginia, to Front Royal. During weekends and holidays it can seem a little too much like city driving— a 35-mph speed limit, rubber-necking leaf-lookers, narrow overlook turnouts, and the occasional black bear sighting can back traffic up uncomfortably. It's best to choose a weekday and allow the entire day; you may want to spend an hour or two resting on one roadside boulder.

■ TIP→ Continue south on Skyline Drive past the park gates and over Interstate 64, and the road becomes the Blue Ridge Parkway, which continues 471 mi south to Cherokee, North Carolina. Unlike Skyline Drive, the parkway is free, and the speed limit is 45 mph.

Luray Caverns. Not only is this the largest cavern in the state, it also features the world's only "stalacpipe organ," composed of stalactites (calcite formations hanging from the ceilings of the caverns) that have been tuned to concert pitch and are tapped to create echoing sound. The organ is played electronically for every tour and may be played manually on special occasions. A one-hour tour begins every 20 minutes. Beyond the organ, Luray Caverns holds plenty of natural beauty, like the Dream Lake that perfectly mirrors back the stalactite formations. It's an easy addition to Skyline Drive, just 9 mi west on U.S. 211. ⊠ *U.S. 211, 101 Cave Hill Rd., Luray* ☎ *540/743–6551* ⊕ *www.luraycaverns. com* 🖃 *$19* ☉ *Mid-Mar.–mid-June, daily 9–6; mid-June–Labor Day, daily 9–7; Labor Day–Oct., daily 9–6; Nov.–mid-Mar., weekdays 9–4, weekends 9–5.*

WHERE TO STAY
PARK-RUN ACCOMMODATIONS

¢–$ 🏨 **Skyland Resort.** At the highest point on Skyline Drive (3,680 feet, milepost 41.7), with views across the Shenandoah Valley, this facility has lodging that ranges from rustic cabins and motel-style rooms to suites. This resort is one of three different properties within the park: **Big Meadows Lodge** (milepost 51.0), originally built by the Civilian Conservation Corps, is in a spectacular setting surrounding by grassy meadows full of deer and wildlife. **Lewis Cabins** (milepost 57.5) is the real deal—very rustic cabins for an authentic outdoor adventure. Since these three properties in the park are in sought-after locations, you'll need to book up to a year in advance. There's no air-conditioning, but days above 80°F are rare at this altitude. **Pros:** stunning scenery; alternative to in-park camping. **Cons:** must plan far in advance; no phones or TVs in many rooms; closed in winter. ✉ *Skyland Resort, Milepost 41.7, Skyline Dr.* ☎ *800/778–2851* ⊕ *www.visitshenandoah.com* ↩ *177 rooms* ♿ *In-room: no phone, no TV (some). In-hotel: restaurant, bar* ▭ *AE, D, DC, MC, V* ⊗ *Closed Dec.–mid-Mar.*

SPORTS AND THE OUTDOORS

CANOEING

At **Downriver Canoe** (✉ *884 Indian Hollow Rd., Rte. 613 near Front Royal, Bentonville* ☎ *540/635–5526 or 800/338–1963* ⊕ *www. downriver.com*), day and overnight trips start at $49 per canoe (or $32 per kayak, $20 per tube, and $79 per raft). **Front Royal Canoe** (✉ *8567 Stonewall Jackson Hwy., U.S. 340, near Front Royal* ☎ *540/635–5440 or 800/270–8808* ⊕ *www.frontroyalcanoe.com*) offers a $20 tube trip as well as canoe, kayak, and raft trips of from one hour up to three days for $45–$150. The company also rents boats and sells fishing accessories. **Shenandoah River Outfitters** (✉ *6502 S. Page Valley Rd., Rte. 684, Luray* ☎ *540/743–4159* ⊕ *www.Shenandoah-river.com*) rents canoes and kayaks for $24 to $90, and tubes from $18.

FISHING

To take advantage of the trout that abound in the 50 streams of Shenandoah National Park, you need a Virginia fishing license; a five-day license costs $16 and it's available in season (early April to mid-October) at concession stands along Skyline Drive. You can purchase them online at ⊕ *www.dgif.virginia.gov/licenses/* or in the park.

HIKING

The **Appalachian Trail** is more than 2,000 mi long, but you don't have to go that far, or even 2,000 feet, along it to see glorious foliage, rock formations, and wildlife. The trail zigzags across Skyline Drive through the park, offering easy access by car, variable hike lengths from a few feet to many miles, and connections with the more than 400 mi of the park's own trail network.

HORSEBACK RIDING

Trail rides leave from the park's Skyland Stables several times daily from April through October, and on weekends in November. The route follows White Oak Canyon trail, which passes several waterfalls; you can choose a one-hour ride or a two-hour ride. It's recommended that you book at least 24 hours in advance. Rides are $30–$50. ✉ *Skyland Lodge, Milepost 41.7, near Luray* ☎ *540/999–2212* ⊗ *Apr.–Oct., daily 8–5; Nov., weekends 8–5.*

SHENANDOAH VALLEY

The fertile hills of the Shenandoah Valley reminded Colonial settlers from Germany, Ireland, and Britain of the homelands they left behind. They brought an agrarian lifestyle and Protestant beliefs that eventually spread across much of the Midwest. Today the valley is full of historic, cultural, and geological places of interest, including Civil War sites; Woodrow Wilson's birthplace and a reproduction of Shakespeare's Globe Theatre, both at Staunton; many beautifully adorned caverns; and the famous hot mineral springs in aptly named Bath County.

ESSENTIALS

Shenandoah Valley Travel Association (✉ I–81, Exit 264 ☐ Box 1040, New Market 22844 ☎ 540/740–3132 or 800/847–4878 ⊕ www.shenandoah.org).

WINCHESTER

129 mi north of Charlottesville, 136 mi northwest of Richmond.

The historic town of Winchester is widely known as the birthplace of one of country music's most beloved stars, Patsy Cline. Cline hit it big when she won the Arthur Godfrey talent show, but died tragically in a plane crash at the peak of her career in 1963. She is buried in Winchester's Shenandoah Memorial Park, where a bell tower was erected in her honor.

Winchester served as a headquarters for Colonel George Washington during the French and Indian War. During the Civil War it was an important crossroads near the front line. It changed hands 72 times during the war, and was General Stonewall Jackson's headquarters for nearly two years.

Today the Old Town features a multiblock pedestrian mall filled with boutiques and restaurants, as well as must-see museums including George Washington's Office Museum and the Old Courthouse Civil War Museum.

GETTING HERE AND AROUND

Since Winchester is only about 75 mi from Washington, D.C., it's a popular weekend retreat for urbanites. In a little over an hour heading west on I–66, visitors are in the beautiful Shenandoah Valley, celebrated for its vast apple orchards during the spring and fall. From Richmond, I–64 runs west to I–81, where there are several exits to Winchester. To reach the historic downtown area, choose the one marked "Route 11 Winchester," as the highway runs through the center of town. Even though the historic downtown with its pedestrian mall is walkable, you'll need a car to visit popular attractions including Belle Grove Plantation, the Museum of the Shenandoah Valley,

TOP CIVIL WAR SITES IN THE REGION

Appomattox Court House National Historical Park (⊕ www.nps.gov/apco)

Cedar Creek and Belle Grove National Park (⊕ www.nps.gov/cebe)

New Market Battlefield State Historical Park (⊕ www2.vmi.edu/museum/nm)

Sailor's Creek Battlefield State Historical Park (⊕ www.dcr.virginia.gov/state_parks/sai.shtml)

Shenandoah Valley Battlefields Foundation (⊕ www.shenandoahatwar.org)

and charming Middletown, all a few miles out of town on Route 11.

TIMING AND PRECAUTIONS
Book early during the spring and fall when the region celebrates the annual Apple Blossom Festival and Apple Harvest. Fog, snow, and ice are common during the winter months, so keep those road conditions in mind when planning a trip.

EXPLORING
Museum of the Shenandoah Valley. Bringing together fine and decorative art collections and multimedia presentations, the Museum of the Shenandoah Valley reflects the region's cultural history. Designed by renowned architect Michael Graves, the museum's modern exterior belies the four centuries of historical artifacts, fine arts, and decorative arts on display inside its mammoth 50,000-square-foot space. In contrast, the Glen Burnie House and gardens, adjacent to the museum, are a gracious walk through the 18th and 19th centuries. The 1736 Georgian country estate that was the home of Winchester's founder, Colonel James Wood, is surrounded by 25 acres of formal gardens. Collections within it include a gallery with furniture, fine arts, and decorative objects gathered by the last family member to live in the house, Julian Wood Glass Jr., who died in 1992. Another gallery assembles shadow-box rooms and miniature furnished houses. ⊠ *901 Amherst St.* ☎ *540/662–1473 or 888/556–5799* ⊕ *www.shenandoahmuseum.org* ⊠ *$12 for museum, house, and gardens; $6–$10 for other combinations* ⊙ *Museum Tues.– Sun. 10–4, house and gardens Mar.–Nov., daily 10–4.*

> **CRAZY ABOUT THE PATSY CLINE TOUR**
>
> Pop in your Patsy Cline greatest hits CD and begin your "Patsy Pilgrimage" at the **Winchester-Frederick Visitors Center** (⊠ *1400 S. Pleasant Valley Rd., Exit 313A I–81)* to peruse their large collection of memorabilia. While you're there, pick up a flyer with directions for a self-guided driving tour to see the country star's childhood home and high school, as well as **Gaunt's Drugstore,** where she worked as teenager manning the soda fountain. The tour takes you throughout Winchester, past the studios of **WINC** where Patsy made her first radio appearance, and ends at **Shenandoah Memorial Park,** her final resting place.

OFF THE BEATEN PATH

State Arboretum of Virginia. This arboretum, 9 mi east of Winchester, has the most extensive boxwood collection in North America. Hands-on workshops and tours are available throughout spring, summer, and fall. You can stroll through the perennial and herb gardens and have a look at more than 8,000 trees. This spot is a wonderful place to bird-watch or to have a picnic. ⊠ *400 Blandy Farm La.* ☎ *540/837–1758* ⊠ *Free* ⊙ *Daily dawn–dusk.*

Stonewall Jackson's Headquarters Museum. The 1854 home of this civil war general is now a museum filled with his personal memorabilia. Jackson used this house as his base of operations during the Valley Campaign in 1861–62. Among the artifacts on display are his prayer book and camp table. The reproduction wallpaper was a gift from the actress Mary Tyler Moore; it was her great-grandfather Lieutenant Colonel Lewis T. Moore who lent Jackson the use of the house. A $10 block ticket purchased at the museum also includes entry to two nearby historic attractions: **George Washington's Office Museum,** a preserved log cabin where Washington briefly lived during the French and Indian War, and **Abram's Delight Museum,** the oldest residence in Winchester. The stone house was owned by Isaac Hollingsworth, a prominent Quaker. ⊠ *415 N. Braddock St.* 🕾 *540/667–3242* ⊕ *www.winchesterhistory.org* 🖙 *$5 each or $10 block ticket* ☼ *Apr.–Oct., Mon.–Sat. 10–4, Sun. noon–4; Nov.–Mar., Fri. and Sat. 10–4, Sun. noon–4.*

WHERE TO EAT

$$$$ ✕**L'Auberge Provencale.** Tucked away in the small town of White Post is
FRENCH a slice of Provence in a historic inn. L'Auberge Provencale is the epicu-
Fodor's Choice rean getaway of choice for Washingtonians, and it's true that Chef Alain
★ Borel has been on the gourmand radar for years. Borel and his wife Celeste grow their own herbs, vegetables, and fruit, and source their other sustainable foods locally from the bounty of the Valley. L'Auberge features not only an excellent list of French vintages, but many of Virginia's top wines as well. Reserve way ahead of time for the authentic Provencale five-course prix-fixe dinner ($90 per person). ⊠ *13630 Lord Fairfax Hwy, Boyce Post* 🕾 *540/837–1375 or 800/638–1702* 🖙 *Reservations essential* 🖃 *AE, D, MC, V* ☼ *Closed Jan.*

$$$ ✕**Violino Ristorante Italiano.** Homemade pasta—about 20 different
ITALIAN kinds—fills the menu in this cheery, yellow-stucco restaurant in the city's Old Town. Owners Franco and Marcella Stocco and their son Riccardo serve up their native northern Italian cuisine, including lobster *pansotti* (lobster-filled ravioli in a sauce of white wine and lemon). Try the Trio Violino, an antipasto platter with duck breast prosciutto, homemade venison bresaola, and duck salami with a raspberry vinaigrette. A strolling violinist entertains diners on weekends. The outdoor patio, enclosed by potted plants, is a quiet spot in the midst of street bustle. ⊠ *181 N. Loudoun St.* 🕾 *540/667–8006* 🖃 *AE, D, DC, MC, V* ☼ *Closed Sun.*

WHERE TO STAY

$ 🖼**The George Washington Hotel.** Located within walking distance of all of the charming town's attractions, this historic hotel once hosted the many celebrities, such as Ed Sullivan, who served as Grand Marshall at the Shenandoah Valley Apple Blossom Parade. Originally built in 1924, the stunning lobby with its original Tennessee marble floors features a pictorial history of the grand hotel, along with a hip new lounge and upscale restaurant called the Dancing Goat. As it's now part of the Wyndham group, guests can expect rooms furnished with period reproductions, luxury bedding, and modern amenities from flat screens to high-speed Internet. **Pros:** great location in historic downtown; pet friendly. **Cons:** smallish rooms; can be noisy when hosting special events in the ballroom. ⊠ *103 E. Picadilly St., Winchester* 🕾 *540/678–4700* ⊕ *www.wyndham.com* 🖙 *90 rooms* 🖙 *In-room: a/c, Wi-Fi, refrigerator (some), safe. In-hotel: Wi-Fi, restaurant, bar, pet-friendly* 🖃 *AE, D, MC, V.*

$$–$$$ 🖼**L'Auberge Provencale.** Chef-owner Alain Borel and his wife Celeste,
Fodor's Choice of Avignon, France, bring the warm elegance of the south of France
★ to this 1750s country inn, originally a sheep farm owned by Lord Fairfax. Rooms are eclectically decorated with French art and fabrics,

5

and Victorian wicker and antiques; some even have fireplaces. Breakfast includes fresh homemade croissants and apple crepes with maple syrup. This is considered one of the most romantic inns in Virginia. The L'Auberge Provencale restaurant itself is also in high demand *(see full review above).* **Pros:** European luxury; stellar cuisine at in-house restaurant. **Cons:** limited number of rooms; must reserve well in advance. ✉ *13630 Lord Fairfax Hwy., Boyce Post* ☎ *540/837–1375 or 800/638–1702* ⊕ *www.laubergeprovencale.com* ⇨ *80 rooms, 6 suites* △ *In-room: Wi-Fi, no phone TV (some). In-hotel: restaurant, pool, Wi-Fi, no kids under 10* ▭ *AE, D, MC, V* ⊘ *Closed Jan.* ⦿| *BP.*

$ 🖼 **Old Waterstreet Inn.** The location, just two blocks from Winchester's pedestrian mall, is a major selling point for this charming historic house. Rooms are furnished with period pieces, and two have working fireplaces. A full breakfast, well-stocked pantry for snacks and sodas, and free parking are included in the rate. **Pros:** good location; great value with free breakfast, snacks, and parking. **Cons:** limited availability; no kids under 12; no pets. ✉ *217 W. Boscawen St., Winchester* ☎ *540/665–6777* ⊕ *www.oldwaterstreetinn.com* ⇨ *5 rooms* △ *In-room: a/c, no phone, TV (some), Wi-Fi. In-hotel: Wi-Fi hotspot, parking (free), no kids under 12* ▭ *MC, V.*

MIDDLETOWN

6 mi south of Winchester.

Middletown has one of the area's loveliest historic homes. The section of Route 11 that makes up this small town's main street contains a few quirky antique shops, as well as the Wayside Theater, home to one of Virginia's oldest regional performing companies.

GETTING HERE AND AROUND

Middletown is just a few miles outside of downtown Winchester on Route 11.

EXPLORING

Belle Grove. Both an elegant farmhouse and 100-acre working farm, Belle Grove is a monument to the rural and the refined, two qualities that exist in harmony in the architecture here and throughout the region. Constructed in 1797 out of limestone quarried on the property, the building reflects the influence of Thomas Jefferson, said to have been a consultant. Originally built for Major Isaac Hite and his wife Nelly (President James Madison's sister), this was the headquarters of the Union general Philip Sheridan during the Battle of Cedar Creek (1864), a crucial defeat for the Confederacy. Part of the battle was fought on the farm. ✉ *336 Belle Grove Rd.* ☎ *540/869–2028* ⊕ *www.bellegrove. org* 🎫 *$5* ⊘ *Apr.–Oct., Mon.–Sat. 10–3:15, Sun. 1–4:15; Nov., Sat. 10–4, Sun. noon–5.*

WHERE TO STAY

$$–$$$ 🖼 **The Inn at Vaucluse Springs.** Midway between Winchester and Belle
★ Grove Plantation, the Inn at Vaucluse Springs sits on 100 acres of rolling orchards. The 200-year-old Manor House serves as the gathering spot for an elegant three-course breakfast and end-of-the-day

socializing. Six private guesthouses sit on the property including the Old Mill House, once an artist's studio, on the spring's edge, and the Gallery Guest House with panoramic meadow views. Innkeepers Neil and Barry Myers offer genial Southern hospitality and elegant accommodations have earned them top accolades for almost two decades. Snacks, tea, and hearty organic breakfast are included in the rate. **Pros:** small retreat in gorgeous apple-orchard setting; first-class organic breakfast. **Cons:** hard to find; a bit removed from local sites. ⊠ *231 Vaucluse Spring La., Stephens City* ☎ *540/862–0200 or 800/869–0525* ⊕ *www.vauclusespring.com* ⟿ *6 guesthouses* ⌂ *In-room: no phone, a/c, no TV. In-hotel: no kids under 10* ⊟ *AE, MC, V.*

EN ROUTE

The **Strasburg Antique Emporium** (⊠ *150 N. Massanutten St., Strasburg* ☎ *540/465–3711* ⊕ *www.strasburgemporium.com* ⊗ *Fri. and Sat. 10–6, Sun.–Thurs. 10–5*), 5 mi south of Middletown, covers 1.4 acres. It's in the quirky and historic downtown of Strasburg, which was settled by Germans. Inside the emporium, more than 100 dealers and artisans sell everything from furniture to jewelry to vintage clothing.

NEW MARKET

35 mi southwest of Middletown via I–81.

Founded primarily by German settlers of the Mennonite and Lutheran faiths, the town's first foray into industry was printing. New Market's Historic District is on the National Register of Historic Places and is also a Virginia Historic Landmark, and the small town played a key role in the Civil War. Stonewall Jackson's troops marched through the small town several times during the war and the 1864 Battle of New Market is reenacted every May on the grounds of the Hall of Valor Civil War Museum.

GETTING HERE AND AROUND

Located about 40 miles southwest of Winchester off I–81, New Market is an easy side trip and is especially interesting for Civil War buffs. You can walk throughout the historic district, but you'll need a car to visit the battlefield.

TIMING

The **Shenandoah Valley Apple Blossom Festival** (☎ *540/662–3864* ⊕ *www.thebloom.com* ✉ *Free*) has been, for more than 80 years, the biggest event of the year. Held in April, the 10-day festival includes more than 30 events including a huge parade led by a celebrity grand marshall. The apple industry, once the largest employer in the valley, is celebrated with food from apple candy to apple butter.

EXPLORING

New Market Battlefield Historical Park. At New Market, the Confederates had a victory at the late date of 1864. Inside the Hall of Valor, in the 260-acre New Market Battlefield Historical Park, a stained-glass window mosaic commemorates the battle, in which 257 Virginia Military Institute cadets, some as young as 15, were mobilized to improve the odds against superior Union numbers; 10 were killed. This circular building contains a chronology of the war, and a short film deals with Stonewall Jackson's legendary campaign in the Shenandoah Valley. A farmhouse that figured in the fighting still stands on the premises. The battle is reenacted at the park each May. ⊠ *8895 George Collins Pkwy.* ☎ *540/740–3101 or 866/515–1864* ⊕ *www.vmi.edu/newmarket* ✉ *$10* ☯ *Daily 9–5.*

NIGHTLIFE AND THE ARTS

The **Shenandoah Valley Music Festival** (⊠ *102 N. Main St.* ☎ *540/459–3396* ⊕ *www.musicfest.org*) brings classical, jazz, and folk music to the Allegheny Mountains on weekends from May to September. The events are held at the Orkney Springs Hotel, an early-19th-century spa that's now an Episcopal retreat. Arts and crafts displays and an ice-cream social precede each concert. Concertgoers can sit on the lawn or in one of two pavilions for around $25–$45; call ahead to reserve tickets.

The Wayside Theatre (⊠ *7853 Main St., Middletown* ☎ *540/869–1776* ⊕ *www.waysidetheatre.org*) is the second-oldest regional theater company in Virginia and the intimate venue has been beautifully restored. Grab a bit to eat at the adjoining Curtain Call Café, open before and after performances and during intermission. Check the Web site for the seasons schedule.

HARRISONBURG

18 mi southwest of New Market via Exit 251 from I–81.

Settled in 1739, Harrisonburg is a stronghold of Mennonites, spotted around town driving horse-drawn buggies. The 10-block historic downtown, listed on the National Register of Historic Places and as one of Virginia's Historic Landmarks, was recognized as a Preserve America Community for its revitalization efforts. It contains locally-owned restaurants, shops, and galleries, as well as several museums. The Harrisonburg Farmer's Market is also held in this district. The city is also a center of higher education, with James Madison University and Eastern Mennonite College in town and Bridgewater College nearby.

The **Hardesty-Higgins House Visitor Center,** located in an 1848 Georgian Greek revival on South Main Street is the center of the historic district and home to the visitor center. Harrisonburg is also the home of James Madison University, where you can stroll through a world of natural beauty at the **Edith J. Carrier Arboretum and Botanical Gardens** (⊕ *www.jmu.edu/arboretum*).

GETTING HERE AND AROUND

Heading south on I–81, Harrisonburg is 18 miles from New Market. Many of the region's Mennonites still drive horse-drawn buggies, so be on the lookout on the secondary roads and highways in this rural region. The city itself, home to James Madison University, combines the energy of the college crowd with its historic past, and the visitor center is located in the heart of town in the historic Hardesty-Higgins House.

EXPLORING

Virginia Quilt Museum. A resource center for the study of the role of quilts and quilting in American culture, the Virginia Quilt Museum hosts exhibits of significant work by both early and contemporary quilt artisans. Located in the historic Warren-Sipe House, there's also a Civil War history room. ⊠ *301 S. Main St.* ☎ *540/433–3818* ⊕ *www. vaquiltmuseum.org* ✉ *$5* ☉ *Tues.– Sat. 10–4.*

WHERE TO EAT AND STAY

$–$$ ✕ **Clementine's Café.** This lively
AMERICAN downtown eatery was voted "Best Live Music Venue" in a reader's poll in a local publication and is also lauded for its great sandwiches and burgers. The dinner menu features steaks, pasta, and seafood

with Southern sides like mashed potatoes and seasonal vegetables. The restaurant is housed in the former Strand Theater in the historic district, and hosts live bands from rockabilly and country to bluegrass and jazz on Friday and Saturday nights. ⊠ *153 S. Main St., Harrisonburg* ☎ *540/801–8881* ⊕ *www.clementinecafe.com* ▤ *AE, MC, V.*

¢–$ ✕ **Dave's Taverna.** Get a bird's-eye view of Harrisonburg from the roof-
GREEK top dining area at Dave's, an award-winnning and family-owned local favorite. Like many casual Greek eateries, the menu runs from American classics like burgers and pizzas to Greek and Italian fare from souvlaki and Greek chicken to caprese salad and linguine. But vegetarians need not worry, as veggie pitas and burgers round out the menu. ⊠ *121 S. Main St.* ☎ *540/564–1487* ▤ *MC, V.*

$$–$$$ ⊞ **By the Side of the Road Inn and Cottages.** This 1789 home features four luxurious suites and three intimate cottages overlooking the rolling hills of Harrisonburg. The inn combines 21st-century amenities with the Old World elegance of featherbeds and fireplaces. The three cottages feature whirlpool spa tubs set in front of the fireplace and 4-inch-thick featherbeds. All rooms and suites are furnished with period antiques and reproductions from Colonial in the 1790s main house to Victorian in the 1840s addition. **Pros:** elegant rooms; fireplaces; gourmet breakfast; close to Skyline Drive and the Blue Ridge. **Cons:** expensive option for the area; limited availability; no pets ⊠ *491 Garbers Church Rd.* ☎ *540/801–0430* ⊕ *www.bythesideoftheroad.com* ⤶ *4 suites, 3 cottages* ♿ *In-room: a/c, refigerator (some), DVD (some), Wi-Fi. In-hotel: Wi-Fi hotspot, no kids under 13* ▤ *D, MC, V.*

¢–$ ⊞ **Joshua Wilton House.** A row of trees guards the privacy of this circa-
★ 1888 B&B decorated in Victorian style and set on a large yard at the edge of the "Old Town" district. The sunroom and back patio are built for relaxation. Ask for Room 4; it has a lace-draped canopy bed and a turret sitting area with a view of the Blue Ridge Mountains looming over Main Street. Room 2 has a fireplace. The restaurant's menu changes daily, its components supplied by many small, local organic farmers. **Pros:** full breakfast; charming decor; nice downtown location. **Cons:** few amenities; limited number of rooms. ⊠ *412 S. Main St.* ☎ *888/294–5866 or 540/434–4464* ⊕ *www.joshuawilton.com* ⤶ *5 rooms* ♿ *In-room: a/c, no TV, Wi-Fi. In-hotel: restaurant, no kids under 12* ▤ *AE, MC, V* ⓘⓞⓘ *BP.*

DAYTON

2 mi west of Harrisonburg via Rte. 33 off I–81.

Dayton is best known for its large Mennonite population, whose black horse-drawn buggies share the road with latter-day SUVs, and for its extensive farmers' market with handcrafted goods and foods from the region.

GETTING HERE AND AROUND

Also home to a large Mennonite population, Dayton is just two miles west of Harrisonburg on Route 33. Be sure to visit its farmers' market a bit south of town on Route 42, also known as John Wayland Highway.

EXPLORING

Harrisonburg–Rockingham Historical Society. Displays of multimedia folk art reflect the largely German and Scotch-Irish culture of the valley. One Civil War exhibit includes an electric map that traces Stonewall Jackson's famous 1862 Valley Campaign. ⊠ *382 High St.* ☎ *540/879–2616 or 540/879–2681* ⊕ *www.heritagecenter.com* ☋ *$5* ⊗ *Mon.–Sat. 10–4.*

The Daniel Harrison House. Listed on the National Register of Historic Landmarks and operated by the historical society, the Daniel Harrison House is named for Dayton's first settler and is the oldest house in the town. It's also called Fort Harrison, a nod to its fortified stone and frontier style. Costumed interpreters discuss how the furnishings—beds with ropes as slats and hand-quilted comforters—were made. Artifacts on display come from recent excavations undertaken adjacent to the house. ⊠ *355 North Main St.* ☎ *540/879–2280* ⊕ *www.heritagecenter. com* ☋ *Donation welcome* ⊗ *Mid-May–Oct., weekends 1–5.*

SHOPPING

The **Dayton Farmers Market** (⊠ *3105 John Wayland Hwy., Rte. 42, south of Dayton* ☎ *540/879–3801* ⊕ *www.daytonfarmersmarket.com*), an 18,000-square-foot area, has homemade baked goods and fresh fruits and vegetables as well as butter churns and ceramic speckle ware, made by the Mennonites who live in the area. Don't be surprised to see locals trotting by in their horse-and-buggy. It's a good place to mingle with the craftspeople, as well as with students from James Madison University in nearby Harrisonburg. It's open Thursday through Saturday from 9 to 6.

STAUNTON

27 mi south of Dayton via I–81, 11 mi west of southern end of Skyline Dr. at Waynesboro off I–64.

Staunton (pronounced *stan*-ton) was once the seat of government of the vast Augusta County, which formed in 1738 and encompassed present-day West Virginia, Kentucky, Ohio, Illinois, Indiana, and the Pittsburgh area. After the state's General Assembly fled here from the British in 1781, Staunton was briefly the state's capital. Woodrow Wilson (1856–1924), the nation's 27th president and the eighth president from Virginia, was a native son, and Staunton is home to the Woodrow Wilson Presidential Library and Museum.

GETTING HERE AND AROUND

Staunton is conveniently located at the intersections of I–64 and I–81 in the Shenandoah Valley. Coming from Skyline Drive, Staunton is just over 10 mi west of the southernmost entrance point at Waynesboro off I–64. Heading south on I–81, it's 27 mi south of Dayton. One of its most popular attractions, the Woodrow Wilson Birthplace and Presidential Library is located in the historic downtown area on North Coalter Street and the visitor center is nearby on New Street.

TOURS

The Historic Staunton Foundation offers free one-hour walking tours Saturday morning at 10, May through October, departing from the Woodrow Wilson Birthplace (24 North Coalter Street). A brochure for a self-guided tour is available from the Staunton/Augusta County Travel Information Center.

ESSENTIALS

Train Station **Train Station** (✉ *1 Middlebrook Ave.*).

Visitor Information **Historic Staunton Foundation** (✉ *20 South New St.* ☎ *540/885–7676* ⊕ *www.historicstaunton.org*). **Staunton Visitor Center** (✉ *116 W. Beverly St.* ☎ *540/332–3865* ⊕ *www.visitstaunton.com*).

EXPLORING

★ **Frontier Culture Museum.** An outdoor living-history museum, the Frontier Culture Museum re-creates agrarian life in America. The four illustrative farmsteads, American, Scotch-Irish, German, and English, were painstakingly moved from their original sites and reassembled on the museum grounds. A West African village and an American Indian village are also among the exhibits. The livestock and plants here resemble the historic breeds and varieties as closely as possible. Special programs and activities, held throughout the year, include soap and broom making, cornhusking bees, and supper and barn dances. ✉ *1250 Richmond Rd., off I–81, Exit 222 to Rte. 250 W* ☎ *540/332–7850* ⊕ *www.frontiermuseum. org* 🎟 *$10* ⊘ *Dec.–Mar., daily 10–4; Apr.–Dec., daily 9–5.*

Seven miles east of Staunton, the **P. Buckley Moss Museum** is a free full-scale gallery of paintings and drawings by one of the Valley's most recognized artists. Moss, who moved to Waynesboro in 1964, was inspired by the quiet dignity and simplicity of the "plain people"—those in the Mennonite communities of the Shenandoah Valley—and has made these neighbors her subject matter. Don't miss the large-scale dollhouse built into a staircase. Her studio, a converted barn about 2 mi from the museum, opens a few times a year to the public. ✉ *150 P Buckley Moss Dr., I–64, Exit 94, Waynesboro 540/949–6473* ⊕ *www.pbuckleymoss. com* 🎟 *Free* ⊘ *Mon.–Sat. 10–6, Sun. 12:30–5:30.*

Woodrow Wilson Presidential Library and Museum. Interactive exhibits and displays children can touch make this museum family-friendly. The collection features period antiques, items from Wilson's political career, and some original pieces that belonged to Wilson's father, a Presbyterian minister. Wilson's presidential limousine, a 1919 Pierce-Arrow sedan, is on display in the garage. An interactive World War I trench exhibit simulates the soldier's experiences and there's also a hands-on kids' corner. ✉ *18 N. Coalter St.* ☎ *540/885–0897 or 888/496–6376* ⊕ *www. woodrowwilson.org* 🖻 *$14* ☉ *Mar.–Oct., Mon.–Sat. 9–5, Sun. noon–5; Nov.–Feb., Mon.–Sat. 10–4, Sun. noon–4.*

WHERE TO EAT

¢–$

SOUTHERN

★

✗ **Mrs. Rowe's Restaurant.** A homey restaurant with plenty of booths, Rowe's has been operated by the same family since 1947 and enjoys a rock-solid reputation for inexpensive and delicious Southern meals. The fried chicken—skillet-cooked to order—is a standout. A local breakfast favorite is oven-hot biscuits topped with gravy (your choice of sausage, tenderloin, or creamy chipped beef). For dessert, try the mince pie in fall or the rhubarb cobbler in summer. ✉ *74 Rowe Rd., I–81, Exit 222* ☎ *540/886–1833* ⊕ *www.mrsrowes.com/index.html* 🖃 *D, MC, V.*

$$$

SOUTHERN

Fodor's Choice

★

✗ **Staunton Grocery.** Featuring contemporary interpretations of Southern classics, the chef here focuses on local produce from the valley, and the menu changes seasonally. The Grocery is in the center of historic downtown Staunton. Look for pork belly with plums in a red-wine reduction or Southern fried quail on braised greens. Tasting menus of four or six courses are also offered, with wine pairings suggested by the house sommelier. ✉ *105 W. Beverly St.* ☎ *540/886–6880* ⊕ *www. stauntongrocery.com* 🖃 *AE, D, MC, V* ☉ *Closed Mon.*

WHERE TO STAY

$$–$$$

🏨 **Stonewall Jackson Hotel.** Built in 1928, this restored hotel in historic downtown combines old-world charm with modern amenities. The charming lobby has a fireplace, but the rooms are definitely contemporary Colonial in style. With more than 100 rooms, the hotel also has an indoor pool, fitness center, business center, lounge, restaurant, and conference facilities. The historic past is reflected in the lobby's period decor. **Pros:** extras like free Internet and daily paper; pet friendly; great location. **Cons:** busy conference hotel; standard room decor. ✉ *24 S. Market St.* ☎ *540/885–4848 or 866/880–0024* ⊕ *www. stonewalljacksonhotel.com* ⤴ *124 rooms* ⚭ *In-room: a/c, Wi-Fi. In-hotel: pool, gym, some pets allowed* 🖃 *AE, D, MC, V.*

NIGHTLIFE AND THE ARTS
THEATER

★ Experience Shakespeare's plays the way the Elizabethans did at the **American Shakespeare Center** (✉ *10 S. Market St.* ☎ *540/885–5588* ⊕ *www.americanshakespearecenter.com*), the world's only re-creation of the bard's indoor playhouse, which has gained acclaim for its attention to detail. Unlike the open-air Globe Theatre styled around a courtyard, this theater was, in its time, an innovative indoor winter venue. As in 17th-century London, most seating consists of benches (modern seat backs and cushions are available), and some stools are right on stage.

LEXINGTON

30 mi south of Staunton via I–81.

Two deeply traditional Virginia colleges sit side by side in this town, each with a memorial to a soldier who was also a man of peace.

GETTING HERE AND AROUND

Lexington is located 30 mi south of Staunton on I–81. From Richmond, take I–64 west to I–81 south, which intersect at Staunton. You'll need a car to visit Natural Bridge, which is actually about 20 mi south of the town, or if you want to explore the campus life at the town's two famous universities, Washington & Lee and the Virginia Military Institute.

TOURS For $16 the Lexington Carriage Company will take visitors around town in a horse-drawn carriage for 45–50 minutes, from April through October. Tours begin and end at the Lexington Visitor Center, where a self-guided walking-tour brochure of the town is also available.

ESSENTIALS

Visitor Information **Lexington Carriage Company** (☎ 540/463–5647 ⊕ www.lexcarriage.com). **Lexington Visitor Center** (✉ 106 E. Washington St. ☎ 540/463–3777).

EXPLORING

George C. Marshall Museum. This museum preserves the memory of the World War II army chief of staff. Exhibits trace his brilliant career, which began when he was aide-de-camp to John "Black Jack" Pershing in World War I and culminated when, as secretary of state, he devised the Marshall Plan, a strategy for reviving postwar Western Europe. Marshall's Nobel Peace Prize is on display; so is the Oscar won by his aide Frank McCarthy, who produced the Academy Award–winning Best Picture of 1970, *Patton.* An electronically narrated map tells the story of World War II. ✉ *VMI campus, Letcher Ave.* ☎ *540/463–2083* ⊕ *www. marshallfoundation.org* ▣ *$5* ⊗ *Tues.–Sat. 9–5, Sun. 1–5.*

Stonewall Jackson House. Confederate general Jackson's private life is on display at the Stonewall Jackson House, where he is revealed as a dedicated Presbyterian who was devoted to physical fitness, careful with money, musically inclined, and fond of gardening. The general lived here only two years, while teaching physics and military tactics to the cadets, before leaving for his command in the Civil War. This is the only house he ever owned; it's furnished now with period pieces and some of his belongings. ✉ *8 E. Washington St.* ☎ *540/463–2552* ⊕ *www. stonewalljackson.org* ▣ *$8* ⊗ *Mon.–Sat. 9–5, Sun. 1–5.*

Virginia Military Institute *(VMI).* Adjacent to Washington and Lee University are the imposing Gothic buildings of the Virginia Military Institute, founded in 1839 and the nation's oldest state-supported military college. With an enrollment of about 1,300 cadets, the institute has admitted women since 1997. After a two-year expansion and renovation effort, the **Virginia Military Institute Museum,** now includes a 3,000-square-foot main exhibit hall in Jackson Memorial Hall, dedicated to the VMI Heritage. Displays include 15,000 artifacts, including Stonewall Jackson's stuffed and mounted horse, Little Sorrel, and the general's coat, pierced by the bullet that killed him at Chancellorsville, and on the lower level, the Henry Stewart antique firearms collection. ✉ *415 Letcher Ave.* ☎ *540/464–7334* ⊕ *www.vmi.edu* ▣ *$3* ⊗ *Daily 9–5.*

Washington and Lee University. The ninth-oldest college in the United States, Washington and Lee University was founded in 1749 as Augusta Academy and later renamed Washington College in gratitude for a donation from George Washington. After Robert E. Lee's term as its president (1865–70), it received its current name. Today, with 2,000 students, the university occupies a campus of white-column, redbrick buildings around a central colonnade. Twentieth-century alumni include the late Supreme Court Justice Lewis Powell, newsman Roger Mudd, and novelist Tom Wolfe. The campus's **Lee Chapel and Museum** contains many relics of the Lee family. Edward Valentine's statue of the recumbent general, behind the altar, is especially moving: the pose is natural and the expression gentle, a striking contrast to most other monumental art. Here you can sense the affection and reverence that Lee inspired. ⊠ *204 W. Washington St.* ☎ *540/458–8400* ⊕ *www.chapelappswlu. edu* ⊒ *Free* ⊙ *Chapel Apr.–Oct., Mon.–Sat. 9–5, Sun. 1–5; Nov.–Mar., Mon.–Sat. 9–4, Sun. 1–4. Campus tours Apr.–Oct., weekdays 10–4, Sat. 9:45–noon; Jan.–Mar., weekdays 10 and noon, Sat. 11.*

OFF THE
BEATEN
PATH

ⓒ

Fodor's Choice
★

Natural Bridge of Virginia. About 20 mi south of Lexington, this impressive limestone arch (which supports Route 11) has been gradually carved out by Cedar Creek, which rushes through 215 feet below. The Monacan Native American tribe called it the Bridge of God. Surveying the structure for Lord Halifax, George Washington carved his own initials in the stone; Thomas Jefferson bought it (and more than 150 surrounding acres) from King George III. The after-dark sound-and-light show may be overkill, but viewing and walking under the bridge itself and along the wooded pathway beyond are worth the price of admission. On the property are dizzying caverns that descend 34 stories, a wax museum, a toy museum, and an 18th-century village constructed by the Monacan Indian Nation. ⊠ *15 Appledore La.* ☎ *540/291–2121 or 800/533–1410* ⊕ *www.naturalbridgeva.com* ⊒ *Caverns $14, Bridge $18, all attractions $26* ⊙ *Mar.–Nov., daily 8 am–dark.*

WHERE TO EAT AND STAY

$

AMERICAN

✕ **The Palms.** The original building, circa 1836, served as a public library and debating hall before becoming a retail space. In the Victorian era, it was an ice cream parlor and today, it houses a full-service restaurant with both indoor and alfresco dining. Wood booths line the walls of the plant-filled room; the pressed-metal ceiling is original. Specialties on the American menu include broccoli-cheese soup, charbroiled meats, and teriyaki chicken. The menu features traditional soups and salads, burgers and sandwiches, and steaks and pasta. The Palms is open for lunch as well. ⊠ *101 W. Nelson St.* ☎ *540/463–7911* ⊕ *www. thepalmslexington.com* ⌂ *Reservations not accepted* ⊟ *AE, D, MC, V.*

$

▥ **Maple Hall.** For a taste of Southern history, spend a night at this country inn dating to 1850. Once a plantation house, it's on 56 acres 6 mi north of Lexington. Individually decorated rooms have period antiques and modern amenities; most have gas log fireplaces as well. On the property are a fishing pond and miles of scenic walking trails. Several marquee names have slept here, from Elizabeth Taylor and Richard Gere to Bill Clinton and Lady Bird Johnson. **Pros:** historic setting; outdoor activities. **Cons:** a bit far from downtown; limited number of rooms. ⊠ *11 N. Main St.* ☎ *540/463–6693 or 877/283–9680* ⊕ *www. lexingtonhistoricinns.com/maplehall.htm* ⬐ *17 rooms, 4 suites* ♿ *In-room: a/c. In-hotel: restaurant, tennis court, pool* ⊟ *D, MC, V* �ⓞ *BP.*

¢–$ ⌂ **Natural Bridge Hotel**. The first hotel on this site was built in 1828, but visitors have been attracted to the Natural Bridge since Colonial times. Within walking distance of the spectacular rock arch of the same name (there's also a shuttle bus), the Colonial-style brick hotel has a beautiful location as well as numerous recreational facilities. The hotel is similar in style to The Homestead resort (⇨ *see below*) but at a fraction of the price. Long porches with rocking chairs allow leisurely appreciation of the Blue Ridge Mountains, and rooms are done in a Colonial Virginia style. **Pros:** walk to the Natural Bridge; budget-friendly; stunning scenery. **Cons:** far from local towns; larger hotel may lack Southern hospitality feel. ✉ *15 Appledore Lane, Natural Bridge* ☎ *540/291–2121 or 800/533–1410* ⊕ *www.naturalbridgeva.com* ➥ *150 rooms* ♿ *In-room: a/c, Wi-FiIn-hotel: restaurant, bar, tennis courts, pool, Wi-Fi hotspot* ▭ *AE, D, DC, MC, V.*

$ ⌂ **Sheridan Livery Inn**. In the heart of downtown, this historic property is within walking distance of shops, restaurants, and attractions. Built in 1887 as the stable and carriage service of prominent Lexington businessman John Sheridan, the historic structure was carefully renovated and opened as an inn in 1997. Rooms are spacious, with high ceilings, and include the charm of 19th-century furnishings along with modern amenities like Wi-Fi. A Continental breakfast is included in the room rate. **Pros:** great location; good breakfast. **Cons:** only 15 rooms; no pets. ✉ *35 N. Main St., Lexington* ☎ *540/464–1887* ⊕ *www.sheridanliveryinn.com* ➥ *12 rooms, 3 suites* ♿ *In-room: a/c, Wi-Fi. In-hotel: restaurant, bar* ▭ *AE, MC, V* ⦿| *BP.*

BATH COUNTY

20 mi northwest of Lexington via Rte. 39.

Bath County, known as the Allegheny Highlands, is where Virginia's rugged outdoors and refined elegance intermingle delightfully. Amid its steep ridges and dense forests is The Homestead, a historic and elegant resort. Forgotten when the C&O Railroad moved its headquarters from Clifton Forge, this region is going through a renaissance. The county's name is fitting: healing thermal springs were what originally brought visitors to town in the 1700s. The sulfurous waters still flow at Warm Springs, Hot Springs, and Bolar Springs, their temperatures ranging from 77°F to 104°F. Thomas Jefferson designed the octagonal buildings that house the Jefferson Pools, now operated by The Homestead.

GETTING HERE AND AROUND

Bath County is about a three-hour drive from Richmond on I–64, but Amtrak also services Clifton Forge. Trains only run a few times a week from Richmond, but daily from Charlottesville and Washington, DC, and they're a wonderful way to soak up the stunning mountain vistas.

TIMING AND PRECAUTIONS

In winter the mountain roads can be treacherous, and throughout the year, keep an eye out for wildlife from deer to badgers.

WHERE TO EAT

$–$$ ✕ **The Company Store.** The 19th-
AMERICAN   century mining company commis-
sary in Low Moor is now a local
gathering spot, with the ambience
of an earlier era supplied by its
jukebox and a broad selection of
merchandise from country ham,
vintage postcards, and penny candy

> **DID YOU KNOW?**
>
> In Virginia, Allegheny is spelled with an "e", but across the border in West Virginia, the mountain range's name is spelled Alleghany with an "a."

to household products, local art, and Virginia wines. Chef Michel Neu-
telings, whose background includes more than two decades of experience at resorts including The Homestead, has turned this spot into a
dining destination worth the drive, featuring a seasonal menu sourced
locally. In fall you might get grilled pork chops in an apple-cider reduc-
tion or butternut squash with chestnuts, while in other seasons updated
classics like rack of lamb or fire-grilled prime sirloin with a red-wine-
and-shallot sauce. There's also a lounge with live music for weekend
entertainment. ⊠ *100 Old Church St., Low Moor* ☎ *540/862–0098*
⊕ *www.thecostorelowmoor.com* ☐ *AE, MC, V.*

$$–$$$ ✕ **Waterwheel Restaurant.** Part of a complex of five historic buildings,
AMERICAN   this restaurant is in a gristmill that dates from 1700. A walk-in wine
★   cellar, set among the gears of the original waterwheel, has 100 wine
selections; diners may step in and choose for themselves. The dining
area is decorated with Currier & Ives and Audubon prints. Some menu
favorites are fresh smoked trout and chicken Fantasio (breast of chicken
stuffed with wild rice, sausage, apple, and pecans). Desserts include such
Old Virginny recipes as a deep-dish apple pie baked with bourbon. On
Sunday look for the hearty but affordable brunch. ⊠ *128 Old Mill Rd.,
Grist Mill Sq., Warm Springs* ☎ *540/839–2231* ☐ *D, MC, V* ⊘ *Closed
Tues. Nov.–May.*

WHERE TO STAY

$$$–$$$$ 🏨 **The Homestead.** For centuries, American glitterati have retreated to
Fodor's Choice   this genteel Southern resort to soak in the healing springs and pur-
★   sue their recreational passions. While the grand lobby still reflects the
elegance and formality of the early 19th century, The Homestead has a
casual atmosphere that caters to outdoor enthusiasts. Daytime activities
include far more than shuffleboard: there are three championship-grade
18-hole golf courses, 4 mi of streams stocked with rainbow trout, 100
mi of riding trails, skeet and trap shooting, and nine ski slopes (The
Homestead was the site of the South's first downhill skiing in 1959).
The venue has evolved from a country spa to a 15,000-acre resort-and-
conference facility. Rooms in the sprawling redbrick building, built in
1891, have Georgian-style furnishings; some have fireplaces. European-
style meal plans are a better value than paying just the room rate. **Pros:**
Southern luxury; outdoor activities; even the spa has history. **Cons:**
daily resort charge; everything costs extra, even coffee; size can be over-
whelming. ⊠ *Rte. 220, Hot Springs* ☎ *540/839–1766 or 800/838–1766*
⊕ *www.thehomestead.com* 🛏 *429 rooms, 77 suites* ⚐ *In-room: a/c,
Wi-Fi. In-hotel: 6 restaurants, golf courses, tennis courts, pools, spa,
bicycles, gym* ☐ *AE, D, DC, MC, V* ⦿ *EP.*

$–$$ ☷ **Inn at Gristmill Square**. Occupying
★   five restored buildings at the same
site as the Waterwheel Restaurant,
the rooms of this state historical
landmark inn are in a Colonial
Virginia style. Four units are in
the original miller's house; others
occupy the former blacksmith's
shop, hardware store, gristmill, and
cottage. Some of the rooms have
fireplaces and patios, and each has
its own unique decor, from Colonial cottage chic to modern rustic
cabin charm. A Continental break-

> ### JEFFERSON POOLS
>
> Don't miss the pools, about 5 mi
> from The Homestead resort:
> designed by Thomas Jefferson
> himself. A host of American nota-
> bles have soaked in the restor-
> ative mineral springs. The resort
> operates the pools and runs a free
> shuttle service to and from them
> several times a day. Day visitors
> can soak in history for $17.

fast is included in the rate. The Inn is at the border of The Homestead
resort property so you can easily walk up and explore that area. It's also
within walking distance of shops and a convenience store. **Pros:** historic;
good location for shoppers; nice in-house restaurant. **Cons:** limited
availability; no pets ⊠ *Old Mill Rd., Warm Springs* ☎ *540/839–2231*
⊕ *www.gristmillsquare.com* ⇨ *12 rooms, 5 suites, 1 apartment* ⚹ *In-
room: a/c, Wi-Fi. In-hotel: restaurant, bar, tennis courts, pool* ▭ *D,
MC, V* ⟦◉⟧ *BP.*

NIGHTLIFE AND THE ARTS

Garth Newel Music Center (⊠ *Rte. 220, Warm Springs* ☎ *540/839–5018*
or *877/558–1689* ⊕ *www.garthnewel.org*) has weekend chamber-music
performances in summer, and hosts more than 50 concerts a year. You
can make reservations and plan to picnic on the grounds, or consider
staying over at The Homestead just down the road.

SPORTS AND THE OUTDOORS

GOLF

The Homestead (⊠ *Rte. 220, Hot Springs* ☎ *540/839–1766* or *800/838–
1766* ⊕ *www.thehomestead.com*) has three excellent 18-hole golf
courses. The par-70, 6,679-yard Cascades course, the site of USGA
and Senior PGA events, has gently sloped fairways amid rugged terrain.
The par-72, 6,752-yard Lower Cascades course, designed by Robert
Trent Jones, has more wide-open fairways with many bunkers and
breaks. The par-72, 6,211-yard Old Course is most famous for its first
tee, established in 1892. It's the oldest tee still in continuous use in the
United States.

HIKING AND MOUNTAIN BIKING

At **Douthat State Park** (⊠ *14239 Douthat State Park Rd., Exit 27, 7 mi
north of I–64 near Clifton Forge* ☎ *540/862–8100*) there are more than
40 mi of well-signed, smoothly groomed, and sometimes steep trails for
hiking and biking. The trails pass by waterfalls and majestic overlooks.
The Warm Springs Ranger District of the **George Washington and Jefferson National Forests** (☎ *540/839–2521*) has information on hundreds of
miles of local trails.

**EN
ROUTE**

The small town of **Clifton Forge** was once the heartbeat of the Chesapeake and Ohio Railway, and generations of travelers sped through the countryside on its trains. In its boom days, the Smith Creek Station saw as many as 100 trains a day passing through on their way west over the Alleghany mountain, east over the Blue Ridge, or down the James River.

Clifton Forge is home to the **C&O Heritage Center,** a railroad museum full of model trains and memorabilia, including an excellent gift shop featuring many items dedicated to the C&O Railway's cuddly kitten mascot, Chessie. Kids love the replica signal tower and the 7½-inch gauge ride-on train that circles the museum. ⊕ *www.cohs.org.*

SOUTHWEST VIRGINIA

Southwest Virginia is a rugged region of alternating mountain ridges and deep valleys. Modern urban life is juxtaposed with spectacular scenery in the Roanoke and New River valleys. Other areas retain the quiet charm of yesteryear: they have many pleasant meadows, old country churches, and towns with just one stop sign. The gorge-incised Appalachian Plateau in far southwest Virginia is abundant in coal. Interstate 81 and Interstate 77 form a kind of "X" across the region, and the Blue Ridge Parkway roughly defines southwest Virginia's eastern edge.

ROANOKE

49 mi south of Lexington (via I–81).

They once called this city "Big Lick." But today Roanoke, with a population of 95,000, is Virginia's largest city west of Richmond, the largest city on the Blue Ridge Parkway, and in many ways, the capital of southwest Virginia. The metropolitan area of 230,000 has enough city flavor to provide a degree of culture and elegance, but its location between the Blue Ridge Parkway and Appalachian Trail means that the wilds aren't too far away either; mountains dominate its horizons in all directions.

GETTING HERE AND AROUND

There is a regional airport in Roanoke (⊕ *www.roanokeairport.com*) or you can fly into Richmond, Charlottesville, or Washington, DC, and drive from there. About 50 mi south of Lexington on I–81, Roanoke is the largest city west of Richmond and also one of the largest accessible from the Blue Ridge Parkway. To access the downtown area, including the Visitor Information Center, Center in the Square, the Civic Center and other major attractions, you'll want to take Exit 143 at the tri-level exchange where I–581 and Route 220 intersect with I–81.

DISCOUNTS AND DEALS

The Roanoke Valley RED Card offers discounts to regional attractions. It's free at the visitor center.

Taxi Companies Liberty Cab (☎ *540/344–1776).* **Yellow Cab Services of Roanoke** (☎ *540/345–7711).*

Visitor Information Roanoke Valley Convention and Visitors Bureau (✉ *101 Shenandoah Ave. NE* ☎ *540/342–6025 or 800/635–5535* ⊕ *www. visitroanokeva.com).*

EXPLORING

Market Square. Market Square is the heart of Roanoke, with Virginia's oldest continuous farmers' market, a multiethnic food court inside the restored City Market Building, and several restaurants, shops, and bars. The building is undergoing a renovation to turn it into a retail complex with shops and restaurants (opening late 2011), but the farmers' market will stay in operation at its current location throughout the construction period. In a restored warehouse, **Center in the Square**(⊠ *1 Market Sq. SE* ☎ *540/342–5700* ⊕ *www.centerinthesquare.org*) contains the Mill Mountain Theatre and regional museums covering science, history, and art, but during the renovation, the museums will be moving into temporary quarters starting in 2011. The finished facade will be upgraded, and a new atrium and green rooftop space with a butterfly habitat will be added. Check the Center's Web site for address and contact information until the construction is completed in 2012. A combined ticket grants access to the science museum, which has many interactive exhibits, as well as the MegaDome theater and Hopkins Planetarium.

Roanoke Star. Even in daylight, the Roanoke skyline is dominated by a star. The 100-foot-tall Mill Mountain Star, constructed in 1949, stands in a city park 1,000 feet above the Roanoke Valley. It is lighted in red, white, and blue each evening. From either of the park's two overlooks, Roanoke, the "Star City of the South," looks like a scale model of a city, framed by wave after wave of Appalachian ridgelines. You can hike or bike the mountain's greenway trail. ⊠ *Mill Mountain Park; follow Walnut St. south 2 mi from downtown Roanoke; or take Pkwy. Spur Rd. 3 mi north from Blue Ridge Pkwy. at milepost 120.3.*

☺ **Mill Mountain Zoo.** Sharing the mountaintop with the star is the Mill Mountain Zoo. Asian animals are center stage here, including a rare Siberian tiger, snow leopards, and red pandas. Ride the Zoo Choo train for $2. ⊠ *Mill Mountain Park; follow Walnut St. south 2 mi from downtown Roanoke; or take Pkwy. Spur Rd. 3 mi north from Blue Ridge Pkwy. at milepost 120.3* ☎ *540/343–3241* ⊕ *www.mmzoo.org* 🎫*$7.50* ☻ *Daily 10–5; gate closes at 4:30.*

★ **O. Winston Link Museum.** You can relive the final days of steam trains at the O. Winston Link Museum, inside a renovated passenger train station. Link spent several years in the late 1950s and early 1960s photographing Norfolk & Western's last steam engines in the railroads of southwest Virginia. The hundreds of stunning black-and-white photographs on display do much more than evoke nostalgia—they also capture day-to-day life: a horse-drawn carriage awaiting an oncoming train, a locomotive rocketing past lovers watching a drive-in movie. ⊠ *101 Shenandoah Ave.* ☎ *540/982–5465* ⊕ *www.linkmuseum.org* 🎫*$5* ☻ *Mon.–Sun. 10–5.*

★ **Taubman Museum of Art.** Opened in the fall of 2008, this Randall Stout–designed faceted-glass structure soars amid the surrounding mountains, the contemporary architecture striking a balance with its natural location. Formerly known as the Art Museum of Western Virginia, the Taubman, with its new 81,000-square-foot home, quadruples its previous exhibit space, housing 19th- and 20th-century American art, modern art, and small special collections of European and ancient Mediterranean art. Norah's Café serves light fare throughout the day. Take advantage of free admission Thursday 5–8 pm. ⊠ *110 Salem Ave. SE* ☎ *540/342–5760* ⊕ *www.taubmanmuseum.org* 🖅 *$10.50* ⊗ *Tues., Wed., Fri.–Sat. 10–5; Thurs. 10–8.*

☺ **Virginia Museum of Transportation.** Near Market Square, just a short stroll along the Railwalk, the Virginia Museum of Transportation has the largest collection of diesel and steam locomotives in the country—not surprising, considering that Roanoke got its start as a railroad town and was once the headquarters of the Norfolk & Western railroad. The dozens of original train cars and engines, some of which can be boarded and many built here in town, include a massive nickel-plate locomotive—just one of the many holdings that constitute an unabashed display of civic pride. The sprawling model-train and miniature-circus setups please young and old alike. ⊠ *303 Norfolk Ave. SW* ☎ *540/342–5670* ⊕ *www.vmt.org* 🖅 *$8* ⊗ *Mon.–Sat. 10–5, Sun. 1–5.*

OFF THE BEATEN PATH

National D-Day Memorial. This site stirs the soul, bringing the sacrifice of D-Day home. When Allied forces landed at Normandy on June 6, 1944, in what would be the decisive military move of World War II, the small town of Bedford lost 19 of its young men, and four more in days to come. The memorial's focal point is a huge granite arch and flag plaza on a hill overlooking the town. There are also granite statues of soldiers in combat and a reflecting pool that periodically shoots up spurts of water, as if struck by bullets. Don't be surprised if you see some D-Day veterans sitting near the memorial. ⊠ *3 Overlord Circle, U.S. 460, 27 mi east of Roanoke, at junction of 122, Bedford* ☎ *540/587–3619* ⊕ *www. dday.org* 🖅 *$7* ⊗ *Tues.–Sun. 10–5.*

Booker T. Washington National Monument. It would have been hard for Booker T. Washington to imagine the farm on which he was born into slavery hosting a national monument. But this restored tobacco farm 25 mi southeast of Roanoke and 21 mi south of Bedford is a fitting tribute to the humble origins of Washington (1856–1915), who broke through the yoke of oppression to become a remarkable educator and author, advising presidents McKinley, Roosevelt, and Taft and taking tea with Queen Victoria. More important, he started Tuskegee Institute in Alabama and inspired generations of African-Americans. Covering 224 acres, the farm's restored buildings; tools; crops; animals; and, in summer, interpreters in period costume all help show what life during slavery was like. ⊠ *12130 Booker T. Washington Hwy. (Rte. 122, 21 mi south of Bedford) Hardy* ☎ *540/721–2094* ⊕ *www.nps.gov/bowa* 🖅 *Free* ⊗ *Daily 9–5.*

QUICK BITES

At the Homestead Creamery (⊠ *7254 Booker T. Washington Hwy. (Rte. 122, just east of intersection with Rte. 116, Wirtz* ☎ *540/721–2045*), you can sample farm-fresh milk and ice cream. No plastic or paper cartons here—the milk is stored and sold in glass bottles, the way milkmen used to bring it. Gulping down the chocolate milk is like drinking a chocolate cake. Unusual milk flavors such as mocha and orange cream are often available.

WHERE TO EAT

\$\$–\$\$\$ ✕ **Carlos Brazilian International Cuisine.** High on a hill with a spectacular
BRAZILIAN sunset view, this lively restaurant has French, Italian, Spanish, and Bra-
★ zilian dishes. Sit in the Olinda Room with its wall of windows. Try the
porco reacheado (pork tenderloin stuffed with spinach and feta cheese)
or the *moqueca mineira* (shrimp, clams, and whitefish in a Brazilian
sauce). Brazilian radio often accompanies the meal. If you love chicken,
try the sautéed version with pineapple and papaya. Carlos is also open
for lunch on weekdays. ✉ *4167 Electric Rd.* ☎ *540/776–1117* ⊕ *www.
carlosbrazilian.com* ⊟ *AE, MC, V* ⊘ *Closed Sun.*

\$ ✕ **The Homeplace.** Bring a big appetite with you on the drive up and
SOUTHERN over Catawba Mountain to get to the Homeplace. Famished Appa-
Fodor's Choice lachian Trail hikers in grimy shorts and suave diners in their Sunday
★ best eat side by side family-style in this farm home in a tiny country
hamlet—come as you are. Old-fashioned cooking is dished up with
all-you-can-eat fried chicken, mashed potatoes and gravy, green beans,
pinto beans, baked apples, and hot biscuits. It's a popular spot, so be
prepared for about a 30-minute wait. ✉ *4968 Catawba Valley Dr., 7 mi
west of Salem on Rte. 311 N, I–81, Exit 141, Catawba* ☎ *540/384–
7252* ⚱ *Reservations not accepted* ⊟ *MC, V* ⊘ *No lunch Thurs.–Sat.,
no dinner Sun.*

\$ ✕ **Mac 'N' Bob's.** The enormous growth in seating since 1980, from 10
AMERICAN to 250, testifies to the popularity of this establishment in downtown
Salem, as does its continual title as "best local restaurant" in an annual
poll. Sports memorabilia line the walls of the attractive redbrick building near Roanoke College, and sporting events are likely to be on the
many TVs near the bar. The menu runs from hamburgers to steak to
seafood to pizza. If you have a big appetite, try a fully loaded cal-
zone, which flops off the sides of your plate. ✉ *316 E. Main St., Salem*
☎ *540/389–5999* ⊕ *www.macandbobs.com* ⊟ *AE, D, MC, V.*

¢–\$ ✕ **The Roanoker.** Fried chicken isn't on the menu every day, but when it
SOUTHERN is, the smell entices you from the parking lot. This local gathering place
has been serving homestyle fare since 1941, from pancakes and chicken
salad sandwiches to blue-plate-style specials. The choice between corn
sticks, biscuits, or wheat rolls can be a tough one. ✉ *2522 Colonial Ave.
SW, Roanoke* ☎ *540/344–7746, 540/772–4834 list of daily specials*
⊕ *www.theroanokerrestaurant.com* ⊟ *MC, V* ⊘ *Closed Mon.*

WHERE TO STAY

\$\$–\$\$\$ ⊞ **Hotel Roanoke and Conference Center.** This elegant Tudor Revival build-
ing, listed on the National Register of Historic Places, was built in
1882 by the Norfolk & Western Railroad. The richly paneled lobby
has Florentine marble floors and ceiling frescos. Its formal restaurant
(\$\$–\$\$\$) serves regional Southern cuisine. A \$6.5-million renovation of
guest rooms and suites includes new furnishings, flat-screens, and Sweet
Dreams beds. The Market Square Bridge, a glassed-in walkway, goes
from the hotel to downtown attractions. **Pros:** historic building with
modern amenities; great Market Square location. **Cons:** fee for Wi-Fi
in room; busy conference hotel. ✉ *110 Shenandoah Ave.* ☎ *540/985–
5900* ⊕ *www.hotelroanoke.com* ⤺ *313 rooms, 19 suites* ⚴ *In-room:*

a/c, refrigerator (some), Wi-Fi. In-hotel: 2 restaurants, bar, pool, gym, Wi-Fi hotspot ⊟ *AE, D, DC, MC, V.*

NIGHTLIFE AND THE ARTS

Roanoke's nightlife centers on the Market Square area of downtown, which is often bustling and lively on weekend nights.

SPORTS AND THE OUTDOORS

HIKING

The **Appalachian Trail** is north and west of Roanoke, crossing the valley at Troutville, 5 mi to the north. Two of the most-photographed formations on the entire 2,000-mi route from Georgia to Maine, McAfee Knob and Dragon's Tooth, are accessible from trailheads on the Virginia 311 highway, west of the valley. The **Star Trail** (⊠ *Trailhead on Riverland Rd., 2 mi southeast of downtown Roanoke*) winds through a forest oasis amid the metropolitan area as it works its way up 1½ mi to the Mill Mountain Star. Other trails can be found along the Blue Ridge Parkway to the east and south and in the George Washington and Jefferson national forests to the north and west. For more information, contact the national forests' **Supervisor's Office** (⊠ *5162 Valleypointe Pkwy., Roanoke* ☎ *540/265–5100 or 888/265–0019*).

BLUE RIDGE PARKWAY

5 mi east of Roanoke.

The Blue Ridge Parkway takes up where Skyline Drive leaves off at Waynesboro, weaving south for 469 mi to the Great Smoky Mountains National Park in North Carolina. The parkway goes up to higher elevations than the drive, up to 4,200 feet at Apple Orchard Mountain, and even higher in North Carolina. In Virginia the parkway is especially scenic between Waynesboro and Roanoke, winding through the George Washington National Forest, visiting numerous ridgetop overlooks that provide views of crumpled-looking mountains and patchwork valleys.

Milepost 0 is at Rockfish Gap. There are no gas stations on the parkway, so you'll have to exit if you need to refuel, and be prepared for a leisurely drive as the speed limit is 45 mph. Go to the **Visitor Center at Explore Park,** open 9–5 daily year-round, 1.5 mi north of milepost 115 near Roanoke, or call the National Park Service's office in Vinton (☎ *540/857–2490*) for information on Virginia's section of the parkway.

GETTING HERE AND AROUND

The Blue Ridge Parkway begins near Waynesboro and Shenandoah National Park (milepost 0), which is also the end point of Skyline Drive. It runs 469 miles and ends at the Great Smoky Mountain National Park. You can access the parkway from all major federal and state highways, and there are explicit directions posted on the Virginia Department of Transportation Web site for access from I–64, I–81, and I–77. The speed limit is 45 mph and since the road is winding, if you're traveling in an RV or large vehicle, be prepared to allow a little extra time for the trip.

EXPLORING

Mabry Mill. Mabry Mill, north of Meadows of Dan and the Blue Ridge Parkway's junction with U.S. 58 at milepost 176, 55 mi south of Roanoke, is one of the parkway's most popular stops for photographers. ✉ *Blue Ridge Pkwy., milepost 176* ☎ *276/952–2947* ☜ *Free* ☉ *May– Oct., daily 8–6.*

Peaks of Otter Recreation Area. Peaks of Otter Recreation Area, 25 mi northeast of Roanoke, offers a close-up view of cone-shaped Sharp Top Mountain, which Thomas Jefferson once called America's tallest peak. At 3,875 feet it's not even the tallest in the park—nearby Flat Top is 4,004 feet. You can hike to both peaks and to little brother Harkening Hill, as well as to Fallingwater Cascades, a thrilling multitier waterfall. For those not up to the climb, a bus heads most of the way up Sharp Top hourly throughout the day in season. The peaks rise about the shores of Abbott Lake, a bucolic picnic spot. A pleasant lakeside lodge and campground along the placid lake below are an ideal base for local trekking. ✉ *Blue Ridge Pkwy., milepost 86* ☎ *540/586–4357* ⊕ *www. peaksofotter.com* ☜ *Free.*

OFF THE BEATEN PATH

Crabtree Falls. A series of cascades fall a distance of 1,200 feet. Taken together, Virginia claims these cascades as the highest waterfall east of the Rockies, though no single waterfall within the series would qualify as such. Whatever the superlatives or qualifications, the falls are a wondrous sight. A trail winds up a steep mountainside all the way to the top, but the first overlook is an easy stroll 700 feet from the lower parking lot. The best time to see the waterfalls is winter through spring, when the water is high. ✉ *11581 Crabtree Falls Hwy. (Rte. 56, 6 mi east of Blue Ridge Pkwy., or 19 mi from Wintergreen by following Rte. 151 south and then Rte. 56 west at Roseland), Montebello* ☎ *540/291–2188* ⊕ *www.crabtreefalls.com.*

WHERE TO STAY

¢–$ 🛏 **Peaks of Otter Lodge.** This unpretentious, peaceful lodge is so popular in the fall that reservations are accepted beginning October 1 for the following year (but it's open year-round). Every room looks out on Abbott Lake from a private terrace or balcony, and their interiors have a folksy quality. Nestled between two of the three peaks of its namesake, the lodge was built in 1964. In non-winter months a complimentary bus takes you to Sharp Top Mountain if you prefer not to hike, and you can see the same mountaintop from the lodge's Lake View Restaurant. **Pros:** restaurant and lounge on-site; ADA-accessible rooms; nice views. **Cons:** may be too rustic for some; must reserve far in advance. ✉ *85554 Blue Ridge Pkwy., milepost 86, Rte. 664, Box 489, Bedford* ☎ *540/586–1081 or 800/542–5927* ⊕ *www.peaksofotter.com* ⟿ *63 rooms* ⌂ *In-room: no phone, a/c, no TV. In-hotel: restaurant, bar* ☰ *MC, V.*

BLACKSBURG AND THE NEW RIVER VALLEY

41 mi southwest of Roanoke via I–81.

Despite its name, derived from being "new" to explorers when it was first discovered, the New River is actually one of the oldest rivers in the world: legend says only the Nile is older. The only river that flows from south to north completely through the Appalachian Mountains, the New River cuts a bluff-graced valley through its Virginia section for 60 mi from Galax near the North Carolina line to Pearisburg, just over the West Virginia line. Visitors will find cozy downtown areas in towns like Blacksburg, Christiansburg, Radford, and Pulaski, and many opportunities for outdoor recreation just outside the towns' limits.

GETTING HERE AND AROUND
You'll need a car to explore Blacksburg and the surrounding outdoor attractions. There are multiple exits of I–81, and if you're coming from the Richmond area, I–64 feeds right onto I–81.

TIMING
It's difficult to get a hotel room on weekends when Virginia Tech University is in session, so book as far in advance as possible if you're visiting on a Friday or Saturday. Also expect crowds on home football weekends and for special events like the fall Radford Highlanders Festival.

EXPLORING
Historic Smithfield Plantation. Almost a century before Virginia Tech's founding in 1872, the Historic Smithfield plantation was built in what was then the frontier wilds. Aristocratic colonist and Revolutionary War patriot William Preston moved his family to the estate in 1774, a year before the war began. Among his descendants were three Virginia governors and four U.S. senators. Today costumed interpreters, authentic period furniture, and Native American artifacts reveal how different life in the New River valley was more than two centuries ago. ⊠ *1000 Smithfield Plantation Rd., Blacksburg* ☎ *540/231–3947* ⊕ *www.smithfieldplantation.org* ⊠ *$7* ⊙ *Mon., Tues., and Thurs.–Sat. 10–5; Sun. 1–5. Closed Wed.*

Virginia Tech. With more than 30,000 students at its nine colleges and graduate school, Virginia Tech is the state's largest university. A small college just a few decades ago, Tech is now known for top-notch research programs and its Hokies football team, regularly ranked in the top 10. The focal point of the sprawling campus is the Drillfield, a vast green space surrounded by hefty neo-Gothic buildings built of what is known locally as "Hokie Stone" masonry. The **Virginia Museum of Natural History**(⊠ *428 N. Main St.* ☎ *540/231–3001*) at Virginia Tech presents rotating exhibits on local and national wildlife; a separate geology museum in Derring Hall displays gems and minerals. ⊠ *Blacksburg* ☎ *540/231–6000* ⊕ *www.vt.edu.*

Wilderness Road Regional Museum. What is now the Wilderness Road Regional Museum was once lodging for settlers making their way west on a Native American route that went from Pennsylvania through the Cumberland Gap. The man who founded the town of Newbern built this house in the same year, and the structure has since served as a private home, a tavern, a post office, and a store. Today the house contains antique dolls, swords and rifles, an old loom, and other artifacts of everyday life. A self-tour map of Newbern, the only Virginia town entirely within a National Register of Historic Places district, is available at the museum. ⊠ *5240 Wilderness Rd., I–81, Exit 98, Newbern* ☎ *540/674–4835* ⊠ *$2* ⊙ *Mon.–Sat. 10:30–4:30, Sun. 1:30–4:30.*

WHERE TO EAT

$–$$ ✕ **Boudreaux's Restaurant.** Ever eaten gator bites or buffalo crawfish? Be
SOUTHERN   sure and try them at Boudreaux's. What started as a project in business
           marketing for a pair of Virginia Tech students is now an established part
           of Blacksburg's downtown. The canopied rooftop is a particularly relax-
           ing place to enjoy jambalaya or Cajun catfish, and they serve brunch
           on both Saturday and Sunday. Live bands often perform in the evening.
           ✉ *205 N. Main St., Blacksburg* ☎ *540/961–2330* ⊕ *www.boudreauxs.*
           com ⊟ *AE, D, MC, V.*

¢–$ ✕ **The Cellar.** A gathering place and watering hole near the Virginia Tech
MEDITERRANEAN campus, this storefront restaurant serves eclectic, inexpensive dishes.
           Try the Greek spaghetti with sautéed feta, garlic, and olives, or the
           "Mac Daddy": a single large meatball in marinara sauce and Parme-
           san. They also offer an extensive list of domestic and imported beers
           and local bands perform here often. ✉ *302 N. Main St., Blacksburg*
           ☎ *540/953–0651* ⊕ *www.the-cellar.com* ⊟ *MC, V.*

WHERE TO STAY

¢–$ ⊡ **Holiday Inn University.** This hotel is across the street from Virginia
           Tech, with a golf course, movie theater, numerous restaurants and shop-
           ping areas, and even a beach volleyball court nearby. The imposing
           entrance made from native stone doesn't look anything like a chain
           hotel. The rooms are modern and comfortable, with two phone lines in
           each one. **Pros:** pet friendly; close to Virginia Tech. **Cons:** no historical
           connection. ✉ *900 Prices Fork Rd., Blacksburg* ☎ *540/552–7001 or*
           888/465–4329 ⤵ *137 rooms, 1 suite* ♺ *In-room: a/c, Wi-Fi. In-hotel:*
           restaurant, bar, tennis court, pools, parking (free) ⊟ *AE, D, DC, MC, V.*

$$$ ⊡ **Mountain Lake.** The 1987 movie "Dirty Dancing" was filmed here,
           and the resort (Kellerman's in the movie) hosts special themed weekends
           with dancing, a movie location tour, and other special events. Centered
           around the highest natural lake east of the Mississippi, accommoda-
           tions range from spartan cottages to plush suites in a majestic sand-
           stone hotel from 1930 (the resort itself predates the Civil War). You
           can also rent two, three, and four-bedroom cottages if you need more
           space for an extended stay. Atop 4,000-foot Salt Pond Mountain, out-
           door activities abound: you can hike, mountain bike, ride horses, swim,
           and boat within the 2,500-acre Mountain Lake Wilderness, which sur-
           rounds the hotel. The adjacent Jefferson National Forest offers even
           more recreation, including a segment of the Appalachian Trail. **Pros:**
           gorgeous scenery; outdoor activities. **Cons:** crowded in summer; far
           from Blacksburg; no pets. ✉ *115 Hotel Circle, 7 mi north of U.S. 460*
           on Rte. 700, Pembroke ☎ *540/626–7121 or 800/346-3334* ⊕ *www.*
           mountainlakehotel.com ⤵ *28 cottages, 16 lodge rooms, 43 hotel rooms*
           ♺ *In-room: a/c, refrigerator (some), no TV (some), Wi-Fi. In-hotel: res-*
           taurant, pool, bicycles ⊟ *AE, D, MC, V* ⦿ *MAP* ☉ *Seasonal May–Oct.,*
           some weekends Nov.–Dec. Closed Jan.–Apr.

5

SPORTS AND THE OUTDOORS
BIKING
Mountain Lake (✉ *115 Hotel Circle, 7 mi north of U.S. 460 on Rte. 700, Pembroke* ☎ *540/626–7121* ⊕ *www.mountainlakehotel.com*) has more than 20 mi of mountain-bike trails, with bicycles available at the hotel. The 52-mi **New River Trail**, Virginia's narrowest state park, runs from Pulaski to Galax following what was once a railroad bed. It parallels the river for 39 of those miles, passing through two tunnels. The trail is also open to hikers and horseback riders. The Jefferson National Forest's **Pandapas Pond Recreation Area**, on the edge of Blacksburg, is a popular place for mountain biking.

HIKING
The **Appalachian Trail** crosses the New River valley, visiting overlook sites such as Angel's Rest and Wind Rock. For more information on area hikes in the Jefferson National Forest, contact the **Blacksburg Ranger Station** (✉ *110 Southpark Dr., Blacksburg* ☎ *540/552–4641*). The 4-mi loop at **Cascades Recreation Area** (✉ *Jefferson National Forest, off U.S. 460, 4 mi north of Pembroke on Rte. 623*) passes a rushing stream and a 60-foot waterfall. This hike is popular locally and becomes crowded on weekends when the weather's good.

ABINGDON

135 mi southwest of Roanoke (via I–81).

Abingdon, near the Tennessee border, is a cultural crossroads in the wilderness: the town of nearly 7,000 draws tens of thousands of people each year because of a fine theater company and exuberant local celebrations.

By far the most popular event here is the **Virginia Highlands Festival** (⊕ *www.vahighlandsfestival.org*) during the first two weeks of August: 200,000 people come to hear live music performances ranging from bluegrass to opera, to visit the exhibitions of mountain crafts, and to browse among the wares of more than 100 antiques dealers. At the **Burley Tobacco Festival** (⊕ *www.washcofair.com*), held in September, country-music stars perform and prize farm animals are proudly displayed.

GETTING HERE AND AROUND
Abingdon is close to the Tennessee state line at Bristol, just off I–81. You will need a car to get around in this area. The closest airport is Bristol, although you could also fly into Roanoke or Knoxville, TN.

ESSENTIALS
Visitor Information Abingdon Convention & Visitors Bureau (✉ *335 Cummings St.* ☎ *276/676–2282* ⊕ *www.abingdon.com/cvb.html*).

WHERE TO STAY
$$$–$$$$ 🏨 **Camberley's Martha Washington Hotel & Spa.** Constructed as a private
★   house in 1832, turned into a college dormitory in 1860, and then used as a field hospital during the Civil War, the Martha Washington finally became an inn in 1935. Across from the Barter Theatre, the inn has rooms furnished with Victorian antiques; some have fireplaces and all have flat-screens and even the odd touch of phones in the bathroom.

Mountain Music

Southwest Virginia's hills and valleys have long reverberated with the sounds of fiddles, banjoes, mandolins, and acoustic guitars. Scotch-Irish settlers brought these sounds with them, and for the generations before radio and television, front-porch gatherings and community dances entertained local families isolated, geographically and culturally, from the rest of civilization.

Virginia has designated a 250-mi route snaking through the hills as **The Crooked Road: Virginia's Music Heritage Trail.** What connects the communities and sites along this route is a passion for traditional mountain music—bluegrass, gospel, roots, and old-time country. Many people point to this region as the birthplace of the country-music industry. In 1927 talent scout Ralph Peer set up a makeshift recording studio in the Virginia-Tennessee border town of Bristol. From these sessions came such seminal acts as the Carter Family and Jimmie Rodgers. For more information, go to ⊕ www.thecrookedroad.org. Sites are listed here from west to east.

Ralph Stanley Museum and Traditional Mountain Music Center (✉ 249 Main St., Clintwood ☎ 276/926–5591 ⊕ www.ralphstanleymuseum.com). The Ralph Stanley Museum opened in 2004 to preserve traditional mountain music. Focusing on the life and career of local legend Ralph Stanley, the exhibits allow visitors to hear the music of Stanley and other artists.

Carter Family Fold (✉ U.S. 58/421, 19 mi west of Bristol, Hiltons ☎ 276/386–6054 or 276/386–9480 ⊕ www.carterfamilyfold.org). At this 1,000-seat auditorium, live music is performed on Saturday night; a two-day festival is held each August. A museum in an adjacent building displays memorabilia from the Carter Family; descendants often perform in the shows.

Old Fiddlers Convention (601 S. Main St., Galax ☎ 276/236–8541 ⊕ www.oldfiddlersconvention.com). Hundreds of musicians and thousands of fans gather at Felts Park the second week of August for performances, contests, and jam sessions.

Rex Theatre (✉ 113 E. Grayson St., Galax ☎ 276/236–0329 or 276/236–0668 ⊕ www.rextheateregalax.com). Bluegrass, country, and gospel music is broadcast from here each Friday night on WBRF, FM–98.1.

Blue Ridge Music Center (✉ 700 Foothills Dr., Galax [Blue Ridge Pkwy. milepost 213, near NC line] ☎ 276/236–5309 ⊕ www.blueridgemusiccenter.net). The center's outdoor amphitheater is the site of an ambitious concert series of regional and national musicians that has included the likes of Ricky Skaggs and Doc Watson. Impromptu jam sessions often break out in the center's plaza area.

Floyd Country Store (✉ 206 S. Locust St., Floyd ☎ 540/745–4563 ⊕ www.floydcountrystore.com 🖃 $3). What were once just sessions have evolved into a Friday Night Jamboree attended by local folks and visitors from far off. In summer, music often breaks out all around the store as well. "Granny Rules" are in effect—"no smokin', no cussin', and no drinkin'." But clogging on the dance floor is fine.

5

A natatorium, pool, and full-service spa add to the old-world luxury. There is a daily resort fee which includes breakfast, morning coffee, afternoon tea, Wi-Fi, access to the fitness center, and shuttle service to the Virginia Highlands Airport. **Pros:** historic luxury; spa and pool facilities. **Cons:** pricey compared to nearby options. ⊠ *150 W. Main St.* ☎ *276/628–3161 or 800/555–8000* ⊕ *www.marthawashingtoninn.com* ⇨ *51 rooms, 11 suites* ⟳ *In-room: a/c, refrigerator, Wi-Fi. In-hotel: restaurant, bar, pool, gym, spa, laundry service, Internet terminal* ⊟ *AE, D, DC, MC, V* ⊚⏐ *BP.*

NIGHTLIFE AND THE ARTS
From February through the Christmas season, audiences flock to the prestigious **Barter Theatre** (⊠ *127 W. Main St.* ☎ *276/628–3991* ⊕ *www. bartertheatre.com*), America's longest-running professional repertory theater. Founded during the Depression by local actor Robert Porterfield, the theater got its name in the obvious way: early patrons who could not afford the 40 tickets could pay in produce. Patricia Neal, Ned Beatty, and Gregory Peck are among the many stars who began their careers at the Barter, which today presents classics, dramas, comedies, musicals, and new and Appalachian works. Although times have changed since Noël Coward was given a Virginia ham for his contributions, patrons can still barter for their seat a few times a year. But don't just show up at the box office with a bag of arugula—all trades must be approved by advance notice.

THE OUTDOORS
HIKING
Wild ponies on open grasslands studded with rocky knobs give the area around **Mt. Rogers** an appearance distinct from any other in Virginia. At 5,729 feet, Mt. Rogers is Virginia's highest point, but you don't need to hike all the way to its summit to experience the grandeur of Western-like terrain—a short walk of about a mile from **Grayson Highlands State Park** (⊠ *829 Grayson Highland Lane [U.S. 58, 20 mi east of Damascus]* ☎ *276/579–7092* ⛁ *$2*) into the adjacent **Mount Rogers Recreation Area** is all that's required. Through the 5,000-acre state park and 120,000-acre recreation area run an extensive network of riding and hiking trails; the Appalachian Trail passes through on its way to North Carolina and Tennessee, just to the south. ⊠ *Mount Rogers National Recreation Area, 3714 Hwy. 16, Marion* ☎ *276/783–5196* ⛁ *Free.*

At the end of Abingdon's Main Street is the beginning of the 34-mi **Virginia Creeper Trail** (⊕ *www.vacreepertrail.com*), a former rail bed of the Virginia-Carolina Railroad. You can hike it, bike it, or take to it on horseback. The trail has sharp curves, steep grades, and 100 trestles and bridges. It joins the Appalachian Trail at Damascus, a town known for its friendly attitude and the many businesses targeted toward hikers and cyclists. In May the town celebrates Trail Days, a festival celebrating hikers. ⊠ *Trailhead at end of Main St.* ☎ *540/676–2282 or 800/435–3440.*

Richmond, Fredericksburg, and the Northern Neck

the Northern Neck

WORD OF MOUTH

"Richmond, and in particular the Shockoe Slip district, has some very nice hotels and restaurants and is lots of fun for music and bars. We really like to stay at the Berkeley down there and have some pampering for a long weekend."

—bgr8ful

Updated
by Ginger
Warder

A host of patriots and presidents have lived and worked in the heart of the Old Dominion, an area that takes in Richmond, Fredericksburg, Petersburg, and the Northern Neck.

Virginia is often called "The Mother of Presidents," since eight of America's leaders, including George Washington, were born here. The birthplaces, boyhood homes, or graves of notable figures such as George Washington, James Monroe, John Tyler, William Henry Harrison, and Robert E. Lee can be found here, and the area has many associations with other leaders, including Patrick Henry and Thomas Jefferson. William Byrd II named the city Richmond in 1737 because the bend in the James River reminded him of the Thames in Richmond, England. George Washington designed the nation's first canal system here, the Kanawha, and Richmond has been home to many other "firsts," including the first African-American governor in the country, the first hospital, and the South's first television station.

Richmond's renovated State Capitol was originally designed by Jefferson, and its rotunda features portraits and statues of Virginia's presidents, including the famous Houdoun marble sculpture of George Washington. At St. John's Church, in one of the city's oldest neighborhoods, Patrick Henry gave his incendiary "Give me liberty or give me death" speech that helped ignite the American Revolution.

ORIENTATION AND PLANNING

GETTING ORIENTED

Richmond is south of Washington, D.C. Interstate 95 runs north–south and easily connects this region of Virginia, bordered by the Chesapeake Bay to the east. Interstate 64, running east–west, offers easy access to Williamsburg, Charlottesville, and most of central Virginia.

Richmond. The capital city of Virginia is easily reached from interstates 95 and 64. Richmond is the former capital of the Confederacy and the home of numerous Civil War sites. It contains several historic neighborhoods including the Fan District, full of 19th-century homes; the Museum District, which contains several world-class Virginia institutions; historic Monument Avenue, the only street in America with a historic designation; the vibrant shopping district known as Carytown; and a wealth of restaurants and nightclubs in Shockoe Slip and Shockoe Bottom. In nearby Ashland (about 20 mi north of Richmond), Patrick Henry honed his oratory skills at the historic Hanover Courthouse. This quaint railroad town is also home to charming shops, the Henry Clay Inn, Randolph Macon College, and Henry's former residence, Scotchtown.

Petersburg. Thirty minutes south of Richmond, Petersburg is a delightful antebellum city with many historic attractions. Besieged by the Union Army in 1864, the townspeople did their best to protect the Confederacy. The Petersburg National Battlefield, Pamplin Park, and the historic

TOP REASONS TO GO

Soak Up Art from around the World: After a massive expansion that doubled its exhibition space, Richmond's Virginia Museum of Fine Arts welcomes visitors to the new James W. and Frances G. McGlothlin Wing. Spectacular expanses of glass allow natural light to pour in, and also give visitors stunning views of the new E. Claiborne and Lora Robins Sculpture Garden and Mary Morton Parsons Plaza.

Experience the Civil War Sesquicentennial: Richmond, with more Civil War battlefields than any other state, will see a host of special events and educational programs running through 2015, emphasizing the experiences and effects of the war on the nation.

Contemplate Colonial Design and Revolutionary History: Patrick Henry delivered his fiery "give me liberty or give me death" speech at historic St. John's Church in Richmond, and several gems of Colonial art and architecture survive at the working river plantations of Stratford Hall, Shirley, and Berkeley.

Visit Presidents of the Past: Tour the boyhood homes, birthplaces, and final resting places of several U.S. presidents. George Washington grew up on Ferry Farm on the Northern Neck, home to the George Washington Birthplace National Monument, and Thomas Jefferson spent some of his boyhood years at Tuckahoe Plantation in Richmond. William Henry Harrison was born at Berkeley Plantation, and James Madison, James Monroe, and John Tyler are buried in Hollywood Cemetery.

Explore the Virginia Wine Trail: With more than 160 wineries throughout the state, Virginia is on the oenophile radar and is considered a top wine region for travelers. The Heart of Virginia Wine Trail is a group of four Virginia Wineries located near Richmond, including Cooper Vineyards, Grayhaven Winery, James River Cellars Winery, and Lake Anna Winery.

6

Blandford Church and Cemetery are must-sees for Civil War buffs. Blandford Church has an incredible collection of 15 stained-glass windows designed by Louis Comfort Tiffany as a tribute to the Confederate states and their soldiers.

Fredericksburg. Less than an hour north of Richmond sits the appealing city of Fredericksburg, a quaint historic city full of both Colonial and Civil War history, with hundreds of impressive 18th- and 19th-century homes and a treasure trove of art and antiques stores. The nearby Fredericksburg/Spotsylvania National Military Park presents the story of the area's role in the Civil War.

The Northern Neck. East of Fredericksburg, away from the blood-soaked and fought-over grounds, peace and quiet reign in a 90-mi-long peninsula Virginians call "The Northern Neck." This outdoorsman's escape was the birthplace of three presidents, including the Father of Our Country. Don't miss George Washington's birthplace and the quintessential seaside town of Irvington. Here wide rivers and the briny Chesapeake Bay entice water lovers and sports anglers.

PLANNING

WHEN TO GO

Richmond's mild climate welcomes visitors year-round. Since Virginia Commonwealth University is spread throughout the downtown area, traffic is more congested from September through May when school is in session.

Spring is spectacular, especially during **Virginia's Annual Garden Week** in April (⊕ *www.vagardenweek.org*). In July the **Hanover Tomato Festival** (⊕ *www.hanovertomatofestival.*

WHAT'S IN A NAME

Did you know that the name Old Dominion originated in Colonial days? King Charles II called Virginia "the best of his distant children" and granted the colony the position of "dominion" in 1663. As the oldest settlement in the New World, it became known as the Old Dominion.

---

com), and in August, the **Carytown Watermelon Festival** (⊕ *www.carytownrva.org/watermelon.php*) celebrates the summer season. In May and September the Richmond International Raceway hosts NASCAR. In September the **Virginia State Fair** (☎ *804/994–2800* ⊕ *www.statefair.com*) is a classic conglomeration of carnival rides, livestock shows, displays of farm equipment, and lots of food for sale. The **Richmond Folk Festival** (⊕ *www.richmondfolkfestival.org*) takes place in October downtown, and Lewis Ginter Botanical Garden is ablaze with 450,000 lights during December's **Garden Festival of Lights** (⊕ *www.lewisginter.org*).

GETTING HERE AND AROUND

Richmond, 100 mi south of Washington, D.C., on the James River, is the state's historic capital. It's easy to get here on I–95. Midway between Washington and Richmond on I–95, Fredericksburg is a lovely place to relax and retrace 18th- and 19th-century history in homes and museums and on nearby battlefields. About 20 mi east of Fredericksburg, the Northern Neck begins. There's no public transportation to this rural area, but a car lets you wander at will among its many historic sites and water views. Ashland, in Hanover County about 20 mi north of Richmond, is the birthplace of Patrick Henry. Petersburg, with its Civil War history, is a mere half hour south of Richmond.

AIR TRAVEL

Richmond International Airport, 10 mi east of the city, Exit 197 off I–64 or Exit 31 off I–295, has scheduled flights by eight major carriers. Other nearby airports include Dulles International and Reagan National in Washington, D.C., as well as Patrick Henry in Newport News and the Charlottesville-Albemarle Airport. A taxi ride to downtown Richmond from the airport costs $26–$32, and the Groom Transportation shuttle is $24 per person.

Air Contacts Richmond International Airport (✉ *Richard E. Byrd Terminal Dr.* ☎ *804/226–3000* ⊕ *www.flyrichmond.com*).

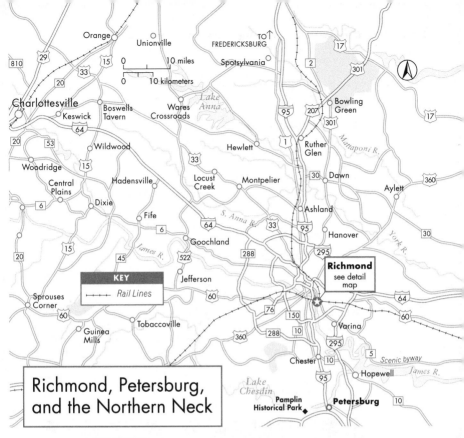

Richmond, Petersburg,
and the Northern Neck

CAR TRAVEL

Having a car is advisable in Richmond and Fredericksburg. It's essential for touring outlying attractions, including historic homes and battle-fields, and the Northern Neck. Avoid the major interstates such as 64 and 95 during morning and evening rush hours if possible.

Richmond is at the intersection of interstates 95 and 64, which run north–south and east–west, respectively. U.S. 1/301 also runs north–south past the city. To drive to Fredericksburg from Washington, D.C., take I–95 south to Route 3 (Exit 130-A), turn left, and follow the signs. The drive takes about an hour one-way; add 45 minutes during rush hour. To reach the Northern Neck from Fredericksburg, either take Route 3 South or U.S. 17 to Route 360, crossing the Rappahannock River at the Tappahannock Bridge. Driving north from Williamsburg and Hampton roads, cross the river at Greys Point by driving north on Route 3. Access from Maryland and Washington, D.C., is over the Potomac River toll bridge on Route 301. If you cross there, you shortly come upon Virginia's Potomac Gateway Visitors Center in King George.

TRAIN TRAVEL

Richmond has two Amtrak stations: Main Street Station downtown and Staples Mill, about 10 mi to the west. Only the trains on the North-east corridor stop at Main Street; more routes are offered from Staples

Mill. Amtrak trains operate between Washington's Union Station, Alexandria, Fredericksburg, Richmond, and a number of commuter stops several times daily. A one-way ticket costs $22 between Fredericksburg and Washington and $30 between Washington and Richmond. Amtrak service between New York City and Newport News or Florida passes through Richmond daily. The Virginia Rail Express, which uses the same tracks and station as Amtrak, provides workday commuter service between Fredericksburg and Washington's Union Station, with additional stops near hotels in Crystal City, L'Enfant Plaza, and elsewhere. A round-trip ticket from Washington's Union Station to Fredericksburg costs $20.60. There's no mass transit to the Northern Neck, but you can take the train to Fredericksburg and rent a car.

Train Information Virginia Rail Express (☎ 703/684–1001 or 800/743–3873 ⊕ www.vre.org).

RESTAURANTS AND HOTELS

Keep in the mind that hotel rooms can be hard to come by during Richmond's NASCAR Nextel Cup races, held over two weekends in May and September. The downtown Broad Street corridor is also crowded during the college school year, since the Virginia Commonwealth University campus is located here. Richmond has a wide variety of restaurants, from Southern comfort food to fine dining, and anything from Thai and Mexican to Dominican and French. Dress is casual at most restaurants; reservations are recommended for most fine dining or during special events. Downtown hotels may be a bit more expensive, but keep in mind that if you stay in an area outside the core, you'll have to pay for parking in the city.

WHAT IT COSTS					
	¢	$	$$	$$$	$$$$
Restaurants	under $10	$10–$16	$17–$23	$24–$30	over $30
Hotels	under $100	$101–$160	$161–$230	$231–$300	over $300

Restaurant prices are per person for a main course at dinner. Hotel prices are for a standard double room, excluding state tax.

PLANNING YOUR TIME

You'll need a minimum of two to three days to see all of the major attractions in Richmond, at least half a day in Petersburg, and two days in the Fredericksburg and Northern Neck regions, which you should see together in one trip. Heading south from D.C., you can stop off in Fredericksburg, head out to Northern Neck, then continue on to Ashland and Richmond. Heading south from Richmond, you can visit Petersburg and continue on to Colonial Williamsburg or Virginia Beach.

VISITOR INFORMATION

Richmond Regional Visitor Center (✉ 401 N. 3rd St. ☎ 800/370–9004 ⊕ www.visitrichmond.com).

RICHMOND

Centered on the fall line of the James River, about 75 mi upriver from the Chesapeake Bay, Richmond completes the transition from Tidewater Virginia into the Piedmont, the central section of rolling plains that reaches toward the mountain barrier in the west. Not only is Richmond the capital of the Commonwealth, but it was also the capital of the Confederacy. As a result, the city is studded with historic sites. At the start of the Civil War, Richmond was the most industrialized city in the South, and it remains an important city for national industries. After years of urban decay, Richmond transformed itself into a lively and sophisticated modern town, adding high technology to traditional economic bases that include shipping and banking.

GETTING HERE AND AROUND

By car, interstates 95 and 64 come directly to Richmond, and state routes 1, 5, and 301 are scenic alternatives. Richmond has two Amtrak stations: one downtown and one on the west side at Staples Mill Road. Cabs are metered in Richmond; they charge $2.50 for the first mile and $1.50 for each additional mile. Greater Richmond Transit operates bus service in Richmond. Buses run daily, 5 am–1 am; fares are $1.25 (exact change required). ■ TIP➜ GRTC (⊕ ridegrtc.com) has extended express routes to Petersburg ($2.50) and to Fredericksburg ($6).

TOURS   Historic Richmond Tours, a service of the Valentine Richmond History Center, offers guided tours that cover such topics as the historic Hollywood Cemetery and the River District and Jackson Ward. You can take either a walking tour or one of the thematic bus tours with topics that change monthly. Richmond Discoveries' excursions include tours that highlight Civil War history and customized trips for large groups or small families. Segway Tours offers a two-hour tour of the historic sites of the city, including a training lesson before departing. Tours meet at the Richmond Visitors Center on 3rd Street.

TIMING AND PRECAUTIONS

Both interstates 95 and 64 are affected by rush-hour traffic. With many major businesses on the West End of Richmond, 64 West will be heavy in the mornings, and 64 East returning to the city will be busy from 4 pm to 6 pm. Similarly, 95 North in the morning and 95 South in the evening will also see increased traffic, and in summer, with many Richmond residents heading to the beaches, both 64 East and 95 South can experience mile-long backups. The Downtown Expressway and the Powhite Parkway are toll roads (🖫25¢–$1.50) that service the suburban areas, especially on the south side of the city, and these will also be busy during rush hours. Most Virginia toll roads accept E-Z Pass, which is also good in 12 additional states.

Also, be aware that since this is a large, urban city, there are some downtown areas that you should visit with caution, especially after dark.

ESSENTIALS

Taxi Companies **Groome Transportation** (☎ 804/222-7222). **Metro Taxicab Service** (✉ 3840 Mastin La. ☎ 804/353-5000). **Yellow Cab Service Inc** (✉ 3203 Williamsburg Rd. ☎ 804/222-7300).

Tour information Historic Richmond Tours (☎ 804/649–0711 ⊕ www. richmondhistorycenter.com). **Richmond Discoveries** (☎ 804/222–8595 ⊕ www. richmonddiscoveries.com). **Segway Tours** (✉ 1301 E. Cary St. ☎ 800/979–3370 ⊕ www.segwayofrichmond.biz 🔖 $68 🕐 Daily tours at 10 am and 2 pm).

Train Stations Richmond train station (✉ 7519 Staples Mill Rd., at Main Street Station ☎ 804/553–2903).

Visitor Information Richmond Regional Visitor Center (✉ 401 N. 3rd St. ☎ 800/370–9004 ⊕ www.visitrichmondva.com). **Virginia Tourism Corporation** (✉ 901 E. Byrd St. ☎ 800/847–4882 ⊕ www.virginia.org ✉ Bell Tower at Capitol Sq., 9th and Franklin Sts. ☎ 800/545–5586 Information by mail: ✉ 401 N. 3rd St.). **Visitor Center at Bass Pro Shop** (✉ 11550 Lakeridge Pkwy. ☎ 804/615–5412). **Visitor Center at Richmond International Airport** (✉ 1 Richard E. Byrd Terminal Dr. ☎ 804/236–3260 ⊕ www.visitrichmondva.com/plan/visitor-center).

RICHMOND'S NEIGHBORHOODS

Richmond is divided into four quadrants: Northside (north of the James River), Southside (south of the James River), West End, and East Richmond. The main attractions, sites, hotels, restaurants, and shopping are spread out between several popular neighborhoods. Starting with Church Hill at the east end of downtown, heading west you'll come to Shockoe Bottom and Shockoe Slip, downtown, the Fan District which is home to Virginia Commonwealth University, the Museum District, the popular shopping area Carytown, and finally to the West End, a major residential and business area.

To the west of downtown, Monument Avenue, the only street in the U.S. designated a National Historic Landmark, is lined with statues of Civil War heroes, as well as a newer one commemorating Arthur Ashe, and the stately homes of some of the first families of Virginia. A block south, a series of streets fanning out southwesterly from Park Avenue near Virginia Commonwealth University creates the Fan District, a treasury of restored turn-of-the-20th-century town houses that has become a popular neighborhood. Adjacent to it is Carytown, a restored area of shops and eateries along Cary Street.

EXPLORING
TOP ATTRACTIONS
Beth Ahabah Museum and Archives. This repository contains articles and documents related to the Richmond and Southern Jewish experience, including the records of two congregations. ✉ 1109 W. Franklin St. ☎ 804/353–2668 ⊕ www.bethahabah.org 🔖 Free, $3 donation suggested 🕐 Sun.–Thurs. 10–3.

🌀 **Children's Museum of Richmond.** A welcoming, hands-on complex for
★ children and families, the museum is a place to climb, explore, experiment, and play. The museum is divided into sections like Art Studio, Tree Climber, Town Square, and Backyard, each with its own activities. The museum also offers classes in painting and music, and hosts special events on holidays. Exhibits and activities are geared to younger children. There's also a satellite museum on the west end of the city. ✉ 2626 W. Broad St. ☎ 804/474–2667 ⊕ www.c-mor.org 🔖 $8

Ⓢ Labor Day–Memorial Day, *Tues.–Sat. 9:30–5, Sun. noon–5*; Memorial Day–Labor Day, daily 9:30–5.

OFF THE BEATEN PATH

Fodor's Choice ★

Lewis Ginter Botanical Garden. You'll find year-round beauty on this historic property with more than 40 acres of spectacular gardens, dining, and shopping. The classical domed conservatory is the only one of its kind in the Mid-Atlantic, and houses ever-changing displays, tropical plants, and more than 200 orchids in bloom. The rose garden features 80 varieties, with more than 1,800 roses, and a pavilion for special events including wine tastings and evening jazz concerts. A Children's Garden offers a wheelchair-accessible tree house—fun for kids and adults—an Adventure Pathway, sand- and water-play areas, as well as an international village. More than a dozen theme gardens include a Healing Garden, Sunken Garden, Asian Valley, and Victorian Garden. The marvelous display of Christmas lights has become a Richmond tradition. Dining options include the Garden Café and the Tea House, and the shop offers an interesting selection of attractive gifts. ⊠ *1800 Lakeside Ave.* Ⓣ *804/262–9887* ⊕ *www.lewisginter.org* ⊠ *$10* Ⓢ *Daily 9–5.*

Ⓒ **Meadow Farm.** This living-history complex has programs, exhibits, and interpretive demonstrations of the life and culture on a working farm in 1860. On weekends, costumed interpreters work in the fields, the barns, the doctor's office, the blacksmith forge, and the farmhouse, offering a glimpse into the daily activities of original owner Dr. John Mosby Sheppard and his family. Special activities for children include storytelling days, Civil War lantern tours, and harvest-picking parties, and best of all, these programs are free. ⊠ *3400 Mountain Rd., Glen Allen* Ⓣ *804/501–5520* ⊕ *www.co.henrico.va.us/rec* ⊠ *Free* Ⓢ *Tues.– Sun. noon–4; closed 1st 2 wks Jan.*

Ⓒ **Science Museum of Virginia.** Aerospace, astronomy, electricity, physical ★ sciences, computers, crystals, telecommunications, and the Foucault pendulum are among the subjects covered in exhibits here. Older children and teens love the Ethyl IMAX Dome and Planetarium, and adults enjoy the Virginia Tech Solar Decathlon House, a working model of a green home of the future. The museum is in a former train station with a massive dome, and you can visit the café or gift shop without paying admission fees. ⊠ *2500 W. Broad St.* Ⓣ *804/864–1400* ⊕ *www. smv.org* ⊠ *Museum $10; IMAX $8.50; IMAX and planetarium $18* Ⓢ *Mon.–Sat. 9:30–5, Sun. 11:30–5; closed Mon.*

Virginia Historical Society Museum of Virginia History. A visitor-friendly museum mounts regularly changing exhibits and has permanent exhibitions that include an 800-piece collection of Confederate weapons and equipment and "The Story of Virginia, an American Experience," which covers 16,000 years of history. The Society also operates the Virginia House, a 16th-century manor house transported to Richmond from England. ⊠ *428 North Blvd., at Kensington Ave.* Ⓣ *804/358–4901* ⊕ *www.vahistorical.org* ⊠ *Free* Ⓢ *Tues.–Sat. 10–5, Sun., galleries only, 1–5. Virginia House $6 by appt. only.*

6

DOWNTOWN

Richmond's historic attractions lie north of the James River, which bisects the city with a sweeping curve. The heart of Old Richmond is the Court End district downtown. This area, close to the Capitol, contains seven National Historic Landmarks, three museums, and 11 additional buildings on the National Register of Historic Places—all within eight blocks. Just a mile east of Court End is historic Church Hill, a neighborhood of 19th-century homes and historic St. John's Church, which offers a free reenactment of Patrick Henry's "Give me liberty" speech on Sunday at 2 pm (Memorial Day through Labor Day).

Running west from the Court End district is Main Street, lined with banks; Cary Street, an east–west thoroughfare, becomes, between 12th and 15th streets, the cobblestone center of Shockoe Slip, and the west end of Cary Street, known as Carytown, is Richmond's most popular shopping district. Shockoe Slip (once the city's largest commercial trading district and the heart of the slave trade) and Shockoe Bottom (on land formerly occupied by a Native American trading post) are unique, restored areas filled with trendy shops, restaurants, and nightlife. Shockoe Bottom landmarks include the 17th Street Farmers' Market, operating since 1775, and Main Street Station, an elaborate Victorian structure capped by red tiles that was Richmond's first train station. Drive west beyond the historic downtown to see a fascinating group of charming and distinctive neighborhoods. Not far from the Capitol is Jackson Ward, called the "Home of Black Capitalism," a cultural and entrepreneurial center after the Civil War.

EXPLORING

TOP ATTRACTIONS

American Civil War Center. This museum weaves the stories of the Union, Confederate, and African-American experiences during the Civil War into a national context. The permanent exhibit *In the Cause of Liberty* is housed in the old Gun Foundry, where more than 1,100 Confederate cannons were made. ⊠ *500 Tredegar St.* ☎ *804/780–1865* ⊕ *www. tredegar.org* ⌨ *$8* ☉ *Daily 9–5.*

Black History Museum & Cultural Center of Virginia. The goal of this museum in the Jackson Ward is to gather visual, oral, and written records and artifacts that commemorate the lives and accomplishments of blacks in Virginia. On display are 5,000 documents, fine art objects, traditional African artifacts, textiles from ethnic groups throughout Africa, and artwork by Sam Gilllam, John Biggers, and P.H. Polk. ⊠ *3 Clay St., at Foushee St.* ☎ *804/780–9093* ⊕ *www.blackhistorymuseum.org* ⌨ *$5* ☉ *Tues.–Sat. 10–5.*

Citie of Henricus. Visit the home of Pocahontas and the second successful English settlement in the New World. Costumed interpreters reenact the lives of Virginia's Native Americans and English settlers who helped create the nation we know today. ⊠ *251 Henricus Park Rd., Chester* ☎ *804/706–1340* ⊕ *www.henricus.org* ⌨ *$8* ☉ *Tues.–Sun. 10–5.*

OFF THE BEATEN PATH

Edgar Allan Poe Museum. Richmond's oldest residence, the Old Stone House in Shockoe Bottom, just west of Church Hill Historic District,

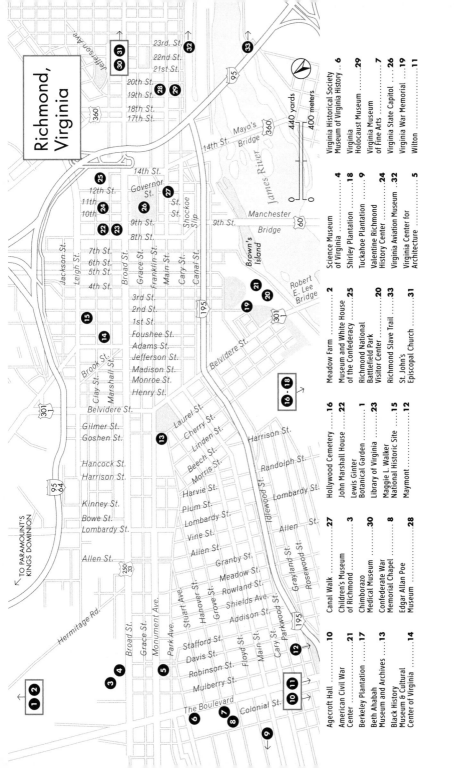

Richmond, Virginia

23rd St.
22nd St.
21st St.
20th St.
19th St.
18th St.
17th St.

14th St.

12th St.
11th St.
10th St.

9th St.
8th St.

7th St.
6th St.
5th St.
4th St.

3rd St.
2nd St.
1st St.
Foushee St.
Adams St.
Jefferson St.
Madison St.
Monroe St.
Henry St.

Jackson St.
Leigh St.
Brook St.
Marshall St.
Clay St.
Belvidere St.

Gilmer St.
Goshen St.

Hancock St.
Harrison St.

Kinney St.
Bowe St.
Lombardy St.

Allen St.

Jefferson Ave.

Governor St.
Shockoe Slip
Broad St.
Grace St.
Franklin St.
Main St.
Cary St.
Canal St.

Mayo's Bridge
James River
Manchester Bridge
Brown's Island
Robert E. Lee Bridge

Belvidere St.

Laurel St.
Cherry St.
Linden St.
Beech St.
Morris St.
Harvie St.
Plum St.
Lombardy St.
Vine St.
Allen St.
Granby St.
Meadow St.
Rowland St.
Shields Ave.
Addison St.

Randolph St.
Lombardy St.
Harrison St.
Idlewood St.
Grayland St.
Rosewood St.

Hermitage Rd.
Broad St.
Grace St.
Monument Ave.
Park Ave.
Stuart Ave.
Hanover Ave.
Grove Ave.
Stafford St.
Davis St.
Robinson St.
Mulberry St.
The Boulevard
Floyd St.
Main St.
Cary St.
Parkwood St.
Colonial St.
Allen St.

TO PARAMOUNT'S KINGS DOMINION

440 yards
400 meters

Agecroft Hall 10
American Civil War
Center 21
Berkeley Plantation 17
Beth Ahabah
Museum and Archives 13
Black History
Museum & Cultural
Center of Virginia 14

Canal Walk 27
Children's Museum
of Richmond 3
Chimborazo
Medical Museum 30
Confederate War
Memorial Chapel 8
Edgar Allan Poe
Museum 28

Hollywood Cemetery 16
John Marshall House 22
Lewis Ginter
Botanical Garden 1
Library of Virginia 23
Maggie L. Walker
National Historic Site 15
Maymont 12

Meadow Farm 2
Museum and White House
of the Confederacy 25
Richmond National
Battlefield Park
Visitor Center 20
Richmond Slave Trail 33
St. John's
Episcopal Church 12

Science Museum
of Virginia 4
Shirley Plantation 18
Tuckahoe Plantation 9
Valentine Richmond
History Center 24
Virginia Aviation Museum .. 32
Virginia Center for
Architecture 5

Virginia Historical Society
Museum of Virginia History .. 6
Virginia
Holocaust Museum 29
Virginia Museum
of Fine Arts 7
Virginia State Capitol 26
Virginia War Memorial 19
Wilton 11

now holds a museum honoring the famous writer. Poe grew up in Richmond, and although he never lived in this early- to mid-18th-century structure, his disciples have made it a monument with some of the writer's possessions on display. ✉ *1914 E. Main St.* ☎ *804/648–5523 or 888/213–2703* ⊕ *www.poemuseum.org* ▣ *$6* ⊙ *Tues.–Sat. 10–5, Sun. 11–5. Guided tours on the hr; last tour departs at 4.*

John Marshall House. John Marshall (1755–1835) was chief justice of the U.S. Supreme Court for 34 years—longer than any other. Appointed to the court by President John Adams, Marshall also served as secretary of state and ambassador to France. The Federal-style red brick house, built in 1790, is fully restored and furnished, with a mix of period pieces and heirlooms. ✉ *818 E. Marshall St.* ☎ *804/648–7998* ⊕ *www.apva.org/marshall* ▣ *$10* ⊙ *Tues.–Sat. 10–5, Sun. noon–5. By appt. only Jan.–Feb.*

Museum and White House of the Confederacy. These two buildings provide a look at a crucial period in the nation's history. The museum (a good place to start) has elaborate permanent exhibitions on the Civil War era. The "world's largest collection of Confederate memorabilia" includes such artifacts as the sword Robert E. Lee wore to the surrender at Appomattox. Next door, the "White House" has in fact always been painted gray. Made of brick in 1818, the building was stuccoed to give the appearance of large stone blocks. Preservationists have painstakingly re-created the interior as it was during the Civil War, when Jefferson Davis lived in the house. ✉ *1201 E. Clay St.* ☎ *804/649–1861* ⊕ *www.moc.org* ▣ *Combination ticket $12; museum only, $9; White House only, $9* ⊙ *Mon.–Sat. 10–5, Sun. noon–5.*

⟳ **Richmond National Battlefield Park Visitor Center.** Inside what was once the
Fodor'sChoice Tredegar Iron Works, this is the best place to get maps and other materi-
★ als on the Civil War battlefields and attractions in the Richmond area. A self-guided tour and optional tape tour for purchase covers the two major military threats to Richmond—the Peninsula Campaign of 1862 and the Overland Campaign of 1864—as well as the impact on Richmond's home front. Three floors of exhibits in the main building include unique artifacts on loan from other Civil War history institutions. Other original buildings on-site are a carpentry shop, gun foundry, office, and company store.

Kids can participate in the Junior Ranger program. They're given a workbook, which leads them through the exhibits in search of "clues." Once they've completed their book, they receive their choice of an embroidered Ranger patch or a Ranger pin.

Built in 1837, the ironworks, along with smaller area iron foundries, made Richmond the center of iron manufacturing in the South. When the Civil War began in 1861, the ironworks geared up to make the artillery, ammunition, and other material that sustained the Confederate war machine. Its rolling mills provided the armor plating for warships, including the ironclad CSS *Virginia*. The works—saved from burning in 1865—went on to play an important role in rebuilding the devastated South; it also produced munitions in both world wars. The center has a pay parking lot ($3), but free parking is available next door at the Belle Isle lot. Also, be aware that the American Civil War Center is also on this site, but is a private museum that charges admission. ⊠ *5th and Tredegar Sts.* ☎ *804/771–2145* ⊕ *www.nps.gov/ rich* 🖾 *Free* ⊗ *Daily 9–5.*

Richmond Slave Trail. Walk in the footsteps of Richmond's slaves from the Manchester Docks, down the Slave Trade path along the James River, past former slave auction houses in cobblestoned Shockoe Bottom and Lumpkin's Jail. Free booklets for a 1.3-mi self-guided walk are available from the city park system, or join in the big Freedom Celebration annually on June 19. ⊠ *Manchester Docks* ☎ *804/646– 8911* ⊕ *www.richmondgov.com/ commissionslavetrail* 🖾 *Free.*

> **AN HISTORIC MARKER**
>
> Not far from Richmond's former slave market in Shockoe Bottom, at the triangle of 15th and East Main streets, stands a 15-foot, half-ton bronze sculpture erected by officials from Liverpool, England, and Benin, West Africa. Both prospered from the slave trade, and Richmond was one of America's busiest slave trading centers. The statue is part of the Richmond Slave Trail, an effort to educate and raise awareness about the city's role in slave trade prior to the Civil War.

Fodor'sChoice ★ **St. John's Episcopal Church.** For security reasons, the rebellious Second Virginia Convention met in Richmond instead of Williamsburg; it was in this 1741 church on March 23, 1775, that Patrick Henry delivered the speech in which he declared, "Give me liberty or give me death!" His argument persuaded the Second Virginia Convention to arm a Virginia militia. The speech is reenacted Memorial Day to Labor Day on Sunday at 2 pm. The cemetery includes the graves of Edgar Allan Poe's mother, Elizabeth Arnold Poe, and many famous early Virginians, notably George Wythe, a signer of the Declaration of Independence. The visitor center, in a restored redbrick schoolhouse, has Colonial crafts and other items for sale. Guided tours are led on the half-hour. ⊠ *2401 E. Broad St., at 24th St.* ☎ *804/648–5015* ⊕ *www.historicstjohnschurch. org* 🖾 *$7* ⊗ *Mon.–Sat. 10–3:30, Sun. 1–3:30*

Valentine Richmond History Center. For more than 100 years, the Valentine Richmond History Center, established in 1898, has celebrated one of America's most historic cities. It has collected more than a million objects—one of the nation's largest collections focusing on a single city—including preserved photographs, textiles, and artifacts, and interprets 400 years of Richmond's history through items of everyday life. **Wickham House** (1812), a part of the Valentine, is more rightly a mansion; it was designed by architect Alexander Parris, the creator of Boston's Faneuil Hall. John Wickham was Richmond's wealthiest citizen of the time, and Daniel Webster and Zachary Taylor were frequent guests. The last owner of the house, Mann Valentine Jr., left a bequest in his will to turn the home into a museum. Mann's brother, sculptor Edward Valentine, worked from his carriage house studio to create the Robert E. Lee memorial at Washington & Lee University, and the famous statue of Thomas Jefferson in Richmond's grand Jefferson Hotel. His studio is one of only four surviving 19th-century sculptors' studios in the United States open to the public. ⊠ *1015 E. Clay St.* ☎ *804/649–0711* ⊕ *www.richmondhistorycenter.com* 🖾 *$10, includes John Marshall House, Black History Museum and Cultural Center, and*

Wickham House ☽ *Tues.–Sat. 10–5, Sun. noon–5; guided Wickham House tours Tues.–Sat. 11–4 and Sun. 1–4.*

Fodor's Choice ★ **Virginia Museum of Fine Arts.** After a $150 million expansion, the Virginia Museum of Fine Arts has doubled its exhibition space, added a casual bistro and fine dining restaurant, and expanded its accessibility with a schedule that will keep it open 365 days a year. Already one of the top contemporary art museums in the nation, the VMFA has a fine collection of American art, British sporting art, and Fabergé. Its collection of 22,000 works also includes Impressionist, Post-Impressionist, Himalayan, and African art. The soaring limestone and glass of the new wing and the whimsy of the adjacent sculpture garden blend the old and new to create a superb arts complex. Updated holiday hours will allow more visitors to take advantage of the free general admission throughout the year. ⊠ *200 North Blvd.* ☎ *804/340–1400* ⊕ *www.vmfa.state. va.us* ☞ *Free* ☽ *Sat.–Wed. 10–5, Thurs.–Fri. 10–9, 12–5 on holidays.*

★ **Virginia State Capitol.** Thomas Jefferson designed this grand edifice in 1785, modeling it on a Roman temple—the Maison Carrée—in Nîmes, France. After an extensive renovation, the Capitol has a handicapped-accessible entrance on Bank Street. A visitor's center is in the adjacent Bell Tower, and the expanded Capitol features an exhibit gallery, gift shop, and Meriwether's Capitol Café. Indoor guided tours last one hour and include the Old House and Senate chambers, the Rotunda, and two restored rooms. A map for self-guided tours is also available. ⊠ *1000 Bank St.* ☎ *804/698–1788* ⊕ *www.virginiacapitol.gov* ☞ *Free* ☽ *Mon.–Sat. 8–5, Sun. 1–4.*

WORTH NOTING

Canal Walk. The 1.25-mi Canal Walk meanders through downtown Richmond along the Haxall Canal, the James River, and the Kanawha Canal, and can be enjoyed on foot or in boats. Along the way, look for history exhibits such as the Flood Wall Gallery, bronze medallions, and other exhibits placed on Brown's Island and Canal Walk by the Richmond Historical Riverfront Foundation. Many sights intersect with Canal Walk, including the Richmond National Battlefield Park Civil War Visitor Center, and 5th, 7th, Virginia, 14th, 15th, and 17th streets meet the water along it.

The James River–Kanawha Canal was proposed by George Washington to bring ships around the falls of the James River, and to connect Richmond to major trade routes. Brown's Island, once the location of an ammunition factory during the Civil War, hosts festivals and concerts in warmer months. **Richmond Canal Cruises** (⊠ *139 Virginia St.* ☎ *804/649–2800*) operates a 40-minute ride on the canal in a 38-seat open boat. Tours, which cost $5, depart from the Turning Basin near 14th and Virginia streets. Tours run from April through mid-November and depart on the hour, but hours and days vary by season. ⊕ *www. venturerichmond.com/experiences/canalcruises.*

Chimborazo Medical Museum. This was once the Confederacy's largest and best-equipped hospital. Chimborazo opened in 1861 and treated more than 76,000 Confederate soldiers between 1862 and 1865. This site—once more than 40 acres—now contains a National Park Service visitor center and a small medical museum that tells the story of the patients, hospital, caregivers, and physicians through uniforms, documents, and other artifacts. ✉ *3215 E. Broad St.* ☎ *804/226–1981* ⊕ *www.nps.gov/rich* 🏷 *Free* ⊙ *Daily 9–5.*

Library of Virginia. As the official state archive, this library preserves and provides access to more than 99.5 million manuscript items documenting four centuries of Virginia history—fascinating to researchers and less so to everyone else. Its collections include 240,000 photographs, prints, engravings, posters, and paintings. The building has free underground parking. ✉ *800 E. Broad St.* ☎ *804/692–3500* ⊕ *www.lva.lib.va.us* 🏷 *Free* ⊙ *Mon.–Sat. 9–5.*

Confederate War Memorial Chapel. Built in 1887 by Confederate veterans, this tiny nondenominational chapel behind the Virginia Museum of Fine Arts was once part of the old Confederate soldiers' home. A video and displays of Confederate memorabilia pay tribute to the soldiers. ✉ *2900 Grove Ave.* ☎ *804/740–4479* ⊕ *www.civilwartraveler.com/east/va/va-central/richmond.html* 🏷 *Free* ⊙ *Wed.–Sun. 11–3.*

Maggie L. Walker National Historic Site. From 1904 to 1934, this restored 28-room brick building was the home of a pioneering African-American businesswoman and educator whose endeavors included banking, insurance, and a newspaper. You can take a 45-minute tour of the house and see a movie about her accomplishments. ✉ *Visitor center, 600 N. 2nd St.* ☎ *804/771–2017* ⊕ *www.nps.gov/malw* 🏷 *Free* ⊙ *Mon.–Sat. 9–5.*

Virginia Aviation Museum. The legendary SR-71 Blackbird spy plane sits proudly outside this museum. The museum, also home to Virginia's Aviation Hall of Fame, has Captain Dick Merrill's 1930s open-cockpit mail plane; airworthy replicas of the Wright brothers' 1900, 1901, and 1902 gliders; a replica 1903 Flyer; and a World War I SPAD VII in mint condition. Kids, especially, love the planes, many of which they can sit in. ✉ *Richmond International Airport, 5701 Huntsman Rd.* ☎ *804/236–3622* ⊕ *www.vam.smv.org* 🏷 *$6* ⊙ *Mon.–Sat. 9:30–5, Sun. noon–5.*

Virginia Center for Architecture. Housed in a Tudor Revival mansion on Monument Avenue designed by John Russell Pope, this museum features rotating exhibitions and a learning center on a self-guided tour. One of the permanent exhibits, "The House that Pope Built," is a tribute to the architect of the Thomas Jefferson Memorial and Richmond's Union Station, which now houses the Science Museum. Touring exhibitions range from American classicism to iconic furniture design. ✉ *2501 Monument Ave.* ☎ *804/644–3041* ⊕ *www.virginiaarchitecture.org* 🏷 *$2* ⊙ *Tues.–Fri. 10–5, weekends 1–5.*

Virginia Holocaust Museum. The city's most poignant museum is housed in the former Climax Warehouse, which stored tobacco in Richmond's Shockoe Bottom. In keeping with the museum's aim to further "tolerance through education," the museum details the experiences of Holocaust survivors from across Virginia who have recorded their stories and shared their memories. After an introductory film in which six Richmond-based survivors tell their stories, visitors receive a book for a self-guided tour; a free audio tour (in English, Spanish, German, French, or Polish) is also available. The museum's auditorium, the Chore Shul, is a replica of the beautiful 18th-century interior of the only surviving synagogue in Lithuania. Because of the nature of the exhibits, the museum is not recommended for young children. ⊠ *2000 E. Cary St.* ☎ *804/257–5400* ⊕ *www.va-holocaust.com* ✉ *Donations accepted* ☉ *Weekdays 9–5, weekends 11–5.*

Virginia War Memorial. A statue called *Memory* overlooks a wall with thousands of names of Virginians who sacrificed their lives in World War II, Korea, Vietnam, and the Persian Gulf. A series of educational programs based on the real-life experiences of Virginians is shown in the Hall of Honor Auditorium, and touch-screen computers in the Visitor's Center provide information on Virginia veterans. Displays of artifacts and memorabilia tell the story of the impact of these conflicts on Virginians and their families. ⊠ *621 South Belvidere St.* ☎ *804/786–2060* ⊕ *www.vawarmemorial.org* ✉ *Free* ☉ *Shrine daily, visitor center Mon.–Fri. 9–4, Sun. 12–4.*

RICHMOND'S PARKS, PLANTATIONS AND ESTATES

Richmond has an abundance of beautiful parks, as well as historic estates and plantations. Many notable citizens, Confederate leaders, and even a few presidents are buried at Hollywood Cemetery, which offers beautiful views of the James River.

EXPLORING

Agecroft Hall. Built in Lancashire, England, in the 15th century during the reign of King Henry VIII, Agecroft Hall was transported here in 1926. It's one of the finest Tudor manor houses in the United States. Set amid gardens planted with specimens typical of 1580–1640, the house contains an extensive assortment of Tudor and early Stuart art and furniture (1485–1660) as well as collector's items from England and elsewhere in Europe. A Tudor kitchen lets visitors learn about the culinary tools of that age. ⊠ *4305 Sulgrave Rd.* ☎ *804/353–4241* ⊕ *www. agecrofthall.com* ✉ *$8* ☉ *Tues.–Sat. 10–4, Sun. 12:30–5.*

Berkeley Plantation. This James River plantation was the birthplace of William Henry Harrison, ninth U.S. President and Benjamin Harrison V, a signer of the Declaration of Independence. It also lays claim to hosting America's first Thanksgiving in December of 1619, long before the Pilgrims arrived. It played a major role in the Civil War, as the headquarters and supply base for McClellan's Union Army. The plantation features five terraced gardens leading from the house to the James River that were dug by hand before the Revolutionary War, and the mansion built in 1726, which is still family-owned. ⊠ *12602 Harrison Landing Rd.* ☎ *804/829–6018* ⊕ *www.berkeleyplantation.com* ✉ *$11* ☉ *Daily 9:30–4:30.*

Hollywood Cemetery. Designed in a garden style along the banks of the James River, the cemetery requires at least an hour to stroll through the grounds. Many noted Virginians are buried here, including presidents John Tyler and James Monroe; Confederate president Jefferson Davis; and generals Fitzhugh Lee, J.E.B. Stuart, and George E. Pickett. Pets are allowed on leashes. ⊠ *412 S. Cherry St., at Albemarle* ☎ *804/648–8501* ⊕ *www.hollywoodcemetery.org* ✉ *Free* ☉ *Daily 8–5.*

☾ **Maymont.** On this 100-acre Victorian estate, one can explore the lavish
★ Maymont House museum, a carriage collection, and elaborate Italian
and Japanese gardens. A true family attraction, Maymont's complex
includes the Nature Visitor Center, native wildlife exhibits, and a children's farm. Kids love the pair of playful otters in the aquarium and
the waterfall above the Japanese garden. A Bald Eagle Habitat and
Raptor Valley are popular additions to the wildlife areas of the park.
Take the hop-on, hop-off tram for $3 to see this huge park and its
exhibits. Guided mansion tours are on the hour and half hour until
4:30 pm. A café is open for lunch. Carriage rides are also available
for $5. ⊠ *2201 Shields Lake Dr.* ☎ *804/358–7166* ⊕ *www.maymont.*
org 🖃 *Free* ⊙ *Grounds Apr.–Oct., daily 10–7; Nov.–Mar., daily 10–5.*
Mansion, nature center, and barn Tues.–Sun. noon–5.

Shirley Plantation. Just 10 mi east of Richmond, Shirley Plantation, on the
James River, is the oldest plantation in Virginia, and the oldest family-
owned business in North America. Founded in 1613 by a grant from
the Crown, Shirley is still a working farm today. The current mansion
was built in 1723 and is known as one of the most architecturally intact
examples of 18th-century homes in the country, with one of the only
surviving "flying staircases." But what brings this plantation to life, and
the main reason for its physical preservation, is the story of the women
of Shirley, who tended the wounded Union soldiers encamped on their
shores after the Battle of Malvern Hill. They took such good care of the
enemy that General McClellan ordered Shirley to be left untouched, and
thus it still thrives today under the management of the 11th generation of
the family. ⊠ *501 Shirley Plantation Rd., Charles City* ☎ *804/829–5121*
⊕ *www.shirleyplantation.com* 🖃 *$11* ⊙ *Daily 9:30–4:30.*

Tuckahoe Plantation. Originally owned by the Randolph family, Tuckahoe is 7 mi west of Richmond, on the James River. Thomas Jefferson
spent his boyhood years, from 1745 until 1752, here. In fact, he began
his studies in the one-room schoolhouse that still stands on the beautifully landscaped grounds, which are open daily for self-guided tours.
Guided tours of the house are by appointment only, except during the
special Christmas tour in December. A working farm, Tuckahoe still
sells beef, chickens, cut flowers, and organic eggs. ⊠ *12601 River Rd.*
☎ *804/784–5736* ⊕ *www.tuckahoeplantation.com* 🖃 *$5* ⊙ *Mon.–Sat.*
9–5, Sun. 12–5.

Wilton. William Randolph III built this elegant Georgian house in
1753, entertaining notable statesmen including George Washington
and Thomas Jefferson. Once 14 mi downriver, the home was moved
brick by brick to its current site when industry encroached upon its
former location. The home's 1815 period furnishings include the family's original desk bookcase and an original map of Virginia drawn
by Thomas Jefferson's father. ⊠ *215 S. Wilton Rd.* ☎ *804/282–5936*
⊕ *www.wiltonhousemuseum.org* 🖃 *$10* ⊙ *Tues.–Sat. 10–4:30, Sun.*
1:30–4:30. Closed Mon.

ASHLAND AND AROUND The historic town of Ashland, where Patrick Henry honed his oratory skills,
is about 20 mi north of Richmond. An easy day trip or stop on the way north
to Fredericksburg, Ashland was home to both Henry and fellow orator

Henry Clay. Visit the historic courthouse and Patrick Henry's plantation, **Scotchtown** (⊠ *16120 Chiswell La., Beaverdam* ☎ *804/227–3500* ⊕ *www. apva.org/scotchtown*). If you plan to stay over, the **Henry Clay Inn** (⊠ *114 N. Railroad Ave., Ashland* ☎ *804/798–3100* ⊕ *www.henryclayinn.com*), a charming Georgina Revival home, is in the heart of the historic town. The **Iron Horse** (⊠ *100 S. Railroad Ave., Ashland* ☎ *804/752–6410*) restaurant is a local favorite for lunch and dinner.

Catch a show at the **Barksdale Theatre** (⊠ *1601 Willow Lawn Dr.* ☎ *804/282–2620* ⊕ *www.barksdalerichmond.org*). The area's oldest not-for-profit theater began in 1953. Performances ranging from classics to innovative new works are staged Thursday through Saturday evening and on Sunday afternoon. And, once again, productions are being staged at the historic Hanover Tavern.

Ⓒ Kids love the nearby 400-acre amusement park, **Paramount Kings Dominion** (⊠ *16000 Theme Park Way, Doswell* ☎ *804/876–5000* ⊕ *www. kingsdominion.com*).

WHERE TO EAT

¢–$

AMERICAN

✕ **Café Gutenberg**. If you're craving a cup of Illy Coffee and a decadent pastry, head for Shockoe Bottom. Directly across the street from the Farmers' Market, this café has a Viennese coffeehouse vibe, complete with loaner books and free Wi-Fi. Richmond residents have been drawn here for years, but now the food is the star. Extensive offerings for vegetarians and vegans include vegan biscuits and gravy and tofu sliders, but there are plenty of choices for carnivores. Chefs Jen Mindel and Garrett Berry use local and seasonal ingredients to create soul-satisfying meals from breakfast to dinner, like a mixed grill of spring lamb and curried chicken satay. There's also a good wine list and selection of beers from Germany and Belgium. ⊠ *1700 E. Main St.* ☎ *804/497–5000* ⊕ *www.cafegutenberg.com* ⚑ *Reservations not accepted* 🖃 *AE, MC, V.*

$–$$

EUROPEAN

✕ **Café Rustica**. Chef/owner Andy Howell is a star on the Richmond culinary scene. His latest success is a European bistro in the heart of downtown. Howell sources his ingredients regionally and whips up European comfort food for breakfast, lunch, and dinner. The roast chicken with vegetables will transport you to the south of France, while the schnitzel is pure Heidelberg. A wine bar and daily cheese plate specials make Café Rustica a great pre- or post-event stop, as well. Seating is limited, and they don't take reservations. Sundays are a bargain with prix-fixe deals. ⊠ *14 E. Main St.* ☎ *804/225–8811* ⚑ *Reservations not accepted* 🖃 *AE, D, MC, V* ⊘ *Closed Mon.*

$–$$

FRENCH

✕ **Can Can Brasserie**. Though it's no tiny Parisian brasserie, Can Can does deliver French comfort food at affordable prices, from a croque monsieur to steak frites. Located in the heart of the Carytown entertainment and shopping district, this is the spot for people-watching from the outdoor tables—whether you're having a croissant and café au lait, or mussels in a white wine and garlic broth. ⊠ *3120 W. Cary St.* ☎ *804/358–7274* ⊕ *www.cancanbrasserie.com* 🖃 *AE, D, MC, V.*

$-$$
EUROPEAN
✕ **Chez Foushee.** This hip bistro just off Broad Street near Virginia Commonwealth University is a popular lunch and brunch spot, and also has a take-out operation. The weekday lunch and weekend dinner menus feature a wide variety of seasonal soups, salads, wraps, and hot entrées. The wine list features French vintages to complement the simple Continental fare. ✉ *203 N. Foushee St.* ☎ *804/648–3225* ⊕ *www.chezfoushee.com* ☰ *AE, D, MC, V* ☻ *Mon.–Fri. lunch 11:30–2:30, Fri.–Sat. dinner 6–10.*

$$
SOUTHERN
✕ **Comfort.** This local favorite is always packed, partly because of its proximity to the National Theater, a popular concert venue. Specializing in Southern comfort food—from fried catfish to macaroni and cheese—each entrée is marked with two prices so you can choose either two or three of the seasonal sides like squash casserole and fried okra. If you're looking for small-batch bourbon, Comfort's whiskey bar stocks more than 40 of the best. ✉ *200 W. Broad St.* ☎ *804/780–0004* ⊕ *www.comfortrestaurant.com* ⌘ *Reservations not accepted* ☰ *AE, D, MC, V* ☻ *Closed Sun. No lunch Sat.*

¢–$
BARBECUE
☺
✕ **Halligan Bar & Grill.** This hole-in-the-wall barbecue joint has taken off like a house on fire. Owned by a 17-year fire service veteran, and staffed by Henrico County's finest, Halligan is a tribute to firefighters with a 1973 Seagrave fire truck that serves as a backdrop to the bar, authentic helmets doubling as pendant lights, and walls covered with memorabilia. Meat is smoked in-house for hearty Southern favorites like the Carolina-style pulled-pork sandwich, classic chicken, and Texas-style beef brisket. Don't be surprised to hear sirens and see lights set off periodically to salute the customers. ✉ *3 N. 17th St.* ☎ *804/447–7981* ☰ *AE, D, MC, V.*

$$-$$$
SEAFOOD
✕ **The Hard Shell.** This fun and unpretentious restaurant has many fresh and local seafood dishes, and those with other tastes can choose from such options as filet mignon and prime rib; even vegetarians are well cared for. Raw bar enthusiasts will be enticed, too, with the option of getting a half-pound of steamed shrimp, Dungeness crab legs, snow crab legs, or littleneck clams. From live Maine lobsters to blue-point oysters, this is the place for any kind of seafood you crave. Although the interior is romantic, with exposed brick and dark wood, if the weather's nice, dine alfresco on one of the city's favorite patios. The Sunday brunch is especially attractive, as are the specialty drinks, particularly the martinis. ✉ *1411 E. Cary St.* ☎ *804/643–2333* ⊕ *www.thehardshell.com* ☰ *AE, D, DC, MC, V* ☻ *No lunch weekends.*

$$-$$$
AMERICAN
✕ **Julep's.** In the River District, and in the city's oldest commercial building (1817), Julep's has a spiral staircase joining the upper and lower dining areas. The specialty here is New Southern cuisine, with seasonal lunch and dinner menus that include tempting dishes such as roasted game hen stuffed with a risotto of country ham, green peas, and mushrooms. The wine list is one to linger over. Try not to leave without sampling one of the restaurant's namesake drinks. ✉ *1719–21 E. Franklin St.* ☎ *804/377–3968* ⊕ *www.juleps.net* ☰ *AE, MC, V* ☻ *Closed Sun. No lunch Sat., no dinner Mon.*

$$-$$$
AMERICAN
Fodor's Choice
★
✕ **Lemaire.** Named after Etienne Lemaire, Maître d'Hôtel to Thomas Jefferson from 1794 until the end of his presidency, this is no ordinary hotel eatery. Jefferson's tastes included adding light sauces and fresh

herbs to dishes prepared with the region's more than abundant supply of ingredients, and Chef Walter Bundy follows suit with his own
urban garden in one of the Jefferson Hotel's parking lots. Today the
farm-to-table menu features updated regional Southern cuisine with
small plates and entrées that feature Virginia ham and sausage, Bundy's
own produce, and regional meats and fishes. Try the shrimp and grits,
Virginia bison rib eye, or homegrown oyster mushroom risotto washed
down with one of more than 200 wines, offered by the glass, bottle or
half-bottle. ⊠ *Jefferson Hotel, 101 W. Franklin St.* ☎ *804/788–8000*
⊕ *www.lemairerestaurant.com* ▤ *AE, D, DC, MC, V.*

$–$$ ✕ **Millie's Diner**. Be prepared to wait in line to check out Richmond's
AMERICAN   favorite diner. Locals often bring lawn chairs and games to pass the
time while waiting for their chance to try the upscale, contemporary
selections at this quirky eatery. This is the place for brunch for everything from huevos rancheros to the signature Devil's Mess kitchen-sink
omelet. Although the vibe is straight out of the '50s, with personal
jukeboxes in every booth, the food is strictly 21st century, with contemporary takes on Southern classics, as well as global offerings like Thai
spicy shrimp. Try the mac 'n' cheese with oyster mushrooms, asparagus, and foie gras butter or the pan-seared venison with black grapes
and Yorkshire pudding. The dinner menu changes every three weeks,
although the most popular lunch and breakfast offerings are always
available. ⊠ *2603 E. Main St.* ☎ *804/643–5512* ⌦ *Reservations not
accepted* ▤ *AE, D, MC, V* ☽ *Closed Mon.*

WHERE TO STAY

$–$$ ⌸ **Berkeley Hotel**. Although built in the style of the century-old ware-
houses and buildings that surround it, this boutique hotel dates from
1988. The majority of rooms are large junior suites with traditional
furnishings and modern amenities including flat-screens, and many have
balconies with panoramic urban views over historic Shockoe Slip area.
Service is personal and friendly, and shops and restaurants are just
steps from the front door. The restaurant offers boxed breakfast and
lunch to go, as well as full service dining. Guests staying here get free
entry to the YMCA health and fitness facilities at the James Center
across the street. **Pros:** valet parking; steps from several restaurants and
shops. **Cons:** extremely busy street; limited parking. ⊠ *1200 E. Cary
St.* ☎ *804/780–1300 or 888/780–4422* ⊕ *www.berkeleyhotel.com* ⌁ *54
rooms, 1 suite* ⌂ *In-room: a/c, Wi-Fi. In-hotel: restaurant, bar, gym,
laundry service, parking (paid)* ▤ *AE, D, MC, V.*

$–$$ ⌸ **Hilton Garden Inn Richmond Downtown**. Located in the historic Miller
and Rhoads Department Store building, this hotel is truly in the heart
of downtown, though there's not much left of the beloved local store
except the sign on the building. The lobby, painted a sunny yellow
with complementary earth tones, is warm and welcoming, with comfy
lounge seating, a bar, and restaurant. The hotel is directly across the
street from the Convention Center and has top amenities for business travelers, as well as a 24-hour on-site convenience store. **Pros:** no
smoking allowed; 24/7 market and business center; downtown location.
Cons: difficult to access; little parking nearby. ⊠ *501 East Broad St.*
☎ *804/344–4300* ⊕ *www.richmonddowntown.hgi.com* ⌁ *235 rooms,*

15 suites ☇ *In-room: a/c, phone, refrigerator, Wi-Fi. In-hotel: restaurant, room service, bar, pool, gym, laundry facilities, laundry service, Internet terminal, Wi-Fi hotspot, parking (paid)* ▭ *AE, D, DC, MC, V.*

$$$

Fodor's Choice

★

🏨 **Jefferson Hotel.** A 70-foot-high ceiling with a stained-glass skylight and 10 of the original Louis Comfort Tiffany stained-glass windows, rich tapestries, and replicas of traditional Victorian furniture make this the most elegant hotel in Richmond. The Palm Court Lobby is home to Edward Valentine's full-size statue of the president and to a magnificent sweeping staircase reminiscent of the one in *Gone With the Wind*. The rooms are done in a total of 57 different styles, and the 1,550-square-foot Presidential Suite has its own private balcony. Since the hotel is older, the rooms are somewhat small, but exquisitely appointed with period furnishings and top-of-the-line amenities including plush robes and flat-screen televisions. **Pros:** excellent concierge service; pet-friendly; complimentary local limousine service. **Cons:** standard rooms are small. ⊠ *101 W. Franklin St., at Adams St.* 🕾 *804/788–8000 or 800/424–8014* ⊕ *www.jeffersonhotel. com* 🛏 *228 rooms, 36 suites* ☇ *In-room: a/c. In-hotel: 2 restaurants, room service, bar, pool, gym, some pets allowed* ▭ *AE, D, DC, MC, V.*

$–$$

🏨 **Omni Richmond.** Part of the historic Shockoe Slip area, this hotel has an elegant lobby that connects to the adjacent James Center, filled with restaurants and shops. Guests also get free access to the YMCA there, can take advantage of the heated indoor pool, and can reserve one of the hotel's Get Fit rooms with their own portable treadmill. The rooms on the club level come with private concierge service and access to a club lounge. **Pros:** close to restaurants and shopping. **Cons:** limited parking. ⊠ *James Center, 100 S. 12th St.* 🕾 *804/344–7000* ⊕ *www.omnihotels. com* 🛏 *353 rooms, 8 suites* ☇ *In-room: a/c, Wi-Fi. In-hotel: 2 restaurants, room service, bar, pool, gym, parking (paid)* ▭ *AE, D, DC, MC, V.*

$$–$$$

🏨 **Richmond Marriott.** Recently renovated, this hotel's lobby is one huge contemporary lounge, with flat-screens, workspaces, an open lobby bar and lounge, and plenty of club seating. T-Millers Sports Bar broadcasts in high definition; the Liberty Bar and a lobby Starbucks offer beverages aplenty. The hotel is connected via a skywalk to the Greater Richmond Convention Center. Rooms are modern and well appointed. **Pros:** walking distance to historic sites and Convention Center; complimentary downtown shuttle service. **Cons:** congested entrance; limited parking; on main artery. ⊠ *500 E. Broad St.* 🕾 *804/643–3400 or 800/228–9290* ⊕ *www.marriotthotels.com/ricdt* 🛏 *410 rooms* ☇ *In-room: a/c, Internet. In-hotel: 2 restaurants, bar, pool, gym* ▭ *AE, D, DC, MC, V.*

NIGHTLIFE AND THE ARTS

The National Theater (⊠ *708 E. Broad St.* 🕾 *804/612–1900* ⊕ *www. thenationalva.com*) hosts everything from the Richmond Symphony to the Black Crowes, with a full schedule throughout the year.

The **Richmond Coliseum** (⊠ *601 E. Leigh St.* 🕾 *804/780–4956* ⊕ *www. richmondcoliseum.net*) has been a Richmond institution since the early 1970s. With 11,330 permanent seats, and nearly 2,000 more for concerts, it hosts top entertainers and artists, the Ringling Brothers circus, Richmond Riverdogs hockey team, wrestling, and other large events.

BARS

From the college bars in the Fan District to upscale martini and wine bars, Richmond has a vibrant nightlife. ■ TIP→ The nonprofit "To the Bottom and Back" Bus offers free service between the Fan and Downtown Thursday–Saturday nights, from 6 pm to 3 am. Call 804/908-2945 or visit 2bnb.org.

One local favorite is **Havana 59** (⊠ *16 N. 7th St.* ☎ *804/780–2822* ⊕ *www.havana59.net*) in Shockoe Bottom. Styled after the Cuban clubs that gave Havana the nickname "the Paris of the '50s," this multilevel club is decked out in palm trees and twinkling white lights, with both outdoor terraces and an open-fronted cavernous ground floor. For dancing, head to **The Tobacco Company** (⊠ *1201 E. Cary St.* ☎ *804/782–9555* ⊕ *www.thetobaccocompany.com* ⊠ *$5* ☉ *Thurs.–Sat. 8 pm–2 am*), where you can disco until the wee hours in Shockoe Slip.

DANCE

The **Richmond Ballet** (⊠ *407 E. Canal St.* ☎ *804/344–0906* ⊕ *www. richmondballet.com*), the city's professional classical ballet company, usually performs at the Carpenter Center and at the Theatre Virginia in the Virginia Museum of Fine Arts.

MUSIC

The **Richmond Symphony** (☎ *804/788–1212* ⊕ *www.richmondsymphony. com*), founded in 1957, often utilizes internationally known soloists at performances in the Carpenter Center. The Richmond Symphony All-Star Pops hosts popular guest artists.

THEATER

Carpenter Theatre (⊠ *600 E. Grace St.* ☎ *804/225–9000* ⊕ *www. carpentercenter.org*), a restored 1928 motion-picture palace, is now a performing-arts center that mounts opera, traveling shows, symphonic music, and ballet. It's the cornerstone of the Center Stage Performing Arts Complex, which also boasts a more intimate venue, Rhythm Hall, for local performers, the Gottwald Playhouse, and a visual arts space called the Showcase Gallery. **Landmark Theatre** (⊠ *6 N. Laurel St.* ☎ *804/646–4213*) was built in an extremely elaborate style with towering minarets and desert murals: when it was built by the Shriners in 1926, it was called "the Mosque," and still is by locals. Just west of downtown, the Landmark is known for its excellent acoustics and has the largest permanent proscenium stage on the East Coast; it hosts the road versions of Broadway shows, symphony performances, ballet, children's theater, concerts, and fashion shows.

SPORTS AND THE OUTDOORS

CAR RACING

Richmond International Raceway (⊠ *600 E. Laburnum Ave. Exit off I–64* ☎ *804/329–0845 or 866/455–7223*) holds two NASCAR Nextel Cup Series races, held on Saturday nights in May and September, as well as other races.

GOLF
In Richmond aficionados tee off most of the year. The area has 24 golf courses open to the public—the **Virginia State Golf Association** (⊕ *www. vsga.org*) has a good handle on them all; its Web site even allows you to book tee times online.

RAFTING
Richmond is the only city within the United States that has rafting within its city limits. **Riverside Outfitters** (☎ *804/560–0068* ⊕ *www. riversideoutfitters.com*) conducts white-water rafting trips through the city on the James River (Class III and IV rapids), as well as canoe and kayak trips.

SHOPPING

Richmond has seven shopping malls, but locals prefer the arty boutiques, shops, and galleries of its unique neighborhoods. **Carytown** (⊠ *West end of Cary St. from the Powhite Pkwy. to Boulevard* ⊕ *www. carytownrva.com*) is a nine-block shopping-and-entertainment district with more than 300 shops and 25 restaurants. Parking is scarce on weekends. The **17th Street Farmers' Market** (⊠ *100 N. 17th St., at Main St.* ⊕ *www.17thstreetfarmersmarket.com*), beside the old Main Street Station, has been a public gathering place since 1737, and is within walking distance of art galleries, boutiques, and antiques shops, many in converted warehouses and factories. Market days are Thursday, Saturday, and Sunday. In the West End, **Libbie Grove** (⊠ *Libbie and Grove avenues* ⊕ *www.libbiegrove.com*) is filled with eclectic boutiques and antique stores. **Shockoe Slip** (⊠ *E. Cary St. between 12th and 15th Sts.*), a neighborhood of tobacco warehouses during the 18th and 19th centuries, has boutiques, antiques stores, and international furniture stores like the multilevel, supermodern La Difference.

PETERSBURG

Historic **Petersburg,** 20 mi south of Richmond on I–95, lies along the Appomattox River. During the Civil War, the city was under siege for 292 days by Union forces from June 1864 to April 1865—the so-called last stand of the Confederacy. A major railroad hub, the city was a crucial link in the supply chain for Lee's army, and its surrender brought about the evacuation of Richmond and the surrender at Appomattox. Lee's Retreat is a 26-stop self-guided driving tour from Petersburg to Appomattox. For a route map and other information, contact the Petersburg Visitor Center.

These days, like many other small Southern towns, it is struggling to overcome decades of depression, and this is readily apparent on the drive from I–95 to the downtown area. However, a great effort has been made in the area around the Petersburg Visitor Center, and there are many beautifully maintained houses in the historic residential area just to the west.

GETTING HERE AND AROUND

Petersburg is off Exit 52 of I–95, and north of the intersection of I–85 and I–95. The Richmond GRTC operates an express bus from the city to Petersburg for $2.50. Amtrak also services Petersburg's Ettrick Station.

SAFETY AND PRECAUTIONS

Although the parks and historic downtown area have been restored and revitalized, be careful in the transitional neighborhoods on the edges of the city.

TIMING

The weather is good from May through October—perfect for exploring the Farmers' Market next to Union Station or walking along the Appomattox River Trail. On the second Friday of the month, Old Towne hosts a Friday for the Arts event from 6 to 10 pm.

EXPLORING

Centre Hill Museum. This, the third home of the Bolling family, was originally built in 1823. Having been remodeled twice since then, it illustrates changing architectural styles; it was and is the grandest home in Petersburg. Inside are ornate woodwork, plaster motifs, period furnishings, and an 1840s service tunnel in the basement that once connected the work area of the house to the street below. For many years, every January 24, the residents of Centre Hill heard the ghosts of Civil War soldiers marching up and down the staircase. You can listen for those boots at the annual Ghost Watch. ✉ *1 Centre Hill Circle* ☎ *804/733–2401* 🖥 *$5* ☉ *Daily 10:30–4:30.*

A parish church from the 18th century, **Old Blandford Church and Cemetery** is a memorial to the Southern soldiers who died during the Civil War. Some 30,000 Confederate soldiers are buried in the churchyard, which is surrounded by ornamental ironwork. The church's 15 spectacular stained-glass windows by Louis Comfort Tiffany are memorials donated by the Confederate states. The Memorial Day tradition is said to have begun in this cemetery in June 1866, inspired by the women's group of the church who not only raised the funds for the memorial, but also decorated the graves every year. ✉ *111 Rochelle La., 2 mi south of town* ☎ *804/733–2396* 🖥 *$5* ☉ *Daily 10–5.*

★ On April 2, 1865, in what is now **Pamplin Historical Park**, Union troops successfully attacked General Robert E. Lee's formerly impenetrable defense line, forcing Lee to abandon Petersburg. Today you are greeted by the 300-foot-long facade of the Battlefield Center, a concrete representation of the Confederate battle lines. Besides the center, which focuses on the April 2 battle, there's a 2-mi battle trail with 2,100 feet of 8-foot-high earthen fortifications, reconstructed soldier huts, and original picket posts. Also on the grounds is Tudor Hall, an 1812 plantation home that served as the 1864 headquarters for Confederate general Samuel McGowan. The **National Museum of the Civil War Soldier** on the grounds has interactive displays and nearly 700 artifacts. You can select an audio guide that includes the actual letters and diaries of a soldier. Allow at least two hours to visit the park and museum. ✉ *6125 Boydton Plank Rd., off U.S. 1, I–85S to Exit 63A*

☎ *804/861–2408 or 877/726–7546* ⊕ *www.pamplinpark.org* ✉ *$12* ⊗ *Open seasonally 9–5.*

Fodor'sChoice
★

To walk **Petersburg National Battlefield** is to be where more than 60,000 Union and Confederate soldiers died during the siege of the city. A pronounced depression in the ground is the eroded remnant of the Crater, the result of a 4-ton gunpowder explosion set off by Union forces in one failed attack. The 1,500-acre park is laced with several miles of earthworks and includes two forts. In the visitor center, maps and models convey background information vital to the self-guided driving tour, during which you park at specified spots on the tour road and proceed on foot to nearby points of interest. ✉ *Rte. 36, 2.5 mi east of downtown* ☎ *804/732–3531* ⊕ *www.nps.gov/pete* ✉ *$5 per car, $3 per cyclist or pedestrian* ⊗ *Daily 9–5.*

The **Petersburg Visitor Center** in the Old Farmer's Bank sells the Fort Henry Pass, which allows admission to the Siege Museum, Centre Hill Mansion, and Blandford Church for $11. The center also has information about Lee's Retreat Trail, a 26-stop driving tour around the area. Free parking is plentiful near the center. ✉ *McIlwaine House, 19 Bollingbrook St.* ☎ *804/733–2400 or 800/368–3595* ⊕ *www. petersburg-va.org.*

★ The **Siege Museum**, inside a former commodities market from 1839, tells the story of how the city's lavish lifestyle gave way to a bitter struggle for survival during the Civil War: a single chicken could cost as much as $50 in Confederate currency. A 16-minute movie narrated by Petersburg-born actor Joseph Cotten dramatizes the upheaval. ✉ *Exchange Bldg., 15 W. Bank St.* ☎ *804/733–2404* ✉ *$5* ⊗ *Daily 10–5.*

WHERE TO EAT

$$–$$$
GREEK

✕ **Alexander's Fine Food**. White tablecloths flare from beneath glass tops at the tables of this Greek-American restaurant, which also has a bar. The souvlaki platter, leg of lamb, and Athenian-style chicken are specialties. Lunch favorites include the "grill and chill" and the variety of hearty salads, while the stuffed chicken breast and the crab cakes are best sellers at dinner. ✉ *101 W. Bank St.* ☎ *804/733–7134* ▬ *No credit cards* ⊗ *Closed Sun. and Wed.–Sat. No dinner Mon. and Tues.*

$–$$
MEXICAN

✕ **Andrades**. Although the faux pergola and grapes might make you think Italian, Andrades is a locally owned eatery in the heart of the historic downtown area featuring classic cuisine from Mexico, Peru, Bolivia, and Spain. Popular for both lunch and dinner, the menu includes such tempting dishes as *Zarzuela de Mariscos*, a seafood casserole, and *Masitas de Puerco*, Cuban-style pieces of pork marinated in criollo sauce and roasted in Sevilla's bitter oranges. The menu is rounded out with traditional selections including tacos and enchiladas. Complimentary tortilla chips and salsa are made fresh daily, and the large outdoor terrace is popular in spring and fall. ✉ *7 Bollingbrook St.* ☎ *804/733–1515* ⊕ *www.andradesinternational.com* ▬ *MC, V.*

$–$$
BRITISH

✕ **The Brickhouse Run**. Tucked away in a small alley in the historic district, this British pub occupies one of the oldest buildings in the city. Traditional and authentic pub grub includes fish-and-chips and shepherd's pie, and of course, a good selection of imported ales. The well-rounded

6

menu includes American favorites like burgers and pasta. Salads are always a good bet, since the chef sources his produce locally, and desserts including crème brûlée are outstanding. Both the chummy bar area and the dining room are filled with British-theme accessories and memorabilia. Reservations are not required and dress is casual. ⊠ *407–409 Cockade Alley* ☏ *804/862–1815* ⊕ *www.brickhouserun.com* ⊟ *AE, MC, V* ⊘ *Closed Sun. and Mon.*

WHERE TO STAY

¢–$ 🏠 **High Street Inn.** In the heart of the historic district, this beautiful, fired-brick Queen Anne mansion, which dates from 1891, was built by wealthy local merchant J.A. Gill. Opened in late 2004, the public areas and rooms—all named after people or places that influenced Petersburg's history—are charmingly classical, and the intricacy of the woodwork on the king-size bed in the BollingBrook Room has to be seen to be believed. **Pros:** in historic district; fireplaces. **Cons:** payment due to confirm reservation; no pets. ⊠ *405 High St.* ☏ *804/733–0271* ⊕ *www.thehighstreetinn.com* ➥ *5 rooms* ⌂ *In-room: a/c, Wi-Fi. In-hotel: parking (free)* ⊟ *AE, D, MC, V* ⦿ *CP.*

¢   🏠 **Howard Johnson Steven Kent.** With an Olympic-size swimming pool and nearly 20 acres of recreational facilities, this is no ordinary two-story motel. Local calls and newspapers are free, and rooms have a coffeemaker, hair dryer, iron, and ironing board. Room rates include a complimentary Continental breakfast. **Pros:** Wi-Fi, on-site amenities, pet friendly; least-expensive option in area. **Cons:** older property; not near historic downtown. ⊠ *12205 S. Crater Rd.* ☏ *804/733–0600 or 800/284–9393* 🖷 *804/862–4549* ➥ *133 rooms* ⌂ *In-room: a/c, Wi-Fi. In-hotel: pool, laundry facilities* ⊟ *AE, D, DC, MC, V* ⦿ *CP.*

¢–$ 🏠 **Ragland Mansion.** This stunningly attractive Italianate villa dates from the 1850s; it was the residence of General "Black Jack" Pershing during World War I. Inside are large formal rooms with crown moldings, French windows, 14-foot ceilings, mosaic parquet floors, and European and American artworks. The rooms and suite are furnished with antique furniture, claw-foot tubs, brass and iron beds, and paintings and engravings. It's a short walk from downtown and the historic district. **Pros:** historic home; period furnishings; good value. **Cons:** no food service on-site other than breakfast. ⊠ *205 S. Sycamore St.* ☏ *804/861–1932 or 800/861–8898* 🖷 *804/861–5943* ⊕ *www.raglandmansion.com* ➥ *6 rooms, 3 suites* ⌂ *In-room: a/c. In-hotel: parking (free)* ⊟ *AE, MC, V.*

FREDERICKSBURG

Halfway between Richmond and Washington, near the falls of the Rappahannock River, Fredericksburg is a popular destination for history buffs. The town's 40-block National Historic District contains more than 350 original 18th- and 19th-century buildings, including the house George Washington bought for his mother; the Rising Sun Tavern; and Kenmore, the magnificent 1752 plantation owned by George Washington's sister.

Although explorer Captain John Smith visited this site as early as 1608, Fredericksburg wasn't founded until 1728. It was named after England's crown prince at the time, Frederick Louis, the eldest son of King George II. The streets still bear names of his family members: George, Caroline, Sophia, Princess Anne, William, and Amelia. Established as a frontier port to serve nearby tobacco farmers and iron miners, Fredericksburg was at one point the 10th largest port in the colonies.

> **FROZEN TREATS**
>
> Family-run Carl's Frozen Custard at 200 Princess Anne Street is a Fredericksburg institution, with a walk-up window and long lines in the summer.

George Washington knew Fredericksburg well, having grown up just across the Rappahannock on Ferry Farm, his residence from age six to 19. The myths about chopping down a cherry tree and throwing a coin (actually a rock) across the Rappahannock (later confused with the Potomac) refer to this period of his life. In later years Washington often visited his mother here on Charles Street.

Fredericksburg prospered in the decades after independence, benefiting from its location midway along the route between Washington and Richmond—an important intersection of railroad lines and waterways. When the Civil War broke out, it became the linchpin of the Confederate defense of Richmond and therefore the target of Union assaults. In December 1862, Union forces attacked the town in what was to be the first of four major battles fought in and around Fredericksburg. In the battle of Sunken Road, Confederate defenders sheltered by a stone wall at the base of Marye's Heights mowed down thousands of Union soldiers who charged across the fields.

At Chancellorsville in April 1863, General Robert E. Lee led 60,000 troops to a brilliant victory over a much larger Union force of 134,000, and this resulted in Lee's invasion of Pennsylvania. The following year, Grant's troops battled Lee's Confederates through the Wilderness, a region of dense thickets and overgrowth south of the Rapidan River, then fought them again at Spotsylvania. Although neither side was victorious, Grant continued heading his troops toward the Confederate capital of Richmond.

By the war's end, fighting in Fredericksburg and at the nearby Chancellorsville, Wilderness, and Spotsylvania Court House battlefields resulted in more than 100,000 dead or wounded. Fredericksburg's cemeteries hold the remains of 17,000 soldiers from both sides. Miraculously, despite heavy bombardment and house-to-house fighting, much of the city remained intact.

A few decades ago Fredericksburg was one of the numerous small Southern cities facing another battle for survival, but today the city is being overrun for a different reason. The charming, historic town appeals to commuters fleeing the Washington, D.C., area for kinder, less-expensive environs. The railroad lines that were so crucial to transporting Civil War supplies now bring workers to and from the nation's capital an hour away, and the sacred Civil War battlegrounds share the area with legions of shopping centers. Tourists aren't scarce either, and not just to visit the historical sights. These days Fredericksburg has reinvented itself as a cute small town chockablock with boutiques and antiques and specialty stores, as well as a lively selection of small cafés and restaurants.

GETTING HERE AND AROUND

By car, Fredericksburg is easily accessible from Interstate 95 or Route 1, about an hour north of Richmond or south of Washington, D.C. The unmanned Fredericksburg train station is two blocks from the historic district. You can ride FRED, Fredericksburg's excellent little bus, for only 50¢. Several lines serve the region and stop at all historic sites as well as shopping malls and other modern areas of the city from 7:30 am to 8 pm.

TOURS   Trolley Tours of Fredericksburg runs a 75-minute narrated tour of Fredericksburg's most important sights. Tours cost $17 and leave from the visitor center.

The tour coordinator at the Fredericksburg Visitor Center can arrange a group walking tour of the city as well as of battlefields and other historic sites to which you can drive. Reservations are required. The Fredericksburg Department of Tourism (in the visitor center) publishes a booklet that includes a short history of Fredericksburg and a self-guided tour covering 29 sights.

TIMING

Fredericksburg is busy during the Christmas and New Year's holiday season, so book hotels and special event tickets in advance for those times.

ESSENTIALS

Taxi Companies **Bumbreys Independent Cab Service** (✉ *209 Lafayette Blvd.* ☎ *540/373–6111*). **City Cab** (☎ *540/372–4484*). **Yellow Cab of Fredericksburg** (✉ *2217 Princess Anne St.* ☎ *540/368–8120*).

Tours **Segway Tours of Fredericksburg** (☎ *800/979–3370* ⊕ *www. otsegtours.com*). **Trolley Tours of Fredericksburg** (☎ *800/979–3370* ⊕ *www. fredericksburgtrolley.com*).

DOWNTOWN FREDERICKSBURG

Fredericksburg, a modern commercial town, includes a 40-block National Historic District with more than 350 original 18th- and 19th-century buildings. No play-acting here—residents live in the historic homes and work in the stores, many of which sell antiques. A walking tour through the town proper takes three to four hours; battlefield tours will take at least that long.

EXPLORING
TOP ATTRACTIONS

Fredericksburg Visitor Center. Beyond the usual booklets, pamphlets, and maps, this visitor center offers a money-saving pass to city attractions ($32 for entry to nine sights including Washington's boyhood home, a better than 40% discount over individual admission prices). Before your

Chatham
Manor **12**

Confederate
Cemetery **7**

Fredericksburg
Area Museum and
Cultural Center ..**9**

Fredericksburg/
Spotsylvania
National Military
Park **14**

Fredericksburg
Visitor Center **1**

Gari Melchers Home
and Studio **13**

George
Washington's
Ferry Farm **11**

Hugh Mercer
Apothecary Shop **2**

James Monroe
Museum and
Memorial Library **8**

Kenmore **5**

Mary Washington
Grave and
Monument **6**

Mary Washington
House **4**

National
Cemetery **15**

Rising Sun
Tavern **3**

University of Mary
Washington
Galleries **10**

Fredericksburg, Virginia

tour, you may want to see the center's 10-minute orientation slide show. The center building itself was constructed in 1824 as a residence and confectionery; during the Civil War it was used as a prison. ✉ *706 Caroline St., Historic District* ☎ *540/373–1776 or 800/678–4748* ⊕ *www.visitfred.com* ⊙ *Daily 9–5; hrs extended in summer*.

QUICK BITES

For freshly made soups, sandwiches, and desserts, drop by **Trolley Stop Deli** (✉ *707 Caroline St., Historic District* ☎ *540/373–2767* ⊙ *Daily 11–4*), in operation for more than a quarter century and directly opposite the Fredericksburg Tourism Center.

Gari Melchers Home and Studio. The last owner of this 1790s Georgian-style house was American artist Gari Melchers, who chaired the Smithsonian Commission to establish the National Gallery of Art in Washington. His wife, Corinne, deeded the 27-acre estate and its collections to Virginia. The home is now a public museum and a Virginia National Historic Landmark administered by the University of Mary Washington. You can take a one-hour tour of the spacious house, which is furnished with a rich collection of the owners' antiques. Galleries in the stone studio, built by the Melchers in 1924, house the largest repository of the artist's work. An orientation movie is shown in the reception area, which was once the carriage house. ✉ *224 Washington*

St. ☎ 540/654–1015 ⊕ www.garimelchers.org ⟐ $10 ☉ Sun.–Mon. and Thurs.–Sat. 10–5.

Goolrick's Pharmacy (⊠ *901 Caroline St., Historic District* ☎ *540/373– 9878* ⊕ *www.goolricks.com*) opened in 1869 and has been in its present location since the late 1890s. In 1912 the soda fountain was installed, and it is now the oldest operating in the United States. In addition to malts and egg creams (made of seltzer, milk, and syrup, but not egg or cream), Goolrick's serves light meals weekdays 8:30–7 and Saturday 8:30–6.

Hugh Mercer Apothecary Shop. Offering a close-up view of 18th- and 19th-century medical instruments and procedures, the apothecary was established in 1761, and demonstrates the work of Dr. Mercer, a Scotsman who served as a brigadier general of the Continental Army (he was killed at the Battle of Princeton). Dr. Mercer may have been more careful than other Colonial physicians, but his methods might still make you cringe. A costumed hostess explicitly describes amputations and cataract operations before the discovery of anesthetics. You can also hear about therapeutic bleeding, see the gruesome devices used in Colonial dentistry, and watch a demonstration of leeching. ⊠ *1020 Caroline St., at Amelia St., Historic District* ☎ *540/373–3362* ⟐ *$5* ☉ *Mar.–Nov., Mon.–Sat. 9–4, Sun. 11–4; Dec.–Feb., Mon.–Sat. 10–3, Sun. noon–4.*

Fodor's Choice
★

Kenmore. Named Kenmore by a later owner, this house was built in 1775 on a 1,300-acre plantation owned by Colonel Fielding Lewis, a patriot, merchant, and brother-in-law of George Washington. Lewis sacrificed his fortune to operate a gun factory and otherwise supply General Washington's forces during the Revolutionary War. As a result, his debts forced his widow to sell the home following his death. The outstanding plaster moldings in the ceilings and over the fireplace in the dining room are even more ornate than those at Mount Vernon. It's believed that the artisan responsible for them worked frequently in both homes, though his name is unknown, possibly because he was an indentured servant. A multiyear renovation returned the grand house to its original state. It is interesting to note that the walls vary in thickness: 36 inches in the basement, 24 inches on the ground floor, and 18 inches upstairs. Guided 45-minute architectural tours of the home are conducted by docents; the subterranean Crowningshield Museum on the grounds displays Kenmore's collection of fine Virginia-made furniture and family portraits as well as changing exhibits on Fredericksburg life. ⊠ *1201 Washington Ave., Historic District* ☎ *540/373–3381* ⊕ *www. kenmore.org* ⟐ *$8, $11 combo ticket with Ferry Farm* ☉ *Mar.–Oct., daily 10–5; Nov.–Dec., daily 10–4.*

★ **Mary Washington House.** George purchased a three-room cottage for his mother in 1772 for £225, renovated it, and more than doubled its size with additions. She spent the last 17 years of her life here, tending the garden where her original boxwoods still flourish today, and where many a bride and groom now exchange their vows. The home has been a museum since 1930. Inside, displays include Mrs. Washington's "best dressing glass," a silver-over-tin mirror in a Chippendale frame; her teapot; Washington family dinnerware; and period furniture. The kitchen, in a rather lopsided wooden house in the pretty gardens, and its spit are original. Tours begin on the back porch with a history of the house. ⊠ *1200 Charles St., Historic District* ☎ *540/373–1569* ⊕ *www. apva.org/marywashingtonhouse* ⌑ *$5* ⊘ *Mar.–Oct., Mon.–Sat. 11–5, Sun. 11–4; Nov.–Feb., Mon.–Sat. 11–4, Sun. noon–4.*

OFF THE BEATEN PATH

Potomac Point Winery. Just 15 mi north of town off Route 1, this winery has a gorgeous tasting room and beautiful restaurant in its French Mediterranean–style building. One of Potomac Point's most notable wines is the viognier. For romantics, it's also got a private "proposal tower" and a dedicated engagement and wedding coordinator. ⊠ *275 Decatur Rd., Stafford* ☎ *540/446–2266* ⊕ *www.potomacpointwinery. com* ⌑ *Free* ⊘ *Sun.–Thurs. 11–6, Fri. and Sat. 11–9.*

Rising Sun Tavern. In 1760 George Washington's brother Charles built as his home what later became the Rising Sun Tavern, a watering hole for such patriots as the Lee brothers (the only siblings to sign the Declaration of Independence); Patrick Henry, the five-term governor of Virginia who said, "Give me liberty or give me death"; and future presidents Washington and Jefferson. Two male indentured servants and a "wench" in period costume lead a tour without stepping out of character. From them, you hear how travelers slept and what they ate and drank at this busy institution. ⊠ *1304 Caroline St., Historic District* ☎ *540/371–1494* ⊕ *www.apva.org/risingsuntavern* ⌑ *$5* ⊘ *Mar.–Oct., Mon.–Sat. 10–5, Sun. 11–4; Nov.–Feb., Mon.–Sat. 11–4, Sun. noon–4.*

6

WORTH NOTING

Confederate Cemetery. This cemetery contains the remains of more than 2,000 soldiers (most of them unknown) as well as the graves of generals Dabney Maury, Seth Barton, Carter Stevenson, Daniel Ruggles, Henry Sibley, and Abner Perrin. ⊠ *1100 Washington Ave., near Amelia St., Historic District* ⊘ *Daily dawn–dusk.*

Fredericksburg Area Museum and Cultural Center. In an 1816 building once used as a market and town hall, this museum's six permanent exhibits tell the story of the area from prehistoric times through the Revolutionary and Civil wars to the present. The museum acquired the historic bank building and added seven permanent exhibitions in the new space, as well as a learning center. The bank annex is home to an exhibit titled "Fredericksburg at War," which details the area's history from the Revolutionary War to World War II. The Civil War exhibits emphasize the civilian experience, although attention is also paid to the soldier. Military items on display include a Henry rifle, a sword with "CSA" carved into the basket, and a Confederate officer's coat. Most weapons and accessories were found on local battlefields. Other displays include dinosaur footprints from a nearby quarry, Native American artifacts, and an 18th-century plantation account book with an inventory of slaves. The first and third floors have changing exhibits. ⊠ *907 Princess Anne St., Historic District* ☎ *540/371–3037* ⊕ *www.famcc.org* ⌑ *$7* ⊘ *Mon.–Sun. 12–5.*

James Monroe Museum and Memorial Library. This tiny one-story building—on the site where Monroe, who became the fifth president of the United States, practiced law from 1787 to 1789—contains many of Monroe's possessions, collected and preserved by his family until the present day. They include a mahogany dispatch box used during the negotiation of the Louisiana Purchase and the desk on which the Monroe Doctrine was signed. ⊠ *908 Charles St., Historic District* ☎ *540/654–1043* ⊕ *www.umw.edu/jmmu* 🖃 *$5* ☾ *Mar.–Nov., Mon.–Sat. 10–5, Sun. 1–5; Dec.–Feb., Mon.–Sat. 10–4, Sun. 1–4.*

Mary Washington Grave and Monument. A 40-foot granite obelisk, dedicated by President Grover Cleveland in 1894, marks the final resting place of George's mother. It was laid at "Meditation Rock," a place on her daughter's property where Mrs. Washington liked to read. ⊠ *1598 Washington Ave. at Pitt St.*

University of Mary Washington Galleries. On campus are two art galleries. The Ridderhof Martin Gallery hosts art exhibitions from various cultures and historical periods. The duPont Gallery, in Melchers Hall, displays paintings, drawing, sculpture, photography, ceramics, and textiles by art faculty, students, and contemporary artists. Free gallery-visitor parking is available in the lot at the corner of College Avenue at Thornton Street. ⊠ *1301 College Ave., Historic District* ☎ *540/654–1013* ⊕ *www.umw.edu/galleries* 🖃 *Free* ☾ *When college is in session, Mon., Wed., and Fri. 10–4, weekends 1–4.*

AROUND FREDERICKSBURG

Surrounding the town of Fredericksburg are historic sites and gorgeous vistas where, in 1862, Union forces once stood. Today you see only the lively Rappahannock and beautiful homes on a lovely drive across the river.

EXPLORING

Chatham Manor. Now part of the Fredericksburg/Spotsylvania National Military Park, Chatham was built between 1768 and 1771 by William Fitzhugh, a plantation owner, on a site overlooking the Rappahannock River and the town of Fredericksburg. Among Fitzhugh's guests were the likes of George Washington and Thomas Jefferson. During the Civil War, Union forces commandeered the house and converted it into a headquarters and hospital. President Abraham Lincoln conferred with his generals here, Clara Barton (founder of the American Red Cross) tended the wounded, and poet Walt Whitman visited for a few hours looking for his brother, who had been wounded in a battle. After the war, the Georgian house and gardens were restored by private owners and eventually donated to the National Park Service. The home itself is now a museum. Five of the 10 rooms in the 12,000-square-foot mansion house exhibits spanning several centuries and are open to the public. ⊠ *120 Chatham La., Falmouth, VA* ☎ *540/370–0802* ⊕ *www.nps.gov/frsp* 🖃 *Free* ☾ *Daily 9–4:30.*

Fodor'sChoice
★
Fredericksburg/Spotsylvania National Military Park. The 9,000-acre park actually includes four battlefields and four historic buildings. At the Fredericksburg and Chancellorsville visitor centers you can learn about the area's role in the Civil War by watching a 22-minute film ($2) and viewing displays of soldiers' art and battlefield relics. In season, park rangers lead walking tours. The centers offer recorded tours

Key Civil War Sites

CLOSE UP

Virginia Civil War Trails: More than 500 historic sites in Virginia are marked and interpreted by easily accessible waysides. Maps and guides are available at visitor centers and museums throughout Virginia or can be downloaded at ⊕ *www.civilwartrails.org.*

Richmond National Battlefield Park: Thirteen sites and four visitor centers tell the story of fighting around Richmond. ⊕ *www.nps.gov/rich.*

Fredericksburg and Spotsylvania County Battlefields Memorial: Four major battlefields (Fredericksburg, Chancellorsville, The Wilderness, and Spotsylvania Court House) are fascinating to explore. ⊕ *www.nps.gov/frsp.*

Petersburg National Battlefield: Thirteen sites and three visitor centers focus on the longest siege of the Civil War. Battle of the Crater site is included. ⊕ *www.nps.gov/pete.*

Pamplin Historical Park & the National Museum of the Civil War Soldier: Interpreted battlefield, museums, antebellum homes, and living history demonstrations. This is one of the most original concepts among Civil War historic sites. ⊕ *www.pamplinpark.org.*

American Civil War Center at Historic Tredegar: First museum to examine the Civil War equally from Union, Confederate, and African-American perspectives. ⊕ *www.tredegar.org.*

Museum and White House of the Confederacy: The largest collection of military artifacts in the America, including uniforms and swords of Confederate high command. The White House has been restored to its wartime appearance and is furnished with many original items. ⊕ *www.moc.org.*

6

($4.95 rental, $7.50 purchase) and maps that show how to reach the battlefields, Chancellorsville (where General Stonewall Jackson was mistakenly shot by his own troops), and Spotsylvania Court House battlefields—all within 15 mi of Fredericksburg.

Just outside the Fredericksburg Battlefield Visitor Center is Sunken Road, where on December 13, 1862, the Confederates achieved a resounding victory over Union forces attacking across the Rappahannock (there were 18,000 casualties on both sides). Much of the stone wall that protected Lee's infantrymen is now a re-creation, but 100 yards from the visitor center part of the original wall overlooks the statue *The Angel of Marye's Heights,* by Felix de Weldon (sculptor of the famous *Marine Corps War Memorial* statue in Arlington). This memorial honors Sergeant Richard Kirkland, a South Carolinian who risked his life to bring water to wounded foes; he later died at the Battle of Chickamauga. ⊠ *Fredericksburg Battlefield Visitor Center, 1013 Lafayette Blvd., at Sunken Rd., Historic District* ☎ *540/373–6122* ⊠ *Chancellorsville Battlefield Visitor Center, Rte. 3 W, 9001 Plank Rd., Chancellorsville* ☎ *540/786–2880* ⊕ *www.nps.gov/frsp* ☞ *Free* ☉ *Visitor centers daily 9–5 with extended hrs in summer; walking tours on a seasonal basis dawn–dusk.*

☾
★
George Washington's Ferry Farm. If it hadn't been for the outcries of historians and citizens, a Wal-Mart would have been built on this site, the boyhood home of our first president. The land was saved by the George Washington's Fredericksburg Foundation, and the megastore found a location farther out on the same road. Recently, archaeologists have uncovered the original fireplaces and four cellars from the house where Washington was raised, as well as thousands of new artifacts. Ferry Farm, which once consisted of 600 acres, is across the Rappahannock River from downtown Fredericksburg and was the site of a ferry crossing. Living here from ages six to 19, Washington received his formal education and taught himself surveying while *not* chopping a cherry tree or throwing a coin across the Rappahannock—legends concocted by Parson Weems. The mainly archaeological site also has an exhibit on "George Washington: Boy Before Legend." The ongoing excavations include a summer program for children and adults, "Digging for Young George." Ferry Farm became a major artillery base and river-crossing site for Union forces during the Battle of Fredericksburg. ⊠ *Rte. 3 E, 268 Kings Hwy., at Ferry Rd., Fredericksburg* ☎ *540/370–0732* ⊕ *www.kenmore.org* ✉ *$5, $11 combo with Kenmore* ☉ *Mar.–Oct., daily 10–5; Nov.–Dec., daily 10–4.*

National Cemetery. The National Cemetery is the final resting place of 15,000 Union dead, most of whom have not been identified. ⊠ *Lafayette Blvd. at Sunken Rd., Historic District* ☎ *540/373–6122* ☉ *Daily dawn–dusk.*

WHERE TO EAT

$$–$$$
AMERICAN
✕**Bistro Bethem.** In an 1833 storefront that served as a general store, buttermilk-color walls display local art. Copper chandeliers and original heart-of-pine floors lend a warm glow; when the weather's fine, tables are brought out onto the sidewalk for alfresco dining. The menu changes with the seasons and features modern American cuisine with a Southern accent, including fresh fish and wild game. The award-winning wine list features the most diverse, multicultural varietal selections in the Fredericksburg region. ⊠ *309 William St.* ☎ *540/371–9999* ⊕ *www.bistrobethem.com* ▭ *AE, D, MC, V* ☉ *Closed Mon.*

$
FRENCH
✕**La Petite Auberge.** Housed in a pre–Civil War brick general store, this white-tablecloth restaurant actually has three dining rooms decorated like a French garden, with numerous paintings by local artists for sale. For more than two decades, this has been a Fredericksburg favorite for its consistently good food and service. The interesting menu changes with the seasons, and the chef sources his products locally. Specialties like house-cut beef, French onion soup, and seafood are all served with a Continental accent. A fixed-price ($23) four-course dinner is served from 5:30 to 7 Monday through Thursday. ⊠ *311 William St., Historic District* ☎ *540/371–2727* ⊕ *www.lapetiteaubergefredericksburg.com* ▭ *AE, D, MC, V* ☉ *Closed Sun.*

¢–$
ITALIAN
✕**Poppy Hill Tuscan Kitchen.** In the heart of the downtown shopping district, you'll have to look down to find this cozy basement eatery, but it's worth the search. A "farm-to-table restaurant," Poppy Hill's regionally sourced produce changes seasonally. Warm earth tones infuse the space and rustic Tuscan favorites include hearty soups and salads, seafood

stew, prosciutto-wrapped tilapia, and balsamic glazed chicken. The antipasto platter, a mountain of artisanal cheeses, crostini, olives, and charcuterie, is big enough to share with four. A nice list of chianti, sangiovese, and other Italian wine favorites, both white and red, complements the menu. It is open for brunch on Sunday. ⊠ *1000 Charles St., Historic District* ☎ *540/373–2035* ⊕ *www.ciaopoppyhill.com* ⊟ *AE, MC, V* ☯ *Closed Mon.*

$$–$$$ ✕ **Ristorante Renato.** This family-owned restaurant, decorated with lace
ITALIAN curtains, red carpeting, and walls covered with paintings, specializes in traditional northern and southern Italian cuisine, including veal, chicken, pasta, and seafood. Standouts include veal Florentine, fettuccine Alfredo, eggplant parmigiana, steamed mussels, and lasagna. The 260-seat restaurant is also open for lunch on weekdays. Save room for the Italian desserts such as cannoli, spumoni, and tiramisu. ⊠ *422 William St., Historic District* ☎ *540/371–8228* ⊕ *www.ristoranterenato. com* ⊟ *AE, MC, V* ☯ *No lunch weekends.*

¢–$ ✕ **Sammy T's.** Vegetarian dishes, healthful foods, and homemade soups
AMERICAN and breads share the menu with hamburgers, oyster and crab-cake sandwiches, and dinner platters at this unpretentious place. Eclectic vegetarian and vegan offerings from tzatziki and tabbouleh to black-bean cakes and veggie chili make this the go-to place for noncarnivores, but it's the list of more than 20 sandwiches and wraps that makes Sammy T's a hot spot for the in-town lunch crowd. The bar is stocked with nearly 50 brands of beer. There's a separate no-smoking section around the corner, but a tin ceiling, high wooden booths, and wooden ceiling fans make the main dining room much chummier. ⊠ *801 Caroline St., Historic District* ☎ *540/371–2008* ⊕ *www.sammyts.com* ⊟ *AE, D, MC, V.*

WHERE TO STAY

$–$$ ☷ **Courtyard Fredericksburg Historic District.** The only hotel in the city's historic district, the Courtyard is conveniently located near the Amtrak station, with many local attractions within walking distance. Modern amenities include a 24-hour gym and business center, indoor pool, and complimentary Wi-Fi, as well as a GoBoard that gives guests current information on weather and airport conditions. The hotel has a full service restaurant called the Bistro and a lounge, and some packages include breakfast. **Pros:** great location; indoor pool; 24-hour gym. **Cons:** fee for parking; not historic; not pet-friendly. ⊠ *620 Caroline St.* ☎ *540/373–8400* ⊕ *www.marriott.com* ⤸ *98* ⌂ *In-room: a/c, refrigerator, Wi-Fi. In-hotel: restaurant, room service, bar, pool, gym, laundry facilities, laundry service, Wi-Fi hotspot, parking (paid)* ⊟ *AE, D, DC, MC, V.*

$$–$$$ ☷ **Homewood Suites.** In a newly developed area locals call the "campus," this new all-suites hotel is a sister property to the Hampton Inn, and in addition to one-bedroom suites, features the only two-bedroom suites in Fredericksburg. A sumptuous complimentary breakfast in the lobby lounge is included in the rate, as is an afternoon happy hour. The spacious suites are like having your own well-appointed apartment making them perfect for families or extended stays since they have full kitchens that include dishes and dishwashers. **Pros:** largest suites in town; free breakfast and happy hour included. **Cons:** not close to historic attractions; 10-minute drive to town. ⊠ *1040 Hospitality*

La. ☎ *540/786–9700* ⊕ *www.homewoodsuites.com* ⬅ *124 suites* ᕯ *In-room: a/c. In-hotel: pool, gym, Wi-Fi hotspot* ☰ *AE, D, DC, MC, V.*

¢–$　🏨 **Inn at the Olde Silk Mill.** This 1920s motel with moss-green siding and forest-green awnings has a beautifully decorated central staircase in the lobby. Each of the 30 rooms is furnished with antiques and appointments from the Civil War period, and the lobby has an old-time upright piano, as well as many historic photographs of Fredericksburg. Efficiency suites for extended stays feature more modern decor and all rooms have high-speed wireless Internet. Breakfast includes beverages, cereal, and coffee cake. The inn is situated just at the edge of the historic district and has private, off-street parking. **Pros:** period rooms; nice breakfast. **Cons:** on the outer edge of the historic district. ✉ *1707 Princess Anne St., Historic District* ☎ *540/371–5666* ⊕ *www.fci1.com* ⬅ *27 rooms* ᕯ *In-room: a/c, refrigerator, Wi-Fi. In-hotel: parking (free)* ☰ *AE, MC, V* ⟊ *BP.*

$–$$　🏨 **Kenmore Inn.** This 18th-century historic home is easily recognizable by its magnificent and inviting front porch. There are two types of rooms. The deluxe ones, in the original part of the house, have working fireplaces and canopy beds; the slightly smaller standard rooms have Colonial furnishings. The English pub, with its mahogany horseshoe bar, serves lighter dishes and imported draft beer; it's open Tuesday to Sunday evenings. **Pros:** charming decor; excellent breakfast, restaurant on-site; high-speed Internet. **Cons:** limited availability; some rooms are small. ✉ *1200 Princess Anne St., Historic District* ☎ *540/371–7622* ⊕ *www.kenmoreinn.com* ⬅ *9 rooms* ᕯ *In-room: a/c, no TV (some), Wi-Fi. In-hotel: restaurant, bar* ☰ *AE, D, MC, V* ⟊ *CP.*

$–$$　🏨 **Richard Johnston Inn.** This elegant B&B was constructed in 1793 and
★　served as the home of Richard Johnston, mayor of Fredericksburg from March 1809 to March 1810. Guest rooms are decorated with period antiques and reproductions, and have working fireplaces, along with high-speed wireless and the purely Southern amenity of complimentary cream sherry. The aroma of freshly baked breads and muffins entices you to breakfast in the large Federal-style dining room, where the table is set with fine china, silver, and linens. The inn is just across from the visitor center and two blocks from the train station. Ample private parking is behind the inn. **Pros:** pet friendly; Wi-Fi in a historic setting; massage therapy; true Southern experience. **Cons:** advance deposit required; expensive. ✉ *711 Caroline St., Historic District* ☎ *540/899–7606 or 877/557–0770* ⊕ *www.therichardjohnstoninn.com* ⬅ *7 rooms, 2 suites* ᕯ *In-room: a/c, Wi-Fi. In-hotel: pets allowed (some), parking (free)* ☰ *AE, MC, V* ⟊ *CP.*

THE NORTHERN NECK

Between Fredericksburg and the Chesapeake Bay is the "Northern Neck," an area attractive to nature lovers, anglers, and boaters. This 90-mi-long peninsula has a 1,200 mi total shoreline and is bathed on three sides by the Potomac and Rappahannock rivers, and the mighty Chesapeake Bay. Settled by Europeans more than 300 years ago, the Northern Neck is the birthplace of presidents George Washington,

James Monroe, and James Madison, as well as General Robert E. Lee and Washington's mother, Mary Ball.

The Northern Neck peninsula is as unspoiled today as when Captain John Smith first visited in 1608. Even at the peninsula's start, the area is forested and tranquil. You can find charming B&Bs; fresh-off-the-boat seafood; excursion boats to islands in the Chesapeake Bay; historic homes and museums; and places to commune with nature.

The sites below are listed in geographical order beginning at the intersection of routes 3 and 301. Though it's unusual that three presidents' birthplaces are in such proximity, those of James Madison and James Monroe are just markers off the highway, whereas Washington's is a national monument. A marker on Highway 301 in Port Conway, King George County, memorializes the onetime plantation where James Madison was born in 1751; an outline of the house and a marker in neighboring Westmoreland County identifies the birthplace of James Monroe, born in 1758, on Highway 205 between Oak Grove and Colonial Beach.

GETTING HERE AND AROUND

The peninsula of land between the Potomac and Rappahannock rivers is called the Northern Neck. From I–95, you'll get off at Fredericksburg and take either Route 3 Route 17 to Tappahannock. Once you get to the Neck, you'll connect to Route 360 East. Most of the attractions and the towns are either on 360 or on routes 3 200. If you like driving on secondary roads, rather than the interstate, you can take 360 all the way from Richmond as well, or take I–64 East from there or Charlottesville to pick up 360.

6

GEORGE WASHINGTON BIRTHPLACE NATIONAL MONUMENT

32 mi east of Fredericksburg on Rte. 3.

EXPLORING

George Washington Birthplace National Monoument. After you pass the town of Oak Grove on Route 3, all signs point to the national park on the Potomac River. At Pope's Creek, George Washington Birthplace National Monument is a 550-acre park mirroring the peaceful rural life our first president preferred. The house in which Mary Ball Washington gave birth to George in 1732 burned in 1779, but native clay was used to make bricks for a representative 18th-century plantation home. Costumed interpreters lead tours through the house, which has items dating from the time of Washington's childhood. The grounds include a kitchen, garden, cemetery with 32 Washington family graves, and the Colonial Living Farm, worked by methods employed in Colonial days. Picnic facilities are available year-round, and children under 15 are admitted free. ⊠ *Rte. 3, 1732 Popes Creek Rd.* ☏ *804/224–1732* ⊕ *www.nps.gov/gewa* ⊠ *Free* ⊙ *Daily 9–5.*

WHERE TO STAY

¢ 🏕 **Westmoreland State Park.** This 1,300-acre, full-service park is one of Virginia's most beautiful campgrounds, with hiking trails winding through marshlands, woods, and meadows and along the Potomac

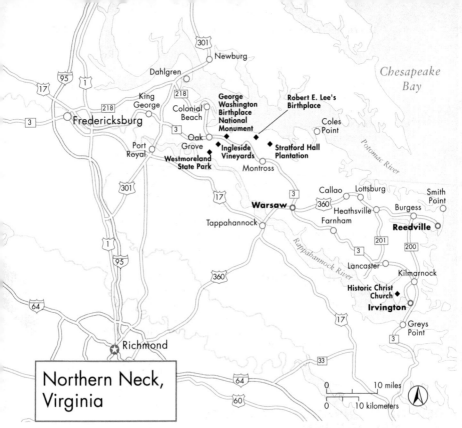

Northern Neck,
Virginia

River. There are also places to fish, rent boats or kayaks, or simply picnic. The comfortable, climate-controlled cabins have complete kitchens with microwave oven and toaster, dishes, silverware, and cooking utensils. Living rooms have a sofa, dining table, and working fireplace. The basic furnishings include linens for four beds. From Memorial Weekend to Labor Day Weekend there is a one-week minimum; at all other times the minimum is two nights. Westmoreland also has 133 campsites available and six camping cabins that provide a shelter but few other amenities. **Pros:** extensive outdoor activities; beautiful setting off the beaten path. **Cons:** no restaurants nearby; limited amenities; minimum stay required. ⊠ *1650 State Park Rd., Rte. 1, Box 600, Montross* ☎ *804/493–8821 or 800/933–7275* ⊕ *www.dcr.virginia.gov/state_parks/wes.shtml* ⬎ *27 cabins, 133 campsites* ⌂ *In-room: no phone, a/c, kitchen, no TV. In-hotel: pool, laundry facilities* ▭ *AE, MC, V.*

STRATFORD HALL PLANTATION

8 mi east of George Washington Birthplace National Monument via Rte. 3.

EXPLORING
Stratford Hall Plantation. Robert E. Lee, who became the commander of the Confederate Army, was born in the Great House of Stratford Hall Plantation, one of the country's finest examples of Colonial architecture.

Eight chimneys in two squares top the H-shaped brick home, built in the 1730s by one of Lee's grandfathers, Colonial governor Thomas Lee. The house contains Robert E. Lee's crib, original family pieces, and period furnishings. The working Colonial plantation covers 1,600 acres and has gardens, a kitchen, smokehouse, laundry, orangery, springhouses, coach house, stables, slave quarters, and a gristmill that grinds from 11 am to 2 pm on the first whole weekend of each month from April through September. The Plantation Dining Room, a log cabin restaurant, serves meals and sandwiches daily from 11 to 3. Its outdoor, screened deck overlooks the woodlands. ⊠ *Rte. 3, 483 Great House Rd., Stratford* ☎ *804/493–8038 or 804/493–8371* ⊕ *www.stratfordhall. org* ⊠ *$10* ⊗ *Visitor center daily 9:30–4, house tours daily 10–4.*

WHERE TO STAY

$ ⊡ **Stratford Hall.** Of the two guesthouses on the plantation property, Cheek, the larger one, has 15 rooms, which come with either two twin beds or a king-size bed. Astor, named after Lady Astor and made from a log cabin, is directly across from the Plantation Dining Room. Both guesthouses have a fully equipped kitchen, a living room with fireplace, and decks, as well as satellite TV, and Astor has been recently renovated. Wi-Fi is available throughout the grounds and guests get a complimentary tour. There are also a few small and very rustic log cabins available for rental. **Pros:** historic property; good on-site restaurant. **Cons:** limited availability, must pre-pay. ⊠ *485 Great House Rd.* ☎ *804/493–8038 or 804/493–8371* ⊕ *www.stratfordhall.org* ⤳ *20 rooms* ♿ *In-room: a/c. In-hotel: restaurant, parking (free)* ☰ *AE, MC, V* ⏏ *CP.*

WARSAW

15 mi southeast of Stratford Hall via Rte. 3.

The county seat of Richmond County, Warsaw is a pleasant town of 7,000 that's shaded by large oak trees. Near the U.S. 360 bridge over the Rappahannock, it's therefore closer to the city of Tappahannock (on the other side) than to its fellow towns on the Northern Neck.

EXPLORING

Ingleside Vineyards. Located near the Washington Birthplace Monument about 40 minutes east of Fredericksburg, this vineyard is one of Virginia's oldest and largest wineries, and has won the prestigious Virginia Governor's Cup more times than any other winery. It produces one of the few sparkling wines from Virginia. There are also white wines (viognier, sauvignon blanc, pinot gris, and chardonnay) and reds (sangiovese, cabernet franc, and sauvignon) as well as specially produced labels. The vineyards cover about 65 acres of gently rolling countryside whose climate and sandy loam soil is similar to that of Bordeaux, France. The winery has a tasting bar, a gift shop with grape-related gifts, a large outdoor patio with umbrella tables and a fountain, and a large indoor room for group tastings. Tours are free. ⊠ *5872 Leedstown Rd., from Rte. 3, turn south on Rte. 638 at winery's signpost, Oak Grove* ☎ *804/224–8687* ⊕ *www.inglesidevineyards.com* ⊗ *Mon.–Sat. 10–5, Sun. noon–5.*

Rappahannock River Cruises. A cruise 20 mi up the river to Ingleside Vineyards leaves from Tappahannock. Rappahannock River Cruises enlists its ship *Capt. Thomas* to take passengers on the narrated day cruise. A buffet lunch is served at the winery ($11), snacks are served on board, or you can bring your own. To reach the dock, take Highway 17 south from Tappahannock to Hoskins Creek. The cruise departs daily at 10, returning at 4:30. They also offer a cruise from Reedville to Tangier Island. ⊠ *Hoskins Creek* ☏ *804/453–2628* ⊕ *www.tangiercruise.com* 🕾 *$25* ⊙ *May–Oct., daily at 10.*

REEDVILLE

31 mi from Warsaw via U.S. 360, 46 mi from Stratford Hall via Rtes. 202 and 360.

This small town at the eastern tip of the Northern Neck was the home of wealthy fishermen and businessmen who made their fortunes from the menhaden fish abundant in the nearby Chesapeake Bay and Potomac waters.

EXPLORING

Reedville Fishermen's Museum. Housed in a restored fisherman's home and a larger building is this educational and activity-oriented museum. Permanent and rotating exhibits document the area's fishing industry, and there are two fishing boats here, a skipjack, the *Claud W.*, and a deck boat, the *Elva C.*, which have been named to the National Register of Historic Places. ⊠ *504 Main St.* ☏ *804/453–6529* ⊕ *www.rfmuseum. org* 🕾 *$5* ⊙ *Early Mar.–Apr., weekends 10:30–4:30; May–Oct., daily 10:30–4:30; Nov–mid-Jan., Fri.–Mon. 10:30–4:30; mid-Jan.–early Mar., by appt. for groups.*

Smith Island and Chesapeake Bay Cruises. Popular cruises to quaint Smith Island in the Chesapeake Bay leave from Reedville. The 150-passenger ship *Captain Evans* and the 139-passenger air-conditioned *Spirit of Chesapeake* of Smith Island and Chesapeake Bay Cruises sail from the KOA Kampground at Smith Point on Route 802. The 13½-mi trip takes 1½ hours and passes a 5,000-acre waterfowl and wildlife refuge. Now a part of Maryland, Smith Island—a Methodist colony settled by British colonists from Cornwall in the early 1700s—can also be reached from Crisfield, on Maryland's Eastern Shore. Lunch is available at several restaurants on the island. Cruise reservations are required. Call ahead for the schedule and fare. ⇨ *For more information on Smith Island, see Chapter 9, The Eastern Shore.* ⊠ *382 Campground Rd., behind KOA Kampground* ☏ *804/453–3430* ⊕ *www.cruisetosmithisland.com* ⊙ *May–mid-Oct.*

Tangier Island & Chesapeake Cruises. Tangier is a Virginia island in the Chesapeake Bay named by Captain John Smith. This largely unspoiled fishing village with quaint, narrow streets also happens to be the soft-shell-crab capital of the nation. There's a small airport here for private planes, and it also can be reached by the ship *Chesapeake Breeze* of Tangier Island & Chesapeake Cruises (ships also leave from Onacock, Virginia, and Crisfield, Maryland, on the Eastern Shore). The ship departs at 10 am and returns at 3:30 pm daily, cruising 1½ hours each way. The island has several restaurants serving lunch. From the intersection of highways 360 and 646, drive 1 mi; then turn left on Highway 656 (Buzzard's Point Road), which leads to the dock. Reservations are required. ⇨ *Also see more Tangier Island information in the Eastern Shore chapter.* ⊠ *468 Buzzard's Point Rd.* ☎ *804/453–2628* ⊕ *www. tangiercruise.com* ⊠ *$25* ⊗ *May–Oct., daily.*

WHERE TO STAY

$–$$ ⊞ **Fleeton Fields**. Set amid beautifully manicured lawns and gardens, this lovely Colonial-style inn also overlooks a tidal pond on which you may be lucky enough to see ospreys, great blue herons, and eagles. Inside the inn, you're greeted by fresh flowers and soothing music before being escorted to one of the three beautifully furnished suites. Cool evenings are warmed by inviting fireplaces, and each morning's breakfast is served using china, crystal, and silver. **Pros:** on-site birding; nearby seafood restaurants. **Cons:** no food on-site except for breakfast. ⊠ *2783 Fleeton Rd.* ☎ *804/453–5014 or 800/497–8215* ⊕ *www.fleetonfields. com* ⊠ *3 suites* ⚭ *In-room: a/c, Wi-Fi* ⊟ *AE, D, DC, MC, V* ⦿ *BP.*

$ ⊞ **The Gables**. A four-story redbrick Victorian mansion, the Gables was built in 1909 by Captain Albert Fisher, one of the founders of the local fishing industry. The house has been lovingly restored and has period antiques throughout. There are two guest rooms in the main house and four more in the adjacent carriage house. The Gables has its own deepwater dock on Cockrell's Creek, with easy access to the Chesapeake Bay. **Pros:** full breakfast; walk to downtown Reedville; marina and boat rides next door. **Cons:** not all rooms have en suite bathroom. ⊠ *859 Main St.* ☎ *804/453–5209* ⊕ *www.thegablesbb.com* ⊠ *6 rooms* ⚭ *In-room: a/c. In-hotel: Wi-Fi hotspot, no kids under 13* ⊟ *AE, D, MC, V* ⦿ *BP.*

EN
ROUTE

After leaving Reedville on Route 360, turn left on Route 200 and drive 13 mi to Kilmarnock. Turn right on Route 3 and drive to the little town of Lancaster, home of the **Mary Ball Washington Museum and Library**. This four-building complex honors George Washington's mother, who was born in Lancaster County. Lancaster House, built about 1798, contains Washington family memorabilia and historic items related to the county and the Northern Neck. The Steuart-Blakemore Building houses a genealogical library, and the Old Jail is a lending library and archives. ⊠ *8346 Mary Ball Rd., Lancaster* ☎ *804/462–7280* ⊕ *www. mbwm.org* ⊠ *$3 museum house and grounds* ⊗ *Tues.–Fri. 10–4; library Tues.–Sat. 10–4.*

IRVINGTON

5 mi south from Kilmarnock.

Although much older than the resort, the lovely town of Irvington has been associated with the Tides Inn for more than 50 years.

EXPLORING

Historic Christ Church. Completed in 1735, this church opened its doors when George Washington was three years old. The Georgian-style structure, on the National Register of Historic Places, was built by Robert "King" Carter and contains a rare "triple-decker" pulpit made of native walnut. Bricks for the church were fired in a great kiln near the churchyard. A 12-minute video is screened in the museum. ✉ *420 Christ Church Rd., from Irvington drive 1.5 mi north on Rte. 200* ☎ *804/438–6855* ⊕ *www.christchurch1735.org* 🎫 *Free* ☉ *Church daily; museum weekdays 10–4; Apr.–Nov., also Sat. 10–4 and Sun. 2–5.*

WHERE TO EAT AND STAY

¢–$ ✕ **White Stone Wine & Cheese.** This French bistro offers sandwiches,
FRENCH   soups, and baked goods as well as a large selection of wine and cheese. There are tables available to eat your picnic, and a good selection of wines for sale. Special wine dinners are held on Saturday, and free wine tastings take place Friday afternoon for happy hour. ✉ *572 Rappahannock Dr.* ☎ *804/435–2000* 🟰 *MC, V* ☉ *Lunch daily 11–5:30; dinner Wed.–Sat. 5:30–9.*

$$$ 🏨 **The Hope and Glory Inn.** This 1890 schoolhouse is now a pale-honey-
Fodor's Choice   color Victorian B&B. The first-floor classrooms have been opened into
★   an expansive, columned lobby with a painted checkerboard floor. The upstairs bedrooms and six small cottages behind the inn are decorated romantically chic, with pastel painted floors and interesting window treatments. In the garden, surrounded by a tall wooden fence, there's a completely open-air bathroom that can be booked by adventurous couples. In 2004 the inn built new cottages, called "tents," in an allusion to turn-of-the-20th-century Methodist tent communities. On wooded bluffs overlooking the headwaters of Carter's Creek, the tents each have three bedrooms and a kitchen, and there's a pool and dock for canoes and kayaks as well as the "Detention" wine bar. **Pros:** free bikes; pet-friendly; designer aesthetic. **Cons:** limited availability. ✉ *65 Tavern Rd.* ☎ *804/438–6053 or 800/497–8228* ⊕ *www.hopeandglory.com* 🛏 *7 rooms, 4 cottages* 🟰 *MC, V* 🍽 *BP.*

🏨 **The Tides Inn.** Surrounded by manicured grounds overlooking Carters Creek, the Tides Inn, here since 1947, is sandwiched between the Potomac and Rappahannock rivers. The resort offers all of the modern amenities travelers have come to expect, and features a wide variety of on-site recreational activities. Many of the rooms and suites, which are luxuriously decorated in a British Colonial style, have spectacular water views. The Golden Eagle Golf course is challenging, the par-3 course less so; the ponds are well stocked with fish; and bird-watchers should take their binoculars. There's also a sailing school that's set up for all ages and experience levels, and you can take a cruise along the Rappahannock River on a 127-foot yacht. **Pros:** full-service resort; golf; sailing lessons; kids' activities. **Cons:** expensive. ✉ *480 King Carter Dr.* ☎ *804/438–5000 or 800/843–3746* ⊕ *www.tidesinn.com* 🛏 *84 rooms, 22 suites* ☖ *In-room: a/c, DVD, Internet. In-hotel: 4 restaurants, bar, golf courses, tennis courts, pools, gym, spa, bicycles, children's programs (ages 4–12), laundry facilities, some pets allowed* 🟰 *AE, D, DC, MC, V.*

Williamsburg and Hampton Roads

WITH VIRGINIA'S EASTERN SHORE

WORD OF MOUTH

"We are planning a first time trip to Colonial Williamsburg . . . visiting Jamestown Settlement and Yorktown [too] . . . Any more 'can't miss' things to do?"

—bob56

"Two other things you might consider while in the area are the car ferry across the James River . . . [and visiting] one of the James River plantations between Williamsburg and Richmond. I am partial to Shirley, still a working plantation. The owners live upstairs, and you tour the downstairs and auxiliary buildings. It has been in one branch or another of the same family since the 17th century, and the house itself, built roughly 1725, has only been painted inside about 6 times in the last 275 years, a good reminder when you feel the 'need' to redecorate your house."

—Ackislander

www.fodors.com/community

Updated by
Alice Powers,
Ramona Settle,
and Nina
Callaway

Perhaps no other region in Virginia contains more variety and options for the traveler than its southeastern coastline. Colonial Williamsburg has evoked the days of America's forefathers since its restoration began during the 1920s. Jamestown and Yorktown make the area one of the most historically significant in the United States. When it's time for pure recreation, you can head to theme parks such as Busch Gardens Williamsburg and resort areas, including Virginia Beach.

At the end of the Virginia peninsula is the enormous Hampton Roads harbor, where the James, Elizabeth, and Nansemond rivers flow together into the Chesapeake Bay and then eastward into the Atlantic Ocean. Hampton Roads has also played a crucial role in the discovery and settlement of the nation, its struggle for independence, and the conflict that nearly dissolved the Union.

This entire area, known as the Tidewater, is land where water in rivers and streams is affected by tides. The cities in southeast Virginia take on different roles depending on their proximity to the Chesapeake Bay and the rivers that empty into it. Hampton contains the world's largest naval base, and enormous shipbuilding yards are in Norfolk and Newport News. The area is also committed to recreation and tourism: there are many resort hotels, a bustling beachfront, and boardwalk attractions. Virginia Beach, which in the 1950s claimed to have the world's longest public beach, has a showy boardwalk.

Finally there's Virginia's Eastern Shore that offers funky waterside hamlets tucked away against the Chesapeake and Atlantic shorelines to either side of the highway. The most celebrated of these is Chincoteague, dominating an island of the same name and famous for its ponies.

ORIENTATION AND PLANNING

GETTING ORIENTED

The Historic Triangle. There is probably no better place in America to study this country's prerevolutionary war history than the Historic Triangle. Between Williamsburg, Jamestown, and Yorktown, visitors get a full picture of life in Colonial times. The lessons are multisensory: museums, battlefields, restorations, and reenactments appeal to history buffs of every age.

Hampton Roads Area. The channel where the James, Elizabeth, and Nansemond rivers meet is surrounded by both small and larger towns that include the historic settlements of Hampton and Portsmouth, and

TOP REASONS TO GO

Colonial Williamsburg: Escape to the 18th century in the world's largest living-history museum. Virginia's capital from 1699 to 1780 and Britain's largest, wealthiest New World outpost was restored so "That the future may learn from the past."

Celebrate early American history: Jamestown was the first permanent English settlement in the Americas. Washington's momentous 1781 Revolutionary War victory at Yorktown secured the country's independence.

Water, Water, Everywhere! From the James River and Chesapeake Bay to the Atlantic Ocean, get in or on the waters of Tidewater Virginia.

Surf the waves, steam past the world's largest naval station, sail on a schooner, or sup on a ship.

Immerse Yourself in Nautical and Military History: Don't miss the Mariners' Museum, the MacArthur Memorial, the Virginia Air and Space Center, and the world's largest naval base at Norfolk Naval Station.

Glimpse the Gracious Gentry Life and the Hard Life of Slaves: Visit America's oldest plantations and historic homes, including one chartered in 1613 and continuously occupied by 11 generations, two homes of presidents, and one claiming to have celebrated the first Thanksgiving.

today's cities Newport News and Norfolk. Linked to the Hampton Roads area by the unusual Chesapeake Bay Bridge-Tunnel is Virginia's "other coastline," the quiet, largely untrafficked Eastern Shore.

Virginia's Eastern Shore. Separated from the rest of Virginia by the Chesapeake Bay, this 70-mi-long stretch of the Delmarva Peninsula is a world apart. The way of life here hasn't changed substantially in hundreds of years, delighting history buffs and nature lovers. Fill relaxing days with strolling through quaint villages, seeing the famous wild ponies on Chincoteague and Assateague, visiting a NASA research center, and especially boating, birding, and fishing.

PLANNING

WHEN TO GO

Fall and spring are the most pleasant times to go to the Historic Triangle. Winters can be chilly and summers in Virginia are damp and hot. Remember that many of the attractions involve walking from building to building or touring battlegrounds. If you go in summer, plan to tour in the morning and evening, reserving the hottest part of the midday for air-conditioned museums or water activities. During December's **Grand Illuminations** (☎ 800/447–8679 ⊕ *www.history.org*) in Williamsburg, Virginia, 18th-century entertainment is performed on several outdoor stages and fireworks are set off at several points through the evening. In March, **Military Through the Ages** (☎ 757/253–4838 ⊕ *www.historyisfun. org*) in Jamestown, Virginia, uses authentic weapons in a series of reenactments of battles from the Middle Ages through the 20th century. **Yorktown Day** (☎ 757/898–2410 ⊕ *www.nps.gov/colo*) observances in Yorktown, Virginia, celebrate the Colonial victory in the American

War of Independence (October 19, 1781) with 18th-century tactical demonstrations, patriotic exercises, and a wreath-laying ceremony.

GETTING HERE AND AROUND

AIR TRAVEL

The three major airports in the region are served by many national and international carriers. Ticket prices are often much less expensive to and from Norfolk and Newport News than nearby Richmond. All three airports are relatively small and easy to navigate.

CAR TRAVEL

Williamsburg is west of I–64, 51 mi southeast of Richmond; the Colonial Parkway joins Williamsburg with Jamestown to the southwest and Yorktown to the east. Interstate 664 forms the eastern part of a beltway through the Hampton Roads area and connects Newport News with Portsmouth. Interstate 264 runs from I–664 to downtown Norfolk, and then extends all the way to Virginia Beach. Interstate 64 runs from Hampton to Portsmouth around the west side of Norfolk to intersect I–664.

Since weekend traffic on I–64 East can be quite heavy, consider leaving that interstate at Exit 205 for Route 60 East—a four-lane highway that leads into Williamsburg past several restaurants as well as outlet shopping centers. ■TIP➔ **If you are coming from the north on I–95 and encountering heavy traffic outside Washington, D.C., you may want to leave I–95 at Fredericksburg and go south to Yorktown on Route 17, a narrower road with stoplights, but less congested.** Because the ragged coastline is constantly interrupted by water, driving from one town to another usually means going through a tunnel or over a bridge, either one of which may create a traffic bottleneck. The entrance to the tunnel between Hampton and Norfolk can get very congested, especially on weekends, so listen to your car radio for updated traffic reports.

In the Tidewater area, with a long list of tunnels and bridges connecting myriad waterways, it's easy to find yourself headed in the wrong direction. Highways have adequate signs, but sometimes it may be too late to merge before entering a tunnel/bridge. Traffic is highly congested during rush hour and during peak summer months, when the beach traffic can grind everything to a halt. Tune in to your car radio for traffic reports, especially during rush hours.

In congested periods, use the less-traveled I–664. The 17.5-mi Chesapeake Bay Bridge-Tunnel is the only connection between the southern part of Virginia and the Eastern Shore; U.S. 13 is the main route up the spine of the Eastern Shore peninsula into Maryland.

TAXI TRAVEL

There are a few taxi companies in Williamsburg, more in Norfolk and Virginia Beach. Unless you're at Newport News/Williamsburg International Airport or Norfolk International Airport, you must phone for a cab. Rates are metered and tipping is expected.

TRAIN TRAVEL

Amtrak trains stop in Williamsburg between Newport News and Richmond, Washington, D.C., and stations to the north. There are two trains daily in each direction. At Newport News, passengers ticketed to Norfolk or Virginia Beach board a chartered bus at the station. The

Williamsburg station is centrally located, sharing a building with the bus station. Service south of Richmond is slow, even for Amtrak. At Fredericksburg, Amtrak meets the Virginia Railway Express, which is cheaper, but only operates on workdays.

ESSENTIALS

Air Contacts **Hampton Roads Transit** (☎ 757/222–6100 ⊕ www.hrtransit.org). **Newport News/Williamsburg International Airport** (*PHF* ✉ *12525 Jefferson Ave., at I-64, Newport News* ☎ *757/877–0221* ⊕ *www.nnwairport.com*). **Norfolk International Airport** (*ORF* ✉ *2200 Norview Ave., Norfolk* ☎ *757/857–3351* ⊕ *norfolkairport.com*). **Richmond International Airport** (*RIC* ✉ *1 Richard E. Byrd Dr., Richmond* ☎ *804/226–3000* ⊕ *www.flyrichmond.com*).

Train Infomation **Virginia Railway Express** (⊕ www.vre.org).

DISCOUNTS AND DEALS

The America's Historic Triangle Vacation Package includes unlimited visits to all five attractions—Colonial Williamsburg, Jamestown Settlement and Historic Jamestowne, Yorktown Victory Center and Yorktown Battlefield—in the Historic Triangle. There is also an America's Historic Triangle Ticket that does not include lodging. For information on the vacation package, visit ⊕ *www.americashistorictriangle.com* or call ☎ *888/882–4156*.

RESTAURANTS

Dining rooms within walking distance of Colonial Williamsburg's restored area are often crowded, and reservations (☎ *800/447–8679*) are necessary. Many nationally known chain eateries line both sides of U.S. 60 on the east side of the city.

■ TIP→ **If you want to dine in one of the Colonial Williamsburg restaurants, make reservations before you arrive.**

HOTELS

There are more than 200 hotel properties in Williamsburg. For a complete list, contact the **Greater Williamsburg Chamber & Tourism Alliance** (✉ *421 N. Boundary St., Box 3495, Williamsburg* ☎ *757/229–6511 or 800/368–6511*⊕ *www.williamsburgcc.com*).

There are many bed-and-breakfasts in the Williamsburg area, especially near the James River Plantations off Route 10. Most are housed in historic properties with charming antiques. Rates usually include a full country breakfast.

Reservations at inns can be made through the following contacts. **Virginia is for Lovers** (⊕ *www.virginia.org*). **Virginia Beach Reservations** (☎ *800/822–3224*) can make a reservation in your choice of about 75 hotels. **Williamsburg Vacation Reservations** (☎ *866/341–4866* ⊕ *www. williamsburgvacations.com*), representing more than 70 hostelries, provides free lodging reservation services.

Apartment and house rentals are not common in the Williamsburg area, but quite the thing to do at Virginia Beach. Rentals vary greatly in size, cost, and degree of luxury, so research possibilities thoroughly. Local agents include **Long and Foster Real Estate** (✉ *317 30th St., Virginia Beach* ☎ *757/428–4600 or 800/941–3333*) and **Siebert Realty** (✉ *601*

Sandbridge Rd., Virginia Beach ☎ *757/426–6200 or 877/422–2200*
⊕ *www.siebert-realty.com).*

WHAT IT COSTS					
	¢	$	$$	$$$	$$$$
Restaurants	under $10	$10–$16	$17–$23	$24–$30	over $30
Hotels	under $100	$100–$160	$161–$230	$231–$300	over $300

Restaurant prices are per person for a main course at dinner. Hotel prices are for a standard double room, excluding state and local taxes.

PLANNING YOUR TIME

Colonial Williamsburg recommends three or four days for their property only, but the entire Historic Triangle can be covered in that time. Try exploring chronologically, starting at the first settlement in Jamestowne, then exploring the Colonial period in Williamsburg, and finally the Revolution at Yorktown.

EXPLORING WILLIAMSBURG AND HAMPTON ROADS

The beginning of both Colonial America and of the United States of America should be required visiting, and this area is home to them both. To keep the chronology straight, visit Virginia's "Historic Triangle," in the order of Jamestown, Williamsburg, and then Yorktown. Although Jamestown is somewhat overshadowed by the much-larger Williamsburg, Jamestown was the first permanent English settlement (1607) in North America, and celebrated its momentous quadricentennial—400th anniversary—in 2007.

Just a short drive along the tree-lined Colonial Parkway is Williamsburg, which subsequently grew into the political and economic center of the Virginia Colony. The 301 acres of modern-day Colonial Williamsburg contain re-created and restored structures peopled with costumed interpreters. Everything from momentous political events to blacksmithing is portrayed. Completing the "Historic Triangle," is Yorktown, 14 mi away from Williamsburg, the site of the battle that ended the war for independence from England. Several 18th- and 19th-century plantations lie west of Williamsburg, along the James River. South of Yorktown are Newport News, the shipbuilding capital of Virginia, and Hampton. To see the rest of this waterfront area of Virginia, you can cross the James River at Hampton and visit Norfolk, Portsmouth, and, to the east, the Virginia Beach resort area.

THE HISTORIC TRIANGLE

Entering Virginia's number one tourist attraction you'll believe you've entered a past century, and you really have. Colonial Williamsburg, a careful, on-the-spot restoration of the former Virginia capital, gives you the chance to walk into the 18th century and see how earlier Americans lived. The streets may be unrealistically clean for that era, and you can find hundreds of other modern-day visitors exploring the buildings with you, but the rich detail of the re-creation and the sheer size of the city never break the spell. A ticket or pass (price is based on the number of attractions and the duration of visit) admits the holder to sites in the restored area, but it costs nothing just to walk around and absorb the atmosphere. ■ TIP→ **Although admission is free to amble around the historic district, you will miss some of the most interesting aspects of Williamsburg by not entering the buildings or seeing the excellent programs staged by skilled reenactors. It is well worth the price of admission.**

Williamsburg anchors three elements of Colonial National Historical Park. The 23-mi Colonial Parkway links Williamsburg to Jamestown and Yorktown, two other significant historical sites on or near the peninsula bounded by the James and York rivers. Historic Jamestowne was the location of the first permanent English settlement in North America—that celebrated its 400th anniversary in 2007—and it's an excellent place to begin a visit to the area; Yorktown was the site of the final major battle in the American Revolutionary War. The sites themselves as well as the parkway are maintained by the National Park Service. Close by are Jamestown Settlement and the excellent Yorktown Victory Center, both run by the Jamestown-Yorktown Foundation. Like Colonial Williamsburg, these two sites re-create the buildings and activities of the 18th century, using interpreters in period dress.

JAMESTOWN

9 mi southwest of Colonial Williamsburg via Colonial Pkwy.

The desperate strivings of Englishmen to stay alive and establish a foothold in the New World become evident when visiting Jamestown, the beginning of English settlement in this country. Its two major sights are places to explore the early relationship between the English and Native Virginia Indians.

GETTING HERE AND AROUND

From April to October, the Jamestown Area Shuttle provides loop service around the Jamestown area every 30 minutes between Historic Jamestowne, the Jamestown Settlement, and the Jamestown Glasshouse (part of Historic Jamestowne).

FERRY TRAVEL The Jamestown–Scotland Ferry began providing service across the James River in 1925. This is the best free ride in Virginia; it takes you back 400 years to when the colonists first spied the site where they founded Jamestown. The ferry leaves the Jamestown dock about every hour on the half hour, leaving the opposite port, Scotland, on the hour 24 hours a day. Wait times vary from 15 to 30 minutes (sometimes longer in summer). Cars, campers, trucks, and motorcycles are allowed on the ferry. Foot passengers may ride, but there's nowhere to park at the ferry landing.

TIMING AND PRECAUTIONS

The least-visited season in the Historic Triangle is winter. During the most popular seasons—summer, fall, and spring break—there may be lines outside the Colonial Williamsburg buildings. The other attractions in the Historic Triangle are not as busy.

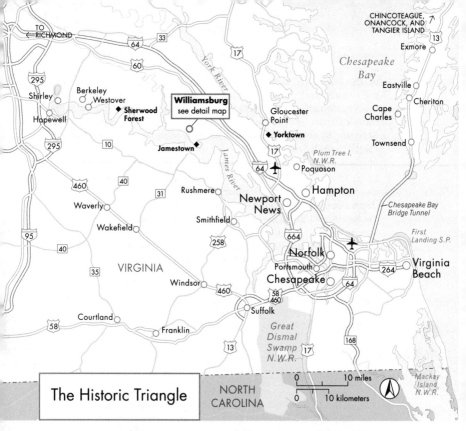

The Historic Triangle

ESSENTIALS

Ferry Information Jamestown–Scotland Ferry (✉ *2317 Jamestown Rd., Rte. 31* ☎ *757/222-6100* ⊕ *www.virginiadot.org/travel/ferry-jamestown.asp*).

Visitor Information Jamestown Settlement and Yorktown Victory Center (☎ *757/253-4838 or 888/593-4682* ⊕ *www.historyisfun.org*).

EXPLORING

Historic Jamestowne. An island originally connected to the mainland by

Fodor's Choice
★

a narrow isthmus, Historic Jamestowne was the site of the first permanent English settlement in North America (1607) and the capital of Virginia until 1699. May 13, 2007, marked the 400th anniversary of its founding. The first settlers' bitter struggle for survival here, on the now uninhabited land, makes for a visit that stirs the imagination. Redbrick foundation walls roughly outline the settlement, and artists' conceptions of the original buildings can be seen at several locations. The only standing structure is the ruin of a church tower from the 1690s, now part of the Memorial Church built in 1907; the markers within indicate the original church's foundations. Other monuments around the site also date from the tercentenary celebration in 1907. Statues portray the founder of Jamestown, Captain John Smith, and his advocate, the Native American princess Pocahontas, whom Smith credited with saving him from being beheaded.

Near the entrance to the park, you can stop at the reconstructed Glasshouse to observe a demonstration of glassblowing, an unsuccessful business venture of the early colonists. The products of today are for sale in a gift shop. Archaeological discoveries from the site are showcased at the Archaearium. You can also observe digs on-site where archaeologists from Preservation Virginia continue to dig up evidence of colonists' and Native Americans' ways of life, including the remains of the original 1607 fort.

A visitor center near the main parking lot tells the history of Jamestown and the Virginia Indians, Europeans, and African peoples who lived here. Ranger-guided tours, held daily, explore many different events in Jamestown's history. Living-history programs are presented daily in summer and on weekends in spring and autumn.

A 5-mi or 8-mi nature drive that rings the island is posted with informative signs and paintings. ⊠ *Off Colonial Pkwy.* ☎ *757/898–2410* ✉ *$10; (under 16 free) includes admission to both Historic Jamestowne and Yorktown Battlefield* ⊙ *Daily 9–5; gates close at 4:30.*

ⓒ **Jamestown Settlement.** Adjacent to but distinct from Historic Jamestowne
Fodor'sChoice is a mainland living-history museum called Jamestown Settlement. The
★ site marries 40,000 square feet of indoor facilities (completed in 2006) with outdoor replicas of the early James Fort, the three ships that brought the founding colonists from England, and a Powhatan Indian village. The introductory film *1607: A Nation Takes Root* is shown in a 250-seat theater. The handsome Tudor-style Great Hall is arranged by decades from 1607 to 1699, when the capital was moved to Williamsburg. Gallery exhibits examine the lives of the Powhatans and their English-born neighbors, their interaction, and world conditions that encouraged colonization. Outdoors within James Fort, interpreters in costume cook, forge metal, and describe what life was like living under thatch roofs and between walls of wattle and daub (stick framework covered with mud plaster). In the Powhatan Indian village you can enter a *yehakin* (house) and see buckskin-costumed interpreters cultivate crops and make tools. At the pier are full-scale reproductions of the ships in which the settlers arrived: *Godspeed, Discovery,* and *Susan Constant.* All the vessels are seaworthy; you may climb aboard the *Susan Constant* and find out more from the sailor-interpreters. Indoor exhibits examine the lives of the Powhatans and their English-born neighbors, their interaction, and world conditions that encouraged colonization. A riverfront discovery area provides information about 17th-century water travel, commerce, and cultural exchange, reflecting Powhatan Indian, European, and African traditions. Dugout-canoe making takes place in this area. Spring and fall bring lots of school groups, so it's best to arrive after 2 pm. ⊠ *Rte. 31 off Colonial Pkwy.* ☎ *757/253–4838 or 888/593–4682* ⊕ *www.historyisfun.org* ✉ *$14; combination ticket with Yorktown Victory Center $19.25* ⊙ *June 15– Aug. 15, daily 9–6; Aug. 16–June 14, daily 9–5.*

Jamestown and John Smith

You can't believe everything you read in travel brochures: "Free land lush with hardwood trees! Food and water abundant! Gold for the taking! Fast side-trip to the Orient! Friendly welcoming committee!"

The real trip: 73 passengers will die. There's no gold. Fresh water and food are difficult to obtain. There is no way to sail to the Orient across North America. The land belongs to the natives, who can be hostile, and disease-carrying mosquitoes are omnipresent.

The men and boys who settled Jamestown in 1607 had little idea of what was in store for them. Most who sailed over were intent on finding riches and hadn't given much thought to how they would survive in Virginia. Almost immediately after landing, the colonists were under attack from the Algonquian natives, and in a little over a month the settlers built a wooden fort named for King James.

One man, Captain John Smith, a soldier and adventurer who had fought in Hungary and Transylvania, was familiar with challenges and worked toward the survival of Jamestown. "America's first hero" made contact with the native chief Powhatan, from whom the colonists obtained much of their food, and became leader of the colony. After being captured by Algonquians, he may or may not have been saved by the 11-year-old princess Pocahontas, but was returned to Jamestown.

Finding the colony languishing due to lack of supplies, a drought, laziness, and conflicts, Smith instituted a policy of rigid discipline and strengthened defenses. He encouraged farming with the admonishment: "He who does not work, will not eat." Because of his strong leadership, the settlement survived and grew during the next year. Unfortunately Smith was injured and returned to England for treatment in October 1609, never to set foot in Virginia again.

Nearly 300 years later, Jamestown was acquired by the Association for the Preservation of Virginia Antiquities (APVA) and the National Park Service. Early archaeologists concluded that James Fort lay completely under the James River. In 1994, however, in preparation for the 400th Anniversary of Jamestown, APVA initiated its own excavations to search for the original 1607 fort. They uncovered evidence that James Fort had not been washed into the river, as most had believed.

Excavation has since uncovered more than 150,000 artifacts dating to the first half of the 17th century. Nearly half date to the first years of English settlement (1607–10). These objects reflect trade between Europe and the New World, patterns of warfare, day-to-day survival, and status in the early colony. You can view a sampling of these artifacts at Historic Jamestowne, whose mission is "to preserve, protect, and promote the original site of the first permanent English settlement in North America and to tell the story of the role of the three cultures—European, North American, and African—that came together to lay the foundation for a uniquely American form of democratic government, language, free enterprise, and society."

COLONIAL WILLIAMSBURG

51 mi southeast of Richmond via I–64.

Williamsburg was the capital of Virginia from 1699 to 1780, after Jamestown and before Richmond. Williamsburg hasn't been politically important for a long time, but now that Colonial Williamsburg is there to represent it in its era of glory, it's a jewel of the commonwealth. Outside the restored area is a modern city with plenty of dining and lodging options and attractions, including outlet shops and a large water park. But the main draw is still time-traveling into a time of tricornered hats.

Fodor's Choice ★

Colonial Williamsburg sells a number of all-inclusive tickets that cost more than a $34 one-day pass. The Freedom Pass ($59) allows you to visit for one full year. The Independence Pass ($72), also valid for a year, includes all the benefits of the Freedom Pass as well as admission to all special events and special discounts.

GETTING HERE AND AROUND

CAR TRAVEL Parking near the Colonial Williamsburg historic area can be difficult during summer months and special events. It's best to park at the visitor center and ride the shuttle to the park. The parking lot behind the Merchants Square shopping area is a good bet if you're planning a short visit or going out to eat around the area.

All vehicular traffic is prohibited within Colonial Williamsburg to preserve the illusion. Shuttle buses run continuously from 9 am to 10 pm to and from the visitor center.

BIKE TRAVEL Biking around Colonial Williamsburg is a wonderful way to explore its 301 acres. Rental bikes are available for those staying at the Williamsburg Inn, Williamsburg Lodge, or Colonial Houses. Bikesmith, in Williamsburg, rents bikes and has especially reasonable multiday rental prices. Bikes Unlimited, close to the Williamsburg Transportation Center, also rents bikes.

TOURS Hour-long guided walking tours of the historic area depart from the Greenhow Lumber House daily from 9 to 5. Reservations should be made on the day of the tour at the Lumber House and can be made only by those with tickets to Colonial Williamsburg. "The Original Ghosts of Williamsburg" Candlelight Tour is based on the book of the same name by L. B. Taylor Jr. The tour is offered every evening at 8 (there's also an 8:45 tour June–August). The 1¼-hour, lantern-lighted guided tour through historic Williamsburg costs $11, and interpreters well versed in Williamsburg and Colonial history are available to lead groups on tours of the historic area. Carriage and wagon rides are available daily, weather permitting. General ticket holders may purchase tickets on the day of the ride at the Lumber House.

■ TIP→ **For walking tours, be sure to park at the visitor center, as cars are not permitted on Duke of Gloucester Street.**

Lanthorn Tours (available in the summer) takes you on an evening walking tour of trade shops where jewelry and other products are made in 18th-century style. The separate ticket required for this program may be purchased at the visitor center or from the Greenhow Lumber House.

Boat tours aboard the 135-foot three-masted topsail schooner *American Rover* cruise Hampton Roads nautical historical landmarks. The *Victory Rover* and *Spirit of Norfolk* cruise the Elizabeth River to the Norfolk Naval Station. The *Spirit* has lunch, early dinner, dinner, and moonlight cruises. The *Carrie B.*, a scaled-down reproduction of a Mississippi riverboat, makes a variety of Hampton Roads cruises, including naval station, sunset, and moonlight cruises. All boats leave the Norfolk waterfront, the *Victory Rover* from beside Nauticus, and the others from beside Waterside. In addition, the *Carrie B.* stops at the Portsmouth waterfront to load passengers.

Three self-guided audio tours of Colonial Williamsburg can be rented at the Colonial Williamsburg Visitor Center: "Highlights of the Historic Area," "Reading the Restoration Architecture," and "Voices of the Revolution." Wander at your own pace; when you stop in front of a numbered location, enter the number into the player and hear all about it. Each recording is about 45 minutes and costs $6 for ticketed guests or $15 for those without tickets.

TIMING AND PRECAUTIONS
Williamsburg can be very warm in summer and even in spring and fall. Be sure to carry water and replenish your bottles at the historic area's water fountains. Wear comfortable clothing and shoes since walking is the primary way to navigate Williamsburg's 301 acres. (There are horse-drawn carriages, not included in the price of admission.)

ESSENTIALS
Bike Rentals **Bikesmith** (⊠ 515 York St. ☎ 757/229–9858). **Bikes Unlimited** (⊠ 141 Monticello Ave., in the Williamsburg shopping area ☎ 757/229–4620 ⊕ www.bikesunlimited.com).

Boat Tours **American Rover** (☎ 757/627–7245 ⊕ www.americanrover.com). **Carrie B** (☎ 757/393–4735). **Spirit of Norfolk** (☎ 757/625–3866 ⊕ www.spiritofnorfolk.com). **Victory Rover** (☎ 757/627–7406 ⊕ www.navalbasecruises.com).

Walking Tours **Greenhow Lumber House** (⊠ Duke of Gloucester St. ☎ 757/220–7645 or 800/447–8679). **Interpreters** (☎ 800/228–8878). **Lanthorn Tours** (☎ 757/229–1000). **"The Original Ghosts of Williamsburg" Candlelight Tour** (☎ 757/253–1058⊕ www.theghosttour.com).

Taxi **Yellow Cab** (☎ 757/722–1111).

Train **Williamsburg Transportation Center** (⊠ 468 N. Boundary St. ☎ 757/229–8750).

Visitor Information **Colonial Williamsburg Dining and Lodging Reservations** (☎ 800/447–8679). **Colonial Williamsburg Visitor Center** (⌕ 102 Visitor Center Dr., Williamsburg 23187-1776 ☎ 800/246–2099 or 757/229–1000 ⊕ www.colonialwilliamsburg.org). **Greater Williamsburg Chamber and Tourism Alliance** (⊠ 421 N. Boundary St., Box 3495, 23187-3495 ☎ 757/229–6511 or 800/368–6511 ⊕ www.williamsburgcc.com).

EXPLORING

TOP ATTRACTIONS

Bruton Parish Church. The lovely brick Episcopal Bruton Parish Church has served continuously as a house of worship since it was built in 1715. One of its 20th-century pastors, W. A. R. Goodwin, provided the impetus for Williamsburg's restoration. The church tower, topped by a beige wooden steeple, was added in 1769; during the Revolution its bell served as the local "liberty bell," rung to summon people for announcements. The white pews, tall and boxed in, are characteristic of the starkly graceful Colonial ecclesiastical architecture of the region. When sitting in a pew, listening to the history of the church, keep in mind that you could be sitting where Thomas Jefferson, Ben Franklin, or George Washington once listened to sermons. The stone baptismal font is believed to have come from an older Jamestown church. Many local eminences, including one royal governor, are interred in the graveyard. The fully operational church is open to the public; contributions are accepted. ■TIP➡ Check *www.brutonparish.org* for free candlelight recitals in the evening at Bruton Parish Church. ⊠ *Duke of Gloucester St. west of Palace Green.*

Capitol. Williamsburg was important because it was the location of the Capitol. It was here that the prerevolutionary House of Burgesses (dominated by the ascendant gentry) challenged the royally appointed council (an almost medieval body made up of the bigger landowners). In 1765 the House eventually arrived at the resolutions, known as Henry's Resolves (after Patrick Henry), that amounted to rebellion. An informative tour explains the development, stage by stage, of American democracy from its English parliamentary roots. In the courtroom a guide recites the harsh Georgian sentences that were meted out: for instance, theft of more than 12 shillings was a capital crime. Occasional reenactments, including witch trials, dramatize the evolution of American jurisprudence.

What stands on the site today is a reproduction of the 1705 structure that burned down in 1747. Dark-wood wainscoting, pewter chandeliers, and towering ceilings contribute to a handsome impression. That an official building would have so ornate an interior was characteristic of aristocratic 18th-century Virginia. This was in telling contrast to the plain town meeting halls of Puritan New England, where other citizens were governing themselves at the same time. ■TIP➡ The stirring Fifes and Drums March leaves from the Capitol to the Palace Green. Don't miss the spectacle of dozens of young men dressed in period costume marching through Williamsburg's streets. Check the program guide for dates and times. ⊠ *East end of Duke of Gloucester St.*

DeWitt Wallace Decorative Arts Museum. This museum adds another cultural dimension that goes well beyond Colonial history. Grouped by medium are English and American furniture, textiles, prints, metals, and ceramics of the 17th to the early 19th century. If you're yawning at the thought of fancy tableware, stop: presentations here tend to be creative and surprising. Prizes among the pieces in the collection are a full-length portrait of George Washington by Charles Willson Peale and a royally commissioned case clock surmounted by the detailed figure of

Colonial Williamsburg Basics

The restoration project that gave birth to Colonial Williamsburg began in 1926, inspired by a local pastor, W.A.R. Goodwin, and financed by John D. Rockefeller Jr. The work of the archaeologists and historians of the not-for-profit Colonial Williamsburg Foundation continues to this day. A total of 88 original 18th-century and early-19th-century structures have been meticulously restored, and another 500 have been reconstructed on their original sites. In all, approximately 225 period rooms have been re-created with the foundation's collection of more than 60,000 pieces of furniture, ceramics, glass, silver, pewter, textiles, tools, paintings, prints, maps, firearms, and carpets. Period authenticity also governs the landscaping of the 301 acres of gardens and public greens. The restored area is surrounded by a greenbelt controlled by the foundation, which guards against development that could mar the illusion of the Colonial city.

Despite its huge scale, Colonial Williamsburg can seem almost cozy. Nearly 1 million people come here annually, and all year hundreds of costumed interpreters, wearing bonnets or three-corner hats, rove and ride through the streets (you can even rent outfits for your children). Dozens of skilled craftspeople, also in costume, demonstrate and explain their trades inside their workshops. They include the shoemaker, the cooper (aka barrel-maker), the gunsmith, the blacksmith, the musical instrument maker, the silversmith, and the wig maker. Their wares are for sale nearby at the Prentis Store. Four taverns serve food and drink that approximate the fare of more than 220 years ago.

Colonial Williamsburg makes an effort to represent not just the lives of a privileged few, and not to gloss over disturbing aspects of history. Slavery, religious freedom, family life, commerce and trade, land acquisition, and the Revolution are portrayed in living-history demonstrations. In the two-hour "Revolutionary City Program" you can become an active citizen in everyday life against the backdrop of momentous, world-changing events. The vignettes that are staged throughout the day take place in the streets and in public buildings. These may include dramatic afternoon court trials or fascinating estate appraisals. Depending on the days you visit, you may see the House of Burgesses dissolve, its members charging out to make revolutionary plans at the Raleigh Tavern.

Because of the size of Colonial Williamsburg and the large crowds (especially in the warmer months), it's best to begin a tour early in the day, so it's a good idea to spend the night before in the area. The foundation suggests allowing three or four days to do Colonial Williamsburg justice, but that will depend on your own interest in the period—and that interest often increases on arrival. Museums, exhibits, and stores close at 5 pm, but walks and events take place in the evening, usually ending by 10 pm. Some sites close in winter on a rotating basis.

■ TIP → Colonial Williamsburg has two common portals for all properties and events under its administration. The Colonial Williamsburg Web sites are ⊕ *www. colonialwilliamsburg.com* and ⊕ *www.history.org.*

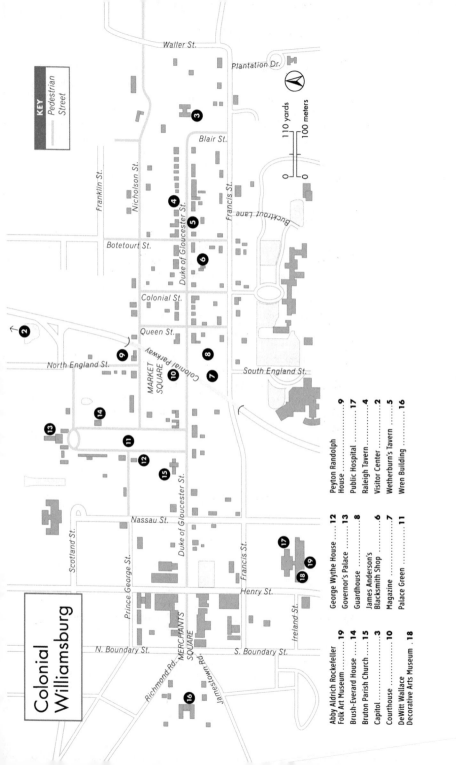

Colonial Williamsburg

KEY

Pedestrian Street

110 yards
100 meters

Waller St.
Plantation Dr.
Blair St.
Francis St.
Botetourt St.
Colonial St.
Queen St.
North England St.
South England St.
Nassau St.
Henry St.
N. Boundary St.
S. Boundary St.
Franklin St.
Nicholson St.
Duke of Gloucester St.
Bucktrout Lane
Colonial Parkway
MARKET SQUARE
Scotland St.
Prince George St.
MERCHANTS SQUARE
Richmond Rd.
Jamestown Rd.
Ireland St.

Abby Aldrich Rockefeller
Folk Art Museum **19**
Brush-Everard House **14**
Bruton Parish Church **15**
Capitol **3**
Courthouse **10**
DeWitt Wallace
Decorative Arts Museum . **18**

George Wythe House **12**
Governor's Palace **13**
Guardhouse **8**
James Anderson's
Blacksmith Shop **6**
Magazine **7**
Palace Green **11**

Peyton Randolph
House **9**
Public Hospital **17**
Raleigh Tavern **4**
Visitor Center **2**
Wetherburn's Tavern **5**
Wren Building **16**

a Native American. You enter the museum through the Public Hospital. ✉ *Francis St.* ⊕ *www.history.org/history/museums/dewitt_gallery.cfm.*

George Wythe House. This home was the residence of Thomas Jefferson's law professor; Wythe was also a signer of the Declaration of Independence. General Washington used the house as a headquarters just before his victory at Yorktown. The large brick structure, built in the mid-18th century, is conspicuously symmetrical: each side has a chimney, and each floor has two rooms on either side of a center hallway. The garden in back is similarly divided. The outbuildings, including a smokehouse, kitchen, laundry, outhouses, and a chicken coop, are reconstructions. ✉ *West side of Palace Green* ⊕ *www.history.org/almanack/places/hb/hbwythe.cfm.*

Governor's Palace. His Majesty's Governor Alexander Spotswood built the original Governor's Palace in 1720, and seven British viceroys, the last of them Lord Dunmore in 1775, lived in this appropriately showy mansion. The 540 weapons, including 230 muskets and pistols, arrayed on the walls of several rooms herald the power of the Crown. Some of the furnishings are original, and the rest are matched to an extraordinary inventory of 16,000 items. Lavishly appointed as it is, the palace is furnished to the time just before the Revolution. During the Revolution, it housed the commonwealth's first two governors, Patrick Henry and Thomas Jefferson. The original residence burned down in 1781, and today's reconstruction stands on the original foundation.

A costumed guide greets you at the door for a tour through the building, offering commentary and answering questions. Notable among the furnishings are several pieces made in Williamsburg and owned by Lord Dunmore. Social events are described on the walk through the great formal ballroom, where you might even hear the sounds of an 18th-century harp, clavichord, or piano. The supper room leads to the formal garden and the planted terraces beyond. ✉ *Northern end of Palace Green.*

Peyton Randolph House. This was the home of a prominent colonist and revolutionary who served as attorney general under the British, then as Speaker of the House of Burgesses, and later as president of the first and second Continental Congresses. The oak-paneled bedroom and Randolph family silver are remarkable. ✉ *Nicholson and. N. England Sts.*

Raleigh Tavern. This gathering place was the scene of prerevolutionary revels and rallies that were often joined by Washington, Jefferson, Patrick Henry, and other major figures. The spare but elegant blue-and-white Apollo Room is said to have been the first meeting place of Phi Beta Kappa, the scholastic honorary society founded in 1776. The French general Marquis de Lafayette was feted here in 1824. In 1859 the original structure burned, and today's building is a reconstruction based on archaeological evidence and period descriptions and sketches of the building. ✉ *Duke of Gloucester St., west of Capitol.*

Visitor Center. This is the logical first stop at Colonial Williamsburg. Here you can park free; buy tickets; see a 35-minute introductory movie, *Williamsburg—the Story of a Patriot*; and pick up *This Week,* which has a list of regular events and special programs and a map of the historic area. Tickets are also sold at the Lumber House in the historic

WILLIAMSBURG: REVOLUTIONARY CITY

In 2006 Williamsburg began its daily programs, Revolutionary City, dramatizations that link issues of Colonial times to those faced by modern Americans. The reenactors are excellent and never break character, illustrating that many of the problems faced by citizens in the United States today could never have been anticipated by our Colonial forebears. As actors impersonating the signers of the Declaration of Independence debate the merits of slavery and women's rights—and engage the audience in their discussion—one must inevitably draw the comparisons to human rights issues today. All Revolutionary City programs are marked with a red star on the weekly program guides and are a "must-see" when visiting Colonial Williamsburg.

area. ■ TIP→ **The best deal for tickets is if you buy in advance off the Historic Williamsburg Web site.** ✉ *102 Information Center Dr., off U.S. 60* ☎ *757/229–1000 or 800/HISTORY* ⊕ *www.history.org* ✉ *$36–$72 (children $18)* ⊙ *Daily 9–5.*

WORTH NOTING

Abby Aldrich Rockefeller Folk Art Museum. This collection, within the DeWitt Wallace Decorative Arts Museum, showcases American "decorative usefulware"—toys, furniture, weather vanes, coffeepots, and quilts—within typical 19th-century domestic interiors. There are also folk paintings, rustic sculptures, and needlepoint pictures. Since the 1920s, the 2,000-piece collection has grown from the original 400 pieces acquired by the wife of Colonial Williamsburg's first and principal benefactor. ✉ *326 West Francis St.*

Brush-Everard House. Built in 1717 by John Brush, a gunsmith, and later owned by Thomas Everard, who was twice mayor of Williamsburg, this wood-frame house contains remarkable, ornate carving work. It is open only for special-focus tours and temporary exhibits, and vignettes on slaves' lives are held here in summer. ✉ *Scotland St. at Palace Green.*

Courthouse. The original Courthouse of 1770 was used by municipal and county courts until 1932. Civil and minor criminal matters and cases involving slaves were adjudicated here; other trials were conducted at the Capitol. The stocks once used to punish misdemeanors are outside the building: they can make for a humorous photo opportunity. The courthouse's exterior has been restored to its original appearance. Visitors often participate in scheduled reenactments of court sessions. ✉ *North side of Duke of Gloucester St., west of Queen St.*

Duke of Gloucester Street. The spine of Colonial Williamsburg's restored area is the broad 1-mi-long Duke of Gloucester Street. On Saturday at 1 pm from March to October, the Fifes and Drums Corps marches the length of the street and performs a stirring drill. Along this artery alone, or just off it, are two-dozen attractions. Walking west on Duke of Gloucester Street from the Capitol, you can find a dozen 18th-century shops—including those of the apothecary, the wig maker, the silversmith, and the milliner.

James Anderson's Blacksmith Shop. At James Anderson's Blacksmith Shop, smiths forge the nails, tools, and other iron hardware used in construction throughout the town. The shop itself was reconstructed by carpenters using 18th-century tools and techniques. ⊠ *Between Botetourt and Colonial Sts., on south side of Duke of Gloucester St.*

Magazine. The original Magazine (1715), an octagonal brick warehouse, was used for storing arms and ammunition—at one time 60,000 pounds of gunpowder and 3,000 muskets. It was used for this purpose by the British and then by the Continental army. Today 18th-century firearms are on display within the arsenal. This is the largest collection of Colonial muskets in the country. Every able-bodied man in Colonial times was expected to have and maintain a musket in his home. Between the ages of 16 and 55 men were expected to be a part of the militia, the civilian army that could be called to arms in defense of hearth and home. ⊠ *West of Queen St. on south side of Duke of Gloucester St.*

Market Square. An open green between Queen and Palace streets along Duke of Gloucester, Market Square was the site where cattle, seafood, dairy products, fruit, and vegetables were all sold—as were slaves. Market auctions are sometimes reenacted.

NEED A BREAK?

At the west end of Duke of Gloucester Street, for a block on both sides, Merchants Square has more than 40 shops and restaurants, including an ice-cream parlor, coffee shop, cheese shop, chocolatier, movie theater, peanut shop, and gourmet food store. Services also include three banks and a drugstore. The William and Mary College bookstore, operated by Barnes and Noble, has a wealth of information on Williamsburg and Virginia history. The Kimball Theatre on Merchants Square shows movies daily and has live family entertainment on weekends. ⊕ *www.kimballtheatre.com.*

Palace Green. The handsome Palace Green runs north from Duke of Gloucester Street up the center of Palace Street, with the Governor's Palace at the far end and notable historic houses on either side.

Public Hospital. A reconstruction of a 1773 insane asylum, the Public Hospital provides an informative, shocking look at the treatment of the mentally ill in the 18th and 19th centuries. It also serves as cover for a modern edifice that houses very different exhibitions; entrance to the DeWitt Wallace Decorative Arts Museum is through the hospital lobby. ⊠ *Francis St.*

Robertson's Windmill. On the outskirts of the historic area is Robertson's Windmill, a Colonial mill for grinding grains. It's currently closed to the public for repairs. ⊠ *N. England St.*

Wetherburn's Tavern. Beginning in 1743 Wetherburn's Tavern offered refreshment, entertainment, and lodging and may be the most accurately furnished building in Colonial Williamsburg, with contents that conform to a room-by-room inventory taken in 1760. Excavations at this site have yielded more than 200,000 artifacts. The outbuildings include the original dairy and a reconstructed kitchen. Vegetables are still grown in the small garden. ⊠ *Duke of Gloucester St. across from Raleigh Tavern.*

Williamsburg Winery. Carrying on a Virginia tradition of wine making that began with early settlers, Virginia's largest winery produces 60,000 cases yearly. The winery offers guided tours, a well-stocked wineshop, a 17th-century tasting room, and a museum of wine-making artifacts. Be sure to give the cabernets and merlots a try. The Gabriel Archer Tavern serves a casual lunch daily and dinner Tuesday to Saturday (April–October only). In 2007 a 28-room country inn, Wedmore Place, opened on the premises. The winery is off Route 199E. To get there, turn east on Brookwood Drive and left onto Lake Powell Road. ⊠ *5800 Wessex Hundred* ☎ *757/229–0999* ⊕ *www.williamsburgwinery.com* 🔁 *$8, includes tasting of 5–7 wines and a souvenir glass* ☉ *Apr.–Oct., Mon.–Sat. 10:30–5, Sun. 11–5; Nov.–Mar., Mon.–Sat. 10:30–4, Sun. 11–4.*

Wren Building. The College of William and Mary, founded in 1693, is the second-oldest college in the United States after Harvard University. The campus extends to the west; the Wren Building (1695) was based on the work of the celebrated London architect Sir Christopher Wren. Its redbrick outer walls are original, but fire gutted the interiors several times, and the current quarters are largely reconstructions of the 20th century. The faculty common room, with a table covered with green felt and an antique globe, suggests Oxford and Cambridge universities, the models for this New World institution. George Wythe became America's first law professor at the college and taught law to Thomas Jefferson, Henry Clay, James Monroe, and John Marshall. Tours, led by undergraduates, include the chapel where Colonial leader Peyton Randolph is buried. Among the portraits of college presidents on the second floor of the Wren Building is an arresting painting of former Prime Minister Margaret Thatcher, who visited William and Mary during her tenure. ⊠ *West end of Duke of Gloucester St.*

WHERE TO EAT

$$
AMERICAN

✕**Aberdeen Barn.** Saws, pitchforks, ox yokes, and the like hang on the barn walls, but the wood tables are lacquered, and the napkins are linen. Specialties include slow-roasted prime rib; baby-back Danish pork ribs barbecued with a sauce of peach preserves and Southern Comfort; and shrimp Dijon. An ample wine list offers a wide variety of domestic and imported choices. After dinner try one their specialty coffees including Tennessee Mud with Jack Daniels or Franciscan Coffee. A children's menu is available. ⊠ *1601 Richmond Rd.* ☎ *757/229–6661* ⊕ *www.aberdeen-barn.com* 🍴 *AE, D, MC, V* ☉ *No lunch.*

$$$
SEAFOOD

✕**Berret's Restaurant and Taphouse Grill.** One of the most reliable seafood spots around, Berret's is in Merchants Square. Upscale but casual, the restaurant lights crackling fires during colder months and opens up its pleasant outdoor patio when it's warm. Entrées and appetizers employ fresh Chesapeake Bay seafood. It's usually a sure bet to try any of the nightly specials of fresh fish, which often include perfectly prepared flounder. The she-crab soup, a house favorite, blends crabmeat, cream, and crab roe with just a hint of sherry. Virginia wines and beers are featured. ⊠ *199 South Boundary St.* ☎ *757/253–1847* ⊕ *www.berrets.com* 🍴 *AE, D, MC, V* ☉ *Closed Mon. in Jan. and Feb.; no lunch in Taphouse Grill.*

7

¢   ✕**College Delly.** It's easy to forget that this is a college town, but this
DELI   cheerful dive keeps up the school spirit. The white-brick eatery with
forest-green canvas awnings is dark and scruffy inside. Walls are hung
with fraternity and sorority pictures, graduation snapshots, and sports-
team photos. Booths and tables are in the William and Mary colors of
green and gold. Deli sandwiches, subs, specialty pizzas, pasta, strom-
boli, and Greek dishes are all prepared with fresh ingredients and are
all delicious, and there's a wide selection of beers on tap. The Delly
delivers free to nearby hotels from 6 pm to 1 am. ⊠ *336 Richmond Rd.*
☎ *757/229–3915* ▭ *MC, V.*

$$$$ ✕**Le Yaca.** A mall of small boutiques is the unlikely location for this
FRENCH   French-country restaurant. The dining room has soft pastel colors,
★   hardwood floors, candlelight, and a central open fireplace. The menu
is arranged in the French manner, with four prix-fixe menus and 10
entrées, including whole duck breast with peach and pepper sauce, leg
of lamb with rosemary garlic sauce, bouillabaisse, and fresh scallops
and shrimp with champagne sauce. Le Yaca is on U.S. 60 East, near
Busch Gardens. ⊠ *Village Shops at Kingsmill, 1915 Pocahontas Trail*
☎ *757/220–3616* ⊕ *www.leyacawilliamsburg.com* ▭ *AE, D, DC, MC,*
V ☾ *Closed Sun. No lunch Sat.*

$ ✕**Old Chickahominy House.** Reminiscent of old-fashioned Virginia tea-
SOUTHERN   rooms, this Colonial-style restaurant has delectable goodies served in
☾   an 18th-century dining room. For breakfast there's Virginia ham and
eggs, made-from-scratch biscuits, country bacon, sausage, homemade
pancakes, and grits. Lunch brings Brunswick stew, Virginia ham biscuits, chicken and dumplings, fruit salad, and homemade pie. There's a
gift shop adjacent to the restaurant. It's a great, inexpensive, and filling
place for families on a budget. ⊠ *1211 Jamestown Rd.* ☎ *757/229–4689*
⊕ *www.oldchickahominy.com* ▭ *MC, V* ☾ *No dinner.*

¢   ✕**Peking.** Tucked away in a K-Mart–anchored shopping center, this
CHINESE   reasonably priced, large Chinese restaurant with a Mongolian grill is
☾   a real treat. The daily buffet offers both stick-to-your-ribs Chinese and
Mongolian dishes. At the grill, choose the ingredients you want in your
entrée, and watch the cooks prepare it in front of you. If your children
don't like Chinese food, there is a children's menu that includes pizza.
Peking is a great value for money and a favorite with locals. The Greene
shopping center location is just outside the historic district. The lunch
special at $7.99 is a good deal. ⊠ *120 J. Waller Mill Rd.* ☎ *757/229–*
2288 ⊕ *www.peking-va.com* ▭ *AE, D, MC, V.*

$$$$ ✕**Regency Room.** This hotel restaurant is known for its elegance, atten-
CONTINENTAL   tive service, and quality cuisine. Among crystal chandeliers, Asian silk-
★   screen prints, and full silver service, you can sample chateaubriand
carved tableside, as well as rack of lamb, Dover sole, lobster bisque,
and house-smoked and -cured salmon. It may almost seem as if you're
treated like royalty. A jacket and tie are required at dinner, but optional
at Sunday brunch. Breakfast or brunch may be good value, but dinner
could be budget-breaking for a family. ⊠ *Williamsburg Inn, 136 E.*
Francis St. ☎ *757/229–1000* ♨ *Reservations essential. Jacket required*
for dinner ▭ *AE, D, DC, MC, V.*

$ ✕ **Sal's Restaurant by Victor.** Locals love this family Italian restaurant and
ITALIAN pizzeria. Victor Minichiello and his staff serve up pasta, fish, chicken,
and veal dinners as well as subs and pizzas. It's a good choice for families who want to please the kids: parents can get quality "adult food"
while their children graze on pizza and subs. An interesting side note:
Chef Victor was on the International Olympics Committee. The restaurant delivers free to nearby hotels. Families rave about Sal's, especially
its family feast that serves five for less than $30. ✉ *1242 Richmond Rd.*
☎ *757/220–2641* ⊕ *www.salsbyvictor.com* ▭ *AE, D, MC, V.*

$$$ ✕ **The Seafare of Williamsburg.** Here in one of the area's few places for
SEAFOOD "fine dining," the waiters are tuxedo-clad, the tablecloths crisp linen.
The menu's offerings resemble those available on a luxury cruise ship.
Rum buns begin the meal, where the highlights include enormous crab
cakes and filet mignon topped with crabmeat and rich béarnaise sauce.
Order one of the showy flambé desserts, which are prepared table-
side. ✉ *1632 Richmond Rd.* ☎ *757/229–0099* ⊕ *www.theseafare.com*
▭ *AE, MC, V.*

$ ✕ **The Trellis.** With vaulted ceilings and hardwood floors, the Trellis is
AMERICAN an airy and pleasant place. The imaginative lunch and dinner menus
change with the seasons. A good wine list complements such dishes as
homemade tomato bisque, wild boar, and soft-shell crabs. The seafood
entrées are particularly good, and many patrons wouldn't leave without
ordering the rich Death by Chocolate, the restaurant's signature dessert.
Prices on the outdoor terrace menu are lower than in the indoor dining
room. ✉ *Merchants Sq., 403 Duke of Gloucester St.* ☎ *757/229–8610*
⊕ *www.thetrellis.com* ▭ *AE, D, DC, MC, V.*

$$ ✕ **The Whaling Company.** Fresh seafood is the drawing card at this large
SEAFOOD wooden building, which wouldn't look out of place in a New England
fishing village. Despite its out-of-town look, the restaurant has an
authenticity sometimes hard to find in touristy towns. Locals come in
for the fresh Virginia scallops, shrimp, fish, and other seafood. Steaks
and lemon herb chicken are available for the non-Whalers. The restaurant is off U.S. 60 near the Route 199 interchange. ✉ *494 McLaws
Circle* ☎ *757/229–0275* ⊕ *www.thewhalingcompany.com* ▭ *AE, MC,
V* ☻ *No lunch.*

COLONIAL TAVERNS

For an authentic dining experience to match the historic setting, it's
nearly a requirement to dine in one of the four reconstructed "taverns"
in Colonial Williamsburg—essentially casual restaurants with beer and
wine available. Colonial-style and modern American fare is served at
lunch, dinner, and Sunday brunch. Although the food can be uneven
(excellent one night and mediocre the next), a meal at any tavern is a
good way to get into the spirit of the era.

■ **TIP→ Dining at the Colonial Taverns can be pricey for families. Consider
having your big meal at lunch at one of the taverns. The menu is cheaper
and you'll escape the heat of a Virginia day.**

No reservations are taken for lunch (or anytime at Chowning's Tavern),
but make dinner reservations up to two or three weeks in advance.
Hours also change according to season, so check by calling the reservations number (☎ *800/447–8679*). Smoking is not permitted in any

of the taverns. To see tavern menus, go to ⊕ *www.history.org/visit/ diningexperience.*

$ ✕**Chowning's Tavern.** A reconstructed 18th-century alehouse, Chown-
AMERICAN ing's serves casual quick fare for lunch, including traditional pit-style barbeque, beef brisket sandwiches, and Smithfield ham and Gloucester cheese on a pretzel roll. You can eat either inside the tavern or under a grape arbor behind the tavern. After 5 pm, Chownings becomes a true Colonial tavern where Gambols (18th-century entertainment), a program presented for 25 years, operates throughout the evening. Cos-tumed balladeers lead family sing-alongs, and costumed servers play popular games of the day. From 8 pm until closing, Chowning's caters to a more mature audience. ⊠ *109 E. Duke of Gloucest St.* ▭ *AE, D, DC, MC, V.*

$$$$ ✕**Christiana Campbell's Tavern.** Across the street from the Capitol, this
AMERICAN tavern serves traditional seafood from the rest of the British colonies of North America. Mrs. Campbell's favorite dishes are sherried shrimp, scallops, and lobster, as well as the Waterman's Supper and lump crab cakes—the tavern's signature dish. Classic sides include cabbage slaw, spoon bread, and sweet potato muffins. An evening's entertainment might include storytelling or traditional music. George Washington often met with local residents at Mrs. Campbell's tavern. ⊠ *Waller St.* ▭ *AE, D, DC, MC, V.*

$$$ ✕**Kings Arms.** This 18th century–style chophouse is where the gentry
AMERICAN dined, and is still the finest of the historic area's four Colonial taverns. Colonial delicacies include roast prime rib of beef, collops of pork, roast duckling, game pie, and favorites such as peanut soup and stuffed mushrooms. Mrs. Vobe's Tavern Dinner, named after the tavern's 18th-century proprietress Jane Vobe, is a fixed-price three-course meal with the trademark peanut soup; chicken and ham with potatoes, mush-rooms, and tarragon; Sally Lunn bread; and a choice of desserts. ⊠ *409 E. Duke of Gloucester St.* ▭ *AE, D, DC, MC, V.*

$$ ✕**Shields Tavern.** Proprietor James Shields served the lesser gentry and
AMERICAN upper middling ranks of locals and travelers in the 1740s. Today, the largest of the colonial taverns now serves more than just light fare, though gumbo soup, salads, wrap sandwiches, and pie are still popu-lar. Heartier food includes traditional 18th-century fare such as welsh rarebit (spicy cheese served over toast) and more modern dishes like bison meat loaf. This tavern closes at 8:30 pm. ⊠ *Duke of Gloucester St.* ☎ *757/229–2141* ⟳ *Reservations essential* ▭ *AE, D, DC, MC, V.*

WHERE TO STAY

$$ ⚏**Colonial Houses.** A stay here seems particularly moving at night, when
★ the town's historic area is quiet and you have Williamsburg pretty much to yourself. Five of the 25 homes and three lodging taverns are 18th-century structures; the others have been rebuilt on their original foun-dations. Antiques and period reproductions furnish the rooms, and the costumed staff reinforces the historical air. Modern amenities include hair dryers, irons, ironing boards, coffeemakers, and a complimentary fruit basket and bottle of wine. The Colonial Houses share the facili-ties of the adjacent Williamsburg Inn and the Lodge. **Pros:** you can't beat the accommodations for the total Colonial experience. **Cons:** some

complain that the houses are noisy; no pool to escape the summer's heat; houses are not handicapped accessible. ⊠ *136 E. Francis St., Box 1776* ☎ *757/229–1000 or 800/447–8679* ⊕ *www.colonialwilliamsburg.com* ⌨ *77 rooms* ⚒ *In-room: a/c, refrigerator (some)* ▤ *AE, D, MC, V* ⦿*BP.*

$$ 🔲 **The Fife and Drum Inn.** On the second floor of Merchant's Square and practically across the street from the historic district stands this family-run B&B (there's no elevator). Each room is stylishly decorated by the owner in a motif that spotlights an aspect of Williamsburg town history. Modern amenities include a hair dryer and in-room phones with voice mail. Rooms have either a shower or a combination tub-shower. Included in the rates are homemade cookies, nonalcoholic beverages, and a full hot breakfast. **Pros:** in the heart of the Williamsburg commercial district and adjacent to the historic district. **Cons:** not handicapped accessible (except for the cottage); children under six are not accepted; minimum two-night stay may be required, especially on the weekends. ⊠ *441 Prince George St.* ☎ *757/345–1776 or 888/838–1783* ⊕ *www. fifeanddruminn.com* ⌨ *7 rooms, 2 suites, 1 cottage* ⚒ *In-room: a/c. In-hotel: restaurant, Wi-Fi hotspot, parking (free), no kids under 6* ▤ *AE, D, DC, MC, V* ⦿*BP.*

$$
★ 🔲 **Kingsmill Resort and Spa.** This manicured 2,900-acre resort on the James River owned by Anheuser-Busch is home to the largest golf resort in Virginia: it hosts the LPGA's Michelob ULTRA Open each May. You can play year-round on three championship courses, including the River Course, renovated in 2005. The 9-hole course is free if you stay here, and so is a shuttle bus to Busch Gardens, Water Country USA, and Colonial Williamsburg. The guest rooms have fireplaces and Colonial-style furniture. The inventive menu at the expensive Bray Bistro emphasizes seafood. **Pros:** lots of space to roam around the resort and away from the hustle and bustle of Colonial Williamsburg. **Cons:** could be too quiet without that hustle and bustle; no rollaways for kids. ⊠ *1010 Kingsmill Rd.* ☎ *757/253–1703 or 800/832–5665* ⊕ *www.kingsmill. com* ⌨ *235 rooms, 175 suites* ⚒ *In-room: a/c, safe, DVD, Wi-Fi. In-hotel: 6 restaurants, room service, bar, golf course, tennis, pool, gym, spa, laundry service, Wi-Fi hotspot, parking (free)* ▤ *AE, MC, V.*

$$ 🔲 **Liberty Rose.** Century-old beeches, oaks, and poplars surround this slate-roof, white-clapboard house on a hilltop acre 1 mi from Colonial Williamsburg. The inn was constructed in the early 1920s; furnishings include European antiques and plenty of silk and damask. Most remarkable is that every room has windows on three sides. The large room on the first floor has a unique bathroom with a claw-foot tub, a red-marble shower, and antique mirrors. Breakfast is served on a sun porch. This two-story bed-and-breakfast does not have an elevator. **Pros:** attentive innkeepers; a cozy bed-and-breakfast experience. **Cons:** may not be appropriate for children; a two-night minimum stay may be required, especially on the weekends; is not handicapped accessible. ⊠ *1022 Jamestown Rd.* ☎ *757/253–1260 or 800/545–1825* ⊕ *www. libertyrose.com* ⌨ *4 rooms* ⚒ *In-room: a/c, Internet. In-hotel: restaurant, parking (free), no kids under 12* ▤ *AE, D, MC, V* ⦿*BP.*

$ 🔲 **War Hill Inn.** This inn was designed by a Colonial Williamsburg architect to resemble a period structure: the two-story redbrick building at the center has a wood-frame wing. Appropriate antiques and repro-ductions decorate the interior. The War Hill is inside a 32-acre oper-ating cattle farm, 4 mi from the Colonial Williamsburg information center. Those in search of privacy may want one of the cottages or the first-floor suite (other rooms open onto a common hallway). **Pros:** children are welcome and may enjoy the farm experience. **Cons:** break-fast, but no restaurant; no handicapped accessibility. ⊠ *4560 Longhill Rd.* ☎ *757/565–0248 or 800/743–0248* ⊕ *www.warhillinn.com* ⤻ *4 rooms, 2 cottages* ♿ *In-room: a/c, kitchen (some), refrigerator (some), Wi-Fi (some). In-hotel: parking (free)* ▭ *MC, V* ☻ *Closed Dec. 23 and 24* ▮⊙▮ *BP.*

¢ ▦ **Williamsburg Hospitality House.** Across the street from the College of William and Mary and two blocks from the historic area, this hotel is a prime site for conferences and reunions, so you won't be the only one standing under the crystal chandelier in the lobby. Guest rooms are furnished in styles ranging from 18th century to art deco; all have hair dryers, irons, ironing boards, and in-room coffeemakers. The large poolside patio is very inviting after a day exploring the Historic Trian-gle. **Pros:** two blocks from the historic district; handicapped accessible with elevator. **Cons:** can be busy as the site of conferences and conven-tions; expensive Wi-Fi fees. ⊠ *415 Richmond Rd.* ☎ *757/229–4020 or 800/932–9192* ⊕ *www.williamsburghosphouse.com* ⤻ *296 rooms, 11 suites* ♿ *In-room: a/c, Wi-Fi. In-hotel: 2 restaurants, room service, pool, gym, laundry facilities, laundry service, parking (free)* ▭ *AE, D, DC, MC, V* ▮⊙▮ *CP.*

$$$$ ▦ **Williamsburg Inn.** This grand hotel from 1937 is owned and operated
★ by Colonial Williamsburg. Rooms are beautifully and individually fur-nished with reproductions and antiques in the English Regency style, and genteel service and tradition reign. Rooms come with such perks as morning coffee and afternoon tea, a daily newspaper, turndown service, and bathrobes. The Providence Wings, adjacent to the inn, are less formal; rooms are in a contemporary style with Asian accents and overlook the tennis courts, a private pond, and a wooded area. **Pros:** this is the most elegant property operated by Colonial Williamsburg. **Cons:** may be pricey for families on a budget. ⊠ *136 E. Francis St., Box 1776* ☎ *757/229–1000* ⊕ *www.colonialwilliamsburg.com* ⤻ *62 rooms, 14 suites* ♿ *In-room: a/c, safe, Internet. In-hotel: restaurant, room service, bar, golf course, tennis court, pool, gym, laundry service, Wi-Fi hotspot, parking (free)* ▭ *AE, D, DC, MC, V* ▮⊙▮ *CP.*

$$ ▦ **Williamsburg Lodge & Conference Center.** The total renovation of this classic hotel and the addition of a conference center were completed in 2006. Charmingly appointed with furnishings inspired by the collec-tions of the Abby Aldrich Rockefeller Folk Art Museum, every room has a hair dryer, iron, ironing board, and clock radio. Rooms with fireplaces are available. Very close to historic district, although the hotel itself lacks the charm of the Colonial Houses. **Pros:** excellent choice for fami-lies; some rooms adjoin. **Cons:** large parties (weddings, conferences) could mean slow check-in or check-out process. ⊠ *310 S. England St.* ☎ *757/229–1000 or 800/447–8679* ⊕ *www.colonialwilliamsburg. com* ⤻ *323 rooms* ♿ *In-room: a/c, safe, Wi-Fi. In-hotel: restaurant,*

room service, bar, pool, gym, laundry service, parking (free), some pets allowed ⊟ AE, D, MC, V ⎮◎⎮ CP.

$ 🏠**Williamsburg Sampler Bed & Breakfast Inn.** Charming and hospitable, this redbrick inn near the historic district is modeled after a plantation-style house from the 1700s. Rooms have 18th- and 19th-century antiques, pewter pieces, four-poster beds, and pleasant views of the city. The suites are particularly inviting: each has a separate sitting room, French doors, and a porch overlooking gardens. There are no phones in the rooms, but local calls are free from the inn's foyer. **Pros:** a trip back in time; great value. **Cons:** not for you if you don't enjoy the B&B experience; two nights required stay on weekends. ⊠ 922 *Jamestown Rd.* ☎ 757/253–0398 or 800/722–1169 ⊕ *www.williamsburgsampler. com* ⬅ 2 rooms, 2 suites ☖ *In-room: a/c. In-hotel: restaurant, no kids under 12* ⊟ *AE, D, DC, MC, V* ⎮◎⎮ *BP.*

$ 🏠**Woodlands Hotel and Suites.** An official Colonial Williamsburg property with contemporary furnishings, this 300-room hotel is adjacent to the HUZZAH! restaurant and the visitor center complex. You can enjoy the extensive free Continental breakfast indoors or on the large patio—kids and adults enjoy making their own homemade waffles. There's gated free parking so you can abandon your car and walk to the free shuttle buses. **Pros:** good choice for families; suites are available; some double rooms have futons for children. **Cons:** if you want luxurious lodgings you might want to book elsewhere. ⊠ 102 *Visitor Center Dr.* ☎ 757/229–1000 or 800/447–8679 ⊕ *www.colonialwilliamsburg. com* ⬅ 204 rooms, 96 suites ☖ *In-room: a/c. In-hotel: restaurant, golf course, pool, gym, laundry facilities, laundry service, Wi-Fi hotspot, parking (free), some pets allowed* ⊟ *AE, D, DC, MC, V* ⎮◎⎮ CP.

NIGHTLIFE AND THE ARTS

Busch Gardens Williamsburg (⊠ *U.S.* 60 ☎ 757/253–3350 ⊕ *www. buschgardens.com*) hosts popular song-and-dance shows (country, gospel, opera, German folk) in several theaters; in the largest, the 5,000-seat Royal Palace, pop stars often perform. Well-known artists on tour play at the 10,000-seat **Phi Beta Kappa Hall** (⊠ 601 *Jamestown Rd. entrance to campus* ☎ 757/221–2674 *box office*) at the College of William and Mary.

SPORTS AND THE OUTDOORS

AMUSEMENT PARKS

🌞 **Busch Gardens** in Williamsburg has been voted the world's most beautiful theme park for 19 consecutive years, and features more than 50 rides and attractions, including five of the world's best roller coasters. Six beautifully landscaped European "countries" re-create the look and feel of France, Germany, England, Scotland, Ireland, and Italy. New for 2009, Sesame Street Forest of Fun brings Elmo and his Sesame Street friends to life. Grover's Alpine Express, the park's newest roller coaster, is one of four new rides designed for children and parents to enjoy together, and is among Busch Gardens' most popular KIDsiderate attractions. Busch Gardens also hosts popular song-and-dance shows (country, Americana, Irish, German folk) in several theaters. ⊠ *U.S.* 60, 3 *mi east of Williamsburg* ☎ 800/343–7946 ⊕ *www.buschgardens.com/ va* ⬅ $59.95, *child* $49.95 (*Prices vary according to ticket package.*

Check the Web site for deals); parking $13 ⊙ *Late Mar.–mid-May, open weekends; mid-May–Labor Day, open daily; early Sept.–Oct., open weekends; late-Nov.–Dec., open weekends. Check Web site or call for exact hrs.*

> **THEME PARKING**
>
> What they don't tell you: even as expensive as they are, tickets don't include parking at either Busch Gardens or Water Country. You must pay $13 per car to enter and park ($6 extra for premium parking that's closer to the entrance). To avoid having to pay for parking, stay at a motel or hotel that offers free shuttle service to the parks.

🌙 At **Water Country USA**, nearly 45 acres of pools, children's play areas, lazy rivers, and water rides have a colorful 1950s and surf theme. Blast down Rock 'n' Roll Island's nearly 600 feet of body slides, ride the 700-foot lazy river, or soak in the 9,000-square-foot pool. Or you can enjoy relaxing by Virginia's largest wave pool in a lounge chair or a private cabana. There are also live entertainment, shopping, and restaurants. ⊠ *Rte. 199, 3 mi off I–64, Exit 242B* ☎ *757/253–3350 or 800/343–7946* ⊕ *www.watercountryusa.com* ✉ *$42.95 for anyone 10 and older, child $36 (Prices vary according to ticket package. Check the Web site for deals); parking $13* ⊙ *Mid-May, weekends only; June–early Sept., open daily. Check Web site or call for exact hrs.*

JOGGING AND WALKING

The historic district as well as the College of William and Mary campus make for a splendid run. The best times for an amble along the sidewalks or cobblestone streets are early in the morning and at sundown. In the district is a 3-mi loop. Some of the nicest paths to run include the main thoroughfare of Duke of Gloucester Street, and the myriad side streets such as Botetourt and Blair streets. A 30-mi path starts at the college and runs all around the Colonial area.

SHOPPING

Merchants Square, on the west end of Duke of Gloucester Street, has both licensed Willliamsburg shops and non-Colonial, upscale shops that include Laura Ashley, the Porcelain Collector of Williamsburg, and the J. Fenton Gallery. There's also Quilts Unlimited and the Campus Shop, which carries William and Mary gifts and clothing.

Williamsburg at Home (⊠ *439 W. Duke of Gloucester* ☎ *757/220–7749*), an official store of Colonial Williamsburg, features the full line of Williamsburg furniture, bedding, rugs, fixtures, and wallpapers. **Celebrations Williamsburg** (⊠ *110 S. Henry St.* ☎ *757/565–8642*) displays seasonal decorations and accessories. The **Williamsburg Craft House** (⊠ *305 S. England St.* ☎ *757/220–7747*) sells a full line of Willliamsburg dinnerware, flatware, glassware, pewter, giftware, and jewelry.

YORKTOWN

14 mi northeast of Colonial Williamsburg via Colonial Pkwy.

It was at Yorktown that the combined American and French forces surrounded Lord Cornwallis's British troops in 1781; this was the end

CLOSE UP

Williamsburg Outlet Shopping

You can find many outlet malls less than 10 minutes west of Colonial Williamsburg, in the tiny town of Lightfoot. If you're driving from Richmond to Williamsburg on I-64, take Exit 234 west to Lightfoot. When you reach U.S. 60 (Richmond Road), the outlets—both freestanding and in shopping centers—are on both sides of the road. Most outlet shops are open Monday–Saturday 10–9, Sunday 10–6. In January and February some stores close weekdays at 6.

The largest of the outlets, **Prime Outlets at Williamsburg** (⊠ *U.S. 60, Lightfoot* ☎ *757/565–0702* ⊕ *www. primeoutlets.com*) has more than 85 stores. Liz Claiborne, L. L. Bean, Waterford-Wedgwood, Eddie Bauer, Coach, Tommy Hilfiger, Brooks Bros., Nike, Guess, Nautica, and Cole Haan are all here.

The **Williamsburg Pottery Factory** (⊠ *U.S. 60 W, Lightfoot* ☎ *757/564–3326* ⊕ *www.williamsburgpottery.com*) is an attraction in itself, and the parking area is usually crammed with tour buses. Covering 200 acres, the enormous store sells luggage, clothing, furniture, food and wine, china, crystal, and—its original commodity—pottery. Individual stores such as Pfaltzgraff are within the compound.

The **Williamsburg Outlet Mall** (⊠ *U.S. 60 W, Lightfoot* ☎ *757/565–3378* ⊕ *www.williamsburgoutletmall. com*) has more than 60 shops, including Pendleton, Lee, Healthtex, Avon, and Lee/Wrangler.

Patriot Plaza (⊠ *3032 Richmond Rd., Lightfoot* ☎ *757/258–0767*) has Lenox, Villeroy & Boch, Orvis, Lenox, and other factory outlets.

7

to the Revolutionary War and the beginning of the United States. In Yorktown today, as at Jamestown, two major attractions complement each other. Yorktown Battlefield, the historical site, is operated by the National Park Service; and Yorktown Victory Center, which has re-creations and informative exhibits, is operated by the state's Jamestown–Yorktown Foundation. As well, a stately Watermen's Museum educates visitors about those who earn their living from the nearby waters.

GETTING HERE AND AROUND

From mid-March through the end of October, the County operates the Yorktown Trolley, providing free service between the Yorktown Battlefield Visitor Center and the Yorktown Victory Center, as well as seven stops between in the historic village. The trolley runs approximately every half hour.

ESSENTIALS

Visitor Information Colonial National Historical Park (⊡ *Box 210, Yorktown 23690* ☎ *757/898–3400* ⊕ *www.apva.org*). **York County Tourism** (☎ *757/890–3300* ⊕ *www.yorkcounty.gov/tourism*).

EXPLORING

Riverwalk Landing is a group of specialty shops, an upscale restaurant, and an outdoor performance venue on the shores of the York River. Two piers for medium-size cruise ships and personal watercraft are also along the waterfront. Yet Yorktown remains a small community of year-round residents. Route 238 leads into town, where along Main Street are preserved 18th-century buildings on a bluff overlooking the York River.

Settled in 1691, Yorktown had become a thriving tobacco port and a prosperous community of several hundred houses by the time of the Revolution. Nine buildings from that time still stand, some of them open to visitors. **Moore House,** where the terms of surrender were negotiated, and the elegant **Nelson House,** the residence of a Virginia governor (and a signer of the Declaration of Independence), are open for tours in summer and are included in the Yorktown Victory Center's entrance fee.

The **Swan Tavern,** a reconstruction of a 1722 structure, houses an

> ### COLONIAL PARKWAY
>
> For a beautiful drive along countryside that's nearly the same as land the Jamestown settlers trod, take the 23-mi scenic Colonial Parkway between Jamestown and Yorktown, a 40-minute drive one-way. The road between Yorktown and Williamsburg, which was aligned along the York River, was completed in 1937, but it wasn't until 1955, for the 350th anniversary of Jamestown, that the road was completed to America's first permanent English settlement. The limited-access highway has broad sweeping curves, is meticulously landscaped, and is devoid of commercial development.

antiques shop. **Grace Church,** built in 1697 and damaged in the War of 1812 and the Civil War, was rebuilt and has an active Episcopal congregation; its walls are made of native marl (a mixture of clay, sand, and limestone containing fragments of seashells). On Main Street, the **Somerwell House,** built before 1707, and the **Sessions House** (before 1699) are privately owned and closed to the public: they're the oldest houses in town. The latter was used as the Union's local headquarters during General George McClellan's Peninsula Campaign of the Civil War.

Watermen's Museum. Sited in a Colonial Revival manor house on Yorktown's waterfront, the Watermen's Museum was floated across the York River on a barge in 1987. In it you can learn more about the generations of men who have wrested a living from the Chesapeake Bay and nearby waters. The five galleries house ship models, dioramas, and artifacts themed on Chesapeake watermen, bay boats, harvesting fish, aquaculture, tools, and treasures. Outdoor exhibits include an original three-log canoe, dredges, engines, and other equipment used by working watermen past and present. ⊠ *309 Water St.* ☎ *757/887–2641* ⊕ *www. watermens.org* ✉ *$5* ⊙ *Apr.–Thanksgiving, Tues.–Sat. 10–5, Sun. 1–5; Thanksgiving–Mar., Sat. 10–5, Sun. 1–5.*

☾   **Yorktown Battlefield.** Yorktown Battlefield preserves the land where
Fodor's Choice   the British surrendered to American and French forces in 1781. The
★   museum in the visitor center has on exhibit part of General George Washington's original field tent. Dioramas, illuminated maps, and a film about the battle make the sobering point that Washington's victory was hardly inevitable. A look around from the roof's observation deck can help you visualize the events of the campaign. Guided by an audio tour purchased from the gift shop, you may explore the battlefield by car,

stopping at the site of Washington's headquarters, a couple of crucial redoubts (breastworks dug into the ground), the field where surrender took place, and the Moore House, where the surrender terms were negotiated. ⊠ *East End of the Colonial Pkwy.* ☎ *757/898–2410* 🖃 *$10 for adults (under 15 free); includes admission to Historic Jamestowne as well as Yorktown Battlefield* ☯ *Visitor center daily 9–5.*

↻ **Yorktown Victory Center.** On the western edge of Yorktown Battlefield, the Yorktown Victory Center has wonderful exhibits and demonstrations that bring to life the American Revolution. Textual and graphic displays along the open-air Road to Revolution walkway cover the principal events and personalities. A renovated *Declaration of Independence* entrance gallery and long-term exhibition, *The Legacy of Yorktown: Virginia Beckons,* debuted in 2006. Life-size tableaux show 10 "witnesses," including an African-American patriot, a loyalist, a Native American leader, two Continental Army soldiers, and the wife of a Virginia plantation owner. ■TIP→ **The "witnesses" testimony is very dramatic and makes the American Revolution real for children. This presentation brings the personal trials of the colonists to life more effectively than the artifacts of the war.**

FodorśChoice
★

The exhibit galleries contain more than 500 period artifacts, including many recovered during underwater excavations of "Yorktown's Sunken Fleet" (British ships lost during the siege of 1781). Outdoors, visitors may participate in a Continental Army drill at an encampment with interpreters costumed as soldiers and female auxiliaries, who reenact and discuss daily camp life. In another outdoor area, a re-created 1780s farm includes a dwelling, kitchen, tobacco barn, crop fields, and kitchen garden, which show how many Americans lived in the decade following the end of the Revolution. ⊠ *Rte. 238 off Colonial Pkwy.* ☎ *757/253–4838 or 888/593–4682* ⊕ *www.historyisfun.org* 🖃 *$9.25; combination ticket for Yorktown Victory Center and Jamestown Settlement $19.95* ☯ *June 15–Aug. 15, daily 9–6; Aug. 16–June 14, daily 9–5.*

7

WHERE TO EAT AND STAY

$$
SEAFOOD

✕ **Nick's Riverwalk Restaurant.** Whether you dine indoors or out, enjoy the view of the York River, the Coleman Bridge, and Gloucester on the opposite shore. Nick's Riverwalk offers casual meals of soups, salads, and sandwiches at the Rivah Café and outdoor courtyard; the Riverwalk Dining Room is more formal, with a menu featuring baked crabmeat imperial, sautéed fillets, and local oysters. Right outside of the café are a boardwalk and a sandy beach. Parking is available across the street. There are many shops just outside the Riverwalk's door. ⊠ *323 Water St.* ☎ *757/875–1522* ▭ *MC, V.*

¢

🏨 **Duke of York Motel.** All rooms in this classic motel face the water and are only a few steps from a sandy public beach on the York River. The furnishings include quilted bedspreads and reproduction wood furniture. The motel also has a swimming pool and a restaurant that serves breakfast and lunch daily and dinner Wednesday–Sunday. It is an easy walk to the riverfront and its shops and restaurants. The free Yorktown Trolley stops right outside the hotel. **Pros:** modestly priced; some rooms have microwaves. **Cons:** the decor is half a century old. ⊠ *508 Water St.* ☎ *757/898–3232* ⊕ *www.dukeofyorkmotel.com* ⇗ *57* rooms ⚂ *In-room: a/c. In-hotel: pool, parking (free)* ▭*AE, D, DC, MC, V* ❙◉❙ *CP.*

CHARLES CITY COUNTY

35 mi northwest of Colonial Williamsburg via Rte. 5.

Colonists founded Charles City County in 1616. This tiny county is unique, being the only U.S. county to have a native president (William Harrison) and his vice president and successor (John Tyler) take office simultaneously, in 1841. Today you can get a taste of those early days by following Route 5 on its scenic way, parallel to the James River, past nine plantations—some of which are now bed-and-breakfasts.

GETTING HERE AND AROUND
The only effective way to get around largely rural Charles City County is by car. The Charles City Web site has an excellent interactive map "Find It in Charles City County," which shows attractions, restaurants, antiques shops, and automobile services.

TIMING AND PRECAUTIONS
Make sure your gas tank is full, and you may want to pack a picnic lunch. Service stations and restaurants are few.

ESSENTIALS
Charles City County (☎ *804/652–4701* ⊕ *www.charlescity.org*).

EXPLORING

★ **Berkeley.** Virginians say that the first Thanksgiving was celebrated at Berkeley in December 1619, not in Massachusetts in 1621. This plantation was the birthplace of Benjamin Harrison, a signer of the Declaration of Independence, and of William Henry Harrison, who became president in 1841. Throughout the Civil War, the Union general George McClellan used Berkeley as headquarters; during his tenure, his subordinate general Daniel Butterfield composed the melody for "Taps" while here in 1862 with 140,000 Union troops. An architectural gem, the original 1726 brick Georgian mansion has been carefully restored and furnished with 18th-century antiques. The gardens are in excellent condition, particularly the boxwood hedges. ⊠ *Rte. 5, 12602 Harrison Landing Rd., Charles City* ☎ *804/829–6018 or 888/466–6018* ⊕ *www. berkeleyplantation.com* 🎫 *$11* ⊙ *Daily tours 9:30–4:30 in summer, 9:30–3:30 in winter.*

Sherwood Forest Plantation. Sherwood Forest Plantation (1720), at 300 feet said to be the longest wood-frame house in the United States, was the retirement home of John Tyler (1790–1862), 10th president of the United States. Tyler, who came into office in 1842 when William Henry Harrison died a month after inauguration, was a Whig who dissented from his party's abolitionist line in favor of the pro-slavery position of the Democrats. He died in 1862, having served briefly in the congress of the Confederate States of America. His house remains in the Tyler family and is furnished with heirloom antiques; it's surrounded by a dozen acres of grounds and the five outbuildings, including a tobacco barn. The house is only open to individuals who have made a reservation in advance, but the grounds are open to the public. ⊠ *Rte. 5, 14501*

John Tyler Memorial Hwy., Charles City ☎ *804/829–5377* ⊕ *www. sherwoodforest.org* 🕮 *Grounds $10, house open to tours of 10 or more with advanced reservation, $10 per person* ⊙ *Grounds daily 9–5.*

★ **Shirley.** Chartered in 1613 and the oldest plantation in Virginia, Shirley has been occupied by a single family, the Carters, for 11 generations. Their claim to the land goes back to 1638, when it was settled by a relative, Edward Hill. Robert E. Lee's mother was born here, and the Carters seem to be related to every notable Virginia family from the Colonial and antebellum periods. The approach to the elegant 1723 Georgian manor is dramatic: the house stands at the end of a drive lined by towering Lombardy poplars. Inside, the "Flying Staircase" rises for three stories with no visible support. Family silver is on display, ancestral portraits are hung throughout, and rare books line the shelves. The family lives on the upper floors, but the main floor, eight original Colonial outbuildings, and gardens of the working farm can be toured. A tour of the Shirley Plantation details stories from the 11 generations of the same family who to this day continue to own and operate it. The guided tour of the first floor of the Great House highlights family stories as well as original furnishings, portraits, silver, and woodwork. Today Shirley continues to be a working plantation, a private family home, and a National Historic Landmark, which includes an on-site gift shop, Lady Cessalye's. ✉ *501 Shirley Plantation Rd., Charles City* ☎ *804/829–5121* ⊕ *www. shirleyplantation.com* 🕮 *$11* ⊙ *Daily 9–5; last tour 4:45.*

Westover. This home was built circa 1720 by Colonel William Byrd II (1674–1744), an American aristocrat and founder of the city of Richmond who spent much of his time and money in London. He was in Virginia frequently enough to serve in both the upper and lower houses of the Colonial legislature at Williamsburg and to write one of the first travel books about the region (as well as a notorious secret diary, a frank account of plantation life and Colonial politics). Byrd lived here with his beloved library of 4,000 volumes. The house, celebrated for its moldings, carvings, and classic proportions is open only during Garden Week in late April. However, it is worth the short drive off Route 5 to walk on the grounds beside the peaceful James River and smell the boxwoods. The grounds are arrayed with tulip poplars at least 100 years old, and other flowers are well tended. Three wrought-iron gates, imported from England by the colonel, are mounted on posts topped by figures of eagles with spread wings. Byrd's grave is here, inscribed with the eloquent, immodest, lengthy, and apt epitaph he composed for himself. ✉ *Rte. 5, 7000 Westover Rd., Charles City* ☎ *804/829–2882* ⊕ *www.jamesriverplantations.org* 🕮 *$2* ⊙ *Grounds daily 9–6, house daily in late Apr.; call for hrs.*

WHERE TO EAT AND STAY

$$
AMERICAN

✕ **Charles City Tavern.** Because this restaurant is the best of only a few places to dine in the area, you may encounter a wait to be seated and served—especially at lunch, when visitors touring the nearby plantations descend. Dinner reservations are recommended, especially on weekends. Housed in a restored farmhouse, the tavern specializes in Southern dishes, especially regional specialties such as crab cakes and bread pudding. Other main dishes include pan-roasted oysters and tavern meat loaf. The tavern (formerly the Indian Fields Tavern) stresses seasonal American regional cuisine. In mild weather, you can eat on the screened porch overlooking gardens. There's brunch on Sunday. ⊠ *9220 John Tyler Memorial Hwy., Charles City* ☎ *804/829–5004* ⊕ *www.charlescitytavern.com* ⊟ *AE, MC, V.*

$ ⊞ **North Bend Plantation Bed & Breakfast.** The road to this historic home winds past trailer homes and cottages before a gravel road turns to the left between farm fields. As a working farm, it stands out from similar B&Bs. The 1819 Greek Revival home was built for Sarah Harrison, sister of President William Henry Harrison, by her husband John Minge. Inside, antebellum-era antiques original to the house, as well as Civil War maps and artifacts, decorate every room. Room amenities include robes and TVs. The Southern breakfast here might include buttermilk biscuits, Smithfield ham, apple butter, bacon and sausage, and strong coffee. Reviewers rave about hospitality of the hosts. **Pros:** generously sized rooms; peaceful surroundings; golf carts available to tour the property; all rooms have DIRECTV and Wi-Fi. **Cons:** may be too quiet for some. ⊠ *12200 Weyanoke Rd., Charles City* ☎ *804/829–5176* ⊕ *www.northbendplantation.com* ⤶ *4 rooms, 1 suite* ⌂ *In-room: a/c, Wi-Fi. In-hotel: restaurant, pool, parking (free), no kids under 6* ⊟ *MC, V* ⑩ *BP.*

HOPEWELL

56 mi northwest of Colonial Williamsburg via Rte. 5 and 24 mi southeast of Richmond off I–295.

City Point, the oldest part of Hopewell, was established in 1613 by Sir Thomas Dale. Across from Charles City County via the Route 106 Benjamin Harrison Bridge, Hopewell is worth a half-day exploration for its 19th-century buildings, nearby plantations, and 44 Sears Roebuck & Co. Catalog houses built from 1926 to 1937.

GETTING HERE AND AROUND

Stop by the Hopewell Visitor Center for maps to the Sears Catalog Homes in the Crescent Hills subdivision near downtown. The visitor center is just off I–295 at Exit 9A, and is open daily 9–5.

A car is necessary to get around Hopewell. The collection of Sears homes is a short drive from the center of town. Tour the homes by driving through the neighborhood.

ESSENTIALS

Visitor Information Hopewell Visitor Center (⊠ *4100 Oaklawn Blvd. [Rte. 36]* ☎ *800/863–8687 or 804/541–2461*) is open 9–5 daily.

EXPLORING

City Point. The history of City Point includes a Revolutionary War skirmish and 10 months as General Ulysses S. Grant's Union headquarters during the Civil War, from which he directed the Siege of Petersburg. It's free to take the open-air, self-guided museum walking tour of 25 wayside exhibits and Grant's Headquarters. The City Point Early History Museum is in a former U.S. Navy church, St. Dennis Chapel. ⊠ *4100*

Oaklawn Blvd. ☎ *804/541–2461 or 800/863–8687* 🖼 *Museum $3, Weston Manor $5, combination ticket for Weston Manor and museum $7* ⊙ *Daily 9–5; closed selected federal holidays.*

Weston Manor. Weston Manor, built in 1789 by the Gilliam family, is a classic example of Virginia Georgian architecture, a formal five-bay manor with hipped roof. The family immigrated to Virginia in the 1600s as indentured servants, eventually acquiring several area plantations. Family members were descendants of Pocahontas, and a cousin married Thomas Jefferson's daughter, Maria. The distinctive interior moldings, wainscoting, and chair rails are 85% original. ⊠ *Weston La. at 21st St.* ☎ *804/458–4682* 🖼 *$5, children under 12 free* ⊙ *Apr.–Oct., Mon.–Sat. 10–4:30, Sun. 1–4:30; Nov.–Mar., by appointment.*

WHERE TO EAT

$$
SEAFOOD ✕ **Dockside**. Broiled fresh seafood of a dozen kinds is the specialty at this casual waterfront restaurant only a quick bridge-crossing from the James River Plantations. You could start with spiced shrimp, and if you're really hungry, order the seafood platter. Other menu items include she-crab soup, Greek salads, and Italian main dishes. One of the few dining choices in the area, the Dockside is set on Big Bay Creek and overlooks the Virginia River. ⊠ *700 Jordan Point Rd.* ☎ *804/541–2600* ⊕ *www.docksideonthejames.com* ▭ *AE, D, MC, V.*

HAMPTON ROADS AREA

7

The region known today as the Hampton Roads Area is made up of not only the large natural harbor, into which five rivers flow, but of the peninsula to the north that extends southeast from Williamsburg, and the Tidewater area between the mouth of the harbor and the Atlantic Ocean. On the peninsula are the cities of Newport News and Hampton; to the south and east are Norfolk, Portsmouth, Chesapeake, and Virginia Beach. These cities have been shaped by their proximity to the Chesapeake Bay and the rivers that empty into it, either as ports and shipbuilding centers or, in the case of Virginia Beach, as a hugely popular beach town. Hampton and Norfolk are the "old" cities of this area; recent development and revival efforts have made them worthy of a second look.

During the Civil War the Union waged its thwarted 1862 Peninsula Campaign here. General George McClellan planned to land his troops on the peninsula in March of 1862 with the help of the navy, and then press westward to the Confederate capital of Richmond. Naval forces on the York and James rivers would protect the advancing army. However, beginning with the blockade that the ironclad CSS *Virginia* (formerly the USS *Merrimack*) held on the James until May, events and Confederates conspired to lengthen and foil the campaign.

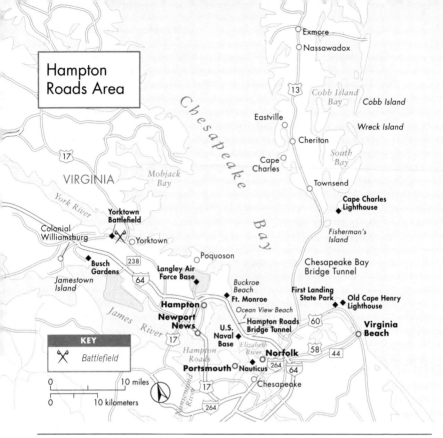

Hampton
Roads Area

Exmore
Nassawadox
Cobb Island
Bay
Cobb Island
Eastville
Wreck Island
Cheriton
South
Bay
Cape
Charles
Townsend
Cape Charles
Lighthouse
Fisherman's
Island
VIRGINIA
Mobjack
Bay
York River
Chesapeake Bay
Colonial
Williamsburg
Yorktown
Battlefield
Yorktown
Poquoson
Chesapeake Bay
Bridge Tunnel
Busch
Gardens
238
Langley Air
Force Base
Jamestown
Island
64
Buckroe
Beach
First Landing
State Park
Old Cape Henry
Lighthouse
Hampton
Ft. Monroe
Ocean View Beach
Newport
News
Hampton Roads
Bridge Tunnel
60
Virginia
Beach
James River
17
U.S.
Naval
Base
Elizabeth
River
Norfolk
58
44
KEY
Battlefield
Hampton
Roads
Portsmouth
Nauticus
Chesapeake
264
64
0   10 miles
0   10 kilometers
17
264

NEWPORT NEWS

23 mi southeast of Williamsburg.

Newport News stretches for almost 35 mi along the James River from near Williamsburg to Hampton Roads. Known mostly for its coal shipping and huge shipbuilding industry, the city is largely residential and is a suburb for both Williamsburg and the Norfolk area. Newport News has a number of Civil War battle sites and a splendid municipal park. The fabulous Mariners' Museum may be the best museum in the state. Close by, the Virginia Living Museum is a pleasant zoo experience for kids.

Newport News first appeared in the Virginia Company's records in 1619. It was probably named after Christopher Newport, captain of the *Susan Constant,* largest of the three ships in the company of Captain John Smith that landed at Jamestown in 1607. Newport News Shipbuilding is one of the largest privately owned shipyards in the world, and with approximately 18,000 employees, probably the second-largest employer in Virginia. It's the only shipyard in the country capable of building nuclear-powered aircraft carriers.

GETTING HERE AND AROUND

The city's small, but busy, airport is convenient to both Williamsburg and the beach, making it a good base from which to visit both areas.

ESSENTIALS

Train **Newport News Amtrak Station** (✉ *9304 Warwick Blvd.* ☎ *757/245–3589*).

Visitor Information **Newport News Tourism and Conference Bureau** (✉ *2400 Washington Ave.* ☎ *757/928–6843 or 888/493–7386* ⊕ *www.newport-news.org*). **Newport News Visitor Information Center** (✉ *13560 Jefferson Ave., I-64, Exit 250B* ☎ *757/886–7777 or 888/493–7386*).

EXPLORING

Endview Plantation. Built in 1769 by William Harwood, the Georgian-style house known as Endview Plantation has witnessed momentous events in American history. Situated atop a knoll near a spring, Endview's land was traversed by Native Americans of the Powhatan Chiefdom a thousand years before the coming of the English. At the outbreak of the Civil War, Endview's owner, Dr. Humphrey Harwood Curtis, formed the Warwick Beauregards, which became Company H, 32nd Virginia Volunteer Infantry. During the subsequent Peninsula Campaign of 1862, Endview served as headquarters for Confederate generals Lafayette McLaws and Robert Toombs. Maintained today as a living-history museum, Endview offers a wide variety of programs; guided tours begin every 30 minutes. ✉ *362 Yorktown Rd., Exit 247 off I-64* ☎ *757/887–1862* ⊕ *www.endview.org* ✎ *$6* ⊗ *Mon., Thurs., and Fri. 10–4, Sat. 10–5, Sun. 12–5.*

Lee Hall. Lee Hall, an Italianate mansion constructed around 1859, was once home to one of Warwick County's leading landowners, Richard Decauter Lee, who achieved prominence using the method of scientific farming. It is the only large mid-19th-century plantation house remaining on Virginia's lower peninsula, and it served as the headquarters for Confederate generals John Bankhead Magruder and Joseph E. Johnston during the spring of 1862. Lee Hall now provides an in-depth review of the 1862 Peninsula Campaign. ✉ *163 Yorktown Rd., Exit 247 off I-64* ☎ *757/888–3371* ⊕ *www.leehall.org* ✎ *$6* ⊗ *Jan.–Mar., Thurs.– Sat. 10–4, Sun. 1–5; Apr.–Dec., Mon. and Wed.–Sat. 10–5, Sun. 12–5.*

☾ **Mariners' Museum.** A world history of seagoing vessels and the people who sailed them occupies the outstanding Mariners' Museum, inside a 550-acre park. An alliance between the museum and the South Street Seaport Museum in New York City allows the two institutions to share collections, exhibitions, and educational programs. Among the more than 50 full-size craft on display are a Native American bark canoe, a sailing yacht, a speedboat, a gondola, a Coast Guard cutter, and a Chinese sampan. In separate galleries you can often watch the progress of a boat under construction; view ornate and sometimes huge figureheads; examine the watermen's culture of the Chesapeake Bay; and learn about the history of the U.S. Navy. The museum also holds artifacts from the RMS *Titanic* and remains of the ironclad USS *Monitor*, which served in the 1862 Peninsula Campaign and was recovered from the coast of North Carolina. A 63,500-square-foot addition, the

Fodor'sChoice
★

USS *Monitor* Center, houses the ironclad ship and Civil War exhibits. ⊠ *100 Museum Dr., I–64, Exit 258A* ☎ *757/595–0368 or 800/581– 7245* ⊕ *www.marinersmuseum.org* 🖃 *$12* ☉ *Wed.–Sat. 10–5, Sun. noon–5; open Mondays that are federal holidays, closed Thanksgiving and Christmas.*

☺ **U.S. Army Transportation Museum.** The U.S. Army Transportation Museum, at Fort Eustis, traces the history of army transportation by land, sea, and air, beginning with the Revolutionary War era. More than 90 vehicles, including experimental craft and numerous locomotives and trains dating to the 1800s, are on display. The museum's Korean War and World War II–era trucks can be toured inside and out. Be prepared to show a driver's license or other identification at the military checkpoint at the base entrance. ⊠ *Besson Hall Bldg. 300, Washington Blvd., I–64, Exit 250A* ☎ *757/878–1115* 🖃 *Free (donations accepted)* ☉ *Tues.–Sun. 9–4:30; closed federal holidays and Easter Sunday; open Memorial Day, July 4, and Labor Day.*

☺ **Virginia Living Museum.** At the Virginia Living Museum, visitors are transported to a steamy cypress swamp and cool mountain cove, the underwater world of the Chesapeake Bay and the underground realm of a limestone cave, all with living exhibits and hands-on activities. The planetarium theater was renovated in 2008. View the sun from the observatory. Outdoors, a 0.75–mi boardwalk features animals native to Virginia in naturalized habitats and wildflower gardens. ⊠ *524 J. Clyde Morris Blvd.* ☎ *757/595–1900* ⊕ *www.thevlm.org* 🖃 *$17* ☉ *Memorial Day–Labor Day, daily 9–5; Labor Day–Memorial Day, Mon.–Sat. 9–6, Sun. 12–5.*

Virginia War Museum. The Virginia War Museum houses more than 60,000 artifacts from all over the world. The collection includes a graffiti-covered section of the Berlin Wall, a Civil War blockade runner's uniform, weapons, uniforms, wartime posters, photographs, and other memorabilia. It traces military history from 1775 to the Gulf War and includes an outdoor exhibition of seven tanks and cannons, and the history of African-Americans and women in the military. Several war memorials are on the grounds of Huntington Park. ⊠ *9285 Warwick Blvd., Rte. 60* ☎ *757/247–8523* ⊕ *www.warmuseum.org* 🖃 *$6* ☉ *Mon.–Sat. 9–5, Sun. 12–5.*

WHERE TO EAT

¢–$ ✕ **Aromas.** The odd name is rather appropriate—if you weren't hungry
COFFEE SHOP   before entering this cozy place, you will be after the enticing smells reach you. A rich looking dining room outfitted with plush leather couches and stone walls makes you want to linger. Breakfast burritos and Belgian waffles are nice ways to start the day. Or end it with Southern caramelized barbecued shrimp over a mound of grits, and snack on fondue. You can even order a colorful cake if you're celebrating a special occasion. ⊠ *706 Town Center Dr., City Center at Oyster Point, Newport News* ☎ *757/240–4650* ⊕ *www.aromasworld.com* 🖃 *MC, V.*

¢   ✕ **Taste Coastal Gourmet Market & Cafe.** Located at City Town Center, this
DELI   is a great place for lunch. The interior has tall ceilings with exposed ducts and shelving with exotic sauces and dips to sample and buy.

Affordable fresh sandwiches, soups, and salads can be made by their suggestions or make up your own. The grilled chicken salad with grapes and celery is very Virginia. Add fresh cucumbers and Balsamic Vinaigrette for a twist. Other choices include Virginia ham, roasted red peppers, and Chesapeake crab cakes. They offer boxed lunches to take while exploring the area and deliveries to hotel rooms. ⊠ *1580 Crossways Blvd., City Center at Oyster Point, Newport News* ☎ *757/596–8651* ⊕ *www.tasteunlimited.com* ▭ *AE, MC, V.*

WHERE TO STAY

$ ⊡ **Hilton Garden Inn Newport News**. Built in 2004, this light and airy motel is within walking distance of a mall, restaurants, and movie theaters. One interesting detail is that the hotel features the latest in "ergonomic" furniture—designed for support and to reduced fatigue. Children will enjoy the heated swimming pool and spa. **Pros:** restaurant in hotel; newer property. **Cons:** keyed to the business traveler with its business center and conference facilities. ⊠ *180 Regal Way, Exit 256B (Victory Blvd.)* ☎ *757/947–1080* ⊕ *hiltongardeninn.hilton.com* ⇗ *122 rooms* ⚅ *In-room: a/c, refrigerator, Wi-Fi. In-hotel: restaurant, pool, gym, spa, laundry service* ▭ *AE, D, DC, MC, V.*

$ ⊡ **Marriott Newport News at City Center**. It's hard to argue with a hotel that presents luxury at a great location. A marble-and-granite lobby with colorful couches, a fireplace, and views of the giant outdoor fountain sets the tone. Rooms have plush beds dressed in yellows and blues and comfort touches like high-speed Internet or flat plasma TVs. There is a beautiful two-story piano room, great for hosting parties and wedding receptions. Marriott is walking distance to the new City Town Center, filled with open air shops and restaurants. A great central location means you'll have access to explore Williamsburg in one direction, Norfolk and Virginia Beach in the other. **Pros:** THE place to stay in Newport News; walk to shops and restaurants, **Cons:** most expensive place to stay in the area. ⊠ *740 Town Center Dr., Newport News* ☎ *757/873–9299* ⊕ *www.marriott.com/phfoy* ⇗ *250 rooms, 6 suites* ⚅ *In-room: a/c, safe, DVD (some), Internet, Wi-Fi (some). In-hotel: 2 restaurants, room service, bar, pool, gym, bicycles, laundry service, Internet terminal, Wi-Fi hotspot, parking (paid), some pets allowed* ▭ *AE, D, DC, MC, V* ⦿❙ *EP.*

$–$$ ⊡ **Omni Newport News Hotel**. Hidden back from traffic noise and fea-
★ turing possibly the most pleasant front desk, the Omni is a stand-out. The burgundy, green, and gold color scheme of the lobby carries over to the guest rooms, which look out on the indoor pool below. Rooms have mahogany furnishings, granite vanities, desks, and sofas. Mitty's Ristorante and Piano Lounge serves regional Italian cuisine and local seafood, with exceptional homemade pasta and veal dishes. Specialties include ziti with broccoli and shrimp Capri (shrimp paired with spinach and fresh Italian herbs). On Friday and Saturday there is a nightclub, Tribeca, with bands and a DJ. On Thursday from 5:30 until 7 there is a manager's reception offering $1 beers and house wines. To reach the hotel, take Exit 258A off I–64 and make the first right. **Pros:** many in-house amenities; convenient to highway. **Cons:** the Omni is half a mile from the center city and there is no shuttle; rooms, while comfortable

and clean, seem a little dated. ✉ *1000 Omni Blvd.* ☎ *757/873–6664 or 800/873–6664* ⊕ *www.omnihotels.com* ⇴ *182 rooms, 4 suites* ♿ *In-room: a/c, Internet. In-hotel: restaurant, bar, pool, gym, laundry facilities* ▤ *AE, D, DC, MC, V.*

¢–$ 🏨 **Point Plaza**. This former Ramada has everything you could want in a hotel: reasonable rates and a location convenient to all the museums, plantation houses, and business centers of Newport News, plus Fort Lee, NASA Langley, Colonial Williamsburg, Yorktown, and Busch Gardens. The rooms, decorated in paisley prints and mahogany furnishings, are loaded with every necessity and convenience, like refrigerators and microwaves. They'll even loan you a wireless card for your computer. Don't overlook the free shuttle for Newport News Williamsburg Airport, the Amtrak station, and Greyhound stop. Ask for a room in the "tower" —recently renovated with plush bedding and flat-screen TV, a bargain for all you get. **Pros:** barbecue pavilion and complementary use of hotel's gas grill; reliable budget option. **Cons:** some rooms still need updating, make sure to ask for one that has been; basic hotel with basic decor. ✉ *950 J. Clyde Morris Blvd., Exit 258 off I-64* ☎ *757/599–4460 or 800/841–1112* ⊕ *www.pointplazasuites.com* ⇴ *78 rooms, 71 suites* ♿ *In-room: a/c, safe, refrigerator, DVD, Wi-Fi. In-hotel: restaurant, room service, bar, pool, gym, laundry facilities, laundry service* ▤ *AE, D, DC, MC, V.*

HAMPTON

5 mi north of Newport News, 16 mi northwest of Norfolk.

Founded in 1610, Hampton is the oldest continuously existing English-speaking settlement in the United States—recently celebrating 400 years. It also holds the country's first aviation research facility, NASA Langley Research Center. The center was headquarters for the first manned space program in the United States: astronauts for the *Mercury* and *Apollo* missions trained here.

Hampton was one of Virginia's major Colonial cities. In 1718 the pirate William Teach (better known as Blackbeard) was killed by Virginia sailors in a battle off North Carolina. As a warning to other pirates, the sailors brought his head back and mounted it on a pole at the entrance to the Hampton River (now Blackbeard Point, a residential area).

The city has been partially destroyed three times: by the British during the Revolution and again during the War of 1812, then by Confederates preempting Union invaders during the Civil War. Since the mid-1990s, Hampton has been undergoing a face-lift. It hosts many summer concerts and family festivals.

GETTING HERE AND AROUND

Hampton Roads is served by the airports of both Newport News and Norfolk. Both the Virginia Railway Express and Amtrak stop there. Traffic during commuting hours, (before 9 am and after 4:30 pm) can try anyone's patience, even more so if you're not familiar with the area. Avoid the roads between Newport News and Virginia Beach on Fridays when it's practically at a stand still.

ESSENTIALS

Visitor Information **Hampton Convention and Visitors Bureau** (✉ *120 Old Hampton La.* ☎ *757/727–1102 or 800/800–2202* ⊕ *www.visithampton.com*).

EXPLORING

C **Cousteau Society.** The Cousteau Society operates a compact gallery displaying underwater photos, models of the research vessels *Calypso* and *Alcyone,* and diving equipment from the past and present. Artifacts from famed explorer-environmentalist Jacques-Yves Cousteau's expeditions are displayed, such as a pair of minisubs, one fully equipped and one reduced to its pressure sphere; a recompression chamber from the 1950s; and a clear plastic shark cage, along with the diver's journal describing his eye-to-eye experiences. Cousteau films from various expeditions run continuously. Free parking is available at the parking garage next door. ✉ *710 Settlers Landing Rd.* ☎ *757/722–9300* ⊕ *www.cousteau.org* 🖾 *Free* ☉ *Nov.–Apr. 14, Wed.–Sat. 10–4, Sun. noon–3; Apr. 15–May 29 and Sept. 5–Oct. 31, Tues.–Sat. 10–4, Sun. noon–3; May 30–Sept. 4, daily 9:30–4.*

Hampton History Museum. The Hampton History Museum opened in 2003 with 10 galleries of permanent and changing exhibits on Native Americans and the early colonists, the city's port, the infamous Blackbeard, contraband and the Civil War, and the development of NASA Langley Research Center. ✉ *120 Old Hampton La.* ☎ *757/727–1610* ⊕ *www.hampton.gov/history_museum* 🖾 *$5* ☉ *Mon.–Sat. 10–5, Sun. 1–5.*

Hampton University. Hampton University was founded in 1868 as a freedmen's school, and ever since has had a distinguished history as an institution of higher education for African-Americans. Booker T. Washington was an early graduate. The **Hampton University Museum,** on the riverfront campus, is notable for its extensive and diverse collection, which includes more than 11,000 African, Native American, Pacific Island, and Asian art objects, as well as items related to the history of the university. Other valuable holdings include Harlem Renaissance paintings. ✉ *Museum, Huntington Bldg., off Tyler St.; I–64, Exit 267, to campus* ☎ *757/727–5308* 🖾 *Free* ⊕ *museum.hamptonu.edu* ☉ *Mon.–Fri. 8–5, Sat. noon–4.*

St. John's Church. Little of early Hampton survived the shellings and conflicts of the past, but the brick walls of St. John's Church (1728) have. Today a stained-glass window honors Pocahontas, the Native American princess who is said to have saved the life of Captain John Smith in 1608. The communion silver on display, made in London in 1618, is the oldest such service still used in this country. The parish, founded in the same year as the city (1610), also claims to be the oldest Protestant church in continuous service in America. You may listen to a taped interpretation or take a guided tour (by arrangement) and visit a small museum in the parish house. ✉ *100 W. Queens Way* ☎ *757/722–2567* ⊕ *www.stjohnshampton.org* 🖾 *Free* ☉ *Weekdays 9–3.*

C **Virginia Air and Space Center.** The Virginia Air and Space Center traces the history of flight and space exploration. The nine-story, futuristic, $30 million center is the visitor center for NASA Langley Research Center and Langley Air Force Base. Its space artifacts include a

3-billion-year-old moon rock, the *Apollo 12* command capsule, and a lunar lander. The center also holds a dozen full-size aircraft, a 3-D IMAX theater that was recently renovated, a variety of flight simulators, and hands-on exhibits that let you see yourself as an astronaut or launch a rocket. ⊠ *Downtown Waterfront, 600 Settlers Landing Rd., I–64, Exit 267* ☎ *757/727–0800* ⊕ *www.vasc.org* ⊠ *IMAX educational films $11.50, IMAX Hollywood films $13, combination ticket $18* ⊙ *Memorial Day–Labor Day, Mon.–Wed. 10–5, Thurs.–Sun. 10–7; Labor Day–Memorial Day, Tues.–Sat. 10–5, Sun. noon–5, closed most Mon.*

WHERE TO EAT

¢ ✕**The Grey Goose Tearoom.** Beside the relocated Hampton History
AMERICAN Museum, you're greeted by an enticing aroma and a gift shop with tea-related items when you enter this cozy room decorated with Victorian tea-party prints in gilded frames, antique teapots, and knick-knacks. Brunswick stew, creamy Hampton blue-crab soup, and biscuits are permanent fixtures on the "everything-homemade" menu, and daily specials, such as chicken and dumplings, are posted on the wall. Desserts are especially good, but avoid the canned fruit salad on iceberg lettuce. The tearoom is open for lunch only. ⊠ *Old Hampton La. at History Museum Way* ☎ *757/723–7978* ⊕ *www.greygooserestaurant. com* ☰ *AE, D, DC, MC, V* ⊙ *Closed Sun. No dinner.*

WHERE TO STAY

$ ▦**Courtyard by Marriott.** The smell of homemade chocolate cookies greets you Monday through Thursday at the front desk of this modern hotel, where the chef refills a bottomless basket. As the naval items on the walls suggest, this Marriott takes in the local influence. Soak in the pool, set amid landscaped grounds. **Pros:** walking distance to Hampton Roads Convention Center and major sports complexes; the price of a room is reduced for long-term stays. **Cons:** Wi-Fi is available in the lobby, but Ethernet is in the rooms; the restaurant serves breakfast only. ⊠ *1917 Coliseum Dr.* ☎ *757/838–3300* ⊕ *www.courtyard.com* ⤸ *146 rooms* ⌂ *In-room: a/c, Internet. In-hotel: restaurant, pool, gym, laundry service* ☰ *AE, D, DC, MC, V.*

¢ ▦**Holiday Inn Hampton.** Halfway between Colonial Williamsburg and Virginia Beach, this complex of buildings stands on 13 beautifully landscaped acres. About half the rooms have a pink-and-green color scheme; others have a darker look, with cherry wood dressers and tables. Some rooms overlook the indoor pool in the atrium, and others have doors that open, motel-style, onto the parking lot. There's free wireless Internet, and it's free to borrow an Ethernet cord. **Pros:** very reasonable rates. **Cons:** basic hotel, could use some updating. ⊠ *1815 W. Mercury Blvd.* ☎ *757/838–0200 or 800/842–9370* ⊕ *www.holidayinn.com* ⤸ *314 rooms, 6 suites* ⌂ *In-room: a/c. In-hotel: restaurant, bar, pools, gym* ☰ *AE, D, DC, MC, V.*

FORT MONROE

Inside Phoebus, at the South end of Mellen St. and Mercury Blvd.

GETTING HERE AND AROUND
The best way to go and get around is by car or walking. Fort Monroe is a tiny "island" with one road that circles it.

ESSENTIALS
All adults must show a picture ID to enter and register their car at the gate.

EXPLORING

🕙 **Fort Monroe.** The channel between Chesapeake Bay and Hampton Roads is the "mouth" of Hampton Roads. On the north side of this passage is Hampton's **Fort Monroe,** built in stages between 1819 and 1834. The largest stone fort in the country, it's also the only one still in operation to be enclosed by a moat. Robert E. Lee and Edgar Allan Poe served here in the antebellum years, and it remained a Union stronghold in Confederate territory throughout the Civil War. After the war, Confederate president Jefferson Davis was imprisoned for a time in one of the fort's casemates (a chamber in the wall); his cell and adjacent casemates now house the Casemate Museum. Exhibits of weapons, uniforms, models, drawings, and extensive Civil War relics retell the fort's history, depict coastal artillery activities, and describe the military lifestyle through the Civil War years and the 20th century. ⊠ *Mellen St., Phoebus* ☎ *757/788–3391* 🎟 *Free* ☉ *Daily 10:30–4:30.*

NORFOLK

16 mi southeast of Hampton.

Like many other old Southern towns, Norfolk has undergone a renaissance, one that's especially visible in the charming shops and cafés in the historic village of Ghent. There's plenty to see in this old navy town.

GETTING HERE AND AROUND
Norfolk is reached from the peninsula by the Hampton Roads Bridge-Tunnel (I–64) as well as Route 460. Norfolk's free shuttle, called NET, covers the downtown area.

ESSENTIALS
Taxis **Black and White Cabs** (☎ *757/855–4444*). **Yellow Cab** (☎ *757/857–8888*).

Visitor Information **Norfolk Convention and Visitors Bureau** (⊠ *232 E. Main St.* ☎ *757/664–6620 or 800/368–3097* ⊕ *www.visitnorfolktoday.com*).

EXPLORING
TOP ATTRACTIONS

★ **Chrysler Museum of Art.** By any standard, the Chrysler Museum of Art downtown qualifies as one of America's major art museums. The permanent collection includes works by Rubens, Gainsborough, Renoir, Picasso, Cézanne, Matisse, Warhol, and Pollock, a list that suggests the breadth available here. Classical and pre-Columbian civilizations are also represented. The decorative-arts collection includes exquisite

English porcelain and art nouveau furnishings. The Chrysler is home to one of the most important glass collections in America, which includes glass objects from the 6th century BC to the present, with particularly strong holdings in Tiffany, French art glass, and English cameo, as well as artifacts from ancient Rome and the Near and Far East. ✉ *245 W. Olney Rd.* ☎ *757/664–6200* ⊕ *www.chrysler. org* ✉ *Free* ☉ *Wed. 10–9, Thurs.– Sat. 10–5, Sun. 12–5.*

MacArthur Memorial. The MacArthur Memorial is the burial place of one of America's most distinguished military officers. General Douglas MacArthur (1880–1964) agreed to this navy town as the site for his monument because it was his mother's birthplace. In the rotunda of the old City Hall, converted according to MacArthur's design, is the mausoleum; 11 adjoining galleries house mementos of MacArthur's career, including his signature corncob pipe and the Japanese instruments of surrender that concluded World War II. However, this is a monument not only to General MacArthur but to all those who served in wars from the Civil to the Korean War. Its Historical Center holds 2½ million documents and more than 100,000 photographs, and assists scholars, students, and researchers from around the world. The general's staff car is on display in the gift shop, where a 24-minute biography is shown. ✉ *Bank St. at City Hall Ave., MacArthur Square* ☎ *757/441–2965* ⊕ *www.macarthurmemorial.org* ✉ *Free (donations accepted)* ☉ *Mon.–Sat. 10–5, Sun. 11–5.*

☺ **Nauticus.** A popular attraction on Norfolk's redeveloped downtown
★ waterfront, Nauticus is a maritime science museum featuring hand-on exhibits, interactive theaters, and high-definition films that celebrate the local connection to the seaport. Visitors can touch a shark, learn about weather and underwater archaeology, and explore the mysteries of the Elizabeth River. A NOAA Environmental Resource Center is an invaluable stop for education materials. Temporary exhibits in both the Changing Gallery and Forecastle Gallery keep things fresh. The Hampton Roads Naval Museum on the second floor and the battleship *Wisconsin* adjacent to the building are also popular attractions operated by the U.S. Navy, and are included in the Nauticus admission. ✉ *1 Waterside Dr.* ☎ *757/664–1000* ⊕ *www.nauticus.org* ✉ *$11.95* ☉ *Daily 10–5.*

☺ **Norfolk Naval Station.** On the northern edge of the city, the Norfolk
Fodor'sChoice Naval Station is an impressive sight, home to more than 100 ships
★ of the Atlantic Fleet. The base was built on the site of the Jamestown Exposition of 1907; many of the original buildings survive and are still in use. Several large aircraft carriers, built at nearby Newport News, call Norfolk home port and can be seen from miles away, especially at the bridge-tunnel end of the base. You may see two, each with a crew

of up to 6,300, beside slightly smaller amphibious carriers that discharge marines in both helicopters and amphibious assault craft. The submarine piers, floating dry docks, supply center, and air station are all worth seeing. The *Victory Rover* and *Carrie B.* provide boat tours from downtown Norfolk to the naval station, and Hampton Roads Transit operates tour trolleys most of the year, departing from the naval-base tour office. Visitor access is by tour only, and photo ID is required to enter the base. ✉ *9079 Hampton Blvd.* ☎ *757/444–7955* ⊕ *www. navstanorva.navy.mil/tour* ✇ *Tour $7.50 (cash only and there is no ATM on premises)* ☉ *Tours: Jan. 1–Mar. 15, Tues. –Sun. at 1:30; Mar. 16–May 17, every ½ hr 11–2; May 18–Aug. 30, every 30 mins 10–2; Aug. 31–Nov. 1, hourly 11–2; Nov. 2–Dec. 31, Tues.–Sun. at 1:30.*

WORTH NOTING

Hermitage Foundation Museum. An early-20th-century estate of the Sloane family, The Hermitage Foundation Museum offers an outstanding presentation of architecture, art, and nature. The Sloanes, educated collectors with broad artistic interests, were among the founders of what is now the Chrysler Museum. Mr. Sloane was a wealthy New York businessman who moved to Virginia to operate textile mills. Docent-led tours are available on the hour. Visitors may also stroll the waterfront and 12-acre gardens and view contemporary art exhibitions. ✉ *7637 N. Shore Rd.* ☎ *757/423–2052* ⊕ *www.thfm.org* ✇ *$5* ☉ *Mon., Tues., and Thurs.–Sat. 10–5; Sun. 1–5.*

Moses Myers House. The Federal redbrick Moses Myers House, built by its namesake between 1792 and 1796, is exceptional, and not just for its elegance. The furnishings, 70% of them original, include family portraits by Gilbert Stuart and Thomas Sully. A transplanted New Yorker as well as Norfolk's first Jewish resident, Myers made his fortune in Norfolk in shipping, then served as a diplomat and a customhouse officer. His grandson married James Madison's grandniece; his greatgrandson served as mayor; and the family kept the house for five generations. ✉ *323 E. Free Mason St.* ☎ *757/333–1086* ⊕ *www.chrysler. org/houses.asp* ✇ *Free* ☉ *Fri.–Sun. noon–5.*

St. Paul's Church. Constructed in 1739, St. Paul's Church was the only building in town to survive the bombardment and conflagration of New Year's Day 1776; a cannonball fired by the British fleet remains embedded in a wall. An earlier church had been built on this site in 1641, and the churchyard contains graves dating from the 17th century. Get a free visitor parking pass in the church office. ✉ *St. Paul's Blvd. at City Hall Ave.* ☎ *757/627–4353* ✇ *By donation* ☉ *Mon. 10–3, Tues.–Fri. 10–4.*

WHERE TO EAT

¢–$ ✕ **Azars Natural Foods.** Lebanese specialties are featured at this casual
MEDITERRANEAN restaurant in Ghent, which also has a Mediterranean food store. Indoor dining is on granite tables under the original tin ceiling and exposed air ducts. Outdoors, the terra-cotta patio has umbrellas. A sampler Mashawee Platter includes *kibbi,* seasoned beef and bulghur patties; *kefta,* spiced lamb meatballs; and lamb kebab with grilled vegetables and side dishes. Vegan and vegetarian selections are noted on the menu, which includes appetizers, wraps, pizza, and kebabs. ✉ *2000 Colley Ave.* ☎ *757/664–7955* ⊕ *www.azarfoods.com* ▭ *AE, D, MC, V.*

¢   ✕**Doumar's.** After he introduced the world to its first ice-cream cone at
BARBECUE   the 1904 World's Fair in St. Louis, Abe Doumar founded this drive-in
institution in 1934. It's still operated by his family. Waitresses carry to
your car the specialties of the house: barbecue, limeade, and ice cream
in waffle cones made according to an original recipe. For breakfast, try
the Egg-O-Doumar, a bargain at $2.70. The Food Network's "Diners,
Drive-Ins, and Dives" featured Doumars twice in 2008. ⊠ *20th St.
at Monticello Ave.* ☎ *757/627–4163* ⊕ *www.doumars.com* ▤ *MC, V*
☾ *Closed Sun.*

$ ✕**Freemason Abbey Restaurant and Tavern.** This former church near the
AMERICAN   historic business district has been drawing customers for a long time,
and not without reason. It has 40-foot-high cathedral ceilings and large
windows, making for an airy, and dramatic, dining experience. You can
sit upstairs, in the large choir loft, or in the main part of the church
downstairs. Beside the bar just inside the entrance is an informal sort of
"diner" area, but with the whole menu to choose from. Regular appetizers include artichoke dip and Santa Fe shrimp. There's a dinner special
every weeknight, such as lobster, prime rib, and wild game (wild boar
or alligator, for example). ⊠ *209 W. Freemason St.* ☎ *757/622–3966*
⊕ *www.freemasonabbey.com* ▤ *AE, D, DC, MC, V.*

$ ✕**No Frill Bar and Grill.** This expansive café is in an antique building in
CAFE   the heart of Ghent. Beneath a tin ceiling and exposed ductwork, a cen-
★   tral bar is surrounded by several dining spaces with cream-and-mustard
walls and wooden tables. Signature items include the ribs; the Funky
Chicken Sandwich, a grilled chicken breast with bacon, tomato, melted
Swiss cheese, and Parmesan pepper dressing on rye; and the Spotswood
Salad of baby spinach, Granny Smith apples, and blue cheese. ⊠ *806
Spotswood Ave., at Colley Ave.* ☎ *757/627–4262* ⊕ *www.nofrillgrill.
com* ▤ *AE, MC, V.*

$$ ✕**Vintage Kitchen.** In its short life, the Vintage Kitchen has racked up
AMERICAN   many accolades for its focus on local foods, artisan cheeses, and micro-
brews. Chef Phillip Craig Thomason is Paris trained, but local, and
knows the specialties of the area. It's a place where you can order
"Five Spice Duck Breast" and also a superb cheeseburger. All the spices
and sauces come from an outdoor herb garden. A special seven-course
tasting meal is available by appointment Monday through Wednes-
day. ⊠ *Dominion Tower, 999 Waterside Dr.* ☎ *757/625–3377* ⊕ *www.
vintage-kitchen.com* ⚏ *Reservations essential* ▤ *AE, D, MC, V* ☾ *No
dinner Mon.–Wed.*

WHERE TO STAY

$–$$ ▦**Marriott Courtyard Downtown.** Built in 2005, this eight-story hotel is
near everything visitors want to see and where business travelers need to
be. It's next door to the MacArthur Memorial and near the MacArthur
Center and Nauticus. A handsome, inviting lobby has a tailored look;
the modern guest rooms have a large desk perfect for spreading out
the free daily newspaper. **Pros:** convenient downtown location. **Cons:**
the hotel has a smoke-free policy. ⊠ *520 Plume St.* ☎ *757/963–6000
or 800/321–2211* ⊕ *www.marriott.com* ↩ *137 rooms, 3 suites* ⚭ *In-
room: a/c, refrigerator, Wi-Fi. In-hotel: restaurant, room service, pool,
laundry facilities, laundry service, parking (paid)* ▤ *AE, D, DC, MC, V.*

$$ ⛐ **Norfolk Marriott Waterside.** Located in the redeveloped downtown area, this hotel is connected to the Waterside Festival Marketplace shopping area by a ramp and it's close to Town Point Park, site of many festivals. The handsome lobby, with wood paneling, a central staircase, silk tapestries, and Federal-style furniture, sets a high standard that continues throughout the hotel. Rooms are somewhat small, but outfitted with everything the business traveler could ask for—including two telephones, voice mail, and Internet access. **Pros:** great central location; two blocks from the Waterside Festival Marketplace. **Cons:** parking is pricey, and a walk with luggage. ⊠ *235 E. Main St.* ☎ *757/627–4200 or 800/228–9290* ⊕ *www.marriott.com* ✍ *396 rooms, 8 suites* ⚐ *In-room: a/c, Wi-Fi. In-hotel: 2 restaurants, bar, pool, parking (paid)* ▭ *AE, D, DC, MC, V.*

$$ ⛐ **Sheraton Norfolk Waterside Hotel.** Modern is the word for this hotel's furnishings, from the bright, spacious lobby to the ample rooms and large suites. A ground-floor bar with dramatic 30-foot windows overlooks the Elizabeth—many rooms also have a beautiful view over the water. This property is convenient to the Waterside Festival Marketplace shopping area. **Pros:** the only hotel that is truly on the waterfront; nice touches such as snacks and cold water served all day; restaurant has a terrific view of Portsmouth. **Cons:** parking—for Norfolk—is pricey; overcrowded rooms may be hard to maneuver for some. ⊠ *777 Waterside Dr.* ☎ *757/622–6664* ⊕ *www.sheraton.com* ✍ *426 rooms, 20 suites* ⚐ *In-room: a/c. In-hotel: restaurant, bar, pool, parking (paid)* ▭ *AE, D, DC, MC, V.*

NIGHTLIFE AND THE ARTS
MUSIC

The **Virginia Opera Company** (⊠ *160 E. Virginia Beach Blvd.* ☎ *757/623–1223* ⊕ *www.vaopera.org*) presents some of the best operatic talent in the nation during its season (September through April) at Norfolk's elegant Harrison Opera House, which is known for its excellent acoustics. Their schedule includes the most popular operas of Europe and the United States.

SHOPPING

You can meet painters, sculptors, glassworkers, jewelers, photographers, and other artists at work in their studios at the **d'Art Center** (⊠ *Selden Arcade, 208 E. Main St.* ☎ *757/625–4211* ⊕ *www.d-artcenter.org*); the art is for sale.

An eclectic mix of chic shops, including antiques stores, bars, and eateries, lines the streets of **Ghent**, a turn-of-the-20th-century neighborhood that runs from the Elizabeth River to York Street, to West Olney Road and Llewellyn Avenue. The intersection of Colley Avenue and 21st Street is the hub.

In Ghent the upscale clothing and shoe boutiques at the **Palace Shops** (⊠ *21st St. at Llewellyn Ave.*) are a good place to search out some finery.

PORTSMOUTH

6 mi southwest of Norfolk via I–264.

Portsmouth, across the Elizabeth River from Norfolk, has a well-maintained historic area called Olde Towne, which has handsome buildings from the 18th and 19th centuries.

GETTING HERE AND AROUND

A five-minute pedestrian ferry makes traveling between Portsmouth and Norfolk easy. The Elizabeth River Ferry carries passengers (but no automobiles) between Waterside Festival Marketplace, in Norfolk, and Portsmouth's Olde Towne weekdays 7:15 am–11:45 pm, weekends 10:15 am–11:45 pm. Bikes and wheelchairs are allowed. Taking the ferry is more fun and normally faster than driving through the bridge; it departs from Norfolk 15 minutes before and after every hour and leaves Portsmouth on the hour and half-hour.

ESSENTIALS

Ferry **Elizabeth River Ferry** (☎ 757/222–6100 🛳 $1).

Visitor Information **Portsmouth Convention and Visitors Bureau** (✉ 6 Crawford Pkwy. ☎ 757/393–5111 ⊕ www.portsmouthva.gov/tourism/vstinfo.html).

EXPLORING

♺ **Children's Museum of Virginia.** The largest children's museum in the state, the Children's Museum of Virginia has more than 90 hands-on exhibits for kids of all ages, including an awesome toy train collection, a planetarium, and tons more. Here kids can learn engineering and scientific principles by playing with bubbles and blocks. ✉ *221 High St.* ☎ *757/393–5258* ⊕ *www.childrensmuseumva.com* 🛳 *$6* ☉ *Tues.–Sat. 9–5, Sun. 11–5.*

OFF THE BEATEN PATH

Great Dismal Swamp National Wildlife Refuge. If you're not a nature lover, hiker, or biker, don't take the time to visit the Great Dismal Swamp. If you are, do take mosquito repellant. The forbidding name was possibly assigned to the area by William Byrd on one of his early-18th-century surveying expeditions. George Washington once hoped to drain it. Today the swamp is a 106,000-acre refuge that harbors bobcats, black bears, and more than 220 varieties of birds. A remarkably shallow lake—3,000 acres, 6 feet deep—is surrounded by skinny cypress trees that lend the scene a primeval quality. One hundred miles of hiking and biking trails, including a wheelchair-accessible boardwalk, stand in stark contrast to nearby downtown Portsmouth and Norfolk. ✉ *Follow signs from Rte. 32, Suffolk* ☎ *757/986–2353.*

Portsmouth Naval Shipyard Museum. One block from the waterfront and about three blocks from the paddle-wheel ferry landing, this museum offers a history of Portsmouth, the Norfolk Naval Shipyard, and the armed forces in Hampton Roads. The exhibitions give visitors the opportunity to learn about this rich history through artifacts, uniforms, ship models, illustrations, and photographs. You can also explore the retired Coast Guard lightship *Portsmouth,* a floating lighthouse just outside the museum, whose quarters below deck have been authentically furnished. ✉ *2 High St.* ☎ *757/393–8591 shipyard museum;*

*757/393–8741 lightship ⊕ www.portsnavalmuseums.com ✉ $3, free
1st Sun. of month ☉ Memorial Day–Labor Day, Mon.–Sat. 10–5, Sun.
1–5; Labor Day–Memorial Day, Tues.–Sat. 10–5, Sun. 1–5.*

WHERE TO STAY

¢–$ 🏨 **Hawthorn Hotel & Suites at the Governor Dinwiddie.** Dating to the 1940s,
★ the Governor Dinwiddie hotel in the center of Portsmouth's Olde Towne
business district was beautifully restored in 2005. Guest rooms are
furnished in reproduction Queen Anne with satin quilted spreads, ecru
walls, and moss woodwork. Museums, restaurants, and the waterfront
are within a few blocks. **Pros:** a Historic Hotel of America, recognized by the National Trust for Historic Preservation; rates include
a Continental breakfast and high-speed Internet. **Cons:** although it's
only 3 mi from the center of Norfolk, it's a little far to compete with
hotels in that city. ✉ *506 Dinwiddie, at High St.* ☎ *757/392–1330 or
800/527–1133* ⊕ *www.governordinwiddiehotel.com* ⬱ *45 rooms, 15
suites* ⚲ *In-room: a/c, refrigerator, Internet, Wi-Fi. In-hotel: restaurant,
bar, gym, laundry service* ▭ *AE, MC, V.*

VIRGINIA BEACH

18 mi east of Norfolk via I–64 to Rte. 44.

The heart of Virginia Beach—a stretch of the Atlantic shore from Cape
Henry south to Rudee Inlet—has been a popular summertime destination for decades. With 6 mi of public beach, high-rises, amusements, and
a busy 40-block boardwalk, Virginia's most populated city is now a place
for communion with nature. The boardwalk and Atlantic Avenue have
an oceanfront park; an old-fashioned fishing pier ($7.50) with shops, a
restaurant, and a bar; and a 3-mi bike trail. The farther north you go,
the more beach you find in proportion to bars, T-shirt parlors, and video
arcades. Most activities and events in town are oriented to families.

GETTING HERE AND AROUND

Virginia Beach has no shortage of parking lots and spaces. The cost
for a day of parking is about $5 to $7 at the central beach lots and
$4 or $5 for the remote beach areas. Municipal lots/decks are at 4th
Street (metered only), 9th Street and Pacific Avenue, 19th Street and
Pacific Avenue, 25th Street and Pacific Avenue, 31st Street and Atlantic
Avenue, and Croatan and Sandbridge beaches. Metered spaces have a
three-hour limit.

Bikes (two- or four-wheel) can be rented at several shops and hotels
along the beach for $4 to $20 per hour. In Virginia Beach there are
numerous locations along the boardwalk where you can rent bikes.
Rental shops away from the boardwalk are more reasonable and have
better bikes. Seashore Bikes & Fitness is near First Landing Park. Back
Bay Getaways is on the other side of Virginia Beach in the Sandbridge
area. They offer bikes and guided biking tours.

Hampton Roads Transit buses have bike racks, and their paddle-wheel
ferries across the Elizabeth River allow bikes, so cyclists can cover a
lot of territory from Newport News through Norfolk and on to Virginia Beach.

TIMING AND PRECAUTIONS

Virginia Beach is one of the prime destinations for college students on spring break. Thousands of them descend on the community in April and may constitute a rowdy crowd. Avoid Virginia Beach during that time—unless you are a college student.

ESSENTIALS

Bike Rental Back Bay Getaways (✉ *3713 S. Sandpiper Rd.* ☎ *757/721–4484*). **Seashore Bikes & Fitness** (✉ *2268 Seashore Shops* ☎ *757/481–5191*).

Bus Hampton Roads Transit (☎ *757/222–6100* ⊕ *www.hrtransit.org*).

Taxis Beach Taxi (✉ *Virginia Beach* ☎ *757/486–6585*). **Yellow Cab of Virginia Beach** (☎ *757/460–0605*).

Visitor Information Virginia Beach Visitor Information Center (✉ *2100 Parks Ave.* ☎ *800/822–3224* ⊕ *www.vbfun.com*).

EXPLORING

Adam Thoroughgood House. Inland from the shore is the early-18th-century Adam Thoroughgood House, named for the prosperous plantation owner who held a land grant of 5,350 acres here in the early 1600s. This 45- by 22-foot brick house, probably constructed by a Thoroughgood grandson, recalls the English cottage architecture of the period, with a protruding chimney and a steeply pitched roof. The four-room early plantation home has a 17th-century garden with characteristic hedges. To get there, take I–264 Exit 17 (Independence Blvd.) 4 mi, turn right on Pleasure House Road, and right on Thoroughgood Drive. ✉ *1636 Parish Rd.* ☎ *757/460–7588* ⊕ *www.vbgov.com/dept/arts* 🖾 *$5* ☉ *Tues.–Sat. 9–5, Sun. 11–5.*

Naval Air Station, Oceana. On the northern edge of the city, this naval station is an impressive sight, home to more than 200 navy aircraft, including the F/A-18 Tomcat (the type of plane flown by the Blue Angels) and other planes assigned to the aircraft carriers of the Atlantic Fleet. From an observation park on Oceana Boulevard at the POW/MIA Flame of Hope Memorial Park, near the runways, you can watch aircraft take off and land. Non–Defense Department visitors can access the base only on the Hampton Roads Transit summer-only tours (photo ID required) or during the annual air show in September. Tours depart at 9:30 am and 11:30 am from the 24th Street transit kiosk on Atlantic Avenue in Virginia Beach and stop at an aviation historical park with 13 aircraft. ✉ *Tomcat Blvd.* ☎ *757/433–3131* ⊕ *www.navy.mil/local/oceana/* 🖾 *Tour $7.50.*

Old Cape Henry Lighthouse. At the northeastern tip of Virginia Beach, on the cape where the mouth of the bay meets the ocean, the historic Old Cape Henry Lighthouse is near the site where the English landed on their way to Jamestown in 1607. This lighthouse, however, didn't light anyone's way until 1792. Across the street to seaward is the replacement to the old lighthouse, but it isn't open to visitors. Be prepared to show a photo ID at the military checkpoint at the Fort Story base entrance. ✉ *U.S. 60* ☎ *757/422–9421* 🖾 *$4* ☉ *Mid-Mar.–Oct., daily 10–5; Nov.–mid-Mar., daily 10–4.*

Old Coast Guard Station. Along the oceanfront, the Old Coast Guard Station, a 1903 Lifesaving Station, contains photographic exhibits, examples of lifesaving equipment, and a gallery that depicts German U-boat activity off the coast during World War II. ⊠ *24th St. at Atlantic Ave.* ☎ *757/422–1587* 🔊 *$3* ⊙ *Tues.–Sat. 10–5, Sun. noon–5.*

☺ **Virginia Aquarium and Marine Science Center.** The sea is the subject at
★ the popular Virginia Aquarium and Marine Science Center, a massive facility with more than 200 exhibits. This is no place for passive museumgoers; many exhibits require participation. You can use computers to predict the weather and solve the pollution crisis, watch the birds in the salt marsh through telescopes on a deck, handle horseshoe crabs, take a simulated journey to the bottom of the sea in a submarine, and study fish up close in tanks that re-create underwater environments. The museum is almost 2 mi inland from Rudee Inlet at the southern end of Virginia Beach. The Virginia Aquarium and Marine Science Center has a nature trail—well worth it, but be sure to wear comfortable shoes. ⊠ *717 General Booth Blvd.* ☎ *757/485–3474* ⊕ *www.virginiaacquarium.com* 🔊 *Aquarium $17; combination ticket for aquarium and IMAX $23* ⊙ *Memorial Day–Labor Day, daily 9–6; Labor Day–Memorial Day, daily 9–5.*

WHERE TO EAT

$$$ ╳**Catch 31.** Located at the Hilton Resort, Catch 31 is one of the nicest
SEAFOOD restaurants on the strip. Order the seafood signature towers that include lobster, crab legs, mussels, and shrimp, made for sharing. Sit outside for atmosphere; the setting is terrific, next to Neptune's statue with fire pits, palm trees, and great people-watching. In summer it gets even better with live music at lunch and in the evenings. ⊠ *3001 Atlantic Ave., Virginia Beach* ☎ *757/213–3472* ▭ *AE, D, MC, V.*

$–$$ ╳**Five 01 City Grill.** Not just a grill in name only, this restaurant has an
AMERICAN open-grill kitchen in the dining room. It can be noisy on the bar side when live bands play in the evening. Locals get comfortable in padded chairs and booths as they quaff the $2 beer of the month or order from the extensive wine vault. The California-inspired fusion menu offers a variety of price ranges: excellent homemade pizza from wood-burning ovens, sandwiches, pasta, chicken, steaks, and seafood followed by sinful desserts such as Homemade Bourbon Chocolate Chip Pecan Pie. ⊠ *501 N. Birdneck Rd.* ☎ *757/425–7195* ⊕ *www.goodfoodgooddrink. com* ▭ *AE, MC, V.*

$ ╳**Murphy's Irish Pub.** This combination Irish pub, sports bar, and res-
IRISH taurant has a large central dining room with an open fireplace in the middle, a bar on one side, and a smaller dining room at one end. The menu includes steaks and Irish, Italian, and seafood entrées as well as snacks and sandwiches. The Sunday brunch is reasonable, and so are the weekday dinner specials. A block from the boardwalk, Murphy's has plenty of easy parking. ⊠ *2914 Pacific Ave.* ☎ *757/417–7701* ▭ *AE, D, DC, MC, V.*

$ ╳**Rockafeller's.** The Down East architecture of this local favorite with
AMERICAN double-deck porches hints at the seafood that's available. The restaurant has a bar, a raw bar, and alfresco dining in good weather (in cool weather, the large window wall still gives you a view of the water).

7

VIRGINIA BEACH PLANNING STRATEGIES

To prepare for your visit to Virginia Beach, there are many webcams to view actual weather and what's going on the week you are traveling. For live webcams of the boardwalk, try Waterman's Restaurant and piers ⊕ www.vbbound.com. To check on fun events, including free concerts on the beach, check out ⊕ www.vbnightlife.com.

And don't forget social media. The VA Beach Facebook page (⊕ www.facebook.com/virginiabeachvirginia) has more than 35,000 fans, and you can often find out about specials, promotions, and other events.

Here's another tip: There are kiosks on every block filled with magazines. Make sure to pick up a *Sunny Day* or a *VB guide*, filled with maps and ideas of excursions, food, and events. They contain coupons for almost everything: percentages off, free gifts with purchase, or double time with rentals. You have to know about the coupons, venders don't offer them to customers.

Seafood, pasta, chicken, and beef share the menu with salads and sandwiches. Rockafeller's (and several others) are on Rudee Inlet. Go on a Thursday night for the lobster special, the best their menu has to offer. To get here, go south on Pacific Avenue and turn right on Winston-Salem immediately before the Rudee Inlet bridge. The street ends at Mediterranean Avenue. ⊠ *308 Mediterranean Ave.* ☎ *757/422–5654* ⊕ *www.rockafellers.com* ⊟ *AE, D, DC, MC, V.*

$–$$ ✕ **Waterman's Beachwood Grill.** The last freestanding restaurant on the
SEAFOOD beach not inside a hotel, this aqua-painted clapboard building houses a
★ family-owned seafood grill. Inside, the ocher walls heighten the sun rays penetrating the ceiling-to-floor windows. Awnings shade the outdoor patio where live musicians perform in season. A local menu favorite is the Crab Ripper, a crab-cake sandwich topped with mozzarella and crisp bacon. A fried seafood sampler, fish and steak platters, steamed fish, appetizers, salads, burgers, and other sandwiches fill out the menu. Banquet facilities are available, and the Beach Nut Gift Shop is also on the premises. ⊠ *1423 N. Great Neck Rd.* ☎ *757/496–3333* ⊕ *www.watermans.com* ⊟ *AE, D, MC, V.*

WHERE TO STAY

$ 🏨 **Cavalier Hotels.** In the quieter north end of town, this 18-acre resort
★ complex combines the original Cavalier Hotel of 1927, a seven-story redbrick building on a hill, with an oceanfront high-rise built across the street in 1973. The clientele is about evenly divided between conventioneers and families. Back in its heyday, the elite spent summers on the hill to escape the city's heat; F. Scott and Zelda Fitzgerald stayed regularly in the original hotel. If you stay in the hilltop building you can see the water—and get to it easily by shuttle van or a short walk. The newer building overlooks 600 feet of private beach. There's a fee for tennis, but the other athletic facilities are free. **Pros:** great choice for people who appreciate historic properties; family friendly with Kid's Café and largest wading pool at the beach. **Cons:** away from the boardwalk; rooms are looking dated. ⊠ *Atlantic Ave. at 42nd St.* ☎ *757/425–8555*

or 888/746–2327 ⊕ *www.cavalierhotel.com* ⟿ *400 rooms* ♿ *In-room: a/c, Internet. In-hotel: 5 restaurants, tennis courts, pools, gym, beachfront* ⊟ *AE, D, DC, MC, V.*

$$$$ ▦ **Hilton Virginia Beach Oceanfront.** This Hilton opened in 2005 and is the only four-star hotel in Virginia Beach. Towering 21 stories over the oceanfront, it has shops, three restaurants, and a rooftop bar and infinity pool. The seafood restaurant Catch 31 receives consistently good reviews, and there is great outdoor seating overlooking the boardwalk. At night the bar is a happening scene for thirtysomethings. Rooms use muted tans textiles to give the space a warm feeling. Flat-screen TVs are in both bedrooms and the bathrooms. Most rooms have balconies with panoramic views, but if yours lacks a beachfront view, you can always hang out at the rooftop pool with rails of glass looking down to the boardwalk. **Pros:** a luxury hotel with all the amenities. **Cons:** the priciest choice in Virginia Beach. ✉ *3001 Atlantic Ave.* ☎ *757/213–3000* ⊕ *www.hiltonvb.com* ⟿ *290 rooms* ♿ *In-room: a/c, Wi-Fi. In-hotel: 3 restaurants, pool, gym, public Wi-Fi* ⊟ *AE, D, MC, V.*

$$–$$$ ▦ **Springhill Suites Virginia Beach Oceanfront.** Yes, this is a hotel chain in the Marriott family, but it still stands out from the pack because all the rooms here are suites—outfitted with two flat-screen TVs, separate living area, and granite top kitchenettes. The rooms have bursts of color: red, blue, and yellow linens and carpets mixed with tropical art on the walls. Its location is close to events on the end of the boardwalk. From the balcony you can see fireworks (when launched) and free beach concerts. Breakfast is always included; the Belgium waffle station is a standout. And parking is free—a rarity on the beach. Although it's a newer property, some of the rooms' carpets are showing damage. Ask to inspect a room before booking it. **Pros:** all suites; great location; colorful; indoor and outdoor pool; parking and breakfast included in rate. **Cons:** long walk to the action on 31st Street; a couple of rooms need updating. ✉ *901 Atlantic Ave., Virginia Beach* ☎ *757/417–3982* ⊕ *www.springhillsuites.com/orfvo* ⟿ *168 suites* ♿ *In-room: a/c, safe, kitchen, refrigerator, Internet, Wi-Fi (some). In-hotel: restaurant, bar, pool, gym, beachfront, Internet terminal, Wi-Fi hotspot, parking (free)* ⊟ *AE, D, DC, MC, V.*

$–$$ ▦ **Wyndham Virginia Beach Oceanfront.** With its 17-story tower, the for-
★   mer Ramada Plaza Resort Oceanfront has been sold to private owners who promise a renovation of the 1960s-era high-rise. Rooms that do not face the ocean directly have either a partial view or overlook the swimming pool. The modern lobby has a skylighted atrium. The Surf Club Ocean Grill serves—predictably—seafood. The hotel's Kids Club is phenomenal, with scavenger hunts and big-screen TVs outside by the beach. With the free shuttle to 31st Street, you can walk the boardwalk daily. **Pros:** the Wyndham Virginia Beach accepts pets (additional fee), but only if the reservation is made directly through the hotel. **Cons:** the hotel is north of the main action on the boardwalk. ✉ *57th St. at oceanfront* ☎ *757/428–7025 or 800/365–3032* ⊕ *wyndham.com* ⟿ *243 rooms* ♿ *In-room: a/c, safe, refrigerator. In-hotel: restaurant, bar, pool, gym, children's programs (ages 5–13), laundry service* ⊟ *AE, D, DC, MC, V.*

7

NIGHTLIFE

Harpoon Larry's (⊠ *24th St. at Pacific Ave.* ☎ *757/422–6000*) is a local watering hole with true character, not a tourist trap. Don't be surprised to see a great white shark staring back at you as you eat a juicy piece of that shark's cousin (mahimahi) stuffed with fresh Chesapeake Bay crabmeat, or enjoy raw oysters and a cold Corona. There's free nightly entertainment from April through Labor Day weekend at the 24th Street stage or **24th Street Park** on the boardwalk. **Murphy's Grand Irish Pub and Restaurant** (⊠ *2914 Pacific Ave.* ☎ *757/417–7701*) has entertainment every night in summer and Tuesday–Saturday during winter—there's typically an Irish musician or two.

SPORTS AND THE OUTDOORS

GOLF

There are several public 18-hole golf courses in Virginia Beach, some with moderate fees. All charge more for nonresidents and have varying fees, depending upon the day of the week and start time. **Honey Bee Golf Club** (⊠ *2500 S. Independence Blvd.* ☎ *757/471–2768*) has greens fees of $30–$60 weekdays and $44–$69 weekends. **Kempsville Greens Municipal Golf Course** (⊠ *4840 Princess Anne Rd.* ☎ *757/474–8441*) is a municipal course and the least expensive: weekdays $18–$23, weekends $24–$28, not including cart.

WATER SPORTS

Back Bay Getaways (⊠ *Sandbridge* ☎ *757/721–4484*) has a variety of kayak rentals and tours, pontoon boats, surfboards, and Jet Skis in the Sandbridge area. **Lynnhaven Dive Center** (☎ *757/481–7949*) leads dives and gives lessons. Their boats are at Rudee Inlet. **Wild River Outfitters** (☎ *757/431–8566 or 877/431–8566*) has guided kayak tours, moonlight paddles, river tours, dolphin tours, and more.

VIRGINIA'S EASTERN SHORE

This is the "-va" in Delmarva, a narrow 70-mi-long tail tacked onto the southern tip of the "Delmar-" Peninsula. It has one main artery bisecting its full length, U.S. 13, its occasional gentle curves interrupting an otherwise straight, flat route through unremarkable landscape. The appeal of Virginia's Eastern Shore is out of sight from the highway, among its barrier islands in the Atlantic to the east, along its wetlands and Chesapeake Bay shoreline to the west. It's the wild ponies, a small slice of NASA, gloriously uncrowded beaches, and waterfront views in every direction that draw thousands of snowbirds here every summer. Tiny hamlets are scattered among farms and protected wildlife habitats, or cling to the edges of the ocean or the Bay where watermen still struggle for their living. Part of the appeal here is its more recent 19th- and early-20th-century history, a welcome change from the Colonial eras that predominate elsewhere.

At its southernmost tip, the extraordinary Chesapeake Bay Bridge-Tunnel sweeps 17.5 mi across the Chesapeake Bay, salted by the close-by Atlantic, to connect with the Virginia Tidewater towns of Hampton Roads, Norfolk, and Virginia Beach.

GETTING HERE AND AROUND

The key to exploring the 70-mi-long peninsula known as Virginia's Eastern Shore is getting off Route 13 onto the byways leading eastward toward the Atlantic and westward toward the Chesapeake Bay.

ESSENTIALS

New Church Welcome Center (✉ 3420 Lankford Hwy. [Rte. 13], New Church ☎ 757/824–5000 ⊕ www.esvatourism.org).

CHINCOTEAGUE

27 mi southeast of Snow Hill, MD, via U.S. 13 to Rte. 175, 43 mi southeast of Salisbury, MD, via U.S. 13 to Rte. 175.

Just south of the Maryland–Virginia line, a few miles east of U.S. 13, the Virginia Eastern Shore's island resort town of Chincoteague (pronounced *shin*-coh-teeg), which means "large stream or inlet"—also known as Chinoteague Island—exudes a pleasant aura of seclusion. Small, but bustling, with affordable eateries and myriad shops, it is eminently walkable. Within a few minutes' drive or an easy bike ride, relatively uncrowded beaches stretch northward for miles. Small inns and B&Bs abound.

GETTING HERE AND AROUND

Chincoteague is about 10 mi east of U.S. 13, just south of the Maryland–Virginia line. Driving is permitted through two picturesque sectors of the Chincoteague National Wildlife Refuge, occupying the southern third of Assateague (Barrier) Island. Appropriate off-road vehicles with special permits may drive to the southernmost tip, known as Tom's Cove Hook. Some 10 mi of pristine beaches to the north are readily accessible on foot.

TIMING AND PRECAUTIONS

Late July's renowned Pony Swim and Auction draws thousands and can create maddening traffic congestion and parking challenges. Follow the signs in regard to the wild horses and do not feed or try to touch them.

ESSENTIALS

Visitor Information **Chincoteague Chamber of Commerce** (✉ 6733 Maddox Blvd. ☎ 757/336–6161 ⊕ www.chincoteaguechamber.com).

EXPLORING

Chincoteague National Wildlife Refuge. Virginia's Chincoteague National Wildlife Refuge occupies the southern third of Assateague Island, directly off Chincoteague Island. (The northern two-thirds, part of Maryland, comprise the Assateague Island National Seashore.) Created in 1943 as a resting and breeding area for the imperiled greater snow goose as well as other birds, this refuge's location makes it a prime "flyover" habitat. It also protects native and migratory non-avian wildlife, including the small Sika deer, which inhabits its interior pine forests. A 3.2-mi self-guided wildlife loop is a great introduction to the refuge. Bike or walk it; it's open to vehicles only between 3 pm and dusk.

The famed Chincoteague ponies occupy a section of the refuge isolated from the public, but they may still be seen in the distance from

Virginia's
Eastern
Shore

MARYLAND

Assateague Island

Chincoteague Island ♦ ○ Chincoteague

New Church

175

Tom's Cove Hook ♦

Wallops Island

Temperanceville ○

Crisfield ○

Cedar Island ○ Bloxom ○

Smith Island Great Fox Island

Tangier Island ♦

Potomac River

Watts Island

Onancock ○ ○ Tasley   Cedar Island

NORTHAMPTON

Pungoteague ○

○ Wachapreague

Parramore Island

○ Quinby

Exmore ○

Nassawadox ○

Hog Island Bay

Hog Island

13

Cobb Island Bay

Cobb Island

Eastville ○

Wreck Island

VIRGINIA MATHEWS

Chesapeake Bay

Rappahannock River

17

Mobjack Bay

Cape Charles ○ ○ Cheriton

South Bay

Townsend ○

York River

Yorktown Battlefield

Colonial Williamsburg ✕ ○ Yorktown

Eastern Shore of VA & Fisherman Island N. W. R.

0   10 miles
0   10 kilometers

KEY	
✕	Battlefield

a number of spots. Swimming, surf fishing, picnicking, and camping are all available on the island. ⊠ *Herbert H. Bateman Educational and Administrative Center and entrance: 8231 Beach Rd.* ☎ *757/336–6122* ⊕ *www.fws.gov/northeast/chinco* ⊡ *$8 per car, or $15 for weekly pass* ☉ *Refuge hrs: May–Sept., daily 5 am–10 pm; Oct. and Apr., daily 6 am–8 pm; Nov.–Mar., daily 6–6. Visitor center hrs vary seasonally; call for information.*

QUICK BITES

From the street, **Sea Star Café Gourmet Carryout** (⊠ *4121 Main St.* ☎ *757/336–5442*) doesn't look very gourmet, but the shacklike exterior of this take-out place belies the delectable salads, sandwiches, and roll-ups, much of it vegetarian, inside. Most items are about $5. Closed Tuesday and Wednesday.

Each of the three ice-cream parlors on the island has its own personality: The **Island Creamery** (⊠ *6243 Maddox Blvd.* ☎ *757/336–6236*), more than a quarter century in business, sells ice cream as well as sorbets, sherbets, and frozen yogurt. On a warm summer night, visit **Muller's Old Fashioned Ice Cream Parlour** (⊠ *4034 Main St.* ☎ *757/336–5894*) for soda-fountain treats, like malted milk shakes, root beer, and warm Belgian waffles served with ice cream, fresh fruit, and homemade whipped cream. Soft-serve shop Mr. Whippy's (✉ *6201 Maddox Blvd.* ☎ *757/336–5122*) is another local favorite.

Museum of Chincoteague Island. Formerly the Oyster and Maritime Museum, this museum chronicles the local oyster trade with displays of mostly homemade tools; elaborate, hand-carved decoys; marine specimens; a diorama; and audio recordings based on museum records. ✉ *7125 Maddox Blvd.* ☎ *757/336–6117* 🖾 *$2, 12 and under, free* ⊙ *Memorial Day–Labor Day daily. In spring and summer, open Fri.– Sun. Hrs vary, call ahead. Closed in winter.*

WHERE TO EAT

$-$$ ✕ **Etta's Channel Side Restaurant.** On the eastern side of the island, happily
SEAFOOD ensconced along the Assateague Channel away from the more heavily trafficked main streets of town, this meticulously maintained family-friendly restaurant has a vista as soothing as its food. Its dishes include pastas and popular meat dishes as well as typical fish and shellfish creations. Its signature dish is flounder stuffed with crab imperial. A trip to Chincoteague is incomplete without a meal at Etta's. ✉ *7452 East Side Dr.* ☎ *757/336–5644* ▭ *D, MC, V* ⊙ *Closed Dec.–Mar. No lunch.*

WHERE TO STAY

$-$$ 🏨 **Channel Bass Inn.** This three-story, beige clapboard house just off
★ Chincoteague Bay was built in the 1870s, then expanded and converted to an inn 50 years later. Its luxurious rooms all have comfortable sitting areas, and outside is a lovely Japanese garden. In addition to its included full breakfast, the inn serves afternoon tea Tuesday, Thursday, and Saturday in the public tearoom, at a reduced rate for inn guests. Delicacies such as *Apfelkuchen* (German apple cake), butterscotch pecan tarts, and firm ginger scones, all homemade, are served on Wedgwood china. The innkeeper herself is charming, personable, and a wealth of information. **Pros:** welcoming hosts; delectable food. **Cons:** not directly on the Bay. ✉ *6228 Church St.* ☎ *757/336–6148 or 800/249–0818* ⊕ *www. channelbass-inn.com* ➪ *7 rooms, 2 suites* ♿ *In-room: no phone, a/c, no TV. In-hotel: some pets allowed* ▭ *AE, D, MC, V* ⅋ *BP.*

$-$$ 🏨 **The 1848 Island Manor House.** The unusual design of the Island Manor
★ House was a result of splitting the home in two, providing adequate privacy for the original owners, who were brothers, and their wives, who were sisters. Most rooms have water views of the channel, and the hotel has an intimate brick courtyard, with a multitier fountain, that makes a nice summer gathering place. Decor is delightfully eclectic, highlighting the regional landscape and history. **Pros:** Chincoteague's largest B&B. **Cons:** streets on three sides; not all rooms have views. ✉ *4160 Main St.* ☎ *757/336–5436 or 800/852–1505* ⊕ *www.islandmanor.com* ➪ *8 rooms, all with private bath* ♿ *In-room: a/c, no phone, no TV (some). In-hotel: no kids under 6* ▭ *AE, D, MC, V* ⊙ *Closed Jan.* ⅋ *BP.*

$-$$ 🏨 **Miss Molly's.** This unassuming 1886 Victorian inn claims fame as the temporary home of author Marguerite Henry, who wrote *Misty of Chincoteague.* Here, in 1946, she spent two of her six weeks in Chincoteague preparing the background for her renowned children's novel. Miss Molly, the daughter of the home's builder, spent most of her life here. Guests have their pick of five bay-front porches loaded with comfy rocking chairs, and traditional English high tea is served every afternoon (for an additional fee). **Pros:** literary history; inviting bay-front porches; Victorian-style home. **Cons:** smaller rooms; afternoon tea costs extra. ✉ *4141 Main St.* ☎ *757/336–6686 or 800/221–5620* ⊕ *www.missmollysinn.com* ⤵ *7 rooms* ♨ *In-room: no phone, a/c, no TV. In-hotel: bicycles, no kids under 6* ☰ *AE, D, MC, V.*

OFF THE BEATEN℧ PATH

Wallops Island. NASA's Wallops Flight Facility Visitors Center fires the imagination with full-scale rockets, films on space and aeronautics, and displays on NASA projects. Although this was the site of early rocket launchings and NASA occasionally sends up satellites here, the facility now focuses primarily on atmospheric research. ✉ *Rte. 175, 20 mi southwest of Chincoteague* ☎ *757/824–2298 or 757/824–1344* ⊕ *www.nasa.gov/centers/wallops/home/index.html* 🎫 *Free* ☉ *July and Aug., daily 10–4; Sept.–Nov. and Feb.–June, Thurs.–Mon. 10–4.*

ONANCOCK

30 mi southwest of Chincoteague via Rte. 175 to U.S. 13.

Four miles from the Chesapeake Bay at the mouth of Onancock Creek, Onancock (pronounced oh-*nan*-cock), which means "foggy place," was once the home of a handful of Algonquian families. It was established by early English settlers as a port in 1690 and later emerged as an important ferry link with the burgeoning waterside cities of Maryland and Virginia. Today, this quiet community of 1,600, the second-largest town on Virginia's Eastern Shore, is worth a short visit for a flavor of its past as a transfer point between water and land. Onancock has a commitment to being Green; all the lodgings here are Virginia Green certified, and recycling bins are abundant.

GETTING HERE AND AROUND

About an hour north of the Chesapeake Bay Bridge-Tunnel, Onancock is just 2 mi from U.S. 13. Rte. 179–Market Street is the main drag, where you'll find ample parking. Most of the sights are easily accessible on foot.

WHERE TO EAT AND STAY

$–$$
SEAFOOD
✕ **Mallards at the Wharf/ Hopkins & Bros. General Store.** Inside a converted 19th-century general store on the National Register of Historic Places, you can imagine yourself waiting for a steamer to Baltimore. Walk past the vintage display cases into a casual dining area overlooking the wharf, or enjoy crab cakes, steamed clams, and fresh fish on the deck outside. On summer Sundays, there's live music playing. ✉ *2 Market St.* ☎ *757/787–8558* ☰ *MC, V.*

$
🏨 **Charlotte Hotel.** Creative funk meets island culture at Onancock's boutique hotel, four blocks from the harbor on Onancock Creek. Built as the White Hotel a century ago, the Charlotte went through a number of permutations before returning full circle to its original role. Rooms and public space are delightfully, imaginatively appointed. (Many of the floors were hand-painted by a co-owner.) In addition to the adjacent Next Door Art Gallery, there is a full-service bar and an intimate dining room. The restaurant's menu features local and regional produce and

seafood. **Pros:** unique character and personality; bar and art gallery on-site. **Cons:** main street location away from the water; not for families (no children under 10 admitted). ⊠ *7 North St.* ☎ *757/787–7400* ⊕ *www.thecharlottehotel.com* ⤳ *8 rooms* ⚐ *In-room: a/c, DVD, Wi-Fi. In-hotel: restaurant, no kids under 10* ☰ *AE, MC, V.*

SPORTS AND THE OUTDOORS

Broadwater Bay Ecotours (⊠ *6035 Killmon Point Rd., Exmore* ⊕ *www. broadwaterbayecotour.com* ☎ *757/442–4363 or 757/710–0568*) schedules custom tours on the flat, quiet waters among the myriad barrier islands stretching the eastern length of Virginia's Eastern Shore aboard one of two comfortable shallow draft boats.

TANGIER ISLAND, VIRGINIA

Crab traps stacked 10 feet high, watermen's shanties on the water, and a landscape virtually devoid of modern commercialization characterize this Virginia island fishing community. Visitors love the unique dialect of English spoken here—a British drawl with some island-specific vocabulary, which resulted from historic isolation from the mainland. Ferry service to Tangier operates from Reedfield or Onancock, Virginia, or from Crisfield, Maryland. Note that Tangier Island is "dry"; you may bring your own alcohol for personal use, but you must use discretion.

GETTING HERE AND AROUND

There are no cars on this small barrier island, so you'll need to catch a boat from Onancock or Reedfield, Virginia or from Crisfield, Maryland. Depending on where you depart from, the trip takes about 1½ hours and costs about $25. Advance reservations are recommended. Be aware that some round-trip tickets require you to return on the same day. You can also take a charter flight to the small airfield. Once on the island, bicycles, golf carts, and your own two feet will easily help you see the charm of Tangier's quarter-square mile.

WHERE TO STAY

$ ⊡ **Bay View Inn.** An overnight on Tangier Island is an experience. A fanciful complex of gingerbread-style cottages, this inn is an enchanting and relaxing place to experience the Bay. Breakfast is served on 100-year-old china, and dinner consists of—what else—crab served up in cakes, soup, or imperial-style. In addition to the Bay View Inn, there are two B&Bs on Tangier Island. **Pros:** unique experience on quiet island. **Cons:** island can feel too remote for some. ⊠ *16408 W. Ridge Rd.* ☎ *757/891–2396* ⊕ *www.tangierisland.net* ⤳ *2 rooms, 9 cottages* ⚐ *In-room: no phone, a/c, refrigerator. In-hotel: beachfront, Internet terminal, some pets allowed* ☰ *No credit cards.*

CAPE CHARLES

30 mi south of Onancock via U.S. 13.

Cape Charles, established in the early 1880s as a railroad-ferry junction, quieted down considerably after its heyday, but in the past few years its very isolation has begun to attract people from farther and farther away. The town holds one of the largest concentrations of late-Victorian and turn-of-the-20th-century buildings in the region. Clean, uncrowded public beaches beckon, as do a marina, a renowned golf course, and two National Wildlife Refuges a dozen miles farther south.

GETTING HERE AND AROUND

At the first stoplight on U.S. 13 after the Chesapeake Bay Bridge-Tunnel, turn left onto Route 184. The town center is just 1 mi away.

ESSENTIALS

TOURS **Bay Creek Railway** (☎ 757/331–8770 ⊕ www.baycreekrailway.com) is a single-car train that meanders through the peninsula flatlands north from Cape Charles for four-course dinner excursions lasting about two hours ($60) and "fun run" pizza trips lasting about one hour ($20 adults, $15 kids ages 2–12).

SPORTS AND THE OUTDOORS

Remote **Bay Creek Resort and Club** (✉ 1 Clubhouse Way ☎ 757/331–9000 ⊕ www.baycreekresort.com) has been a popular public course since it opened in 2001. Some of the "front 9" of the 18-hole Arnold Palmer course play right along the edge of the Chesapeake Bay. It's a view rivaled by few other courses. A second course, the Jack Nicholas, opened in 2006. They offer Stay-and-Play golf packages, which include lodging at nearby three-bedroom condos. There are also a full-service marina, restaurants, and shops.

SouthEast Expeditions (✉ 32218 Lankford Hwy. ⊕ www.southeastexpeditions.net ☎ 757/331–2680 or 877/225–2925) offers kayak rentals and instruction, as well as tours among the wetlands of the still-pristine shoreline of the Chesapeake Bay.

NATIONAL WILDLIFE REFUGES

13 mi south of Cape Charles.

GETTING HERE AND AROUND

Located at the southern tip of the Delmarva Peninsula, the Wildlife Refuges are just off of Route 13, north of the Chesapeake Bay Bridge-Tunnel.

EXPLORING

National Wildlife Refuges. At the southernmost tip of the Delmarva Peninsula, the unique Eastern Shore of Virginia and the Fisherman Island National Wildlife Refuges—including nearby Skidmore Island—established in 1984, are among the most untrammeled havens for winged wildlife, resident and migrating alike, in the region.

Each fall, between late August and early November, a vast migration of monarch butterflies and songbirds descend by the thousands on these forests and wetlands in myrtle and bayberry thickets, grasslands and croplands, on their voyage south. ✉ 5003 Hallett Circle ☎ 757/331–2760 ⊕ www.fws.gov/northeast/easternshore 🎟 Free.

Baltimore

WORD OF MOUTH

"The water taxi service on the harbor is a great way to get around quickly—especially in the heat. However, it really doesn't take long to walk to a lot of the places. Fell's Point is a must and we spent our last day in Baltimore exploring the cobblestone streets. Great shopping!"

—Tanya

Updated by
Evan Serpick

Baltimore's charm lies in its neighborhoods. While stellar downtown attractions such as the National Aquarium and the Inner Harbor draw torrents of tourists each year, much of the city's character can be found in bergs like Hampden (the "p" is silent) and Federal Hill. Scores of Baltimore's trademark narrow redbrick row houses with white marble steps line the city's East and West sides. Some neighborhood streets are still made of cobblestone, and grand churches and museums and towering, glassy high-rises fill out the growing skyline.

After World War II, as manufacturing jobs dried up and its populace moved to the suburbs, Baltimore declined. But in the 1970s real-estate development surged in some areas, and new arts and cultural events such as the city's ethnic festivals began to spring up. Homesteaders started moving into once-abandoned row houses, and city tourism grew dramatically when the National Aquarium opened in the early 1980s. Further development of the Inner Harbor, including Oriole Park at Camden Yards and M&T Bank Stadium, continued to fuel the city's resurgence.

Now the city's blue-collar past mixes with present urban-professional revitalization. Industrial waterfront properties are giving way to high-end condos, and corner bars formerly dominated by National Bohemian beer—once made in the city—are adding microbrews to their beverage lists. And with more and more retail stores replacing old, run-down buildings and parking lots, Baltimore is one of the nation's up-and-coming cities. Though Baltimore has seen a spike in development, signs of the city's pockmarked past still persist. Boarded-up row houses sit just west of downtown, and abandoned factory shells still dot the landscape—signs of the troubles the city still faces.

ORIENTATION AND PLANNING

GETTING ORIENTED

Laid out in a more-or-less regular grid pattern, Baltimore is fairly easy to navigate. Pratt Street runs east along the Inner Harbor; from there the major northbound arteries are Charles Street and the Jones Falls Expressway (I–83). Cross-street addresses are marked "East" or "West" according to which side of Charles Street they are on; similarly, Baltimore Street marks the dividing line between north and south. Residents refer to areas of the city by the direction of these major arteries: thus, South Baltimore, North Baltimore, East Baltimore, West Baltimore,

ıNG

WHEN TO GO

Summer is the ideal time to explore Baltimore. It's also tourist season, which means the Inner Harbor fills up with foot traffic. Though the rest of Baltimore can be humid in the summer months, there's usually a breeze blowing in from the water, which helps cool the harbor. Summer is also festival season, with a number of ethnic celebrations taking place around the city. Check ⊕ *www.bop.org* for more information, as dates and locations change from year to year.

The Inner Harbor is a must-see, and try to squeeze in a baseball or football game if you can. If you spend a long weekend in Baltimore, you can see most of the Inner Harbor attractions and get out to a few neighborhoods, too. Weekends are by far the busiest time for the Inner Harbor, but weekdays are often the best time to explore the boutiques in neighborhoods like Hampden and Federal Hill.

New Year's Eve (☎ *410/752–8632* ⊕ *www.bop.org*) festivities in Baltimore include a concert at the Harborplace amphitheater and a 9 pm fireworks display over Inner Harbor. **The American Craft Council Retail Show** (☎ *800/836–3470*), held each February is the largest indoor, juried craft show in the country, drawing more than 800 exhibitors for three days of artful displays and sales. The **Maryland Preakness Celebration** (☎ *410/542–9400* ⊕ *www.preakness.com*) is a weeklong festival that includes parades, street parties, fund-raisers, and hot-air balloons. The celebration culminates in the annual running of the Preakness Stakes at Pimlico Race Course, on the third Saturday in May. **Artscape** (⊕ *www. artscape.org*), the country's largest free arts festival, takes over several blocks in the middle of the city for several days each July and is a must-visit for residents and tourists alike, featuring a half-dozen music stages, endless art displays, and live theater. In late August the **Maryland State Fair** (☎ *410/252–0200* ⊕ *www.marylandstatefair.com*), in Timonium (15 mi north of Baltimore), is 10 days of horse racing, livestock judging, live entertainment, agricultural displays, farm implements, and plenty of food. **Defenders' Day** (☎ *410/962–4290* ⊕ *www.nps.gov/fomc*) celebrations in September at Fort McHenry commemorate—with music, drilling, mock bombardment, and fireworks—the battle that led to the writing of the national anthem.

GETTING HERE AND AROUND

Baltimore is not particularly known for great public transportation, but things are improving. The bus system is a bit convoluted, especially for visitors. A light-rail train runs north–south along Howard Street from Baltimore-Washington International Airport to Camden Yards and up into northern suburbs such as Hunt Valley. In 2010, the city introduced the Charm City Circulator, a free bus service with four lines that run through Baltimore's most popular tourist areas, including Mount Vernon, Fells Point, and Johns Hopkins. Cabs are still your quickest option, though you will have to call for a pickup in most neighborhoods. Water taxis are a great alternative when visiting sites around the harbor.

TOP REASONS TO GO

Relive American History: Take a water taxi to see Fort McHenry, the site of a relentless British attack during the war of 1812. The fort never fell and the sight of its flag after the battle inspired the words that later became the national anthem.

Explore a Revitalized Addition to the Inner Harbor: The former industrial zone just east of the tourist-oriented Inner Harbor, now called Harbor East, has become a chic destination with some of the city's best restaurants, shopping, and people-watching.

Visit the Country's Most Inspiring Museum: The American Visionary Art Museum, which highlights artists outside the mainstream, is a glorious ode to the creative impulse, a family-friendly joy to behold both inside

and out. out the h. on wheels!

Get Wild and Zany a. one weekend each June, . gussy up to celebrate Honfest . Hampden in the traditional attire o. a Baltimore "hon": beehive hairdos and cat's-eye glasses.

Crack 'Em and Eat 'Em like a Baltimorean: Baltimore loves crabs, especially at Bo Brooks in Canton—one of the city's best crab houses—where you can crack into a piping-hot crustacean year-round.

Taste the Country's First Tiramisu: Piedigrotta Bakery, on the edge of historical Little Italy, claims to have invented tiramisu. Try it for yourself—a big wedge is only a couple of bucks.

Northeast Baltimore, Northwest Baltimore, etc. The major downtown north–south thoroughfares are Charles and Saint Paul (north of Baltimore Street) and Light Street (south of Baltimore). Downtown, east–west traffic depends heavily on Pratt and Lombard streets. The downtown area is bounded by Martin Luther King Boulevard on the west and by the Jones Falls Expressway (President Street) on the east.

Mount Vernon. Baltimore's arts and culture scene is focused in Mount Vernon. Some of the city's grandest architecture can be seen on Charles Street.

Charles Village. Students, professors, writers, and artists are drawn to the area's intellectual environment, centered around Johns Hopkins University.

Inner Harbor and Harbor East. South of the city center, the Inner Harbor is the city's biggest destination, filled with popular attractions like the National Aquarium, Harborplace shopping centers, and the Maryland Science Center.

Fells Point. To the east of Inner Harbor, Fells Point is just a water taxi away. Shops, two small museums, and the neighborhood's many pubs—most of which host live local bands daily, attract both locals and tourists.

Station North. The formerly blighted area around Penn Station has become a hub for galleries, theaters, artist studios, and hipster bars and restaurants.

AIR TRAVEL

Traveling to Baltimore by air is fairly simple. The main airport is Baltimore-Washington International Airport (BWI), just south of town. BWI is easily reached by car, taxi, or light rail; for most agencies, rental cars are returned to lots off the airport premises.

BWI SuperShuttle provides van service between the airport and downtown hotels every half-hour 4 am–midnight. Travel time is about 30 minutes; the fare is $23 for the first person, $12 per additional passenger. Hotel vans, which operate independently of the hotels, take 30 minutes on average.

Carey Limousines provides sedan service, which costs $80; make reservations 24 hours in advance. Private Car/RMA Worldwide Chauffeured Transportation has sedans, limos, and vans; the cost to the Inner Harbor is about $40 for a sedan.

Airport Taxis stand by to meet arriving flights. The ride into town on I–295 takes 20 minutes; a trip between the airport and downtown costs about $25. Airport Taxi service is available only *from* BWI; for transportation to the airport, consult a local cab company such as Jimmy's Cab Co. or Arrow Taxicab.

Airport Information **Baltimore-Washington International Thurgood Marshall Airport** (BWI ✉ *10 mi south of Baltimore off Rte. 295/Baltimore-Washington Pkwy., Hanover, MD* ☎ *410/859–7111 for information and paging* ⊕ *www.bwiairport.com*).

Airport Transfers **Airport Taxis** (☎ *410/859–1100* ⊕ *www.bwiairporttaxi.com*). **Arrow Taxicab** (☎ *410/358–9696*). **BWI Airport rail station** (☎ *410/672–6167* ⊕ *www.mtamaryland.com*). **BWI SuperShuttle** (☎ *800/258–3826* ⊕ *www.supershuttle.com*). **Carey Limousines** (☎ *410/880–0999 or 888/880–0999* ⊕ *www.carey.com*). **Maryland Area Rail Commuter** (MARC ☎ *800/325–7245 or 410/539–5000* ⊕ *www.mtamaryland.com*). **Penn Station** (✉ *1515 N. Charles St., Mount Vernon* ☎ *800/523–8720*). **Private Car/RMA Worldwide Chauffeured Transportation** (☎ *410/519–0000 or 800/878–7743* ⊕ *www.rmalimo.com*).

BUS TRAVEL

Travel to Baltimore by bus is easy and convenient. Passengers can arrive at the downtown bus terminal or at the Baltimore Travel Plaza just off I–95; the plaza has long-term parking and local bus service to downtown and other destinations. Greyhound Lines has scheduled daily service to and from major cities in the United States and Canada. Peter Pan/Trailways Bus Lines offers slightly nicer (more leisurely) travel to many destinations in the Northeast, including Washington, D.C., New York, and Boston.

In 2010, in an effort to improve transportation options for tourists and residents, Baltimore introduced the Charm City Circular, a free bus service running along four lines around major attractions and destinations in the downtown area.

Maryland Transit Authority (MTA) buses provide an inexpensive way to see much of Baltimore beyond the Circulator routes, though you may have to transfer several times. Route and schedule information is available by contacting the Maryland Transit Administration (⊕ *www.mtamaryland.com*).

Bus and transit schedules are sometimes available inside the Charles Center metro station (Charles and Baltimore streets downtown). Fare is $1.60 (exact change is required). All-day passes are $3.50 and can be used with light-rail or metro travel. Some routes have service 24 hours daily.

CAR TRAVEL

From the northeast and south, I–95 cuts across the city's east side and the harbor; Route 295, the Baltimore–Washington Parkway, follows a similar route farther to the east, and is the best route downtown from the airport. From the north, I–83, also called the Jones Falls Expressway, winds through Baltimore and ends downtown, near the Inner Harbor. Interstate 395 serves as the primary access to downtown from I–95. From the west, I–70 merges with the Baltimore Beltway, I–695. Drivers headed downtown should use I–395.

Parking in downtown Baltimore can be difficult; on weekdays many garages fill up early with suburban commuters. When the Orioles or Ravens play a home game, parking around the Inner Harbor can be nearly impossible to find. Best bets for parking are hotel garages, which often have spaces available. Attended parking lots are around the downtown periphery and cost less than garages.

It's hard to find a metered parking spot downtown, though in other areas it's much easier. Most meters in well-traveled areas charge 25¢ per 15-minute period and have a two-hour limit; around the Inner Harbor vicinity meters are in effect 24 hours a day.

METRO TRAVEL

The Baltimore metro subway serves those coming into the city from the suburban northwest. Stops include Charles Center and Lexington Market, both within walking distance of the Inner Harbor. The single line runs from Owings Mills to Johns Hopkins Hospital, east of downtown. There's also a light rail that runs between points north and south in the city (⇨ *By Train below*). Fare is $1.60; day passes, which also count for bus and light-rail fares, are $3.50. Trains run weekdays 5 am–midnight, weekends 6 am–midnight.

TAXI TRAVEL

It can be hard to catch a cab on the street in Baltimore. The best places to flag one down are at Pratt and Light streets in the Inner Harbor, Cross and South Charles streets in Federal Hill, O'Donnell Square in Canton, and at Broadway and Thames Street in Fells Point. Otherwise, your best option is to phone ahead and ask for a pickup, or ask your hotel concierge or doorman to summon one for you. Meters determine local fares, which average $7–$15, depending on how far you go.

Ed Kane's Water Taxis and the Seaport Taxi are fun and convenient ways to get around the Inner Harbor. They make stops at 12 points along the waterfront, including Fells Point, the National Aquarium, museums, restaurants, and Fort McHenry. All-day tickets for both services are $9 for adults and $4 for children 10 and under. Look for stops, marked with signs, all along the waterfront; depending on season, boats arrive every 10–15 minutes, or you can call to be picked up at a particular location.

Taxi Contacts Arrow Taxicab (☎ 410/358–9696). **Ed Kane's Water Taxis** (☎ 410/563–3901 ⊕ www.thewatertaxi.com). **Seaport Taxi** (☎ 410/675–2900).

TRAIN TRAVEL

All Amtrak trains on the northeast corridor between Boston and Washington stop at Baltimore's Penn Station. Maryland Area Rail Commuter (MARC) trains travel between Baltimore's Penn Station and Washington, D.C., Camden Station, and Washington, and BWI Airport and Penn Station. The trip to Washington, D.C., takes about one hour and costs $7; the trip to BWI Airport from Penn Station takes about 20 minutes and costs $4. Trains run several times per hour, weekdays 4:45 am–9:30 pm (note that MARC trains do not run on weekends).

Light rail is an easy, comfortable (if slow) way to reach downtown from the northern and southern suburbs. Stops near downtown include Oriole Park at Camden Yards, Howard Street, and Centre Street near Mount Vernon. The city's cultural center can be reached by the Cathedral Street stop. Light rail extends to Hunt Valley, BWI Airport, and Glen Burnie. The fare is $1.60 (exact change is required); day passes are $3.50.

Train Contacts Amtrak Penn Station (✉ 1515 N. Charles St., Mount Vernon ☎ 800/523–8720). **Maryland Area Rail Commuter** (MARC ☎ 800/325–7245 or 410/539–5000 ⊕ www.mtamaryland.com). **Maryland Transit Administration** (MTA ☎ 800/325–7245 or 410/539–5000 ⊕ www.mtamaryland.com).

TOURS

Tours of Baltimore, on foot or four wheels, run from traditional surveys of historic buildings and sites to quirkier explorations such as the Fells Point Ghost Tour. Baltimore Sightseeing Tours offers a 90-minute narrated trolley tour of the city; tours are $24.95 for adults ($15.95 for children 6–12; 5 and under free) and depart at 10:30 am, 11 am, 12:30 pm, and 1 pm on weekdays, 10:30 am and 12:30 pm on weekends, from the visitor center at the Inner Harbor.

For an overview of downtown's many historic sights, the Baltimore Heritage Walk is a 90-minute on-foot trail of 20 downtown sites including City Hall and the Phoenix Shot Tower, which, when completed in 1828, was the tallest structure in the United States. Free guided tours begin at the visitor center at the Inner Harbor.

For a general overview of Baltimore, energetic, irrepressible Zippy Larson offers many different walking tours with historic, cultural, and architectural themes. Zippy's witty, well-researched tours take you outside the tourist bubble.

A particularly fascinating experience is local historian Wayne Schaumburg's guided tour to Greenmount Cemetery. Baltimore's largest and most prestigious burial ground is the final resting place of John Wilkes Booth, Johns Hopkins, and other native sons and daughters. Tours take place Saturday mornings in May and October and are $15 per person.

Baltimore Ghost Tours interweave narratives about city neighborhoods' colorful pasts with tales of its spectral inhabitants. Tours, which are suitable for children, run Friday and Saturday evenings (depending on the neighborhood) at 7 pm from March to November; the cost is $15 per adult; reservations are recommended. The Fells Point Visitors Center also offers a Fells Point Ghost Walk as well as tours focusing on such topics as maritime history and immigration.

A far less pedestrian way to see downtown is atop a Segway, the motorized upright two-wheel scooters. Segs in the City offers one- and two-hour historic city safaris for $45 and $70, respectively.

Most cruise and tour boats depart from docks in the Inner Harbor. Spirit Cruises, Ltd. and Pintail Yachts present lunch, dinner, and evening cruises around the harbor.

Tour Information **Baltimore Ghost Tours** (🕾 410/522–7400 ⊕ www. fellspointghost.com). **Baltimore Sightseeing Tours** (🕾 410/254–8687 ⊕ www. baltimoresightseeingtours.com). **Baltimore Heritage Walk** (🕾 443/514–5900 ⊕ www.heritagewalk.org). **Greenmount Cemetery Tours** (🕾 410/256–2180 ⊕ home.earthlink.net/~wschaumburg). **Spirit Cruises, Ltd.** (🕾 866/312–2469 ⊕ www.spiritcruises.com/metro/Baltimore-metro). **Mount Vernon Cultural District** (✉ 217 N. Charles St., Mount Vernon 🕾 410/605–0462 ⊕ www.mvcd. org). **Pintail Yachts** (✉ Pier 5, Inner Harbor 🕾 410/539–3485). **Segs in the City** (🕾 410/276–7347 ⊕ www.segsinthecity.com). **Zippy Larson's Shoe Leather Safaris** (🕾 410/522–7334 ⊕ zippytours.com).

VISITOR INFORMATION

Contacts **Baltimore Convention Center** (✉ 100 W. Pratt St., Inner Harbor 🕾 410/649–7000 ⊕ www.bccenter.org). **Baltimore Office of Promotion** (🕾 410/752–8632 ⊕ www.bop.org). **Baltimore Visitor Center** (✉ 401 Light St, Inner Harbor 🕾 877/225–8466 ⊕ www.baltimore.org). **Fells Point Visitors Center** (✉ 808 S. Ann St., Fells Point 🕾 410/675–6750 ⊕ www.preservationsociety.com).

DISCOUNTS AND DEALS

The Baltimore Visitor Center offers the three-day Harbor Pass, which saves you on admission to local attractions and gives you discounts on parking, hotels, and tours.

EXPLORING BALTIMORE

Visiting Baltimore without seeing the Inner Harbor is like touring New York City and skipping Manhattan. The harbor and surrounding area are home to a good number of the city's most popular sites: the National Aquarium in Baltimore, Camden Yards, M&T Bank Stadium, the American Visionary Arts Museum, and The Science Center.

The neighborhoods themselves are fun to explore. Historic Federal Hill, just south of the Inner Harbor, is home to some of the oldest houses in the city. Fells Point and Canton, farther east, are lively waterfront communities. Mount Vernon and Charles Village have wide avenues lined with grand old row houses that were once home to Baltimore's wealthiest residents. Farther north are Roland Park (Frederick Law Olmsted Jr. contributed to its planning), Guilford, Homeland, and Mt. Washington, all leafy, residential neighborhoods with cottages, large Victorian houses, and redbrick Colonials. It's easy to tour the Inner Harbor and neighborhoods such as Mount Vernon, Federal Hill, Charles Village, and Fells Point on foot. To travel between areas or farther out, however, the light rail or a car is more efficient. Most of the Inner Harbor's parking is in nearby garages, though meters can be found along Key Highway. In other neighborhoods, you can generally find meters and two-hour free parking on the street.

MOUNT VERNON

Baltimore's arts and cultural center, Mount Vernon is home to the Walters Art Museum and the Peabody Institute conservatory—one of the country's top music schools—as well as some of the city's grandest architecture.

The Walters and nearby Mount Vernon Place, a wonderfully designed park, are two of the neighborhood's must-sees. A good plan is to visit the Walters first then rest for a while in Mount Vernon Place. You'll need a breather before and after climbing the Washington Monument, which sits in the middle of the park. After, there are plenty of restaurants on or near Charles Street, the neighborhood thoroughfare. From the Inner Harbor, you can walk up Charles Street into the heart of Mount Vernon in about 25–30 minutes. You can also drive or take the No. 3 bus.

The area was named for the nation's first significant monument to George Washington, erected at the neighborhood's center in Mount Vernon Place. In the 19th century Mount Vernon was home to some of Baltimore's wealthiest residents, including Enoch Pratt, a wealthy merchant who donated funds for the first public library; Robert Garrett, of the Baltimore & Ohio Railroad; and Henry and William Walters, who founded the art gallery that bears their names. Though some of the grand houses here remain single-family residences, many have been turned into apartments or offices.

TOP ATTRACTIONS

Fodor's Choice ★ **Basilica of the Assumption.** Completed in 1821, the Catholic Basilica of the Assumption is the oldest cathedral in the United States. Designed by Benjamin Latrobe, architect of the U.S. Capitol, it stands as a paragon of neoclassicism, with a grand portico fronted by six Corinthian columns that suggest an ancient Greek temple. Two towers are surmounted by cupolas. The church, including 24 original skylights in the dome, which were covered over after World War II, were restored in November 2006, the bicentennial of the laying of the church's cornerstone. ⊠ *Mulberry and Cathedral Sts., Mount Vernon* ☎ *410/727–3564* ☾ *Call for hrs.*

Contemporary Museum. Artists come from around the world to collaborate with local communities and institutions and produce artwork that is relevant to Baltimore. The museum's minimalistic interior shifts all of your focus to the unconventional art within. Works are shown both on-site and off, using traditional mediums and innovative approaches. ⊠ *100 W. Centre St., Mount Vernon* ☎ *410/783–5720* ⊕ *www.contemporary.org* ✉ *$5 suggested donation* ☾ *Wed.–Sun. noon–5.*

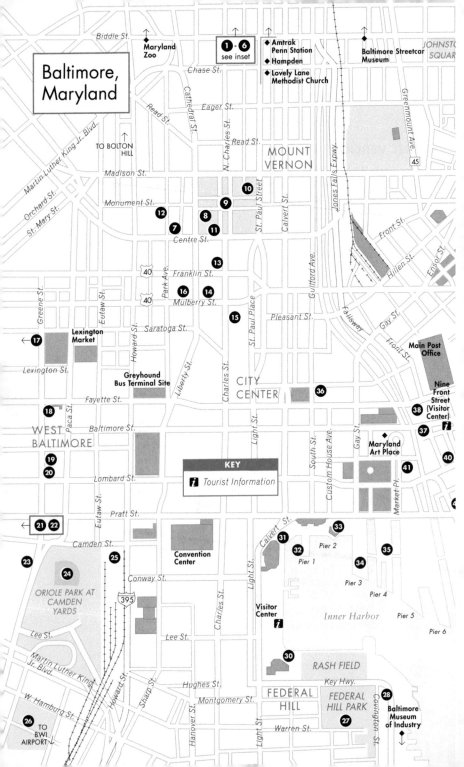

Great Blacks in Wax Museum ◆

MADISON SQUARE

CHARLES VILLAGE

WYMAN PARK

TO WAVERLY FARMER'S MARKET

HISTORIC JONESTOWN

LITTLE ITALY

FELLS POINT

TO CANTON →

Fell's Point Visitor Center

0   220 yards
0   200 meters

American Visionary Art Museum **28**

B&O Railroad Museum **22**

Babe Ruth Birthplace and Museum **23**

Baltimore City Hall **36**

Baltimore Civil War Museum-President Street Station **45**

Baltimore Museum of Art **6**

Baltimore Public Works Museum **44**

Basilica of the Assumption **14**

Broadway Market **46**

Carroll Mansion **40**

Contemporary Museum **7**

Davidge Hall **20**

Dr. Samuel D. Harris National Museum of Dentistry **19**

Enoch Pratt Free Library **16**

Evergreen House **2**

Federal Hill Park **27**

Fells Point Maritime Museum **47**

First Unitarian Church **13**

Fort McHenry **29**

Garrett-Jacobs Mansion **8**

Geppi's Entertainment Museum **25**

Harbourplace and the Gallery **31**

Homewood House Museum **5**

Jewish Museum of Maryland **39**

Johns Hopkins University **4**

Lacrosse Museum and National Hall of Fame **3**

M&T Bank Stadium **26**

Maryland Historical Society **12**

Maryland Science Center **30**

Mount Clare Museum House **21**

Mount Vernon Place **10**

National Aquarium in Baltimore **34**

Nine Front Street **37**

Oriole Park at Camden Yards **24**

Phoenix Shot Tower **38**

Poe House **17**

Port Discovery—The Baltimore Children's Museum **41**

The Power Plant **35**

Reginald F. Lewis Museum **42**

Robert Long House Museum **48**

Sherwood Gardens **1**

Star-Spangled Banner House **43**

USS *Constellation* **32**

Walters Art Museum **11**

Washington Monument **9**

Westminster Cemetery and Catacombs **18**

Woman's Industrial Exchange **15**

World Trade Center **33**

8

Maryland Historical Society. More than 200,000 objects serve to celebrate Maryland's history and heritage at this museum. One major attraction is the original manuscript of "The Star-Spangled Banner." The first floor is devoted to an exhibit about Marylanders' pursuit of liberty, with a focus on religious freedom, voting rights, labor, and war. Featured on the second floor are portrait paintings by the Peale family and Joshua Johnson, America's first African-American portrait artist, as well as 18th- and 19th-century Maryland landscape paintings juxtaposed against present-day photographs of the same places. Furniture manufactured and designed in Maryland from the 18th century to the present is on the third floor. There's also a library with 7 million works that relate to the state's history. ✉ *201 W. Monument St., Mount Vernon* ☎ *410/685-3750* ⊕ *www.mdhs.org* 💲 *$8* ⊙ *Museum: Wed.–Sun. 10–5; library: Wed.–Sat. 10–4:30.*

★ **Mount Vernon Place**. One of the country's more beautifully designed public spaces, Mount Vernon Place is a prime spot for relaxing. It was established when John Eager Howard donated the highest point in Baltimore as a site for a memorial to George Washington. With the monument as its center, the square is composed of four parks, each a block in length, that are arranged around Mount Vernon Place (which goes east–west) and Washington Place (north–south). Benches near the monument are great for watching water calmly trickle from the fountains. The sculptures in the parks deserve a close look; of special note is a bronze lion by Antoine-Louis Barye in the middle of West Mount Vernon Place. Northeast of the monument is Mount Vernon Methodist Church, built in the mid-1850s on the site of Francis Scott Key's home and place of death. Free concerts are held here monthly in the summertime. Take a moment to admire the brownstones along the north side of East Mount Vernon Place. They're excellent examples of the luxurious mansions built by 19th-century residents of Baltimore's most prestigious neighborhood.

Fodor'sChoice **Walters Art Museum**. The Walters' prodigious collection of more than
★ 30,000 artworks provides an organized overview of human history over 5,500 years, from the 3rd millennium BC to the early 20th century. ■TIP➜ Thanks to a grant by the city, admission is free. The original museum (1909) houses major collections of Renaissance and baroque paintings as well as a sculpture court. Two other buildings contain Egyptian, Greek and Roman, Byzantine, and Ethiopian art collections— among the best in the nation—along with many 19th-century paintings. There are also medieval armor and artifacts; jewelry and decorative works; Egyptology exhibits; a wonderful gift shop; great kids activities in the basement; and a café. ✉ *600 N. Charles St., Mount Vernon* ☎ *410/547-9000* ⊕ *www.thewalters.org* 💲 *Free* ⊙ *Wed.–Sun. 10–5.*

Washington Monument. Completed on July 4, 1829, the impressive monument was the first one dedicated to the nation's first president. An 18-foot statue depicting Washington caps the 160-foot white marble tower. The tower was designed and built by Robert Mills, the first architect born and educated in the United States; 19 years after completing Baltimore's Washington Monument, Mills designed and erected the national Washington Monument in D.C. ✉ *Mt. Vernon Pl., Mount Vernon.*

WORTH NOTING

Enoch Pratt Free Library. Donated to the city of Baltimore in 1882 by its namesake, a wealthy merchant, the Enoch Pratt Free Library was one of the country's first free-circulation public libraries; it remains one of the country's largest. The Pratt was remarkable for allowing any citizen to borrow books at a time when only the wealthy could afford to buy them. When the collection outgrew its original fortresslike rococo structure in 1933, Pratt's democratic ideals were incorporated into the new building's grand yet accessible design. Innovations such as a sidewalk-level entrance and department store–style exhibit windows set the standard for public libraries across the country. The building is still a treat to explore. A huge skylight illuminates the Central Hall's marble floors, gilded fixtures, mural panels depicting the history of printing and publishing, and oil portraits of the Lords Baltimore. The Children's Department, with a fishpond, puppet theater, and a large selection of books, is a real gem for little ones. An audio architecture tour of the museum is available at the circulation desk. ✉ *400 Cathedral St., Mount Vernon* ☎ *410/396–5500* ⊕ *www.pratt.lib.md.us* ☉ *June–Sept., Mon.– Wed. 10–8, Thurs. 10–5:30, Fri. and Sat. 10–5, Sun. 1–5; Oct.–May, Mon.–Wed. 11–7, Thurs. 10–5:30, Fri. and Sat. 10–5, Sun. 1–5.*

First Unitarian Church. Designed by Maximilian Godefroy in 1819, the church that year was the site for the sermon that definitively established Unitarianism as a denomination (the sermon was given by the church's founder, Dr. William Ellery Channing). ✉ *Charles and Franklin Sts., entrance at 1 W. Hamilton St., Mount Vernon* ☎ *410/685–2330* ☉ *Tues.–Fri. 10–4:30.*

QUICK BITES

Donna's (✉ *800 N. Charles St., Mount Vernon* ☎ *410/385-0180*) is a relaxing Mount Vernon spot for coffee; soups, salads, and sandwiches are also served. At artsy and elegant **Sascha's 527** (✉ *527 N. Charles St., Mount Vernon* ☎ *410/539-8880*) you can choose from a selection of salads and sandwiches.

Garrett-Jacobs Mansion. Originally built in 1893 by Stanford White for Robert Garrett, the president of the Baltimore & Ohio Railroad, this mansion was the largest and most expensive ever constructed in Baltimore (the neighbors objected to its size). After Garrett died in 1896, his widow, Mary, and her second husband, Dr. Henry Barton Jacobs, had John Russell Pope build an extension of equal size. Call ahead to book a tour. ✉ *11 W. Mt. Vernon Pl., Mount Vernon* ☎ *410/539–6914* 💲*$5* ☉ *Group tours by appointment; reservations required.*

OFF THE BEATEN PATH

Great Blacks in Wax Museum. Though not as convincing as the likenesses at a Madame Tussauds, the more than 100 wax figures on display here do a good job of recounting the triumphs and trials of Africans and African-Americans. The wax figures are accompanied by text and audio. Baltimoreans honored include Frederick Douglass, who as a youth lived and worked in Fells Point; singer Billie Holiday; and jazz composer Eubie Blake. To get here from Mount Vernon, take Charles north and turn left at North Avenue. ✉ *1601 E. North Ave., East Baltimore* ☎ *410/563–3404* ⊕ *www.greatblacksinwax.org* 💲*$12; $10*

8

children ⏱ *Mid-Jan.–mid-Oct., Tues.–Sat. 9–6, Sun. noon–6; mid-Oct.–mid-Jan., Tues.–Sat. 9–5, Sun. noon–5. Closed Mon. except in Feb., July, Aug., and most federal holidays.*

Woman's Industrial Exchange. This Baltimore institution was organized in the 1880s as a way for destitute women, many of them Civil War widows, to support themselves in a ladylike fashion through sewing and other domestic handiworks. To this day you can still purchase handmade quilts, embroidered baby clothes, sock monkeys, and many other arts and crafts. ⊠ *333 N. Charles St., Mount Vernon* ☎ *410/685–4388* ⊕ *www.womansindustrialexchange.org* ⏱ *Tues.–Fri. 11–6, Sat. 11–5.*

CHARLES VILLAGE

Though Johns Hopkins University anchors Charles Village, the Baltimore Museum of Art is the neighborhood's prime tourist draw—especially since admission is free. Students, professors, writers, and artists are drawn to the area's intellectual environment. Row houses along Charles, St. Paul, and Calvert streets—some of them quite large—were built in the late 1890s and early 1900s for merchants, bankers, and other professionals. These early developments were constructed on old family estates, one of which became the basis for the present-day Johns Hopkins campus. Some of the old mansions are now museums, including Johns Hopkins's Homewood House and the Evergreen House, which also belongs to the university. On the eastern and northern sides of the Johns Hopkins campus are the neighborhoods of Tuscany-Canterbury and Roland Park. Farther to the north and east are Homeland and Guilford, tony areas worth exploring for their beautiful homes and lovely, tree-lined streets.

TOP ATTRACTIONS

Fodor'sChoice
★

Baltimore Museum of Art. Works by Matisse, Picasso, Cézanne, Gauguin, van Gogh, and Monet are among the 90,000 paintings, sculptures, and decorative arts on exhibit at this impressive museum near Johns Hopkins University. Particular strengths include an encyclopedic collection of postimpressionist paintings donated to the museum by the Cone sisters, Baltimore natives who were pioneer collectors of early-20th-century art. The museum also owns the world's second-largest collection of Andy Warhol works, and many pieces of 18th- and 19th-century American painting and decorative arts. The museum's neoclassical main building was designed by John Russell Pope, the architect of the National Gallery in Washington; the modern aluminum and concrete wing houses the contemporary art collection. From Gertrude's, the museum restaurant, you can look out at 20th-century sculpture displayed in two landscaped gardens. ⊠ *10 Art Museum Dr., Charles Village* ☎ *410/396–7100* ⊕ *www.artbma.org* ▱ *Free* ⏱ *Wed.–Fri. 10–5, weekends 11–6.*

Evergreen House. Built in the 1850s, this 48-room Italianate mansion was the home of the 19th-century diplomat and collector John Work Garrett, whose father was president of the Baltimore & Ohio Railroad (the Garrett family continued to live here until the 1950s). Garrett bequeathed the house, its contents (an exquisite collection of books, paintings, and porcelain), and 26 acres of grounds to Johns Hopkins University. He required that the estate remain open to "lovers of music, art, and beautiful things." A tour of the mansion is a fascinating look at the luxury that surrounded a rich American family at the turn of the 20th century. ⊠ *4545 N. Charles St., Homeland* ☎ *410/516–0341* 🖃 *$8* 🕙 *Tues.–Fri. 11–4, weekends noon–4.*

Homewood House Museum. This elegant Federal-period mansion was once the home of Charles Carroll Jr., son of Charles Carroll of Carrollton, a signer of the Declaration of Independence. Deeded to Johns Hopkins University in 1902 along with 60 acres, the house served as faculty club and offices before being fully restored to its 1800 grandeur (it's one of the finest examples of the neoclassical architecture of the period). ⊠ *3400 N. Charles St., Charles Village* ☎ *410/516–5589* 🖃 *$8* 🕙 *Tues.– Fri. 11–4, weekends noon–4.*

Johns Hopkins University. The school was founded in 1876 with funds donated by Johns Hopkins, director of the Baltimore & Ohio Railroad. Much of the neo-Colonial architecture of the Homewood campus dates from the early 1900s, when the present-day campus was laid out. Dominating the school's main quad is Gilman Hall, which was built in 1904 and named for the university's first president, Daniel Coit Gilman. Pathways lead through campus; maps throughout can help you find your way. The medical school and hospital are in East Baltimore. ⊠ *3400 N. Charles St., Charles Village* ☎ *410/516–8000* ⊕ *www.jhu.edu.*

WORTH NOTING

Lacrosse Museum and National Hall of Fame. Photos, objects, and videos tell the story of the history of lacrosse, a very popular sport in Maryland. One room is dedicated to outstanding players who have been honored by the U.S. Lacrosse Association since 1957. ⊠ *113 W. University Pkwy., Tuscany-Canterbury* ☎ *410/235–6882* ⊕ *www.uslacrosse.org* 🖃 *$3* 🕙 *June–Jan., weekdays 10–3; Feb.–May, Tues.–Sat. 10–3.*

Lovely Lane Methodist Church. Built in 1882, Lovely Lane Methodist Church is honored with the title "The Mother Church of American Methodism." Stanford White designed the Romanesque sanctuary after the basilicas of Ravenna, Italy; the stained-glass windows are excellent examples of Italian mosaic art. The buildings to the north that resemble the church are the original campus of the Women's College of Baltimore, now called Goucher College (the school moved to Towson in the 1950s). Dr. Goucher, the college's founder, was a pastor at Lovely Lane. Today the building next to the church is occupied by the Baltimore Lab School. Tours of the church and the Methodist Historical Society are by appointment. ⊠ *2200 St. Paul St., North Charles* ☎ *410/889–1512* ⊕ *www.lovelylane.net* 🕙 *Weekdays 9–3.*

QUICK BITES

With great vegetarian food, cocktails, and doors that stay open until 2 am every day but Sunday, it's no surprise that students love the **One World Cafe** (⊠ *100 W. University Pkwy., North Charles* ☎ *410/235–5777*). In summer, take advantage of the café's sidewalk seating.

Sherwood Gardens. A popular spring destination for Baltimore families, this 6-acre park contains more than 80,000 tulips that bloom in late

8

April. Azaleas peak in late April and the first half of May. The gardens are usually at their best around Mother's Day. ⊠ *Stratford Rd. at Greenway, east of St. Paul St., Guilford* ▨ *Free* ⊗ *Daily dawn–dusk.*

INNER HARBOR/DOWNTOWN

The Inner Harbor has come a long way in the past 20-odd years. Before it was transformed into the city's biggest destination, the harbor consisted mostly of run-down warehouses. Now it includes the National Aquarium, Harborplace shopping centers, the Maryland Science Center, fountains, and high-rise offices. Oriole Park at Camden Yards and M&T Bank Stadium, where the NFL's Ravens play, are only a couple of blocks away. The harbor is still a working port, and visitors can get on the water with sailboat tours, water taxis, and boat rentals. Just south of the Inner Harbor and best accessed by car or water taxi, Fort McHenry was bombarded by the British during the War of 1812. Despite a long night's siege by cannon and artillery the fort never fell, and the sight of the American flag flying above the walls inspired Francis Scott Key to pen a poem that became the national anthem.

TOP ATTRACTIONS

Fodor's Choice
★
American Visionary Art Museum. The nation's primary museum and education center for self-taught or "outsider" art has won great acclaim by both museum experts and those who don't even consider themselves art aficionados. Seven galleries exhibit the quirky creations—paintings, sculptures, relief works, and pieces that defy easy classification—of untrained "visionary" artists working outside the mainstream art world. In addition to the visual stimulation of amazingly intricate or refreshingly inventive works, reading the short bios of artists will give you insight to their often-moving spiritual and expressive motivations. The museum's unusual, playful philosophy extends outside its walls, with large exhibits installed in a former whiskey warehouse and a 55-foot whirligig twirling in the museum's plaza. ⊠ *800 Key Hwy., Federal Hill* ☎ *410/244–1900* ⊕ *www.avam.org* ▨ *$12* ⊗ *Tues.–Sun. 10–6.*

☾ **Historic Ships in Baltimore.** Consisting of three docked vessels and a restored lighthouse, this museum gives a good sense of Baltimore's maritime heritage as well as American naval power. On the west side of the pier, the submarine USS *Torsk,* the "Galloping Ghost of the Japanese Coast," is credited with sinking the last two Japanese warships in World War II. The lightship *Chesapeake,* built as a floating lighthouse in 1930 and now out of commission, remains fully operational. The *Taney* is a Coast Guard cutter that saw action at Pearl Harbor. Built in 1856 the Seven Foot Knoll Lighthouse marked the entrance to Baltimore Harbor from the Chesapeake Bay for 133 years before its move to the museum. ⊠ *Pier 1, 301 E. Pratt St., Inner Harbor* ☎ *410/539–1797* ⊕ *www. historicships.org* ▨ *$10–$18* ⊗ *All boats and the lighthouse open at 10 am year-round (except Jan.–Feb., when the Torsk and the Lighthouse are closed weekdays); closing time varies by attraction and by month.*

☾ **Baltimore Museum of Industry.** Housed in an 1865 oyster cannery, the fascinating and kid-friendly Baltimore Museum of Industry covers the city's industrial and labor history and is well worth the 0.5-mi walk south of the Inner Harbor along Key Highway. Here you can watch and help operate the functional re-creations of a machine shop circa 1900, a print shop, a cannery, and a garment workroom. A restored steam-driven tugboat that plied the waterfront for the first half of the 20th century is docked outside. ⊠ *1415 Key Hwy., Federal Hill* ☎ *410/727–4808* ⊕ *www.thebmi.org* 🔖 *$10* ⊙ *Tues.–Sat. 10–4, Sun. 11–4.*

★ **Federal Hill Park**. If you want to snap a photo of the Inner Harbor, Federal Hill Park is the place to do it. On the south side of the harbor, the park was named in 1788 to commemorate Maryland's ratification of the U.S. Constitution. Until the early 1900s, a signal tower atop Federal Hill displayed the "house" flags of local shipping companies, notifying them of the arrival of their vessels. Some of the oldest homes in Baltimore surround the park, and its summit provides an excellent view of the Inner Harbor and the downtown skyline. The park is also a favorite spot for watching holiday fireworks. ⊠ *Battery Ave. and Key Hwy., Federal Hill.*

Fodor'sChoice
★ **Fort McHenry**. This star-shaped brick fort is forever associated with Francis Scott Key and "The Star-Spangled Banner," which Key penned while watching the British bombardment of Baltimore during the War of 1812. Key had been detained onboard a truce ship, where he had been negotiating the release of one Dr. William Beanes, when the bombardment began; Key knew too much about the attack plan to be released. Through the next day and night, as the battle raged, Key strained to be sure, through the smoke and haze, that the flag still flew above Fort McHenry—indicating that Baltimore's defenders held firm. "By the dawn's early light" of September 14, 1814, he saw the 30- by 42-foot "Star-Spangled Banner" still aloft and was inspired to pen the words to a poem (set to the tune of an old English drinking song). The flag that flew above Fort McHenry that day had 15 stars and 15 stripes, and was hand-sewn for the fort. A visit to the fort includes a 15-minute history film, guided tour, and frequent living-history displays on summer weekends. To see how the formidable fortifications might have appeared to the bombarding British, catch a water taxi from the Inner Harbor to the fort instead of driving. ⊠ *E. Fort Ave., from Light St., take Key Hwy. for 1½ mi and follow signs, Locust Point* ☎ *410/962–4290* ⊕ *www. nps.gov/fomc* 🔖 *$7* ⊙ *Memorial Day–Labor Day, daily 8–8; Labor Day–Memorial Day, daily 8–5.*

Geppi's Entertainment Museum. Fans of comic books and pop culture have plenty to take in at this museum since it opened in 2006. A stone's throw from the baseball park in Camden Yards, it boasts thousands of comic books, toys, and collectibles from as far back as the 1700s. It has won awards from parents and local publications as a destination for kids (and adults with inner kids). For adults, it's a trip down memory lane. Kids will marvel at how their favorite superhero evolved over the years. ⊠ *301 W. Camden St., Inner Harbor* ☎ *410/625–7060* ⊕ *www. geppismuseum.com* 🔖 *$10* ⊙ *Tues.–Sun. 10–6.*

Harborplace and the Gallery. Inside two glass-enclosed marketplaces are a plethora of shops and eateries: the Light Street Pavilion has two stories of food courts and restaurants, and the Pratt Street Pavilion is dedicated mainly to retail stores. More than a dozen restaurants, including Edo Sushi, Phillips, and Tir Na Nog, offer waterfront dining, and such local specialty shops as Best of Baltimore and Maryland Bay Company carry interesting souvenirs. In summer, performers entertain at an outdoor amphitheater between the two pavilions, and paddleboats are available for rent south of the Pratt Street building. A skywalk from the Pratt Street Pavilion leads to **The Gallery**, a four-story shopping mall with 70 more shops, including Bebe, J. Crew, Coach, and Godiva Chocolatiers. ⊠ *100 Pratt St., Inner Harbor* ☎ *410/332–4191* ⊕ *www.harborplace. com* ⊗ *Mon.–Sat. 10–9, Sun. 11–7. Harborplace and the Gallery have extended summer hrs; some restaurants open earlier for breakfast, and most close late.*

Maryland Science Center. Originally known as the Maryland Academy of Sciences, this 200-year-old scientific institution is one of the oldest in the United States. Now housed in a contemporary building, the three floors of exhibits on the Chesapeake Bay, Earth science, physics, the body, dinosaurs, and outer space are an invitation to engage, experiment, and explore. The center has a planetarium, a simulated archaeological dinosaur dig, an IMAX movie theater with a screen five stories high, and a playroom especially designed for young children. ⊠ *601 Light St., Inner Harbor* ☎ *410/685–5225* ⊕ *www.mdsci.org* ⊠ *$14.95* ⊗ *Memorial Day–Labor Day, Thurs.–Sat. 10–8, Sun.–Wed. 10–6; Labor Day– Memorial Day, Tues.–Fri. 10–5, Sat. 10–6, Sun. 11–5.*

National Aquarium in Baltimore. The most-visited attraction in Maryland has more than 10,000 fish, sharks, dolphins, and amphibians dwelling in 2 million gallons of water. The Animal Planet Australia: Wild Extremes exhibit mimics a river running through a gorge. It features lizards, crocodiles, turtles, bats, and a black-headed python, among other animals from Down Under. The aquarium also features reptiles, birds, plants, and mammals in its rain-forest environment, inside a glass pyramid 64 feet high. The rain-forest ecosystem harbors two-toed sloths in calabash trees, parrots in the palms, iguanas on the ground, and red-bellied piranhas in a pool (a sign next to it reads "do not put hands in pool"). Each day in the Marine Mammal Pavilion, Atlantic bottlenose dolphins are part of several entertaining presentations that highlight their agility and intelligence. The aquarium's famed shark tank and Atlantic coral reef exhibits are spectacular; you can wind through an enormous glass enclosure on a spiral ramp while hammerheads and brightly hued tropical fish glide by. Hands-on exhibits include such docile sea creatures as horseshoe crabs and starfish. ■ TIP➔ **Arrive early to ensure admission, which is by timed intervals; by noon, the wait is often two or three hours.** ⊠ *Pier 3, Inner Harbor* ☎ *410/576–3800* ⊕ *www. aqua.org* ⊠ *$24.95* ⊗ *Nov.–Feb., Sat.–Thurs. 10–5, Fri. 10–8; Mar.– June, Sept., and Oct., Sat.–Thurs. 9–5, Fri. 9–8; July–Aug. 19, daily 9–8; Aug. 20–31, Sat.–Thurs. 9–6, Fri. 9–8; visitors may tour for up to 1½ hrs after closing. Timed tickets may be required on weekends and holidays; purchase these early in the day.*

Fodor'sChoice

Port Discovery—The Baltimore Children's Museum. At this interactive museum, adults are encouraged to play every bit as much as children. A favorite attraction is the three-story KidWorks, a futuristic jungle gym on which the adventurous can climb, crawl, slide, and swing their way through stairs, slides, ropes, zip lines, and tunnels, and even cross a narrow footbridge three stories up. In Miss Perception's Mystery House, youngsters help solve a mystery surrounding the disappearance of the Baffeld family by sifting through clues; some are written or visual, and others are gleaned by touching and listening. Changing interactive exhibits allow for even more play. ⊠ *35 Market Pl., Inner Harbor* ☎ *410/727-8120* ⊕ *www.portdiscovery.com* ⊠ *$12.95* ☉ *Memorial Day–Labor Day, Mon.–Sat. 10–5, Sun. noon–5; Labor Day–Memorial Day, Tues.–Fri. 9:30–4:30, Sat. 10–5, Sun. noon–5.*

> ### BEST VIEW OF THE INNER HARBOR
>
> From the "Top of the World"—the observation level on the 27th floor of the World Trade Center— you can see for miles in any direction, or peer through binoculars for a closer look. Best free view of the Inner Harbor: Federal Hill Park, across the water from the National Aquarium, offers a good vantage point for photos and picnics.

Reginald F. Lewis Museum of Maryland African American History & Culture. Named for the former CEO of TLC Beatrice International, the Reginald F. Lewis Museum is dedicated to the African-American experience in Maryland. The contemporary, predominantly red-and-black building holds exhibits on African-American history, art, and culture as told through the lives of such individuals as Frederick Douglass, Billie Holiday, and civil rights leader Kweisi Mfume. The collections are divided into three sections: Family and Community, Labor that Built a Nation, and Art and Enlightenment. Facilities include an oral history recording and listening studio and an information resource center. ⊠ *830 E. Pratt St., Inner Harbor* ☎ *443/263-1800* ⊕ *www.africanamericanculture.org* ⊠ *$8* ☉ *Wed.–Sat. 10–5, Sun. noon–5.*

☺ **USS *Constellation*.** Launched in 1854, the USS *Constellation* was the last—and largest—all-sail ship built by the U.S. Navy. Before the Civil War, as part of the African Squadron, she saw service on antislavery patrol; during the war, she protected Union-sympathizing U.S. merchant ships from Confederate raiders. The warship eventually became a training ship for the Navy before serving as the relief flagship for the Atlantic Fleet during World War II, finally arriving in Baltimore in 1955 for restoration to her original condition. You can tour the USS *Constellation* for a glimpse of life as a 19th-century navy sailor, and children can muster to become Civil War–era "powder monkeys." Recruits receive "basic training," try on replica period uniforms, participate in a gun drill, and learn a sea chantey or two before being discharged and paid off in Civil War money at the end of their "cruise." ⊠ *Pratt and Light Sts., Inner Harbor* ☎ *410/539-1797* ⊕ *www.constellation.org* ⊠ *$10* ☉ *Mar.–Oct., daily 10–5:30; Nov.–Feb., daily 10–4:30.*

Visitor Center. Stop by the sweeping, all-glass center for information on the city, brochures, tickets, and hotel and restaurant reservations. ⊠ *401 Light St., Inner Harbor* ☎ *877/225-8466* ⊕ *www.baltimore.org* ☉ *Daily 9–6.*

★ **World Trade Center**. With 32 stories, this building, designed by I. M. Pei's firm, is the world's tallest pentagonal structure. The 27th-floor "Top of the World" observation deck allows an unobstructed view of Baltimore and beyond from a height of 423 feet. ⊠ *401 E. Pratt St., Inner Harbor* ☎ *410/837–8439* ⊕ *www.wtci.org* ☏ *$5* ☽ *Memorial Day–Labor Day, weekdays and Sun. 10–6, Sat. 10–8; Apr., May, Sept., and Oct., Wed.–Sun. 10–6.*

WORTH NOTING

Baltimore City Hall. Built in 1875, Baltimore City Hall consists of mansard roofs and a gilt dome over a 110-foot rotunda, all supported by ironwork. Inside you can get tours of the chambers and view exhibits on Baltimore's history. Directly across the street is **City Hall Plaza,** on what was originally the site of the Holliday Street Theatre. The theater was owned and operated by the Ford brothers; they also operated Ford's Theatre in Washington, D.C., where President Lincoln was assassinated. "The Star-Spangled Banner" was first publicly sung here. ⊠ *100 N. Holliday St., Downtown* ☎ *410/396–3100* ☏ *Free* ☽ *Weekdays 8:30–4:30.*

Baltimore Civil War Museum-President Street Station. President Street Station offers a glimpse of the violence and divided loyalties that the war caused in Maryland, a state caught in the middle. Originally the Baltimore terminus of the Philadelphia, Wilmington & Baltimore Railroad, the relocated station, built in 1849, contains exhibits that depict the events that led to mob violence. It began when troops from the Sixth Massachusetts Regiment bound for Washington, D.C., walked from this station to the Camden Station (near Oriole Park). In what would be the first bloodshed of the Civil War, four soldiers and 12 civilians were killed; 36 soldiers and a number of civilians were wounded. The riot lasted for several hours and inspired the secessionist poem "Maryland, My Maryland," today the state song. ⊠ *601 President St., Inner Harbor East* ☎ *410/461–9377* ⊕ *www.angelfire.com/biz/presidentststation* ☏ *Free* ☽ *Weekends 10–5, tours available by appointment.*

Carroll Mansion. This was once the winter home of Charles Carroll, one of the signers of the Declaration of Independence. It's now a museum dedicated to the history of the city and the neighborhood, Historic Jonestown, as told by the various occupants of the house through the years. ⊠ *800 E. Lombard St., Historic Jonestown* ☎ *410/605–2964* ⊕ *www.carrollmuseums.org* ☏ *$5* ☽ *Sat.–Sun. noon–4 and by appointment.*

Jewish Museum of Maryland. Sandwiched between two 19th-century synagogues, the Jewish Museum of Maryland has changing exhibits of art, photography, and documents related to the Jewish experience in Maryland. The Lloyd Street Synagogue, to the left of the museum was built in 1845 and was the first in Maryland and the third in the United States. The other, B'nai Israel, was built in 1876 in a uniquely Moorish style. Tours of both synagogues are available. ⊠ *15 Lloyd St., Historic Jonestown* ☎ *410/732–6400* ⊕ *www.jewishmuseummd.org* ☏ *$4* ☽ *Tues.–Thurs. and Sun. noon–4 and by appointment.*

Nine Front Street. This cute two-story brick town house, built in 1790, was once the home of Mayor Thorowgood Smith, the second mayor of Baltimore. The Women's Civic League, which has its home here, gives tours of the house and of city hall; call for an appointment. ✉ *9 Front St., Historic Jonestown* ☎ *410/837–5424* ⊙ *Tues.–Thurs. 9–2:30, Fri. 9–2; call ahead.*

Phoenix Shot Tower. The only remaining tower of three of this type that once existed in Baltimore, this brick structure was used to make shot pellets by pouring molten lead from the top. As the drops fell, they formed balls that turned solid in cold water at the bottom. In the summer months the tower may close due to heat. ✉ *801 E. Fayette St., Historic Jonestown* ☎ *410/605–2964* ⊙ *Tours, leaving from Carroll Mansion, offered Sat.–Sun. at 4.*

☾ **The Power Plant.** What actually was the city's former power plant is now a retail and dining complex that includes a Hard Rock Cafe and a Barnes & Noble. Next door is the **Pier 4 Building,** which houses a Chipotle Mexican Grill and Blu Bamboo, a fast-casual Mongolian grill. The cutting-edge **Maryland Art Place** (✉ *8 Market Pl., Suite 100, Inner Harbor* ☎ *410/962–8565* ⊕ *www.mdartplace.org* ✍ *Free* ⊙ *Tues.–Sat. 11–5*) gallery highlights works by contemporary local and regional artists. ✉ *Pier 5, 601 E. Pratt St., Inner Harbor* ☎ *No phone.*

QUICK BITES | Espresso, cannolis, and other delicious Italian pastries can be found at **Vaccaro's** (✉ *222 Albemarle St., Little Italy* ☎ *410/685–4905*). **Whole Foods** (✉ *1001 Fleet St., Inner Harbor East* ☎ *410/528–1640*) has tables and chairs inside and out for eating pre-made sandwiches, sushi, and salads.

Star-Spangled Banner House. Built in 1793, this Federal-style home was where Mary Pickersgill hand-sewed the 15-star, 15-stripe flag that survived the British bombardment of Fort McHenry in 1814 and inspired Francis Scott Key to write "The Star-Spangled Banner." The house contains Federal furniture and American art of the period, including pieces from the Pickersgill family. Outdoors, a map of the United States has been made of stones from the various states. A museum connected to the house tells the history of the War of 1812. ✉ *844 E. Pratt St., Historic Jonestown* ☎ *410/837–1793* ⊕ *www.flaghouse.org* ✍ *$7* ⊙ *Tues.–Sat. 10–4.*

FELLS POINT

Fells Point is a gathering ground for blue- and white-collar locals and tourists. Plenty of bars and small craft shops line Broadway, running north–south, and Thames (pronounced with a long "a" and thick "th"), running east–west along the water. Head here in the afternoon and tour the shops and two small museums; afterward stay for dinner and drinks at one of the neighborhood's many pubs—most of which host live local bands daily. From the Inner Harbor it takes about five minutes to reach Fells Point by car. You can also opt for the water taxi, a much more fun way to get there.

Standing in the heart of Fells Point, you get the feeling little has changed since it was founded several hundred years ago. Englishman William Fell purchased the peninsula in 1726, seeing its potential for shipbuilding and shipping. Starting in 1763 his son Edward and his wife, Ann

Bond Fell, divided and sold the land; docks, shipyards, warehouses, stores, homes, churches, and schools sprang up, and the area quickly grew into a bustling seaport. Fells Point was famed for its shipyards (the notoriously speedy clipper ships built here annoyed the British so much during the War of 1812 that they tried to capture the city, a move resulting in Fort McHenry's bombardment). Frederick Douglass worked at a shipyard at the end of Thames Street in the 1830s. Around the 1840s the shipbuilding industry started to decline, in large part because of the rise of steamships, which were being constructed elsewhere.

TOP ATTRACTIONS

Broadway Market. Head to the market's two pavilions to grab a drink or light snack or stock up on ethnic deli meats. You can also find pizza, sandwiches, and oysters at a raw bar. ⊠ *Broadway between Fleet and Lancaster Sts., Fells Point.*

Fells Point Maritime Museum. For the history of the shipbuilding industry in Fells Point and the people involved in it, go to this small museum. You can find out about the speedy Baltimore clipper schooners, which once made this area famous; the cargoes they carried; and the shipbuilders, merchants, and sailors who sought their fortunes. ⊠ *1724 Thames St., Fells Point* ☎ *410/732–0278* ⊕ *www.mdhs.org* ✉ *$4* ۩ *Thurs.–Mon. 10–5.*

Fell's Point Visitor Center. Be sure to take a neighborhood walking tour brochure from the gift shop. The tours depart from here on Friday evening and Saturday morning (April–October) and focus on topics such as ghosts, the War of 1812, mritime history, or slavery and Frederick Douglass's tenure in Fells Point. ⊠ *808 S. Ann St., Fells Point* ☎ *410/675–6750 Ext. 16* ⊕ *www.preservationsociety.com* ۩ *Apr.–Nov. 25, Sun.–Thurs. 10–5, Fri. and Sat. 10–8; Nov. 26–Mar., Tues.–Sun. noon–4.*

QUICK BITES

The Daily Grind (⊠ *1720 Thames St., Fells Point* ☎ *410/558–0399*) is the neighborhood spot for coffee and Wi-Fi.

Robert Long House Museum. The city's oldest residence still standing, this small brick house was built in 1765 as both home and business office for Robert Long, a merchant and quartermaster for the Continental Navy who operated a wharf on the waterfront. Furnished with Revolutionary War–era pieces, the parlor, bedroom, and office seem as if Long himself just stepped away. A fragrant, flowering herb garden flourishes in warm months. ⊠ *812 S. Ann St., Fells Point* ☎ *410/675–6750* ⊕ *www.preservationsociety.com* ✉ *$3* ۩ *Tours daily Apr.–Nov. at 1 and 2:30.*

WEST BALTIMORE

Though some sections are still dodgy, Baltimore's West Side is undergoing a much-needed transformation for the better. A multimillion-dollar renovation turned the old Hippodrome movie house and its neighboring buildings into an elegant performing arts center. Up and down Eutaw and Howard streets, once-abandoned buildings are being converted into high-end loft apartments.

But the neighborhood's most popular draws are the Oriole Park at
Camden Yards and M&T Bank
Stadium, where the Baltimore
Ravens football team plays. West
Baltimore is also home to birthplaces and former residences of
historic figures such as Babe Ruth,
Edgar Allan Poe, and Charles Carroll, a member of the Continental
Congress. The University of Maryland medical campus, including
the Dr. Samuel D. Harris National
Museum of Dentistry, occupies a
large swath of the neighborhood.

> ## WEST BALTIMORE TIPS
>
> Set aside several hours for a tour
> of West Baltimore, and at least a
> half-hour for lunch at Lexington
> Market. Because the sights are
> scattered throughout the neigh-
> borhood and the streets are less
> safe than those in downtown Bal-
> timore, parts of this area are best
> visited by car. It's safer to avoid
> walking through West Baltimore
> alone at night.

A few blocks west of the school, the B&O Railroad Museum, with
more than 100 trains on display, is captivating to most small children
(and the inner kid in train-loving adults).

TOP ATTRACTIONS

Babe Ruth Birthplace and Museum. This plain brick row house, three blocks
from Oriole Park at Camden Yards, was the birthplace of "the Bam-
bino." Although Ruth was born here in 1895, his family never lived
here; they lived in a nearby apartment, above a tavern run by Ruth's
father. The row house and the adjoining buildings make up a museum
devoted to Ruth's life and to the local Orioles baseball club. Film
clips and props, rare photos of Ruth, Yankees payroll checks, a score
book from Ruth's first professional game, and many other artifacts
can be found here. ⊠ *216 Emory St., West Baltimore* ☎ *410/727–1539*
⊕ *www.baberuthmuseum.com* ✉ *$6* ☉ *Apr.–Oct., daily 10–5, until 7
before Oriole home games; Nov.–Mar., daily 10–5.*

B&O Railroad Museum. The famous Baltimore & Ohio Railroad was
★ founded on the site that now houses this museum, which contains more
than 120 full-size locomotives and a great collection of railroad memorabilia, from dining-car china and artwork to lanterns and signals. The
1884 roundhouse (240 feet in diameter and 120 feet high) adjoins one
of the nation's first railroad stations. Train rides are available every day
but Monday. The Iron Horse Café serves food and drinks. ⊠ *901 W.
Pratt St., West Baltimore* ☎ *410/752–2490* ⊕ *www.borail.org* ✉ *$14*
☉ *Mon.–Sat. 10–4, Sun. 11–4.*

M&T Bank Stadium. The Baltimore Ravens football team hosts home games
in this state-of-the-art stadium from August to January. ⊠ *1101 Russell St., West Baltimore* ☎ *410/261–7283* ⊕ *www.baltimoreravens.com.*

Oriole Park at Camden Yards. Home of the Baltimore Orioles, Camden
★ Yards and the nearby area bustle on game days. Since it opened in 1992,
this nostalgically designed baseball stadium has inspired other cities to
emulate its neotraditional architecture and amenities. The Eutaw Street
promenade, between the warehouse and the field, has a view of the
stadium; look for the brass baseballs embedded in the sidewalk that
mark where home runs have cleared the fence, or visit the Orioles Hall

8

of Fame display and the monuments to retired Orioles. Daily 90-minute tours take you to nearly every section of the ballpark, from the massive, JumboTron scoreboard to the dugout to the state-of-the-art beer-delivery system. ✉ *333 W. Camden St., Downtown* ☎ *410/685–9800 general information; 410/547–6234 tour times; 888/848–2473 tickets to Orioles home games* ⊕ *www.theorioles.com* ✆ *Eutaw St. promenade free; tour $7* ☉ *Eutaw St. promenade daily 10–3, otherwise during games and tours; tours Mar.–Sept., Mon.–Sat. at 11, noon, 1, and 2; Oct., weekdays at 11:30 and 1:30, Sat. at 11, noon, 1, and 2, Sun. at 12:30, 1, 2, and 3; Nov., Mon.–Sat. at 11:30 and 1:30, Sun. at 12:30 and 2:30.*

Westminster Cemetery and Catacombs. The city's oldest cemetery is the final resting place of Edgar Allan Poe and other famous Marylanders, including 15 generals from the American Revolution and the War of 1812. Dating from 1786, the cemetery was originally known as the Old Western Burying Grounds. In the early 1850s a city ordinance demanded that burial grounds be part of a church, so a building was constructed above the cemetery, creating catacombs beneath it. In the 1930s the schoolchildren of Baltimore collected pennies to raise the necessary funds for Poe's monument. Each year on Poe's birthday a mysterious stranger leaves three roses and a bottle of cognac on the writer's grave. ✉ *W. Fayette and Greene Sts., Downtown* ☎ *No Phone* ☉ *Daily 8–dusk.*

WORTH NOTING

Davidge Hall. Built in 1812 for $35,000, this green-dome structure has been used for teaching medicine for nearly two centuries. Part of the downtown campus of the University of Maryland at Baltimore, Davidge Hall is a relic of the days when dissection was illegal; the acoustically perfect anatomy theater was lighted by skylights instead of windows so that passersby would not witness students working on cadavers. ✉ *522 W. Lombard St., West Baltimore* ☎ *410/706–7454* ✆ *Free* ☉ *Weekdays 8:30–4:45.*

Dr. Samuel D. Harris National Museum of Dentistry. This unusual museum, which has a set of George Washington's dentures, is on the Baltimore campus of the University of Maryland, the world's first dental school. Housed in a Renaissance Revival–style building, the museum has exhibits on the anatomy and physiology of human and animal teeth and the history of dentistry; you can also play a tune on the "Tooth Jukebox." One popular exhibit displays the dental instruments used in treating Queen Victoria in the mid-19th century. ✉ *31 S. Greene St., West Baltimore* ☎ *410/706–0600* ✆ *$7* ☉ *Wed.–Sat. 10–4, Sun. 1–4.*

Mount Clare Museum House. One of the oldest houses in Baltimore, this elegant mansion was begun in 1754. It was the home of Charles Carroll, author of the Maryland Declaration of Independence, member of the Continental Congress, and one of Maryland's major landowners. The state's first historic museum house has been carefully restored to its Georgian elegance; more than 80% of the 18th-century furniture and artifacts, including rare pieces of Chippendale and Hepplewhite silver, crystal, and Chinese export porcelain, were owned and used by the Carroll family. Washington, Lafayette, and John Adams were all guests here. The greenhouses are famous in their own right: they provided rare trees and plants for Mount Vernon. ✉ *1500 Washington Blvd., Southwest Baltimore* ☎ *410/837–3262* ⊕ *www.mountclare.org* 🎫 *$6* ⏱ *Tues.–Sat. 10–4; tours every hr until 3.*

Poe House. Though the "Master of the Macabre" lived in this tiny row house only three years, he wrote "MS Found in a Bottle" and his first horror story, "Berenice," in the tiny garret chamber that's now furnished in an early-19th-century style. Besides visiting this room, you can view changing exhibits and a video presentation about Poe's short, tempestuous life. Because of the possibility of crime, it's best to visit this neighborhood during daylight hours as part of a group. ✉ *203 N. Amity St., West Baltimore* ☎ *410/396–7932* ⊕ *www.eapoe.org/balt/ poehse.htm* 🎫 *$4* ⏱ *Thurs.–Fri. noon–3:30; Sat. noon–3:45; call ahead.*

<table>
<tr><td>

**QUICK
BITES**

</td><td>

Lexington Market (✉ *400 W. Lexington St., West Baltimore* ☎ *410/685– 6169*) is in a slightly sketchy area, but a trip there for Faidley's crab cakes and other famous food is definitely worth it. **Trinacria Foods** (✉ *406 N. Paca. St., West Baltimore* ☎ *410/685–7285*) is an authentic Italian grocery store a few blocks from Lexington Market that sells meat, cheese, fresh-baked bread, pastries, and wine. There's no better sandwich in the area.

</td></tr>
</table>

DRUID HILL PARK

The areas surrounding Druid Hill Park—the largest park in Baltimore and the third oldest landscaped park in America—actually encompasses parts of several neighborhoods, including Reservoir Hill and Wood-berry. The park itself includes some of the city's best attractions, including the Maryland Zoo, the Howard Peters Rawlings Conservatory and Botanic Gardens, an 18-hole disc golf course, and the beginning of the Jones Falls Trail, the best route for hiking and biking within city limits. The surrounding areas include some of the areas best and oldest examples of Victorian architecture.

TOP ATTRACTIONS

☺ **Baltimore Streetcar Museum**. This often-overlooked museum lets you travel back to an era when streetcars dominated city thoroughfares. A film traces the vehicle's evolution, there are beautifully restored streetcars to explore, and, best of all, you can take unlimited rides. ■ TIP➜ **Come in December and ride to "The North Pole" (nearby piles of street salt) to visit with Santa!** ✉ *1901 Falls Rd., Midtown* ☎ *410/547–0264* ⊕ *www. baltimorestreetcar.org* 🎫 *$7; $5 children and seniors* ⏱ *June–Oct., weekends noon–5; Nov.–May, Sun. noon–5.*

☺ **Maryland Zoo in Baltimore**. The 150 acres of the Maryland Zoo in Baltimore—the third-oldest zoo in the country—are a natural stomping ground for little ones seeking out the spectacle of elephants, lions, giraffes, hippos, and penguins, among the more than 2,000 animals that make this their home. Favorite spots include the giraffe-feeding station, the polar bear arctic pool, and a petting zoo with a re-created barnyard. Also, don't miss the new (opened in 2010) Jones Falls Zephyr, a locomotive modeled on an 1863 locomotive that takes visitors on

8

a 10-minute ride alongside the African Journey exhibit. ■TIP→ **Book online and save $2 per ticket.** Surrounding the zoo is grand, leafy Druid Hill Park, which was designed by Frederick Law Olmsted Jr. ⊠ *Druid Hill Lake Dr., Druid Hill* ☎ *410/366–5466* ⊕ *www.marylandzoo.org* ✉ *$16 on weekdays; $16 weekends ($10; $11 for children)* ⊙ *Mar.– Dec., daily 10–4.*

WHERE TO EAT

Baltimore loves crabs. Soft- or hard-shell crabs, crab cakes, crab dip— the city's passion for clawed crustaceans seems to have no end. Flag down a Baltimore native and ask them where the best crab joint is and you'll get dozens of different options. In addition to crabs and seafood, Baltimore's restaurant landscape includes Afghan, Greek, American, tapas, and other ethnic cuisines. The city's dining choices may not compare to those of New York, or even Washington, but it does have some real standouts and surprises.

Since most of the Inner Harbor only has chain and hotel restaurants, you'll want to head north up Charles Street to Mount Vernon—the city's center for fine dining. Or, you can go south down Light Street to try Federal Hill's trendy pubs, sushi bars, and bistros. A few blocks east of the Inner Harbor, Little Italy has a host of Italian restaurants, most of which serve classic southern Italian, spaghetti-with-garlic-bread fare. Yet father east, Fells Point has some renowned local restaurants. Charles Village, near Johns Hopkins University, and Hampden, just west, also have some funky casual options. Note that most places generally stop serving by 10 pm, if not earlier.

WHAT IT COSTS				
¢	$	$$	$$$	$$$$
At dinner	under $10	$10–$16	$17–$23	$24–$30	over $30

Prices are per person for a main course at dinner.

MOUNT VERNON

$$$

AMERICAN

✕ **Abacrombie.** When new owners took over Abacrombie, local foodies wondered if they could sustain the high standards set by previous chef Sonny Sweetman. They have. Patrons of the nearby opera house and symphony hall still flock to the simple, elegant basement dining room for seafood dishes, rich traditional entrées, and lighter fusion fare. Highlights include the lamb served with mint chutney rather than mint jelly, smashed chickpeas, and deep-fried potato wedges. The milk-chocolate panna cotta is a tasty way to top off a meal. If you can, ask to sit in the skylighted atrium section. Hosts and servers are skillful and accommodating—even during the crush of pre-opera customers. Under its new leadership, Abacrombie is undoubtedly still one of the city's best restaurants. ⊠ *58 W. Biddle St., Mount Vernon* ☎ *410/837–3630*

⊕ *www.abacrombie.net* ⚘ *Reservations essential* ▤ *AE, D, DC, MC, V* ✆ *Closed Mon.–Wed.* ✢ *1B.*

$ ╳ **Akbar.** A few steps below street level, this small restaurant is usu-
INDIAN ally crowded and always filled with pungent aromas and the sounds of Indian music. Among the vegetarian dishes, *alu gobi masala,* a potato-and-cauliflower creation, is prepared with onions, tomatoes, and spices. Tandoori chicken is marinated in yogurt, herbs, and strong spices, then barbecued in a charcoal-fired clay oven. Akbar also makes a good choice for Sunday brunch. ✉ *823 N. Charles St., Mount Vernon* ☎ *410/539–0944* ⊕ *www.akbar-restaurant.com* ▤ *AE, D, DC, MC, V* ✢ *2C.*

$$ ╳ **The Brewer's Art.** Part brewpub, part restaurant, and part lounge, this
AMERICAN spot in a redone mansion feels young but urbane, with an ambitious menu, a clever wine list, and the Belgian-style beers it brews itself: try the potent, delicious Resurrection ale. The upstairs dining room serves seasonal dishes with high-quality, locally available ingredients to create European-style country fare that is both hearty and sophisticated. In the dungeonlike downstairs dining room and bar the menu and decor are more casual. Made with rosemary and garlic, the classic steak frites are a best bet. ✉ *1106 N. Charles St., Mount Vernon* ☎ *410/547–6925* ⊕ *www.belgianbeer.com* ▤ *AE, D, DC, MC, V* ✢ *1C.*

$ ╳ **City Cafe.** The lofty space and black-and-white tile floors give this
AMERICAN casual spot a feeling of classic grandeur. Come here for basic American fare—sandwiches, salads, pasta, big brunches—and stick to that: the more creative, ambitious attempts on the menu often fall short. But City Cafe handles breakfast, lunch, and dinner staples with ease—a feat of flexibility few Baltimore restaurants can match. The service could be sharper, but the seasonal items hit the spot. In summer the frozen cappuccino is a sweet, creamy treat. ✉ *1001 Cathedral St., Mount Vernon* ☎ *410/539–4252* ⊕ *www.citycafebaltimore.com* ▤ *AE, D, DC, MC, V* ✢ *1C.*

$–$$ ╳ **Donna's.** Basic black and light wood are the backdrop for this casual
AMERICAN American café and restaurant, part of a local chain (other locations are on St. Paul Street in Charles Village and in Cross Keys in Roland Park). For breakfast, bagels and muffins are served on weekdays and brunch is available on weekends; sandwiches, soups, and salads are the lunchtime offerings; dinner might include balsamic-glazed salmon, herb chicken breast with artichoke hearts, or a daily pasta dish. You can also just stop in for a cup of coffee any time of the day. ✉ *800 N. Charles St., Mount Vernon* ☎ *410/385–0180* ⊕ *www.donnas.com* ▤ *AE, D, MC, V* ✢ *2C.*

$–$$ ╳ **The Helmand.** Owned by Hamid Kharzai's brother, Qayum Karzai,
MIDDLE EASTERN Helmand serves outstanding Afghan fare in a casual yet elegant space.
Fodor's Choice Beautiful woven textiles and traditional dresses adorn the walls, adding
★ color to the simple white table settings. Try one of the many outstanding lamb dishes such as *sabzy challow* (spinach sautéed with chunks of lamb) or the vegetarian *aushak* (Afghan ravioli). For starters, *kaddo,* a sweet-and-pungent pumpkin dish, is unforgettable. ✉ *806 N. Charles St., Mount Vernon* ☎ *410/752–0311* ⊕ *www.helmand.com* ▤ *AE, DC, MC, V* ✆ *No lunch* ✢ *2C.*

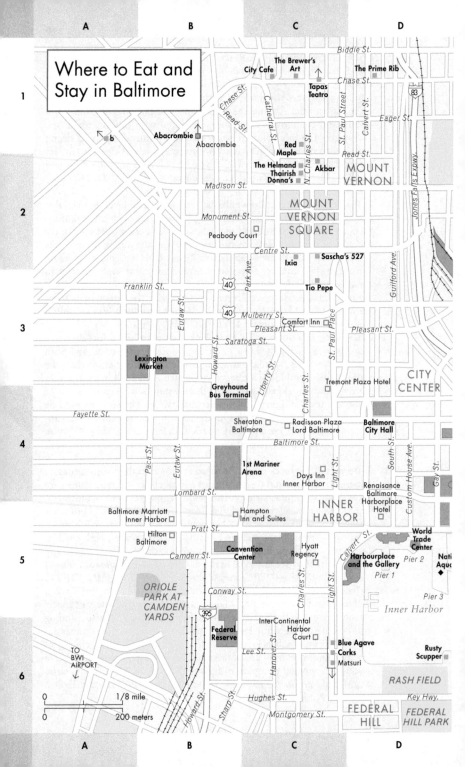

Where to Eat and Stay in Baltimore

Biddle St.

City Cafe
The Brewer's Art
The Prime Rib
Chase St.
Tapas Teatro

b
Abacrombie
Abacrombie

Read St.
Chase St.

Eager St.

83

Read St.

Red Maple
The Helmand
Thairish
Donna's
Akbar

MOUNT VERNON

Madison St.

MOUNT VERNON SQUARE

Monument St.

Peabody Court

Centre St.
Ixia
Sascha's 527

Franklin St.
40

Tia Pepe

40
Mulberry St.
Comfort Inn
Pleasant St.
Pleasant St.
Saratoga St.

Lexington Market

Greyhound Bus Terminal

Tremont Plaza Hotel

CITY CENTER

Fayette St.

Sheraton Baltimore
Radisson Plaza Lord Baltimore
Baltimore City Hall

Baltimore St.

1st Mariner Arena
Days Inn Inner Harbor

Renaisance Baltimore Harborplace Hotel

Lombard St.

Baltimore Marriott Inner Harbor
Hampton Inn and Suites

INNER HARBOR

Hilton Baltimore

Pratt St.

World Trade Center

Camden St.
Convention Center
Hyatt Regency
Harbourplace and the Gallery
Pier 2
Nati Aqu

ORIOLE PARK AT CAMDEN YARDS

Conway St.

395

Pier 1

Pier 3

Inner Harbor

InterContinental Harbor Court

Federal Reserve

Lee St.
Blue Agave
Corks
Matsuri

Rusty Scupper

TO BWI AIRPORT

RASH FIELD

0   1/8 mile
0   200 meters

Hughes St.
Montgomery St.

Key Hwy.

FEDERAL HILL

FEDERAL HILL PARK

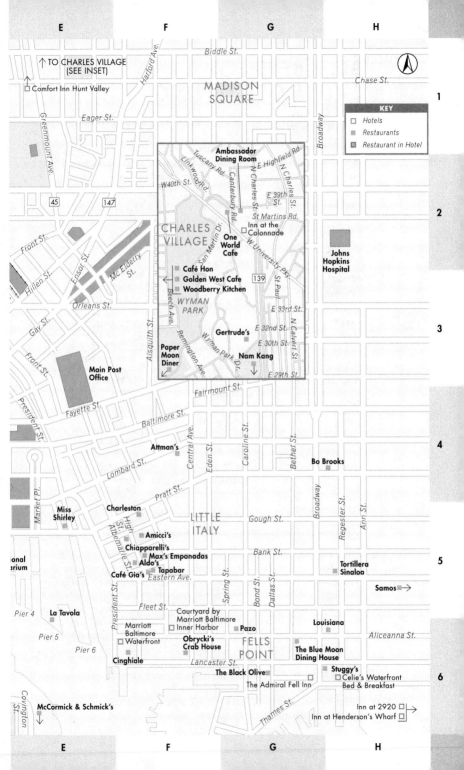

E   F   G   H

Biddle St.

↑ TO CHARLES VILLAGE
(SEE INSET)

□ Comfort Inn Hunt Valley

Chase St.

MADISON
SQUARE

Eager St.

Greenmount Ave.

Hatford Ave.

Broadway

KEY
□ Hotels
■ Restaurants
■ Restaurant in Hotel

1

Front St.

45   147

Mc Elderry St.

Ensor St.

W40th St.

Tuscany Rd.

Linkwood Rd.

Canterbury Rd.

N Charles St.

E Highfield Rd.

N. Charles St.

**Ambassador
Dining Room**

E 39th
St.

St Martins Rd.

**Inn at the
Colonnade**

2

Hillen St.

Orleans St.

Gay St.

CHARLES
VILLAGE

San Martin Dr.

Beech Ave.

W. University Pkwy.

St. Paul

■ **One
World
Cafe**

■ **Café Hon**
■ **Golden West Cafe**
■ **Woodberry Kitchen**

←

**WYMAN
PARK**

139

Johns
Hopkins
Hospital

E 33rd St.

Front St.

Aisquith St.

Remington Ave.

Wyman Park Dr.

Gertrude's

**Paper
Moon
Diner**

□

Nam Kang

E 32nd St.

N. Calvert St.

E 30th St.

E 29th St.

3

**Main Post
Office**

Fairmount St.

President St.

Fayette St.

Baltimore St.

Central Ave.

Eden St.

Caroline St.

Bethel St.

Attman's

Bo Brooks

4

Market Pl.

**Miss
Shirley**

Lombard St.

Pratt St.

Charleston

High St.

Albemarle St.

LITTLE
ITALY

Gough St.

Broadway

Regester St.

Ann St.

■ **Amicci's**

■ **Chiapparelli's**
■ **Max's Empanadas**
■ **Aldo's**
Café Gia's ■ **Tapabar**

Eastern Ave.

Bank St.

Spring St.

Bond St.

Dallas St.

**Tortillera
Sinaloa**

Samos ■→

5

onal
arium

Pier 4

La Tavola

Pier 5

Pier 6

President St.

Fleet St.

**Marriott
Baltimore
Waterfront** □

Cinghiale

Courtyard by
Marriott Baltimore
□ Inner Harbor

**Obrycki's
Crab House**

Lancaster St.

Pazo

FELLS
POINT

The Black Olive ■

The Admiral Fell Inn

Louisiana

**The Blue Moon
Dining House**

Aliceanna St.

Stuggy's
□ **Celie's Waterfront
Bed & Breakfast**

6

Covington St.

McCormick & Schmick's

Thames St.

Inn at 2920 □→
Inn at Henderson's Wharf □

E   F   G   H

BEST BETS FOR BALTIMORE DINING

Fodor's Choice ★

Charleston, p. 335
The Helmand, p. 329
Pazo, p. 339
The Prime Rib, p. 332
Woodberry Kitchen, p. 335

Best by Price

¢

Attman's, p. 335
Café Hon, p. 335
Golden West Café, p. 335
Max's Empanadas, p. 338
Paper Moon Diner, p. 334
Pazo, p. 339
Stuggy's, p. 339
Tortilleria Sinaloa, p. 339

$

b, p. 334
Café Gia's, p. 338
The Helmand, p. 329
Samos, p. 339

$$

The Brewer's Art, p. 329
Gertrude's, p. 334

McCormick & Schmick, p. 336
Tapas Teatro, p. 333
Woodberry Kitchen, p. 335

$$$

The Black Olive, p. 338
Charleston, p. 335
Cinghiale, p. 336
Corks, p. 337
Tio Pepe, p. 333

$$$$

The Prime Rib, p. 332

Best by Cuisine

AMERICAN

The Brewer's Art, p. 329
Café Hon, p. 335
City Cafe, p. 329
Corks, p. 337
Gertrude's, p. 334
Paper Moon Diner, p. 334
The Prime Rib, p. 332
Woodberry Kitchen, p. 335

ECLECTIC

b, p. 334

Golden West Café, p. 335

GREEK

The Black Olive, p. 338
Samos, p. 339

INDIAN

Akbar, p. 329
Ambassador Dining Room, p. 334

ITALIAN

Café Gia's, p. 338
Cinghiale, p. 336

MEXICAN

Blue Agave, p. 336
Tortilleria Sinaloa, p. 339

SEAFOOD

Bo Brooks, p. 340
McCormick & Scmick, p. 336
Obrycki's Crab House, p. 339
Rusty Scupper, p. 336

SPANISH

Tio Pepe, p. 333
Tapas Teatro, p. 333

$$$$
AMERICAN
Fodor's Choice
★

✕ **The Prime Rib.** Bustling and crowded, this luxuriously dark dining room is just north of Mount Vernon Square and a five-minute drive from the Inner Harbor. Tables are set close together under a low ceiling, keeping things intimate for the bankers and lawyers who often eat here, as well as couples on expensive dates. The leopard-print carpet and live pianist lend a swanky 1960s feel to a place that seems untouched by time. The traditional menu is headed by a superb prime rib and an even better filet mignon; the jumbo lump crab cakes are also great. The wine list is predominantly California-centric. ⊠ *1101 N. Calvert St., Mount Vernon* ☎ *410/539–1804* ⊕ *www.theprimerib.com* ⌔ *Reservations essential* ▭ *AE, D, DC, MC, V* ⊕ *1D.*

$–$$
ASIAN

✕ **Red Maple.** Theatrical, stylish Red Maple doesn't even have a sign out front. Instead, it's only marked with a small maple-tree icon on the front door. Inside, the striking, minimalist space is warmed by a fireplace, candlelight, and sumptuous suede banquettes. The food is equally arresting: Asian-inspired tapas, artfully conceived and beautifully presented. Small plates such as wild mushroom and asparagus dumplings and shrimp and mango tapas are inexpensive, but it's easy to run up your tab because each is so compelling. ✉ *930 N. Charles St., Mount Vernon* ☎ *410/547–0149* ⊕ *www.930redmaple.com* ▭ *AE, DC, MC, V* ⊙ *No lunch* ✛ *1C.*

$–$$
ECLECTIC
✗ **Sascha's 527.** High ceilings, warm yellow walls hung with paintings, and a giant crystal chandelier add drama to this spacious, artsy spot near the Walters. Choose from an eclectic menu of "tastes" (appetizer-size plates), "big plates" (chicken, lamb, or fish) served with a selection of unusual sauces, and other American fare with a twist. At lunch there's counter service only, with a choice of fancy sandwiches and salads on a rotating menu. If you go for dinner, be sure to check out the lengthy wine list. ✉ *527 N. Charles St., Mount Vernon* ☎ *410/539–8880* ⊕ *www.saschas.com* ▭ *AE, DC, MC, V* ⊙ *Closed Sun. No lunch Sat.* ✛ *2C.*

$$–$$$
SPANISH
✗ **Tapas Teatro.** Connected to the Charles Theater, the place for art and indie films in Baltimore, the Tapas Teatro is a popular pre- and post-movie spot. It's often a scene, especially in warm weather, when the glass front is open and tables spill onto the street. Tapas include roasted potatoes, spinach sautéed with crab, and lamb tenderloin. There's also an extensive list of wines by the glass, and if you don't finish them with dinner, you can carry drinks into the Charles. But be careful: it's so much fun to keep sampling that it's easy to run up a hefty bill. ✉ *1711 N. Charles St., Station North Arts District* ☎ *410/332–0110* ⊕ *www.tapasteatro.com* ▭ *AE, MC, V* ⊙ *Closed Mon. No lunch* ✛ *1C.*

¢
THAI
✗ **Thairish.** Twenty years ago, Thai chef-owner Kerrigan Kitikul named his hole-in-the-wall dive in deference to his Irish wife and adopted Irish first name, but the food is as authentically Thai as anything you'll find in Baltimore. All entrées on the limited menu are $8.95, from the spot-on Pad Thai to the sizzling-hot Panang with just-barely-steamed vegetables in a perfect red curry. There are a few tables, but the business is mostly carryout. For the quickest service—this is a one-man kitchen—avoid the lunch and dinner rushes. ✉ *804 N. Charles St., Mount Vernon* ☎ *410/752–5857* ▭ *AE, MC, V* ⊙ *Closed for dinner, Mon.–Fri.; Closed for lunch, Sat.–Sun.* ✛ *2C.*

$$–$$$
SPANISH
✗ **Tio Pepe.** Candles light up the whitewashed walls of these cellar dining rooms, where the menu covers all regions of Spain. The staple is *paella à la Valenciana* (chicken, sausage, shrimp, clams, and mussels with saffron rice); a less-well-known Basque preparation is red snapper with clams, mussels, asparagus, and boiled egg. Make dinner reservations well in advance; walk-in weekday lunch seating is usually available. ✉ *10 E. Franklin St., Mount Vernon* ☎ *410/539–4675* ⊕ *www.tiopeperestaurant.com* ⌦ *Reservations essential* ▭ *AE, D, DC, MC* ✛ *3C.*

8

BOLTON HILL

$–$$ ✕ **b.** In a residential neighborhood of lovely, large row houses, this casual
ECLECTIC   corner bistro serves imaginative, Mediterranean-influenced fare. The seasonal menu includes such dishes as roasted vegetable ravioli in sage butter and sesame-encrusted salmon with honey horseradish crème fraîche. Or choose from one of the chalkboard specials, such as the risotto of the day or the "butcher's special." On Sunday b is a popular spot for brunch. ✉ *1501 Bolton St., Bolton Hill* ☎ *410/383–8600* ⊕ *www.b-bistro.com* ▭ *AE, D, MC, V* ⊗ *Closed Mon. No lunch Tues.–Sat.* ✛ *1A.*

CHARLES VILLAGE

$$–$$$ ✕ **Ambassador Dining Room.** A Tudor-style dining room in a 1930s apartment building is the setting for superb Indian fare. Go for the classics such as chicken *tikka masala* (grilled chicken in a sauce of red pepper, ginger, garlic, and yogurt) or *alu gobi* (spicy potatoes and cauliflower), or sample more creative options such as lamb tenderloin with fennel-and-chive sauce. In summer the lovely garden is a favorite spot for outdoor dining. The service does not disappoint. ✉ *3811 Canterbury Rd., Tuscany-Canterbury* ☎ *410/366–1484* ⊕ *www.ambassadording. com* ▭ *AE, MC, V* ✛ *2G.*
INDIAN

$$ ✕ **Gertrude's.** In the Baltimore Museum of Art, this casual yet classy spot cooks up creative Maryland cuisine. Crab cakes, served in many forms, are one option, as are cornmeal-encrusted catfish or one of the many daily specials. In warm weather the outdoor terrace overlooking the sculpture garden makes for very pleasant dining. During the day, large windows brighten up the main dining space, which has a nautical theme. John Shields, the chef and owner, has won accolades for his homey, regional menu. ✉ *10 Art Museum Dr., Charles Village* ☎ *410/889–3399* ⊕ *www.gertrudesbaltimore.com* ✑ *Reservations essential* ▭ *AE, MC, V* ⊗ *Closed Mon.* ✛ *3G.*
AMERICAN

¢–$ ✕ **One World Cafe.** A favorite of Johns Hopkins students, this low-key restaurant, café, and bar is open morning until night for tasty vegetarian fare. Settle onto a couch or at one of the small tables for a portobello sandwich with caramelized onions and feta cheese, tofu baked with ginger and served with steamed vegetables, or One World's version of that Baltimore specialty: a crabless crab cake. Smoothies, espresso drinks, microbrews, and mixed drinks from the full bar fill out the menu. ✉ *100 W. University Pkwy., Tuscany-Canterbury* ☎ *410/235–5777* ⊕ *www. one-world-cafe.com* ▭ *AE, DC, MC, V* ✛ *2G.*
VEGETARIAN

¢–$ ✕ **Paper Moon Diner.** The ceilings and walls of this funky, colorful diner are plastered with toys and other interesting objects. People come at all hours (it's open 24/7) for the overstuffed omelets, big stacks of pancakes, burgers, and other classic fare. Stop by at 3 am on a Friday or Saturday night to nosh on sweet potato fries with hipsters and students from nearby Johns Hopkins University. The servers have a diner attitude—they don't always seem too interested in serving, and the food might take a while—but the place is always lively and entertaining. ✉ *227 W. 29th St., Charles Village* ☎ *410/889–4444* ⊕ *www. papermoondiner.com* ▭ *MC, V* ✛ *3F.*
AMERICAN

HAMPDEN

¢–$ ✕**Café Hon**. This funky eatery, specializing in comfort food and kitsch,
AMERICAN is the centerpiece of Hamden's main drag of restaurants and shops,
called The Avenue. Entrées like meatloaf, crabcake sandwiches, and
thick hamburgers, all served with thick hand-cut french fries, are nothing fancy, but solid and filling. Equally as enticing are the giant Elvis
statue and the gift shop with cat's-eye "Hon" glasses. In case you get
lost, you can always spot this place by the giant pink flamingo out front
(an ode to hometown hero John Waters, director of Pink Flamingos).
⊠ *1002 W. 36th St., Hampden* ☎ *410/243–1230* ⊕ *www.cafehon.com*
▤ *AE, MC, D, V* ✛ *2F.*

¢–$ ✕**Golden West Café**. On "The Avenue," funky Hampden's main com-
ECLECTIC mercial street, Golden West is the go-to spot for breakfast, lunch, and
dinner. The place is colorful and eclectic, and so is the menu of diner
fare with a Tex-Mex and Asian twist. Try the cold Vietnamese salad
with shrimp or the hefty *huevos montuleños*—fried eggs with yellow
corn cakes covered in beans, feta, salsa, and a fried banana (and served
at all hours). Large tables make it a good spot for groups, and the bar
makes it good for pre- or post-dinner drinks. Occasionally, the café
hosts local folk and indie rock bands. ⊠ *1105 W. 36th St., Hampden*
☎ *410/889–8891* ⊕ *www.goldenwestcafe.com* ▤ *AE, D, MC, V* ✛ *2F.*

$$ ✕**Woodberry Kitchen**. This restaurant is in such high demand that it
AMERICAN books up weeks in advance. Swathed in wood and aged brick, Wood-
Fodor'sChoice berry Kitchen has a cozy, relaxed atmosphere and the menu harks back
★ to a simpler era. The best items are often the most basic: Eastern Shore
popcorn, cheddar potato gratin, and cast-iron rib-eye steak. Diners
range in age from thirtysomethings to senior citizens. Ask for a table
on the mezzanine, where you can peer down to the floor below and
people-watch between courses. ⊠ *2010 Clipper Park Rd., Hampden*
☎ *410/464–8000* ⊕ *www.woodberrykitchen.com* ⌁ *Reservations
essential* ▤ *AE, MC, V* ☺ *No lunch* ✛ *3F.*

INNER HARBOR

¢–$ ✕**Attman's**. Open since 1915, this authentic New York–style deli near
DELI the Jewish Museum is the king of Baltimore's "Corned Beef Row." Of
the three delis on the row, Attman's has the longest waits and steepest
prices, but delivers the highest-quality dishes. Don't be put off by the
long lines—they move fairly quickly, and the outstanding corned beef
sandwiches are worth the wait, as are the pastrami, homemade chopped
liver, and other oversize creations. Attman's closes at 6:30 pm daily.
⊠ *1019 Lombard St., Historic Jonestown* ☎ *410/563–2666* ⊕ *www.
attmansdeli.com* ▤ *AE, DC, MC, V* ✛ *4F.*

$$$–$$$$ ✕**Charleston**. Chef-owner Cindy Wolf's inspired cuisine rivals anything
SOUTHERN in the region. The kitchen here may have a South Carolina Low Country
Fodor'sChoice accent, but it's also skilled in the fundamentals of French cooking. Inside
★ the glowingly lighted dining room, such classics as she-crab soup, crisp
cornmeal-crusted oysters, and spoon bread complement more elegant
fare, such as squab roasted with apples. Best bets are Southern-inspired
dishes such as shrimp sautéed with andouille and Cajun ham served

8

over creamy grits. ✉ *1000 Lancaster St., Harbor East* ☎ *410/332–7373* ⊕ *www.charlestonrestaurant.com* ⌕ *Reservations essential* ▭ *AE, D, MC, V* ☉ *Closed Sun.* ✛ *5F.*

$$$
ITALIAN

✕ **Cinghiale.** The spotlight is on wine at Cinghiale (pronounced "ching-GYAH-lay"), one of Baltimore's best upscale spots for northern Italian fare. The restaurant is an open, inviting space with tall, wide windows. The wine list is vast—more than 400 bottles, listed on the menu by region. The service is sharp and unpretentious, but can be slightly overbearing at times. Cinghiale is split into two sections, the elegant osteria and the less-formal enoteca. Opt for the latter, where you can nibble on small plates, sample one of the city's best wine collections, and rub elbows with the professional set. ✉ *822 Lancaster St., Inner Harbor* ☎ *410/547–8282* ⊕ *www.cgeno.com* ▭ *AE, D, MC, V* ☉ *Closed Sun.* ✛ *6F.*

$$
SEAFOOD

✕ **McCormick & Schmick's.** It may be a chain restaurant, but it's a very good one. From its expansive location at the end of Pier 5, on the east side of the waterfront, there's a terrific harbor view; ask to be seated on the patio. More than two dozen varieties of fish and seafood, available on a daily basis, are flown in from all over the world: the large menu changes daily. Choose from the more than half-dozen varieties of oysters on the half shell, or go for the signature cedar-plank wild Oregon king salmon. ✉ *711 Eastern Ave., Inner Harbor* ☎ *410/234–1300* ⊕ *www. mccormickandschmicks.com* ▭ *AE, D, MC, V* ✛ *6E.*

$–$$
AMERICAN

✕ **Miss Shirley's.** With amazing pancakes, omelets, and French toast, this upscale cafe, now with two locations, at the Inner Harbor and in North Baltimore's Roland Park, has become the go-to destination for unbeatable breakfast and brunch (neither outlet serves dinner). Lunch entrées like the Chesapeake Club (crab cake, shrimp salad, lettuce, bacon, red and yellow tomatoes, avocado, and Old Bay remoulade on sourdough toast, dusted with more Old Bay) are also excellent. There's also a second location at 513 W. Cold Spring Lane in Roland Park. ✉ *750 E. Pratt St., Inner Harbor* ☎ *410/528–5373* ⊕ *www.missshirleys.com* ▭ *AE, D, MC, V* ✛ *5E.*

$$–$$$
SEAFOOD

✕ **Rusty Scupper.** A tourist favorite, the Rusty Scupper undoubtedly has the best view along the waterfront; sunset here is magical, with the sun sinking slowly into the harbor as lights twinkle on the city's skyscrapers. The interior is decorated with light wood and windows from floor to ceiling; the house specialty is seafood, particularly the jumbo lump crab cake, but the menu also includes beef, chicken, and pasta. Reservations are essential on Friday and Saturday; service can be spotty. ✉ *402 Key Hwy., Inner Harbor* ☎ *410/727–3678* ▭ *AE, D, DC, MC, V* ✛ *6D.*

FEDERAL HILL

$–$$
MEXICAN

✕ **Blue Agave.** At this authentic regional Mexican and American Southwestern restaurant every sauce and salsa is made daily to create pure, concentrated flavors—the traditional mole sauces here are delicious. Dishes such as grilled quail served with both green and spicy yellow moles, or the more familiar chicken enchiladas with mole poblano, demonstrate the kitchen's command of this rich, complex concoction. More than 80 different kinds of tequila are available, and you would be hard-pressed to find a better margarita in the city. ✉ *1032 Light St.,*

Federal Hill ☎ *410/576–3938* ⊕ *www.blueagaverestaurant.com* 🖃 *AE, D, MC, V* ☉ *Closed Mon.* ⊹ *6C.*

$$$
AMERICAN

✕ **Corks.** The creative American cuisine here is as stellar as the impressive wine list, and the waitstaff are adept at pairing wines with dishes. Corks helped up the ante in Federal Hill fine dining. Start with a made-in-house mozzarella on top of a salad or the artisan macaroni and cheese. Other outstanding options on the seasonal menu might include monkfish osso buco or braised veal breast with woodland mushrooms. It's so cozy in the dimly lighted, wood-panel dining room that you may never want to leave. ✉ *1026 S. Charles St., Federal Hill* ☎ *410/752–3810* ⊕ *www.corksrestaurant.com* ⌖ *Reservations essential* 🖃 *AE, D, MC, V* ☉ *No lunch* ⊹ *6C.*

$–$$
JAPANESE

✕ **Matsuri.** Sit down at the counter or make your way to one of the tables as this small sushi place, a Federal Hill favorite. And it's not just popular among Baltimoreans; the walls are covered with awards from local and national press. You can order by the roll, or opt for one of the bento boxes, udon soups, or tempura dishes like the signature crab and shrimp, wrapped in rice and seaweed and deep fried. The narrow, two-story corner row house is cozy but not cramped, and the servers are quick and accommodating. ✉ *1105 S. Charles St., Federal Hill* ☎ *410/752–8561* ⊕ *www.matsuri.us* 🖃 *AE, D, MC, V* ☉ *No lunch weekends* ⊹ *6C.*

LITTLE ITALY

$$$
ITALIAN

✕ **Aldo's.** It's easy to see why Aldo's has won so many awards in the past decade. Have a meal under the skylight in the pillared two-story central dining room and you'll swoon over both the decor and food. Chef Aldo Vitale prepares unabashedly rich Italian fare, from pasta tossed in Italian black truffle butter to heavenly hunks of veal topped with melt-in-your-mouth spinach and mozzarella. The service is charming and the wine list comprehensive. A go-to for visiting celebrities and the city's upper crust, Aldo's is undeniably Little Italy's most romantic restaurant. ✉ *306 S. High St., Little Italy* ☎ *410/727–0700* ⊕ *www. aldositaly.com* 🖃 *AE, D, DC, MC, V* ☉ *No lunch* ⊹ *5F.*

$–$$
ITALIAN

✕ **Amicci's.** At this self-proclaimed "very casual eatery," you don't have to spend a fortune to get a satisfying taste of Little Italy. Blue jean–clad diners and walls hung with movie posters make for a fun atmosphere. Service is friendly and usually speedy, and the food comes in large portions. Try the chicken Lorenzo: breaded chicken breast covered in a marsala wine sauce, red peppers, prosciutto, and provolone. ✉ *231 S. High St., Little Italy* ☎ *410/528–1096* ⊕ *www.amiccis.com* 🖃 *AE, D, DC, MC, V* ⊹ *5F.*

$$–$$$
ITALIAN

✕ **Chiapparelli's.** At this neighborhood favorite, families come to celebrate milestones—baptisms, communions, graduations, and such. Pictures of the Baltimore landscape adorn the redbrick walls, and some white-cloth tables overlook one of Little Italy's main streets. The reasonably priced pasta selections rely on standards, but there's also more upscale fare such as chicken Giuseppe: breaded chicken breast with spinach, crabmeat, and provolone in a lemon wine sauce. ✉ *237 S. High St., Little Italy* ☎ *410/837–0309* ⊕ *www.chiapparellis.com* 🖃 *AE, D, DC, MC, V* ⊹ *5F.*

8

$-$$ ✕**Café Gia's**. The painted retro facade invites visitors to this casual
ITALIAN family-owned cafe in the middle of Little Italy, and the simple, well-
prepared cuisine only adds to the experience. Downtown professionals
and savvy tourists fill the place for lunch entrées, all under $10, includ-
ing hearty pastas like rigatoni bolognese or sandwiches like La Spiaggia
(eggplant parmigiana) and La Adriatica (chicken parmigiana), served
on perfectly toasted bread. Delicate dinner entrées like penne Gorgon-
zola and Shrimp & Scallop Alberto (named after the father of owner
Giovanna Aquia) are only a bit more pricey but significantly larger.
✉ *410 S. High St., Little Italy* ☎ *410/685–6727* ⊕ *www.cafegias.com*
🗖 *AE, MC, V* ✛ *5F.*

$-$$ ✕**La Tavola**. Specializing in homemade, inventive pasta dishes, La Tavola
ITALIAN is a cut above other Little Italy spaghetti houses. Don't miss the *mafalde
alla fiorentina*, wide pasta with spinach, ricotta, pine nuts, and raisins
in a nutmeg-flavor cream sauce. Veal cannelloni in béchamel tomato
sauce is another standout. If you're still hungry after one of La Tavola's
generous plates of pasta, the fresh fish is a good bet, as is the roasted
veal chop. ✉ *248 Albemarle St., Little Italy* ☎ *410/685–1859* ⊕ *www.
la-tavola.com* 🗖 *AE, D, DC, MC, V* ✛ *5E.*

¢ ✕**Max's Empanadas**. This casual Argentinian spot is a welcome new
ARGENTINIAN addition to Little Italy, with delicious delicate empanadas filled with
a broad range of ingredients ranging from beef, chicken, spinach, and
ham and cheese to more unique creations on a rotating specials list,
including chorizo and barbecue, all for $3.15 each. The specials are
often the freshest, but the mainstays are more reliable. ✉ *313 S. High
St., Little Italy* ☎ *410/547–7900* ⊕ *www.maxempanadas.com* 🗖 *AE,
MC, V* ☽ *Closed Mon.* ✛ *5F.*

FELLS POINT

$$$-$$$$ ✕**The Black Olive**. One of the best Greek restaurants in the country,
GREEK the Black Olive specializes in impeccably fresh seafood. Let the waiter
give you a guided tour of the catch of the day, which reclines on a bed
of ice in the kitchen case. You can have your selection simply grilled,
lightly dressed, and filleted for you table-side, accompanied by a glass
of wine from the list's thoughtful selection of oft-neglected Greek vin-
tages. For an appetizer be sure to try the *kakavia*, a spicy Greek bouil-
labaisse served with irresistible bread warm from the brick oven. ✉ *814
S. Bond St., at Shakespeare St., Fells Point* ☎ *410/276–7141* ⊕ *www.
theblackolive.com* ⌂ *Reservations essential* 🗖 *AE, D, MC, V* ✛ *6G.*

¢-$ ✕**Blue Moon Dining House**. A cozy café with a celestial motif appropriate
ECLECTIC to its name, the Blue Moon is a favorite for breakfast, served until 3 pm
daily. Start with one of the enormous house-made cinnamon rolls, but
save room for excellent brunch fare such as crab Benedict and sky-high
French toast with fruit compote. On Friday and Saturday the Moon
reopens at 11 pm and stays open all night, attracting revelers from
Fells Point's many clubs and bars. On weekend mornings there's often
a line, but it's well worth the wait. ✉ *1621 Aliceanna St., Fells Point*
☎ *410/522–3940* ⌂ *Reservations not accepted* 🗖 *AE, D, MC, V* ✛ *6G.*

$$-$$$ ✕**Louisiana**. Fells Point's most elegant dining room feels like a spacious,
SOUTHERN opulent antebellum parlor. The menu mixes creole and French with a

touch of New American, and is accompanied by an expansive, thoughtful wine list. The lobster bisque, with a dollop of sherry added at the table by one of Louisiana's servers, is sublime, and crawfish étouffée is a worthy follow-up course. ☒ *1708 Aliceanna St., Fells Point* ⊕ *www. louisianasrestaurant.com* ☎ *410/327–2610* ▭ *AE, DC, MC, V* ⊙ *No lunch* ✛ *6H.*

$$–$$$ ╳ **Obrycki's Crab House.** For more than 50 years Obrycki's has served
SEAFOOD steamed crabs with its unique black pepper seasoning. Politicians and lawyers meet at Orbrycki's after hours to talk business. It feels as though little has changed inside the dark dining room in decades. Service can be sluggish and prices steep, but that doesn't deter its fans. ■ **TIP**➔ **Ask any native of Maryland—eating crabs is an art. If you're unsure how to approach a bushel of hardshells, go to** ⊕ *www.obryckis.com* **for a demonstration.** Go for the crabs; beyond that, the seafood menu is standard and the food just fair. ☒ *1727 E. Pratt St., Fells Point* ☎ *410/732–6399* ⊕ *www.obryckis. com* ▭ *AE, D, DC, MC, V* ⊙ *Closed mid-Dec.–early Mar.* ✛ *6F.*

¢–$ ╳ **Pazo.** An expansive 19th-century warehouse is now home to this
MEDITERRANEAN fashionable, two-level restaurant serving Mediterranean-influenced
Fodor's Choice fare. Enjoy tapas and large plates in the rich, red-hue setting lighted by
★ giant wrought-iron chandeliers and smaller candles on tables, or head upstairs to the mezzanine and watch the crowd below. Service can be pretentious at times but is always quick with orders. Tasty tapas and warm, stylish decor make Pazo one of the city's better dinner destinations. ☒ *1425 Aliceanna St., Fells Point* ☎ *410/534–7296* ⊕ *www. pazorestaurant.com* ▭ *AE, DC, MC, V* ⊙ *No lunch* ✛ *6G.*

$–$$ ╳ **Samos.** East of Fells Point is Greektown (20 minutes by car from Inner
GREEK Harbor hotels), home to Baltimore's Greek population. An informal restaurant, done in clean, classic blue and white, Samos serves excellent Greek fare. Portions are generous, with lamb souvlaki and tender, juicy gyros leading the menu. Be warned: the folks at Samos often take the phone off the hook and stop offering carryout during the lunchtime rush. Samos doesn't offer beer or wine, but you can bring your own. ☒ *600 Oldham St., Greektown* ☎ *410/675–5292* ⊕ *www. samosrestaurant.com* ▭ *AE, D, DC, MC, V* ⊙ *Closed Sun.* ✛ *5H.*

¢ ╳ **Stuggy's.** This hot dog specialist a block from the Fells Point water-
AMERICAN front earns a large share of the lunch and late-night crowds with specialties like the Bmore Dog, with grilled baloney and deli mustard, and the Wild Thing, a Bison dog with blue cheese and diced raw onions. For dessert, the fried Oreo cookies have a certain charm. ☒ *809 S. Broadway, Fells Point* ☎ *410/327–0228* ⊕ *www.stuggys.com* ▭ *AE, MC, V* ⊙ *Closed for dinner Sun.* ✛ *6G.*

¢ ╳ **Tortilleria Sinaloa.** The Latino enclave just north of Fells Point, called
MEXICAN Upper Fells Point, is fast becoming a foodie destination with many low-cost, authentic variations on Mexican and South American cuisine. This tiny but charming hole in the wall—mostly a take-out operation, although the counter space and in-house food presentations are lovely—is the best of the bunch. The homemade corn tortillas are the perfect platform for delectable tacos with fresh fish, pork, chorizo, or tongue. This is also the city's best place for tamales. ☒ *1716 Eastern Ave., Upper Fells Point* ☎ *410/276–3741* ⊕ *www.tortilleria-sinaloa. com* ▭ *AE, MC, V* ✛ *5H.*

8

CANTON

$$–$$$ ✕ **Bo Brooks.** Picking steamed crabs on Bo Brooks's waterfront deck as
SEAFOOD   sailboats and tugs ply the harbor is a quintessential Baltimore pleasure.
Locals spend hot summer days cracking into warm, spicy crabs and
enjoying a refreshing pitcher of beer while a cool breeze blows in from
the harbor. Brooks serves its famous crustaceans year-round, along with
a menu of Chesapeake seafood classics. Locals know to stick to the
Maryland crab soup, crab dip, jumbo lump crab cakes, and fried oysters. ✉ *2701 Boston St., Canton* ☎ *410/558–0202* ⊕ *www.bobrooks.
com* ▭ *AE, D, MC, V* ⊹ *4H.*

MIDTOWN

$$–$$$ ✕ **Nam Kang.** The once grimy area in central Baltimore called Midtown
KOREAN   has buoyed in recent years by the sprouting of several restaurants and
stores catering to the city's burgeoning Korean community. Nam Kang
is the oldest and best of the eateries in this area, increasingly called Little
Korea (Nak Won, around the corner on 20th Street, is also excellent).
Ornate, clean decor greets you, along with a series of complimentary,
shared appetizers, including pickled veggies, edamame (soy beans), and
kimchi. From there, all of the traditional Korean specialties are on offer,
bibimbap, bulgogi, and barbecue—and all are excellent. The noodle
soups, like the very spicy seafood-filled *samsung jampong*, are a sinus-
clearing delight. ✉ *2126 Maryland Ave., Midtown* ☎ *410/685–6237*
▭ *AE, D, MC, V* ⊹ *4H.*

WHERE TO STAY

When booking a hotel or bed-and-breakfast in Baltimore, focus on the
Inner Harbor, where you're likely to spend a good deal of time. The
downside to staying in hotels near downtown is the noise level, which
can rise early in the morning and stay up late into the night—especially
if there's a baseball or football game. For quieter options, head to neighborhoods like Fells Point and Canton. All of the hotels listed are within
a half-hour drive of the harbor. If you're coming to Baltimore in summer or near Preakness (the third weekend in May), reserve your rooms
well in advance. Hunt Valley, a suburb about a 25-minute drive north
of Baltimore on I–83, has several convenient budget options.

WHAT IT COSTS				
	¢	$	$$	$$$	$$$$
For two people	under $100	$100–$160	$161–$230	$231–$300	over $300

Prices are for a standard double room in high season, excluding 14.5% room tax.

BEST BETS FOR BALTIMORE LODGING

Fodor's Choice ★	**Best by Price**	Celie's Waterfront Bed & Breakfast, p. 346
Abacrombie Bed and Breakfast, p. 341	**$**	Inn at 2920, p. 346
The Admiral Fell Inn, p. 346	**Abacrombie Bed and Breakfast**, p. 341	Inn at the Colonnade, p. 347
InterContinental Harbor Court, p. 345	**Sheraton Baltimore City Center**, p. 343	**$$$**
Tremont Plaza Hotel, p. 343	**Tremont Plaza Hotel**, p. 343	Baltimore Marriott Inner Harbor, p. 343
	$$	Hyatt Regency, p. 345
	The Admiral Fell Inn, p. 346	InterContinental Harbor Court, p. 345
		Renaissance Baltimore Harborplace Hotel, p. 345

MOUNT VERNON

$
Fodor's Choice
★
🏨 **Abacrombie Bed and Breakfast.** In a large, late-19th-century building, once a private house, this intimate inn has rooms furnished in Victorian style and an outstanding restaurant. It's across the street from the Meyerhoff Symphony Hall and in walking distance of MICA, the University of Baltimore, and Amtrak's Penn Station. Breakfast is served in the parlor room. **Pros:** within walking distance of the opera and symphony. **Cons:** the four-story inn has no elevator. ⊠ *58 W. Biddle St., Mount Vernon* ☎ *410/244–7227 or 888/922–3437* ⊕ *www.abacrombie.net* ⤸ *12 rooms* ⚲ *In-room: a/c, Wi-Fi. In-hotel: restaurant, bar, parking (free)* ⊟ *AE, D, MC, V* ⅢⓄⅠ *CP* ✢ *1B.*

$$$
🏨 **Peabody Court.** Built as a luxury apartment house in 1924, this 13-story hotel faces the Washington Monument. The hotel retains its original distinguished lobby and other period touches such as marble bathrooms. Rooms have desks and two-line speakerphones with data ports; a lobby business center has a fax machine, copier, and computer station. Rooms with park views are the best choice. A courtesy shuttle will ferry you to destinations within a 2-mi radius. The hotel bistro, George's on Mount Vernon Square, serves American and Italian cuisine. **Pros:** in the heart of Mount Vernon. **Cons:** semi-steep prices. ⊠ *612 Cathedral St., Mount Vernon* ☎ *410/727–7101* ⊕ *www.peabodycourthotel.com* ⤸ *104 rooms* ⚲ *In-room: a/c, safe, refrigerator, Internet, Wi-Fi. In-hotel: restaurant, gym, parking (paid)* ⊟ *AE, D, DC, MC, V* ⅢⓄⅠ *CP* ✢ *2C.*

CITY CENTER

$$
🏨 **Comfort Inn.** Built in the 1960s as an apartment house, the 13-story Comfort Inn is now an affordable all-suites near Mount Vernon and the Inner Harbor. The suites come in two sizes, and, although they're

WHERE SHOULD I STAY?

	NEIGHBORHOOD VIBE	PROS	CONS
Mount Vernon	Bustling with a refined shade of city life, packed with restaurants, shops, and bars.	Convenient to many of the best eateries and cultural institutions in town, great locale for an evening stroll.	Can get very noisy at night; a bit of a walk to the harbor and downtown attractions.
City Center	Baltimore's Times Square, the center of it all; very tourist-focused.	Close to convention center, stadiums; easy transportation.	Lacks the charm found in less chaotic parts of the city; a bit overwhelming; can be unsafe as the night goes on.
Inner Harbor	Similar to City Center, with the cool breezes and calming influence of the Chesapeake Bay.	Close to all major tourist destinations; beautiful harbor views.	Expensive; little interaction with locals; removed from museums, etc.
Fells Point	Combination sea-faring working town and bar-hopping wonderland.	The cobblestone streets and 100-year-old buildings breathe history; lots of great bars and restaurants.	Very noisy at night; a bit of a schlep to the Inner Harbor, a bigger schlep to the stadiums and museums.
Canton	A combination residential neighborhood for young professionals and hub for bars and seafood.	Get a glimpse of residential life, with some of the safest streets downtown; plenty of nightlife.	Far from typical tourist attractions, inconvenient transportation options.
Roland Park	Beautiful, large homes and estates on the north end of the city; refined and quiet.	A retreat from urban life, lovely parks, hiking, gourmet food and specialty shop options; close to Johns Hopkins University.	A car ride away from most significant tourist attractions; the few lodging options are expensive.
Northern Suburbs	Land of strip malls and chain restaurants.	Much more affordable than downtown hotels with similar amenities.	A substantial car ride to any of the city's tourist attractions and better restaurants.

not exactly spacious, the bigger ones are probably worth the extra few dollars. **Pros:** an affordable option close to downtown and other attractions. **Cons:** few amenities, no wireless Internet in the rooms—just Ethernet cables. ✉ *8 E. Pleasant St., City Center* ☎ *410/576–1200 or 800/873–6668* ⊕ *www.choicehotels.com* ⇨ *60 suites* ⌂ *In-room: a/c, kitchen, Internet. In-hotel: gym* ▤ *AE, D, DC, MC, V* ✢ *3C.*

$$ ⓣ **Hampton Inn and Suites.** The free breakfast and the logo may be the same, but this Hampton Inn tries to be more urban and chic than others in the chain. In an early-1900s office building that lay vacant for many years, the hotel follows the historical direction of the structure, but keeps things contemporary. Rooms, done in warm mauve and beige and dark wood, have a clubby, streamlined look. The biggest and most expensive rooms, on the top floor, are studio suites in the former executive offices. **Pros:** trendier than most other Hampton Inns. **Cons:** patrons can get loud from time to time. ✉ *131 E. Redwood St., City Center*

☎ 410/539–7888 ⊕ *www.baltimorehamptoninn.com* ↩ *116 rooms, 10 studio suites* ☧ *In-room: a/c, Wi-Fi. In-hotel: pool, gym, Internet terminal, parking (paid)* ▤ *AE, D, DC, MC, V* ⊹ *5B.*

$ ☷ **Radisson Plaza Lord Baltimore**. Baltimore's historic landmark hotel, the Radisson extends its Jazz Age elegance to the guest rooms, which have been restored to their original style. Built in 1928, this 23-story hotel is distinguished by an elegantly gilded art deco lobby. Rooms on the south side have the best view, and from the top three floors you can see the harbor. The hotel is quiet and comfortable, and the location is central, three blocks from the Baltimore Convention Center or Harborplace. **Pros:** centrally located. **Cons:** somewhat dated rooms and amenities. ✉ *20 W. Baltimore St., City Center* ☎ *410/539–8400* ⊕ *www.radisson. com/lordbaltimore* ↩ *439 rooms, 3 suites* ☧ *In-room: a/c, Wi-Fi. In-hotel: restaurant, bar, gym, Internet terminal, parking (paid)* ▤ *AE, D, DC, MC, V* ⊹ *4C.*

$ ☷ **Sheraton Baltimore City Center**. One of Baltimore's largest, this hotel (four blocks from the harbor) divides its rooms between two towers and also houses the largest ballroom in the city, which makes it especially popular with conventioneers. Rooms, decorated in light colors, have a contemporary flair and marble-floor bathrooms. Amenities include in-room voice mail, Internet access, hair dryers, and ironing boards. The hotel restaurant is Don Shula's Steak House, where the menu is presented on an official NFL football autographed by Shula, a former coach for the Baltimore Colts. **Pros:** easy access to the convention center. **Cons:** service can be sluggish. ✉ *101 W. Fayette St., City Center* ☎ *410/752–1100* ⊕ *www.sheraton.com* ↩ *707 rooms, 21 suites* ☧ *In-room: a/c, refrigerator (some), Internet, Wi-Fi. In-hotel: restaurant, bar, pool, gym, Internet terminal, parking (paid)* ▤ *AE, D, DC, MC, V* ⊹ *4C.*

$ ☷ **Tremont Plaza Hotel**. This 37-story all-suites hotel, once an apartment
Fodor's Choice building, is in the densest part of the business district. Its plain facade
★ and minuscule brass-and-marble lobby belie the tasteful earth-tone guest rooms, which are a favorite of musicians and actors performing at local theaters. The suites come in six sizes. The best views of the city and the small park in the center of St. Paul Place are from rooms with numbers ending in 06. The restaurant, Tugs, has a nautical theme and a menu rich in seafood. **Pros:** renovated rooms; kitchens in suites. **Cons:** a somewhat long walk from the Inner Harbor. ✉ *222 St. Paul Pl., City Center* ☎ *410/727–2222 or 800/873–6668* ⊕ *www.tremontsuitehotels. com* ↩ *303 suites* ☧ *In-room: a/c, kitchen, Internet. In-hotel: restaurant, bar, pool, gym, Wi-Fi hotspot, parking (paid)* ▤ *AE, D, DC, MC, V* ⊹ *4C.*

8

INNER HARBOR

$$$ ☷ **Baltimore Marriott Inner Harbor**. This 10-story hotel is a block away from Oriole Park at Camden Yards, Harborplace, and the convention center. The public areas are nondescript but surprisingly tranquil, as are the rooms, decorated in teal, mauve, and gray. The best views are from rooms facing the Inner Harbor and the ballpark. Rooms on the 10th floor come with concierge-level privileges. Staff is generally friendly

and eager to please, and some of the views are top-notch. **Pros:** some rooms have stunning views of historic landmarks like the Bromo Seltzer Tower; easy access to Oriole Park. **Cons:** adjacent fire department and rowdy ballpark crowds can make for a noisy night. ⊠ *110 S. Eutaw St., Inner Harbor* ☎ *410/962–0202 or 800/228–9290* ⊕ *www.marriott.com* ↪ *524 rooms, 2 suites* ⚒ *In-room: a/c, Internet. In-hotel: 2 restaurants, bar, pool, gym, Internet terminal, Wi-Fi hotspot, parking (paid)* ▭ *AE, D, DC, MC, V* ✛ *5B.*

$–$$ 🏨 **Courtyard by Marriott Baltimore Inner Harbor.** Close to the Inner Harbor waterfront and adjacent to Little Italy, this lodging is the farthest east of the Inner Harbor hotels. With sunny rooms in soothing neutral tones, the Courtyard Inner Harbor is a comfortable and attractive alternative to more central hotels with similar amenities and higher rates. Most downtown attractions are still within walking distance, though the stadiums and convention center are more comfortably reached by car or cab. **Pros:** less expensive than most downtown hotels; situated in the newly swanky Harbor East, a block from some of the best restaurants in town. **Cons:** a decent walk to many Inner Harbor attractions. ⊠ *1000 Aliceanna St., Inner Harbor East* ☎ *443/923–4000* ⊕ *www.marriott. com/bwidt* ↪ *205 rooms* ⚒ *In-room: a/c, Wi-Fi. In-hotel: restaurant, pool, gym, parking (paid)* ▭ *AE, D, DC, MC, V* ✛ *6F.*

$–$$ 🏨 **Days Inn Inner Harbor.** Less than three blocks from the Inner Harbor, this nine-story redbrick building provides reliable and relatively economical accommodations in the center of town. The utilitarian, pastel-hue guest rooms are sparsely furnished, but each has a small desk and phone with voice mail and Internet access. It's also close to the 1st Mariner Arena venue, which makes it an easy pick for concert-goers. **Pros:** you will not find less expensive accommodations this close to the major downtown attractions. **Cons:** this street can be sketchy at night. ⊠ *100 Hopkins Pl., Inner Harbor East* ☎ *410/576–1000* ⊕ *www. daysinnerharbor.com* ↪ *250 rooms* ⚒ *In-room: a/c, refrigerator. In-hotel: restaurant, bar, gym, pool, public Wi-Fi, parking (paid)* ▭ *AE, D, DC, MC, V* ✛ *4C.*

$$$–$$$$ 🏨 **Hilton Baltimore.** Location, location, location: One of Baltimore's newest hotels has an unparalleled view of Camden Yards and a skywalk that connects to the city convention center. Opened in 2008, the towering 20-story hotel is mostly boring gray metal on the outside, in stark contrast with the brick-clad ballpark. Inside, the hotel has a nautical feel, with wave-shaped fixtures hanging from the ceiling and pillars of dark wood and blue tiles. Ask for a room on the south side, where you can peer down into the ballpark. Or you can watch the games from the fitness center on the fourth floor. Hotel staff is friendly and accommodating and the amenities are new. **Pros:** connected to the convention center; excellent ballpark view. **Cons:** rooms are considerably smaller than those at similarly priced hotels in town. ⊠ *401 W. Pratt St., Inner Harbor* ☎ *443/573–8700* ⊕ *www.baltimore.hilton.com* ↪ *757 rooms* ⚒ *In-room: a/c, Internet, Wi-Fi. In-hotel: restaurant, bar, pool, gym, Internet terminal, Wi-Fi hotspot, parking (paid)* ▭ *AE, D, DC, MC, V* ✛ *5B.*

$$$-$$$$ ⊞**Hyatt Regency.** This stretch of Light Street is practically a highway, but the unenclosed skyways allow ready pedestrian access to both Inner Harbor attractions and the convention center. Rooms have rich gold and black-purple prints and cherrywood furniture; most rooms have views of the harbor or the city. The lobby has glass elevators and the chain's trademark atrium. The 12th floor is the Club level, with complimentary breakfast, evening hors d'oeuvres, and a private concierge available. Atop the hotel, the Pisces restaurant and lounge provides stunning city views, especially at night. **Pros:** the Inner Harbor is just a skywalk away. **Cons:** service can be slow and unhelpful. ⊠ *300 Light St., Inner Harbor* ☎ *410/528–1234 or 800/233–1234* ⊕ *baltimore. hyatt.com* ⇆ *488 rooms, 26 suites* ⚒ *In-room: a/c, Wi-Fi. In-hotel: restaurant, bars, tennis courts, pool, gym, parking (fee)* ⊟ *AE, D, DC, MC, V* ⊹ *5C.*

$$$-$$$$

Fodor's Choice

★

⊞**InterContinental Harbor Court.** The entrance to the most prestigious hotel in Baltimore is set back from the street by a brick courtyard that provides an immediate sense of tranquillity. A grand spiral staircase dominates the lobby, which is decorated in English country opulence. All guest rooms include such deluxe touches as twice-daily maid service, plush bathrobes, and TVs in the bathrooms; upscale suite amenities also include 6-foot marble tubs, canopied four-poster beds, and CD players. Waterside rooms have a commanding view of the harbor, but courtyard rooms are quietest. **Pros:** the city's nicest hotel. **Cons:** also city's most expensive hotel. ⊠ *550 Light St., Inner Harbor* ☎ *410/234–0550 or 800/824–0076* ⊕ *www.harborcourt.com* ⇆ *195 rooms, 23 suites* ⚒ *In-room: a/c, refrigerator, Internet, Wi-Fi. In-hotel: 2 restaurants, bar, tennis court, pool, gym, Internet terminal, parking (paid)* ⊟ *AE, D, DC, MC, V* ⊹ *6C.*

$$$-$$$$ ⊞**Marriott Baltimore Waterfront.** The city's tallest hotel and the only one directly on the Inner Harbor itself, this upscale 31-story Marriott has a neoclassical interior that uses multihue marbles, rich jewel-tone walls, and photographs of Baltimore architectural landmarks. Although it's at the eastern end of the Inner Harbor, all downtown attractions are within walking distance; there's also a water-taxi stop right by the front door. Most rooms offer unobstructed views of the city and harbor; ask for one that faces west toward downtown for a splendid panorama of the waterfront and skyscrapers. **Pros:** nice amenities; great location and view. **Cons:** pricey compared to nearby hotels. ⊠ *700 Aliceanna St., Inner Harbor East* ☎ *410/385–3000* ⊕ *www.marriotthotels.com/bwiwf* ⇆ *751 rooms* ⚒ *In-room: a/c, safe, refrigerator, Internet. In-hotel: restaurant, bar, pool, gym, parking (paid)* ⊟ *AE, D, DC, MC, V* ⊹ *6F.*

$$$ ⊞**Renaissance Baltimore Harborplace Hotel.** The most conveniently located of the Inner Harbor hotels—across the street from the shopping pavilions—the Renaissance Harborplace meets the needs of tourists, business travelers, and conventioneers. Guest rooms are light and cheerful, with amenities that include coffeemakers, terry robes, hair dryers, and ironing boards. Rooms have a view of the harbor, the downtown landscape, or the indoor courtyard. The hotel adjoins the Gallery, a four-story shopping mall. **Pros:** snappy service. **Cons:** some rooms are a bit threadbare. ⊠ *202 E. Pratt St., Inner Harbor* ☎ *410/547–1200 or*

8

800/468–3571 ⊕ www.renaissancehotels.com/bwish ⌦ 562 rooms, 60 suites ♿ In-room: a/c, Internet. In-hotel: restaurant, bar, pool, gym, Wi-Fi hotspot, parking (paid) ▭ AE, D, DC, MC, V ✛ 5D.

FELLS POINT

$$

Fodor'sChoice

★

The Admiral Fell Inn. This inn is an upright anchor at the center of the action in funky Fells Point. By joining together buildings constructed between the late 1770s and the 1920s, the owners created a structure that resembles a small, European-style hotel, with lots of character and quirks. The rooms, which vary in shape, all have four-poster canopy beds. Three suites and eight rooms have whirlpool baths. Some hallways have a few stairs, and some rooms face a quiet, interior courtyard; if steps or street noise bother you, let the reservation agent know. **Pros:** a good sense of history; close to nightlife. **Cons:** neighborhood noise can be loud. ⊠ 888 S. Broadway, Fells Point ☎ 410/522–7377 or 800/292–4667 ⊕ www.admiralfell.com ⌦ 80 rooms ♿ In-room: a/c, Internet, Wi-Fi. In-hotel: 2 restaurants, bars, Internet terminal, parking (fee) ▭ AE, D, DC, MC, V ⏉| CP ✛ 6G.

$$

Celie's Waterfront Bed & Breakfast. Proprietors Nancy and Kevin Kupec oversee every detail of this small inn in the heart of Fells Point. Guest rooms, all with private bath, are furnished in Early American style; two suites accommodate large groups. Upscale amenities include down comforters, terry robes, fireplaces, and whirlpool baths. Continental breakfast is served in the cozy dining room. The rooftop deck provides a wonderful view of Baltimore's skyline and harbor. **Pros:** intimate accommodations; situated next to an entertainment district. **Cons:** it can get noisy late at night. ⊠ 1714 Thames St., Fells Point ☎ 410/522–2323 or 800/432–0184 ⊕ www.celieswaterfront.com ⌦ 7 rooms, 2 suites ♿ In-room: a/c, Wi-Fi. In-hotel: restaurant, parking (paid) ▭ AE, D, MC, V ⏉| CP ✛ 6H.

$$–$$$

Inn at Henderson's Wharf. Built in the mid-1800s as a B&O Railroad tobacco warehouse, this richly decorated, warmly inviting B&B–style inn has harbor or garden views from all of its rooms. The inn is at the water's edge, on the very peninsula that gave Fells Point its name. Adjacent to the inn is a marina with slips to 150 feet; all possible amenities are available to visiting yachters. It's a short, scenic walk from the shops, bars, and restaurants of central Fells Point. **Pros:** sweeping waterfront views. **Cons:** slightly pricey for the level of accommodations; a considerable hike from downtown attractions. ⊠ 1000 Fell St., Fells Point ☎ 410/522–7777 or 800/522–2088 ⊕ www.hendersonswharf. com ⌦ 37 rooms ♿ In-room: a/c, Wi-Fi. In-hotel: gym, Internet terminal, parking (free) ▭ AE, DC, MC, V ⏉| CP ✛ 6H.

CANTON

$–$$

Inn at 2920. In the heart of one of the city's liveliest neighborhoods, this stylish B&B is dedicated to tranquil, luxurious living. Low-allergen surroundings (natural fiber carpeting, low-chemical cleaning products, purified air) and high-thread-count sheets are standard amenities, and each room has a Jacuzzi bathtub, satellite television, and CD player.

Full-course breakfasts generally include fresh-fruit salad, omelets, and waffles or pancakes, but different dietary needs can be accommodated. **Pros:** stylish and eco-friendly. **Cons:** limited availability. ⊠ *2920 Elliott St.* ☎ *410/342–4450* ⊕ *www.theinnat2920.com* ⬎ *5 rooms* ♨ *In-room: no phone, a/c. In-hotel: Wi-Fi hotspot, no kids under 13* ▤ *AE, D, MC, V* ⎟⊙⎟ *BP* ✢ *6H.*

ROLAND PARK

$$ ☷ **Inn at the Colonnade.** Directly across the street from Johns Hopkins and within walking distance of the Baltimore Museum of Art and the charming Charles Village neighborhood, this hotel is 15 minutes north of downtown. Rooms are welcoming, with rich, warm furnishings, and there are extras such as a glass-dome swimming pool and whirlpool baths. **Pros:** close to Johns Hopkins University; removed from the tourist glut downtown. **Cons:** some rooms can feel run-down; requires a cab ride to most attractions. ⊠ *4 W. University Pkwy., Tuscany-Canterbury* ☎ *410/235–5400* ⊕ *www.doubletree.com* ⬎ *125 rooms, 19 suites* ♨ *In-room: a/c, Wi-Fi. In-hotel: restaurant, bar, pool, gym, parking (paid)* ▤ *AE, D, DC, MC, V* ✢ *2G.*

NORTHERN SUBURBS

$ ☷ **Comfort Inn Hunt Valley.** Guest rooms at this suburban hotel are brightly decorated with basic furnishings. The property is within walking distance of a light-rail station for transportation to downtown Baltimore; the city is an easy 25-minute drive directly down I–83. Although there's no restaurant in the hotel, a free breakfast bar is available every morning, and many restaurants are nearby. A note to outdoor enthusiasts: This hotel is only a short drive from Loch Raven Reservoir. **Pros:** near a light-rail station; budget-friendly. **Cons:** no hotel restaurant; long drive to downtown. ⊠ *11200 York Rd., Hunt Valley* ☎ *410/527–1500* ⊕ *www.choicehotels.com* ⬎ *125 rooms* ♨ *In-room: a/c, refrigerator. In-hotel: gym, Internet terminal, public Wi-Fi, parking (free)* ▤ *AE, D, DC, MC, V* ⎟⊙⎟ *CP* ✢ *1E.*

NIGHTLIFE AND THE ARTS

The *City Paper* (⊕ *www.citypaper.com*), a free weekly distributed in shops and yellow street-corner boxes, has the most comprehensive and complete calendar of Baltimore events; it's published every Wednesday. Other event listings appear in the Thursday edition of the *Baltimore Sun* (⊕ *www.baltimoresun.com*), the monthly *Baltimore* magazine (⊕ *www. baltimoremagazine.net*), and the daily *b* magazine.

Fells Point, just east of the Inner Harbor; Federal Hill, due south; and Canton, due east, have hosts of bars, restaurants, and clubs that draw a rowdy, largely collegiate crowd. If you're seeking quieter surroundings, head for the upscale comforts of downtown or Mount Vernon clubs and watering holes.

BARS AND LOUNGES

Upstairs at **The Brewer's Art** (✉ *1106 N. Charles St., Mount Vernon* ☎ *410/547–6925* ⊕ *www.belgianbeer.com*) is an elegant bar and lounge with armchairs, marble pillars, and chandeliers, plus a dining room with terrific food; downstairs, the dark basement bar specializes in Belgian-style beers. With its stylized art deco surroundings, the funky **Club Charles** (✉ *1724 N. Charles St., Station North Arts District* ☎ *410/727–8815*) is a favorite hangout for an artsy crowd, moviegoers coming from the Charles Theater across the street, and, reputation has it, John Waters. **Club Hippo** (✉ *1 W. Eager St., Mount Vernon* ☎ *410/547–0069* ⊕ *www. clubhippo.com*) is Baltimore's longest-reigning gay bar. The **Dog Pub** (✉ *20 E. Cross St., Federal Hill* ☎ *410/727–6077*) has no TVs, so you focus more on conversation. About 10 beers are made from in-house recipes, and always served two at a time in 10-ounce glass mugs. The patio at the waterside **DuClaw Brewery** (✉ *901 S. Bond St., Fells Point* ☎ *410/563–3400*) is a great spot for an early-evening pint; the restaurant serves bar fare with a twist, but stick to the standards. The well-heeled gather at the Harbor Court Hotel in the **Explorer's Lounge** (✉ *550 Light St., Inner Harbor* ☎ *410/234–0550*), where there are antique elephant-tusk lamps and faux leopard-skin chairs. Enjoy a cigar and pick a single-malt Scotch from one of the largest selections in town. A pianist performs every night, and on Friday and Saturday nights there's a jazz trio. A dance club, martini bar, and pub have all helped make **Grand Central** (✉ *1003 N. Charles St., Mount Vernon* ☎ *410/752–7133*) into a hip gay hot spot. The **Horse You Came In On** (✉ *1626 Thames St., Fells Point* ☎ *410/327–8111*) is a dim, quiet neighborhood tavern during the day and a raucous bar with live music almost every night. The arty, funky **Idle Hour** (✉ *201 E. Fort Ave., Federal Hill* ☎ *410/468–0357*) is a low-key hangout with some of the city's best indie DJs. Beer lovers should visit **Max's Taphouse** (✉ *737 S. Broadway, Fells Point* ☎ *410/675–6297* ⊕ *www.maxs.com*), which has more than 70 brews on tap and about 300 more in bottles. At **Pickles Pub** (✉ *520 Washington Blvd., Inner Harbor* ☎ *410/752–1784*) sports fans banter about trivia, dispute scores, and commiserate over scandals. This is a favorite postgame hangout for Orioles and Ravens fans. **Red Maple** (✉ *930 N. Charles St., Mount Vernon* ☎ *410/547–0149* ⊕ *www.930redmaple.com*) is one of the city's most stylish spots for drinks and tapas. At the top of the Belvedere Hotel, the **13th Floor** (✉ *1 E. Chase St., Mount Vernon* ☎ *410/347–0888*) offers a great view, a long martini list, and live dance music.

CLASSICAL MUSIC

An die Musik (✉ *409 N. Charles St., Mount Vernon* ☎ *410/385–2638* ⊕ *www.andiemusiklive.com*) is an intimate space for classical, jazz, and world music. **Friedberg Hall** (✉ *E. Mount Vernon Pl. at Charles St., Mount Vernon* ☎ *410/659–8124* ⊕ *www.peabody.jhu.edu*), part of the Peabody Institute, is the scene of recitals, concerts, and opera performances by students, faculty, and distinguished guests. **Meyerhoff Symphony Hall** (✉ *1212 Cathedral St., Mount Vernon* ☎ *410/783–8000* ⊕ *www.baltimoresymphony.org*) is the city's principal concert hall and home of the Baltimore Symphony Orchestra. At the outdoor **Pier Six Concert Pavilion** (✉ *731 Eastern Ave., Inner Harbor* ☎ *410/783–4189*

⊕ *www.piersixpavilion.com*) there's both pavilion and lawn seating for concerts showcasing top national musicians and groups. Concerts run from June to September.

COMEDY CLUBS

The Comedy Factory (✉ *36 Light St., Inner Harbor* ☎ *410/752–4189*) is the best local spot to see live standup.

FILM

The **Charles Theater** (✉ *1711 N. Charles St., Mount Vernon* ☎ *410/727–3456* ⊕ *www.thecharles.com*) is Baltimore's preeminent venue for first-run, foreign, and art films. The sleek **Landmark Theatres** (✉ *645 S. President St., Inner Harbor* ☎ *410/624–2622* ⊕ *www.landmarktheatres.com*) offer mainstream films within walking distance of the Inner Harbor. You can order a drink at the bar, take it into the auditorium, and relax in one of the black leather seats. **Rotunda Cinematheque** (✉ *11 W. 40th St., Roland Park* ☎ *410/235–4800*) has two small theaters showing independent films.

POP MUSIC

For some of the city's best and most authentic live blues and rockabilly, head to the **Cat's Eye Pub** (✉ *1730 Thames St., Fells Point* ☎ *410/276–9866* ⊕ *www.catseyepub.com*), which hosts live music every night. **The 8x10 Club** (✉ *8–10 E. Cross St., Federal Hill* ☎ *410/625–2000* ⊕ *www.the8x10.com*) is one of the city's premier spots for live music, from rock and reggae, to jazz, blues, and soul. The spring-loaded dance floor bounces under large crowds, and there is barely a bad place to stand inside. **The Ottobar** (✉ *2549 N. Howard St., Mount Vernon* ☎ *410/662–0069* ⊕ *www.theottobar.com*) is the city's venue for live alternative music—a hipster magnet. **Rams Head Live** (✉ *20 Market Pl., in Power Plant Live, Inner Harbor* ☎ *410/244–8854* ⊕ *www.ramsheadlive.com*) is one of the city's newest live music venues, regularly featuring international and local bands. **Sonar** (✉ *407 E. Saratoga St., Mount Vernon* ☎ *410/327–8333* ⊕ *www.sonarbaltimore.com*) has three separate spaces: a warehouse with a large stage, a club room, and a smaller lounge.

THEATER

The **Baltimore Theatre Project** (✉ *45 W. Preston St., Mount Vernon* ☎ *410/752–8558* ⊕ *www.theatreproject.org*) is dedicated to showing original and experimental theater, music, and dance. **Center Stage** (✉ *700 N. Calvert St., Mount Vernon* ☎ *410/332–0033* ⊕ *www.centerstage.org*) performs works by Shakespeare and Samuel Beckett as well as contemporary playwrights. The intimate **Fells Point Corner Theater** (✉ *251 S. Ann St., Fells Point* ☎ *410/276–7837* ⊕ *www.fpct.org*), an 85-seat venue focused on acting and directing workshops, stages eight off-Broadway productions a year, along with readings and poetry slams. A beautifully restored 1914 movie palace is home to the **France-Merrick Performing Arts Center at the Hippodrome** (✉ *12 N. Eutaw St., West Baltimore* ☎ *410/837–7400* ⊕ *www.france-merrickpac.com*), a stage for concerts, Broadway musicals, and other big productions. **Lyric Opera House** (✉ *140 W. Mt. Royal Ave., Mount Vernon* ☎ *410/685–5086*) hosts plays and musicals in addition to opera productions. **Spotlighters Theater** (✉ *817*

St. Paul St., Mount Vernon ☎ *410/752–1225* ⊕ *www.spotlighters.org*)
is a true community theater, staging locally produced (and cast) works
that include original productions, Shakespeare, and musicals; there's
one production a month, with performances on weekends. The **Vaga-
bond Players** (✉ *806 S. Broadway, Fells Point* ☎ *410/563–9135* ⊕ *www.
vagabondplayers.org*) hosts performances of recent Broadway hits and
theater favorites every weekend.

SPORTS AND THE OUTDOORS

PARTICIPANT SPORTS

BICYCLING

Due to the lack of street-side paths and angry motorists, exploring inner
city Baltimore on two wheels is a bad idea. But the city's most defined
network of bicycling paths is the Gwynns Falls Trail, which connects
2,000 acres of public land in and around Baltimore. The trail, which
was completed in the past couple of years, stretches for about 15 mi.
Maps are available at ⊕ *www.gwynnsfallstrail.org.* Or you could head
to one of the city's parks or out of town to dedicated cycling trails.
Bikes can be rented from **Light Street Cycles** (✉ *1015 Light St., Federal
Hill* ☎ *410/685–2234*); ask for a map of local trails.

Just south of the city is the **Baltimore and Annapolis Trail** (☎ *410/222–
6244*); to get on the trail near BWI airport, follow I–695 to I–97 south,
take Exit 15 onto Dorsey Road, heading west away from the airport.
Look for signs for Saw Mill Creek Park, which has 13 mi of paved
trails, open space, bridges, and woodlands. North of the city, the 21-mi
Northern Central Railroad Hike and Bike Trail (☎ *410/592–2897* ⊕ *www.
dnr.state.md.us/publiclands/central/gunpowder.html*) extends along the
old Northern Central Railroad to the Maryland–Pennsylvania line. It
begins at Ashland Road, just east of York Road in Hunt Valley, and
heads north 20 mi to the Pennsylvania border. Parking is available at
seven points along the way.

GOLF

The *Baltimore Sun*'s **golf guide** (⊕ *www.baltimoresun.com/golfguide*)
gives a detailed and thorough overview of local courses.

Public **Forest Park** (✉ *2900 Hillsdale Rd., North Baltimore* ☎ *410/448–
4653*) has 18 challenging holes (par 71), with a tight, tree-lined front 9
and open back 9. Greens fees are $30 weekdays and $33 on weekends;
reservations are accepted. Designed in 1936, **Mount Pleasant** (✉ *6001
Hillen Rd., North Baltimore* ☎ *410/254–5100*) was for many years the
site of the Eastern Open. It has 18 holes of par-71 golf on bent grass.
Greens fees are $36 on weekdays and $42 on weekends.

HEALTH AND FITNESS CLUBS

A few clubs offer temporary membership to visitors. Your hotel may
provide this as a courtesy, so ask the concierge. Among hotels, the **Harbor Court** has by far the best athletic facilities.

RUNNING

Scenic places to run around the Inner Harbor include the promenade around the water; Rash Field, on the south side, adjacent to the Science Center and Federal Hill Park; and the path at the water's edge at Fort McHenry. If you're staying in Mount Vernon, head north up Charles Street toward Charles Village and Johns Hopkins University.

> ### DUCKPIN BOWLING
>
> Invented in Baltimore in 1900, duckpin bowling uses smaller balls and pins. For some fun and some real Baltimore character, head to the **Patterson Bowling Center** (✉ *2105 Eastern Ave., Fells Point* ☎ *410/675–1011*), the oldest duckpin bowling center in the country.

TENNIS

Courts can be found in the city's public parks, though if you're a serious player, you may be better off using hotel courts or tennis clubs.

Open year-round, the **Cross Keys Tennis Club** (✉ *5100 Falls Rd., Roland Park* ☎ *410/433–1800*) has courts available for $27–$37 per hour. **Druid Hill Park** (✉ *Druid Hill Lake Dr., West Baltimore* ☎ *410/396–6106*) has 24 courts. The courts at the **Orchard Indoor Tennis Club** (✉ *8720 Loch Raven Blvd., Towson* ☎ *410/821–6206*) are available to nonmembers for $25 per hour. **Patterson Park** (✉ *Eastern Ave., East Baltimore* ☎ *410/396–3774*) has 10 courts.

SPECTATOR SPORTS

BASEBALL

The **Baltimore Orioles** (✉ *Oriole Park at Camden Yards, 333 W. Camden St., West Baltimore* ☎ *410/685–9800 general information; 410/481–7328 for tickets* ⊕ *www.theorioles.com*) play in their beautiful ballpark from early April until early October. Think twice about settling on a hot dog and Budweiser for your meal: the stadium also sells lump-meat crab cakes, former Orioles first baseman Boog Powell's barbecued pork loin and beef, and local microbrews, such as Clipper City's Ft. McHenry Lager.

Fodor's Choice ★

8

FOOTBALL

The **Baltimore Ravens** (✉ *1101 Russell St., West Baltimore* ☎ *410/261–7283* ⊕ *www.baltimoreravens.com*) play in state-of-the-art M&T Stadium from August to January.

HORSE RACING

On the third Saturday in May the prestigious Preakness Stakes, the second race in the Triple Crown, is run at Baltimore's **Pimlico Race Course** (✉ *5204 Park Heights Ave., Northwest Baltimore* ☎ *410/542–9400* ⊕ *www.marylandracing.com*). The course has additional Thoroughbred racing. Call ahead for days and times.

LACROSSE

The **Johns Hopkins University Blue Jays** (✉ *Homewood Field, Charles St. at University Pkwy., Charles Village* ☎ *410/516–7490* ⊕ *hopkinssports. cstv.com*) are a perennial favorite.

The **Loyola Greyhounds** (✉ *Charles St. at Cold Spring La., North Baltimore* ☎ *410/617–5014*) play on their college's campus.

SHOPPING

Baltimore isn't the biggest shopping town, but it does have some malls and good stores here and there. Hampden (the "p" is silent), a neighborhood west of Johns Hopkins University, has funky shops selling everything from housewares to housedresses along its main drag, 36th Street (better known as "The Avenue"). Some interesting shops can be found along Charles Street in Mount Vernon and along Thames Street in Fells Point. Federal Hill has a few fun shops, particularly for furnishings and vintage items.

SHOPPING MALLS

About 7 mi north of downtown, at Northern Parkway and York Road, is **Belvedere Square** (✉ *E. Belvedere Ave. at York Rd.* ☎ *410/464–9773*), a small, open-air mall with shops for women's and children's clothing, furniture, and gifts, as well as a number of gourmet food shops (the soup at Atwater's is delicious). At the Inner Harbor, the Pratt Street and Light Street pavilions of **Harborplace and the Gallery** (☎ *410/332–4191*) contain almost 200 specialty shops that sell everything from business attire to children's toys. The Gallery has J. Crew, Banana Republic, and the Gap, among others. **Towson Town Center** (✉ *Dulaney Valley Rd. at Fairmount Ave., 0.5 mi south of I–695 at Exit 27A, Towson* ☎ *410/494–8800* ⊕ *www.towsontowncenter.com*) has nearly 200 shops, including Hecht's, Nordstrom, the Gap, and Anthropologie. **Village of Cross Keys** (✉ *5100 Falls Rd., North Baltimore* ☎ *410/323–1000*), about 6 mi north of downtown, is an eclectic collection of 30 stores, including Talbot's, Chico's, Williams-Sonoma, Ann Taylor, and some small, high-end boutiques for women's clothing and gifts.

DEPARTMENT STORES

For deals on designer clothes, head to **Filene's Basement** (✉ *600 E. Pratt St., Baltimore* ☎ *410/685–2637*), the city's first new department store in decades. Shop for top-name designer goods accompanied by courteous, service-oriented sales staff and live music from a grand piano at **Nordstrom** (✉ *Towson Town Center, 825 Dulaney Valley Rd., Towson* ☎ *410/494–9111*).

FOOD MARKETS

Baltimore's indoor food markets, all of which are at least 100 years old, are a mix of vendors selling fresh fish, meat, produce, and baked goods and a food court, with stands for street food such as crab cakes, sausages, fried chicken, and pizza. Lexington Market is the largest and most famous, and the Broadway and Cross Street markets are close behind in terms of local, taste-tempting foods. City markets are generally open year-round, every day but Sunday. Closing times depend on the market.

Broadway Market (✉ *Broadway at Fleet St., Fells Point*) has many stalls with fresh fruit, prepared foods, a raw bar, and baked goods that can be eaten at counters or taken outside for picnics along the waterfront. **Cross Street Market** (✉ *Light and Cross Sts., Federal Hill*) has stands selling produce, sandwiches, steamed crab, and baked items. Cross Street is open late on Friday and Saturday, when the market hosts one of the city's most popular happy-hour scenes, attracting crowds of youngish professionals. Be sure to stop by Piedigrotta Bakery, where you can sample what the owners claim to be the country's first-ever tiramisu. The city's oldest and largest public market, **Lexington Market** (✉ *400 W. Lexington St., between Paca and Eutaw Sts., Downtown* ☎ *410/685–6169* ⊕ *www.lexingtonmarket.com*) has more than 150 vendors selling meat, produce, seafood, baked goods, delicatessen items, poultry, and food products from around the world. Don't miss the world-famous crab cakes at Faidley's Seafood; other local specialties with market stalls are Rheb's chocolates, Polock Johnny's Polish sausages, and Berger's Bakery's chocolate-iced vanilla wafer cookies.

SPECIALTY STORES

ANTIQUES

Many of Baltimore's antiques shops can be found on historic Antiques Row, which runs along the 700 and 800 blocks of North Howard Street. Shops include cluttered kitsch boutiques as well as elegant, high-end galleries of furniture and fine art. Fells Point shops are concentrated on Eastern, Fleet, and Aliceanna streets. Hampden shops are found primarily on 36th Street.

Avenue Antiques (✉ *901 W. 36th St., Hampden* ☎ *410/467–0329*) is a collection of multiple dealers, selling antiques from Victorian to mid-century modern. **Second Chance** (✉ *1645 Warner St., Southwest Baltimore* ☎ *410/385–1101* ⊕ *www.secondchanceinc.org*) salvages unique architectural pieces from old buildings being renovated or destroyed; the five large warehouses are open Tuesday–Saturday 9–5. The **Turnover Shop** (✉ *3855 Roland Ave., Hampden* ☎ *410/235–9585* ⊕ *www.theturnovershop.com*) is a consignment shop selling high-end antiques.

BOOKS

The **AIA/Baltimore Bookstore** (✉ *11½ W. Chase St., Mount Vernon* ☎ *410/625–2585*) carries all kinds of architecture books. **Atomic Books** (✉ *3620 Falls Rd., Hampden* ☎ *410/366–1004* ⊕ *www.atomicbooks.com*) specializes in obscure titles and small-press publications, including independent comics and 'zines, along with videos. There's also a formidable selection of pop-culture toys such as lunch boxes, cookie jars, and stickers. **Book Thing** (✉ *3001 Vineyard La., Waverly* ☎ *410/662–5631* ⊕ *www.bookthing.org*) takes donations and gives away free books—as many as you like, as long as you promise not to resell them; it's open weekends 9–6. The **Children's Bookstore** (✉ *737 Deepdene Rd., Roland Park* ☎ *410/532–2000* ⊕ *www.thecbstore.com*) is a cozy, well-stocked resource for current and classic children's literature. The **Kelmscott**

8

Bookshop (⊠ *32 W. 25th St., Charles Village* ☎ *410/235–6810* ⊕ *www. kelmscottbookshop.com*) is known for its enormous, well-preserved stock of old and rare volumes in every major category, especially art, architecture, American and English literature, and travel. **Mystery Loves Company** (⊠ *1730 Fleet St., Fells Point* ☎ *410/276–6708* ⊕ *www. mysterylovescompany.com*) specializes in books and gifts for whodunit fans; the shop stocks an excellent selection of works by Baltimore native son (and inventor of the genre) Edgar Allan Poe.

CHILDREN'S CLOTHING

Raw Sugar (⊠ *524 E. Belvedere Ave., Belvedere Square* ☎ *410/464– 1240*) carries clothing for the funky, fashionable six-and-under set as well as maternity wear and toys.

GIFTS

Many of the city's museums have excellent shops, which are good sources for gifts. **Best of Baltimore** (⊠ *301 S. Light St., Inner Harbor* ☎ *410/332–4191*) carries city-related souvenirs and local specialty products. For unique, truly local mementos of Baltimore, like crab-shaped twinkle lights and a kit for cleaning row-house marble steps, **Hometown Girl** (⊠ *1001 W. 36th St., Hampden* ☎ *410/662–4438*) is the place to go. It also stocks local history books and Baltimore guidebooks. The **Store Ltd.** (⊠ *Village of Cross Keys, Roland Park* ☎ *410/323–2350*) has an eclectic mix of top-quality (and pricey) jewelry, women's sportswear, glassware, and other high-design gifts. The **Tomlinson Craft Collection** (⊠ *The Rotunda, 711 W. 40th St., Roland Park* ☎ *410/338–1572*) is a gallery of local artisan handiworks, from fine jewelry to ceramics and metalwork.

JEWELRY

Amaryllis (⊠ *The Gallery, 200 E. Pratt St., Inner Harbor* ☎ *410/576– 7622*) specializes in handcrafted jewelry from more than 400 artists. Designers come from all over the world for the incredibly wide selection of beads at **Beadazzled** (⊠ *501 N. Charles St., Mount Vernon* ☎ *410/837–2323*); there's also a selection of already-made jewelry.

MEN'S CLOTHING

Jos. A. Bank's Clothiers (⊠ *100 E. Pratt St., Inner Harbor* ☎ *410/547– 1700*) is a century-old Baltimore source for men's tailored clothing and casual wear. **Samuel Parker Clothier** (⊠ *6080 Falls Rd., Northern Suburbs* ☎ *410/372–0078* ⊕ *www.samuelparker.com*) carries a fine selection of updated traditional clothing by the likes of Ralph Lauren and Samuelson.

WOMEN'S CLOTHING

Jones & Jones (⊠ *Village of Cross Keys, Roland Park* ☎ *410/532–9645*) carries stylish sportswear and business attire. **Ma Petite Shoe** (⊠ *832 W. 36th St., Hampden* ☎ *410/235–3442*) sells chocolates as well as funky, fabulous shoes. **Oh! Said Rose** (⊠ *832 W. 36th St., Hampden* ☎ *410/235–5170*) carries fun, feminine clothing with a vintage look. **Ruth Shaw** (⊠ *Village of Cross Keys, Roland Park* ☎ *410/532–7886*) sells the work of European designers like Gaultier and Paul Smith as well as chic evening wear. **Something Else** (⊠ *1611 Sulgrave Ave., Mt. Washington* ☎ *410/542–0444*) is the source for sophisticated hippie wear:

Side Trips from Baltimore

Flax-brand clothes, flowing skirts, big scarves, and colorful sweaters. The **Shine Collective** (⊠ 1007 W. 36th St., Hampden ☎ 410/366–6100) carries hip accessories and clothing made by a group of local young designers.

SIDE TRIPS FROM BALTIMORE

Not far from Baltimore, Maryland's landscape is dotted with well-preserved 18th- and 19th-century towns. Harford County's Havre de Grace, at the top of the bay, and nearby Aberdeen, with a legacy of military history, make for an ideal day trip. Historic Ellicott City, southwest of Baltimore in Howard County, is a fun place to explore, have lunch, and shop.

HAVRE DE GRACE

40 mi northeast of Baltimore (via I–95).

On the site of one of Maryland's oldest settlements is the neatly laid-out town of Havre de Grace, reputedly named by the Marquis de Lafayette. This "harbor of mercy," on the Chesapeake Bay at the mouth of the Susquehanna River, was shelled and torched by the British in the War of 1812, and few structures predate that period.

TIMING AND PRECAUTIONS

Depending on the season, you'll want to budget about a half day for Havre de Grace. The waterfront town has gardens and museums to tour, but none of them take too much time. It's a pleasant way to see firsthand some of the area's history. Be sure to stroll down the half-mile boardwalk and stop for a picnic in the park.

ESSENTIALS

Visitor Information **Havre de Grace Visitor Center** (✉ *450 Pennington Ave.* ☎ *410/939–2100).*

EXPLORING

The conical **Concord Point Lighthouse** is the oldest continuously operated lighthouse on the Chesapeake Bay. Built in 1827, it was restored in 1980. You can climb up 30 feet for views of the bay, river, and town. ✉ *700 Concord St.* ☎ *410/939–9040* ✉ *Free* ☉ *Apr.–Oct., weekends 1–5.*

The **Havre de Grace Decoy Museum**, housed in a converted power plant, has 1,200 facsimiles of ducks, geese, and swans made from wood, iron, cork, papier-mâché, and plastic. Three classes—decorative, decorative floater, and working decoys—are represented. A festival during the first full weekend in May includes carving contests and demonstrations by retriever dogs. ✉ *215 Giles St.* ☎ *410/939–3739* ⊕ *www.decoymuseum. com* ✉ *$6* ☉ *Mon.–Sat. 10:30–4:30, Sun. noon–4.*

★ The **Ladew Topiary Gardens** displays the life's work of Harvey Smith Ladew. The trees and shrubs are sculpted into geometric forms and lifelike renditions of animals such as a fox and hounds, swans, and even a sea horse. The 15 formal gardens cover 22 acres. Besides the amazing topiary displays are rose, berry, and herb gardens, and a tranquil Japanese garden with pagoda, lily ponds, and lush flowers. In summer there are special events such as concerts and polo matches. The 18th-century manor house is filled with English antiques, paintings, photographs, and fox-hunting memorabilia. The café serves lunch and light snacks. ✉ *3535 Jarrettsville Pike, 14 mi north of I–695, Monkton* ☎ *410/557– 9466* ⊕ *www.ladewgardens.com* ✉ *House and gardens $13, gardens only $10* ☉ *Mid-Mar.–Oct., weekdays 8–4, weekends 10:30–5.*

One of the few 18th-century structures in Havre de Grace, **Rodgers House** (✉ *226 N. Washington St.*) is a two-story redbrick Georgian town house topped by a dormered attic. The town's most historically significant building, it was the home of Admiral John Rodgers, who fired the first shot in the War of 1812. Like most of the other historic houses in Havre de Grace, it's closed to the public but still worth a drive past.

The **Steppingstone Museum** is a 10-acre complex of seven restored turn-of-the-20th-century farm buildings plus a replica of a canning house. Among the 12,000-plus artifacts in the collection are a horse-drawn tractor and an early gas-powered version, manual seeders and planters, and horse-drawn plows. A blacksmith, a weaver, a wood-carver, a cooper, a dairymaid, and a decoy artist regularly demonstrate their trades in the workshops. ✉ *Susquehanna State Park, 461 Quaker Bottom Rd.* ☎ *410/939–2299* ⊕ *www.steppingstonemuseum.org* ✉ *$3* ☉ *May–Sept., weekends 1–5.*

The **Susquehanna Museum**, at the southern terminal of the defunct Susquehanna and Tidewater Canal, tells the history of the canal and the people who lived and worked there. From 1839 until 1890 the canal ran 45 mi north to Wrightsville, Pennsylvania. It was a thoroughfare for mule-drawn barges loaded with iron ore, coal, and crops. The museum, in a lock tender's cottage built in 1840, is partially furnished with modest mid-century antiques that recall its period of service. ⊠ *Erie and Conesto Sts.* ☎ *410/939–5780* ⊕ *www.thelockhousemuseum.org* ☜ *Donations accepted* ☽ *Weekends 1–5.*

WHERE TO EAT AND STAY

$$–$$$
ECLECTIC
✕ **Chipparelli's.** The owners of Baltimore Little Italy mainstay Chipparelli's recently opened up a second outlet in the Old Chesapeake Hotel, an elegant historic building in the heart of Havre de Grace that dates back to the 1890s. In addition to serving up old-school favorites like Homemade Gnocchi and Spaghetti Toscanini, the location offers guest accommodations—not a bad idea after all that pasta. ⊠ *400 N. Union Ave.* ☎ *410/939–5440* ⊕ *www.chiapparellishdg.com* ▤ *AE, MC, V.*

$$–$$$
SEAFOOD
✕ **MacGregor's.** Behind the redbrick facade of a bank built in 1928, MacGregor's occupies two dining rooms on two levels, with glass walls on three sides looking onto the Chesapeake Bay. The interior is adorned with carved duck decoys, mounted guns, and antique prints of the town; there's also outdoor dining on a deck with a gazebo. Seafood is the specialty, and the kitchen claims to have the best crab cakes on the bay. ⊠ *331 St. John's St.* ☎ *410/939–3003* ⊕ *www.macgregorsrestaurant. com* ▤ *AE, D, DC, MC, V.*

¢–$
🏠 **Spencer-Silver Mansion.** This house was built in 1886 from gray granite quarried at nearby Port Deposit—the same kind of granite was used to build the Brooklyn Bridge. Characteristic Victorian details include stained-glass windows, a wraparound porch, and a turret. The carriage house is a lovely two-story stone cottage with loft bedroom, Jacuzzi, and fireplace; it sleeps up to four but is ideal for couples seeking a romantic hideaway. All rooms are furnished with period antiques supplemented by select reproductions. **Pros:** classic, romantic atmosphere. **Cons:** few amenities; no elevator. ⊠ *200 S. Union Ave.* ☎ *410/939– 1485 or 800/780–1485* ⊕ *www.spencersilvermansion.com* ⇱ *4 rooms, 1 suite* ☖ *In-room: a/c, Wi-Fi* ▤ *AE, MC, V* ⑩ *BP.*

¢–$
🏠 **Vandiver Inn.** This three-story wood house, built in 1886 and listed on the National Register of Historic Places, is 1½ blocks from the bay. Green with dark green trim on the outside, the inn has a Victorian look, with antique beds and other period pieces. A porch extends the width of the house front, and the gazebo in the backyard is as old as the house itself. **Pros:** accommodations with historic charm; budget-friendly. **Cons:** rooms can be dusty and unkempt. ⊠ *301 S. Union Ave.* ☎ *410/939–5200 or 800/245–1655* ⊕ *www.vandiverinn.com* ⇱ *17 rooms* ☖ *In-room: a/c, Internet. In-hotel: Wi-Fi hotspot* ▤ *AE, D, MC, V* ⑩ *BP.*

8

ELLICOTT CITY

12 mi southwest of Baltimore.

Ellicott City was founded in 1772 by three Quaker brothers—John, Andrew, and Joseph Ellicott. By the 1860s Ellicott City had become one of the most prominent milling and manufacturing towns in the east. Today the town retains its historical flavor and is a pleasant place to stroll and browse the many stores and antiques shops. The Howard County Office of Tourism offers walking tours of the town. It's easy to spend a day browsing shops and stopping for meals on the town's main drag. There's a large free parking lot that's well marked and within walking distance from all the stores.

ESSENTIALS

Visitor Information **Howard County Office of Tourism** (⊠ *8267 Main St.* ☎ *410/313–1900 or 800/288–8747* ⊕ *www.visithowardcounty.com*).

EXPLORING

Ellicott City was the B&O Railroad's first stop. The **Ellicott City B&O Railroad Station Museum**, built in 1831, is the oldest surviving railroad terminal in America. Exhibits focus on the history of the railroad and on its role in the Civil War. ⊠ *2711 Maryland Ave.* ☎ *410/461–1945* ⊕ *www.ecborail.org* 🎟 *$5* ☉ *Wed.–Sun. 11–4.*

Frederick and Western Maryland

WORD OF MOUTH

"The artillery re-enactment we wanted to see was in a remote field near the high point at Fox's Gap . . . A battery of four period cannon surrounded by fully costumed re-enactors were in the field facing east. About 400 yards away across a small valley, two cannon faced back at us . . . When the guns fired, the concussion was stunning, actually reverberating through our bones and organs. The booms rolled across the small valley, echoing for seconds like thunder . . . The thought of men charging directly at such artillery during a battle was unfathomable. We then headed to Antietam National Battlefield itself—the site of the greatest single day loss of life in combat in American history . . ."

—MRand

Updated by
Donna M.
Owens

Although just a short drive from Washington, Baltimore, and Pittsburgh, western Maryland and Frederick County feel a world apart, with their postcard-perfect vistas and vintage feel. Sometimes called "The Mountain Side of Maryland," travelers are drawn here by sweeping views of the Allegheny Mountains, especially when the foliage turns rich shades of gold and russet. Others come to explore the area's historic Civil War past at Harpers Ferry, Monocacy, and Antietam National Battlefield, scene of the bloodiest one-day battle in the nation's history. The past is inescapable here: everywhere there are reminders of the men in blue and gray who clashed during the Civil War, and the steam engines that chugged through mountainous passes into the wilderness.

Many of the area's most verdant regions were once home to coal mines, lumber mills, factories, and railroad stations. Indeed, the crossroads of the Baltimore & Ohio Railroad, the Chesapeake & Ohio Canal, and the National Road, kept western Maryland alive with industry in centuries past. As transportation patterns changed businesses pulled out, workers left, and whole towns died. Mother Nature reclaimed the land with dense stands of hickory, oak, and pine trees. The state and federal government took advantage of the remote space and today have preserved great swaths of parkland.

The lush woods of Swallow Falls State Park on the western edge of the state and Catoctin Mountain National Park in Frederick are ideal for long hikes. Swimmers and boaters can explore the dark blue waters of man-made Deep Creek Lake, where there's freshwater fishing in warm months and even ice fishing in winter. As the weather chills, skiers, snowboarders and tubers can zip down the slopes of the Wisp Resort. The Potomac and Shenandoah rivers can be explored by kayak, canoe, or inner tube, and white-water rafting is popular. Cyclists bike along the historic C&O Canal (built in 1828) and its towpath that stretches from Cumberland to the nation's capital. Nestled among the region's cool, fresh forests is the nation's most famous retreat—Camp David—where every president from Franklin D. Roosevelt to Barack Obama has sought refuge.

Western Maryland and Frederick County are both changing in some ways, however. In recent years, Washingtonians have flocked to Frederick, making the historic environs more contemporary and hip. Although housing developments and strip malls have replaced farmland on the

TOP REASONS TO GO

Explore Civil War History: Visit Harpers Ferry, scene of abolitionist John Brown's famous raid; view patriot Barbara Fritchie's home in Frederick; learn about slaves and free persons who helped heal the Civil War wounded; and walk the hallowed Antietam National Battlefield.

Sea and Ski: Swim, boat, and water-ski all summer in Deep Creek Lake, Maryland's largest man-made body of water. Come back in winter to ski or relax by a blazing fire at a lodge.

Bike the Canal: Follow the trail along the old Chesapeake & Ohio Canal towpath and take in the spectacular panoramic views. Bike between Washington, D.C., and Cumberland, stopping for coffee and conversation off the beaten path.

Fall in Love: Snuggle by the fireplace at a Victorian mansion turned B&B. Dine by candlelight at first-class restaurants. Stroll hand-in-hand and window-shop along the cobblestone streets of revitalized Main Streets that date back centuries. Sip vino and enjoy tastings at family-owned wineries and local breweries.

outside of town, the newer residents have also sparked an artistic revival and the opening of trendy boutiques. Staid diners have been replaced with sushi bars and restaurants featuring the tastes of India, Ethiopia, Thailand, and award-winning American nouveau cuisine. Frederick's neighbors—Hagerstown, Cumberland, and Oakland among them—have also revitalized their downtowns with brick facades, eateries, antiques stores, and quaint shops.

ORIENTATION AND PLANNING

GETTING ORIENTED

There's been good-natured debate as to just where western Maryland officially begins. State tourism officials define Western Maryland as Washington, Allegany, and Garrett Counties. Then there's Frederick County—less than an hour from Washington, D.C., and Baltimore—a place where the landscape begins to transform from rolling hills to more rugged terrain in the north and west. Many see this as the beginning of the Western Maryland region, but these days, state highway maps and the state visitor guide, designate it as part of the Capital region. Despite that "official" designation, calling Frederick County part of Western Maryland isn't too far off the mark.

For many residents of Allegany and Garrett counties, western Maryland begins just west of a man-made cut in a mountain called Sideling Hill. This unusual geological formation has become an attraction among motorists tooling along I–68. As one drives past rock formations that are several million years old, the highway opens to sweeping views of mountain ridges, shaded blue in the fading sunset. These are the Alleghenies, Maryland's majestic mountains.

Frederick. Maryland's fourth-largest city (according to recent Census data) is surrounded by rolling farmland and rugged mountains. Top attractions include everything from fine dining to history lessons to outdoor activities like kayaking and cross-country skiing.

Hagerstown. Located in Washington County, northwest of Frederick, Hagerstown is the county seat. Nicknamed the "Hub City" for its transit and commerce reputation, it's got everything from Civil War sites to outlet shopping and golf. It's a great base for excursions to the C&O Canal, various state parks, and the Appalachian Trail.

Western Maryland. Farther west, the rugged mountains of Allegany County are crossed by the "Historic National Road," also known as the Old National Pike: once a route that numerous westward pioneers traveled in covered wagons. Today it's the site of a scenic railroad excursion. Maryland's westernmost county, Garrett County, was once the vacation destination of railroad barons and Washington's high society; it's now a major destination for boaters, fishermen, and other outdoor enthusiasts. Like its neighbor Frederick County, Washington County boasts historic arch bridges, most built before the end of the Civil War.

PLANNING

WHEN TO GO

Most of Washington County's main historical attractions are busiest during the spring and summer months. The many special events found in the area happen sometime between May and December. Spring and fall offer milder temperatures and are ideal for taking in the sights—and in fall you get the added bonus of the colorful foliage.

At the **Antietam National Battlefield Memorial Illumination** (☎ *301/432–5124* ⊕ *www.nps.gov/anti/planyourvisit/luminary.htm*) in early December (weather permitting), a sea of flickering luminaries—23,110 in all—glow in poignant tribute to Union and Confederate soldiers who were killed or wounded on September 17, 1862—the nation's single bloodiest day of battle. The annual event draws lines of cars up to two hours long, according to the National Park Service. On the first weekend in June, hundreds of fine artists and skilled craftspeople sell their wares to large crowds at the **Frederick Festival of the Arts** (☎ *301/662–4190* ⊕ *www.frederickarts.org*). Held along Carroll Creek Linear Park, the popular, two-day juried festival features theater groups, a film festival, children's performances, and more. The city's numerous galleries extend their hours, too. When the forests of western Maryland turn rich shades of umber, it's time for October's **Autumn Glory Festival** (☎ *301/387–4386* ⊕ *www.visitdeepcreek.com*). Held in quaint Oakland since 1967, the huge Garrett County event typically features an Appalachian-style fiddle and banjo competition, antiques and craft shows with everything from homemade quilts to stained-glass demonstrations, a parade, and an Oktoberfest-themed dinner.

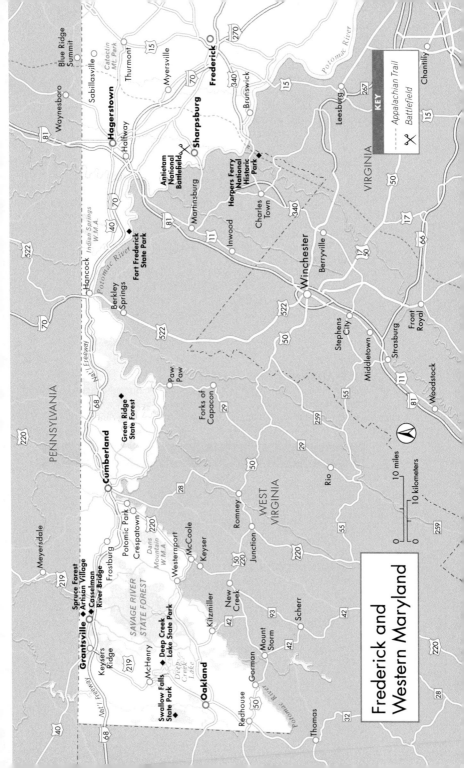

Frederick and Western Maryland

KEY
- - - - Appalachian Trail
✗ Battlefield

PENNSYLVANIA

VIRGINIA

WEST VIRGINIA

Blue Ridge Summit
Waynesboro
Sabillasville
Catoctin Mt. Park
Thurmont
Myersville
Frederick
Hagerstown
Halfway
Sharpsburg
Brunswick
Leesburg
Chantilly
Anietam National Battlefield
Harpers Ferry National Historic Park
Martinsburg
Charles Town
Meyersdale
Hancock
Berkley Springs
Fort Frederick State Park
Indian Springs W.M.A.
Inwood
Winchester
Berryville
Stephens City
Middletown
Strasburg
Front Royal
Woodstock
Green Ridge State Forest
Paw Paw
Forks of Capacon
Rio
Cumberland
Potomic Park
Crespatown
Dans Mountain W.M.A.
Westernport
McCoole
Keyser
Romney
Junction
New Creek
Scherr
Mount Storm
Gorman
Thomas
Redhouse
Oakland
Swallow Falls State Park
Deep Creek Lake State Park
McHenry
Keysers Ridge
Frostburg
Grantsville
Spruce Forest Artisan Village
Casselman River Bridge
SAVAGE RIVER STATE FOREST
Kitzmiller
Potomac River

National Freeway

10 miles
10 kilometers

GETTING HERE AND AROUND
AIR TRAVEL
Most travelers land at one of the three main airports in the Washington-Baltimore area: Dulles, Reagan National, or Baltimore/Washington International Thurgood Marshall (aka BWI-Marshall). All three airports are about two hours from Frederick and Hagerstown by car. Both cities, along with Cumberland have their own small airports.

CAR TRAVEL
The best way to explore the verdant mountain roads of western Maryland is by car. Interstate 70 links Frederick to Hagerstown and intersects with Route 15 and I–270 (the main highway to Washington, D.C.). West of Hagerstown, I–68 (the main road through western Maryland) passes through some of the most picturesque stretches of the state. Follow Route 219 off I–68 to reach Deep Creek Lake and the more remote areas of Garrett County.

TRAIN TRAVEL
The Maryland Area Rail Commuter (MARC) system has a line that runs from Frederick southwest to Point of Rocks on the Potomac River and then onto Washington, D.C. Amtrak service is available from Washington, D.C., to Cumberland. The schedules seem designed for commuters versus tourists, so call ahead.

Train Contacts Maryland Transit Administration (☎ *410/539–5000 or 866/743–3682* ⊕ *www.mtamaryland.com*).

RESTAURANTS AND HOTELS
Chain hotels are found in most larger cities and along the highways, but the best way to soak up the region's tranquil ambience is at an elegant B&B. For more rugged accommodations, spacious rental homes are available along the shores of Deep Creek Lake.

WHAT IT COSTS				
	¢	$	$$	$$$	$$$$
Restaurants	under $10	$10–$16	$17–$23	$24–$30	over $30
Hotels	under $100	$100–$160	$161–$230	$231–$300	over $300

Restaurant prices are per person for a main course at dinner. Hotel prices are for a standard double room, excluding state tax.

PLANNING YOUR TIME
If your time is limited to a weekend, spend a few hours touring somber Antietam; in Frederick, check out the downtown historic district's shops, museums, and restaurants; and hike or bike along one of the many mountain trails. If you're in search of serious relaxation, it's easy to pass the time exploring the area's peaceful small towns, historic homes, and scenic lakes and forests.

FREDERICK

With roots dating back to the 1700s, Frederick was once known mostly for its American history, museums, and federal-style architecture. But in recent years, the city has undergone a renaissance. Thanks in part to new residents from nearby Washington, D.C., the downtown is now lauded for its thriving arts community, and upscale boutiques and restaurants.

In fact, Frederick has emerged as a dining destination, fueled in part by fresh produce from some of the region's best farms, and a growing selection of local beers and wines. The Frederick Wine Trail, even has a stop at a winery in downtown. There are some 60 restaurants, specialty food shops, cafés, bakeries, and coffee and teahouses within just a few short blocks of one other.

You could spend a day or more meandering the cobblestone streets of the leafy, expansive historic district and admiring the city's famed "clustered" spires. Be sure to browse the antiques stores and assortment of artsy shops.

GETTING HERE AND AROUND

Frederick is easy to navigate by car and street parking is plentiful. Frederick TransIT, run by the county, provides shuttle bus service within Frederick and to outlying towns, including Thurmont, Emmitsburg, Jefferson, and Walkersville. It does not run on Sunday. There is a MARC train station in Downtown Frederick, Point of Rocks, and Brunswick. The MARC train to Washington, D.C., runs Monday through Friday, departing Frederick three times in the morning and returning three times in the evening. (Travelers coming from DC should plan to arrive on an evening train, and depart on a morning train, Monday through Friday; there is no weekend service). The Downtown Frederick station (⊠ *100 S. East St., Frederick, MD*), which is also the Greyhound bus station, and is very convenient to shops, restaurants, and accommodations. Taxis are available as well.

TOURS Guided walking tours of the city's historic district ($7) depart on Saturday and Sunday mornings in the spring, summer, and fall, from the new visitor center. Maps are also available for self-guided walks. At night, costumed guides leading the Candlelight Ghost Tour spin tales of gory history as you walk the city's dark streets and alleys. The tours depart from Brewer's Alley restaurant and brewery, and take place from June through November. Cost is $8 for adults and $4 for children.

Frederick tourism officials and partners have recently unveiled an updated African-American Heritage brochure, with a suggested walking tour itinerary. It includes points of interest and properties designated on the Underground Railroad Network to Freedom and more, including the recent discovery of an intact slave village at Monocacy National Battlefield.

ESSENTIALS

Transportation Information Frederick TransIT (☎ *301/694–2065* ⊕ *www. co.frederick.md.us/transit*). **Frederick Train Station** (⊠ *100 S. East St.* ☎ *301/663–3311*).

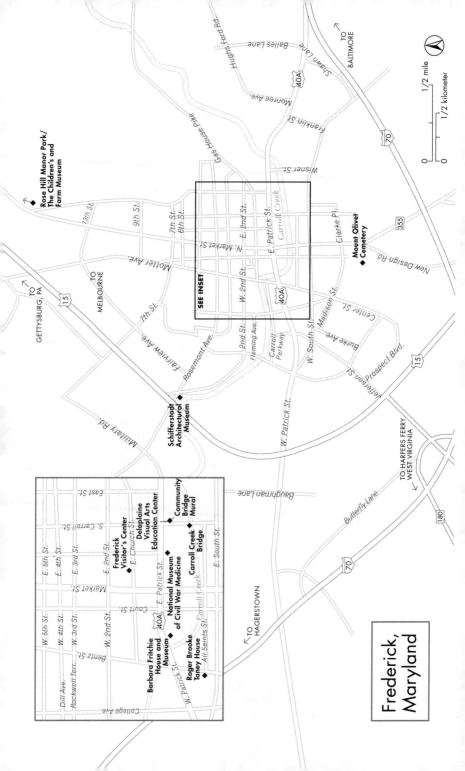

Frederick, Maryland

Visitor Information **Tourism Council of Frederick County** (✉ *151 S. East St.* ☎ *301/600–4047 or 800/999–3613* ⊕ *www.fredericktourism.org*).

EXPLORING

TOP ATTRACTIONS

★ **Barbara Fritchie House**. According to legend, 95-year-old Barbara Fritchie—the wife of a glove maker and neighbor of Francis Scott Key—defiantly hung the Union Jack from her window as Confederate troops marched through Frederick in 1862. This reproduction of her home, constructed from original bricks, is furnished with Fritchie's belongings, including the tea set from which she served George Washington. The patriot's story caught the imagination of poet John Greenleaf Whittier, who penned "The Ballad of Barbara Fritchie." When Winston Churchill visited the home en route to a meeting at Camp David with President Franklin D. Roosevelt, he recited Whittier's poem, "Shoot if you must this old gray head, but spare your country's flag." The home is privately owned and is not open to the public. There are interpreter markers outside. ✉ *154 W. Patrick St.*

Frederick Visitor Center. After more than three decades in a previous location, a new Frederick Visitor Center is expected to open in early 2011 near the new I–70 interchange on East Street. The Tourism Council of Frederick County is renovating the circa-1899 industrial warehouse; as of this writing, construction was well underway. In addition to maps, brochures, and displays highlighting regional attractions and amenities, the new center will boast a 2,200-square foot exhibit area, an orientation film about Frederick County, and expanded restroom facilities. Guided 90-minute walking tours will leave from the center on weekends (Saturday at 11 am; Sunday at 1:30 pm), from May through October. ✉ *151 S. East St.* ☎ *301/600–4047 or 800/999–3613* ⊕ *www. fredericktourism.org* 🎫 *Tour $7* ⊙ *Daily 9–5.*

9

National Museum of Civil War Medicine. The critical role that early medicine played in the Civil War is front and center at this museum, believed to be the only one of its kind. Housed in a former funeral home that prepped the bodies of soldiers who died at Antietam, it's said that ghostly footsteps sometimes echo in the night. By day, a soundtrack of moans and groans plays as visitors wander past a life-size tableau of soldiers preparing to amputate a comrade's leg. A Civil War ambulance, hospital tent, and various surgical instruments testify to the advances in technology that the war fostered. The museum also highlights the documented but barely-known role of black Civil War doctors and nurses, and camp life for black soldiers. Finally, letters written by wounded patients illustrate humanity amid the tragedies of war. ✉ *48 E. Patrick St.* ☎ *301/695–1864* ⊕ *www.civilwarmed.org* 🎫 *$6.50, $4.50 children, $6 seniors and military* ⊙ *Mon.–Sat. 10–5, Sun. 11–5.*

Roger Brooke Taney House. Taney began his law career in Frederick, but is best known as the Chief Supreme Court Justice who wrote the controversial 1857 Dred Scott decision. Taney's opinion, which said that slaves were not citizens and therefore had no Constitutional rights, helped move the country toward Civil War. The brick Federal-style home turned museum offers insight into Taney's life (his wife was the sister of his law partner, Francis Scott Key), middle-class life in the late 1800s, and the slaves he owned. A bust of Taney stands at Frederick's City Hall Plaza, a few feet from a plaque explaining the Dred Scott ruling. ⊠ *121 S. Bentz St.* ☎ *301/663–7880* ⊿ *$3* ☉ *Apr.–mid-Dec., Sat. 10–4, Sun. 1–4.*

WORTH NOTING

Community Bridge Mural. From an outstretched hand to a Constellation shaped like a drinking gourd, dozens of images and symbols are woven into this sweeping and remarkable trompe-l'oeil mural, which makes a humble concrete bridge appear ivy-covered and made of intricately carved stone. The public art is the work of nationally known artist William Cochran who used ideas submitted by Frederick residents and others nationwide as inspiration. The bridge and the waterway it spans are part of the multimillion-dollar construction, development, and renovation efforts that revitalized the Carroll Creek Park area. Restaurants offer outside seating along the walkways that flank the creek and bands play during summer festivals. Thousands of visitors now enjoy this area's charms year-round. ⊠ *Carroll Street Bridge between E. Patrick and E. All Saints Sts.* ☎ *301/228–2888* ⊕ *bridge.skyline.net.*

The Delaplaine Visual Arts Education Center. Named for a prominent family that helped settle Frederick, this former historic flour mill overlooking Frederick's Community Bridge now houses art exhibits as well as art classes and programs—and admission is free. A gift shop sells fine jewelry and local crafts and the new sculpture garden is well worth a visit. ⊠ *40 S. Carroll St.* ☎ *301/698–0656* ⊕ *www.delaplaine.org* ☉ *Mon.– Sat. 9–5, Sun. 1–4.*

☼ **Rose Hill Manor Park/The Children's and Farm Museum.** The home of Maryland's first governor, Thomas Johnson, the mansion has been reinvented as a children's museum. Costumed interpreters lead kids through the house and grounds, where they can dress up in period clothing, weave on a loom, and play with reproductions of toys from the 1700s and 1800s. Visitors can also explore a collection of carriages, a log cabin and blacksmith shop, herb gardens, and a smokehouse. ⊠ *1611 N. Market St.* ☎ *301/600–1646* ⊕ *www.rosehillmuseum.com* ⊿ *$5* ☉ *Apr.– Oct., Mon.–Sat. 10–4, Sun. 1–4; Nov., Sat. 10–4, Sun. 1–4.*

Mount Olivet Cemetery. Francis Scott Key—who penned "The Star Spangled Banner"—Barbara Fritchie, and the state's first governor, Thomas Johnson, rest in this cemetery, which dates to the 1850s. Tidy rows of graves (some inscribed to unknown children), pay tribute to Union and Confederate troops who perished in the battles of Antietam and Monocacy. ⊠ *515 S. Market St.* ☎ *301/662–1164* ⊕ *www. mountolivetcemeteryinc.com* ☉ *Daily dawn–dusk.*

Schifferstadt Architectural Museum. Believed to be the oldest house in Frederick, this unusual stone structure was built in 1756 by German immigrants. Spared from the wrecking ball two decades ago by preservation-minded citizens, the house-turned-museum is considered one of the finest examples of German architecture in Colonial America. The privately owned home is staffed by volunteers; open days and hours vary. ⊠ *1110 Rosemont Ave.* ☎ *301/663–3885* ⊜ *$3* ⊙ *Call for days/ hours of operation.*

WHERE TO EAT

$ ✗ **Brewer's Alley.** With more than a dozen beers brewed on the premises,
AMERICAN a menu featuring locally grown and organic produce, plus a bright, airy dining room and outdoor patio, Frederick's original brewpub is a crowd-pleaser that draws families, local office workers, and a Happy Hour crowd. The Germanic brews include an award-winning golden Kölsch, a spicy Hefeweizen, and a malty Maibock. Try the upscale twists on pub favorites like creamy Maryland crab dip with poblano chilies, a pulled-pork sandwich made with local hickory smoked pork, and grilled chicken served in a rosemary peach sauce with toasted pecans. ⊠ *124 N. Market St.* ☎ *301/631–0089* ⊕ *www.brewers-alley. com* ⊟ *AE, DC, MC, V.*

$$$ ✗ **Danielle's.** From the elegant black-and-red dining room to the lush
ITALIAN plants and trickling waterfall in the bricked courtyard, you'll want to dress snazzily for this upscale American and Italian restaurant. Signature dishes like the decadent "exploding" shrimp appetizer and the baked *radiatore*—lobster, scallops, and shrimp in a creamy sherry tomato sauce—are a hit. End your meal with bananas Foster, prepared tableside with flaming liqueur. The cheerful high-ceiling bar area offers a menu of updated pub favorites like sliders as well as excellent happy-hour specials. Musicians play in the garden on Thursday and Friday during warm weather. ⊠ *6 East St.* ☎ *301/663–6600* ⊕ *www.danielles-restaurant.com* ⊟ *AE, DC, MC, V.*

$$$ ✗ **Firestone's.** With its embossed tin ceiling, dark-wood bar, and cheer-
AMERICAN ful service, Firestone's serves up old-fashioned elegance with a nou-
★ velle menu and a telephone book of a wine list. Locals rave about the food. Start with the lobster, mango, and avocado salad tossed with ginger-shallot vinaigrette and move on to the veal strip steak with tangy goat cheese gnocchi and oyster mushrooms, or the "shank of swine" braised in hard cider and served with sautéed bacon and bok choy. An easy, but sophisticated Sunday brunch can be kicked off with a bottomless mimosa. ⊠ *105 N. Market St.* ☎ *301/663–0330* ⊕ *www. firestonesrestaurant.com* ⊟ *AE, D, MC, V* ⊙ *Closed Mon.*

$$ ✗ **Isabella's.** A touch of Andalusia in historic Frederick, Isabella's draws
SPANISH lively crowds with a dazzling selection of both hot and cold tapas—
★ small plates intended to be shared. They incorporate the farm to table concept with local produce. Dishes include saffron-infused buttered artichokes stuffed with lumps of crab, delicately flavored chicken mousse alongside rich roasted quail, and goat cheese and almond frit-ters. Savory paellas, steaks, and seafood cooked with Mediterranean spices satisfy heartier appetites. ⊠ *44 N. Market St.* ☎ *301/698–8922* ⊕ *www.isabellas-tavern.com* ⊟ *AE, D, DC, MC, V* ⊙ *Closed Mon.*

$ ✗ **La Paz.** On summer evenings, locals and tourists crowd onto the
MEXICAN elegant brick patio to sip raspberry and pomegranate-flavor margari-tas and munch on overstuffed quesadillas and blackened tilapia tacos. Year-round, the cozy dining room evokes a hacienda with rustic wooden beams and brightly colored paintings by Mexican artists. The marinated

strip steak, creamy chicken La Paz, and crab cakes served with jalapeño tartar sauce are, as they say in Spanish, delicioso. ⊠ *51 S. Market St.* ☎ *301/694–8980* ⊕ *www.lapazmex.com* ▤ *AE, MC, V.*

$$$ ✕ **The Red Horse.** Anyplace with a cheerful red horse perched on the roof
STEAK has got to be interesting, right? Indeed, this restaurant is not a hokey tourist trap but a popular local institution known for sizzling, thick-cut steaks. The dining room decor with its wagon-wheel chandelier isn't for everyone, but the service is good, the wine and spirits list is extensive, and the menu, though not fancy, features time-honored favorites such as bacon-wrapped scallops and broiled flounder stuffed with crab imperial. ⊠ *996 W. Patrick St.* ☎ *301/663–3030* ⊕ *www.redhorseusa. com* ▤ *AE, D, DC, MC, V.*

$$$$ ✕ **VOLT.** Award-winning Chef Bryan Voltaggio returned home to Fred-
NEW AMERICAN erick in 2008 to launch this inventive restaurant in downtown's historic district. Since then, it's had national food writers gushing and gourmands vying for coveted reservations. Situated in an 1890s brownstone mansion, VOLT offers contemporary haute-cuisine, built on seasonal ingredients and local agriculture. Chef Voltaggio, a Culinary Institute of America grad who gained reality TV fame on *Top Chef,* definitely pushes the culinary envelope. Fare ranges from seven-course vegetarian menus to savory molecular gastronomy. For the latter, he may prepare sweetbreads with flavors of picata, meyer lemon, and kalamata olive; or a sophisticated dessert, like "Textures of Chocolate." Besides an à la carte menu in the 38-seat main dining room, VOLT also features a sleek bar/lounge, a 14-seat Kitchen Dining Room, and "Table 21" located in the kitchen. The extensive wine list includes nearly 500 choice labels. Brunch is served Sunday. As of this writing, buzz had begun about plans (though incomplete) for a second, more casual Voltaggio restaurant in town. In the meantime, lunch offers a three-course tasting menu at a more economic price. ⊠ *228 N. Market St., Frederick* ☎ *301/696–8658* ⊕ *www.voltrestaurant.com* ☌ *Reservations essential* ▤ *AE, MC, V* ☾ *Closed Mon.–Tues.*

WHERE TO STAY

$$$–$$$$ ▦ **Antrim 1844.** The graceful antebellum mansion, charming outbuild-
★ ings, and immaculate gardens here comprise one of the region's premier countryside hotels. Once the centerpiece of a massive plantation, the mansion has been lovingly renovated into nine guest rooms. Nearly three-dozen additional suites are tucked into smaller, but equally lovely, adjoining buildings, including an icehouse, carriage house, and barn. Each has a unique feeling, but all include luxurious details, whether a wood-burning fireplace, private balcony, whirlpool, steam shower, or canopy feather bed. A swimming pool, gazebo, tennis court, croquet field, and putting greens are interspersed with the elegant topiary gardens. Just 15 minutes from Gettysburg, the inn is a popular choice for weddings and romantic getaways. Note: it's technically outside of Western Maryland in Caroll County. **Pros:** opulent setting; restaurant on-site. **Cons:** pricier than other area B&Bs. ⊠ *30 Trevanion Rd., Taneytown* ☎ *410/756–6812 or 800/858–1844* ⊕ *www.antrim1844. com* ☞ *9 rooms, 31 suites* ☖ *In-room: no phone, a/c, no TV (some).*

In-hotel: restaurant, bar, tennis court, pool, no kids under 12 ▭ *AE, MC, V* ❏ *BP.*

$–$$ 🏠 **Hill House B&B.** Built circa 1870, this three-story Victorian house has been lovingly restored by owners Taylor and Damian Branson. The result is a cozy place to slumber right in the historic district. The four rooms are uniquely and individually decorated (from romantic canopied beds to twin beds with a Mexican theme) and have private baths. Bring your appetite: the hosts serve a full Southern breakfast. **Pros:** within walking distance of dozens of restaurants. **Cons:** limited number of rooms. ✉ *12 W. 3rd St., Frederick* ☎ *301/682–4111* ⊕ *www. hillhousefrederick.com* ⇆ *4 rooms* ⚹ *In-room: no phone, a/c, safe (some), refrigerator (some), DVD (some), Internet, Wi-Fi. In-hotel: Internet terminal, Wi-Fi hotspot, parking (free), no kids under 13* ▭ *MC, V* ❏ *BP.*

$ 🏠 **Hollerstown Hill B&B.** Built circa 1900, this Victorian home-turned-inn is embellished with lace and chintz wallpaper. Claw-footed tubs and pull-chain toilets add to the vintage feel, but the home also features modern amenities like wireless Internet throughout the mansion. Guests can amuse themselves wandering the gardens, playing billiards, enjoying a game of chess on a set that has Civil War pieces, or admiring the owner's collection of antique dolls. A hearty country-style breakfast with home-baked breads and casseroles is served each morning. **Pros:** quaint ambience and Wi-Fi. **Cons:** the kids can't come along. ✉ *4 Clarke Pl.* ☎ *301/228–3630* ⊕ *www.hollerstownhill.com* ⇆ *4 rooms* ⚹ *In-room: a/c, Wi-Fi. In-hotel: Wi-Fi hotspot, no kids under 15* ▭ *AE, MC, V.*

$$ 🏠 **Inn at Stone Manor.** Situated on a sweeping 114-acre estate that houses the Stone Manor Country Club, this posh Bed & Breakfast and guest house offers serene accommodations with an aura of European elegance. Suites have whirlpool baths and fireplaces, plus private balconies. There's free Wi-Fi and a full breakfast. The scenic environs are also suitable for weddings or corporate hobnobbing. **Pros:** intimate and cozy. **Cons:** your favorite TV show will have to wait. ✉ *5820 Carroll Boyer Rd., Middletown* ☎ *301/371–0099* ⊕ *www.stonemanorcountryclub. com* ⇆ *6 rooms* ⚹ *In-room: no phone, a/c, no TV, Wi-Fi. In-hotel: spa, bicycles, Wi-Fi hotspot, parking (free)* ▭ *D, MC, V* ❏ *BP.*

NIGHTLIFE AND THE ARTS

Thanks to new development projects and new residents in the last decade or so, Frederick's downtown has become positively vibrant. Galleries open their doors on First Saturdays, and restaurants often run specials. The group *Celebrate Frederick* hosts a Sunday night concert series from June through August at the Baker Park bandshell, a few blocks from the main drag. They also host a SummerFest Family Theatre program (also free) on Thursdays from June through August. To learn more visit ⊕ *www.celebratefrederick.com.*

Frederick Coffee Company. At this intimate little spot that was once a 1930s filling station, one can sip a latte and nibble on a sandwich while taking in the casual, artsy scene. It's open weekdays 7–9 and weekends 9–9. Feeling inspired? Tuesday is open-mic night. ✉ *Shab*

Row–Everedy Sq., 100 East St. ☎*301/698–0039 or 800/822–0806* ⊕ *www.fredcoffeeco.com.*

Weinberg Center for the Arts. A 1920s movie marquee heralds the entrance to this downtown cultural hub for plays, musical performances, and more. Past performers have included singer Emmy Lou Harris, South African a cappella singing group Ladysmith Black Mambazo, the Second City comedy troupe, and the Baltimore Symphony Orchestra (BSO). ✉ *20 W. Patrick St.* ☎ *301/228–2828* ⊕ *www.weinbergcenter.org.*

SPORTS AND THE OUTDOORS

HIKING

The famed **Appalachian Trail** crosses the spine of South Mountain just west of Frederick, from the Potomac River to the Pennsylvania line. Several well-known and scenic viewpoints along Maryland's 40-mi stretch include Annapolis Rocks and Weverton Cliffs. The best access points are Gathland State Park, Washington Monument State Park, and Greenbrier State Park—and they even have parking. For more information, contact the **Appalachian Trail Conference** (✉ *799 Washington St., Harpers Ferry, WV* ☎ *304/535–6331* ⊕ *www.appalachiantrail.org*).

SHOPPING

Downtown Frederick has blossomed with a profusion of boutiques in recent years, and has emerged as one of the state's best shopping destinations. Storefronts where livestock, feed and bolts of gingham were sold in the not-too-distant past are now filled with trendy and designer clothing, eclectic home furnishings, and quirky novelties.

Cross a magician's workshop with a child's daydream and you'd get something like **Dancing Bear Toys and Gifts** (✉ *12 N. Market St.* ☎ *301/631–9300*), where you can find tooth-fairy boxes, a bowling set with bunny-shaped pins, musical stacking boxes, and paintings with secret doors that open into mirrors. **Everedy Square & Shab Row** (✉ *Corner of East and Church Sts.* ☎ *301/662–4140*) is a complex of former factories turned into artsy shops and galleries. Bring home a punchy-patterned pillow or sinuously shaped salt shaker from **Home Essentials** (✉ *38 E. Patrick St.* ☎ *301/696–9070*). Yummy-smelling soaps are handmade on the premises at **Le Savon: The Soap Factory** (✉ *10 E. Church St.* ☎ *301/694–5002*). Fragrances include spicy Japanese Dusk, sweet O Honey Fairest, and Frederick—a fresh woodsy scent. Wanna deck out your home like a Victorian B&B? Then visit **Molly's Meanderings** (✉ *17 N. Market St.* ☎ *301/668–8075*) for lacy linens, sweet tea-scented soaps, and ornate silver lockets. The trendier set head toward **Velvet Lounge** (✉ *201 N. Market St.* ☎ *301/695–4472*) for jeans from Chip & Pepper, and cute hoodies and tees from Volcom and Obey. Browsing the hundreds of thousands of books that crowd the shelves of **Wonder Book and Video** (✉ *1306 W. Patrick St.* ☎ *301/694–5955*) is rather like walking through the physical equivalent of an online used-book clearinghouse: a true bibliophile's dream.

OFF THE
BEATEN
PATH

Brunswick and Middletown. Located on the Potomac River and the Chesapeake & Ohio Canal, Brunswick is a small town of about 5,200 residents. A Main Street Maryland community that is steeped in early railroad history, the town was once a hub for the Baltimore and Ohio Railroad. Today, historic downtown Brunswick offers the Brunswick Railroad Museum (a major city-wide event is "Railroad Days" in early October), the C&O Canal National Historic Park Visitor's Center, shopping, antiquing, and unique dining experiences. Its location on the Potomac makes it ideal for hiking, biking, canoeing, kayaking, fishing, and other outdoor pursuits.

Middletown sits in a valley framed by the Catoctin Mountains and South Mountain—hence its name—on the Historic National Road. A young George Washington reportedly called this area one of the most lovely he'd seen. During the Civil War, Union and Confederate armies both passed through the town en route to the battles of South Mountain and Antietam, and townsfolk cared for the wounded in the aftermath. Today, the historic town has stately Victorian-style homes and church steeples that point heavenward, picturesque views of fertile fields, architectural history, a variety of specialty shopping and dining experiences, and heritage events throughout the year. While in Middletown, visit South Mountain State Battlefield Park and related Civil War sites and Washington Monument State Park.

SIDE TRIPS FROM FREDERICK

Frederick is a great home base for exploring the region's lush mountain forests, powerful national battlefields, and quaint historic towns.

MONOCACY NATIONAL BATTLEFIELD

2 mi south of Frederick via Rte. 355.

In the summer of 1864, Confederate general Jubal Early (who has perhaps the most memorable name in Civil War history), marched 15,000 troops toward Frederick in hopes of capturing the capital. At Monocacy Junction, a stop on the B&O Railroad, they encountered a force of Union soldiers about a third their size. Despite being outnumbered, the Union troops managed to stall the Rebels by burning a key bridge across the Monocacy River, thereby thwarting a takeover of Washington, D.C. Roam the fields surrounding the park with an audio tour, available in the visitor center, to better understand what's sometimes called "The battle that saved Washington, D.C." Recently, Monocacy has been making headlines for a major new discovery: National Park Service archeologists have uncovered the site of the largest known slave habitation site in the Mid-Atlantic region. The remains of several dwelling houses and artifacts dating back to the 1790s have been uncovered. The site is associated with L'Hermitage, a plantation established by French planters who came to Maryland from Saint-Domingue (known today as Haiti). By 1800, it was home to 90 enslaved laborers—the second largest slave population in Frederick County at the time, and

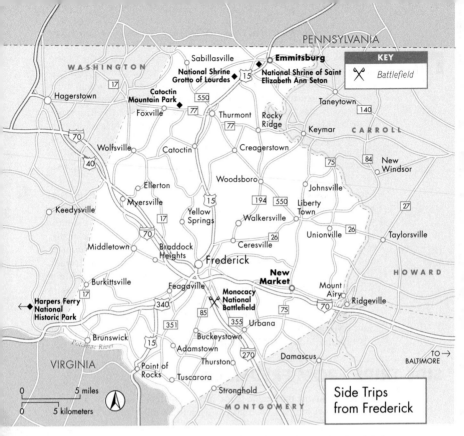

Side Trips from Frederick

among the largest in Maryland. ✉ *5201 Urbana Pike* ☎ *301/662–3515* ⊕ *www.nps.gov/mono* 🎟 *Free* 🕐 *Daily 8:30–5.*

GETTING HERE AND AROUND

There is no public transportation to the Monocacy battlefield but the site is easily accessed by car from both Baltimore and the Washington, D.C., region. From D.C., take I–270 north to I–70 east. Take exit 54 and bear right. Turn left onto Rte. 355 south, and the Monocacy Battlefield Visitor Center will be on the left (about 1–2 mi). From the Baltimore area, take I–70 east and follow the same directions. Once you arrive, information about driving and/or walking tours of the site can be found at the visitor center.

HARPERS FERRY NATIONAL HISTORICAL PARK

24 mi southwest of Frederick via Rte. 340.

At the stunning convergence of the Potomac and Shenandoah rivers, the town of Harpers Ferry—just over the border in West Virginia—played a key role in the events leading to the Civil War. This historical park brings to life details of the famous raid led by John Brown, a radical abolitionist. His plan—to take control of the town and commandeer weapons from the arsenal for the fight against slavery—was ultimately foiled and Brown was later tried and hanged. Still, historians cite the incident as the spark that helped ignite the conflict between North and South. The town, at the crossroads of Maryland, Virginia, and West Virginia, has been restored to its appearance during Brown's time, and various exhibits highlight early American life and Civil War history. The breathtaking rivers, shrouded by wooded cliffs, are popular spots for rafting and tubing during the warmer months.

GETTING HERE AND AROUND

A car is probably your best bet for getting to and around Harpers Ferry. The site is about 65 mi from Baltimore and Washington, D.C.; drive time is about an hour. Amtrak's "Capitol Limited" train between D.C. and Chicago stops in Harpers Ferry seven days a week. Additionally, MARC commuter trains operate Monday through Friday between Union Station in D.C., and Martinsburg, WV, on the Brunswick Line. Once at Harpers Ferry, guests can park near the Visitors Center. Shuttle buses run approximately every 15 minutes and provide easy access to a three-block pedestrian area with museums and exhibits. Other outlying areas are accessible to hikers and cars.

EXPLORING

Harpers Ferry. Along the cobblestone streets of the town abolitionist John Brown made famous, costumed interpreters in 19th-century homes and storefronts demonstrate period activities such as candle-dipping. Lectures and special tours are offered on weekends. Several hikes meander through the shady mountains that surround the sprawling park, passing over stone bridges and past the remains of homes and churches. There's plenty of parking at the Cavalier Heights Visitor Center along with the free shuttle buses that depart approximately every 15 minutes. ⊠ *Visitor Center and Parking: 171 Shoreline Dr., Harpers Ferry, WV* ☎ *304/535–6029* ⊕ *www.nps.gov/hafe* ☒ *$6 per vehicle, $4 per person arriving by other means* ☼ *Daily 8–5.*

SPORTS AND THE OUTDOORS

The Shenandoah and Potomac rivers are idyllic spots to kayak or canoe. Drift along the refreshing waters in an inner tube or raft through the rivers' rapids. Local favorite **Butt's Tubes** (⊠ *10985 Harpers Ferry Rd., Purcellville, VA* ☎ *877/723–8284* ⊕ *www.buttstubes.com*) drops you off at the river and picks you up downstream a few hours later. They offer patriotic-theme excursions in summer and "haunted" raft tours in October. **River Riders** (⊠ *408 Alstadts Hill Rd., Harpers Ferry, WV* ☎ *800/326–7238* ⊕ *www.riverriders.com*) offers everything from tranquil tubing to adventurous river-rafting tours on the Shenandoah River for all ages. They also rent mountain bikes.

CATOCTIN MOUNTAIN PARK

15 mi north of Frederick via Rte. 15.

GETTING HERE AND AROUND

There is no public transportation to or near Catoctin Mountain Park. Drive time is about 90 minutes north from Dulles International Airport in northern Virginia; approximately 2 hours from Reagan International in D.C.; and about 90 minutes from BWI Thurgood Marshall near Baltimore. Hagerstown MD Regional Airport is 45 minutes west of Catoctin.

EXPLORING

Catoctin Mountain Park. Nearly 6,000 acres of thick pine forests, rocky ledges, and magnificent views make Catoctin a true retreat. America's presidents apparently think so, too—Camp David is hidden within the park, although, of course, it is not open to the public. Catoctin also rents rustic cabins built during the era of the federal Works Progress Administration, and there's a dining hall that seats 120 people. ⊠ *6602 Foxville Rd., Thurmont* ☎ *301/663–9388* ⊕ *www.nps.gov/cato* ☜ *Free* ⊙ *Daily dawn–dusk.*

Cunningham Falls State Park. Located in the Catoctin Mountains, this state park is a haven for outdoor enthusiasts: there's hiking, fishing, and a crystal clear man-made lake for swimming and boating. The showpiece for many is a 78-foot waterfall (hence the name, although some locals call it McAfee Falls)—the largest cascading waterfall in the state. The park also features an aviary, the historic Catoctin Iron Furnace, campgrounds, and activities such as maple syrup making, and a bird and reptile program for kids. Picnic tables and grills are available, and campsites/cabins can be rented from April through October. ⊠ *14039 Catoctin Hollow Rd., Thurmont* ☎ *301/271–7574* ⊕ *www. dnr.state.md.us* ☜ *Memorial Day–Labor Day $5 per person; Labor Day–Memorial Day $3 per vehicle.*

↻ **Catoctin Wildlife Preserve & Zoo.** About 6 mi from Catoctin Mountain Park, this preserve/zoo holds more than 350 animals on some 30 acres. The zoo is easily navigated by children, and the tall trees and winding paths make for comfortable walking. Exotic animals here include tigers, macaws, monkeys, and boas. A petting zoo allows kids to mingle with goats and other small animals. Throughout summer there are interactive shows, when the little ones can touch snakes and learn about grizzlies. ⊠ *13019 Catoctin Furnace Rd., Thurmont* ☎ *301/271–3180* ⊕ *www. cwpzoo.com* ☜ *$14.95* ⊙ *Mar., weekends 10–4; Apr. and Oct., daily 10–5; early to late May and early to late Sept., daily 9–5; Memorial Day–Labor Day, daily 9–6.*

WHERE TO EAT

$ ✕ **Cozy Restaurant.** Family-owned and -operated since 1929, this legend-
AMERICAN   ary establishment boasts a bustling restaurant and pub with 11 dining rooms, an adjacent inn, shops, and a museum—reportedly the only one in the nation—that pays homage to nearby presidential retreat Camp David. The spot is well patronized by members of the media, and posted newspaper clippings and photographs recall the 1979 Camp David accords and other major news stories. Cozy has home-baked treats and several all-you-can-eat buffet nights to refuel after a long day of hiking. On Wednesday and Thursday it's steak and shrimp; Friday and Saturday feature a gut-busting land-and-sea spread that includes steamed oysters, clams casino, shrimp, scallops, barbecued ribs, steaks, and fried chicken. You can ratchet up the heat with one of the 200 hot sauces from the restaurant's "Wall of Fire." ⊠ *103 Frederick Rd., Thurmont* ☎ *301/271–7373* ⊕ *www.cozyvillage.com* ▭ *AE, MC, V.*

EN
ROUTE
Two of Frederick County's three covered bridges span creeks near Thurmont and make a lovely detour, especially in fall. Rustic and painted red, **Loy's Station Covered Bridge** rattles when cars roll across. Snap pictures of the bridge, built in 1848 and renovated in the 1990s, then picnic at the adjacent park's tables and let the kids splash in the stream or roam about the playground. **Roddy Road Covered Bridge**, built in 1856, is north of Thurmont, just off Route 15. The smallest of the covered bridges, it's surrounded by a cooling canopy of trees on either side and there's a small picnic area where you can have a bite while enjoying the view.

EMMITSBURG

24 mi north of Frederick via Rte. 15.

Founded in the 1700s and tucked among the blooming foothills of the Blue Ridge Mountains, Emmitsburg is a quaint small town known for its Catholic shrines, which draw visitors from all over the world. Elizabeth Ann Seton, the first American-born saint, founded the country's first order of nuns here in the early 1800s. Today the historic downtown has antiques shops, a railroad museum, and well-maintained historic homes. Students from Mount St. Mary's University enliven the town.

GETTING HERE AND AROUND

Emmitsburg is near the Pennsylvania border. It's about 50 mi from Baltimore, 65 mi from D.C., and 10 mi from Historic Gettysburg. A MARC commuter train stops in Frederick and Frederick TransIT, run by Frederick County (⊕ *www.frederickcountymd.gov/transit*), provides shuttle bus service to Emmitsburg every day except Sunday.

EXPLORING

National Shrine Grotto of Lourdes. Surrounded by shaded walkways and trickling brooks, the National Shrine Grotto of Lourdes is a meditative spot for Catholics and non-Catholics alike, in use since 1805. The grotto itself is a re-creation (from about 1875) of the spot in France where Bernadette Soubirous saw visions of the Virgin Mary. Today it attracts hundreds of thousands of visitors annually who come to pray or ask for healing. Many leave photographs, flowers, or handwritten prayers and take spring water from the grotto. The paved paths are safe for children, the elderly, or disabled. ⊠ *U.S. Rte. 15* ☎*301/447–5318* ⊕ *www.msmary.edu/grotto* ☑ *Free* ⊗ *Daily dawn–dusk.*

National Shrine of St. Elizabeth Ann Seton. Located on the campus of Mount St. Mary's College, the National Shrine of St. Elizabeth Ann Seton honors the country's first native-born saint. Born to a wealthy New York family, Elizabeth Ann Seton (1774–1821) was a widow with five children when she converted to Catholicism. Charismatic and tireless, she started the nation's first parochial school and first order of nuns. Today, her legacy lives on at the numerous churches and schools, including Seton Hall University, that bear her name. A small white clapboard house at the shrine is a re-creation of the home where she lived with fellow religious sisters and relatives surrounded by near-total wilderness. St. Elizabeth's body is entombed at the magnificent on-site basilica where masses are held several times a week. Only the Basilica

is open on Monday. ⊠ *333 S. Seton Ave.* ☏ *301/447–6606* ⊕ *www.
setonshrine.org* ✉ *Donations requested* ⊙ *Tues.–Sun. 10–4:30.*

WESTERN MARYLAND

Past Frederick, the highways of western Maryland twist along wooded
mountainsides offering sweeping views. Hikers and bikers prize the
unspoiled trails along the C&O Canal towpath and the South Mountain
section of the Appalachian Trail. Many of the oldest cities have seen
their downtowns revitalized through the state's Main Streets program.
To wit: upscale eateries and shops now coexist alongside important
Civil War sites.

HAGERSTOWN

25 mi west of Frederick via I–70, 75 mi west of Baltimore via I–70.

Hagerstown has always had a bit of an identity crisis. In Colonial times
it was considered the last bastion of civilization before the frontier. During the Civil War, Union and Confederate troops played a protracted
game of tug-of-war with the city. The railroad brought a flurry of industry here, but slowly drifted away as other modes of transportation
gained prominence. Now the once sleepy mountain city is reinventing
itself with a renovated downtown, a recently opened children's museum,
and a burgeoning arts district centered around the historic Maryland
Theater. There's also outlet shopping, golf, and of course, history all
around. Despite raising its profile, the city remains a boon for travelers.
Bed-and-breakfasts offer tremendous value for money and the charming museums clustered around the leafy City Park are rarely crowded.

GETTING HERE AND AROUND

Several federal highways lead to Hagerstown, which is about 75 mi
from Baltimore and 85 mi from Washington, D.C. Washington County
Commuter service and Greyhound buses travel here, and there is daily
Amtrak service and weekday MARC commuter train service from Martinsburg, WV, about 23 mi south of Hagerstown. There is ample parking in downtown Hagerstown—two parking garages and a metered
lot—and the area is easily explored on foot, though there's also a downtown taxi service.

ESSENTIALS

Taxis **Antietam Cab** (☏ *301/393–8811*). **City Cab** (☏ *301/662–2250*).

Visitor Information **Hagerstown/Washington County Convention & Visitor's Bureau** (⊠ *Elizabeth Hager Center, 16 Public Sq.* ☏ *301/791–3246* ⊕ *www.
marylandmemories.org*).

EXPLORING

↺ **Discovery Station and Hagerstown Aviation Museum.** A full-size model of
a triceratops skull welcomes you to the Discovery Station and Hagerstown Aviation Museum, the first hands-on science museum in Western
Maryland. Set in a former bank building, the museum allows kids to
work the controls in the cockpit of a Cessna plane, squeeze through a

model of an artery, and dig in sand for dinosaur fossils. Other popular attractions include a National Institutes of Health–sponsored exhibit on the eye and a model of the solar-powered NEAR spacecraft which traveled more than 200 million miles from the sun to explore asteroids. ✉ *101 W. Washington St.* ☎ *301/790–0076* ⊕ *www.discoverystation. org* ✉ *$7 $* ☉ *Tues.–Sat. 10-4, Sun. 2–5.*

Hager House and Museum. In 1739 Jonathan Hager, an adventurous young German immigrant, built a stone home over two springs in a virgin forest. The Hager House and Museum still stands, a testament to Hagertown's founder and early-American life. The thick-walled home includes bedrooms, a sewing room, and a kitchen furnished with pieces from the 18th and 19th centuries, as well as a replica of the trading post that Hager operated. Guided tours include the indoor springhouse where the family preserved food and kept cool in summer. Coins, pottery, and buttons excavated from the property are on display, and Colonial-style gardens of fragrant rosemary, lavender, and thyme surround the home. ✉ *110 Key St.* ☎ *301/739–8393* ⊕ *www.hagerhouse.org* ✉ *$3* ☉ *Apr.–Dec., Thurs.–Sat. 10–4; Sun.–Wed. by appointment only.*

☾ ★ **Hagerstown Roundhouse Museum.** Dubbed "Hub City" due to its importance to the Western Maryland and Baltimore & Ohio railroads, Hagerstown has a rich railway history. It's been more than a decade since the city demolished the roundhouse (a circular building used for repairing steam locomotives), but the museum preserves several cabooses, locomotives, and trolley cars as well as other railroad artifacts and memorabilia. During the Christmas season the elaborate train gardens are particularly enchanting. ✉ *300 S. Burhan's Blvd. (US 11)* ☎ *301/739–4665* ⊕ *www.roundhouse.org* ✉ *$3.50* ☉ *Fri.–Sun. 1–5.*

★ **Washington County Museum of Fine Arts.** Shaded by trees near a placid lake at Hagerstown's **City Park**, the airy galleries of Washington County Museum of Fine Arts hold an eclectic mixture of American painting, from Whistler's moody *La Mere Gerard* to Norman Rockwell's folksy *The Oculist.* Portraits by members of the Peale family and Joshua Johnson, the famed African-American portrait artist, bring depth to the collection, which also includes European, Asian, and African paintings, sculptures, and prints. ✉ *91 Key St.* ☎ *301/739–5727* ⊕ *www.wcmfa. org* ✉ *Free* ☉ *Tues.–Fri. 9–5, Sat. 9–4, Sun. 1–5.*

WHERE TO EAT AND STAY

$ GERMAN ✕ **Schmankerl Stube.** The area's German roots may have you hankering for schnitzel, knockwurst, or a cold Oktoberfest beer. If so, head to Schmarkerl Stube. Waitresses dressed in traditional dirndls (recall those St. Pauli Girl beer commercials?) carry heaping plates of homemade sausages, veal and noodles, and sweet and sour beef with dumplings. The house favorite *Knusperige Schweinshaxe* (marinated pork shank with sauerkraut, apple-flavored red cabbage, and homemade Bavarian bread dumplings) must be ordered 24 hours in advance so that the pork has ample time to marinate. Intricate wood carvings and red-and-white checked tablecloths complete the theme. ✉ *58 S. Potomac St.* ☎ *301/797–3354* ⊕ *www.schmankerlstube.com* ▭ *AE, D, MC, V* ☉ *Closed Mon.*

9

$–$$ ⊞ **Inn on Potomac.** Just a few blocks from the City Park, with restaurants and shopping, this restored century-old mansion is a gem. Ornately carved wooden beds and period furnishings coexist with flat-screen TVs in each of the four rooms, and two suites have Jacuzzi bathtubs. Breakfast is complimentary and might include quiche seasoned with herbs from the inn's garden. Visit the attached Tranquility Salon and Spa for a comforting warm stone massage, reviving rosemary mint body wrap, facial, or hair services with Aveda products. Afterwards, relax a bit more on the comfortable porch. **Pros:** spa on-site; business center; complimentary wine nightly. **Cons:** few rooms, so may book up fast. ⊠ *400 N. Potomac* ☎ *301/739–5679* ⊕ *www.innonpotomac. com* ⤵ *4 rooms* ⌂ *In-room: a/c, Wi-Fi. In-hotel: parking (free), spa* ⊟ *AE, DC, MC, V.*

SHOPPING

Hagerstown Premium Outlets (⊠ *495 Prime Outlets Blvd.* ☎ *301/790–2031*), open daily, is a bargain hunter's bonanza. The hundreds of stores featuring apparel, footwear, and more include Banana Republic, BCBG, Puma, kate spade, Coach, and Ralph Lauren.

NIGHTLIFE AND THE ARTS

Ava Lounge A (⊠ *28 S. Potomac St.* ☎ *301/745–6648* ⊕ *www. avaloungehagerstown.com*) brings cosmopolitan panache to Hagerstown. This hip little spot could easily exist in New York City. Sip sophisticated cocktails at the sinuous brushed-metal bar, or nosh on gourmet pizzas in a private room with mod white leather couches. The lounge hosts weekly open mic nights, live jazz and acoustic music, and a dance party with a DJ spinning on weekends. Be sure to slip up to the city's only rooftop deck where urbane pleasures meet the distinctly rural pleasure of a sky crowded with stars. **The Maryland Theatre** (⊠ *21 S. Potomac St.* ☎ *301/790–3500* ⊕ *www.mdtheatre.org*), built in 1915 by renowned architect Thomas W. Lamb (who also designed Madison Square Garden), stands in the heart of the city's burgeoning arts district. The refurbished theater welcomes big-name country singers, doo-wop groups, comedians, and classical musicians to its stage. On Monday night, art-house films are shown, and throughout the year, there are theatrical offerings for kids.

SHARPSBURG

10 mi south of Hagerstown via Rte. 65, 20 mi west of Frederick via Alt. Rte. 40 to Rte. 34.

East of the Potomac River, Sharpsburg is a small town (the last census counted nearly 700 people) that was settled in the 1740s. Known at one time in its history for industry, it is now famous as the place where the historic Battle of Antietam (aka the Battle of Sharpsburg) took place. The town also hosts a large Memorial Day celebration (said to be the nation's first) and an annual Sheep and Wool Festival.

GETTING HERE AND AROUND

You'll need a car to reach and explore Sharpsburg. The town is approximately 65 mi by car from Baltimore, 70 mi from Washington, D.C., and 23 mi from Frederick.

EXPLORING

Fodor's Choice ★ **Antietam National Battlefield.** Time has returned Antietam National Battlefield, the site of the bloodiest one-day battle of the Civil War, to its tranquil antebellum appearance, with woodlands giving way to sloping cornfields bound by rough-hewn fences. On September 17, 1862, more than 23,000 Union and Confederate troops were killed, wounded, or missing here. The gruesome battle led Abraham Lincoln to issue the preliminary Emancipation Proclamation. A self-guided tour by car follows 8½ mi of well-preserved battlefield including Dunkard Church and Bloody Lane. An hour-long documentary is shown at the visitor center at noon each day, and there is an exhibit of Civil War artifacts. You can also hike the battlefields with an audio tour or accompanied by a ranger. Stop at the **Pry House Field Hospital Museum** (an extension of Frederick's National Museum of Civil War Medicine), where a re-created operating room and implements used to care for the wounded are displayed.

At the historic Newcomer House, **The Heart of the Civil War Heritage Area Exhibit and Visitor Center** (⊠ *18422 Shepherdstown Pike, Keedysville* ☎ *301/432–6402* ⊕ *www.heartofthecivilwar.org* ☉ *Open Sat. and Sun., May–Oct. 11–5; open daily Nov. and Apr. 11–5*), a new addition to the battlefield site, aims to promote stewardship of historic, cultural, and natural Civil War resources across the region and features interpretive exhibits that play on key themes such as On the Home Front, In the Heat of Battle, and Beyond the Battlefield. Brochures, maps, county visitor guides, and other materials are available, and center volunteers can help visitors tailor their plans for exploring the heritage area. ⊠ *Rte. 65, Sharpsburg Pike* ☎ *301/432–5124* ⊕ *www.nps.gov/anti* ☒ *Battlefield $4 for individuals; $6 for families; Pry House $2 suggested donation* ☉ *Battlefield: daily dawn–dusk. Visitor center: Labor Day–Memorial Day, daily 8:30–5; Memorial Day–Labor Day, daily 8:30–6. Pry House: Labor Day–Memorial Day, daily 11–5.*

★ **Boonsborough Museum of History.** Doug Bast, a local historian and founder of the Boonsborough Museum of History, never gave up his boyhood habit of collecting unusual curios. Besides extensive Civil War artifacts (including a cannonball), among the quirky finds crammed into this small house are a wooly mammoth tusk, a moonshine still, mummified animals, a piece of the White House discarded during a mid-20th-century renovation, patent medicines, and Geronimo's walking stick. ⊠ *113 Main St., Boonsboro* ☎ *301/432–6969* ☒ *$4* ☉ *May–Sept., Sun. 1–5 and by appointment.*

WHERE TO EAT AND STAY

$$
CONTINENTAL
✕**Old South Mountain Inn.** Since 1732, this sturdy bluish gray stone home has welcomed travelers along a road called by turns the National Trail, the National Road, the Old National Pike, and (least romantically) Route 40. Historic figures Daniel Webster and Henry Clay stopped

here, and during the Civil War, John Brown's followers seized control of the building for a day. Just prior to the Battle of Antietam, it served as the headquarters for a Confederate general. The menu is as elegant as the setting: highlights include fillet Mona Lisa, a seared filet mignon with a cabernet sauvignon demi-glace, served over crispy fried leeks. The extensive dessert list includes peanut butter, fresh apple, and bourbon pecan pies; Godiva chocolate cake; and ice cream sundaes. ⊠ *6132 Old National Pike, Boonsboro* ☎ *301/432–6155 or 301/371–5400* ⊕ *www.oldsouthmountaininn.com* ▤ *AE, DC, MC, V* ⊗ *Closed Mon.*

$–$$ ⌦ **Inn at Antietam.** Perched on a ridge next to Antietam National Cemetery, this turn-of-the-20th-century B&B makes a lovely home base for exploring Sharpsburg's history. The four suites and a penthouse all have a distinctive feel—the Rose Suite features a four-poster bed and chintz wallpaper, while the rustic Gen. Burnside Smokehouse Suite is dominated by an enormous brick fireplace. Enjoy a hearty breakfast in the dining room, sit a spell on the wrap-around porch, or meander through the 8 acres of land that surround the inn. If you're lucky, owners Bob LeBlanc and Charles Van Metre, showbiz vets, will sing and play for guests on the parlor's baby grand. **Pros:** lovely gardens; convenient location. **Cons:** no phone in rooms; individual decor may not appeal to all. ⊠ *220 E. Main St.* ☎ *301/432–6601 or 877/835–6011* ⊕ *www. innatantietam.com* ▱ *4 suites, 1 penthouse* ⌂ *In-room: no phone, a/c, no TV (some). In-hotel: no kids under 6* ▤ *AE, MC, V* ⊗ *Closed Jan.*

$–$$ ⌦ **Jacob Rohrbach Inn.** A veritable textbook of American history is packed into this more than 200-year-old structure, now an elegant inn within walking distance of Antietam National Battlefield. For starters, the home had ties to the Calvert family, Maryland's founders. Later, during the Civil War, a small cannonball, fired during the Battle of Antietam, flew into a wall in the summer kitchen. The house was later used as a field hospital to aid the wounded. Each of the five elegantly appointed rooms pays tribute to an aspect of this home's rich history, and four rooms have private porches that look onto the inn's lush flower gardens. Breakfast includes herbs and produce from the inn's garden, fresh pastries baked on-site, and breads from nearby Mennonite bakeries. **Pros:** fascinating history; Federal-style inn. **Cons:** unconfirmed reports of ghostly footsteps being heard. ⊠ *138 W. Main St.* ☎ *301/432–5079 or 877/839–4242* ⊕ *www.jacob-rohrbach-inn.com* ▱ *5 rooms* ⌂ *In-room: no phone, a/c, no TV (some), Wi-Fi. In-hotel: no kids under 10* ▤ *AE, D, MC, V.*

FORT FREDERICK STATE PARK

17 mi west of Hagerstown via I–70, 40 mi west of Frederick via I–70.

GETTING HERE AND AROUND

Fort Frederick State Park is 1 mi south of I–70 near Big Pool (Rte. 56, exit 12). The park is 88 mi from Baltimore and 81 mi from Washington, D.C.

Fort Frederick State Park. Along the Potomac River stands the only remaining stone fort from the French and Indian War. Built in 1756 and named after Frederick Calvert, the sixth Lord of Baltimore, Fort Frederick's stone walls protected Maryland's frontier settlers. Today, a visitor center displays artifacts from the French and Indian War and several times a year, staff and volunteers dressed in 18th-century period clothing give visitors a taste of life in the Colonial era. The park also offers hiking trails, skiing, boating, and canoeing. ☒ *11100 Fort Frederick Rd., Big Pool* ☏ *301/842–2155* ☒ *$3* ☉ *Apr.–Oct., daily 8 am–dusk; Nov.–Mar., weekdays 8 am–dusk, weekends 10 am–dusk.*

GREEN RIDGE STATE FOREST

23 mi west of Fort Frederick State Park via I–70 to I–68, 62 mi west of Frederick via I–70 to I–68.

GETTING HERE AND AROUND

You will need a car to access and explore Green Ridge State Forest.

Green Ridge State Forest. At 46,000 acres, Green Ridge—part of the Allegheny Mountain chain—is the state's second-largest forest, stretching from Pennsylvania nearly to the West Virginia border. A century ago, this land was home to iron, sawmill, and other workers. Remains of their mossy cemeteries and crumbling stone homes can be found among vast stands of hickory and oak trees. A victory for Maryland and Mother Nature, the second-growth forest is a beautiful spot to camp, hike, ride mountain bikes, and fish at a stocked lake. ☒ *28700 Headquarters Dr. NE, Flintstone* ☏ *301/478–3124* ☒ *Free* ☉ *Park office daily 8–4.*

CUMBERLAND

17 mi west of Green Ridge State Park via I–68, 89 mi west of Frederick via I–70 to I–68, 142 mi west of Baltimore via I–70 to I–68.

Surrounded by the deep blue Allegheny Mountains, Cumberland appears plucked from a Currier-and-Ives print. Tall steeples grace the skyline and elegant 19th-century mansions line the hillsides. In the 1800s Cumberland, the county seat, was a major transportation hub where the Chesapeake & Ohio Canal, the Baltimore & Ohio Railroad, and the National Pike met. Railroad barons built lavish mansions, and the city bustled with tourists. But as transportation patterns shifted, so too did Cumberland's fortunes.

In 2008, a multimillion-dollar tourism project restored the city's pulse. The stately brick Western Maryland Station (built circa 1900) has been renovated and a steam-powered antique locomotive puffs through the red shale cliffs to Frostburg (where you can stop for lunch and museum tours) and back each day. The Western Maryland Scenic Railroad also has special murder mystery trains and a North Pole and Santa Express around the Christmas holidays. At nearby Canal Place, you can follow markers from youthful George Washington's headquarters to scenic bridges, cycle over the canal towpath, and wander into shops and restaurants. A few blocks away, the cobblestone pedestrian mall feels like a small European town.

TOURS Mountain Getaway Tours offers guided bus tours of the mountains and historic sites in Allegany and Garrett counties, as well as West Virginia and Pennsylvania. Westmar Tours conducts group bus tours of the Allegheny Mountain region and the Shenandoah Valley, led by guides in Colonial and 19th-century garb.

GETTING HERE AND AROUND

Historic Route 40 (aka the Old National Road) runs through the middle of Cumberland. Allegany County Transit offers public transportation in the area. Amtrak also has a stop here that comes through twice a day. Drive times from both Baltimore and Washington, D.C., are about 2½ hours, one-way. Once in town, the city is pedestrian friendly.

ESSENTIALS

Tours **Mountain Getaway Tours** (☎ 800/459–0510). **Westmar Tours** (✉ 13 Canal St. ☎ 301/777–0293 ⊕ www.wstmr.com).

Visitor Information **Allegany County Tourism Department** (✉ Western Maryland Station, 13 Canal St. ☎ 301/777–5132 or 800/425–2067 ⊕ www. mdmountainside.com).

EXPLORING

Washington Street Historic District. In the mid- to late 19th century, Cumberland's railroad barons built homes in the Washington Street Historic District, which stretches along Washington Street from Wills Creek to Allegany Street and from Greene Street to Fayette Street. The six-block district, on the National Register of Historic Places, features an eclectic mix of Federal, Greek Revival, Italianate, Queen Anne, and Georgian Revival homes and is a dream come true for architecture lovers. Of particular interest is the **Emmanuel Episcopal Church and Parish Hall** (✉ 16 Washington St.). Built in 1849–50 on the site of the former Fort Cumberland, this historic church was a frontier outpost during the French and Indian War. The Gothic Revival church is built of native sandstone and contains three large Tiffany windows.

C&O Canal National Historical Park. This park is the starting point for walking and biking the towpath, and taking tours on replica canal boats. Markers set occasionally along the towpath explain the railroad's role in the development of the town and the region's coal industry. There are even mules on hand, since the history of the canal includes these hardy 1,000-pound animals who once pulled canal boats. At nearby Canal Place, you can grab a bite, browse through the small shops, or listen to a summer concert on the water. ✉ Western Maryland Railway Station, 13 Canal St. ☎ 301/722–8226 ⊕ www.canalplace.org 🎫 Free ⏰ Daily 9–5.

George Washington's Headquarters. In a log cabin about the size of an ice-cream stand, the man who would become America's first president mapped out strategies during the French and Indian War (1754–63). George Washington's Headquarters, the only remaining structure from Fort Cumberland, was used by the patriot when he was an aide to General Braddock. The 250-year-old cabin contains a simple bed, desk, and fireplace, which can be viewed from outside through large windows. A walking tour that continues along the canal begins here. ✉ Washington and Greene Sts. ☎ 301/777–5132 🎫 Free ⏰ By appointment.

Gordon-Roberts House. Josiah Roberts, the one-time president of the C&O Canal, commissioned this Second Empire–style house on fashionable Washington Street in 1867, a few years after he was released from prison for being an alleged secessionist. The Allegany County Historical Society has its headquarters here today, and costumed guides lead guests through rooms of Victorian furnishings. A courting couch in the parlor has three sitting compartments—the young lady and her caller sat on opposite ends while two chaperones were perched between them. The museum hosts themed teas throughout the year. ✉ *218 Washington St.* ☎ *301/777–8678* ⊕ *www.historyhouse. allconet.org* 🎫 *$5* ⊙ *Tues.–Sat. 10–5.*

Thrasher Carriage Collection Museum. This unique museum has more than 100 carriages amassed by James R. Thrasher, a local blacksmith's son who made a small fortune in business. The vehicles vary from those meant to carry royalty to ones typical of a fruit seller. ✉ *19 Depot St., Frostburg* ☎ *301/689–3380* ⊕ *www.thrashercarriagemuseum.com* 🎫 *$4* ⊙ *May–Dec., Wed.–Sun. 10–3; Jan.–Apr. by appointment.*

Ⓒ **Western Maryland Scenic Railroad.** Puffing through dark stone tunnels and
★ along majestic cliffs, this scenic rail excursion allows passengers to relive the glory days of trains in Cumberland and beyond. A 1916 Baldwin locomotive carries you uphill through the Narrows and scenic mountains as a narrator explains the region's history. The journey is 32 mi (3½-hours) round-trip to Frostburg. A 90-minute layover in Frostburg, a college town, allows time for lunch at one of the many restaurants on the city's main street, just up the hill. A diesel engine typically runs on weekdays, with the more popular steam engine saved for weekends. For a fun twist, try dinner and drinks on a murder-mystery train or take the kids on the North Pole Express at Christmastime. ✉ *13 Canal St.* ☎ *301/759–4400 or 800/872–4650* ⊕ *www.wmsr.com* 🎫 *$25; more for 1st-class seating or theme trains* ⊙ *Departures at 11:30 am: May–Sept., Wed.–Sun; Oct., daily; Nov.–mid-Dec., weekends.*

WHERE TO EAT

$$$ ✕ **City Lights.** Set near a fountain on the brick pedestrian walkway, City
AMERICAN Lights brings urbane charm to downtown Cumberland. The menu of upscale American classics features seafood with a distinctively Chesapeake touch, hand-cut steaks, freshly made pies, and espresso drinks. Lunch includes an assortment of salads and sandwiches—the portobello Reuben on rye is an unexpected twist on an old standby. ✉ *59 Baltimore St.* ☎ *301/722–9800* ⊕ *www.citylightsamericangrill.com* ▤ *AE, D, DC, MC, V* ⊙ *Closed Sun.*

$$ ✕ **Ristorante Ottaviani.** Owned by a charismatic family from Italy by
ITALIAN way of Baltimore, this restaurant and wine bar is a favorite of locals and tourists. Black-and-white photos of Italy hang on a textured wall painted warm shades of gold and orange, and candles flicker on tables in the covered patio. Try the slow-cooked chicken Ottaviani, the owner's Italian grandmother's signature dish, or Pasta Chivitella, penne and wild mushrooms in a rich cream sauce. There's an impressive wine list, and decadent deserts—try the tiramisu—complete the experience. ✉ *25 N. Centre St.* ☎ *301/722–0052* ▤ *MC, V.*

$$ ✕ **Warner's Restaurant.** This historic establishment was founded in 1928
GERMAN (as Warner's German Restaurant), closed in 2003, and re-opened by two new owners—one the grandson of the late proprietor—in 2010.

9

Judging from the local buzz and busy servers, the restaurateurs are already reminding customers of tasty meals from decades past. Besides German cuisine (one specialty pizza features knockwurst and sauerkraut), the restaurant boasts a book-sized international menu, fresh baked breads, an extensive wine list, imported beers, and sophisticated cocktails. Ask about the famous Bee Sting, a rum flavored dessert so beloved in these parts that in his day, President John F. Kennedy bought dozens from the original restaurant to serve to members of Congress. ⊠ *14514 McMullen Hwy. SW, Cumberland* ☎ *240/362–7242* ⊕ *www. warnersgermanrestaurant.com* ▭ *AE, MC, V.*

WHERE TO STAY

$$ ⊡ **Rocky Gap Lodge and Golf Resort.** With Evitts Mountain as a backdrop, this lovely resort is in one of the state's most idyllic spots. The lobby, dining room, and lounge overlook a 243-acre man-made lake, Lake Habeeb. In keeping with the natural environs outside, natural shades like green and brown are used throughout the six-story hotel. Rooms, larger than usual, are appointed with Shaker-style furniture and flat-screen TVs, and most have views of a breathtaking ridge of mountains. If traveling with your pet, request a special "V.I.P." room, which greets your furry one with a special treat basket. Suites include a gas fireplace and sitting area. Try a spa treatment, 18 holes on the Jack Nicklaus signature golf course, a hike along the park's trails, or boating, fishing, and swimming. **Pros:** one of the region's best golf courses and a first-rate spa. **Cons:** not as intimate an experience as staying at a small B&B. ⊠ *Rocky Gap State Park, 16701 Lakeview Rd., Box 1199, Flintstone* ☎ *301/784–8400 or 800/724–0828* ⊕ *www.rockygapresort.com* ⤶ *215 rooms, 15 suites* ⛅ *In-room: a/c. In-hotel: 2 restaurants, bar, Wi-Fi, golf course, tennis courts, pool, gym, spa, beachfront, some pets allowed* ▭ *AE, D, DC, MC, V.*

$$ ⊡ **Savage River Lodge.** Halfway between Grantsville and Frostburg,
★ this upscale lodge is tucked away in Maryland's largest state forest. Nestled on the wooded 45-acre plot are 18 cozy, two-level log cabins and an excellent restaurant that includes vegetarian menus and a nationally-recognized wine list. The handsome three-story lodge, with a towering stone fireplace that splits the room, is a short walk from the cabins. They boast oversize furniture, queen-size beds draped with down quilts, gas log fireplaces, oversize soaking tubs, and porches with rocking chairs. Muffins, orange juice, and newspapers are delivered to your room each morning. Activities range from birding, sleigh rides, and horseback riding to stargazing. **Pros:** lots of privacy; quiet. **Cons:** no air-conditioning in rooms, although ceiling fans cool the air. ⊠ *1600 Mount Aetna Rd., 5.2 mi off I–68, Exit 29, Frostburg* ☎ *301/689–3200* ⊕ *www.savageriverlodge.com* ⤶ *18 cabins* ⛅ *In-room: no a/c, no TV. In-hotel: restaurant, bar, bicycles, some pets allowed* ▭ *AE, D, MC, V.*

SPORTS AND THE OUTDOORS

Allegany Expeditions Inc. (⊠ *10310 Columbus Ave. NE* ☎ *301/722–5170* ⊕ *www.alleganyexpeditions.com*) offers guided backpacking, caving, canoeing, fishing, and kayaking tours. The company also rents out camping equipment.

Western Maryland Adventures (✉ *16701 Lakeview Rd. NE, Flintstone* ☎ *301/784–8403* ⊕ *www.wmdadventures.com*) is an excellent choice for outdoorsy types. Sure many companies can take you white-water rafting, fishing, rock climbing, or zip lining, but how many do all that and more, plus offer Segway tours through the woods?

EN ROUTE Along the Old National Road out of Cumberland stands the only remaining tollhouse in Maryland. Built in 1836, the historic **LaVale Toll Gate House** is a unique, seven-sided, four-room building that housed the gatekeepers who collected tolls until the early 1900s. ✉ *Historic National Rd., 14302 National Hwy., LaVale* ☎ *301/777–5132* ⊗ *May–mid-Oct., weekends 1:30–4:30.*

GRANTSVILLE

21 mi west of Cumberland via I–68.

Two miles south of the Mason-Dixon Line, Grantsville is a tiny village (population about 600) that was incorporated in 1864. It's nestled amid some of the most productive farmland in the region—no surprise as this is the heart of the county's Amish and Mennonite farming communities. To the west and south is Maryland's largest forest, the 53,000-acre Savage River State Forest. Mostly undeveloped, it's used by hikers, campers, anglers, and, in winter, cross-country skiers. Also nearby is New Germany State Park, which has hiking trails, campsites, and cabins.

GETTING HERE AND AROUND

You'll need a car to access Grantsville and its neighboring parks. To reach the town, head toward the Casselman River Bridge. From I–68, take exit 22 and turn north on U.S. 219. At the first light, make a left onto National Highway/U.S. 40 Alt. Follow 2 mi, pass Penn Alps, cross over Casselman River, and make an immediate right.

EXPLORING

Casselman River Bridge. By the time you spot the picturesque Casselman River Bridge, you're almost in Grantsville. This single-span stone arch bridge ½ mi east of town was built in 1813; at the time it was the largest of its kind. Though the bridge is no longer in use, it serves as the backdrop for a small state park and picnic area. ✉ *Rte. 40.*

New Germany State Park. In the northern end of Savage River State Forest, this 455-acre park was established by German immigrants in the 19th century. The park contains stands of hemlocks and pines planted in the late 1950s and a 13-acre man-made lake. You can swim, fish, and boat here, although low water levels and a profusion of aquatic plants have made parts of the lake unusable. In winter the park's 8 mi of hiking trails are groomed for cross-country skiing. Picnic shelters, 39 campsites, and 11 rental cabins fully equipped for year-round use are also on-site along with a grand lake house that is suitable for weddings or meetings. ✉ *349 Headquarters La., 25 mi southwest of Cumberland via I–68 and Lower New Germany Rd., Exit 24* ☎ *301/895–5453* ⊕ *www. dnr.state.md.us* ▦ *$2 Memorial Day–Labor Day; $3 during ski season* ⊗ *Daily dawn–dusk.*

9

Spruce Forest Artisan Village and Penn Alps. The history and craftsmanship of Upper Appalachia are exhibited at this rustic village where spinners, weavers, potters, stained-glass workers, wood sculptors, and bird carvers demonstrate their artistry and skills. The Winterberg House, a log stagecoach stop, is the last remaining log tavern along the Old National Pike. It's now used as a crafts store and restaurant. ⊠ *177 Casselman Road., at Rte. 40* ☎ *301/895–3332* ⊕ *www.spruceforest.org* ✉ *Free* ⊙ *Mon.–Sat. 10–5.*

SHOPPING

Yoder Country Market (⊠ *Rte. 669* ☎ *301/895–5148*), open Monday through Saturday, began as a butcher shop on a Mennonite family farm in 1947. Today the market sells breads, cookies, pies, and pastries baked on the premises. There's also a nice selection of bulk groceries, local food products, meats, and homemade jams and jellies. A Mennonite kitchen serves a limited menu.

DEEP CREEK LAKE

21 mi southwest of Grantsville via I–68 and Rte. 219.

Garrett County's greatest asset, the 3,900-acre Deep Creek Lake, was created in the 1920s as a water source for a hydroelectric plant on the Youghiogheny (pronounced "Yok-a-gainy") River—a favorite among kayakers and white-water rafters. Deep Creek Lake State Park offers public access for fishing, swimming, and boat/kayak launching and picnicking is available in the park's waterfront area (a service charge applies). Area restaurants and motels offer docks so you can sail to your lodging of choice, or use your boat to grab a quick bite.

GETTING HERE AND AROUND

You'll need a car to access Deep Creek Lake. From Washington, D.C., Take I–270 north to I–70 west to I–68 west. Take exit 14A (Rte. 219 South Deep Creek Lake). Continue on Rte. 219 south approximately 15 mi until you reach McHenry & Deep Creek Lake. Once here, you can get around on foot, by bike, or by boat/kayak. In fact, you can go shopping, dining, or even to the movies by boat. Pick up a Travel by Boat brochure at the Visitors Center. Local maps and information about recreation (including hiking), dining, and lodging can also be found at the Visitors Center.

ESSENTIALS

Taxi Contact Deep Creek Lake Taxi Cab (☎ *301/616–7407*).

Visitor Information Garrett County Chamber of Commerce (⊠ *15 Visitors Center Dr., McHenry* ☎ *301/387–4386* ⊕ *www.garrettchamber.com*).

EXPLORING

Deep Creek Lake State Park. The 1,818-acre Deep Creek Lake State Park hugs the eastern shore of the lake and has a public boat launch, small beach with lifeguards (in summer), and picnic and camping sites. The lake's indigo waters are breathtaking—literally. Even in summer the water can be chilly. At the park's Discovery Center are hands-on educational activities for children, a freshwater aquarium, native animals on display, and a small gift shop. The center is also a staging area for organized outdoor activities, including boat tours. ✉ *898 State Park Rd.* ☎ *301/387–5563* ⊕ *www.dnr.state.md.us.*

Wisp Resort. The two biggest attractions in the area are Deep Creek Lake and Marsh Mountain, and the Wisp Resort takes advantage of both. Called "the Wisp" by locals, the mountain has a humble history: its eastern face was once a cow pasture. Today it's one of the area's most popular destinations. Not only does the resort boast Maryland's only alpine ski slopes, it's also a veritable amusement park with water and snow tubing, mountain biking, a mountain coaster, skate park, paintball course, climbing wall, paddleboarding, canopy tours, and waterskiing, to name a few activities. Instructors teach skiing and snowboarding to all ages and ability levels, and afterwards you can stop into one of several restaurants and bars to warm up and relax after a day on the slopes.

WHERE TO EAT AND STAY

¢ ✕ **Canoe on the Run.** Deep Creek's best spot for sophisticated café food
AMERICAN serves breakfast burritos and homemade granola and scones in the morning. Lunch brings on an assortment of appetizers and sandwiches, including chicken breast with basil mayo, and fresh mozzarella on ciabatta bread and quesadillas with smoked Gouda, portobello mushrooms, and caramelized onions. Salads feature crisp vegetables and grilled meats. Beer and wine are available when a cappuccino just won't cut it. Best of all, the eatery is just a short walk uphill from the lake, near the public park access, and opens bright and early at 8 am. ✉ *2622 Deep Creek Dr., McHenry* ☎ *301/387–5933* ▭ *AE, D, DC, MC, V.*

$ ✕ **Jearbryo's.** Above the county fairgrounds, this homey diner serves
AMERICAN affordably priced breakfasts, lunches, and dinners. Try the sweet-potato pancakes or sausage gravy and biscuits for breakfast. Homemade potato chips, cut thick and still hot from the fryer, are a mouth-watering treat. Desserts, made in-house, are a hit, particularly the choco-fabulous Sinful Seven Cake. Free Wi-Fi is available throughout the restaurant. ✉ *145 Bumble Bee Rd., just off Rte. 219* ☎ *301/387–7667* ⊕ *www.jearbryos. com* ▭ *MC, V.*

$$ ✕ **Santa Fe Grille & Cantina.** A taste of the Southwest meets Appalachia
AMERICAN at this restaurant and bar where a large wooden bear and bar stools carved from saplings greet guests. Hearty portions are welcome after a long day of skiing or swimming. Try the Painted Desert Soup with layers of pureed red peppers, corn, and beans, mesquite-grilled breast of chicken, or the huge rack of ribs slow-roasted in habanero sauce. ✉ *75 Visitors Center Dr., McHenry* ☎ *301/387–2182 or 301/387–2202* ⊕ *www.dclsantafe.com* ▭ *AE, DC, MC, V.*

$ ⛺ **Savage River Inn.** Way off the beaten path within the Savage River State Forest, this quaint B&B began as a farmhouse in 1934. Today the bed in breakfast portion is closed, but the owner welcomes visitors to the on-site Fox Den Log Cabin. It's well furnished with rustic but modern decor, and splendid views of mountain scenery. Outside, enjoy a landscaped garden, pool, and hot tub. Rooms are decorated with country furnishings, and two have sitting areas and fireplaces. **Pros:** bikes, paddleboats, and canoes to borrow. **Cons:** difficult to access in icy weather. ✉ *Rte. 495 S to Dry Run Rd., Box 147, McHenry* ☎ *301/245–4440*

9

⊕ *www.savageriverbandb.com* ↻ *4 rooms* ♿ *In-room: a/c, no TV. In-hotel: pool, bicycles, parking (free)* ⊟ *MC, V* ⊠○⊩ *BP.*

$–$$ 🎿 **Wisp Resort Hotel.** Western Mary-
☾ land's biggest draw features activities that run the gamut from skiing and fly-fishing to a spa, skatepark, and paintball arena. All of the rooms are ski-in, ski-out, and they all include modern appliances, fluffy comforters, and comfortable lodge furniture to sink into after a long day on the slopes, or the water. Parents can take advantage of the Club Wisp Kids' Night Out program as they take a break at the spa or enjoy a round of golf. All activities are arranged through the hotel. **Pros:** fun activities all in one spot. **Cons:** big crowds and lots of kids may be too much for some. ⊠ *290 Marsh Hill Rd., McHenry* ☎ *800/462–9477 or 301/387–5581* ⊕ *www.wispresort.com* ↻ *102 suites, 67 rooms* ♿ *In-room: a/c, kitchen (some), refrigerator. In-hotel: restaurant, room service, bar, golf courses, tennis courts, pool, gym, spa, bicycles, children's programs (ages 3–14), Wi-Fi hotspot, parking (free), some pets allowed* ⊟ *AE, D, DC, MC, V.*

> ## LOCAL VACATION RENTALS
>
> **Railey Mountain Lake Vacations**
> (☎ 800/846–7368 or 301/387–2124 ⊕ rentals.deepcreek.com).
> The area's most popular lodging choice is the ski resort, but vacation rental homes are a good choice for families and groups of friends. This company offers year-round options that include everything from lakefront chalets to log cabins in the woods. Many of the rentals have amenities like outdoor hot tubs, double balconies, game rooms, stone fireplaces, whirlpool tubs, and private piers.

SPORTS AND THE OUTDOORS

BICYCLING

High Mountain Sports (⊠ *21327 Garrett Hwy., Oakland* ☎ *301/387–4199* ⊕ *www.highmountainsports.com*) rents mountain bikes, snow and water skis, kayaks, and snowboards, and sells outdoor gear and equipment. Kayak, mountain-bike, and other outdoor tours are available as well.

BOATING

At the docks at Deep Creek Lake State Park, **Nature Lake Tours** (⊠ *898 State Park Rd.* ☎ *301/746–8782*) runs sunrise, nature, dinner, and family-oriented tours of the lake daily, from April through October. **Deep Creek Lake Boat Rentals** (⊠ *2030 Deep Creek Dr., McHenry* ☎ *301/387–9130* ⊕ *www.deepcreeklakeboatrentals.com*) rents pontoon and paddleboats and Jet Skis.

SKIING

Wisp Resort has 132 acres of ski terrain ranging from beginner to difficult; most are open for night skiing. Three terrain parks are geared toward beginners, advanced, and/or extreme skiers. The Bear Claw Tubing Park has 750-foot-long tubing lanes. Peak-season lift rates (mid-December through early March) are $39 for a full day on weekdays, $59 on weekends; prices go up about $6 on holidays. Ski/snowboard rentals are $36 each. Tubing sessions run in two-hour blocks; rates are $15–$25 per person. ⊠ *296 Marsh Hill Rd., McHenry* ☎ *800/462–9477* *or 301/387–4911 ⊕ www.wispresort.com ⊟ AE, D, MC, V ⊘ Closed Apr.–mid-Dec.*

OAKLAND

11 mi southwest of Deep Creek Lake State Park via Rte. 219.

Tiny Oakland, perched on a mountain plateau at the far western end of the state, is a true escape from the big-city bustle. Its heyday was in the late 1800s, when a number of opulent hotels catered to vacationers brought by the Baltimore & Ohio Railroad. Saunter through the quaint antiques shops that line downtown's recently restored brick paths and you'll feel that you've traveled to another time.

GETTING HERE AND AROUND

You'll need a car to access Oakland. From Washington, D.C., take I–270 north to I–70 west to I–68 west. Take exit 14A (Rte. 219 South Deep Creek Lake). Continue on Route 219 south approximately 25 mi until you reach Oakland. Visitors can park in the Oakland Town parking lot (at the end of 2nd Street behind Newman's Funeral Home) and then set off on foot or bike (best to bring your own) to explore all that downtown Oakland has to offer.

EXPLORING

Swallow Falls State Park. At Swallow Falls State Park, paths wind along the Youghiogheny River, past shaded rocky gorges and rippling rapids, to a 53-foot waterfall. One of Maryland's hidden gems, the park is also known for its assemblage of 300-year-old hemlocks and for excellent camping, hiking, and fishing facilities. ⊠ *222 Herrington La., off Rte. 219* ☎ *301/334–9180* ⊕ *www.dnr.state.md.us* ⊠ *$2 Memorial Day–Labor Day, $1 Labor Day–Memorial Day* ⊘ *Daily dawn–dusk.*

WHERE TO EAT AND STAY

$$

FRENCH

✕ **Cornish Manor**. In its long life, this spectacular Victorian mansion, built just after the Civil War, has been a judge's summer home, and a speakeasy, to name a few incarnations. Today the restaurant is a local landmark known for the elegant dishes prepared by the owner, a native of France. Try the delicately flavored rainbow trout pan fried in almond butter, an immense 10-ounce crab cake, tortellini swimming in a rich Newburg sauce and topped with chunks of crab, or the zesty green peppercorn steak with brandy sauce. After dinner take a stroll around the manor, set on 7 lovely acres. ⊠ *830 Memorial Dr.* ☎ *301/334–6499* ⊕ *www.cornishmanor.net* ⌦ *Reservations not accepted* ⊟ *AE, D, MC, V* ⊘ *Closed Sun.*

$$$

FRENCH

✕ **Deer Park Inn**. Within the Deer Park Inn B&B, the proprietor prepares an exceptional French menu with ingredients procured from local Amish farms. Duck confit is marinated overnight and served with savory braised red cabbage. Beef tenderloins are served with a tantalizing sun-dried cherry sauce. Desserts—such as a tart of local strawberries and rhubarb with whipped cream, or local organic blueberries with crème fraiche—are simple and elegant. During the area's off-season months, the inn and restaurant may be closed Monday–Wednesday,

9

so call ahead. ⊠ *65 Hotel Rd., Deer Park* ☎ *301/334–2308* ⊕ *www. deerparkinn.com* ⊟ *AE, D, MC, V* ☹ *Closed Sun. No lunch.*

$$ 🛏 **Carmel Cove Inn.** This former monastery retreat sits on a ridge above a
★ Deep Creek Lake cove. The chapel has been converted into an English-style great room, where you can play billiards or board games, watch movies, listen to music, or browse through magazines. Guests have free use of on-site sporting equipment, and a communal refrigerator is stocked with wine and beer. Breakfast can be taken in the small, bright dining room, in your room, or on the deck, weather permitting. Some rooms have private decks and fireplaces. **Pros:** sports equipment; fireplaces; complimentary wine and beer. **Cons:** fewer amenities than larger local resorts. ⊠ *105 Monastery Way, Stanton* ☎ *301/387–0067* 🖷 *301/387–4127* ⊕ *www.carmelcoveinn.com* ⇆ *10 rooms* ♿ *In-room: a/c, DVD. In-hotel: room service, tennis court, bicycles, no kids under 12* ⊟ *D, MC, V* ℗ *BP.*

SPORTS AND THE OUTDOORS

Ten minutes from Deep Creek Lake, **Precision Rafting Expeditions** (⊠ *715 Morris Ave., Friendsville* ☎ *301/746–5290* ⊕ *www.precisionrafting. com*) provides kayaking instruction and guided white-water rafting trips on the Upper Youghiogheny, Savage, Gauley, and Cheat rivers. Serious river rats can get decked out at **Upper Yough Whitewater Expeditions** (⊠ *Macadam Rd., Friendsville* ⊕ *www.upperyoughexpeditions. com* ☎ *800/248–1893*), which specializes in white-water rafting.

SHOPPING

A bonus of Oakland's off-the-beaten-track location is that antiques are much more reasonably priced here than in the big cities. Many shops line Second and Alder streets. **Alder Haus Antiques and Uniques** (⊠ *229 E. Alder St.* ☎ *301/334–3233*) is packed with elegant rugs, stained glass, and all manner of furniture. Call for hours. Housed inside a former pharmacy, **Englander's Antiques and Collectibles** (⊠ *205 E. Alder St.* ☎ *301/533–0000*) features dozens of vendors selling everything from hand-stitched quilts to glassware, handcrafted toys, and furniture. The best antique to be found here is in the back—the shop's original soda fountain, **Dottie's Fountain and Grill** (open daily). Diners sit at pale-green stools around a wave-shaped counter and drink old-fashioned thick milk shakes while enjoying buckwheat pancakes and sausages, or hamburgers—all of which cost less than $4—just as they have for the past 40 years.

Annapolis and Southern Maryland

THE CHESAPEAKE BAY'S WESTERN SHORE

WORD OF MOUTH

"It didn't take long before I decided that Annapolis was the unsung jewel of the mid-Atlantic, so charmed was I by the compactness of the city, with its narrow, red-brick sidewalks, streets and roundabouts à la England, not to mention the delightfully-named alleyways like Chancery Way surrounded continually by the rows of early-13-colonies window-shuttered architecture. While this may seem reminiscent of a Colonial Williamsburg, the presence of the harbor on the mouth of the Severn River/Spa Creek offers a delightful, scenic bonus."

—Daniel_Williams

Updated by
Alice Powers

The past is never far away from the present among the coves, rivers, and creeks of the Chesapeake Bay's lesser-known *western* shore. In the lively port of Annapolis, Colonial Maryland continues to assert itself. Today "Crabtown," as the state capital is sometimes called, has one of the highest concentrations of 18th-century buildings in the nation, including more than 50 that predate the Revolutionary War.

The region's counties—Anne Arundel, Calvert, Charles, and St. Mary's—have been supported since their 17th-century founding through tobacco fields and fishing fleets. More recently, the northern parts of the counties have emerged as prime residential satellites for the Annapolis–Baltimore–D.C. metro triangle; but despite the subdivisions and concomitant shopping centers, southern Maryland maintains much of its rural character. With the exception of the fair-weather getaway enclave Solomons Island and the archaeological site-in-progress Historic St. Mary's City, the region remains largely undiscovered. All the better for travelers who come to enjoy stunning water vistas, miles of scenic roads, dozens of historic sites, and a plethora of inns and bed-and-breakfasts on the water, in tiny towns, and in the fields and woodlands of its unspoiled countryside.

ORIENTATION AND PLANNING

GETTING ORIENTED

The region south of Annapolis and D.C. is a peninsula broken in two by the Patuxent River, a 110-mi-long tributary to the Bay. Until the middle of the 20th century, the so-called Western Shore was the main vacation spot for families from Baltimore and Washington. When the Bay Bridge was completed in the 1950s and people could easily get to shore points like Rehoboth and Bethany Beach, towns like North Beach and Chesapeake Beach fell out of favor. However, in recent years the closer-in "Western Shore" has become popular again.

Annapolis. People in Annapolis live to sail on the Chesapeake Bay; its picturesque harbor with hundreds of boats is the epicenter of town. Add the Naval Academy and you have a definite nautical theme. The town is a lovely warren of historic homes and quaint shops.

Calvert County. Like the calm, nearly wave-free Bay itself, the shore resorts of Calvert County are tranquil getaways. Relatively undiscovered, Calvert County lacks the boardwalk life of the ocean resorts and its towns are often just collections of fishermen's cottages and holiday homes.

St. Mary's County. Across the Governor Thomas Johnson Bridge from Calvert County's Solomons Island is St. Mary's City, once (briefly) the

TOP REASONS TO GO

Experience Colonial History: The U.S. Congress met in the Maryland State House from 1783 to 1784, and two significant events occurred during that time: General George Washington resigned as commander-in-chief of the Continental Army and the Treaty of Paris was ratified.

Salute the Navy at Annapolis: The U.S. Naval Academy is the most important site in town. Don't miss its centerpiece, the bright copper-clad dome of the U.S. Naval Academy Chapel, beneath which lies the crypt of the Revolutionary War naval officer John Paul Jones.

Return to the Golden Age of the Railroad: At the Chesapeake Bay Railway Museum, housed in the railroad's 1898 track-side terminus, check out a glass-enclosed model of the town of Chesapeake Beach and a gleaming, black Ford Model T that once carried guests from the station to their hotels.

Visit a 17th-Century British Settlement: At Historic St. Mary's, the fourth permanent settlement in British North America and eventually the first (albeit short-lived) capital of Maryland, you can view ongoing restoration work in this much smaller, and less-refined, version of Williamsburg, Virginia.

capital of Maryland. The historic city is gradually being restored, and is the center point of the mostly rural county.

Charles County. Charles County is slowly becoming a bedroom community to Washington, D.C.—especially for those who want acres and acres of land and don't mind a long commute. But there's still plenty of relatively unspoiled parkland.

PLANNING

WHEN TO GO

Each season has its charms in southern Maryland. In the heat of summer the Chesapeake Bay provides boating and swimming. In fall, the changing colors of the trees and smaller crowds attract hikers and bird-watchers. The shops of Annapolis offer unique seasonal gifts in winter and many of the historic homes have special holiday events. And in spring, sailors ready their boats for the season and the Naval Academy graduates another class during Commissioning Week.

Maryland's three-day **Historic Annapolis Antiques Show** (🖀 *410/267–8146* ⊕ *www.annapolis.com*) in January is one of the major Mid-Atlantic events of its kind. On the last Saturday in April, rain or shine, the **Celtic Festival and Highland Gathering of Southern Maryland** (🖀 *443/404–7319* ⊕ *www.cssm.org*) takes place south of Annapolis in St. Leonard. It includes piping and fiddling competitions, dancing, games, and the foods and crafts of the United Kingdom, Ireland, and Brittany. Fifty Celtic clans are represented. In the second week of May, **Commissioning Week** (🖀 *410/293–0263* ⊕ *www.usna.edu/specialevents/commweek. htm*) at the U.S. Naval Academy in Annapolis, Maryland, is a time of dress parades, traditional stunts such as the Herndon Monument Climb,

10

and a spectacular aerobatics demonstration by the navy's famous Blue Angels precision flying team.

The **United States Sailboat and Powerboat Shows** (☎*410/268–8828* ⊕*usboat.com*), the world's largest events of their kind, take place in Annapolis in October. In the second week of December more than 70 sailboats and powerboats get decked out in lights for the holidays and sail into Annapolis Harbor for the **Eastport Yacht Club Lights Parade.** Spectators watch from the center of town at City Dock. ⊠ *Annapolis Harbor* ☎*410/263–0415* ⊕ *www.eastportyc.org* ✉ *Free* ☉ *6 pm.*

GETTING HERE AND AROUND

Baltimore-Washington International Airport is convenient to Annapolis and attractions in southern Maryland. The most convenient way to get to Annapolis is by car or taxi (the fare is roughly $50). From BWI, follow airport exit signs and then take I–97 south to Route 50 East. Take Exit 24 onto Rowe Boulevard and follow signs to the Annapolis Visitor Center.

You can also reach Annapolis by bus or shuttle. The Sky Blue Bus route runs from the International Terminal Bus Stop to Annapolis. You can transfer from the Spa Road stop to other routes, several of which stop near the visitor center. BWI Ground Transportation has information on SuperShuttle and Airport Vans

ESSENTIALS

Transportation Information Baltimore–Washington International Airport (*BWI* ⊠ *Exit 2 off Baltimore-Washington Pkwy.* ☎ *410/859–7111* ⊕ *www. bwiairport.com).* **SuperShuttle** (☎ *800/258–3826* ⊕ *www.supershuttle.com).*

RESTAURANTS

In the beginning, there was crab: crab cakes, crab soup, whole crabs to crack. These days, most likely because of overfishing and habitat changes, crabs from the Bay are pretty scarce. Maryland's favorite crustacean is still found in abundance on menus, but most arrive from out of state. In addition, Annapolis has broadened its horizons to include eateries—many in the historic district—that offer many sorts of cuisines. Dinner reservations in Annapolis are recommended throughout summer and at times of Naval Academy events.

HOTELS

There are many places to stay near the heart of Annapolis, as well as at area B&Bs and chain motels a few miles outside town. A unique "Crabtown" option is Boat & Breakfasts, in which you sleep, eat, and cruise on a yacht or schooner; book ahead. During the sailboat and powerboat shows in spring and fall and at Naval Academy commencement in May, hotel reservations are necessary, even a year in advance. Like most places on the water, prices are lower in the cooler months.
■ TIP→ **You can save money on a hotel by booking a room away from the City Dock. To avoid relying on your car (and dealing with the limited parking in the historic area) ask if your hotel has a free shuttle service.**

Two reservation services operate in Annapolis. **Annapolis Accommodations** (⊠ *41 Maryland Ave.* ☎ *410/280–0900 or 800/715–1000* ⊕ *www. stayannapolis.com*) specializes in long-term rentals. The office is open

9–5 weekdays. **Annapolis Bed & Breakfast Association** (☎ *No phone* ⊕ *www.annapolisbandb.com*) books lodging in the old section of town, which has many restaurants and shops as well as the Maryland State House and the City Dock. The U.S. Naval Academy and St. John's College serve as the northern and western boundaries of the territory.

WHAT IT COSTS					
	¢	$	$$	$$$	$$$$
Restaurants	under $10	$10–$16	$17–$23	$24–$30	over $30
Hotels	under $100	$100–$160	$161–$230	$231–$300	over $300

Restaurant prices are per person for a main course at dinner. Hotel prices are for a standard double room, excluding state and local taxes.

PLANNING YOUR TIME

A trip through southern Maryland could be a leisurely three-day journey, including one day in quaint Annapolis, one day in bay-side towns like North Beach and Chesapeake Beach, and one day in the southern part of the region, including Solomons Island and Historic St. Mary's. Depending on your interests—sailing and water sports, hiking or birding, sightseeing in historic homes, or simply sitting dockside and digging into the region's famous crab cakes—you could spend much more time there.

EXPLORING ANNAPOLIS AND SOUTHERN MARYLAND

Annapolis and southern Maryland encompass the Western Shore of the Chesapeake Bay, an area within easy driving distance of Baltimore and Washington, D.C. Annapolis, on a peninsula bounded by the Severn and South rivers and the Chesapeake Bay, is a Mid-Atlantic sailing capital and the gateway to southern Maryland. Calvert County, just south of Annapolis, promises compelling bay-side scenery that includes the imposing Calvert Cliffs and several miles of Bay beaches. Beyond the Patuxent River, across the 1.3-mi Governor Thomas Johnson Bridge, lies St. Mary's County, a peninsula that protrudes farther into the Chesapeake, with the Patuxent and the Potomac rivers on either side of it.

10

ANNAPOLIS

In 1649 a group of Puritan settlers moved from Virginia to a spot at the mouth of the Severn River, where they established a community called Providence. Lord Baltimore, who held the royal charter to settle Maryland, named the area around this town Anne Arundel County, after his wife; in 1684 Anne Arundel Town was established across from Providence on the Severn's south side. Ten years later, Anne Arundel Town became the capital of Maryland and was renamed Annapolis after Princess Anne, who later became queen. It received its city charter in 1708 and became a major port, particularly for the export of tobacco.

In 1774, patriots here matched their Boston counterparts (who had thrown their famous tea party the previous year) by burning the *Peggy*

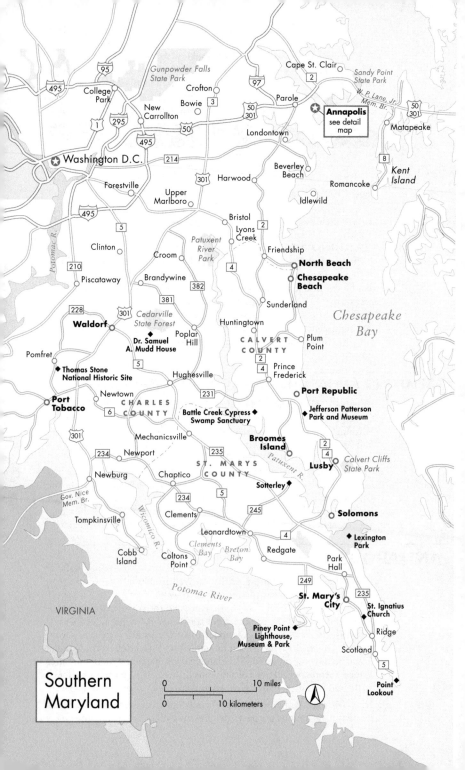

Stewart, a ship loaded with taxed tea. Annapolis later served as the nation's first peacetime capital (1783–84). The city's considerable Colonial and early republican heritage is largely intact, and because it's all within walking distance, highly accessible.

Although it has long since been overtaken by Baltimore as the major Maryland port, Annapolis is still a popular pleasure-boating destination. On warm sunny days the waters off City Dock become center stage for an amateur show of powerboaters maneuvering through the heavy traffic. Annapolis's enduring nautical reputation derives largely from the presence of the U.S. Naval Academy, whose strikingly uniformed midshipmen throng the city streets in crisp white uniforms in summer and navy blue in winter.

GETTING HERE AND AROUND

CAR TRAVEL Annapolis is normally 35–45 minutes by car from Washington, D.C., on U.S. 50 (Rowe Boulevard exit). During rush hour (weekdays 3:30–6:30 pm), however, it takes about twice as long. From Baltimore, following routes 3 and 97 to U.S. 50, travel time is about the same. To tour southern Maryland, follow Route 2 South from Annapolis, and Route 4, which continues through Calvert County.

■ **TIP➔ In the summertime avoid going to Annapolis from Washington on Saturday morning or returning to Washington on Sunday evening— traffic slows to a crawl, as many Washingtonians spend their weekends on the Eastern Shore.**

PARKING Parking spots on Annapolis's historic downtown streets are scarce, but you can pay $5 to park at the Navy–Marine Corps Stadium (to the right of Rowe Boulevard as you enter town from Route 50) and ride a free shuttle bus downtown. Parking garages on Main Street and Gott's Court (adjacent to the visitor center) are free for the first hour and $1.25 an hour thereafter with a $10 maximum—but note that they are often full on weekdays. On weekends these garages cost $4 a day. Street parking in the historic area is metered (in effect 10–7:30 daily) or limited to two hours for those without a residential parking permit.

ON FOOT Downtown Annapolis is accessible on foot, but to reach the malls and outlying attractions a car or taxi is necessary. To get around the Annapolis waterfront, call the Annapolis Water Taxi, which runs from mid-May to mid-September.

TOURS Walking tours are a great way to see Annapolis's historic district. HistoryQuest rents two self-guided (with audiotapes and maps) walking tours: "Historic Annapolis Walk with Walter Cronkite" and "Historic Annapolis African-American Heritage Audio Walking Tour." The cost for each is $5. Guides from Three Centuries Tours wear Colonial-style dress and take you to the State House, St. John's College, and the Naval Academy. The cost is $13. Tours depart daily April through October at 10:30 from the visitor center and at 1:30 from the information booth, City Dock. From November through March one tour a week leaves on Saturday at 1:30 from the information booth.

Discover Annapolis Tours leads one-hour narrated minibus tours ($18) that introduce you to the history and architecture of Annapolis. Tours

10

leave from the visitor center daily April through November and most weekends December through March.

From April through November, Discover Annapolis runs 40-minute motorized Historic Annapolis Trolley Tours through the historic district of Annapolis. Sightseeing includes the State House, City Dock, and Colonial and Victorian homes. Tickets are sold at HistoryQuest, at 99 Main Street. Tours leave from the Annapolis Visitor Center at Northwest and Calvert streets. There is paid parking adjacent to the center.

The schooners *Woodwind* and *Woodwind II* are twin 74-foot boats that make two to four trips Tuesday through Sunday between April and October, with some overnight trips. Two-hour sails are $31 to $34. For more information, ⇨ *the Sailing on the Chesapeake box, below.* When the weather's good, Watermark Journeys runs boat tours that last from 40 minutes to 7½ hours and go as far as St. Michaels on the Eastern Shore, where there's a maritime museum, yachts, dining, and boutiques. Prices range from $10 to $60. Watermark also runs land tours that depart from the information booth at the City Dock. The tours include a 90-minute "Colonial Stroll" and a two-hour "African-American Heritage Tour." Tours run from April through October, and not every tour is given every day. Check the Watermark Journey Web site for information. Prices range from $12 to $16.

If you'd rather see Annapolis from a horse-drawn carriage, board "Annapolis Carriage" at the City Dock outside the Market House. The historic tours last either 25 minutes or 50 minutes and the carriages carry four adults comfortably.

TIMING AND PRECAUTIONS

Swim at your own risk in the calm waters of the Chesapeake Bay. The Bay contains sea nettles that can sting like jellyfish. Some beaches are netted, but ask before you take a plunge.

ESSENTIALS

Taxis **Annapolis Cab Company** (☎ *410/268–0022*). **Annapolis Water Taxi** (☎ *410/263–0033* ⊕ *www.watermarkcruises.com*).

Tours **Annapolis Carriage** (✉ *99 Main St., Historic District* ☎ *410/349–1660* ⊕ *www.annapoliscarriage.com*). **Discover Annapolis Tours** (✉ *31 Decatur Ave., Historic District* ☎ *410/626–6000* ⊕ *www.discover-annapolis.com*). **Historic Annapolis Foundation Walking Tours** (✉ *18 Pinkney St., Historic District* ☎ *410/267–7619 or 800/603–4020* ⊕ *www.annapolis.org*). **Schooner Woodwind Cruises** (✉ *Annapolis Marriott Hotel dock, City Dock* ☎ *410/263–7837* ⊕ *www.schooner-woodwind.com*). **Historic Annapolis Trolley Tours** (✉ *99 Main St. at HistoryQuest, Historic District* ☎ *410/626–6000* ⊕ *www.discover-annapolis.com/transportation/trolley.html*). **Three Centuries Tours** (✉ *48 Maryland Ave., Historic District* ☎ *410/263–5401* ⊕ *www.annapolis-tours.com*). **Watermark Journeys** (🖃 *Box 3350, Annapolis, Historic District 21403* ☎ *410/268–7600* ⊕ *www.watermarkjourney.com*).

Visitor Information **Annapolis & Anne Arundel County Conference and Visitors Bureau** (✉ *26 West St., West Side* ☎ *410/280–0445 or 888/302–2852* ⊕ *www.visit-annapolis.org* ⊗ *Daily 9–5*). **Information Booth** (✉ *Dock St. parking lot* ☎ *410/280–0445*).

Annapolis & Anne Arundel Country Conference & Visitors Bureau ..**2**

Banneker-Douglass Museum **3**

Hammond-Harwood House **8**

HistoryQuest .. **10**

Historic London Town and Gardens **1**

Information Booth **12**

Kunta Kinte–Alex Haley Memorial **11**

Maryland State House **6**

St. Anne's Church **4**

St. John's College **7**

Thurgood Marshall Memorial **5**

United States Naval Academy **13**

William Paca House and Garden **9**

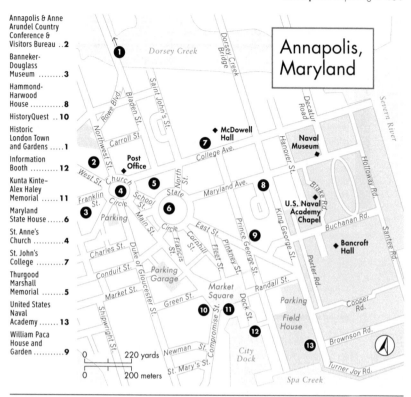

EXPLORING

Start your visit at Annapolis's main visitor center. Here you can pick up maps and brochures or begin a guided tour. From April to October the information booth on City Dock, adjacent to the harbormaster's office, is open and stocked with maps and brochures.

TOP ATTRACTIONS

☺ ★ **Banneker-Douglass Museum.** Named for abolitionist Frederick Douglass and scientist Benjamin Banneker, this former church and its next-door neighbor make up a museum that tells the stories of African-Americans in Maryland through programming, art, and interactive historical exhibits. The church hosts performances, lectures, and educational programs, while the four-floor addition houses changing exhibits and permanent shows. Audio and visual presentations and hands-on exhibits make the museum engaging for kids, while also bringing home the hardships of slave life. ⊠ *84 Franklin St.* ☎ *410/216–6180* ⊕ *www.bdmuseum.com* 🖅 *Free* ☉ *Tues.–Sat. 10–4.*

▌ **NEED A BREAK?**

The Annapolis Bookstore (⊠ *35 Maryland Ave.* ☎ *888/339–7370* ⊕ *www. annapolisbookstore.com*) has recently relocated to a spot not far from the State Capitol. In its expanded Maryland Avenue quarters it has a café and a garden for reading and storytelling. With its carefully selected collection of

10

CLOSE UP

Sailing on the Chesapeake

Of course, one of the main attractions of Annapolis is the Bay itself. Short of owning your own boat, there are many ways for visitors to sample the sailing life on the Chesapeake. Many cruises—from as short as 40 minutes to as long as the entire day—leave from the City Dock. **Watermark Cruises** (⌧ *City Dock, Historic District* ☎ *410/268-7601* ⊕ *www. watermarkcruises.com*) is Annapolis's biggest charter and tour service, with many themed tours of varying lengths. Children might especially enjoy Watermark's "Pirates of the Chesapeake" cruise. This "high-seas adventure" is good for short attention spans and is just one hour. Private charters are also available from Watermark.

Probably the most economical way to get out on the water is on the **Water Taxi** (⌧ *City Dock, Historic District* ☎ *410/263-0033*) that runs from Annapolis Harbor to Back Creek. For less than $5 per person you can get out on the water for a short trip. For a long trip, consider a Boat & Breakfast on the **Schooner *Woodwind*** (⌧ *80 Compromise St., at the Annapolis Marriot Waterfront Hotel* ☎ *410/263-7837* ⊕ *www.schoonerwoodwind. com*). Take a two-hour sail and then spend the night dockside in double-berth staterooms. A comprehensive listing of all of the sailing possibilities is available on the Visitors Bureau Web site (⊕ *www.visitannapolis.org*).

both new and rare books, the store is an oasis from the ubiquitous chains. As befits its Annapolis location, it specializes in maritime books. It is open daily except Wednesday.

★ **Hammond-Harwood House.** Based on a plate of the Villa Pisani in Montagnana, Italy, by Andrea Palladio, this 1774 home was designed by premier Colonial architect William Buckland and is considered America's greatest colonial high-style residence. Called the architectural "Jewel of Annapolis," the residence was greatly admired by Thomas Jefferson when he sketched the house in 1783. The wood carvings surrounding the front door and enriching the dining room are some of the best surviving of their kind in America. Set on 4 acres, the site today exhibits famous Colonial art by Charles Willson Peale, Rembrandt Peale, James Peale, John Trumbull, John Hesselius, Jeremiah Theus, and John Beale Bordley, as well as an extensive decorative arts collection covering everything from Chinese export porcelain to Georgian period silver. Also on display is the world's largest collection of inspired Colonial cabinetwork by the Annapolis native John Shaw. Noted landscape architect Alden Hopkins from Colonial Williamsburg created the property's Colonial Revival garden. Tours leave on the hour; the last begins at 4. Regular tours may be a bit dry for children under 12, but children's tours are available by special appointment. ■TIP➔ **Call ahead to see if special children's programs are planned for the day of your visit.** ⌧ *19 Maryland Ave.* ☎ *410/263-4683* ⊕ *www.hammondharwoodhouse.org* ⌧ *$6* ☉ *Apr.–Oct., Tues.–Sun. noon–5; Nov–Mar., by appointment only.*

★ **Historic London Town and Gardens.** This National Historic Landmark, a short car ride from Annapolis, is on the South River and has dramatic river views. The three-story waterfront brick house, built by William Brown between 1758 and 1764, is one of two remaining original Colonial structures. The 17th-century tobacco port of London, made up of 40 dwellings, shops, and taverns, disappeared in the 18th century, its buildings abandoned and left to decay. The excavation of the town is underway, and some buildings have been restored. Docents conduct 30- to 45-minute house tours; allow more time to wander the grounds. From March 15 to December, house tours leave on the hour (the last is at 3). ⊠ *839 Londontown Rd., Edgewater* ☎ *410/222–1919* ⊕ *www. historiclondontown.com* ⊠ *$10, children 7–17 $5, under 7 free* ☉ *Mid-Mar.–Dec., Wed.–Sat. 10–4, Sun. noon–4.*

Fodor's Choice   **Maryland State House.** Completed in 1780, the State House is the old-
★ est state capitol in continuous legislative use; it's also the only one in which the U.S. Congress has sat (1783–84). It was here where General George Washington resigned as commander in chief of the Continental Army and where the Treaty of Paris was ratified in 1784, ending the Revolutionary War. Both events took place in the Old Senate Chamber, which is filled with intricate woodwork (attributed to Colonial architect William Buckland), including the ubiquitous tobacco motif. Also decorating this room is Charles Willson Peale's painting *Washington at the Battle of Yorktown,* a masterpiece by the Revolutionary War period's finest portrait artist. The Maryland Senate and House hold their sessions in two other chambers in the building. Also on the grounds is the oldest public building in Maryland, the tiny redbrick Treasury, built in 1735. Note that you must have a photo ID to enter the State House. ⊠ *One Hundred State Circle* ☎ *410/974–3400* ⊠ *Free* ☉ *Welcome center weekdays 9–5, weekends 9–4; tour is half hour, daily, on demand.*

QUICK
BITES

Chick and Ruth's Delly (⊠ *165 Main St.* ☎ *410/269–6737* ⊕ www. chickandruths.com) is a longtime counter-and-table institution where the waitstaff is friendly and the deli sandwiches are named after local state politicos. Burgers, subs, milk shakes, and other ice-cream concoctions are also on offer. Built in 1901, it's been run by Baltimoreans Chick and Ruth Levitt since 1965.

10

St. John's College. Students at St. John's, home to the Great Books curriculum, all follow the same four-year, liberal-arts curriculum, which includes philosophy, mathematics, music, science, Greek, and French. Students are immersed in the classics, through small classes conducted as discussions rather than lectures. Start a visit here by climbing the gradual slope of the long, brick-paved path to the cupola of **McDowell Hall.** The Annapolis campus of St. John's, the third-oldest college in the country (after Harvard and William and Mary), once held the last Liberty Tree, under which the Sons of Liberty convened to hear patriots plan the Revolution. Damaged in a 1999 hurricane, the 400-year-old tree was removed; its progeny stands to the left of McDowell Hall. The **Elizabeth Myers Mitchell Art Gallery** (☎ *410/626–2556* ⊕ *www. stjohns.edu/events/an/art/main.shtml*), on the east side of Mellon Hall, presents world-class exhibits and special programs that relate to the fine arts. Down King George Street toward the water is the **Carroll-Barrister House,** now the college admissions office. Once home to Charles Carroll (not the signer of the Declaration but his cousin), the house was built in 1722 at Main and Conduit streets and moved onto campus in 1955. ⊠ *60 College Ave., at St. John's St.* ☎ *410/263–2371* ⊕ *www.sjca.edu.*

Fodor's Choice ★ **United States Naval Academy**. Probably the most interesting and important site in Annapolis, the Naval Academy runs along the Severn River and abuts downtown Annapolis. Men and women enter from every part of the United States and foreign countries to undergo rigorous study in subjects that include literature, navigation, and nuclear engineering. The USNA, established in 1845 on the site of a U.S. Army fort, occupies 329 waterfront acres. The centerpiece of the campus is the bright copper-clad dome of the interdenominational **U.S. Naval Academy Chapel.** Beneath it lies the crypt of the Revolutionary War naval officer John Paul Jones, who, in a historic naval battle with a British ship, uttered the inspirational words, "I have not yet begun to fight!"

Adjoining Halsey Field House is the **USNA Armel-Leftwich Visitor Center** (⊠ *52 King George St.* ☎ *410/263–6933*). Its exhibits include a mock-up of a midshipman's room and the *Freedom 7* space capsule flown by astronaut Alan Shepard, an Academy graduate. Walking tours of the Naval Academy leave from the center. Don't miss the award-winning film *To Serve and to Lead.* You must have a photo ID to be admitted through the Academy's gates. **■ TIP→ Park on the street or in Annapolis public parking and walk through Gate 1 or 3—on foot is the only way you can enter unless you're driving a car used for official Department of Defense business..**

Near the chapel in Preble Hall is the **U.S. Naval Academy Museum & Gallery of Ships** (⊠ *118 Maryland Ave.* ☎ *410/293–2108*), which tells the story of the U.S. Navy through displays of model ships and memorabilia from naval heroes and fighting vessels. The U.S. Naval Institute is also in this building. The Rogers Ship Model Collection has 108 models of sailing ships built for the British Admiralty. Admission for the museum and institute is free; hours are Monday through Saturday from 9 to 5 and Sunday from 11 to 5. On the grounds, midshipmen (the term used for women as well as men) go to classes, conduct military drills, and practice or compete in intercollegiate and intramural sports. **Bancroft Hall,** closed to the public, is one of the largest dormitories in the world—it houses the entire 4,200-member Brigade of Midshipmen. The **Statue of Tecumseh,** in front of Bancroft Hall, is a bronze replica of the USS *Delaware*'s wooden figurehead, "Tamanend." It's decorated by midshipmen for athletics events; and for good luck during exams, students pitch pennies into his quiver of arrows. **■ TIP→ If you're there at noon on weekdays in fair weather, you can see midshipmen form up outside Bancroft Hall and parade to lunch accompanied by the Drum and Bugle Corps.** *U.S. Naval Academy* ⊕ *www.navyonline.com* *Grounds tour $7.50* ⏲ *USNA Armel-Leftwich Visitor Center: Mar.–Dec., daily 9–5; Jan. and Feb., daily 9–4. Guided walking tours generally leave Mon.–Sat. 10–3 on the hr and Sun. 12:30–3 on the ½ hr; call ahead to confirm and for Jan. and Feb. tour times.*

William Paca House and Garden. A signer of the Declaration of Independence, Paca (pronounced "PAY-cuh") was a Maryland governor from 1782 to 1785. His house was built from 1763 through 1765, and its original garden was finished by 1772. Inside, the main floor (furnished with 18th-century antiques) retains its original Prussian blue and soft gray color scheme. The second floor contains 18th-century pieces. The adjacent 2-acre garden provides a longer perspective on the back of the house, plus worthwhile sights of its own: upper terraces, a Chinese Chippendale bridge, a pond, a wilderness area, and formal arrangements. An inn, Carvel Hall, once stood in the gardens. After the inn was demolished in 1965, it took eight years to rebuild the gardens, which are planted with 18th-century perennials. You can take a self-guided tour of the garden, but to see the house you must go on the docent-led tour, which leaves every hour at half past the hour. The last tour leaves 1½ hours before closing. ⊠ *186 Prince George St.* ☎ *410/990–4543* ⊕ *www.annapolis.org* 🎫 *House and garden $8, house only $6, garden only $6* ⊗ *House and garden mid-Mar.–Dec., Mon.–Sat. 10–5, Sun. noon–5; Jan.–mid-Mar., Fri. and Sat. 10–4, Sun. noon–4.*

WORTH NOTING

HistoryQuest. In a redbrick building at the base of Main Street, the store occupies the site of a warehouse that held supplies for the Continental Army during the Revolutionary War. Today it's filled with maps, Maryland history books, ceramics, and nautical knickknacks. You can rent taped narrations here for 90-minute walking tours and also buy tickets for the Historic Trolley ride (⇨ *see Tours above*). Run by the Historic Annapolis Foundation, HistoryQuest is the source for many of the historic venues, tours, and events in town. ⊠ *77 Main St.* ☎ *410/268–5576* ⊕ *www.annapolis.org* 🎫 *Free* ⊗ *Mon.–Thurs. 10–5, Fri. and Sat. 10–6, Sun. 11–5; fewer hrs in winter.*

Kunta Kinte–Alex Haley Memorial. A series of plaques along the waterfront recounting the story of African-Americans in Maryland lead to a sculpture group depicting the famed author reading to a group of children. On the other side of the street, a three-sided obelisk and plaque commemorates the 1767 arrival of the African slave immortalized in Alex Haley's *Roots*. This is a lovely place to reflect on African-American history and the importance of family, reading, and passing oral history from one generation to another. ⊠ *Market Sq.* ⊕ *www.kintehaley.org.*

St. Anne's Church. Residing in the center of one of the historic area's busy circles, this brick building is one of the city's most prominent places of worship. King William III donated the communion silver when the parish was founded in 1692, but the first St. Anne's Church wasn't completed until 1704. The second church burned in 1858, but parts of its walls survived and were incorporated into the present structure, built the following year. The churchyard contains the grave of the last Colonial governor, Sir Robert Eden. ⊠ *Church Circle* ☎ *410/267–9333* 🎫 *Free* ⊗ *Weekdays 9–5, Sat. 6–2; services on Sun.*

Thurgood Marshall Memorial. Born in Baltimore, Thurgood Marshall (1908–93) was the first African-American Supreme Court Justice and one of the 20th century's foremost leaders in the struggle for equal rights

10

under the law. Marshall won the decision in 1954's *Brown v. Board of Education,* in which the Supreme Court overturned the doctrine of "separate but equal." Marshall was appointed as U.S. Solicitor General in 1965 and to the Supreme Court in 1967 by President Lyndon B. Johnson. The 8-foot statue depicts Marshall as a young lawyer. ⊠ *State House Sq., bordered by Bladen St., School St., and College Ave.*

WHERE TO EAT

$$ ✕ **aqua terra.** This funky restaurant gives history-minded Annapolis an
SEAFOOD alternative to the Colonial flavor found at most other downtown eateries. Inside are blond-wood furniture, an open kitchen, and a handsome granite counter. The menu features ingredients from the water (aqua) and the earth (terra), with additional small plates, soups, and salads. Offerings change with the season but include seafood, beef, and pasta as regular features. ⊠ *164 Main St.* ☎ *410/263–1985* ⊕ *www.aquaterraofannapolis.com* ⊟ *AE, MC, V.*

$$ ✕ **Buddy's Crabs & Ribs.** Family owned and operated since 1988, with
SEAFOOD a great location overlooking Annapolis Harbor, this fun and informal
☉ restaurant features all kinds of seafood and shellfish, including their famous "Big Buddy" crab cakes and all-you-can-eat buffets. Buddy's is the biggest restaurant in Annapolis. With each full-price entrée, one child 10 and under can eat free from the kids' menu. ⊠ *100 Main St.* ☎ *410/626–1100* ⊕ *www.buddysonline.com* ⊟ *AE, D, DC, MC, V.*

$$$ ✕ **Café Normandie.** Ladder-back chairs, wood beams, skylights, and a
FRENCH four-sided fireplace make this French restaurant homey. Out of the open kitchen comes an astonishingly good French onion soup, made daily from scratch. Bouillabaisse, puffy omelets, crepes, and seafood dishes are other specialties. The restaurant's breakfast, served only on weekends, includes poached eggs in ratatouille; eggs Benedict; seafood omelets; and crepes, waffles, and croissants. All offerings are sustainable and local. ⊠ *185 Main St.* ☎ *410/263–3382* ⊟ *AE, D, DC, MC, V.*

$$ ✕ **Cantler's Riverside Inn.** Opened in 1974, this local institution was
SEAFOOD founded by Jimmy Cantler, a native Marylander who worked as a waterman on the Chesapeake Bay. The no-nonsense interior has wooden blinds and floors and nautical items laminated beneath tabletops. Food is served on disposable dinnerware; if you order steamed crabs, they'll come served atop a "tablecloth" of brown paper. Waterview outdoor dining is available seasonally. Boat owners can tie up at the dock; free parking spaces are rare during the busy summer season and carpooling is encouraged if you drive. Specialties include steamed mussels, clams, and shrimp as well as Maryland vegetable crab soup, seafood sandwiches, oysters, crab cakes, and numerous fin fish. Jimmy Buffett claims that it is one of his top 10 favorite places to have a drink waterside. This place is easiest to find by boat, so if you're coming by car, check the Web site for directions. ■TIP➜ Cantler's gets very crowded on summer weekends—prepare to wait. Reservations are accepted for parties of ten or more. ⊠ *458 Forest Beach Rd.* ☎ *410/757–1311* ⊕ *www.cantlers.com* ⊟ *AE, DC, MC, V.*

$$$ ✕ **Carrol's Creek.** You can walk, catch a water taxi from City Dock, or
AMERICAN drive over the Spa Creek drawbridge to this local favorite in Eastport.

Whether you dine indoors or out, the view of historic Annapolis and its harbor is spectacular. The all-you-can-eat Sunday brunch ($21.95) is worth checking out, as are the seafood specialties. Any of the entrées, including the herb-encrusted rockfish or Southwestern blackened prime rib, can be turned into a four-course meal with the addition of soup, salad, and dessert for $12 more. ⌧ *410 Severn Ave., Eastport* ☎ *410/263–8102* ⊕ *www.carrolscreek.com* ⊟ *AE, D, DC, MC, V.*

$$ ✕**El Toro Bravo.** A local favorite, this authentic Mexican restaurant is
MEXICAN family-owned. The wooden Colonial exterior conceals colorful, south-of-the-border scenes hand painted on the interior walls, hanging plants, and padded aqua booths. There's often a line, but takeout is available. Lunch and dinner specials include a variety of enchiladas, fish tacos, grilled shrimp, and steak. The guacamole is made on the premises. ⌧ *50 West St., 1 block from visitor center* ☎ *410/267–5949* ⊟ *AE, D, DC, MC, V.*

$$ ✕**49 West Coffeehouse and Gallery.** In what was once a hardware store,
ECLECTIC this eclectic, casual eatery has one interior wall of exposed brick and another of exposed plaster; both are used to hang art for sale by local artists. Daily specials are chalked on a blackboard. Menu staples include a large cheese-and-pâté plate, deli sandwiches, and soups and salads. There's free Wi-Fi, and live music every night but Sunday. ⌧ *49 West St.* ☎ *410/626–9796* ⊕ *49westcoffeehouse.com* ⊟ *AE, MC, V.*

$$$ ✕**Harry Browne's.** In the shadow of the State House, this understated
SEAFOOD establishment has a reputation for quality food and attentive service that ensures bustle year-round, especially during the busy days of the legislative session (early January into early April) and special weekend events at the Naval Academy. The menu clearly reflects the city's maritime culture, but also has seasonal specialties such as rack of lamb and wild mushroom ravioli. Live Irish music is performed in the lounge once a month. The sidewalk café is open, weather permitting, April through October. There is a champagne brunch on Sunday. ⌧ *66 State Circle* ☎ *410/263–4332* ⊕ *www.harrybrownes.com* ⊟ *AE, D, DC, MC, V.*

$ ✕**McGarvey's Saloon and Oyster Bar.** An Annapolis institution since 1975,
AMERICAN this dockside eatery and watering hole is full of good cheer, great drink, and grand food. A heritage of seasonal shell- and fin-fish dishes, the finest burgers and steaks, as well as unstinting appetizers, make McGarvey's menu one of the most popular in the area. The full menu is available daily until 11 pm. Choose to eat outside in good weather, at the bar, or in the light-filled atrium. ⌧ *8 Market Space* ☎ *410/263–5700* ⊕ *www.mcgarveys.net* ⊟ *AE, MC, V.*

$$ ✕**Middleton Tavern.** Horatio Middleton began operating this "inn for
AMERICAN seafaring men" in 1750; Washington, Jefferson, and Franklin were among his guests. Today two fireplaces, wood floors, paneled walls, and a nautical theme make it cozy. Seafood tops the menu; the Maryland crab soup and pan-seared rockfish are standouts. Try the tavern's own Middleton Pale Ale, perhaps during happy hour or during a weekend blues session in the upstairs piano bar. Brunch is served on weekends, and you can dine outdoors in good weather. ⌧ *City Dock at Randall St.* ☎ *410/263–3323* ⊕ *www.middletontavern.com* ⊟ *AE, MC, V.*

10

$ ✗ **Rams Head Tavern.** A traditional English-style pub also houses the
BRITISH   Fordham Brewing Company, which you can tour. The Rams Head
★   serves better-than-usual tavern fare, including spicy shrimp salad, crab
cakes, beer-battered shrimp, and daily specials, as well as more than 100
beers—15 on tap—including six Fordham beers and others from around
the world. Brunch is served on Sunday. The nightclublike Rams Head
Tavern, On Stage, brings in nationally known folk, rock, jazz, country,
and bluegrass artists. Dinner-show specials are available; the menu has
light fare. ⊠ *33 West St.* ☎ *410/268–4545* ⊕ *www.ramsheadtavern.com*
⊟ *AE, D, MC, V.*

WHERE TO STAY

$$$ ⊡ **The Annapolis Inn.** An extraordinarily elegant B&B, this circa-1770
house has richly colored rooms decorated in the formal style of the
home's original era. The master suite has a sitting room and two fire-
places. Each suite has a king-size bed with luxury linens and a bath-
room with hand showers, bidets, and heated towel holders and marble
floors. From the third-floor suite's sundeck there's a close-up view of
the domes of the Naval Academy Chapel and the state capitol and the
harbor. Breakfast is a sumptuous three-course event served in the stately
dining room. TVs are placed in the rooms on request. **Pros:** in the heart
of the historic district; you'll feel like you've truly gone back in time.
Cons: no elevator; children are not welcome; no parking except down
the street in a public lot. ⊠ *144 Prince George St.* ☎ *410/295–5200*
⊕ *www.annapolisinn.com* ↪ *3 suites* ⌂ *In-room: a/c, Wi-Fi. In-hotel:
restaurant, parking (free), no kids under 17* ⊟ *AE, MC, V* ⦶ *BP.*

$$$ ⊡ **Annapolis Marriott Waterfront.** You can practically fish from your room
♻   at the city's only waterfront hotel. Rooms have either balconies over
the water or large windows with views of the harbor or the historic
district. The outdoor bar by the harbor's edge is popular in nice weather.
Pros: a "pure room" is available for the allergy sensitive; handicapped
accessible; a great place for children (offers Nintendo Wii). **Cons:** it's
a chain hotel, so it lacks the charm of some of Annapolis's bed-and-
breakfasts; parking is pricey. ⊠ *80 Compromise St.* ☎ *410/268–7555*
⊕ *www.annapolismarriott.com* ↪ *150 rooms* ⌂ *In-room: a/c, Wi-Fi.
In-hotel: restaurant, bars, gym, bicycles, laundry service, parking (paid)*
⊟ *AE, D, DC, MC, V.*

¢   ⊡ **Country Inn & Suites.** True to its name, a cozy, country mood, as well
as the gentle aroma of potpourri, permeates this suburban hotel. Rooms
all have standard chain-hotel decor, but a large fireplace, wooden floors,
and overstuffed sofas make the lobby an inviting place to linger. Exterior windows, trimmed with shutters and latticework, look out at a
wooded area or a shopping plaza. Within walking distance of Annapolis's largest mall, the hotel also has a free shuttle that can take you
to the historic district and to business parks. Four rooms have whirlpool tubs and two have fireplaces. **Pros:** complimentary hot breakfast
included; reliable and inexpensive option; near shopping. **Cons:** 4 mi
from the dock. ⊠ *2600 Housely Rd.* ☎ *410/571–6700 or 800/456–4000*
⊕ *www.countryinns.com* ↪ *100 rooms* ⌂ *In-room: a/c, refrigerator,*

DVD (some), Wi-Fi. In-hotel: pool, gym, laundry facilities ▭ *AE, D, DC, MC, V* ⦿❙ *CP.*

$$ ⌂ **Gibson's Lodgings.** Three detached houses from three centuries—1780, 1890, and 1980—are operated together as a single inn. One of the house's hallways is strikingly lined with mirrors. Guest rooms are furnished with pre-1900 antiques. One first-floor room, which has a private bath and porch, is designed for universal access. Free parking in the courtyards is a big advantage in the heart of this small Colonial-era city (the houses are opposite the U.S. Naval Academy). Continental breakfast is served in the formal dining room of the 18th-century Patterson House. **Pros:** conveniently located between the Naval Academy and downtown; some rooms have free Wi-Fi. **Cons:** children under five are not permitted; not handicapped accessible. ✉ *110–114 Prince George St.* ☎ *410/268–5555 or 877/330–0057* ⦿ *www.gibsonslodgings. com* ⟿ *21 rooms, 17 with bath* ♿ *In-room: a/c, Wi-Fi (some). In-hotel: parking (free), no kids under 5* ▭ *AE, MC, V* ⦿❙ *CP.*

$ ⌂ **Historic Inns of Annapolis.** Three 18th-century properties in the historic district are now grouped as one inn with registration for all three at the **Governor Calvert House.** Built in 1727, Calvert House is steps from the capitol. Also on State Circle, **Robert Johnson House** was built for the Annapolis barber in 1772. At the **Maryland Inn,** on nearby Church Circle, all rooms date back to the Revolutionary era. The Treaty of Paris Restaurant and two pubs serve all three inns. Guest rooms are individually decorated with antiques and reproductions; all have hair dryers, some have sitting suites or whirlpools. **Pros:** historic properties; recent renovations include new bathrooms; within walking distance of activities. **Cons:** prices vary greatly; some rooms are too small. ✉ *58 State Circle* ☎ *410/263–2641 or 800/847–8882* ⦿ *www. historicinnsofannapolis.com* ⟿ *124 rooms, 14 suites* ♿ *In-room: a/c, Wi-Fi. In-hotel: restaurant, bar, gym, laundry service, parking (paid)* ▭ *AE, D, DC, MC, V.*

$$ ⌂ **Loews Annapolis Hotel.** Although its redbrick exterior blends with the city's 1700s architecture, this hotel's interior is airy, spacious, and modern. Guest rooms, decorated in a sailing theme, include coffeemakers and terry robes. A free hotel shuttle bus takes you anywhere you want to go in Annapolis, and a complimentary breakfast is served in the Breeze restaurant for concierge-level guests. **Pros:** many amenities; more reasonable than some of the closer-in locations. **Cons:** a mile from the dock, it's a bit removed from the action of the historic center. ✉ *126 West St.* ☎ *410/263–7777* ⦿ *www.loewsannapolis.com* ⟿ *216 rooms, 15 suites* ♿ *In-room: a/c, Wi-Fi. In-hotel: restaurant, room service, bar, gym, spa, children's programs (all ages), laundry service, parking (paid), some pets allowed* ▭ *AE, D, DC, MC, V.*

¢ ⌂ **Scotlaur Inn.** On the two floors above Chick and Ruth's Delly, rooms in this family-owned B&B are papered in pastel Colonial prints. The high beds are topped with fluffy comforters and lots of pillows. Chandeliers in each room and marble floors in the private bathrooms bring this place a long way from its first days as a boardinghouse with only two bathrooms. Check-in as well as breakfast are held in the famous deli downstairs. **Pros:** a chance to stay above one of Annapolis's landmarks

10

right in the center of town. **Cons:** might not be your style if you prefer modern decor and don't like chintz; rooms are on the smaller side. ✉ *165 Main St.* ☎ *410/268–5665* ⊕ *www.scotlaurinn.com* ⇨ *10 rooms* ⚴ *In-room: a/c, Wi-Fi. In-hotel: restaurant* ▭ *MC, V* ❚◯❘ *CP.*

$ 📺 **Sheraton Annapolis Hotel.** Next to Westfield Shoppingtown, and near numerous chain restaurants, this large Sheraton has a free hourly shuttle bus to and from downtown Annapolis. (Traffic and parking there can be difficult.) The lobby is outfitted with marble floors, fresh flowers and ferns, and two sitting areas among marble columns. The café is adjacent to the lobby. Rooms are furnished with blond woods, geometric carpeting, and burgundy-print bedspreads. **Pros:** reliable Sheraton experience; many in-hotel amenities. **Cons:** despite its name, the hotel is 5 mi from downtown. ✉ *173 Jennifer Rd.* ☎ *410/266–3131 or 888/627–8980* ⊕ *www.starwoodhotels.com/sheraton* ⇨ *196 rooms* ⚴ *In-room: a/c, Internet. In-hotel: restaurant, room service, bar, pool, gym, Wi-Fi hotspot, parking (free)* ▭ *AE, D, DC, MC, V.*

$$$ 📺 **The Westin Annapolis Hotel.** The new Westin Annapolis is part of a large redevelopment complex about a mile from the City Dock. Park Place will contain not only the hotel, but offices, condominiums, and shops and the future site of the Maryland Theater of the Performing Arts. This luxury hotel offers complete spa services, a business center, and four varied restaurants, both within the hotel and outside in the larger complex. **Pros:** the complete Starwood hotel experience, including the comfortable Heavenly Bed; modern hotel with modern amenities. **Cons:** about a mile from the City Dock in a rapidly gentrifying neighborhood; Wi-Fi only free in public areas. ✉ *100 Westgate Circle, Park Place* ☎ *410/972–4300* ⊕ *www.westin.com/annapolis* ⇨ *225 rooms* ⚴ *In-room: a/c, Wi-Fi. In-hotel: 4 restaurants, bar, pool, gym, Wi-Fi hotspot* ▭ *AE, D, MC, V.*

$$ 📺 **William Page Inn.** Built in 1908, this dark-brown, cedar-shingle, wood-frame structure was the local Democratic Party clubhouse for 50 years. Today its wraparound porch is furnished with Adirondack chairs—a nice place to relax if the weather is nice. The third-floor suite, with dormer windows and a sloped ceiling, includes an Italian-marble bathroom with whirlpool. A hot breakfast is served in the common room. **Pros:** a nice alternative to large hotels; only half a block from the dock; free Wi-Fi. **Cons:** no elevator; two-night minimum stay on weekends; not for families with young kids. ✉ *8 Martin St.* ☎ *410/626–1506 or 800/364–4160* ⊕ *www.williampageinn.com* ⇨ *5 rooms, 3 with bath; 1 suite* ⚴ *In-room: a/c, no TV (some), Wi-Fi. In-hotel: parking (free), no kids under 12* ▭ *MC, V* ❚◯❘ *BP.*

NIGHTLIFE AND THE ARTS

BARS AND CLUBS

The lounge at **Harry Browne's** (✉ *66 State Circle* ☎ *410/263–4332* ⊕ *harrybrownes.com*) gives people something fun to do on Tuesday night: listen to live Irish music. **Middleton Tavern** (*2 Market Space* ☎ *410/263–3323* ⊕ *www.middletontavern.com*) presents local and regional acoustic musicians nightly at its Oyster Bar lounge. The Oyster Shooter—raw oysters served in a shot glass with vodka and cocktail sauce and washed down with beer—supposedly originated here. The upstairs piano bar is open on Friday and Saturday nights. The **Rams Head Tavern on the Stage** (⌧ *33 West St.* ☎ *410/268–4545* ⊕ *www.ramsheadtavern.com*) hosts nationally known folk, rock, jazz, country, and bluegrass groups. Past performers include Lyle Lovett, Ralph Stanley, and Linda Thompson. Dinner combinations are available; the tavern is no-smoking.

MUSIC AND THEATER

Annapolis Summer Garden Theater (⌧ *143 Compromise St., at Main St.* ☎ *410/268–9212* ⊕ *www.summergarden.com*) stages a mix of musicals and plays outdoors (May–September), including occasional works by local playwrights. The **Colonial Players** (⌧ *108 East St.* ☎ *410/268–7373* ⊕ *www.thecolonialplayers.org*), active since the 1940s, are the city's principal theater troupe.

Entertainment at the **Naval Academy** (☎ *410/293–2439 for schedules; 800/874–6289 for tickets*) includes the Distinguished Artists Series, the Masqueraders (the Academy's theatrical club), chamber music recitals, and glee club concerts. **Naval Academy Band** (☎ *410/293–0263*) concerts, many held outside during fair weather, are free.

SPORTS AND THE OUTDOORS

PARTICIPANT SPORTS

BIKING

The **Baltimore and Annapolis (B&A) Trail** (⌧ *Early Height Ranger Station, 51 W. Early Height Rd., Severna Park* ☎ *410/222–6244* ⊕ *www.dnr.state.md.us/greenways/ba_trail.html*) runs through 13 mi of farmland and forests as well as urban and suburban neighborhoods, from Annapolis to Glen Burnie. It follows the old Baltimore and Annapolis Railroad and is linked directly to the 12.5-mi trail encircling Baltimore-Washington International Airport. The trail is open sunrise to sunset to hikers, bikers, runners, and in-line skaters. Access to the northern end of the trail is via Dorsey Road off I–97 Exit 15 near Friendship Park. Parking is free but limited. **Pedal Pushers Bike Shop** (⌧ *546 Baltimore, at Annapolis Blvd., Rte. 648, Severna Park* ☎ *410/544–2323* ⊕ *www.pedalpushersmd.com*) rents bikes for the B&A Trail.

FISHING

Anglers (⌧ *1456 Whitehall Rd.* ☎ *410/757–3442*) sells equipment for archery and hunting as well as for fresh- and saltwater fishing. Anglers is also a full-service Orvis fly-fishing dealer.

SAILING

Annapolis Sailing School (⌧ *7040 Bembe Beach Rd.* ☎ *410/267–7205 or 800/638–9192* ⊕ *www.annapolissailing.com*) bills itself as America's oldest and largest sailing school. The inexperienced can take a two-hour basic lesson. In addition, live-aboard, cruising, and advanced-sailing programs are available, as are boat rentals. **Womanship** (⌧ *137 Conduit St.* ☎ *410/267–6661 or 800/342–9295* ⊕ *www.womanship.com*) is a sailing school with programs for women, for mother–daughter partners, and for couples. Classes can be custom-designed for special needs or desires. Men are welcome to take classes as half of a couple

10

or as part of a group. The Young Womanship program is for grades 7 to 12. Started in 1984 in Annapolis, Womanship now has 16 locations around the world.

SPECTATOR SPORTS

The teams of the **United States Naval Academy Athletic Association (NAAA)** (☎ *800/874–6289 ticket office* ⊕ *www.navysports.com*) compete in about 20 varsity sports, most notably football. The team plays home games in fall at the Navy–Marine Corps Stadium on Rowe Boulevard in Annapolis.

BOAT RACES

Annapolis Yacht Club (☎ *410/263–9279* ⊕ *www.annapolisyc.org*) sponsors sailboat races at 6 pm each Wednesday from mid-May through early September in Annapolis Harbor, starting at the Eastport bridge.

CALVERT COUNTY

The long, narrow peninsula between the Patuxent River and the Chesapeake Bay is Calvert County, an area that has not yet been completely overrun by tourism. Two principal routes—Route 2 from Annapolis and Route 4 from Washington, D.C.—merge near Sunderland and continue on together to the county's southern tip. Exploring the bay-side and riverside communities to either side of the highway, as well as the inland sites and attractions, will immerse you quickly in the tangible history and heritage of agriculture and fishing. ■TIP➜ Although southern Maryland is best known as a fishermen and boaters' paradise, it is also popular with cyclists. Its flat terrain and relatively uncongested roads make for perfect conditions to tour the area by bike.

ESSENTIALS

Calvert County Dept. of Economic Development & Tourism (✉ *175 Main St., Prince Frederick* ☎ *410/535–4583 or 800/331–9771* ⊕ *www.ecalvert.com*).

NORTH BEACH

31 mi south of Annapolis, via Rte. 2, Rte. 260, and Rte. 261.

In some ways a quieter, more-residential extension of Chesapeake Beach, North Beach has a fishing pier and a quiet boardwalk. When it was founded in 1900, it was a resort for family summer vacations, and amusement centers, bingo halls, theaters, and bathhouses defined the town until the Great Depression. Then in 1933 a hurricane ravaged the beach and destroyed many of its buildings. Post–World War II programs sponsored by the Veterans Administration facilitated a building boom, turning North Beach into a year-round community. Although sea nettles are a problem when swimming in the Chesapeake Bay, North Beach has a small, netted beach and a nearly waveless shore. Walk out on the pier where many of the benches are dedicated to the victims of September 11.

GETTING HERE AND AROUND

A little over an hour from Washington and less than an hour from Annapolis, North Beach is not for those who want exciting shore resorts like Ocean City or Rehoboth. There are only a few places to eat or even get a cup of coffee, and a handful of antiques and gift shops. The main activity in North Beach is simply sitting on the shore watching the Bay or going fishing.

> ### BEACH TROLLEY
>
> In 2008 Beach Trolley Association inaugurated a regular route of motorized trolleys between North Beach and Chesapeake Beach. The trolleys run on Friday and the weekend from June through August and cost 25¢ a ride (⊕ www.beachtrolleyassociation. org).

Access to the beach is free for North Beach residents only. In summer, out-of-county visitors must pay $7. Fishing passes are also free for North Beach residents, but out-of-county residents pay $5 or $65 for a season pass.

ESSENTIALS

North Beach Welcome Center (☎ 410/286–3799 ⊕ www.ci.north-beach. md.us).

EXPLORING

Free summer concerts are held on the second Saturday of the month from June through August on the boardwalk. Local crafts are featured at the annual Bayfest held on the fourth weekend in August. In 2008 the town inaugurated a seasonal Friday night farmers' market from 6 pm to 9 pm.

WHERE TO EAT

$$
SEAFOOD
✕**Neptune's.** Modest Neptune's claims of preparing "the world's best mussels" rings true with many, making the trip to this tiny town just north of Chesapeake Beach worthwhile. Attached to the small bar, a glass-enclosed dining room with a brick floor is a friendly, informal spot to dig in to its signature dish—it's also a great place for nice views. Also on the menu are seafood pastas, burgers, and cuts of Angus beef. Don't let the "divey" atmosphere dissuade you; order the mussels (sold by the pound) and enjoy. This is the best restaurant (and there are few choices) in town. ⊠ 8800 Chesapeake Ave., at 1st St. ☎ 410/257–7899 ⊟ AE, D, MC, V.

CHESAPEAKE BEACH

1 mi south of North Beach via Rte. 261; 32 mi south of Annapolis via Rte. 2, Rte. 260, and Rte. 261.

This charming little town beside the Bay was founded at the close of the 19th century as a resort to rival those along the French Riviera. It was served by steamboats from Baltimore and by a railroad from Washington, D.C. Steamboat service diminished over time and the railroad failed in 1935, but the town survived as private automobiles became more readily available. It boomed again in 1948 with the legalization of slot machines, although they lasted only 20 years. Today Chesapeake

Beach is once again staging a tourism comeback with the addition of a water park and a new waterfront hotel.

Joined almost seamlessly to North Beach, Chesapeake Beach is the more exciting of the two relatively quiet towns. While North Beach retains the low profile of a collection of beachfront cottages, Chesapeake Beach has been built up with hotels and condominiums. Development also means that there is more to do in Chesapeake Beach—restaurants, a good museum, a hotel with a spa, a water park, and a greater number and variety of shops.

GETTING HERE AND AROUND

The Beach Trolley Association provides transportation between Chesapeake Beach and nearby North Beach, Herrington Harbor, and Deale. The trolley runs on weekends from Memorial Day to Labor Day. It arrives at each stop about once every hour hour. Visit ⊕ *www.beach-trolleyassociation.org* for a route map, schedule, and other information. The fare is 25¢.

North Beach is reached by car. The town itself is easily walked in an hour. Metered parking is available adjacent to the boardwalk.

ESSENTIALS

Chesapeake Beach (☏ *410/257–2230 town hall* ⊕ *www.chesapeake-beach. md.us*).

EXPLORING

☾ **Chesapeake Beach Railway Museum.** Housed in the railroad's 1898 track-
★ side terminus, this museum provides memorable glimpses of the one-time resort's turn-of-the-20th-century glory days. Among its exhibits are a glass-enclosed model of the town of Chesapeake Beach and a hand-carved kangaroo from the magnificent carousel, as well as a slot machine and photos of early vacationers. One of the railroad's passenger cars rests nearby. ✉ *4155 Mears Ave., Rte. 261* ☏ *410/257–3892* ⊕ *www.cbrm.org* 🎟 *Free* ⊗ *May–Sept., daily 1–4; Apr. and Oct., weekends 1–4 and by appointment.*

☾ **Chesapeake Beach Water Park.** Families make a day of it at Chesapeake Beach Water Park, which has a children's pool, beach, and many slides. The park is open from Memorial Day until the first day of school. Admission is $18 (it's less for locals). ✉ *4079 Gordon Stinnett Ave. at Rte. 261* ☏ *410/257–1404 or 301/855–3803.*

WHERE TO EAT AND STAY

$$ ✕ **Rod 'n' Reel.** This family-owned restaurant opened optimistically in
SEAFOOD 1936, the year after the demise of the railroad from Washington. Since then it has remained synonymous with superb seafood. Now part of the Chesapeake Beach Resort & Spa, its bay-side location still provides stunning views. The extensive menu includes succulent southern Maryland specialties such as rockfish stuffed with crab imperial, fried oysters, and the region's ubiquitous crab cakes. ✉ *Rte. 261 at Mears Ave.* ☏ *410/257–2735 or 877/763–6733* ⊕ *www.rodnreelinc. com* ▭ *AE, D, MC, V.*

$$$ ▦ **The Chesapeake Beach Resort & Spa.** Opened in 2004, this luxury hotel
★ and spa is a key part of the revitalization of the town's tourism business.

The public spaces pay homage to the beachfront community's history. A mural in the lobby depicts the old roller coaster that once thrilled vacationers, and framed photographs line the corridors, tracing the town's changes from its Victorian heyday to the present. The whitewashed oak furniture and sand-color walls give the rooms an elegant yet beachy style. The resort was built right on the water's edge, and its suites and deluxe rooms have balconies that seem to hang over the Bay. There are also three dining options, a boardwalk, and a fishing charter company at the hotel's full-service marina. **Pros:** a full-service resort with boating, an indoor pool, and spa services; a sandy beach. **Cons:** don't expect a "jumping the waves" experience at the beach—the Chesapeake is placid compared to the beach properties on the Atlantic. ☒ *4165 Mears Ave.* ☎ *410/257–5596 or 301/855–0096* ⊕ *www.cbresortspa.com* ➪ *72 rooms, 6 suites* ⌂ *In-room: a/c, Internet. In-hotel: 3 restaurants, pool, gym, spa, parking (free)* ☐ *AE, D, DC, MC, V* ⦿*BP.*

PORT REPUBLIC

17 mi south of Chesapeake Beach.

Two sites in Port Republic, Christ Church and Port Republic School No. 7, are easy to miss simply because the sign for Port Republic from Route 765 points north, but the attractions are actually south. From Route 765 turn onto Broomes Island Road. If you plan on dining near Port Republic you may have to continue to Lusby or Solomons Island.

GETTING HERE AND AROUND

Port Republic is accessible by car. The town is easy to miss and the sites listed below are not in the town limits.

EXPLORING

☺ ★ **Battle Creek Cypress Swamp Sanctuary.** With the northernmost naturally occurring stand of bald cypress trees in the United States, the 100-acre Battle Creek Cypress Swamp Sanctuary provides close-up looks at the forest primeval. A 0.25-mi elevated boardwalk at the bottom of a steep but sturdy set of steps gives you a good vantage point to see the swamp, thick with 100-foot-tall trees that are 75 to 100 years old. Guides at the nature center can alert you to the seasonal permutations of the vegetation and the doings of squirrels, owls, and other wildlife. Indoor exhibits focus on the area's natural and cultural history. The swamp is about 5 mi west of Port Republic. ☒ *Sixes Rd., Rte. 506, Prince Frederick* ☎ *410/535–5327* ⊕ *www.calvertparks.org* ☒ *Free* ⊙ *Tues.–Sat. 10–4:30, Sun. 1–4:30.*

Christ Church. Tracings its origins to 1672, when a log-cabin church stood at the site, Christ Church received a brick replacement in 1772, coated with plaster, is notable for its biblical garden, planted with species mentioned in the scriptures. Port Republic School No. 7 is on the church's property. Since immediately after the Civil War the grounds have been a venue for jousting (Maryland's state sport) on the last Saturday in August. ☒ *3100 Broomes Island Rd., Rte. 264* ☎ *410/586–0565* ☒ *Free* ⊙ *Daily dawn–dusk.*

10

Jefferson Patterson Park and Museum. Behind 2.5 mi of scenic Patuxent riverfront stretch 544 acres of woods and farmland. The 70-odd archaeological sites have yielded evidence of 9,000 years of human habitation—from prehistory on through to colonial times. At the Jefferson Patterson Park and Museum you can follow an archaeology trail to inspect artifacts of the successive hunter-gatherer, early agricultural, and plantation societies that once roamed and settled this land. Displays include primitive knives and axes, fragments of Native American pottery, and Colonial glassware. Stroll along the nature trails to take a look at wildlife, antique agricultural equipment, and fields of crops. The park is 2 mi south of Port Republic. ⊠ *10115 Mackall Rd., Rte. 265, St. Leonard* ☎ *410/586–8501* ⊕ *www.jefpat.org* ☛ *Free* ⊙ *Mid-Apr.–mid-Oct., Wed.–Sun. 10–5.*

Port Republic School No. 7. Port Republic School No. 7, a classic one-room schoolhouse built in the 1880s, looks for all the world as if today's lesson could begin any minute. Here, you can find a restored classroom with archetypal desks, inkwells, and a school bell. Until 1932 a single teacher taught children in seven grades here. ⊠ *3100 Broomes Island Rd., Rte. 264* ☎ *410/586–0767* ☛ *Free* ⊙ *Memorial Day–Labor Day, Sun. 2–4 and by appointment.*

BROOMES ISLAND

7 mi south of Port Republic, via Rte. 264.

An area without specific boundaries, Broomes is not even an island per se, except during a very high tide or in a strong storm. It's made up of little more than a few houses and stores, a post office, and a church. This little area at the mouth of Island Creek is a portrait of a water-dependent community amid change: weather-beaten structures of its past now mingle with new, expensive waterfront homes.

GETTING HERE AND AROUND

Broomes Island is only accessible by car or boat. A blink-and-you'll-miss-it kind of place, Broomes Island has just one road going into and out of it. It takes about 10 minutes to walk the town. Visitors (especially boaters) come here for Stoney's.

WHERE TO EAT

$$$

SEAFOOD

★

✕ Stoney's Seafood House. Popular with boaters who tie right up to the dock, this restaurant overlooking Island Creek has one dining room that actually juts out over the water and another on higher ground with great views from its floor-to-ceiling windows. There's also ample seating—and a tiki bar—outside. Stoney's hefty crab cakes are made with plenty of back-fin meat and little filler. Oyster sandwiches and Stoney's Steamer—handpicked selections of fresh seafood—are also good choices. The intense, house-made desserts, such as the strawberry shortcake and Kim's key lime pie, are not for the faint of heart. If you miss Stoney's in Broomes Island, there are two other locations in Solomons Island. ⊠ *3939 Oyster House Rd.* ☎ *410/586–1888* ⊕ *www. stoneysseafoodhouse.com* ▭ *AE, D, MC, V* ⊙ *Closed Nov.–early Mar.*

LUSBY

☺ *12 mi southeast of Broomes Island.*

Lusby is larger than either Port Republic or Broomes Island and has a town center as well as some of the big, convenience stores on its perimeter that are lacking in some of the smaller shore towns. And if you want to do anything after 8 pm other than watching the sunset over the dock, you might find it in Lusby.

GETTING HERE AND AROUND

A car is essential in Lusby. With a population of nearly 2,000 it is the largest town in the area and has several shopping centers and a downtown that has grown in the last several years. There is no mass transit.

EXPLORING

Flag Ponds Nature Park. Like its better-known neighbor Calvert Cliffs State Park, Flag Ponds Nature Park has spectacular views of the cliffs, but with just a short stroll to the beach, this county park is the more accessible of the two. Until the 1950s the area was a busy fishery, and some of the buildings from that era still stand. Today it beckons with bathhouses, a fishing pier, 3 mi of gently graded hiking trails, observation decks at two ponds, a boardwalk through wetlands, and indoor wildlife exhibits. Soaring cliffs, flat marshland, and wildflowers (including the blue flag iris, for which the park is named) provide stunning contrasts. ■ TIP→ A shark's tooth, which scientists date at more than 10 million years, is the big prize in a fossil hunt on the beach, one of the park's most popular activities. ⊠ *Rte. 2/4* ☎ *410/586–1477* ⊕ *www. calvertparks.org* ⊇ *$6 per vehicle Apr.–Oct., $3 per vehicle Nov.–Mar.* ☺ *Memorial Day–Labor Day, weekdays 9–6, weekends 9–8; Labor Day–Memorial Day, weekends 9–5.*

NIGHTLIFE AND THE ARTS

For a taste of the tropics *and* the South Pacific along St. Leonard's Creek, wet your lips with an umbrella-topped cocktail at **Vera's Beach Club** (⊠ *1200 White Sands Dr., Lusby* ☎ *410/586–1182* ⊕ *verasbeachclub. com* ☺ *Closed Nov.–Apr.*). Vera's offers weekly entertainment and no cover charge. With an exotic environment and fantastic location with open-air decks overlooking a deepwater marina and delightful river views—not to mention a swimming pool—it's well worth a visit, despite its difficult-to-find location west off Route 2/4.

10

SOLOMONS

8 mi south of Lusby.

On the tip of the peninsula, Solomons is where the Patuxent empties into the Chesapeake. The town has become a popular getaway for sailors, boaters, and affluent professionals. But it's still a laid-back waterfront town—at least when compared with, say, Annapolis or St. Michaels. Several excellent boatyards and marinas cater to powerboaters and sailors, with nautical services from the simplest to the most sophisticated. There are several antiques, book, gift, and specialty shops and galleries side by side, parallel to the boardwalk. Wherever you go, stunning views surround you at nearly every turn.

GETTING HERE AND AROUND

Solomons Island is reached by either boat or car. Once you arrive public parking is plentiful; spend a pleasant few hours either walking or biking the town's flat terrain.

EXPLORING

Annmarie Garden. A world-class sculpture and botanical venue, Annmarie Garden Sculpture Park and Arts Center is a 30-acre property on the St. John Creek. The sculptural art is by artists both local and from around the world. One of the more intriguing installations is a series of 13 "Talking Benches."

> ### KIM'S KEY LIME PIE
>
> Many of the restaurants in southern Maryland serve **Kim's pies** (⊠ *14618 Solomons Island Rd.* ☎ *410/326–8469*)—especially the key lime. The bakery is located in Solomons Island in a cottage that is a combination café, Kim's Key Lime Pie and Coffee Shop, and gift shop, Kim's Riverwalk Gifts. Although the key lime is the most popular, we also highly recommend the carrot cake.

Each tells an ecological story by depicting a plant that grows in southern Maryland, including dogwood, loblolly pines, papaw trees, and tobacco. Smooth, user-friendly pathways curve through the grounds. Don't miss the lyrical brass statue of a crabber in front of the museum. The figure and water feature perfectly captures the dependence of the area on the seafood industry. Little here is off-limits, and picnickers are welcome to settle in virtually anywhere. Be sure to visit the mosaic-filled restrooms. ■TIP➔ Annemarie Garden has a special Christmas display, "The Garden in Lights," from mid-December through New Year's Eve. Children get in free and there are many specialized programs that provide a hands-on art experience. ⊠ *13480 Dowell Rd.* ☎ *410/326–4640* ⊕ *www. annmariegarden.org* ⊠ *$3* ⊙ *Daily 9–5.*

WHERE TO EAT AND STAY

$$
ITALIAN
✕ **DiGiovanni's Dock of the Bay.** It's rare to be able to enjoy elegant waterside dining and professional service at budget prices. The chef creates succulent northern Italian dishes using fresh herbs and spices. The *cacciucco* (seafood soup) alone is worth a special trip, as is the homemade lasagna. Italian music is played during meals. There are many excellent seafood restaurants in southern Maryland, but DiGiovanni's is one of the few to give the fruit of the Bay an ethnic spin. ⊠ *14556 Solomons Island Rd.* ☎ *410/394–6400* ▭ *AE, D, MC, V* ⊙ *Closed Mon. Jan.– May. No lunch.*

$
★
🛏 **Back Creek Inn.** Built for a waterman in 1880, this blue wood-frame house sits in a residential neighborhood on well-tended grounds at the edge of Back Creek. You can lounge on the deck next to a beautiful perennial garden. Four rooms have water views, and one opens onto the garden. Breakfast is served in the dining room. The Lavender Cottage in the rear of the Inn costs a little more and boasts water views and a king-size bed, but it is a favorite for couples. The Back Creek Inn is in a residential neighborhood, but easily within walking distance to town. Kayaking and bikes are nearby for rental. **Pros:** very friendly management; well-tended property. **Cons:** no elevator; only children 12 and older are welcome; a two-night stay is mandatory April through October. ⊠ *Calvert and Alexander Sts.* ☎ *410/326–2022* ⊕ *www.*

backcreekinnbnb.com ⤴ *4 rooms, 2 suites, 1 cottage* ⚓ *In-room: a/c, Wi-Fi. In-hotel: bicycles, no kids under 12* ➡ *MC, V* ⏲ *BP.*

$ ⊞ **Hilton Garden Inn Solomons.** This relatively new inn and convention center has the standard amenities, including a heated indoor pool and a modern fitness center. The business crowd fits right in here, as the hotel's expansive lobby and corporate look signal the expectation of convention and meetings clientele. Large rooms have desks with ergonomically designed chairs and plenty of outlets There are six rooms with Jacuzzis available. **Pros:** everything is modern and up-to-date; it has many handy amenities like laundry and a convenience store; Wi-Fi is free. **Cons:** 2 mi from the center of town and along a highway. ⊠ *13100 Dowell Rd., Dowell* ☎ *410/326–0303* ⊕ *www.hiltongardeninn.hilton. com* ⤴ *100 rooms, 8 suites* ⚓ *In-room: a/c, Wi-Fi. In-hotel: restaurant, bar, pools* ➡ *AE, D, MC, V.*

$ ⊞ **Solomons Victorian Inn.** On the Back Creek side of narrow Solomons Island this three-story, yellow frame house was built in 1906 by the foremost shipbuilder on the Chesapeake Bay. Six rooms look onto Solomons Harbor and two have garden views. All are furnished with period antiques and reproductions, and every room has an ornate armoire. Afternoon refreshments and breakfast are served on an enclosed porch. **Pros:** the great room in the common area has stunning water views; all the necessary modern amenities but with 19th-century decor. **Cons:** only one room is handicapped accessible; no elevator; a two-night minimum stay on weekends. ⊠ *125 Charles St.* ☎ *410/326–4811* ⊕ *www. solomonsvictorianinn.com* ⤴ *8 rooms* ⚓ *In-room: a/c, Wi-Fi. In-hotel: no children under 12* ➡ *AE, MC, V* ⏲ *BP.*

ST. MARY'S COUNTY

"Just at the mouth of the river, we observed the natives in arms. That night, fires blazed through the whole country and since they had never seen such a large ship, messengers were sent in all directions, who reported that a 'canoe' like an island had come with as many as there were trees in the woods."—Father Andrew White, recounting the arrival of the *Ark* and the *Dove* in 1634.

10

Father White arrived in the New World in 1634 as a member of Lord Baltimore's contingent of 140 colonists. The two "canoes" the Native Americans spotted were the tiny sailing vessels that had just crossed the Atlantic to reach the southernmost tip of Maryland's Western Shore, where the Potomac River meets the Chesapeake Bay. The peninsula between the Potomac and the Patuxent rivers is today St. Mary's County—easily one of the state's most beautiful regions. It is gradually attracting development because of its easy access to Washington, D.C., to the north.

Like so much of Maryland south of Annapolis and Washington, many scenic drives throughout St. Mary's County bring together charming inland and waterside towns and historic sites. Hearty food and homey places to stay are easy to find.

■TIP→ Looking for an unusual find? Numerous liquor stores in St. Mary's
County sell popular brands of U.S. beer in rare 8-ounce and 10-ounce cans.

ESSENTIALS

St. Mary's County Tourism (⊠ 23115 Leonard Hall Dr., Leonardtown
☎ 800/327–9023 ⊕ www.co.saint-marys.md.us).

LEXINGTON PARK

9 mi southeast of Solomons, 68 mi south of Annapolis, via Rte. 2/4
to Rte. 235.

This military town is dominated by the Patuxent River Naval Air Station, which covers 25 mi of the shoreline at the mouth of the epony-
mous river. The station assists naval aviation operations by its research,
development, and testing of aircraft and things associated with them.
Its facilities are also utilized by private industry, academic institutions,
and foreign governments.

GETTING HERE AND AROUND

All of the attractions listed here are outside of the town limits, so you
don't actually need to go into Lexington Park.

EXPLORING

**OFF THE
BEATEN
PATH**

Sotterley. The distinguished house on the grounds of this 18th-century
plantation is the earliest (1703) post-in-ground structure known to
exist in the United States; in place of a foundation, cedar timbers driven
straight into the ground support it. The house is a sampler of architectural styles and interior design from the last two centuries. On the
grounds of this National Historic Landmark are other buildings from
the 18th through early 20th century: a Colonial customs warehouse, a
smokehouse, a "necessary" (an outhouse), and a restored slave cabin
from the 1830s. The house also has Colonial Revival gardens and
nature trails overlooking the Patuxent River. Admission, which is less
for children, includes a tour. ⊠ Rte. 245 near Hollywood, 12 mi north
of Lexington Park via Rtes. 235 and 245 ☎ 301/373–2280 ⊕ www.
sotterley.com ≊ $10, museum $3, grounds ⊙ May–Oct., Tues.–Sat.
10–4, Sun. noon–4. Grounds open year-round.

POINT LOOKOUT STATE PARK

20 mi south of Lexington Park, 88 mi south of Annapolis, via Rte. 2/4
and Rte. 235 to Rte. 5.

GETTING HERE AND AROUND

Point Lookout can be reached by car. Once in the park there are boating, swimming, and abundant trails for hiking.

EXPLORING

Point Lookout State Park. When Father Andrew White came to Point
Lookout and saw the Potomac at its side, he mused that the Thames
was a mere rivulet in comparison. But instead of being overwhelmed
by the wildness of the New World, he observed that "fine groves of
trees appear, growing in intervals as if planted by the hand of man."

On the approach to Point Lookout State Park, two memorial obelisks remind travelers of the dark later history of this starkly alluring point of land. Beginning in 1863 a Union prison stood at the farthest tip of the peninsula, just across the Potomac from Confederate Virginia. During those last two years of the conflict, nearly 4,000 Confederate soldiers died here because of disease and poor conditions. Point Lookout is a reminder that many men from southern Maryland fought on the side of the Confederates during the Civil War. After the Battle of Gettysburg, 20,000 prisoners crowded the Point Lookout facilities—a space built for only half that. All that remains of the prison are some earthen fortifications, partially rebuilt and known as Fort Lincoln, with markers noting the sites of hospitals and other buildings. A small museum supplies some of the details.

The 1,046-acre state park has boating facilities, nature trails, and a beach for swimming. The RV campground, with hookups, is open year-round; tent camping facilities are open from April through October. Be sure to visit the lighthouse at the southern end of the park. Built in 1830 and used until 1965, the lighthouse also served as a depot. ■TIP→ **Bring plenty of bug spray. Mosquitoes can be a problem.** ⊠ *Point Lookout State Park, 11175 Point Lookout Rd., Scotland, Md.* ☎ *301/872–5688* ⊕ *www.dnr.state.md.us* ✉ *May–Sept., weekends and holidays $5 per person, all other times $3 per vehicle* ⊗ *Year-round, daily 6 am–sunset.*

▌ **OFF THE BEATEN PATH**	**St. Ignatius Church.** Built in 1758, this beautiful church—one of the most beautiful in Maryland—is all that survives of a prerevolutionary plantation. In addition to stunning stained-glass windows, parishioners have adorned each kneeler with scenes from Maryland culture. The adjacent graveyard, one of the oldest in the United States, is a history in stone of the families of the church and the region. Several veterans of the Revolution are buried here, alongside Jesuit priests who served here. A stop here is well worth a detour. ■TIP→ **To see inside the church, ask for the key at the sentry box of the naval installation next door.** ⊠ *Villa Rd. off Rte. 5, St. Inigoes* ☎ *301/872–5590* ✉ *Free.*

ST. MARY'S CITY

73 mi south of Annapolis, via Rte. 2/4 to Rte. 5 North.

An intrepid group of 140 English settlers sailed the *Ark* and the *Dove* up the Potomac and into one of its tributaries, the St. Mary's River. About halfway up, on an east bank, they founded St. Mary's City, the fourth permanent settlement in British North America and eventually the first (albeit short-lived) capital of Maryland.

Long before a Constitution or a Bill of Rights, the first law of religious tolerance in the New World was enacted in St. Mary's City, guaranteeing the freedom to practice whatever religion one chose. Here, too, almost three centuries before American women achieved suffrage, Mistress Margaret Brent challenged the status quo and requested the right to vote (she didn't get it). The settlement served as Maryland's capital city until 1695, when the legislature moved to Annapolis and the county seat moved to Leonardtown. St. Mary's City virtually vanished, its existence acknowledged only in historical novels and textbooks.

10

Today the city is home to a living-history park and a small liberal-arts college that shares its name, St. Mary's College of Maryland.

GETTING HERE AND AROUND

The St. Mary's Transit System connects St. Mary's City to other towns in the county. For a schedule or more information, go online to ⊕ *www.co.saint-marys.md.us/dpw/ststransportation.asp* or call ☎ *301/ 863–8400.*

EXPLORING

⟲ **Historic St. Mary's City**. When you visit the 800-plus acres here, with a liberal arts college serving at the cultural center, don't expect Colonial Williamsburg. St. Mary's is an ongoing archaeological dig and a work in progress. In 1934, in commemoration of the 300th anniversary of Maryland, the colony's imposing State House, originally built in 1676, was reconstructed. In the early 1970s a vast archaeological-reconstruction program began in earnest, a project that has revealed nearly 200 individual sites. In 2009 St. Mary's marked its 375th anniversary of the founding of Maryland. A living history museum of sorts, the historic town includes several notable reconstructions and reproductions of buildings. The **State House of 1676**, like its larger and grander counterpart in Williamsburg, has an upper and a lower chamber for the Council and General Assembly. This 1934 reproduction is based on court documents from the period; the original was dismantled in 1829, with many of the bricks used for Trinity Church nearby. The square-rigged ship *Maryland Dove*, docked behind the State House, represents the smaller of the two vessels that conveyed the original settlers from England. The **Godiah Spray Tobacco Plantation** depicts life on a 17th-century tobacco farm in the Maryland wilderness, with interpreters portraying the Spray family—the real family lived about 20 mi away—and its indentured servants, enlisting visitors in such household chores as cooking and gardening or in working the tobacco field. The buildings, including the main dwelling house and outbuildings, were built with period tools and techniques.

Other sites to see in town are the town center, the location of the first Catholic church in the English Colonies, a "victualing" and lodging house, and the Woodland Indian Hamlet. Historic interpreters in costume—some in character—add realism to the experience. Admission is about a third of the price for kids. ⊠ *Rte. 5* ☎ *240/895–4990 or 800/762–1634* ⊕ *www.stmaryscity.org* ⊡ *$10* ☉ *Wed.–Sun. 10–5.*

Fodor's Choice
★

OFF THE BEATEN PATH

Piney Point Lighthouse, Museum & Historic Park. The first permanent lighthouse constructed on the Potomac River is now the center of a small, 6-acre park. The grounds, which are free, have a boardwalk, pier, and picnic tables. The 1990 lighthouse is a replica of the 1861 original. ⊠ *44720 Lighthouse Rd., Piney Point* ☎ *301/494–1471* ⊕ *www. stmarysmd.com/recreate/museums* ⊡ *$3* ☉ *Mid-May–Oct., daily.*

WHERE TO STAY

$
★

Brome-Howard Inn. Set on 30 acres of farmland, this farmhouse provides a trip through time to life on a tobacco plantation in the 19th century. Rooms are decorated with original family furnishings. Relax on one of the big outdoor porches or patios and watch the St. Mary's

River running lazily nearby. In the evening there are two candlelit dining rooms—the foyer or the formal parlor. Five miles of hiking trails lead to St. Mary's City, and the inn has bikes for the use of guests. The in-house restaurant specializes in seafood and occasionally serves such exotic items as bison, ostrich, or shark. **Pros:** breathtaking setting overlooking the St. Mary's River—the reason that many couples pick it as a wedding site; featherbeds and fireplaces keep you cozy. **Cons:** the inn is remote and is a destination itself, so unless you get in your car, you will not be strolling to other sites. ✉ *18281 Rosecroft Rd.* ☎ *301/866–0656* ⊕ *www.bromehowardinn.com* ⤴ *3 rooms, 1 suite* △ *In-room: a/c. In-hotel: restaurant, bicycles, Internet terminal* ⊟ *AE, MC, V* ⦿ *BP.*

CHARLES COUNTY

To the north of St. Mary's County and about 35 mi southwest of Annapolis, relatively rural Charles County is flanked on its west by the Potomac River's big bend as it flows south from Washington, D.C. In what used to be tobacco country, the pristine countryside, crisscrossed by less-traveled county and state roads, is dotted with depot towns, riverfront ports-of-call, wildlife preservation centers, and unsung historic sites.

ESSENTIALS

Visitor Information **Charles County Office of Tourism** (✉ *103 Centennial St., Suite C, La Plata* ☎ *800/766–3386*). **Crain Memorial Welcome Center** (✉ *U.S. Rte. 301, 12480 Crain Hwy., near Newburg, 1 mi north of Governor Nice bridge over the Potomac River* ☎ *301/259–2500*).

WALDORF

40 mi south of Annapolis on Rte. 301.

The lovely rural fields of other parts of eastern Maryland give way to developments and higher-density traffic when you reach Waldorf.

GETTING HERE AND AROUND

Waldorf is now a suburb of Metropolitan D.C. The Maryland Commuter Bus offers more than 60 trips from Waldorf to stops in downtown Washington or connecting Metro Stops.

EXPLORING

Dr. Samuel A. Mudd House. The Dr. Samuel A. Mudd House is where John Wilkes Booth ended up at 4 am on Holy Saturday, 1865, his leg broken after having leaped from the presidential box at Ford's Theater. Most likely, the 32-year-old Dr. Mudd had no idea his patient was wanted for the assassination of Abraham Lincoln. Nonetheless, Mudd was convicted of aiding a fugitive and sentenced to life in prison. (His time behind bars was cut short when President Andrew Jackson pardoned him in 1869.) Today the two-story house, set on 197 rolling acres, looks as if the doctor is still in. The dark purple couch where Mudd examined Booth remains in the downstairs parlor, 18th-century family pieces fill the rooms, and the doctor's crude instruments are on display. There's a 30-minute guided tour of the house, an exhibit building, and

10

Mudd's original tombstone. They also have a farm museum and tobacco museum. ⊠ *3725 Dr. Samuel Mudd Rd.* ☎ *301/645–6870* ⊠ *$6* ⊙ *Late Mar.–late Nov., Wed. and weekends 11–4.*

PORT TOBACCO

11 mi southwest of Waldorf via Rte. 301 and Rte. 6.

One of the oldest communities in the East, Port Tobacco first existed as the Native American settlement of "Potopaco." (The similarity between this Native American name—meaning "the jutting of water inland"— and the name for the plant that was to become a cornerstone of the region's economy is purely coincidental.) Potopaco was colonized by the English in 1634, and later in the century emerged as the major seaport of Port Tobacco. The historic district includes the reconstructed early-19th-century courthouse; Catslide House, one of the area's four surviving 18th-century homes; and a restored one-room schoolhouse, dating to 1876 and used as such until 1953.

■ TIP→ Unlike the restoration in St. Mary's City that has a town with dining and lodging amenities, Port Tobacco is remote. Plan on eating or staying in a nearby location.

GETTING HERE AND AROUND

Getting to or around Port Tobacco requires a car as the main site, The Thomas Stone National Historic Site, is several miles away.

EXPLORING

★ **Thomas Stone National Historic Site.** Set in a lovely rural setting and built in the 1770s, this site marks the Charles County home of Thomas Stone, one of four Maryland signers of the Declaration of Independence. It has been painstakingly rebuilt after a devastating fire left it a shell in the late 1970s. The restoration re-created the distinctive five-part Georgian house inside and out. The two-story main plantation house is linked to the two wings and adjoining hallways in an arc rather than a straight line. All the rooms have exquisite details, such as built-in cabinets, elaborate moldings, a table set in fine china, gilded mirrors, and a harpsichord. The house and family grave site are just a short stroll from the parking lot and visitor center, where you can examine a model of the house or watch a video about Stone. This is one of the least-visited National Park Service sites. ⊠ *6655 Rose Hill Rd., between Rtes. 6 and 225, 4 mi west of La Plata* ☎ *301/392–1776* ⊕ *www.nps.gov/thst* ⊠ *Free* ⊙ *Mid-June–Aug. daily 9–5; Sept.–mid-June, Wed.–Sun. 9–5.*

Maryland's Eastern Shore

WORD OF MOUTH

"Be sure and get some Fisher's caramel popcorn, which is served hot, and also Thrasher's french fries. All are located within blocks of each other on the [Ocean City] boardwalk."

—Katie 2

"We are to a degree a crab culture here on the Shore . . . crabs (always eaten with cold beer), crab cakes, and crab soup."

—GeorgeW

Updated by
Alice Powers

Sailing the Chesapeake Bay nearly four centuries ago in search of new territory for his English king, Captain John Smith wrote that "heaven and earth never agreed better to frame a place for man's habitation." The eastern side of the Bay retains today its landscape of calm despite its proximity to Baltimore and Washington, D.C.

An early-American aura pervades most of the Eastern Shore. The peninsula is rich with maritime heritage (you will see many boats!), and the area's architecture reflects its colonial and pre-colonial history (view the stately homes in Chestertown and Oxford). The Eastern Shore's first permanent English settlement—indeed the first in Maryland and one of the earliest along the Atlantic—took root on Kent Island, now Queen Anne's County, in 1631. Many Eastern Shore families have been here for generations; residents of Smith Island still speak with an Elizabethan lilt.

A visit to the Eastern Shore might consist of exploring historic sites, strolling through wildlife parks and refuges, pausing at a few of the myriad shops, dining at third-generation-owned waterfront restaurants, and overnighting at inns and bed-and-breakfasts in one of the region's enchanting communities. It you prefer the ocean to the bay, a different experience all together awaits at the popular summertime destination of Ocean City. Clinging to a narrow barrier island off the southeastern edge of Maryland's Eastern Shore, Ocean City has high-rise condos, a boardwalk, multiple restaurants and bars, and theme park-like attractions. The bustling, ocean-side culture differs dramatically from that of the Chesapeake.

ORIENTATION AND PLANNING

GETTING ORIENTED

Maryland's Eastern Shore shares the Delmarva Peninsula stretching southward from easternmost Pennsylvania with virtually all of Delaware and with the two counties of Virginia's Eastern Shore. Although Maryland's eight Eastern Shore counties share a similar culture as well as their early history, traveling through them reveals individual characteristics unique to each.

To understand the Eastern Shore, look to the Bay. The Chesapeake is 195 mi long and the nation's largest estuary (a semi-enclosed body of water with free connection to the open sea). Freshwater tributaries large and small flow south and west into the Bay, ensuring the agricultural wealth of the peninsula as well as the bounty of the Bay ("Chesapeake" is an Algonquian word meaning "great shellfish"). At day's end look west across the Chesapeake Bay and you can see the sun set over water—a rare sight for any East Coast resident.

■ **TIP→** The Bay Bridge, just past Annapolis on Route 50, is both the entry point and a bottleneck to the Eastern Shore communities. It is not unusual for hours long backups, especially on summer weekends.

Cecil County. The northern gateway to the Eastern Shore caps the headwaters of the Chesapeake Bay, including some 12,000 acres of park- and forestland as well as a National Resource Area of more than 5,600 acres. It is known best, however, for its world-renowned horse farms.

Kent County. Immediately to the south of Cecil County lies a delightful blend of agriculture and maritime culture. The principal towns here are successful combinations of colonial-era history and 21st-century modernity.

Queen Anne's County. Best known as the eastern gateway to Maryland's Eastern Shore, Queen Anne's Kent Island is the site of the eastern end of the double-span William Preston Lane Jr. Bridge—known colloquially as the "Bay Bridge." On the island's eastern shore, Kent Narrows, with its variety of lodging, restaurant, and water-related recreation opportunities has emerged as an attractive travel destination.

Talbot County. Much of this county is threaded with waterways of various sizes that yield myriad untrammeled peninsulas and almost-islands that welcome explorers. Its county seat, Easton, is a vibrant small town.

Dorchester County. Dorchester exudes an aura of gentility reminiscent of the Southern states. Home of one of the region's largest wildlife refuges, it, too, has a wildly ragged western shoreline, undeveloped and unsung, and a mix of agriculture and maritime heritage.

Lower Eastern Shore. Maryland's southernmost shore comprises three counties: Wicomico, whose county seat, Salisbury, is the area's second-largest port city (after Baltimore); Worcester, which includes the ever-popular year-round Atlantic resort destination Ocean City; and quiet Somerset, with the state's southernmost locales (opposite the mouth of the Potomac River).

PLANNING

WHEN TO GO

Traditional summertime months, i.e. school vacation time, are the busiest throughout the region. Ocean City attracts not only visitors for weeks-long stays but also day-trippers, particularly on weekends, and that means heavy traffic. July and August are the hottest and humidity can be high, but literally thousands of miles of water's edge produce cooling breezes.

Shallower edges of the Chesapeake Bay can freeze over in January and February. However, the relatively temperate climate of this region—winters without any snow at all are not uncommon—means year-round appeal. Many large and small towns celebrate winter months as heartily as the warmer ones with regional festivals and local tours.

In May a weekend-long festival called the **Chestertown Tea Party** (☎410/778–0416 ⊕ *www.chestertownteaparty.com*) commemorates a little-known Colonial rebellion in 1774 that includes an authentic

TOP REASONS TO GO

Sail on a Historic Skipjack: Though they once dominated the Chesapeake Bay waterways, these traditional fishing vessels are now nearly extinct—but you can hop aboard one of the few remaining ones and experience a bit of history.

Crack into Maryland's Trademark Crustacean: Don't leave the Eastern Shore without sampling the slightly sweet taste of the Chesapeake renowned blue crab at a down-home eatery, cracking shells with your own wooden mallet.

Get Back to Nature: Bike the Blackwater National Wildlife Refuge or paddle the tidal marsh pathways of the Fishing Bay Water Trail and look for bald eagles.

Be Touristy in Ocean City: Maryland's barrier island has year-round leisure-time opportunities—mid-summer for 24/7 activity and unparalleled people-watching, mid-winter for bracing coastal solitude, or idyllic moments in the months in between.

reenactment of their hurling British tea into the Chester River, in support of a similar event in Boston a year earlier. In September, Crisfield's **National Hard Crab Derby** (☎ 410/968–2500 ⊕ www.crisfieldchamber. com/crab_derby.htm) celebrates the Eastern Shore's crabs with a crab race, steamed crabs, and all things crabby, including the crowning of a Miss Crustacean.

Ocean City, Maryland, celebrates the quest for endless summer in mid-September with **Sunfest Kite Festival** (☎ 800/626–2326 ⊕ www.kiteloft. com/events.asp), a four-day blowout with all sorts of entertainment, kite contests, and a crafts show. On or close to the first weekend in November, a small fleet of vessels—from historic working boats and traditional sailing ships to majestic "tall ships"—gathers in the Chester River's broad waters in front of Chestertown for **Downrigging Weekend** (☎ 410/778–5954 ⊕ www.sultanaprojects.org/downrigging.htm), hosted by the town's resident schooner *Sultana.*

GETTING HERE AND AROUND

In general, this is a driving and walking region—you arrive by car and either walk or bike around your destination. Taxis are few and far between. One of the most thorough transportation resources is the non-profit Chesapeake Bay Gateways Network (⊕ www.baygateways.net).

AIR TRAVEL

The most convenient major airport for travel throughout eastern Maryland is Baltimore-Washington Thurgood Marshall Airport (BWI), approximately 30 minutes' drive from the Chesapeake Bay Bridge. There are several municipal airports catering to private and small charter aircraft, including Ocean City Airport in Berlin, Maryland and Easton-Newnam Field in Easton, Maryland. Salisbury (Wicomico County) is served by US Airways.

CAR TRAVEL

A car is indispensable for touring the region. To reach the Eastern Shore from Baltimore or Washington, D.C., travel east on U.S. 50/301 and cross the 4.5-mi Chesapeake Bay Bridge northeast of Annapolis (toll, $2.50, eastbound only). The extraordinary 17.5-mi Chesapeake Bay Bridge-Tunnel goes to Tidewater-area towns like Ocean City. The bridge-and-tunnel complex comprises 12 mi of trestled roadway, two tunnels, two bridges, almost 2 mi of causeway, among four man-made islands (toll, $12, in either direction).

Weekend traffic going to the beach can be exceptionally heavy during summertime months. Times to avoid if possible are Friday afternoon and evening as well as Saturday morning, eastbound, and Sunday afternoon and evening, westbound. You can see live webcams of bridge traffic at ⊕ *www.baybridge.com*. Your trip over the bridge will be expedited by using EZPass, allowing you to drive in designated lanes (⊕ *www. ezpass.com*).

ESSENTIALS

Transportation Information Chesapeake Bay Gateways Network (⊕ *www. baygateways.net*). **Chesapeake Bay Bridge-Tunnel** (☎ *757/331-2960 in Maryland 410/974-0341 in Virginia* ⊕ *www.cbbt.com*). **William Preston Lane Jr. Bridge—Chesapeake Bay Bridge** (☎ *866/713-1596* ⊕ *www.baybridge.com*).

RESTAURANTS

Clearly "seafood"—finned fish and shellfish from the Chesapeake and its tributaries—reigns. Many menus include local dishes and seasonal highlights, such as corn and cantaloupe ("'lopes") in the summertime.

HOTELS

Outside of Cambridge's singular Hyatt Regency and Ocean City's approximately 10,000 hotel rooms—the great majority of accommodations throughout this region are B&Bs, inns, and budget chain hotels. The scope of choice is broad, yet as might be expected, the quality and level of service of these smaller enterprises varies dramatically. Many B&Bs and inns have teamed up with other tourism enterprises to create packages that include boating, golf, and tennis, visits to art galleries and museums, and more.

Of note: B&Bs and inns throughout Maryland's and Virginia's Eastern Shore commonly require two-night minimum stays on weekends during periods of high demand, most often throughout the summer months, sometimes in late spring and early fall, and during special events such as town-wide festivals.

WHAT IT COSTS				
	¢	$	$$	$$$	$$$$
Restaurants	under $10	$10–$16	$17–$23	$24–$30	over $30
Hotels	under $100	$100–$160	$161–$230	$231–$300	over $300

Restaurant prices are per person for a main course at dinner. Hotel prices are for a standard double room, excluding state tax.

PLANNING YOUR TIME

Considering there are eight counties comprising Maryland's Eastern Shore, planning a circuitous, nonrepetitive route can be difficult. Most travelers follow the county roads from small town to town along the Chesapeake Bay. The north–south orientation of the region, bridges and ferries, narrow roads, and small towns require getting off the highway and slowing down. The Bay's enigmatic islands are easy day trips, but an overnight on one of them means planning within the limited schedules of the ferries that serve them.

EXPLORING THE EASTERN SHORE

Maryland's Eastern Shore is readily accessible from the north via any number of routes out of eastern Pennsylvania and northern Delaware and from the east out of Delaware. The William Preston Lane Jr. Bridge, "the Bay Bridge," crosses the Chesapeake Bay northeast of Annapolis; its dual spans stretch 4.5 mi across.

QUEEN ANNE'S COUNTY

The eastern landfall of the Bay Bridge, which carries U.S. 50/301, is Kent Island, home to historic Stevensville and a small cluster of waterside restaurants, bars, lodging, art galleries, and several marinas surrounding the slim Kent Narrows channel. This island gateway is 5.5 mi wide where U.S. 50/301 crosses it, and 14 mi long. William Claiborne established Maryland's first permanent settlement here in 1631 as part of Virginia.

Beyond Kent Island and its waning fishing towns, Queen Anne's stretches mostly northward as well as eastward to the Delaware line, its agricultural heritage readily apparent among burgeoning residential development, many designed as retirement communities.

ESSENTIALS

Queen Anne's County Office of Tourism & Exploration Hall (⊠ 425 *Piney Narrows Rd., Chester* ☎ *410/604–2100* or *888/400–7787* ⊕ *www. discoverqueenannes.com*)

STEVENSVILLE

10 mi east of Annapolis via U.S. 50/301.

Stevensville, just north of the Bay Bridge's eastern landfall, is a growing village of artists and craftspeople. Its galleries and studios sell original pottery, stained glass, and painted furniture as well as antiques and fine art. Its historic center has been on the National Register since 1986.

GETTING HERE AND AROUND

Stevensville is just a short jog from Route 50 after you cross east on the Bay Bridge. Blink and you might miss it, but it's worth a stop. You can walk the town in 10 minutes. Park near the art galleries, which is basically the center of town.

EXPLORING

The Cray House. Completed in 1809 this is a glimpse into middle-class life of the early 19th century. The two-story cottage, furnished with period pieces, sits in a little yard surrounded by a picket fence. ⊠ *Cockey La.* ☎ *410/758–2502* ⊕ *www.historicqac.org* 🖾 *Donations accepted* ⊙ *May–Oct., 1st Sat. of month noon to 4 pm and by appointment.*

The Stevensville Train Depot. From the early 1900s, this was the western terminus of the old Queen Anne's Railroad Company system. ⊠ *Cockey La.* ☎ *410/758–2502* ⊕ *www.historicqac.org* 🖾 *Donations accepted* ⊙ *May–Oct., 1st Sat. of month and by appointment.*

NEED A BREAK?

With its glow-in-the-dark green and yellow exterior colors, the **Jetty** (⊠ *201 Wells Cove Rd., Grasonville* ☎ *410/827–4959* ⊕ *www.jettydockbar. com*) strives for an aura of the tropics among its very laid-back crowd. Popular with area residents and visitors alike, its large, partially covered outdoor seating area juts out over the waters of Kent Narrows—hence its name. It's a prime spot to watch boat traffic, both commercial and leisure, traversing under a drawbridge between the Chester River and the Eastern Bay. Drinks are strong and most of the food is bad for your health, but it's fun and (relatively) family-friendly. There are periodic karaoke nights and occasional live music on weekends.

WHERE TO EAT AND STAY

$$$ ✕**Hemingway's.** Perched near the eastern end of the Bay Bridge, the
SEAFOOD upper-level indoor dining area and the broad veranda of this restaurant provide panoramic views westward across the Bay and of the city of Annapolis beyond. Sunsets can rival those off Key West, home of the restaurant's namesake. Entrées include Atlantic salmon and coconut sesame shrimp. In summer an informal bar and grill, Lola's, opens at 5 pm Thursday through Sunday on the lower level, with tables on the lawn adjacent to its private dock. Live music on weekends enhances its simple soup-and-sandwich menu. ⊠ *357 Pier 1 Rd.* ☎ *410/643–2722* ⊕ *www.hemingwaysmaryland.com* 🖃 *AE, D, MC, V.*

$ 🏠 **Kent Manor Inn.** A summer hotel since 1898, this imposing antebellum
SEAFOOD manor house is on 226 acres of farmland along Thompson Creek near the Chesapeake Bay. Many guest rooms have cozy window seats, others boast Italian marble fireplaces. All rooms on the upper floors open onto semiprivate verandas. The in-house restaurant serves breakfast daily and lunch and dinner, Wednesday through Sunday in two elegant Victorian dining rooms or in an enclosed porch. **Pros:** pleasant, relaxed environment; waterside setting is perfect for wandering around; unique alternative to many chains in the area. **Cons:** as a popular wedding venue, it is often busy weekends, so book well in advance. ⊠ *500 Kent Manor Dr.* ☎ *410/643–7716 or 800/820–4511* ⊕ *www.kentmanor.com* ⇖ *20 rooms, 4 suites* ⚏ *In-room: a/c, Internet, Wi-Fi. In-hotel: restaurant, bar, tennis court, pool, bicycles* 🖃 *AE, D, MC, V.*

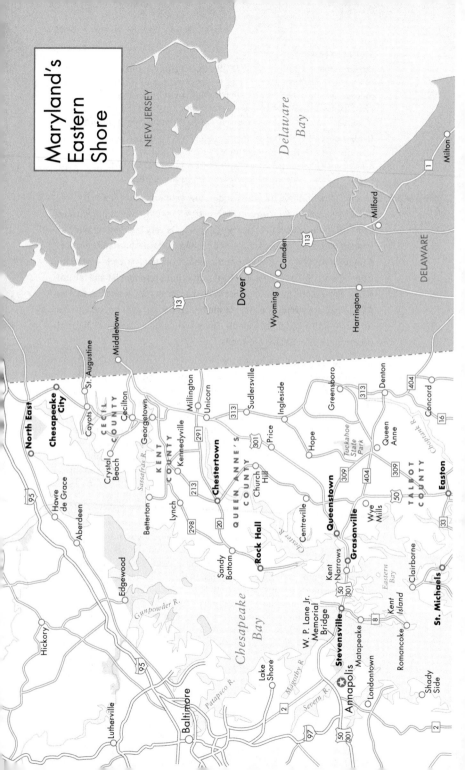

Maryland's Eastern Shore

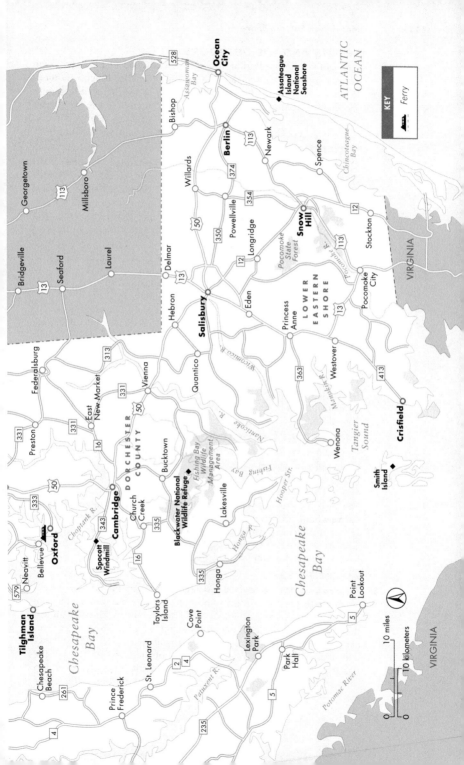

KEY

⚓ Ferry

SPORTS AND THE OUTDOORS

You can stroll or roll along the 6-mi **Cross Island Trail** between Kent Narrows on the western edge of Kent Island and Bay beachfront on its eastern side. Here the flat, smoothly paved or hard-packed trail joins the **Terrapin Nature Area,** 279 lush acres composed of five identifiable habitats: wetlands, woodlands, wildflower meadows, tidal ponds, and sandy beaches. There is ample parking at both ends of the trail.

SHOPPING

Old Stevensville's popular art gallery, the **Kent Island Federation of Art** (✉ *405 Main St.* ☎ 410/643–7424), showcases local artists. **Ye Olde Church House** (✉ *426 Love Point Rd.* ☎ 410/643–6227) in old Stevensville is just that, a de-sanctified church, but now it's a shop filled with crafts and hand-spun yarn, hand-dipped candles, old-fashioned soap and candy, and the occasional antique. With sheep grazing in the pasture next door, it's hard to miss and worth seeking out.

GRASONVILLE

7 mi east of Stevensville, 21 mi east of Annapolis via U.S. 50/301.

Follow the scenic byway, old two-lane Route 18, across Kent Island and over an aging drawbridge across Kent Narrows to reach quiet Grasonville. The modest homes and shops of the town are a pleasant alternative to the east–west U.S. 50 highway route. Most restaurants and lodging are clustered around scenic Kent Narrows, the waterway between Kent Island's eastern side and the mainland.

GETTING HERE AND AROUND

Grasonville can be reached by car or by boat. Many of the restaurants have dockage for diners.

SPORTS AND THE OUTDOORS

Operated by the Wildfowl Trust of North America, the 500 acres of the **Chesapeake Bay Environmental Center** will open your eyes, ears, and mind to the wildfowl and waterscapes that characterize Maryland's Eastern Shore. The aviary and waterfowl ponds are full of ducks, geese, swans, and birds of prey. Pause a moment in a secluded blind and explore native woodlands, marshes, and meadows along 4 mi of trails. A visitor center and picnic facilities are on the grounds. ✉ *600 Discovery La., Grasonville* ☎ 410/827–6694 ⊕ *www.bayrestoration.org* 🖼 *$5* ☉ *Daily 9–5, except major holidays.*

WHERE TO EAT

$$ ✕ **Harris Crab House & Seafood Restaurant.** On the mainland side of Kent
AMERICAN Narrows, this family-friendly institution serves fresh catch directly from local watermen, some of whom are Harris family members. Nautical decor prevails in the large dining room, including an intriguing collection of oyster cans from an adjacent abandoned oyster house. Views over the shallow, twisting northern end of the Narrows toward the Eastern Neck National Wildlife Refuge can be stunning. Cream-of-crab soup and back-fin crab cakes are among the best around—the cakes are spicy enough to promote plenty of beer drinking. ✉ *433 Kent Nar-*

BOATING IN QUEEN ANNE'S COUNTY

Queen Anne's County has 18 public landings for boats of all sizes. Of these, nine have trailer-launching ramps, but the others are "unimproved" and can be used only for canoes, kayaks, and other small boats that can be carried to the water. A seasonal or daily permit is required to launch a boat from public landing ramps and for parking at these sites. For locations where permits may be purchased, contact **Parks and Recreation** (☎ 410/758–0835 ⊕ www.parksandrec.com).

Experienced and hospitable, **C&C Charters** (✉ Mears Point Marina, 506 Kent Narrows Way N ☎ 410/827–7888 or 800/733–7245 ⊕ www.ccccharters.com) has a fleet of power- and sailboats over 30 feet for bare-boat or captained charter.

Tuna the Tide Charter Service (✉ 404 Greenwood Creek La. ☎ 410/827–5635 or 410/827–6188 ⊕ www.exploredelmarva.com) has two boats for light tackle and fly-fishing expeditions as well as for crabbing or a sightseeing cruise.

rows Way N, Grasonville ☎ 410/827–9500 ⊕ www.harriscrabhouse. com ⊟ AE, D, MC, V.

$
SEAFOOD
☺
★
✗ **Holly's Restaurant.** This family-style restaurant is reason enough to stop in Grasonville. Watch for its sign off Route 50. Holly's specializes in all the Eastern Shore favorites, including a spectacular crab soup and crab cakes, but the fried chicken is the real attraction. Down-home and unpretentious, this is the real thing. ✉ 108 Jackson Creek Rd., Grasonville ☎ 410/827–8711 ⊕ www.hollysrest.com ⚓ Reservations not accepted ⊟ MC, V ☉ Daily, 7 am–9:30 pm.

$$$
SEAFOOD
Fodor's Choice
★
✗ **The Narrows.** The spacious contemporary dining room, its porch-like extension, and an adjacent bar all face southward to the Eastern Bay and across this restaurant's slim namesake waterway separating Kent Island from the Eastern Shore mainland. One of the region's largest commercial fishing fleets is harbored next door. Specialties include a Caesar salad with fried oysters and grilled peppered tuna, served over sautéed spinach; and Crab Imperial, lump crabmeat, and select oysters baked with imperial sauce, topped with bacon. The Narrows' dinner menus include "Light Suppers," that encourage a second look at the to-die-for—or -from—desserts listing. ✉ 3023 Kent Narrows Way S, Grasonville ☎ 410/827–8113 ⊕ www.thenarrowsrestaurant. com ⚓ Reservations essential ⊟ AE, D, DC, MC, V.

QUEENSTOWN

11 mi east of Stevensville

The cove of Queenstown's harbor is protected by a bend of the mouth of the Chester River. Established in 1707 as "Queen Anne's Town," it became an important-enough port to be attacked by the British during the War of 1812. An erstwhile fishermen's community, it's worth a quick visit—drive along its north-side water's edge and through town, where there's a pretty, central square, a coffee shop, and a few good restaurants. Note the statue in the center of the square of Queen Anne of England that was dedicated by Princess Anne.

GETTING HERE AND AROUND

With only a few more than 600 people in the town there is no public transportation. If you choose to get out and explore, the town can be walked in about 10 minutes.

SPORTS AND THE OUTDOORS

Queenstown is home to a pair of the finest golf courses in the region, both of which are part of **Queenstown Harbor Golf Links** (✉ *32 Links La., off Rte. 301, just beyond Rte. 50/301 split* ☎ *410/827–6611 or 800/827–5257* ⊕ *www.mdgolf.com*).

SHOPPING

A major lure to discount seekers year-round, **Prime Outlets Queenstown** (✉ *441 Outlet Center Dr., at the U.S. 50/301 split* ☎ *410/827–8699* ⊕ *www.primeoutlets.com* ☉ *Apr.–Dec., daily 9–9; Jan.–Mar., daily 10–9*), just 10 mi east of the Bay Bridge at the Routes 50/301 split, has 60 upscale factory outlet stores, including Coach, Calvin Klein, Eddie Bauer, and L.L. Bean.

KENT COUNTY

Not unlike most of Maryland's Eastern Shore, Kent County is steeped in history and determined to preserve it. Its idyllic location between the Chester and Sassafras rivers is enhanced by a long, ragged Chesapeake Bay shoreline, many of its hidden hamlets untouched by time and savoring their quiet anonymity, while others struggle to balance their discovery by immigration from northern states with their heritage of 300 years.

In the summertime, both Kent and Cecil County are dotted with family-run farmstands. In addition to corn and tomatoes, locals grow cantaloupes, watermelon (including a yellow variety) peppers, squash, and many other fruits and vegetables—at a fraction of supermarket prices. **Lockbriar Farms** (☎ *410/778–9112* ⊕ *www.lockbriarfarms.com*) has several locations in Kent County—call or go online for the harvest schedule and other information.

ESSENTIALS

Kent County Tourism Development Office (✉ *400 High St., Chestertown* ☎ *410/778–0416* ⊕ *www.kentcounty.com*).

CHESTERTOWN

47 mi northeast of Annapolis via U.S. 50/301 to Rte. 213, 24 mi north of Queenstown via U.S. 301 to Rte. 213.

Second only to Annapolis in its concentration of 18th-century houses, Chestertown was a major international port in Colonial days: a tall, brick customhouse continues to dominate the High Street waterfront. Still the home of families whose local roots go back many generations, the town has its share of newer residents, many of them retirees. Today inns and good restaurants, fine-art galleries, three independent bookstores, and antiques shops line the brick pavements of High Street, Chestertown's broad, tree-lined main street. To walk along its narrow streets, some of them cobbled, is to commune quietly with some of the country's earliest history. At the northern edge of Chestertown is **Washington College,** one of the nation's oldest liberal-arts institutions. George Washington helped found the college in 1782 through a gift of 50 guineas.

GETTING HERE AND AROUND

Walking the cobbled streets of Chestertown is a wonderful way to spend an afternoon. There are plenty of shops and restaurants. Wander to the harbor or around Washington College's beautiful campus. There are a few restaurants or sites—like Crumpton Auction—that are farther afield and require a car, but in general this is a walker's town.

ESSENTIALS

TOURS **Historic Chestertown and Kent County Tours** (☎ 410/778–2829) schedules guided, narrated walking tours (by appointment only) that focus on history and architecture.

EXPLORING

Geddes-Piper House, home of the Historical Society of Kent County, is a splendid Federal-style home containing 18th-century furniture and an impressive teapot collection, a historical library, and a shop. It's a good place to begin a visit to Chestertown. ⊠ *101 Church Alley* ☎ *410/778–3499* ⊕ *www.kentcountyhistory.org* 🕮 *Donation suggested* 🕑 *Hrs. vary seasonally.*

♻ ★ **Sultana.** This reproduction of a 1768 Colonial schooner by the same name was launched in 2001. With a length of 97 feet, the original *Sultana* was the smallest schooner ever registered on the Royal Navy Lists. The modern mission of this "Schoolship of the Chesapeake" is to provide unique, hands-on educational experiences in Colonial history and environmental science. Several two-hour public sails are available each month from April through November. Daylong public sails are scheduled on occasion. The *Sultana* can be seen close-up when she is anchored in the Chester River, at the end of Cannon Street (⇨ *see also When to Go, above*). Additionally, half-day guided paddle tours operated by Sultana management are also available a few times a year in various Kent Count rivers. ⊠ *105 S. Cross St.* ☎ *410/778–5954* ⊕ *www. sultanaprojects.org* 🕮 *$30* 🛶 *Reservations essential.*

OFF THE BEATEN PATH ★ About a 10-minute drive east of Chestertown is **Dixon's Furniture Auction (Crumpton Auction)** (⊠ *1921 Dudleys Cr. Rd., at intersection of Rtes. 290 and 544, Millington* ☎ *410/928–3006* ⊕ *www.crumptonauctions.com*), a Maryland Eastern Shore institution—with much more than just furniture (although there are literally a couple of acres of that). Hundreds of pieces, "other people's junk" and real treasures, are sold out in the open, regardless of the weather. A huge shed houses smaller items defying easy description, from atlases to zithers. The auction is held every Wednesday of the year (Christmas week excepted) beginning at 8 am.

WHERE TO EAT

$$$　✕ **Blue Heron Café.** This relaxed, contemporary dining room has high,
SEAFOOD　sloped ceilings and skylights. Among its crab offerings and pasta, as
well as chops and steaks, the café's most sought-after entrée is baked
rockfish, but don't overlook the oyster fritters, a signature dish. Week-
end nights are busy, and the service here is genuine and attentive. ⊠ *236
Cannon St.* ☎ *410/778–0188* ⊕ *www.blueheroncafe.com* ⊟ *AE, D,
MC, V* ⊘ *Closed Sun.*

$$$　✕ **Brooks Tavern.** A pair of seasoned professionals have converted
ECLECTIC　Colonial-era Radcliffe Mill—"the old mill"—into one of the finest res-
Fodor's Choice　taurants in the area. In an atmosphere rustic and casual, yet chic, diners
★　sit between solid wooden floors and exposed supporting beams. The
superbly talented chef co-owner describes his cuisine as evolutionary
and ever-changing, his ingredients as local, seasonal, and fresh. Favorite
entrées include roast and stir-fried duck with rice noodles and vegetables
in a coconut curry sauce and a trademarked crab steak in lemon-butter
sauce. There is also a "kitchen table," where you can watch the preparations, and a small separate bar. ⊠ *870 High St.* ☎ *410/810–0012*
⊕ *www.brookstavern.com* ⊟ *AE, MC, V* ⊘ *Closed Sun. and Mon.*

¢　✕ **Play It Again, Sam.** This is the place to mingle with C'town residents
AMERICAN　as well as with Washington College students and local pols, for good
conversation—indoors or alfresco—over fresh coffee (including excellent espresso) or fine wine, by the glass or bottle, to accompany hearty,
healthy soups, salads, and sandwiches. Friday night is "wine night"
with complimentary hors d'oeuvres, often accompanied by live music.
Wi-Fi's in the air here. ⊠ *108 S. Cross St.* ☎ *410/778–2688* ⊟ *AE, D,
MC, V.*

WHERE TO STAY

$$$　▦ **Brampton Bed & Breakfast Inn.** On 20 wooded acres between the Ches-
ter River and the Chesapeake Bay, about 1 mi south of downtown Ches-
tertown, this mid-19th-century inn, known for its gracious hospitality,
still resembles the plantation house it once was. The brick building's
entrance has a 3½-story walnut-and-ash staircase, pine floors, and plas-
ter ceiling medallions. All of the spacious, well-appointed guest rooms
have working fireplaces (but only lit October through April), and five
have hot tubs. Classic movies, available from the innkeepers' private
collection, can be viewed in the library, which also has an extensive sup-
ply of books. Rates include a full country breakfast and afternoon tea
with homemade pastries. **Pros:** exceptional waterside locale; hospitable
B&B experience. **Cons:** not in the center of Chestertown; two-night
stays required on weekends. ⊠ *25227 Chestertown Rd., Rte. 20 W*
☎ *410/778–1860* ⊕ *www.bramptoninn.com* ⇆ *10 rooms* ♿ *In-room:
no phone, a/c, DVD. In-hotel: some pets allowed, no kids under 12*
⊟ *AE, D, MC, V* ⊚| *BP.*

$$$　▦ **Great Oak Manor.** On 12 acres sloping gently to a gazebo on the edge
of its private Chesapeake beach, this stately 18th-century Georgian
brick manor house provides a taste of Eastern Shore gentility. Its antique
furnishings and Oriental rugs, along with an airy sunporch, re-create
a bygone era. Of its 11 impeccably decorated guest rooms, five have
working fireplaces. The manor's formal library is well stocked with

both books and films. If needed, guests are provided transportation to the restaurant of their choice for dinner. Golf and tennis are available at neighboring Great Oak Landing. **Pros:** stunning waterside location. **Cons:** formal period decor may be stuffy; cancellations must be made 14 days prior to arrival; cell phone coverage is spotty. ⊠ *10568 Cliff Rd.* ☎ *410/778–5943 or 877/502–6892* ⊕ *www.greatoak.com* ⤴ *11 rooms* ⟨ *In-room: no phone, a/c. In-hotel: beachfront, pool, bicycles, no kids under 18* ⊟ *AE, D, MC, V* ⊩❑ *BP.*

$ ⛉ **Imperial Hotel.** This three-story brick structure on Chestertown's main street was built in 1903 for traveling salesmen. Today it is a gathering center for residents and visitors alike. Guest rooms and suites with authentic period furnishings, as well as custom-designed and hand-crafted pieces, some of which hide TVs and telephones, strive for a blend of 20th-century eras. The hotel's four dining areas ($$$), including one outside in the summertime, all serve traditional Eastern Shore fare like crab cakes as well as locally sourced poultry, meat, and vegetables. **Pros:** a pleasant alternative to pervasive colonial historical sites; good on-site dining; a heated towel rack in every room. **Cons:** historic property's amenities may not be up to modern travelers' expectations. ⊠ *208 High St.* ☎ *410/778–5000* ⊕ *www.imperialchestertown. com* ⤴ *11 rooms, 2 suites* ⟨ *In-room: a/c, Wi-Fi. In-hotel: restaurant* ⊟ *AE, MC, V.*

$$ ⛉ **White Swan Tavern.** Step back in time at this inn restored to its appear-
★ ance circa 1790. Built as a home in 1733, it was a tavern, then a general store; it may be the town's oldest building. Brick fireplaces and deep window seats, an old writing desk, and pewter candleholders are all in keeping with its Colonial past. The original kitchen, shaded by a giant elm, is the inn's most requested guest room—its rough ceiling beams, brick floor, and large fireplace attest to its antiquity. Afternoon tea is served in the dining room, on the rear stone patio, or in guest rooms. **Pros:** historic inn; in the heart of the historic district. **Cons:** small rooms; few amenities. ⊠ *231 High St.* ☎ *410/778–2300* ⊕ *www. whiteswantavern.com* ⤴ *4 rooms, 2 suites, 2 apartments* ⟨ *In-room: no phone, a/c, no TV. In-hotel: public Wi-Fi* ⊟ *MC, V* ⊩❑ *CP.*

NIGHTLIFE AND THE ARTS

Younger and older C'town residents alike head to **Andy's** (⊠ *337½ High St.* ☎ *410/778–6779* ⊕ *www.andys-ctown.com*) when they're looking for an unpretentious nightspot with the aura of an "everybody-knows-your-name" neighborhood pub. Bands play on Friday and Saturday.

ROCK HALL

13 mi southwest of Chestertown via Rte. 291 to Rte. 20.

No longer just a side trip, Rock Hall, its hardy maritime character intact, has emerged as a viable destination in its own right, to be reached either by road or by boat. It reveres its heritage, despite the pleasure boats anchored in its waters and moored at its docks—which far out-number actual working fishing boats.

GETTING HERE AND AROUND

Like Stevenville and Queenstown, Rock Hall is tiny. Many people feel that it is one of the most "authentic" places in the area because it lacks the conventional draws of intimate shops and high-end restaurants. Boating here is king. There is a small town beach about a mile west from the center of town where locals swim in the bay. Rock Hall is only reachable by car or private boat.

EXPLORING

Fodor's Choice   **Eastern Neck National Wildlife Refuge.** At the tip of the Eastern Neck ★ peninsula, 8 mi south of Rock Hall, and at the mouth of the Chester River, this 2,285-acre park is superb. It's a prime place to spot migratory waterfowl, wild turkeys, Delmarva fox squirrels, and southern bald eagles, undeterred by the experimental power-generating solar panels and wind turbines installed nearby. Nearly 6 mi of roads and trails and an observation tower provide excellent vantage points. ⊠ *1730 Eastern Neck Rd.* ☎ *410/639–7056* ⊕ *www.fws.gov/northeast/easternneck* ☉ *Daily dawn–dusk.*

Waterman's Museum. This interesting place profiles the hard life on the Bay in absorbing detail, celebrating a Chesapeake way of life that is dying out. On display are exhibits on oystering and crabbing that include historical photos and local carvings, as well as preserved examples of the watermen's all-important boats and a reproduction of a waterborne shanty. ⊠ *20880 Rock Hall Ave.* ☎ *410/778–6697* ☒ *Free* ☉ *May–Sept., daily 8–5; Oct.–Apr., weekdays 8–5, Sat. 9–5, Sun. 10–4.*

WHERE TO EAT AND STAY

$$ ✕ **Waterman's Crabhouse.** This casual dockside restaurant looking south-
SEAFOOD   ward toward the Chesapeake Bay Bridge in the distance has lots of local color. The menu includes ribs, steaks, and fried oysters, but its crab dishes are legendary, as are its homemade cheesecake and key lime pie. Warm summer weekends mean live entertainment and seating on the 40-foot deck. There's a deep-draft dock for diners arriving by boat. Waterman's gets very busy on the weekends, so be prepared to wait. ⊠ *21055 Sharp St.* ☎ *410/639–2261* ⊕ *www.watermanscrabhouse.com* ☒ *AE, D, MC, V* ☉ *Closed Jan. and Feb.*

$$$ ▦ **The Inn at Osprey Point.** On 30 lush acres along Swan Creek, this stately Colonial-era building welcomes guests with brick fireplaces and exposed beams; four-poster, canopied beds; and a spacious two-room Escapade suite with French doors and a marble bath with a whirlpool hot tub. Yet it's worth staying here for the views alone. At the inn's restaurant ($28) regional fare is served—the cream-of-crab soup with sherry is a favorite among regulars, as are entrées such as Maryland jumbo lump crab cakes and pan-seared duck breast. It serves dinner Wednesday through Saturday and brunch on Sunday. Osprey Point Marina, with 160 slips, welcomes transient boaters year-round. **Pros:** great views; quintessential Chesapeake Bay elegance. **Cons:** some visitors may find modern marina clashes with historical ambience. ⊠ *20786 Rock Hall Ave.* ☎ *410/639–2194* ⊕ *www.ospreypoint.com* ⤶ *15 rooms, 1 suite* ☖ *In-room: no phone, a/c. In-hotel: restaurant, pool, bicycles* ☒ *D, MC, V* ❢◉❢ *CP.*

SPORTS AND THE OUTDOORS

Canoeing and kayaking on quiet creeks and rivers throughout the Eastern Shore's ragged western shorelines are popular pastimes here. Two firms in Kent County provide rentals, tours, and lessons for the area: there are also good sources for waterside camping advice.

The folks at **Chester River Kayak Adventures** (✉ *5758 Main St., Rock Hall* ☎ *410/639–2001* ⊕ *www.crkayakadventures.com*) also operate two B&Bs. Gear up at **KayakCanoe** (✉ *7280 Swan Creek Rd., 4 mi north of Rock Hall* ☎ *410/639–9000*).

CECIL COUNTY

Cecil County includes the northern extremities of Chesapeake Bay. Its western boundary with Harford County, the Susquehanna River, is the Bay's principal northern tributary. Its southern boundary with Kent County is another tributary, the Sassafras River. The all-important Chesapeake and Delaware (C&D) Canal is cut between Cecil's third major river, the Elk, and the Delaware River, a major shipping route that connects Chesapeake Bay with Delaware Bay and the Atlantic Ocean. Its many acres of public parks and forests and well-known horse farms help preserve connections to the land.

ESSENTIALS

Cecil County Tourism (✉ *1 Seahawk Dr., Suite 114, North East* ☎ *410/996–6290 or 800/232–4595* ⊕ *www.seececil.org*).

CHESAPEAKE CITY

31 mi north of Chestertown via Rte. 213.

As it's a town split dramatically in two by the Chesapeake and Delaware (C&D) Canal, Chesapeake City homes and businesses face each other across the busy waterway. Those sitting at the restaurants and taverns next to the canal often marvel at the giant oceangoing vessels that slide by—seemingly within arm's reach.

GETTING HERE AND AROUND

Chesapeake City is a beautiful community, split in two. Other than navigating the intervening canal by boat, you must drive over the sculptural Chesapeake City Bridge in order to explore both sides.

QUICK BITES

Kilby's Canal Creamery (✉ *9 Bohemia Ave., Chesapeake City* ⊕ *www. kilbycream.com*) is the richest ice cream around. It is made from Kilby's herd of Holstein cows on a dairy located in nearby Rising Sun, which is why the motto is "from cow to cone in two days." Flavors include Holstein Cream, Cow Dough, and Chocotopia. Located in the historic district on the canal, it is open daily from 11:30 am to 9 pm.

WHERE TO EAT AND STAY

$$$

SEAFOOD

★

✕ **The Bayard House.** One of the few restaurants in Chesapeake City, the Bayard House has cuisine and service that would stand out anywhere. Patrons in the know travel to this canal-shop eatery for dishes such as tournedos Baltimore, twin fillets of beef topped with crab and lobster; stuffed Anaheim pepper, chilies stuffed with lobster, crabmeat, and shrimp; and de rigueur Maryland crab cakes. The Maryland crab soup is even more widely renowned. ⊠ *11 Bohemia Ave.* ☎ *410/885–5040* ⊕ *www.bayardhouse.com* ▭ *AE, D, MC, V.*

$$ ⬚ **Ship Watch Inn.** Three levels of broad decks mean that every room has a place from which to relax and watch all manner of watercraft, including international shipping vessels, sail in and out of the Chesapeake & Delaware Canal just yards away. (A canal-side hot tub offers an even closer view.) Built as a residence in 1920, this elegant, waterfront B&B blends eclectic furnishings with modern amenities. The decades-old black-and-white photos hanging in the public areas reveal much about the roles the owner-innkeepers' families played in the history of Chesapeake City. The Ship Watch is one of several B&Bs in Chesapeake City. **Pros:** extraordinary location literally on the edge of the C&D Canal; two-night stay not required. **Cons:** few amenities. ⊠ *401 1st St.* ☎ *410/885–5300* ⊕ *www.shipwatchinn.com* ↰ *8 rooms, 2 suites* ⬙ *In-room: a/c, DVDs, refrigerators* ▭ *AE, MC, V* ⦿ *BP.*

NORTH EAST

12 mi northwest of Chesapeake City via Rte. 213 and Rte. 40.

Uncommon neighborliness along a main street of antiques and collectibles shops and homey eateries gives Cecil's riverside county seat its welcoming charm.

GETTING HERE AND AROUND

Reachable by car, North East is a main street with homey shops and a few good restaurants. It would take a quarter of an hour to walk from one end of town to another. Unlike Chesapeake City, it does not have a stunning view. Its main commodity is small town neighborliness.

EXPLORING

Day Basket Factory. You can often watch the crafting of oak baskets by hand, done here since 1876. Skilled craftspeople and weavers use techniques passed down through the generations. ⊠ *714 S. Main St.* ☎ *410/287–6100* ⊕ *www.daybasketfactory.com* ☉ *Wed.–Fri. 10:30–5, Sat. 10–5 (until 6 in summer), Sun. 1–5.*

Elk Neck State Park. About 6 mi south of the town of North East, this park juts into the headwaters of the Chesapeake Bay to its west, with the Elk River flowing along its eastern flank. You can drive almost the length of the peninsula and then walk about a mile through pleasant woodlands to the cliffs on its tip. There you can find the sparkling-white Turkey Point Lighthouse, albeit no longer in use. The 270-plus-degree view from Turkey Point is stunning. Campsites are available here, as are some charming 1950s-era wooden cabins that are admirably well maintained. Elk Neck is a prime location for picnicking as well as for fishing and swimming off sandy beaches. ⊠ *4395 Turkey Point Rd.* ☎ *410/287–5333 or 888/432–2267* ⊕ *www.dnr.state.md.us/ publiclands/central/elkneck.asp.*

5&10 Antique Market. Originally the Hotel Cecil, this market became Cramer's 5&10, an old-fashioned variety store operated by a pair of proprietors who themselves became historic treasures. The building's enterprising current owner created an antiques mart, but fully restored the building's exterior and retained its well-worn wood flooring, candy jars, and display counters. You could spend a weekend here! ⊠ *111 S. Main St.* ☎ *410/287–8318.*

Upper Bay Museum. The two spacious buildings here, at the head of the North East River, preserve the rich heritage of both the commercial and recreational hunter. This unusual museum houses an extensive collection of boating, fishing, and hunting artifacts native to the Upper Chesapeake Bay: sleek sculling oars, rare working decoys, and the outlawed "punt" gun and "gunning" rigs. ⊠ *Walnut St. at Rte. 272* ☎ *410/287–2675* ⊙ *Sat. 10–3, Sun. 10–4.*

WHERE TO EAT AND STAY

$$ SEAFOOD   ☺ ✕ **Woody's Crab House.** You can buy crabs here, of course, and have them served any number of imaginative ways. But slurp one of the thick homemade soups, or down the famous Carolina shrimp burger, to understand why this funky little eatery is so popular. The children's menu is a thoughtful extra. But go easy on the real food: Woody's ice-cream parlor, next door, includes seasonal favorite flavors such as apple, pumpkin, and Fourth of July (a celebration of red, white, and blue ice creams). Call ahead if you want traditional crabs. Woody's is quite hopping, so they occasionally run out. ⊠ *29 S. Main St.* ☎ *410/287–3541* ⊕ *www.woodyscrabhouse.com* ⚓ *Reservations not accepted* ⊟ *D, MC, V.*

$$ ★ **Elk Forge B&B Inn and Retreat.** A 20-minute drive from North East, Elk Forge is nestled among 5 acres of woods and gardens along Big Elk Creek. Each of the 12 guest units is beautifully furnished and uniquely decorated, inspired by area locales and cultures, and creature comforts are plentiful. A daily afternoon tea includes the innkeepers' own herbal blends; services at the Spa in the Garden include Swedish massage and aromatherapy facials. With easy access to sites of interest in Delaware and Pennsylvania as well as Maryland, Elk Forge is indeed a mini-resort. **Pros:** attractively priced considering available spa amenities. **Cons:** might seem somewhat remote to some. ⊠ *807 Elk Mills Rd., Elk Mills* ☎ *410/392–9007 or 877/355–3674* ⊕ *www.elkforge.com* ⮎ *7 rooms, 5 suites* ⚘ *In-room: a/c, Wi-Fi. In-hotel: gym, spa* ⊟ *AE, MC, V* ⦿ *BP.*

TALBOT COUNTY

Water defines the landscape of Talbot County, which has some of the region's most vibrant little towns, including Easton and St. Michaels. The Chesapeake Bay forms its western border, and the meandering Choptank River slices through the Delmarva Peninsula to form its southern and eastern borders. Waterfront hamlets that started as fishing villages now include comfortable inns and downtown B&Bs. Fine waterside restaurants and folksy main-street taverns are also part of this comfortably refined region.

ESSENTIALS
Talbot County Office of Tourism (⊠ *11 S. Harrison St., Easton* ☎ *410/770–8000* ⊕ *www.tourtalbot.org*).

EASTON

★ *79 mi south of North East and 36 mi south of Chestertown via Rte. 213 and U.S. 50, 36 mi southeast of Annapolis via U.S. 50/301 to U.S. 50.*

Well-preserved buildings dating from Colonial through Victorian times still grace this affluent, genteel town. Fine art galleries, high-quality antiques shops, and gift boutiques sit side by side along North Harrison Street as well as the small midtown mall called Talbottown. Downtown Easton's tree-lined streets present an eclectic collection of boutique-style shops. Strolling Harrison Street—between the Talbottown shopping complex and the Academy Art Museum—and parts of parallel Washington Street, as well as their cross streets, can be at once eminently rewarding and soberingly expensive.

GETTING HERE AND AROUND
At more than 14,000 citizens, Easton is the largest town in the area. It does not have a system of public transportation and the best way to get around is on foot. Park in one of the plentiful, public, and reasonably priced lots in the center of town and explore.

EXPLORING

★ **Academy Art Museum.** This nice local museum houses a permanent collection of fine art by such American artists as James McNeil Whistler, Grant Wood, Lichtenstein, and Rauschenberg, as well as Chagall and Dürer. Special exhibitions often cover local artists, and the juried art show held here in early October is one of the finest in the region. ⊠ *106 South St.* ☎ *410/822–2787 or 410/822–0455* ⊕ *www.art-academy.org* ☞ *$3* ⊙ *Mon., Fri., and Sat. 10–4; Tues.–Thurs. 10–8.*

Historical Society of Talbot County. The Society maintains a small museum of local history and manages Tharpe Antiques. Housed in a three-story Federal brick house restored by a Quaker cabinetmaker in 1810, the society also operates Three Centuries Tours, a one-hour overview of authentically furnished homes of the 17th through 19th centuries. ⊠ *25 S. Washington St.* ☎ *410/822–0773* ⊕ *www.hstc.org* ☞ *$5* ⊙ *Mon.–Sat. 10–4. Guided house tours Tues.–Sat. 11:30 and 1:30.*

Talbot County Courthouse. The gathering point for citizens who protested the Stamp Act in 1765 and where people rallied to adopt the Talbot Resolves, this 1712 courthouse was a forerunner of the Declaration of Independence. The courthouse was expanded in 1794 and two wings were added in the late 1950s. It is still in use. ⊠ *11 N. Washington St.* ☎ *410/770–8001* ⊙ *Weekdays 8–5.*

WHERE TO EAT

$$$$ ✕ **Bartlett Pear Inn.** Consistently rated the top restaurant in Easton, The
AMERICAN Bartlett Pear Inn Restaurant calls itself an "upscale Amerian Bistro." However, its roots are European and the menu features truffle butter paparadelle, braised snails, and paella. The decor and service are impeccable, as is the inn. ⊠ *28 S. Harrison St., Easton* ☎ *410/770–3300*

⊕ *bartlettpearinn.com* ▭ *AE, D, MC, V* ⊗ *Closed Tues. Open for dinner Wed.–Mon. and brunch on Sun.*

$$ ✕ **General Tanuki's.** A most unusual and exciting blend of Pacific Rim,
ECLECTIC California surf, and grandma's kitchen await adventurous taste buds in this intimate venue. A *tanuki* is akin to a Japanese leprechaun, and the creative flavors here play tricks on traditional dishes. Imagine a restaurant serving buttery sushi and sashimi, lamb lettuce wraps, thai mussels simmered in Woodpecker cider, and a classic Hawaiian pizza under one roof. Run, don't walk, to this place, and make sure to check out happy hour (4 pm–6 pm) at the U-shaped bar. ⊠ *25 Goldsborough St.* ☏ *410/819–0707* ⊕ *www.generaltanukis.com* ▭ *MC, V.*

$$$ ✕ **Mason's.** A family-run landmark for more than 30 years, Mason's
AMERICAN uses fresh ingredients from its own garden. The chef brings bold flavors like pan-seared crab cakes topped with a corn and soybean succotash, crispy-skin red snapper surrounded by braised artichokes, and gentle rockfish stuffed with lump crab meat, a local delicacy. Sip a classic martini in the swanky lounge while waiting for a table—make sure to ask for one on the porch in warm weather. Next door are a coffee bar and a food store that sells hard-to-find cheeses and meats, wonderful handcrafted chocolates, and all manner of esoteric edibles. ⊠ *42 E. Dover St.* ☏ *410/822–3204* ⊕ *www.masonsgourmet.com* ▭ *AE, D, MC, V* ⊗ *Closed Sun.*

$$$$ ✕ **Scossa.** Surrounded by shops, lodging, and other eateries so very
ITALIAN American, sophisticated Scossa almost seems out of place. From its
Fodor's Choice sidewalk patio with wall-mounted fountains to its superb menus, Scossa
★ Café is unmistakably northern Italian. The well-trained co-owners create lunch and dinner dishes with an Italian influence that does not overwhelm the fine ingredients. Samples of daily specials include braised lamp shank with artichokes, short ribs with Borolo wine sauce, roast rabbit *campagnola*, and soft-shell crabs *alla provinciale*. Brunch is available on weekends. Jackets are not required, but the cosmopolitan style of Scossa definitely attracts a well-dressed clientele who reserve ahead. ⊠ *8 N. Washington St.* ☏ *410/822–2202* ⋐ *Reservations essential* ⊕ *www.scossarestaurant.com* ▭ *AE, MC, V* ⊗ *Closed Mon.*

WHERE TO STAY

$$ ▦ **Bartlett Pear Inn.** Natives Jordan and Alice Lloyd returned to their
★ hometown and bought a 220-year-old home (the former Inn at Easton) right in the center of town. They restored the inn, creating seven guest rooms and suites, each named after a different variety of pear. Impeccable hosts, the Lloyds considered every detail, from the luxurious sheets to the brightly colored walls. **Pros:** central location; beautiful garden; on-site Bartlett Pear Restaurant. **Cons:** lacks some of the amenities of a large hotel, such as a swimming pool; pets are allowed with a $50 deposit. ⊠ *28 S. Harrison St.* ☏ *410/770–3300* ⊕ *www.bartlettpearinn. com* ⮑ *7 rooms* ⌂ *In-room: a/c, Wi-Fi. In-hotel: restaurant, Wi-Fi hotspot, some pets allowed* ▭ *AE, D, DC, MC, V* ⦿I *BP.*

$ ▦ **The Tidewater Inn & Conference Center.** Beyond the entry archways of this stately, four-story brick hotel, an early-20th-century aura pervades its spacious common areas, which are enhanced by huge fireplaces and paintings of old Easton. Mahogany reproduction furniture fills the guest rooms, most in greens and golds. In the hotel's full-service dining room a "hunting breakfast" is available early every morning in season. To one side of the porte cochere, broad awnings shade an alfresco lobby and sometime dining area. A small on-site spa offers manicures and massages. Built in 1949, the Tidewater is a member of the Historic Hotels of America. **Pros:** welcome contrast to ubiquitous colonial-era lodging; large property has more amenities than local B&Bs; valet parking. **Cons:** if inn is hosting a conference, individual guests may feel marginalized. ✉ *101 E. Dover St.* ☎ *410/822–1300 or 800/237–8775* ⊕ *www.tidewaterinn.com* ⥀ *114 rooms, 7 suites* ⌂ *In-room: a/c, Internet. In-hotel: restaurant, bar, pool, spa, Wi-Fi hotspot, some pets allowed* ▤ *AE, D, MC, V.*

NIGHTLIFE AND THE ARTS

Avalon Theatre (✉ *40 E. Dover St.* ☎ *410/822–0345* ⊕ *www.avalontheatre. com*), a former vaudeville house built in 1921, has been restored as a venue for the Talbot Chamber Orchestra and the Eastern Shore Chamber Music Festival, as well as films and other performances.

The **Washington Street Pub** (✉ *20 N. Washington St.* ☎ *410/822–9011* ⊕ *www.wstpub.com*) has a raw bar, 19 beers on tap, hardwood floors, a brick wall behind a bar that stretches on and on, and serves the town's legendary "pub chips."

SPORTS AND THE OUTDOORS

BICYCLING

Easton Cycle & Sports (✉ *723 Goldsborough St.* ☎ *410/822–7433* ⊕ *www. eastoncycleandsport.com*) specializes in bike rentals as well as kayaks and canoes.

BOATING

Most of the fishing and boating tours depart a few miles away in the towns of St. Michaels and Tilghman Island.

GOLF

One of the best public courses in the state, **Hog Neck Golf Course** (✉ *10142 Cordova Rd.* ☎ *410/822–6079 or 800/280–1790* ⊕ *www. hogneck.com*) has an 18-hole, par 72 championship course and a 9-hole, par 32 "Executive" course ($25 walk/$35 ride). Nonresident greens fees are $60–$70.

ST. MICHAELS

9 mi west of Easton via Rte. 33, 49 mi southeast of Annapolis.

St. Michaels, once a shipbuilding center, is today one of the region's premier leisure-time destinations. Its ever-growing popularity has resulted in more and more shops, cafés, waterfront restaurants, and inns. In warmer months, tourists and boaters crowd its narrow streets and snug harbor. Talbot Street is lined with restaurants, galleries, and all manner of shops, including a hardware store that doubles as a retro gift shop.

Stroll between Mill Street, the lane to the Chesapeake Bay Maritime Museum, and Willow Street, or head just beyond to Canton Alley Artiste Locale, Broken Rudder Sportswear, Chesapeake Trading Company, and The Minds Eye Craft Collection cut.

GETTING HERE AND AROUND

Parking is a little problematic in crowded St. Michaels. There is a public lot in the south end of Talbot Street. Walking is the order of the day in this compact town. St. Michaels is probably the "cutest" of the adjacent communities, and many of the shops and restaurants are geared towards day tourists. The **St. Michaels Trolley Company** (☎ *410/745–5870* ⊕ *www.saintmichaelstrolley.com*) was started in the summer of 2010 and has a continuous circuit tour of the historic district. It's $10 for adults and $5 for children for an all-day pass.

Besides any number of tours by boat from several of the waterside towns on Maryland's and Virginia's Eastern Shore, there are day-trip tours into the region from Annapolis and Baltimore. Larger towns, including Annapolis as well as St. Michaels, are home port for diesel- or gasoline-powered tour boats and yachts.

EXPLORING

The Patriot. This 65-foot steel-hull yacht departs four times daily, from March through September, for one-hour cruises on the Miles River. The tour covers the ecology and history of the area as it passes along the tranquil riverfront landscape. ⊠ *Docked near Crab Claw Restaurant and Chesapeake Bay Maritime Museum, End of Mill St., at Harbor* ☎ *410/745–3100* ⊕ *www.patriotcruises.com.*

☾ **Chesapeake Bay Maritime Museum.** One of the region's finest, this nine-
★ building complex chronicles the Bay's rich history of boatbuilding, commercial fishing, navigating, and hunting in compelling detail. Exhibits on the 18-acre waterfront site include two of the Bay's unique skipjacks among the museum's more than 80 historic regional boats. There are also the restored 1879 Hooper Strait Lighthouse, a working boatyard, and a "waterman's wharf" with shanties plus oystering and crabbing tools. In the Bay Building you can see a crabbing skiff as well as a dug-out canoe hewn by Native Americans. The Waterfowl Building contains carved decoys and stuffed birds, including wood ducks, mallards, and swans. ⊠ *End of Mill St. at Navy Point, near harbor* ☎ *410/745–2916* ⊕ *www.cbmm.org* ⌦ *$13* ☾ *Open daily year-round—except Tues.–Thurs. Nov. 14–Jan. 14, but hrs vary seasonally.*

WHERE TO EAT

$$$ ✕ **Crab Claw Restaurant.** Owned and operated by the same family since
SEAFOOD 1965, this St. Michaels landmark started as a clam- and oyster-shucking house for watermen long before that. Diners at both indoor and outdoor tables have panoramic views over the harbor to the river beyond, but dockside tables are the best. As the name suggests, this is *the* down-home place for fresh steamed and seasoned blue crabs. But the extensive menu also includes sandwiches and other light fare as well as other seafood and meat dishes. Children's platters are available, too. ⊠ *End of Mill St., at harbor* ☎ *410/745–2900 or 410/745–9366* ⊕ *www. thecrabclaw.com* ▭ *No credit cards* ☾ *Closed Dec.–early Mar.*

$$ ✕ **Rupert's Bar and Tea Room.** In a town dominated by crab places,
BRITISH Rupert's is completely different. First, the decor is British pub, filled with interesting antiques, including taxidermied animals. Ruperts provides nightlife—a well-stocked bar and dancing—in a town that's

known to close up around 7. It's not the traditional Eastern shore, crab shack experience, but then the owner's a British expat. Specials range from American comfort food like meat loaf to lobster ravioli. Try the "killer guacamole." ✉ *407 S. Talbot St.* ☎ 410/745–9090 ▭ *MC, V.*

$$ SEAFOOD ✕ **Town Dock Restaurant.** Every seat in this vast restaurant overlooks St. Michaels Harbor and the Miles River, every window framing its own scene; the deck is also open. Favorites among patrons are fresh seafood dishes like sesame-seared tuna and grilled Atlantic salmon, as well as roast duck with dried cherry glaze—their preparation carefully supervised by award-wining restaurateur Michael Rork. If you just can't decide, tackle the Land and Sea Buffet. For a finale, sample some strawberries hand-dipped in chocolate. Keep in mind that the price of entrées vary with the cost of crabs, going up and down with the season. ✉ *125 Mulberry St.* ☎ *410/745–5577* ▭ *AE, D, DC, MC, V* ⏲ *Closed Mon.–Thurs. Nov.–Mar.*

$$$ SEAFOOD ✕ **208 Talbot Restaurant & Wine Bar.** Unobtrusively situated on St. Michaels' busy main street, 208 Talbot, long a favorite among discriminating diners, has several intimate dining rooms with exposed brick walls and brick floors. Specialties include such original first-course dishes as house-cured gravlax served with fresh mango, avocado, jalapeño pesto, and grilled flat bread; and more-traditional second-course entrées such as whole grilled rockfish accompanied by braised greens, grape tomato relish, and hush puppies; as well as a welcome variety of meat dishes. Small plates ($8–$14) are available for more conservative appetites, and on Saturday there's a four-course prix-fixe menu available ($55). ✉ *208 N. Talbot St.* ☎ *410/745–3838* 🌐 *www.208talbot.com* ▭ *D, MC, V* ⏲ *Closed Sun.–Tues.*

WHERE TO STAY

$ ★ **Five Gables Inn & Spa.** Three circa-1860 houses have been turned into an elegant and comfortable getaway. All rooms have a private porch or balcony, and all are decorated with antique furnishings, fine linens and towels, and down comforters. The hot stone massage and invigorating rosemary mint body wrap are treatments in the spa. Refreshments are served daily at 3. The bed-and-breakfast home also emcompasses a fine needlepoint shop, B's Stitches, and an upscale pet boutique, Flying Fred's. **Pros:** allows for easy walking throughout St. Michaels thanks to its main-street location; on-site shopping and spa options; fireplace in the room. **Cons:** true resort feel challenged by main-street location. ✉ *209 N. Talbot St.* ☎ *410/745–0100 or 877/466–0100* 🌐 *www.fivegables.com* *12 rooms, 8 suites* *In-room: a/c, no phone (some), DVD. In-hotel: restaurant, pool, spa, bicycles, some pets allowed* ▭ *AE, MC, V* *CP.*

$$$$ ★ **Inn at Perry Cabin.** On 25 acres beside the Miles River, this luxury inn—operated by the world-renowned Orient Express Hotels group—employs a nautical theme throughout to elegant effect. Each unique guest room has elegant appointments; amenities include heated towel racks, fresh flowers in all rooms, and afternoon tea. Above all, staying here means impeccable service. Dining at the inn's restaurant with its exquisite cuisine and stellar wine selection is an event. The signature crab spring roll with pink grapefruit, avocado, and toasted almonds,

and the lamb shank glazed with honey and tarragon are both exquisite. **Pros:** great customer service; riverside location; movies are available for guest rooms. **Cons:** expensive for the area. ⊠ *308 Watkins La.* ☎ *410/745–2200 or 866/278–9601* ⊕ *www.perrycabin.com* ↬ *54 rooms, 27 suites* ⚲ *In-room: a/c, Wi-Fi. In-hotel: restaurant, bar, pool, spa, bicycles, some pets allowed* ⊟ *AE, DC, MC, V.*

$$ 🏨 **The Oaks, a Country Inn.** Antebellum grace defines this 1748 mansion on 17 acres along the banks of Oak Creek, 3 mi from St. Michaels. The antique-filled inn has a stunning black-and-white tile foyer; its best rooms have fireplaces, private porches, and hot tubs. The day starts with a full country breakfast served in the sunny yellow-and-red dining room. After that, you might want to go fishing off the pier, or head no farther than one of the rockers in the screened porch overlooking the water. **Pros:** affordable; waterside location; fireplaces in most rooms. **Cons:** some decor clashes with inn's heritage; a short drive from downtown. ⊠ *Rte. 329 at 329 Acorn La., Royal Oak* ☎ *410/745–5053* ⊕ *www.the-oaks.com* ↬ *22 rooms, 1 cottage* ⚲ *In-room: a/c. In-hotel: restaurant, pool, water sports, bicycles* ⊟ *MC, V* ⫶◯⫶ *BP.*

$$$ 🏨 **Victoriana Inn.** Adirondack chairs line a sloping expanse of lawn leading to the formal gardens of what was once a Civil War army officer's home. Set on the town's harbor and across a footbridge from the Maritime Museum, this inn is a relaxing haven. All rooms include queen-size beds; two have fireplaces, and three overlook the water. The suite has a private water-view deck and a fireplace as well as a TV. There's a nightly happy hour that includes wine, beer, and light hors d'oeuvres. No children under 13 are allowed on weekends. **Pros:** a revered St. Michaels institution among many favored town sites; most rooms have a fireplace. **Cons:** minimum of a two-night stay; location near the harbor can be heavily trafficked. ⊠ *205 Cherry St.* ☎ *410/745–3368* ⊕ *www. victorianainn.com* ↬ *6 rooms, 1 suite* ⚲ *In-room: no phone, a/c, no TV (some). In-hotel: bicycles, Wi-Fi hotspot* ⊟ *MC, V* ⫶◯⫶ *BP.*

SPORTS AND THE OUTDOORS

Town Dock Marina. Rent bicycles here as well as surrey-top electric boats and small powerboats. The marina is open from 8 am until dusk during warm-weather months, typically March or April through November. ⊠ *305 Mulberry St.* ☎ *410/745–2400 or 800/678–8980.*

★ *HM Krentz.* The 1955 32-passenger skipjack, captained by owner Edward Farley, is available to the public for sails between early April and late November. ⊠ *Docked at the Chesapeake Bay Maritime Museum* ☎ *410/ 745–6080* ⊕ *www.oystercatcher.com.*

TILGHMAN ISLAND

13 mi southwest of St. Michaels via Rte. 33.

A visit to Tilghman Island provides intriguing insight into the Eastern Shore's remarkable character. Leave your car and explore by bike or kayak. A handful of B&Bs and inns provide excellent accommodations here. A small fleet of working fishing boats, including a few of the region's remaining skipjacks, call Dogwood Harbor their home port.

GETTING HERE AND AROUND

Tilghman Island is for nature lovers. Once you arrive there by car, get on your hiking boots or swim gear and explore the island, slowly and without a car.

WHERE TO STAY

$$ ⊞ **Tilghman Island Inn.** Warm and welcoming conviviality and casual elegance define this compact, modern resort overlooking the Chesapeake Bay and a waterfowl marsh. Decor and furnishings throughout are bright and modern, with lots of white enhanced by splashes of color. Five deluxe waterside suites have hot tubs, fireplaces, and spacious decks. The 5-acre complex includes a 20-slip transient marina and a small fleet of tandem and single kayaks available for rent. Dishes served at the Gallery Restaurant ($$–$$$) are at once innovative and traditional, enhanced by a well-selected wine list. **Pros:** truly panoramic Bay views; aura of a mini-resort. **Cons:** not historic setting; lacks the small B&B feel of the island's other options. ⊠ *Coopertown Rd. (2nd right after Knapps Narrows Bridge)* ☎ *410/886–2141 or 800/866–2141* ⊕ *www.tilghmanislandinn.com* ⇆ *15 rooms, 5 suites* ⚴ *In-room: a/c, Wi-Fi. In-hotel: restaurant, bars, tennis court, pool, spa, water sports, some pets allowed* ⊟ *AE, D, DC, MC, V* ⦿ *CP.*

SPORTS AND THE OUTDOORS

★ *Rebecca T. Ruark.* Built in 1886, this 49-passenger ship, captained by owner Wade Murphy Jr., offers hands-on learning charters from early April into late October. She is the oldest working skipjack on the Bay, and is one of several skipjacks designated as National Historic Landmarks. Captain Murphy is as much the entertainment as the skipjack itself. Legend has it that he captained James Michener when the author was doing research for his blockbuster Chesapeake. Tickets are $30 for adults, $15 for those under 12. ⊠ *21308 Phillips Rd., at Dogwood Harbor* ☎ *410/829–3976 or 410/886–2176* ⊕ *www.skipjack.org.*

OXFORD

7 mi southeast of St. Michaels via Rte. 33 and Rte. 333.

Tracing its roots to 1683, tiny Oxford remains secluded and untrammeled. Robert Morris, a merchant from Liverpool, lived here with his son, Robert Morris Jr., a signer of the Declaration of Independence. The younger Morris helped finance the Revolution but ended up in debtor's prison after losing at land speculation.

Oxford is very pretty, but there isn't much to do in town, and there aren't many shops (St. Michaels or Easton are better options). But reserve time for Oxford, via the Oxford-Bellevue Ferry, its Bellevue terminus near St. Michaels, if early U.S. history is paramount and if time permits you to take in some of the scenery here.

GETTING HERE AND AROUND

Oxford's best mode of transportation is the **Oxford-Bellevue Ferry** (☎ *410/745–9023* ⊕ *www.oxfordbellevueferry.com*), which gives spectacular views of the bay as it takes you on its 20-minute voyage to St.

CLOSE UP

Chesapeake Bay's Skipjacks

11

Settlement along the fertile shores of the Chesapeake Bay was an obvious choice for 17th-century English immigrants, who soon farmed the cash crop of tobacco and plucked plentiful blue crabs and plump oysters from its bottom. Among the reminders of the Bay's fishing culture, which endures, is its dwindling fleet of native skipjacks: broad, flat-bottom wooden sailing vessels for dredging oysters. Economical to build, skipjacks had the shallowest draft—the distance from the waterline to the lowest point of the keel—of any boat in the bay. This made them excellent for cruising above the grassy shoals favored by oysters.

At first, oyster harvesters would stand in small boats and use simple, long-handle tongs, to grasp clumps of oysters from the bottom and bring them aboard. It was tiresome, difficult work. In the early 1800s, sturdy Yankee schooners, having left the depleted waters of New England, entered the Chesapeake Bay with dredges, iron contraptions that dragged up oysters along the bottom. With their first large harvest, Chesapeake's fishing industry changed forever.

Dredging was initially banned as being exploitative and intrusive, first by Virginia and later by Maryland. However, after the Civil War drained the region's economy, Maryland legalized the practice, allowing it under certain conditions for boats powered only by sails. By 1875 more than 690 dredging licenses were issued. Soon more-sophisticated dredgers emerged; all were loosely called *bateaux*, French for "boats."

The oyster bounty was not to last. After peaking in 1884 with 15 million bushels, less than a third of that amount was caught in 1891. Despite the growing use of steam and gasoline power on land and water, "only under sail" dredging laws prevailed in the Bay. As the 19th century drew to a close, boatbuilders were forced to experiment with boat designs that were cheap to build yet had sails that would provide enough power for dredging and transporting the harvests. In 1901 one of these new bateaux appeared in Baltimore's harbor. She caught the eye of a *Baltimore Sun* newspaper reporter, who wrote that their "quickness to go about may have earned for them the name of skipjack." The name stuck. On occasion, skipjacks have been compared to bonito tuna because, like the great Atlantic fish, they seem to skip over the surface of the water.

Oysters—and the Chesapeake's renowned blue crab—are still harvested by a diminishing number of watermen, their fleets of small, flat-bottom boats—sometimes powered by modified automobile engines—concentrated in locales such as Crisfield and Kent Narrows as well as Smith and Tangier islands, but less than a dozen sail-powered skipjacks are still working. Sailing on one of them (generally from early April through October, when they're not dredging) is an exhilarating way to fully experience the culture and history of the Chesapeake. The *Herman M. Krentz,* built in 1955, sails from St. Michaels, and the 80-foot *Rebecca T. Ruark,* originally built in 1886, from Tilghman Island. An authentic replica skipjack, the *Nathan of Dorchester,* also available for sails by the public, is berthed in Cambridge.

Michaels. It is the region's smallest ferry and can accommodate less than half a dozen cars.

Oxford is tiny and can be handled in less than half an hour by foot. Another option is to explore by bike. The flat, empty streets are ideal for riding.

ESSENTIALS
Oxford Business Association (⊕ www.portofoxford.com).

EXPLORING
Oxford-Bellevue Ferry. Begun in 1683, the ferry may be the oldest privately owned ferry in continuous operation in the United States. It crosses the Tred Avon River between Bellevue, 7 mi south of St. Michaels (via Routes 33 and 329), and Oxford in seven to 10 minutes. ⊠ *2756 Oxford Road, Oxford* ☎ *410/745–9023* ⊕ *www.oxfordbellevueferry. com* ⊠ *Ferry: $7 car and driver one-way, $4 motorcycle, $3 bicycle, $2 pedestrian* ☉ *Mar.–Memorial Day and Labor Day–Nov., weekdays 7 am–sunset, weekends 9 am–sunset; Memorial Day–Labor Day, weekdays 7 am–9 pm, weekends 9–9.*

Oxford Museum. View displays, models, and pictures of sailboats. Some boats were built in Oxford, site of one of the first Chesapeake regattas (1860). Check out the full-scale racing boat by the door. Other artifacts include the lamp from a lighthouse on nearby Benoni Point, a sailmaker's bench, and an oyster-shucking stall. Docents elaborate on the exhibits, which set the context for a walking tour of nearby blocks. ⊠ *100 S. Morris* ☎ *410/226–5122* ⊠ *Suggested donation* ⊕ *www. oxfordmuseum.org* ☉ *Apr.–Oct., Fri.–Sun. 2–5.*

WHERE TO EAT AND STAY

$$$

AMERICAN

✕ **Latitude 38.** A whimsical red, white, and green color scheme; painted vines climbing the walls; and polished wooden floors distinguish this bistro. Weather permitting, you can eat outdoors at wrought-iron tables in a brick courtyard. The creative and diverse menu changes twice a month, with such dishes offered as veal fettuccine Montrachet topped with goat cheese and a tomato cream sauce, and sauté of seafood including lobster, shrimp, and scallops. ⊠ *26342 Oxford Rd.* ☎ *410/226– 5303* ⊕ *www.latitude38.org* ☐ *AE, D, MC, V* ☉ *Closed Mon.*

$$$

★

▦ **Combsberry.** This 1730 brick manor house, together with the carriage house and the Oxford cottage, is set amid magnolias and willows on the banks of Island Creek, a few minutes' drive from Oxford. Inside are five arched fireplaces, floral chintz fabrics, and polished wood floors. All the rooms and suites of this luxurious B&B have water views and are furnished with English manor–style antiques, including four-poster and canopy beds. Some also have hot tubs and working fireplaces; the two-bedroom carriage house has a kitchen. **Pros:** elegantly appointed inn; impeccable service. **Cons:** expensive option, no telephones or televisions in bedrooms. ⊠ *4837 Evergreen Rd.* ☎ *410/226– 5353* ⊕ *combsberryinn.com* ⊅ *2 rooms, 2 suites, 1-bedroom cottage, 2-bedroom carriage house* ⚖ *In-room: no phone, a/c, no TV. In-hotel: restaurant, some pets allowed, no kids under 12* ☐ *AE, MC, V* ⦿ *BP.*

$$

▦ **Robert Morris Inn.** In the early 1700s this building on the banks of the Tred Avon River was crafted as a home by ships' carpenters using ship nails, hand-hewn beams, and pegged paneling. In 1738 it was bought by an English trading company as a house for its Oxford representative, Robert Morris. Four guest rooms have handmade wall paneling and fireplaces built of English bricks used as boat ballast. Other buildings in the complex include a newer manor house on a private beach. Breakfast is included. Several years ago the inn closed its famous restaurant (with its reputed "best crabcakes on the bay"), but in 2010 it reopened, redecorated, and rehabilitated, under celebrity chef Mark Seller, who promotes locally sourced food. The kitchen has regained its former glory. **Pros:** whiffs of history exude from every corner; riverfront setting. **Cons:** three-centuries-old accommodations are difficult to maintain. ✉ *314 N. Morris St.* ☎ *410/226–5111* ⊕ *www.robertmorrisinn.com* ⌨ *35 rooms* ⌂ *In-room: no phone, a/c, no TV (some). In-hotel: restaurant, beachfront, Wi-Fi hotspot, parking (free)* ▭ *AE, MC, V* ⦿ *BP.*

DORCHESTER COUNTY

One of the larger, yet more sparsely populated, counties on Maryland's Eastern Shore, Dorchester retains bits of early America in its picture-postcard towns and waterfront fishing villages. The expansive Choptank River, its northern boundary, and the rambling 28,000-acre Blackwater National Wildlife Refuge are idyllic locales for biking and boating, hiking and camping, and hunting, fishing, and crabbing.

GETTING HERE AND AROUND

Most people get to Dorchester County by car or boat, but **Shore Transit** provides limited route public bus transportation around Dorchester County and the Delmarva Peninsula. An unlimited ride seven-day pass is $25.

ESSENTIALS

Dorchester County Tourism Department (✉ *2 Rose Hill Pl., Cambridge* ☎ *410/228–1000 or 800/522–8687* ⊕ *www.tourdorchester.org*). **Shore Transit** (☎ *410/221–1910* ⊕ *www.shoretransit.org*).

CAMBRIDGE

15 mi southeast of Oxford via U.S. 50, 55 mi southeast of Annapolis via U.S. 50/301 to U.S. 50.

Once upon a time renowned resident Annie Oakley would shoot waterfowl from the ledge of her waterfront home here. Today graceful Georgian, Queen Anne, and Colonial Revival buildings abound, and with an art gallery here and a museum there, a night or two in this county seat can be very refreshing. Cambridge has gained residents—both weekenders from Washington and Baltimore and permanent urban refugees—who have taken advantage of housing prices that are lower than surrounding bay communities. The town's revitalization was slowed by the recent recession, but its fortunes continue on an upward trend. There is a lively scene here, especially on the weekend and events are published in an online newsletter at ⊕ *www.cambridgemainstreet.com.*

GETTING HERE AND AROUND

You may have to do some backtracking to reach Cambridge, but the trip is worth it. Cambridge can only be reached by car and has no public transit within the town. △ **Cambridge's downtown is still undergoing gentrification. Be a little cautious, especially after dark.**

EXPLORING

La Grange Plantation. Headquarters to the Dorchester County Historical Society, this property houses two historic homes. The three-story, 18th-century Georgian **Meredith House** is rich with Chippendale, Hepplewhite, and Sheraton period antiques, and the Children's Room holds an impressive doll collection, cradles, miniature china, and baby carriages. Portraits and effects of seven former Maryland governors from Dorchester County adorn the Governor's Room. In the **Neild Museum** are agricultural, maritime, and Native American artifacts. There's also a restored smokehouse, blacksmith's shop, and medicinal herb garden on the grounds. Fall is ablaze with vibrant leaves and many family activities. ⊠ *902 La Grange Ave.* ☎ *410/228–7953* ⊡ *Free* ⊘ *Weekdays 10–3, and by appointment.*

**OFF THE
BEATEN
PATH**

Old Trinity Church. Seven miles southwest of Cambridge stands this tiny church that was built around 1675. In the churchyard are the graves of four governors of Maryland and several members of the distinguished political and clerical Carroll family. Services are still held here every Sunday at 11. Extensively altered in the 1800s, the church has been restored to its 17th-century appearance. ⊠ *Rte. 16 near Church Creek* ☎ *410/228–2940* ⊕ *www.oldtrinity.net* ⊘ *Tours by appointment.*

WHERE TO EAT AND STAY

$$$

FRENCH

✗ **Bistro Poplar.** Young chef Ian Campbell, formerly of California's French Laundry, returned to his native Cambridge in 2007 to open Bistro Poplar. In the past few years it has been hailed as not only the best restaurant in town but one of the best on the East Coast. Campbell specializes in well-prepared, simple French food. Gourmands rave about his steak frites. The menu changes seasonally so no chance of either the chef or his followers getting bored. A definite must if you travel to this area. ⊠ *535 Poplar St., Cambridge* ☎ *410/228–4884* ⊕ *www.bistropoplar.com* ⊟ *AE, DC, MC, V* ⊘ *Closed Tues. and Wed.*

$$

AMERICAN

✗ **Snappers Waterfront Cafe.** Join regulars at this casual waterside restaurant and bar on the edge of town that has a wide-ranging menu with a Southwestern flavor. Mexican quesadillas are a Snappers specialty, but there is also an array of burritos, enchiladas, and fajitas. Jamaican jerk spices enhance burgers and crab cakes. From waters close to home, there's shrimp, stuffed or simply fried. Sandwiches, wraps, and pasta also satisfy the local lunch crowd. ⊠ *112 Commerce St.* ☎ *410/228–0112* ⊕ *www.snapperswaterfrontcafe.com* ⊟ *AE, D, MC, V.*

$$$

▦ **Hyatt Regency Chesapeake Bay Golf Resort, Spa and Marina.** This 370-acre complex is the Eastern Shore's first full-service, year-round resort, and one that takes full advantage of the soothing natural light and spectacular views of the Choptank River. The resort encompasses an 18-acre Blue Heron rookery, an 18,000-square-foot spa, and a golf course designed by Keith Foster. All rooms and suites have a private balcony; those on the upper level have raised ceilings. The resort's restaurants include the self-service Bay Country Market and the Blue Point Provision Company for seafood. Two outdoor sandstone fireplaces make perfect s'more hubs, and a 30-foot-high wall of windows welcomes you to Michener's Library. **Pros:** features and amenities worthy of any world-class resort; expensive. **Cons:** strangely isolated in a region devoid of comparable lodging; can be overwhelmingly large. ⊠ *100 Heron Blvd.* ☎ *410/901–1234* ⊕ *www.chesapeakebay.hyatt.com* ⊅ *384 rooms, 16 suites* ⌂ *In-room: a/c, safe, refrigerator, Wi-Fi. In-hotel: 5 restaurants, room service, bar, golf course, tennis courts, pool, gym, spa, children's programs (4–12), some pets allowed* ⊟ *AE, D, MC, V.*

$$ ⛱ **Lodgecliffe on the Choptank.** Located on a rise overlooking the river, this elegant turn-of-the-20th-century country home was the first bed-and-breakfast in the county (1986) and remains one of the most charming. Accommodations include the delightfully contemporary second-floor room called Sarah's Loft, named for the original innkeeper. Don't sleep through breakfast or you might miss cranberry French Toast made with sourdough bread, Chesapeake puff pancakes, or phyllo dough egg blossoms, freshly made and hot from the oven and often served out on the screened-in porch. Guests feel like personal guests of the innkeepers and their two young sons. **Pros:** traditional B&B in the truest sense; less expensive option. **Cons:** almost too personalized an enterprise for some. ⊠ *103 Choptank Terr.* ☎ *866/273–3830* ⊕ *www.lodgecliffeonthechoptankbandb.com* ⊅ *4 rooms* ⌂ *In-room: a/c, Wi-Fi. In-hotel: restaurant* ⊟ *AE, D, MC, V.*

$ ⛱ **Mill Street Inn Bed & Breakfast.** Several years ago Skip and Jenny Rideout left their jobs in suburban Washington to open the Mill Street Inn in Cambridge. They bought a house just a half a block from the water and transformed it to a B&B with three guest rooms, one of which is a suite. The rooms—named Edward, Winifred, and the Cambridge Suite—are decorated gaily in bright colors and chintz. The Rideouts get high marks as hosts and they serve guests breakfast as well as a daily high tea. **Pros:** the quintessential personal B&B experience. **Cons:** no in-room Wi-Fi; a little too personal for the guest who wants more anonymity or modern amenities; not suitable for children. ⊠ *114 Mill St., Cambridge* ☎ *410/901–9144* ⊕ *www.millstinn.com* ⊅ *3 rooms* ⌂ *In-room: no phone (some), a/c, DVD (some). In-hotel: Wi-Fi hotspot, parking (free), no kids under 12* ⊟ *AE, D, DC, MC, V* ⧈ BP.

SPORTS AND THE OUTDOORS

All of the land of the **Fishing Bay Wildlife Management Area**, bordering Blackwater National Wildlife Refuge, is along Fishing Bay at the southern end of Dorchester County. Here you can take a pair of "water trails" through some scenic rivers and streams—it's reminiscent of Florida's Everglades. A short canoeing or kayaking trek down one of these water trails—recommended only for experienced paddlers—is an exceptional way to experience a salt marsh and the wildlife that lives in one. Contact the **Dorchester County Department of Tourism** (☎ *410/228–1000* ⊕ *www.tourdorchester.org*) for more information, as well as for a waterproof map.

Rent kayaks and bikes at **Blackwater Paddle & Pedal Adventures** (⊠ *4303 Bucktown Rd.* ☎ *410/901–9255* ⊕ *www.blackwaterpaddleandpedal. com*), which also provides guided instruction.

★ *Nathan of Dorchester.* This skipjack replica, commissioned in 1994, cruises the Choptank River from the foot of High Street in Cambridge. In summer the 28-passenger *Nathan* sets sail on most Saturday evenings and Sunday afternoons for two-hour cruises. ⊠ *Long Wharf, 526 Poplar St.* ☎ *410/228–7141* ⊕ *www.skipjack-nathan.org.*

BLACKWATER NATIONAL WILDLIFE REFUGE

8 mi south of Cambridge via Rte. 16 to Rte. 335, 63 mi southeast of Annapolis.

GETTING HERE AND AROUND

The Blackwater National Wildlife Refuge is just a few miles from Cambridge. Most people drive to the refuge and then drive the 5-mi loop around the park. However, the terrain is very flat and a bicycle is certainly a viable alternative. Fit hikers would find it an easy route as well.

EXPLORING

Blackwater National Wildlife Refuge. The largest nesting bald eagle population north of Florida makes Blackwater its home. You can often see the birds perching on the lifeless tree trunks that poke from the wetlands here, part of nearly 28,000 acres of woods, open water, marsh, and farmland. In fall and spring, some 35,000 Canada and snow geese pass through in their familiar V formations to and from their winter home, joining more than 15,000 ducks. The rest of the year, residents include endangered species such as peregrine falcons and silver-hair Delmarva fox squirrels. Great blue heron stand like sentinels while ospreys dive for meals and tundra swans preen endlessly. By car or bike you can follow a 5-mi road through several habitats or follow a network of trails on foot. Exhibits and films in the visitor center provide background and insight. ⊠ *2145 Key Wallace Dr., at Rte. 335* ☎ *410/228–2677* ⊕ *www. fws.gov/blackwater* 🖃 *$3 car, $1 pedestrian or cyclist* ⊙ *Wildlife drive daily dawn–dusk. Visitor center weekdays 8–4, weekends 9–5.*

OFF THE BEATEN PATH	**East New Market.** Believed to have been first settle on the Choptank Native American trail in the 1660s, the East New Market contains some 75 buildings of historic significance—churches, schools, businesses, and residences—representing three centuries. In this living museum of architecture, every exhibit is in its original location. An illustrated walking-tour map is available from the Dorchester County Tourism office (☎ *410/228–1000*).

THE LOWER EASTERN SHORE

The three counties of Maryland's Lower Eastern Shore—Wicomico, Worcester, and Somerset—contain the contrasting cultures of the Chesapeake Bay and the Atlantic coast but still share a common history.

The Nanticoke River flows out of southern Delaware across fertile farmland between Dorchester and Wicomico counties into the Chesapeake

Bay's Tangier Sound near the Blackwater National Wildlife Refuge. To the east the Atlantic alternately caresses and pounds Worcester County's sturdy shorelines and fragile barrier islands stretching from the Delaware Bay to easternmost Virginia. Somerset County, comprising the Eastern Shore's southeastern corner, includes a few communities clinging to the shoreline of Tangier Sound among sprawling Wildlife Management Areas and an island State Park.

The Main Street shops, early-American inns, and unsung restaurants of the small towns in this region seem a century removed from the boutiques and galleries, high-rise hotels and condos, myriad eateries, and nightlife of nearby Ocean City.

SALISBURY

32 mi southeast of Cambridge via U.S. 50, 87 mi southeast of Annapolis via U.S. 50/301 to U.S. 50.

Barges still ply the slow-moving Wicomico River between the Bay and Salisbury, the Eastern Shore's second-largest port after Baltimore. This urban center is a hub of commercial activity in the region and the home of Salisbury University, but its leisure options pale compared to the excitement of nearby Ocean City. The tree-shaded waterfront draws bikers and shoppers. Antiques shops and galleries, along with some exemplary Victorian architecture, fill its downtown six blocks.

GETTING HERE AND AROUND

The Salisbury-Ocean City Wicomico Regional Airport is the only airport with scheduled airline service on the Delmarva Peninsula and therefore is the hub of air transportation for the entire region. Once you arrive in Salisbury, walking the six-block downtown makes a pleasant afternoon.

EXPLORING

★ **Ward Museum of Wildfowl Art.** Operated in partnership with Salisbury University, the Ward Museum of Wildfowl Art presents realistic marshland and wildfowl displays. Two brothers from Crisfield, Lem and Steve Ward, helped transform decoy making from just a utilitarian pursuit to an art form; their re-created studio is a must-see exhibit. Besides the premier collection of wildfowl art, the 30,000-square-foot museum has some 2,000 other artifacts as well as a gift shop and library. ⊠ *909 S. Schumaker Dr.* ☎ *410/742–4988* ⊕ *www.wardmuseum.org* ✉ *$7* ☾ *Mon.–Sat. 10–5, Sun. noon–5.*

WHERE TO EAT

$$ ✕ **The Red Roost.** Inside a former chicken barn about 15 mi from Salis-
AMERICAN   bury, inverted bushel baskets now serve as light fixtures at this down-home crab house, where hammering mallets rival the beat of piano and banjo sing-alongs. The Red Roost gets rave reviews for its seafood specialties and ribs, as well as its meaty steamed crabs. ⊠ *Rtes. 352 and 362, Whitehaven* ☎ *410/546–5443 or 800/953–5443* ⊕ *www.theredroost.com* ☐ *AE, MC, V* ☾ *Closed Nov.–Mar. and Mon. and Tues. Labor Day–Memorial Day. No lunch.*

EN
ROUTE
Delmarva Discovery. Opened in 2009, this modern structure on the banks of the Pocomoke River delivers hands-on experiences of the region's history. Exhibits focus on the work- and lifestyles of indigenous communities and early settlers, on local wildlife, and on the river as a fishing and shipbuilding industry hub and a major port for Chesapeake Bay steamers during the 19th century. The center's aquarium has a 6,000-gallon tank containing fish found in the Pocomoke River. ✉ *2 Market St. (BR 13 at Riverside Dr.), Pocomoke* ☎ *410/957–9933* ⊕ *www.delmarvadiscoverycenter.org* 🖾 *$10* ۞ *Wed.–Sat. 10–4, Sun. 12–4.*

SNOW HILL

19 mi southeast of Salisbury via Rte. 12, 106 mi southeast of Annapolis.

The streets of Snow Hill, the Worcester County seat, are lined with huge sycamores and stately homes that reflect its days as a shipping center in the 18th and 19th centuries. Today's visitors are often drawn to kayak on the Pocomoke River.

GETTING HERE AND AROUND

Snow Hill is only accessible by car, but once you are there you have several low-tech choices: bike its quiet streets, take a walking tour of its residential neighborhoods with their stately clapboard homes, stroll through the small but quaint downtown, or rent a canoe and glide along the Pocomoke River.

WHERE TO STAY

$$ 🏠 **River House.** With its welcoming icon, the prancing carousel horse on the front porch, this Victorian home and its adjacent cottages are on two lovely acres on the banks of the Pocomoke River. This small inn, on the National Register, is impeccably appointed and maintained, including the lovely gardens. Decor is traditional Early American. A free day of canoeing is offered with any stay of two nights or more, courtesy of the Pocomoke River Canoe Company (⇨ *see Sports and the Outdoors*). **Pros:** relaxing riverside setting; attractive for paddlers; complimentary breakfast. **Cons:** may be too quiet for some. ✉ *201 E. Market St.* ☎ *410/632–2722* ⊕ *www.riverhouseinn.com* 🛏 *2 private cottages, 2 rooms* ⌂ *In-room: no phone, a/c, refrigerator. In-hotel: pool, bicycles, some pets allowed* ⊟ *AE, D, MC, V* ۞ *Closed Dec.–Feb.*

SPORTS AND THE OUTDOORS
CANOEING

Pocomoke River Canoe Company (✉ *312 N. Washington St., Snow Hill* ☎ *410/632–3971* ⊕ *www.atbeach.com/amuse/md/canoe*) rents canoes, offers lessons, and leads tours along the Pocomoke River, a habitat for bald eagles, blue herons, and egrets.

BERLIN

15 mi northeast of Snow Hill via Rte. 113, 22 mi east of Salisbury via U.S. 50; 7 mi west of Ocean City via U.S. 50.

Berlin—named not for the German city, but evolving from Burleigh Inn, a Colonial-era way station—is a short drive from Ocean City, yet it could not be more different. Magnolias, sycamores, and ginkgo trees line streets filled with predominantly Federal- and Victorian-style buildings, of which 47 are on the National Register of Historic Places.

Berlin still clings to its now decade-long claim to fame as the principal location for the filming of *Runaway Bride,* in which several of the town's shops were featured along with the bride's home and half the residents "starred" as extras.

PADDLING INN-TO-INN

You can canoe miles of pristine woodland in the Bald Cypress tidal river on an **inn-to-inn tour** (☎ 410/632–2722 ⊕ www.inntours.com) arranged by the River House B&B. After a full breakfast at a participating inn, you spend the day drifting past waterside homes, hidden landings, and abundant wildlife. Have a picnic lunch on a quiet bank or in a riverside park. Dinner awaits at your next overnight inn; then continue on for a second day (luggage transfers are included).

A delightful short-visit destination onto itself, Berlin is also a great break from the hoopla of Ocean City, particularly when inclement weather precludes beach time.

Viewtrail 100, a marked 100-mi biking circuit, runs along less-traveled secondary roads between Berlin and Pocomoke City. For a brochure and map, contact the Worcester County Tourism Office.

GETTING HERE AND AROUND

Berlin is easily accessible from Ocean City by car. Once you arrive, park and walk around the charming downtown. A self-guided walking tour of Berlin, including a cup of coffee in one of its cafés, should take about an hour.

WHERE TO EAT AND STAY

$ ✕ **The Globe.** Housed inside a brilliantly converted theater, with its stage
ECLECTIC   area is retained and periodically used for a variety of presentations, this eclectic eatery is well worth a meal, from vegetable risotto and jerk pork plate to, of course, crab cakes. Allow some extra time to wander the upper-level art gallery, its works all for sale. And you might luck into one of the periodic screenings of *Runaway Bride.* Sunday brunch and weekend dinners are popular with locals. On the weekends the stage has live entertainment. ✉ *12 Broad St., Historic District* ☎ 410/641–0784 ⊕ *www.globetheater.com* ▭ *AE, MC, V.*

$ ⊞ **Atlantic Hotel.** This fully restored 1895 inn blends the taste of grand
★   living with modern conveniences. Spacious, hardwood-floor guest rooms all offer four-poster beds. The second-floor parlor, done in bold red-and-green hues with ornate furnishings, is a perfect place to escape with a fat book or a stack of magazines. The curved entry drive has

been closed to vehicles and landscaped into a delightful people-watching alfresco lobby. Beneath sparkling chandeliers, the The Drummer's Café ($$$) serves scrumptious entrées that may include crab cakes, rack of New Zealand lamb, and Grandma's Twin Chicken. **Pros:** excellent in-house restaurant; historic inn with modern updates. **Cons:** style may be too formal for some. ⊠ *2 N. Main St., Historic District* ☎ *410/641–3589 or 800/814–7672* ⊕ *www.atlantichotel.com* ⏎ *18 rooms* ⌂ *In-room: a/c, Wi-Fi. In-hotel: restaurant, no kids under 4* ▤ *AE, MC, V.*

OCEAN CITY

7 mi east of Berlin and 29 mi east of Salisbury via U.S. 50.

Stretching some 10 mi along a narrow barrier island off Maryland's Atlantic coast, Worcester County's Ocean City draws millions from neighboring states (New Jersey, Pennsylvania, Virginia, and Delaware) and the District of Columbia virtually year-round to its broad beaches and the innumerable activities and amenities that cling to them, as well as to the quiet bay side between the island and the mainland. "O.C." is a premier mid-Atlantic leisure travel destination, at once big and small, sprawling and congested, old and new, historic and hip, noisy and quiet, sophisticated and tacky, expensive and not, and everything in between.

The town grew into a city south to north. On the older, southern end of the island a restored 19th-century carousel and other traditional amusement park rides churn near a long fishing pier along the inlet connecting the Atlantic and Assawoman Bay. On the opposite side of the inlet is the northern tip of the pristine 37-mi-long Assateague Island, federally and state-protected lands devoid of man-made elements beyond the most rudimentary.

From this southern end, O.C.'s renowned and brilliantly maintained 3-mi-long boardwalk reaches northward as far as 27th Street, nothing but sand to one side, everything else—hotels and eateries and shops—crowding every available square inch lining the other. Beyond 27th Street, the cross streets climb to 145th at the Delaware state line. High-rise condominium complexes prevail farther to the north, interspersed with more hotels and shopping complexes. While it seems a little less hectic toward O.C.'s northern end, beaches are not necessarily less crowded, depending on the season and on the presence of condominium residents. The western side, along the Bay, tends to be made up of smaller enterprises, including cruise and fishing-boat firms.

GETTING HERE AND AROUND

You can avoid the aggravation of driving in often heavy traffic by taking **The Bus,** which travels the 10-mi-long Coastal Highway 24 hours a day in its own lane. Service is about every 10 minutes from bus stops located every other block. A $2 ticket is good for 24 hours. A park-and-ride facility on the mainland—on Route 50 just west of Ocean City—has free parking for some 700 vehicles. It's on the bus route. A walking map of Ocean City's historic sites is available at its Visitor Information Center. In addition to The Bus there is a continuous loop **Ocean City Trolley** that has both a boardwalk and a downtown route. One-way fare is $2.50 and an all-day, unlimited ride ticket is $3.50.

TIMING AND PRECAUTIONS

A year-round destination, Ocean City is particularly appealing in fall and spring, when the weather is mild. Most hotels and better restaurants remain open year-round, although the latter may operate on fewer days and/or shorter schedules. Furthermore, many festivals and other special events are scheduled for the off-season. Weekend traffic to and from Ocean City on U.S. 50 and MD 404 can be exceptionally heavy, not only during summertime months but often from late spring into early fall as well.

⚠ Don't underestimate the force of the currents off the Delmarva Peninsula. Every year unfortunate swimmers are caught in the dangerous riptide.

ESSENTIALS

Bus and Trolley Contacts **The Bus** (☎ 410/723–1607). **Ocean City Trolley** (⊕ www.gatrolley.com/h_fm1-ocean-city.html).

Taxi Contacts **Light Up Your Night** (☎ 410/289–9700). **Sunshine Cab** (☎ 410/208–2828).

Visitor Information **Ocean City Department of Tourism** (✉ 4001 Coastal Hwy., at 41st St., Ocean City ☎ 410/289–2800 or 800/626–2326 ⊕ www. ococean.com).

EXPLORING

○ **Dumser's Dairyland.** Jacob Fussell began a wholesale ice-cream business in Baltimore in 1851, the first in the United States. Today privately owned and operated ice-cream parlors abound along Maryland's Eastern Shore, but Dumser's Dairyland, established in 1939, is the choice for longtime beachgoers; its vast "factory" and parlor are open from noon to midnight in the summertime. In addition to its main South Atlantic Avenue outfit, it also operates branch locations at 49th Street and Coastal and 124th Street and Coastal, as well as three smaller outlets on the boardwalk. ✉ 601 S. Atlantic Ave. ☎ 410/524–1588 ⊕ www. beach-net.com/dumsers.

★ **Ocean City Life Saving Station Museum.** This attraction on the southernmost tip of the island traces the resort to its days as a tiny fishing village in the late 1800s. Housed in an 1891 building that once held the U.S. Lifesaving Service and the Coast Guard, the museum's exhibits include models of the grand old hotels, artifacts from shipwrecks, boat models, five saltwater aquariums, an exhibit of sands from around the world, and even itchy wool swimsuits and an old mechanical laughing lady from the boardwalk. Press the button, and you can be laughing with her. ✉ Boardwalk at inlet ☎ 410/289–4991 ⊕ www.ocmuseum.org ☞ $3 ⊙ June–Sept., daily 11–10; May and Oct., daily 11–4; Nov.–Apr., weekends 10–4.

○ **Trimper's Amusement Park.** At the south end of the boardwalk, this thrill center has a "boomerang" roller coaster; the rickety and terrifying "Zipper" wood coaster; and the Hirschell Spellman Carousel, from 1902. The park has been owned by the Trimper family since it opened in 1890. ✉ Boardwalk at S. 1st St. ☎ 410/289–8617 ☞ Pay per ride or attraction ⊙ Memorial Day–Labor Day, weekdays 1 pm–midnight, *weekends noon–midnight. Labor Day–Memorial Day indoor portion only, weekends noon–midnight.*

WHERE TO EAT

"Fresh catch" is the magic phrase, but note that this is the one area of Maryland's and Virginia's Eastern Shore region in which crab is not king. Many diners like to time their meals with the view: don't forget that the sun rises over the Atlantic and sets behind Assawoman Bay.

■TIP→ Eating hard-shell crabs is an art. Novices can find step-by-step instructions and a helpful video at 🌐 *www.atlanticbreezes.com/crabpicking.htm.*

$$ AMERICAN ★ ✕ **Fager's Island.** This fine-dining restaurant, adjacent to and operated by the same owners as the Lighthouse Club and the Edge hotels, gives you white-linen treatment and views of soothing wetlands and the Bay, and stunning sunsets through its large windows. In addition to ubiquitous fresh-catch seafood, Fager's is renowned for its prime rib. There's an outside deck for more informal dining and a raw bar with lighter fare. **■TIP→ Tchaikovsky's *1812 Overture* is played every evening, with the tumultuous finale timed to coincide with the setting of the sun.** ✉ *60th St. at Bay* ☎ *410/524–5500* 🌐 *www.fagers.com/restaurant* ♨ *Reservations essential* ▭ *AE, D, DC, MC, V.*

$$ SEAFOOD ✕ **Fish Tales Bar and Grill.** When the children need a break from the standard boardwalk fare, take 'em to this incredibly family-friendly restaurant, where children are part of the action. Youngsters can play on an awesome pirate ship or on the soft beach with the Frisbee that comes with their meals. The food is as easygoing as the atmosphere, from a fried chicken and barbecued ribs combo to skewered surf and turf. There's also a slew of economical offerings "From the Dock" and "From the Farm," as well as an extensive menu for "L'il Skippers," like pizza and mac and cheese. At night, a bit of a rowdy (yet civilized) older bar crowd likes to congregate on the waterfront benches. ✉ *2207 Herring Way* ☎ *410/289–7438* 🌐 *www.ocfishtales.com* ▭ *AE, D, DC, MC, V.*

$$$ AMERICAN ✕ **Galaxy 66 Bar & Grill.** This unusual watering hole is a welcome breeze of creative cuisine. Appetizers are light and delicate, like seared foie gras and asparagus shrimp risotto. Equally innovative mains include homemade manchego cheese gnocchi, seared duck with sun-dried cherries, and a pistachio-encrusted rockfish. The second and third floors open up to outdoor seating and views of the Bay. The cosmic Star Bar is a hot spot for local celebs and those looking for creative cocktails in a dark hideaway—and it serves tapas until midnight. ✉ *66th St. at Bay* ☎ *410/723–6272* 🌐 *www.galaxy66barandgrille.com* ▭ *AE, D, DC, MC, V.*

$$$ SEAFOOD ✕ **Phillips Crab House & Seafood Buffet.** Feast on crab cakes, crab imperial, or stuffed and fried shrimp at the 1956 home of an O.C. institution that is the original of three Phillips locations here and has since grown into a regional chain (✉ Phillips By the Sea *1301 Atlantic Ave.* ✉ Phillips Seafood House *14101 Coastal Hwy.*). Considered the city's most popular dining site, the restaurant has a dark-panel dining area with decorative stone floors, Tiffany-style hanging lamps, stained-glass windows, and funky wall art. Expect big crowds in the summer months. Its seafood buffet is served in an upstairs dining room. ✉ *21st St. at Philadelphia*

Ave. ☎ *410/289–6821 or 800/549–2722* ⊕ *www.phillipsseafood.com* ⊟ *AE, D, MC, V.*

$$ ✕ **The Shark on the Harbor.** Don't let the name scare you: The namesake
SEAFOOD shark is meant to be your dinner, prepared any way you like. This off-the-beaten-path place in West Ocean City is worth the trek and takes advantage of every bay view, including from the sweeping rooftop bar. Dishes experiment with unusual flavors like the tuna with wasabi-cream sauce and pineapple meringue. Go for the Eggplant Tower stuffed with layers of shrimp, lump crab, and wild mushrooms with fresh-shaved Parmesan. Entrées are $5 from 3 pm to 5 pm, and a live jazz band plays on Thursday nights. ⊠ *12924 Sunset Ave., West Ocean City* ☎ *410/213–0924* ⊕ *www.ocshark.com* ⊟ *AE, D, DC, MC, V.*

WHERE TO STAY

Ocean City's narrow barrier island means that no lodging is far from either the ocean or the Bay. Rates vary dramatically through the year, the lowest typically between mid-November and mid-March, and the highest during July and August. Ocean-view rooms are always considered premium.

$ ☷ **Atlantic Hotel.** Family-owned and -operated since 1923, the three-story, H-shaped frame hotel—Ocean City's oldest—is a replacement of the original Victorian hotel, opened on July 4, 1875, that was destroyed as part of the Great Ocean City fire of 1925. The present structure was quickly rebuilt by 1926, its rooms today plainly furnished and decorated just as they were originally, but now with modern comforts, such as private baths and air-conditioning throughout. A rooftop deck affords truly panoramic views over the ocean and the Bay. **Pros:** ocean side; classic vacationing spot. **Cons:** in a noisy area. ⊠ *Boardwalk at Wicomico St.* ☎ *800/328–5268 or 410/289–9111* ⊕ *www.atlantichotelocmd. com* ➥ *90 rooms* ♿ *In-room: a/c, Wi-Fi. In-hotel: pool, parking (free)* ⊟ *MC, V* ☯ *Closed Oct.–Apr.*

$ ☷ **Castle in the Sand Hotel.** This compound of castles is a popular family
♧ destination for its sheer amount of kid-friendly amenities. "Castle Kid" activities include tales of pirates and ghosts of Assateague Island told by Captain J. one night a week in summer, and Lady Sunshine is on hand to pamper young princesses. All rooms are basic, with pastel walls and random, motel-esque furniture. But all are oceanfront, looking onto a wide swath of beach, with some overlooking the largest pool in Ocean City. Two off-site cottages a block away provide a cozy home-away-from-home atmosphere. **Pros:** ideal for families with younger children; oceanfront location. **Cons:** simple rooms; "kid-friendly" focus not for everyone. ⊠ *3701 Atlantic Ave.* ☎ *410/289–6846 or 800/552–7263* ⊕ *www.castleinthesand.com* ➥ *179 rooms* ♿ *In-room: a/c, kitchen (some), refrigerator. In-hotel: restaurant, bar, pool, beachfront, parking (free)* ⊟ *AE, D, DC, MC, V.*

$$$ ☷ **The Lankford Hotel & Apartments.** Opened in 1924, the Lankford is still owned by the family of the original owners. Many combinations of rooms in the hotel and the adjacent lodge are available for small groups of friends and families. Bicycle storage and Ocean City Golf Course privileges are included in the rate. Lazing in a rickety rocking chair on the front porch off the small (un-air-conditioned) lobby,

cooled by overhead fans, is a true throwback to quieter times. (All guest rooms are air-conditioned.) Pros: good for groups; a genuine aura of classic seashore vacations; weekly rates are available. Cons: small in size; little privacy from boardwalk and beachfront activity; no a/c in the lobby. ⊠ *8th St. at boardwalk* ☎ *410/289–4041; 800/282–9709 late May–Sept.; 410/289–4667 Oct.–late May* ⊕ *www.lankfordhotel.com* ⌨ *23 rooms, 28 suites* ⌂ *In-room: a/c. In-hotel: beachfront, laundry facilities, Wi-Fi hotspot, parking (free)* ▭ *No credit cards* ☺ *Closed Columbus Day–Apr.*

$$$ ⊡ **Lighthouse Club Hotel.** This elegant boutique hotel is a Chesapeake Bay
★ lighthouse lookalike of quiet luxury, just blocks from the busy Coastal Highway. Its airy, contemporary suites have high ceilings and views of sand dunes that slope to Assawoman Bay. Suites have white-cushion rattan furniture and marble bathrooms, some with two-person hot tubs, and the allure of wet bars and fireplaces. Sliding glass doors lead to private decks with steamer chairs. Pros: comfortably luxurious; quiet bay-side location; Continental breakfast. Cons: pricey in high season; not beachfront. ⊠ *56th St. at Bay* ☎ *410/524–5400 or 888/371–5400* ⊕ *www.fagers.com* ⌨ *23 suites* ⌂ *In-room: a/c, refrigerator, Wi-Fi. In-room: restaurant, bar, pool* ▭ *AE, D, DC, MC, V* ⧖ *BP.*

$$$ ⊡ **Park Place.** Filling a need for more affordable, family- and child-
☺ friendly accommodations, this small, multistory hotel on the boardwalk is owned and operated by a family with over a century of experience. All rooms are efficiencies with fully equipped kitchenettes and sofa beds. Some have extra-long beds and hot tubs. Conner's Beach Café, a full-service restaurant, and Conner's Sail Loft Deck Bar, a beach-side bar and restaurant, are part of the complex. Pros: prime location for lower OC activities; on the boardwalk; some rooms have ocean views. Cons: "family-friendly" features not for everyone. ⊠ *2nd and 3rd Sts. at boardwalk* ☎ *410/289–6440 or 888/212–7275* ⊕ *www. ocparkplacehotel.com* ⌨ *89 rooms* ⌂ *In-room: a/c, kitchen, refrigerator, Wi-Fi. In-hotel: restaurant, bar, pool, beachfront, parking (free)* ▭ *AE, D, MC, V.*

NIGHTLIFE AND THE ARTS

In summer Ocean City provides enough entertainment for everyone, ranging from refined to rowdy. Some bars and clubs close in midwinter, but most of those with live music remain open year-round.

BARS

Open since 1976, the large sports saloon known as the **Greene Turtle** (⊠ *Coastal Hwy. at 116th St.* ☎ *410/723–2120*) is a beach landmark and a must for casual drinks to soothe the afterburn. The waterside **Seacrets Bar and Grill** (⊠ *117 49th St.* ☎ *410/524–4900*) often presents four live bands at four different entertainment venues. The crowds run in age from those in their early 20s on through baby boomers, proving that you're never too old to sip a piña colada while on an inner tube.

DANCE CLUBS

The huge **Bonfire Restaurant & Nightclub** (⊠ *71st St. at Ocean Hwy.* ☎ *410/524–7171*) serves an all-you-can-eat buffet and an à la carte menu. It caters to thirties-and-over diners enjoying the live Top 40 music played by local groups. It's closed Monday–Thursday mid-October–mid-March. One of the most versatile complexes for twenty-one-plus-somethings, the **Party Block** (✉ *Coastal Hwy. at 17th St.* ☎ *410/289–6331*) encompasses a handful of somewhat raunchy yet crazy-popular nightclub venues: **Big Kahuna**, a DJ-driven "party place"; the **Paddock,** pumping out heart-thumping recorded and live music with a bit more volume and flash; and **Rush,** a Miami-style dance club for a well-dressed clientele.

SPORTS AND THE OUTDOORS

Although Ocean City is primarily a beach resort, there are ample outdoor activities beyond bathing and tanning—from fishing, powerboating, and sailing to kiteboarding, parasailing, and jet-skiing, as well as the more peaceful pursuits of kayaking and canoeing (ideal in the gentle Bay wetlands). On-land fun includes biking, tennis, volleyball, and (especially) golf. For many of the area's sports, classes are offered for first-timers.

BICYCLING

A portion of Coastal Highway has been designated for bus and bicycle traffic. Bicycle riding is allowed on the Ocean City boardwalk from 5 am to 10 am in summer and 5 am to 4 pm the rest of the year. The bike route from Ocean City to Assateague Island, to the south (U.S. 50 to Route 611), is a 9-mi trek, and Assateague itself is crisscrossed by a number of clearly marked, paved trails.

FISHING

No fishing licenses are required in Ocean City. Public fishing piers on the Assawoman Bay and Isle of Wight Bay are at (south to north) 3rd, 9th, 40th, and 125th streets and at the inlet in Ocean City. Other fishing and crabbing areas include the U.S. 50 bridge, Oceanic Pier, and Ocean City Pier, at Wicomico Street and the boardwalk. Crabbing is especially good at Northside Park.

Bahia Marina (✉ *21st St. at Bay* ☎ *410/289–7438 or 888/575–3625* ⊕ *www.bahiamarina.com*) is a great venue for sportfishing enthusiasts. It has spotless charter boats, live bait and tackle, and opportunities for bottom fishing. **Ocean City Fishing Center** (✉ *U.S. 50 at Shantytown Rd., West Ocean City* ☎ *410/213–1121* ⊕ *www.ocfishing.com*) is Ocean City's largest deep-sea charter-boat marina, with some 30 vessels and Coast Guard–licensed professional captains. In addition to catering to preformed groups, the Fishing Center will form fishing groups of individuals who are on their own.

GOLF

Now rivaling premier golfing destinations around the United States, Ocean City is within easy driving distance of more than 21 golf courses. The Web site **Ocean City Golf Getaway** (⊕ *www.oceancitygolf.com*) provides thorough information about courses.

SHOPPING

Ocean City's 3-mi-long boardwalk is lined with retail outlets for food, souvenirs, more food, and more souvenirs, with a smattering of surprising specialty stores. Side streets are filled with still more shops, as are the avenues parallel to the beachfront in the older, southern end of the island. Farther north, the atmosphere changes; the beaches a block away become almost incidental. Shopping plazas—several composed of factory outlets—vie for attention behind acres of parking.

🗱 **The Kite Loft** (✉ *11 Boardwalk Ave.* ☎ *410/289–6852* ✉ *45th Street Village* ☎ *410/524–0800* ✉ *Coastal Hwy. at 131st St.* ☎ *410/250–4970*), with its dazzling line of kites as well as banners, flags, wind socks, hammocks, sky chairs, whirligigs, and wind chimes, is more than just a store. It's symbolic of Ocean City: the kites, thriving on the ocean-side winds and flying high over the boardwalk all day long, and visible for long distances, are an iconic welcome to the beachfront.

ASSATEAGUE ISLAND

11 mi south of Ocean City.

GETTING HERE AND AROUND
The only way to reach Assategue Island is by car or bicycle. However, once you are there the best way to explore it is by canoe or kayak.

EXPLORING
Fodor'sChoice **Assateague Island.** The Assateague Island National Seashore, estab-
★ lished in 1962, occupies the northern two-thirds of a 37-mi-long barrier island, encompassing a small portion operated as Assateague State Park. ("Assateague" means "a marshy place across.") Although most famous for the small, shaggy, wild horses (adamantly called "ponies" by the public) that roam freely along the beaches and roads, this stunning island is also worth getting to know for its wildland, wildlife (including the beautiful sika deer), and for simply enjoying a pristine ocean-side environment. In summer the seashore's mild surf is where you can find shorebirds tracing the lapping waves back down the beach. There are three self-guided nature trails behind the dunes that encourage exploration of the island's forests and bay-side marshes.

Driving is permitted the length of—and several miles south of—the state park. Appropriate off-road vehicles with special permits may drive the length of the National Seashore as far as the Maryland-Virginia line. Remember that the animals here are wild, and follow the signs about not feeding or trying to pet the horses (or ponies).

Swimming, biking, hiking, surf fishing, picnicking, and camping are all available on the island. The visitor center at the entrance to the park has aquariums and hands-on exhibits about the seashore's birds and ocean creatures as well as the famous ponies. ✉ *7206 National Seashore La., Rte. 611, south of Ocean City, southeastern extremity of Rte. 611* ☎ *410/641–1441* ⊕ *www.assateagueisland.com* 🎫 *7-day pass MD/VA section $3–$10 per vehicle; no fee for bicycles or pedestrians* ⊙ *Visitor center daily 9–5, park daily 24 hrs.*

CRISFIELD

33 mi southwest of Salisbury via U.S. 13 to Rte. 413.

In William W. Warner's study of the Chesapeake Bay, *Beautiful Swimmers,* Crisfield was described as a "town built upon oyster shells, millions of tons of it. A town created by and for the blue crab, Cradle of the Chesapeake seafood industries, where everything was tried first." Unfortunately, visitors can see the creeping hand of development changing the face of this charming, end-of-the-road town with the sprawling condominium complex at the end of Main Street. Workers at the bustling seafood processing plants here—down to just three from more than 150—pick crabs and shuck oysters by hand, just as those plying the trade here more than a century ago did.

GETTING HERE AND AROUND

It is easy to walk around town. If you want to explore, take a guided tour with the visitor's center. Crisfield is also where you can board a ferry to Smith Island.

EXPLORING

J. Millard Tawes Museum & Visitor's Center. There is not a lot to do in town, but to learn about its history, stop by this center operated by the Crisfield Heritage Foundation. Guided tours of Crisfield are run from here; from May through October the tours include a visit to a crab processing plant. ⊠ *3 9th St.* ⊙ *Weekdays 9 am–3 pm; Sat. 9 am–4 pm* ☎ *410/968–2501* ⊕ *www.crisfieldheritagefoundation.org.*

Smith Island Sweet Shoppe. Don't skip the area's nationally known cakes—stacked eight to 10 layers high and frosted—and recently designated Maryland's state cake by lawmakers. (They can be purchased in person or online.) ⊠ *41 W. Main St.* ☎ *410/968–2200* ⊕ *www. smithislandcakes.net.*

SHOPPING

The **Ice Cream Gallery** (⊠ *5 Goodsell Alley* ☎ *410/968–0809*), a seasonally store, is a sweets emporium that doubles as a crafts outlet for local artisans. From here there's a pleasant view out over the Bay.

SMITH ISLAND

12 mi west of Crisfield by boat.

Chesapeake Bay's Smith Island has an intriguing heritage dating back more than three centuries. The residents are descendents of late-17th-century English settlers who made a living coaxing creatures from the Chesapeake Bay. They speak with a charmingly distinct accent, echoing the speech patterns of their forebears, among the earliest Europeans to have ventured across the Atlantic.

The tiny island's three villages (Tylerton, Ewell, and Rhodes Point) are fiercely independent, made up of simple homes, churches, and a few stores; and they remain reachable only by boat and fairly remote (cable TV didn't arrive here until 1994). A midday visit by passenger ferry allows ample time for a stroll around the island and a leisurely meal overlooking watermen's shanties and workboats.

GETTING HERE AND AROUND

The island is readily accessible by ferry from Crisfield. The air-conditioned Smith Island Cruises leave Crisfield's Somers Cove Marina for the 60-minute trip to Smith Island (ferry docks are at Tylerton and Ewell; one ferry runs to both and one runs just to Ewell) at 12:30 pm daily, returning at 4 pm, from Memorial Day to mid-October. Another way to get to Smith Island is via the mail boat, *Island Belle*. There are two departures daily (12:30 and 5 pm). Two freight boats, *Captain Jason I* and *Captain Jason II*, also take passengers to Smith Island. All three boats (including the above-mentioned *Island Belle*) depart daily at 12:30 pm and return to Crisfield at 5:15 pm, year-round, weather permitting. You can ride back to Smith Island later in the evening; both captains live on the island.

ESSENTIALS
Ferry Services *Captain Jason I & II* (☎ 410/425–4471 ⚓ $22 round-trip). *Island Belle* (☎ 410/968–1118 ⚓ $22 round-trip). **Smith Island Cruises** ✉ 4065 Smith Island Rd., Crisfield ☎ 410/425–2771 ⊕ www.smithislandcruises. com ⚓ $25 round-trip.

EXPLORING
Weather permitting—and, mid-winter excepted, it usually does—exploring the creeks and inlets of Smith Island (actually a mini-archipelago) by canoe or kayak is truly memorable. See ⊕ *www.paddlesmithisland. com* for photos and detailed information—including a map—on exploring by water. Waterproof copies of *Smith Island Water Trails Paddlers Guide* are available from ✎ *dlitedirector@comcast.net*. For town information, see also ⊕ *www.visitsmithisland.com*.

Smith Island Crabmeat Co-op Inc. Started in 1996 by 12 gutsy Smith Island women, this co-op produces the finest, shell-less-quality crabmeat, with all proceeds going straight back to the women and their families. Visitors can drop by and see the lightning-fast pickers at work. Don't forget to pick up a pound before you leave, and ask Janice (the founder and president) about her secret crab-cake ingredient. ✉ *21128 Wharf St., Tylerton* ☎ *410/968–1344* ⊕ *wwwcrabs.maryland.com*.

Stop by **Ruke's** (☎ *410/425–2311*), a venerable general store across from the ferry dock that serves excellent fresh seafood.

WHERE TO STAY
An overnight on Smith Island gives new meaning to the term "getaway." Your neighbors include more egrets, heron, osprey, and pelicans than people.

Inn of Silent Music. Located in a town that's separated by water from the other two villages on Smith Island, this remote English cottage–style inn takes its soothing name from a phrase in a poem by the mystic St. John of the Cross, a Carmelite monk. The rooms are small with antique linens and big windows. Tylerton has no restaurants, but, for an extra charge, the eclectic innkeepers will cook a fresh seafood dinner for guests. **Pros:** on the quietest end of a very quiet island. **Cons:** location can be vulnerable to the whims of Chesapeake weather patterns; no restaurants in town. ✉ *2955 Tylerton Rd., Tylerton* ☎ *410/425–3541* ⊕ *www.innofsilentmusic.com* ⚑ *3 rooms* ⚐ *In-room: no phone, a/c, no TV. In-hotel: restaurant, bicycles, no kids under 12* ☐ *No credit cards* ☾ *Closed mid-Nov.–early Mar.* ⦿*BP*.

Travel Smart Virginia and Maryland

WORD OF MOUTH

"What is the cheapest way from one [D.C.] airport to the other?"

—karamia

"From National Airport take the blue line metro (right at the airport) to the Rosslyn metro stop. From there transfer to the 5A bus which will go to IAD. Time wise this will take between 1–1.5 hours. Depending upon whether u go during rush hour or non rush hours fare will range between $4.05 and $4.50. You can look at the Metro/Bus Web site to see times and exact fares."

—yestravel

GETTING HERE AND AROUND

▌ AIR TRAVEL

Flying time to Baltimore-Washington International (BWI) Airport is just over one hour from New York; approximately two hours from Chicago, and five hours from Los Angeles. Flying time to Richmond International Airport is approximately 1½ hours from New York, 2 hours from Chicago, and 7 to 9 hours from Los Angeles (because there are no nonstop flights). A flight to D.C. is a little more than an hour from New York, about two hours from Chicago, and five hours from San Francisco. Those flying from London can expect a trip of about six hours. A trip from Sydney takes about 20 hours.

Flying into BWI Airport could save money; airlines, including Southwest, often have good deals to this airport. Good sales can sometimes be found to Dulles and occasionally to Reagan National. Fares into Richmond International are sometimes more expensive.

Airlines and Airports Airline and Airport Links.com (⊕ www.airlineandairportlinks.com) has links to many of the world's airlines and airports.

Airline Security Issues Transportation Security Administration (⊕ www.tsa.gov) has answers for almost every question that might come up.

AIRPORTS

Virginia has Richmond International Airport (RIC), 10 mi east of Richmond; the busy Ronald Reagan Washington National Airport (DCA), 3 mi south of downtown Washington; and Washington Dulles International Airport (IAD), 26 mi northwest of Washington. There is considerable service nationwide into and out of Norfolk (ORF) and even Newport News (aka Patrick Henry, PHF). Maryland's Baltimore-Washington Thurgood Marshall International Airport (BWI) is about 25 mi northeast of Washington and

10 mi south of Baltimore. Amtrak and commuter trains stop at BWI.

Most travelers fly to the nearest major airport and rent a car to get to areas covered by smaller regional airports. Many smaller airports have flights or connections to Washington, Baltimore, Richmond, Norfolk, and Philadelphia. Hagerstown Regional Airport has flights to Pittsburgh and other Pennsylvania airports (but not to Washington or Baltimore). Salisbury-Ocean City-Wicomico Regional Airport serves the lower Eastern Shore with service to Philadelphia. Airports at Staunton, Charlottesville, Lynchburg, and Roanoke have scheduled service.

Airport Information Newport News/Williamsburg International Airport (PHF ☎ 757/877–0221 ⊕ www.nnwairport.com). Norfolk International Airport (ORF ⊠ 2200 Norview Ave., Norfolk ☎ 757/857–3351 ⊕ norfolkairport.com). Richmond International Airport (RIC ☎ 804/226–3000 ⊕ www.flyrichmond.com). Ronald Reagan Washington National Airport (DCA ☎ 703/417–8000 ⊕ www.metwashairports.com/reagan/reagan.htm). Thurgood Marshall Baltimore-Washington International Airport (BWI ☎ 410/859–7111 or 800/435–9294 ⊕ www.bwiairport.com). Washington Dulles International Airport (IAD ☎ 703/572–2700 ⊕ www.metwashairports.com/dulles).

Secondary Airports Charlottesville Albemarle County (CHO ☎ 434/973–8342). Hagerstown Regional (HGR ☎ 240/313–2777). Lynchburg Regional (LYH ☎ 434/455–6090). Roanoke Regional Airport (ROA ☎ 540/362–1999). Salisbury-Ocean City-Wicomico Regional (SBY ☎ 540/548–4827).

GROUND TRANSPORTATION

Reagan National, Dulles, and BWI airports are served by SuperShuttle, which takes passengers to or from a hotel or residence. Buy tickets and request service at the SuperShuttle counter, or book online for returns to the airports.

The most reasonable way to BWI is by Maryland Transit Administration (MTA) train, MTA light rail, Washington Metropolitan Transit Authority (WMATA) bus, or a combination thereof. All northbound Amtrak and MTA Penn Line trains from Washington's Union Station or southbound from Baltimore Penn Station make a BWI stop, where there's a free shuttle bus to the terminal. MTA costs about a third of the Amtrak fare, but only operates on workdays. MTA light trains run from BWI to downtown Baltimore and the suburbs daily. WMATA has an express bus (B30) to BWI every 40 minutes from its Greenbelt, MD, Metrorail station.

Taxi fare to Baltimore's Inner Harbor is about $25.

Dulles is served by Washington Flyer bus and WMATA's Metrobus. Washington Flyer operates between Dulles and the West Falls Church Metrorail station every half hour from 5:45 am (7:45 on weekends) until 10:15 pm for $10 one-way and $18 round-trip. WMATA Metrobuses and trains operate from the Metrorail station.

■TIP→ The little-known express Metrobus, route 5A, runs hourly between Dulles and L'Enfant Plaza Metrorail station in downtown Washington. It costs $6, and exact change is required.

Taxi fares from Dulles to downtown Washington range from $57 to $61; drivers accept major credit cards.

Reagan National has its own Metrorail station just outside the main terminal. There is virtually no bus service to the airport. Taxi drivers must accept credit card payment, and they charge a $1.75 airport-access fee. Fare to the U.S. Capitol is about $10, though a small gas surcharge may also apply.

TRANSFERS BETWEEN AIRPORTS
Taxi service is by far the most expensive option between airports; sample fares are $100 between BWI and National, $120 between BWI and Dulles, and $55 between Dulles and National.

Travel between BWI and National for $11: Take WMATA's $6 express bus from BWI to the Greenbelt Metrorail station, then switch to the Metrorail and transfer at Gallery Place. Between BWI and Dulles, take WMATA's express bus, then the Metrorail to L'Enfant Plaza, then switch to the 5A express bus; total fare is $17. Note that Metrorail rates rise slightly during rush hour.

For a little more comfort on weekdays, take the MTA train to or from BWI via Union Station. The fare is $6 one-way.

Contacts BWI Airport Taxi (☎ 410/859–1100 ⊕ www.bwiairporttaxi.com).

Maryland Transportation Administration (☎ 410/539–5000 ⊕ www.mtamaryland. com). **SuperShuttle** (☎ 800/258–3826 ⊕ www.supershuttle.com). **Washington Flyer** (☎ 888/927–4359 ⊕ www.washfly.com). **WMATA** (☎ 202/637–7000 ⊕ www.wmata.com).

∎ BOAT TRAVEL

Water sports and activities are popular recreational pursuits in Virginia and Maryland, which share the expansive Chesapeake Bay and the Potomac River. Harbor and river cruises are offered in Baltimore, St. Michaels, Annapolis, Washington, D.C. (along the Potomac), Hampton, and Norfolk, to name a few starting points. Sailboats and other pleasure craft can be chartered for trips on the Chesapeake Bay or inland rivers. Popular ports include Rock Hall, Havre de Grace, and Solomons in Maryland, and Newport News and Chincoteague in Virginia.

For a complete list of ferries operating in Virginia, including commercial ferries and those operating to the Maryland shore, see ⊕ *www.virginiadot.org/travel/ferry.asp*.

■TIP→ If you're over 60, chances are you qualify for greatly discounted transit fares in Virginia and Maryland. If you're over 60 in the Norfolk area, they almost pay you to ride their excellent system of buses and ferries. And if you're over 65, Maryland and

WMATA let you ride their trains, buses, and subways at half price. All state-operated ferries in Virginia are free. The Elizabeth River ferry between Portsmouth and Norfolk costs $1.50 per person, and half that for seniors. Ferries to Tangier and Smith islands cost about $25 round-trip, but be sure to confirm the price in advance.

Information Hampton Roads Transit (☎ 757/222–6100 ⊕ www.gohrt.com). **Smith Island Cruises** (☎ 410/425–2771 ⊕ www. smithislandcruises.com). **Tangier Island Cruises** (☎ 410/968–2338 or 800/863–2338 ⊕ www.tangierislandcruises.com). **Virginia Department of Transportation** (☎ 804/786–2801 ⊕ www.virginiadot.org/travel/ferry.asp).

▌ BUS TRAVEL

A bus is a very practical way to get to a one-stop resort destination such as Ocean City or Virginia Beach, but many of Maryland's and Virginia's more scenic attractions lie outside the cities served by bus routes. Municipal buses do provide point-to-point transportation in Baltimore, Richmond, the Hampton Roads area, and metropolitan Washington, D.C.

Greyhound Lines has extensive service to Virginia and Maryland, supplemented by Peter Pan from Washington to points north to Massachusetts. Unfortunately, there is no system for reserving or assigning seats, so even ticket holders may not get a seat or may lose their seat during stops to change buses. Buses in Virginia and Maryland tend to be quite crowded, so competition is fierce for seats.

A low-cost alternative is the system of "Chinatown" buses, which operate primarily between little travel agencies in northeastern cities. Reservations can be made in person or online, and the price is about half the equivalent Greyhound ticket or less. Chinatown Bus Lines has information for some (but by no means all) "Chinatown" bus companies on the East Coast.

Two newer arrivals, BOLTBUS and Megabus, run discounted trips several times a day between Washington and New York. Fares are cheapest when you reserve well in advance.

Bus Information Chinatown Bus Lines (⊕ www.staticleap.com/chinatownbus). **Greyhound Lines** (☎ 800/231–2222 ⊕ www. greyhound.com). **Peter Pan Trailways** (☎ 800/343–9999 ⊕ www.peterpanbus.com). **BOLTBUS** (⊕ www.boltbus.com). **Megabus** (⊕ www.megabus.com).

▌ CAR TRAVEL

A car is by far the most convenient means of travel throughout Maryland and Virginia, and in many areas it's the only practical way to get around. (Where it exists, public transportation is clean, reasonable, and comfortable, but too often it bypasses or falls short of travel high points.)

HIGHWAYS

Interstate 95 runs north–south through Maryland and Virginia, carrying traffic to and from New England and Florida and intermediate points. U.S. 50 links I–95 with Annapolis and Maryland's Eastern Shore. U.S. 97 links Baltimore with Annapolis. Interstate 695 forms a beltway around Baltimore, and I–495 and I–95 form a beltway around Washington. The Baltimore-Washington Parkway is an old four-lane road that parallels I–95 between the two beltways. Interstate 895 parallels I–95 near Baltimore, offering an alternative route around the city (a $2 toll applies to tunnels on both roads). Interstate 64 intersects I–95 at Richmond and runs east–west. At Staunton, I–64 intersects I–81, which runs north–south. Interstate 70 runs west from Baltimore's Beltway, I–695, to Hancock in western Maryland. Interstate 270 stretches north from the Washington beltway to I–70 at Frederick, Maryland. Interstate 68 connects Hancock to Cumberland and Garrett County. U.S. 40—the National Pike—travels east and west, the entire length of Maryland. Interstate 83 journeys south from Pennsylvania to the top of I–695, the Baltimore Beltway.

ROAD MAPS

The state tourist offices of Maryland and Virginia (⇨ *Visitor Information*) publish official state road maps (and special-interest maps like bike maps and scenic highway maps), free for the asking, that contain directories and other useful information. For the excellent, free *Maryland Scenic Byways* guide, call ☎ 877/632–9929 or look for one at a state welcome center.

RULES OF THE ROAD

The maximum speed limit is 65 mph on stretches of major highways in both states. Radar detectors are legal in Maryland, but are not permitted in D.C. or Virginia. Front-seat passengers in all jurisdictions must wear seat belts.

In Virginia, D.C., and Maryland, you may usually turn right at a red light after stopping if there's no oncoming traffic and no pedestrians present. Watch the signs.

In both states, HOV (high-occupancy vehicle) lanes are restricted to a minimum of two (three in some places) people during rush hour. Look for the diamond on the highway and on signs telling you when the restrictions are in effect.

Talking on cell phones while driving is not allowed in D.C.

In D.C., Maryland, and Virginia, children must travel in approved child restraints if they are under the age of eight. In Maryland, an exception is made for kids who are at least 4 feet, 9 inches tall or weigh more than 65 pounds.

▌TRAIN TRAVEL

Amtrak trains run out of Baltimore, Maryland, north toward Boston and south toward Washington, D.C., along the busy "northeast corridor." A rail station at Baltimore-Washington International Airport serves both Baltimore (about 15 mi to the north) and Washington, D.C. (about 30 mi to the south). Some trains running between New York and Chicago stop at Charlottesville, Virginia, and at two locations in western Virginia. Trains run between Newport News, Virginia, and New York City, stopping in northern Virginia, Richmond, and Williamsburg in between. Stops in Richmond and northern Virginia are also made on runs between New York City and Florida.

The Maryland Transit Administration operates commuter trains (on weekdays only) between Baltimore's Penn Station and D.C.'s Union Station. It also operates trains from Baltimore's downtown Camden Station and from Union Station in Washington, D.C. There's free bus transportation between the Baltimore-Washington International Airport Rail Station and the airport passenger terminal.

Virginia Railway Express, or VRE, provides workday commuter service between Union Station in Washington and Fredericksburg and Manassas, with additional stops near hotels in Crystal City, Alexandria, and elsewhere.

Information Amtrak (☎ *800/872-7245* ⊕ *www.amtrak.com*). **Maryland Transit Administration** (*MTA* ☎ *800/325-7245* ⊕ *www. mtamaryland.com*). **Virginia Railway Express** (*VRE* ☎ *800/743-3873* ⊕ *www.vre.org*).

ESSENTIALS

■ ACCOMMODATIONS

The lodgings we list are the cream of the crop in each price category. We always list the facilities that are available, but we don't specify whether they cost extra; when pricing accommodations, always ask what's included and what costs extra.

■TIP→ Assume that hotels operate on the European Plan (EP, no meals) unless we specify that they use the Breakfast Plan (BP, with full breakfast), Continental Plan (CP, Continental breakfast), Full American Plan (FAP, all meals), Modified American Plan (MAP, breakfast and dinner), or are all-inclusive (AI, all meals and most activities).

APARTMENT AND HOUSE RENTALS

At shoreline resorts, as well as Deep Creek Lake in western Maryland, real estate agents generally handle apartment, condo, and town-house rentals. For rentals in Deep Creek Lake, contact Railey Mountain Lake Vacations or Coldwell Banker. Call Atkinson Realty for Virginia Beach and Bud Church Coldwell Banker for Ocean City. Seashore homes usually rent by the week.

Online Booking Resources **Atkinson Realty** (📞 757/428-4441 ⊕ www.atkinsonrealty.com). **Bud Church Coldwell Banker** (📞 800/851-7326 ⊕ www.coldwellbankerbudchurch.com). **Coldwell Banker** (📞 301/387-6187 ⊕ www.deepcreekrealty.com). **Hideaways International** (📞 603/430-4433 or 800/843-4433 ⊕ www.hideaways.com). **Interhome** (📞 954/791-8282 or 800/882-6864 ⊕ www.interhome.us). **Railey Mountain Lake Vacations** (📞 800/544-2425 ⊕ realty.railey.com). **Vacation Home Rentals Worldwide** (📞 201/767-9393 or 800/633-3284 ⊕ www.vhrww.com). **Villas International** (📞 415/499-9490 or 800/221-2260 ⊕ www.villasintl.com).

BED AND BREAKFASTS

Houses in this region make it a natural area for bed-and-breakfast accommodations. The majority of B&Bs in Virginia and Maryland are Victorian structures with fewer than 10 rental units; a full or a Continental breakfast is typically included in the lodging rate, and rooms rarely have their own TV. Most rooms, however, have private bathrooms.

Reservation Services **Bed & Breakfast.com** (📞 512/322-2710 or 800/462-2632 ⊕ www.bedandbreakfast.com) also sends out an online newsletter. **Bed & Breakfast Accommodations Ltd. of Washington, DC** (📞 877/893-3233 ⊕ www.bedandbreakfastdc.com). **Bed & Breakfast Association of Maryland** (📞 301/432-5079 ⊕ www.marylandbb.com). **Bed & Breakfast Inns Online** (📞 310/280-4363 or 800/215-7365 ⊕ www.bbonline.com). **BnB Finder.com** (📞 888/469-6663 ⊕ www.bnbfinder.com). **Maryland Office of Tourism** (📞 410/767-3400 or 866/639-3526 ⊕ www.visitmaryland.org). **Virginia Tourism Corporation** (📞 804/786-2051 or 800/847-4882 ⊕ www.virginia.org).

CAMPING

Camping is popular in the Shenandoah and Blue Ridge mountains—particularly on the Appalachian Trail, which crosses Virginia and Maryland—and at state forests and parks in western Maryland. The Maryland Department of Natural Resources sells trail guides online. You can reserve sites at Virginia state parks online or by phone.

Assateague Island State Park in Maryland, the Assateague Island National Seashore (in Maryland and Virginia), and the state park at Cape Henry in Virginia are popular campgrounds. State-maintained sites include primitive and full-service sites (with showers, bathrooms, and hookups). Private campgrounds offer more amenities.

FOR INTERNATIONAL TRAVELERS

CURRENCY

The dollar is the basic unit of U.S. currency. It has 100 cents. Coins are the penny (1¢); the nickel (5¢), dime (10¢), quarter (25¢), and half-dollar (50¢). In 2010, the U.S. mint began distributing a line of presidential $1 coins. There's also the very rare golden $1 coin and even rarer silver $1. Bills are denominated $1, $5, $10, $20, $50, and $100, all mostly green and identical in size; designs and background tints vary. You may come across a $2 bill, but the chances are slim.

CUSTOMS

U.S. Customs and Border Protection (⊕ www.cbp.gov).

DRIVING

Driving in the United States is on the right. Speed limits are posted in miles per hour (usually between 55 mph and 70 mph). Watch for lower limits in small towns and on back roads (usually 25 mph to 40 mph). Most states require front-seat passengers to wear seat belts; many states require children to sit in the backseat and to wear seat belts. In major cities rush hour is between 7 am and 10 am; afternoon rush hour is between 4 pm and 7 pm. The traffic around Washington, though, is some of the worst in the country, often extending rush hour in the Maryland and Virginia suburbs well beyond these windows. To encourage carpooling, some freeways have special lanes, ordinarily marked with a diamond, for high-occupancy vehicles (HOV)—cars carrying two people or more.

Highways are well paved. Interstates—limited-access, multilane highways designated with an "I–" before the number—are fastest. Interstates with three-digit numbers circle urban areas, which may also have other limited-access expressways, freeways, and parkways. Tolls may be levied on limited-access highways. U.S. and state highways aren't necessarily limited-access, but may have several lanes.

Gas stations are plentiful. Most stay open late (24 hours along major highways and in big cities) except in rural areas, where Sunday hours are limited and where you may drive for long stretches without a refueling opportunity. Along larger highways, roadside stops with restrooms, fast-food restaurants, and sundries stores are well spaced. State police and tow trucks patrol major highways. If your car breaks down on an interstate, pull onto the shoulder and wait for help, or have your passengers wait while you walk to an emergency phone (available in most states). If you carry a cell phone, dial *55, noting your location on the small green roadside mileage marker.

ELECTRICITY

The U.S. standard is AC, 110 volts/60 cycles. Plugs have two flat pins set parallel to each other.

HOLIDAYS

New Year's Day (Jan. 1); Martin Luther King Jr. Day (3rd Mon. in Jan.); Presidents' Day (3rd Mon. in Feb.); Memorial Day (last Mon. in May); Independence Day (July 4); Labor Day (1st Mon. in Sept.); Columbus Day (2nd Mon. in Oct.); Thanksgiving Day (4th Thurs. in Nov.); Christmas Eve and Christmas Day (Dec. 24 and 25); and New Year's Eve (Dec. 31).

MAIL

You can buy stamps and send letters and parcels in post offices. The United States no longer makes aerograms. Stamp-dispensing machines can occasionally be found in airports, bus and train stations, office buildings, drugstores, and convenience stores. U.S. mailboxes are stout, dark-blue steel bins; pickup schedules are posted inside the bin (pull down the handle to see them).

CON OR CONCIERGE?

Good hotel concierges are invaluable—for arranging transportation, getting reservations at the hottest restaurant, and scoring tickets for a sold-out show or entrée to an exclusive nightclub. They're in the know and well connected. That said, sometimes you have to take their advice with a grain of salt.

It's not uncommon for restaurants to ply concierges with free food and drink in exchange for steering diners their way. Indeed, European concierges often receive referral *fees*. Hotel chains usually have guidelines about what their concierges can accept. The best concierges, however, are above reproach. This is particularly true of those who belong to the prestigious international society of Les Clefs d'Or.

What can you expect of a concierge? At a typical tourist-class hotel you can expect him or her to give you the basics: to show you something on a map, make a standard restaurant reservation (particularly if you don't speak the language), or help you book a tour or airport transportation. In Asia, concierges perform the vital service of writing out the name or address of your destination for you to give to a cab driver.

Savvy concierges at the finest hotels and resorts can arrange for just about any good or service imaginable—and do so quickly. You should compensate them appropriately. A $10 tip is enough to show appreciation for a table at a hot restaurant. But the reward should really be much greater for tickets to that U2 concert that's been sold out for months or for those last-minute sixth-row-center seats for *The Lion King*.

There are 30 free National Park Service campsites along the C&O Canal towpath in Maryland with water, chemical toilets, and grills. At some sites, however, the water might not be potable. Bike camping is a very practical way to travel the towpath, and five drive-in campsites rent for $10. For large groups, two additional drive-in campsites are available for $20 a night.

Information C&O National Historical Park (⊕ *www.nps.gov/choh/planyourvisit/camping.htm*). **Go Camping America** (⊕ *www.gocampingamerica.com*). **Maryland Department of Natural Resources** (☎ *410/260–8367* ⊕ *www.dnr.state.md.us*). **Virginia Department of Conservation and Recreation** (☎ *804/786–1712* ⊕ *www.dcr.virginia.gov*).

HOSTELS

With few exceptions, hostels in Virginia and Maryland are near popular outdoor spots or resort communities. In Maryland, the HI-Harpers Ferry is near the Appalachian Trail in Knoxville, across the Potomac River from Harpers Ferry. Virginia's Bears Den Lodge is near the Appalachian Trail in Bluemont, HI-Galax is near the Blue Ridge Parkway, and HI-Angie's Guest Cottage is in Virginia Beach.

Information Bears Den Lodge (☎ *540/554–8708* ⊕ *www.bearsdencenter.org*). **HI-Angie's Guest Cottage Hostel** (☎ *757/491–1830* ⊕ *www.angiescottage.com*). **HI-Galax** (☎ *276/236–4962*). **HI-Harpers Ferry** (☎ *310/834–7652* ⊕ *www.harpersferryhostel.org*). **Hostelling International–USA** (☎ *301/495–1240* ⊕ *www.hiusa.org*).

HOTELS

The large hotels of Baltimore, Richmond, Norfolk, D.C., and the Virginia suburbs of Washington, D.C., are in competitive markets for business travelers: standards and prices are high. The beach and mountain resorts in the region are among the oldest and largest in the country, and on the expensive side. Accommodations at beach resorts in Maryland and Virginia can be difficult to find during summer holiday weekends—be sure to make reservations. Off-season, rates often go down in both metropolitan areas and resorts.

All hotels listed have a private bath unless otherwise noted.

▌ COMMUNICATIONS

INTERNET

Local Internet cafés are listed in the Contacts section of each chapter. Larger hotels often have Wi-Fi available but some smaller B&Bs may not.

Contacts Cybercafes (⊕ *www.cybercafes. com*) lists more than 4,000 Internet cafés worldwide.

▌ EATING OUT

The restaurants listed are the cream of the crop in each price category.

The treasure of the Chesapeake Bay is the blue crab. In Maryland, Virginia, and D.C., the locals like crabs steamed in the shells, seasoned by the bushel, and dumped on brown-paper-covered tables in spartan crab houses. Diners use wooden mallets to crack the shells, and nimble fingers to reach the meat. Crab cakes, soft-shell crab, crab imperial (enriched crabmeat stuffed back into shells), crab soup, and a host of other such dishes can be found throughout the region. Following a decade-long decline, Bay crabs made a comeback in 2010, raising hopes that Maryland's signature critter will be gracing crab house menus for many years to come. Rockfish (striped bass) is another seafood delicacy, harvested in summer and fall.

In Virginia, country ham, biscuits, collard greens, and fried chicken—Southern staples—are popular Sunday meals. Grits (often served for breakfast) and pecan and sweet-potato pies are other popular Southern foods.

MEALS AND MEALTIMES

Unless otherwise noted, the restaurants listed in this guide are open daily for lunch and dinner.

RESERVATIONS AND DRESS

Regardless of where you are, it's a good idea to make a reservation if you can. In some places (Washington, D.C., for example), it's expected. We only mention them specifically when reservations are essential (there's no other way you'll ever get a table) or when they are not accepted. For popular restaurants, book as far ahead as you can (often 30 days), and reconfirm as soon as you arrive. (Large parties should always call ahead to check the reservations policy.) We mention dress only when men are required to wear a jacket or a jacket and tie.

Online reservation services make it easy to book a table before you even leave home. OpenTable covers most states, including 20 major cities, and has limited listings in Canada, Mexico, the United Kingdom, and elsewhere. DinnerBroker has restaurants throughout the United States as well as a few in Canada.

Contacts OpenTable (⊕ *www.opentable.com*). **DinnerBroker** (⊕ *www.dinnerbroker.com*).

WINE, BEER, AND SPIRITS

In Maryland and Virginia, restaurants and bars can serve wine, beer, and spirits seven days a week.

■ TIP→ **In Virginia the state-run ABC liquor stores are open daily. In Maryland, some** counties prohibit liquor sales on Sunday, but some restaurants and bars package alcohol to go, even on Sunday. Beer and wine are sold throughout the region in convenience stores, markets, drugstores, and even gas stations every day. Sunday liquor sales in D.C. are limited to wine and beer.

▌ HOURS OF OPERATION

The business week runs from 9 to 5 weekdays, and in some instances, on Saturday in the metropolitan regions of Virginia and Maryland, and in Washington, D.C. Stores, restaurants, and other services maintain longer hours. Hours vary in small towns and resort areas, especially those dependent on seasonal visitors. In rural areas many retail establishments close on Sunday.

Most businesses in the area close for many religious holidays and all holidays that are celebrated on a Monday. However, shopping malls and plazas, as well as restaurants, remain open.

Most art and historical museums in the region are open Monday through Saturday from 10 or 11 to 5 or 6, and Sunday noon to 5. Some museums are closed Monday and/or Tuesday. Many parks and historic homes tend to have later closing hours in summer, and some close during the winter months. In this book's sight reviews, open hours are denoted by a clock icon.

In the metropolitan areas, retail stores and shopping malls are open Monday through Saturday 10–9 and Sunday 11–6. In suburban Baltimore, Washington, and Richmond, grocery stores and superstores often are open 24 hours. Retailers in small towns and in the downtown office districts close earlier and are often not open on Sunday.

▌ MONEY

Generally, lodging, restaurants, and attractions are most expensive in Washington, D.C., Baltimore, Richmond,

WORST-CASE SCENARIO

All your money and credit cards have just been stolen. In these days of real-time transactions, this isn't a predicament that should destroy your vacation. First, report the theft of the credit cards. Then get any traveler's checks you were carrying replaced. This can usually be done almost immediately, provided that you kept a record of the serial numbers separate from the checks themselves. If you bank at a large international bank like Citibank or HSBC, go to the closest branch; if you know your account number, chances are you can get a new ATM card and withdraw money right away.

suburban Washington, and resort areas, especially Ocean City and Virginia Beach. Gas prices tend to be higher in the mountainous regions. Lodging and restaurant costs are considerably lower in the western Maryland mountains and rural Virginia.

Coupons for hotel discounts and services in Maryland and Virginia can be printed at ⊕ *www.travelcoupons.com.*

Prices throughout this guide are given for adults. Substantially reduced fees are almost always available for children, students, and senior citizens.

CREDIT CARDS

Throughout this guide, the following abbreviations are used: **AE**, American Express; **D**, Discover; **DC**, Diners Club; **MC**, MasterCard; and **V**, Visa.

It's a good idea to inform your credit-card company before you travel. Otherwise, the credit-card company might put a hold on your card owing to unusual activity—not a good thing halfway through your trip. Record all your credit-card numbers—as well as the phone numbers to call if your cards are lost or stolen—in a safe place, so you're prepared should something go wrong. Both MasterCard and Visa have general numbers you can call if your card is lost, but you're better off calling the number of your issuing bank, since

MasterCard and Visa usually just transfer you to your bank; your bank's number is usually printed on your card.

Reporting Lost Cards American Express (☎ *800/992-3404 in U.S.* ⊕ *www.americanexpress.com*). **Diners Club** (☎ *800/234-6377 in U.S.* ⊕ *www.dinersclub.com*). **Discover** (☎ *800/347-2683 in U.S.* ⊕ *www.discovercard.com*). **MasterCard** (☎ *800/622-7747 in U.S.* ⊕ *www.mastercard.com*). **Visa** (☎ *800/847-2911 in U.S.* ⊕ *www.visa.com*).

TIPPING

Tipping is expected in restaurants and bars. Waiters receive 15%–20% of the total bill, depending on the level of service; for groups of six or more, a 15%–20% gratuity may be tacked onto the bill (if gratuity is covered, additional tips aren't necessary). Bartenders get $1–$2 or more, depending on the number of drinks and the number of people in the party. Taxi drivers are generally tipped 15% of the total price of the ride; more if they have been particularly helpful. Doormen carrying bags to the registration desk and porters carrying bags between the lobby and the room are usually tipped $1 per bag, as are Red Caps at the airport or the train station. Chambermaids are generally tipped $1 to $3 a night for inexpensive-to-average hotels and up to $5 a night per guest for high-end properties. Barbers, hairdressers, and masseuses are usually tipped 10%–20% of the total cost of the service, depending on the place and the amount of time spent.

TIPPING GUIDELINES FOR VIRGINIA AND MARYLAND	
Bartender	$1–$5 per round of drinks, depending on the number of drinks
Bellhop	$1–$5 per bag, depending on the level of the hotel
Hotel Concierge	$5 or more, if he or she performs a service for you
Hotel Doorman	$1–$5 for help with bags or hailing a cab

TIPPING GUIDELINES FOR VIRGINIA AND MARYLAND	
Hotel Maid	$1–$3 a day (either daily or at the end of your stay, in cash)
Hotel Room-Service Waiter	$1–$2 per delivery, even if a service charge has been added
Porter at Airport or Train Station	$1 per bag
Skycap at Airport	$1–$3 per bag checked
Taxi Driver	15% but round up the fare to the next dollar amount
Tour Guide	10% of the cost of the tour
Valet Parking Attendant	$1–$2, but only when you get your car
Waiter	15%–20%, with 20% being the norm at high-end restaurants; nothing additional if a service charge is added to the bill
Spa Personnel	10%–20% of the cost of your service
Restroom Attendants	$1 or small change
Coat Check	$1–$2 per item checked unless there is a fee, then nothing

▮ PACKING

If you're visiting the mountains and the caverns of Virginia, prepare for colder-than-average temperatures. Hiking along the Appalachian Trail, even in spring and fall, frequently requires a coat.

Where dress is concerned, Washington, Baltimore, and Richmond are relatively conservative. In the more expensive restaurants men are expected to wear a jacket and tie.

At the Bay and ocean resorts, "formal" means long trousers and a collared shirt for men, and shoes for everybody. A tie might never get tied during a stay in these areas.

▌ TAXES

Sales tax is 6% in D.C.; 6% in Maryland; and 4% in Virginia, though a 1% local tax is often added, bringing Virginia's total sales tax to 5% for most purchases. The hotel tax varies because a local tax is added to the state tax. The result in Maryland varies from 6% to 13.5% and in Virginia from 6.5% to 12.5%; in D.C. it's 14.5%.

▌ TIME

Maryland, Virginia, and Washington, D.C., are in the Eastern Time Zone. The area is 3 hours ahead of Los Angeles, 1 hour ahead of Chicago, 5 hours behind London, and 14 hours behind Sydney.

▌ VISITOR INFORMATION

State Tourism Offices **Maryland Office of Tourism Development** (☎ *410/767-3400 or 866/639-3526* ⊕ *www.visitmaryland.org*). **Virginia Tourism Corporation** (☎ *804/786-2051 or 800/847-4882* ⊕ *www.virginia.org*). **Washington, DC Convention and Visitors Association** (☎ *202/789-7000 or 800/422-8644* ⊕ *www.washington.org*).

National Park Service The **National Park Service** (☎ *202/208-3818* ⊕ *www.nps.gov/findapark/index.htm*).

Weather **Accuweather.com** (⊕ *www.accuweather.com*) is an independent weather-forecasting service with especially good coverage of hurricanes. **Weather.com** (⊕ *www.weather.com*) is the Web site for the Weather Channel.

For Civil War buffs, ⊕ *www.civilwartraveler.com* has information on battlefields and war-related sites and events. Wine enthusiasts can learn the basics of Maryland and Virginia wines (including winery locations) at ⊕ *www.marylandwine.com* and ⊕ *www.virginiawine.org*, respectively.

Find arts and entertainment listings online for Baltimore at the *Baltimore Sun*, for Richmond at the *Richmond Times-Dispatch*, and for D.C. at the *Washington Post*. For D.C. gay bars and clubs, click on the Web site for the gay newspaper *Washington Blade* or the bar guide *Metro Weekly*.

All About Virginia and Maryland **Baltimore Sun** (⊕ *www.baltimoresun.com*). **Metro Weekly** (⊕ *www.metroweekly.com*). **Richmond Times-Dispatch** (⊕ *www2.timesdispatch.com*). **Washington Blade** (⊕ *www.washingtonblade.com*). **Washington Post** (⊕ *www.washingtonpost.com*).

INDEX

A

Abacrombie Bed and Breakfast ⬚ , *341*
Abby Aldrich Rockefeller Folk Art Museum, *261*
Abingdon, VA, *200, 202*
Abram's Delight Museum, *179*
Academy Art Museum, *444*
Accokeek, MD, *149–150*
Accommodations, *474, 476–477*
Adam Thoroughgood House, *292*
Admiral Fell Inn, The ⬚ , *346*
African-American history
Annapolis and Southern Maryland, *401, 405–406, 420*
Baltimore, *315–316, 321*
Central and Western Virginia, *171–172*
Frederick and Western Maryland, *367–368*
Northern Virginia, *89, 102*
Richmond, Fredericksburg, and the Northern Neck, *212, 217*
Agecroft Hall, *218*
Air Force Memorial, *101*
Air travel, *470–471*
Annapolis and Southern Maryland, *396*
Baltimore, *307*
Central and Western Virginia, *156*
D.C.'s Maryland Suburbs, *125*
Fredrick and Western Maryland, *364*
Maryland's Eastern Shore, *428*
Northern Virginia, *82*
Richmond, Fredericksburg, and the Northern Neck, *206*
Washington, D.C., *25–26*
Williamsburg and Hampton Roads, *248*
Alexandria, VA, *80, 85–87*
Alexandria Black History Museum, *89*
Alexandria Convention & Visitors Association, *88*
American Civil War Center, *156, 212, 235*
American Craft Council Retail Show, *306*
American Film Institute Silver Theatre and Cultural Center, *139–140*
American Market, *150*

American Shakespeare Center, *186*
American Visionary Art Museum, *318*
Amusement parks
Annapolis and Southern Maryland, *414*
D.C.'s Maryland Suburbs, *136, 147*
Maryland's Eastern Shore, *461–462*
Richmond, Fredericksburg, and the Northern Neck, *220*
Williamsburg and Hampton Roads, *269–270*
Annapolis and Southern Maryland, *8, 393–424*
Annapolis, *13, 394, 395, 397, 399–412*
beaches, *413–415, 421*
Calvert County, *394, 412–419*
Charles County, *395, 423–424*
children's activities, *401, 404, 406, 408, 414, 415, 417, 418, 422*
essential information, *396, 400, 412, 413, 420, 423*
exploring Annapolis and Southern Maryland, *397*
festivals and seasonal events, *395–396*
guided tours, *399–400, 405*
lodging, *396–397, 408–410, 414–415, 418–419, 422–423*
nightlife and the arts, *410–411, 417*
price categories, *397*
restaurants, *396, 401–402, 403, 406–408, 413, 414, 416, 418*
St. Mary's County, *394–395, 419–423*
sports and outdoor activities, *402, 411–412*
transportation, *396, 399*
Anne Spencer House and Gardens, *171–172*
Annmarie Garden, *418*
Antietam National Battlefield, *12, 16, 362, 381*
Antietam National Battlefield Memorial Illumination, *362*
Antique Row (Kensington, MD), *138–139*
Antrim 1844 ⬚ , *370–371*
Apartment rentals, *474*
Appomattox Confederate Statue, *87*

Appomattox Court House, *156, 172–173*
Appomattox Court House National Historical Park, *177*
Aquariums, *293, 320, 458, 466*
Arlington, VA, *80, 97–99, 101–106*
Arlington House, *98*
Arlington National Cemetery, *81, 98–99, 101*
Art Whino exhibition, *150–151*
Arthur M. Sackler Gallery, *34*
Artscape, *306*
Ash Lawn-Highland, *160*
Ashland, *219–220*
Assateague Island, *466*
Athenaeum, *89*
Atlantic Hotel ⬚ , *459–460*
Audubon Naturalist Society, *130*
Autumn Glory Festival, *362*
Awakening, The (sculpture), *151*

B

B&O Railroad Museum, *325*
Babe Ruth Birthplace and Museum, *325*
Back Creek Inn ⬚ , *418–419*
Baltimore, MD, *8, 303–358*
Bolton Hill, *334*
Canton, *340, 346–347*
Charles Village, *305, 316–318, 334*
City Center, *341–343*
children's activities, *318–319, 320–321, 323, 325–326, 327–328, 351*
discounts and deals, *310*
Druid Hill Park, *327–328*
Ellicott City, *358*
exploring Baltimore, *310–311*
Federal Hill, *336–337*
Fells Point, *305, 323–324, 338–339, 346*
festivals and seasonal events, *305, 306*
guided tours, *309–310*
Hampden, *335*
Havre de Grace, *355–357*
Inner Harbor/Downtown, *13, 305, 318–323, 335–336, 343–346*
Little Italy, *337–338*
lodging, *340–347, 357*
Midtown, *340*

Mount Vernon, 305, 311, 314–316, 328–329, 332–333, 341
nightlife and the arts, 347–350
Northern Suburbs, 347
price categories, 328, 340
restaurants, 315, 323, 324, 327, 328–329, 332–340, 357
Roland Park, 347
shopping, 352–355
side trips from, 355–358
sports and outdoor activities, 350–352
Station North, 305
transportation, 306–309
visitor information, 310, 321
West Baltimore, 324–327
when to go, 306
Baltimore City Hall, *322*
Baltimore Civil War Museum–President Street Station, *322*
Baltimore Museum of Art, *316*
Baltimore Museum of Industry, *318–319*
Baltimore Streetcar Museum, *327*
Bancroft Hall (United States Naval Academy), *404*
Banneker-Douglass Museum, *401*
Barbara Fritchie House, *367*
Barboursville Vineyards, *155, 169*
Barksdale Theatre, *220*
Bartlett Pear Inn ⊠ , *445*
Barton, Clara, *135–136*
Baseball
Baltimore, 15, 325–326, 351
D.C.'s Maryland Suburbs, 147
Washington, D.C., 74
Basilica of the Assumption, *311*
Basket factory, *442*
Basketball, *74, 75*
Bath County, VA, *189–192*
Battle Creek Cypress Swamp Sanctuary, *415*
Battlefields, *16*
Antietam National Battlefield, 12, 16, 362, 381
City Point, 276–277
Fort McHenry, 16, 319
Fredericksburg/Spotsylvania National Military Park, 156, 235
Manassas National Battlefield Park (Bull Run), 16, 113
Monocacy National Battlefield, 373–374
New Market Battlefield Historical Park, 156, 177, 181–182

Pamplin Historical Park, 156, 226–227, 235
Petersburg National Battlefield, 156, 227, 235
Richmond National Battlefield Park Visitor Center, 156, 214–215, 235
Yorktown Battlefield, 16, 272–273
Bayard House, The ✕ , *441–442*
Beaches, *12*
Annapolis and Southern Maryland, 413–415, 421
Maryland's Eastern Shore, 434, 437, 441, 465, 466
Williamsburg and Hampton Roads, 12, 291–296
Bed and breakfasts, *85, 157, 397, 474*
Belair Mansion, *146–147*
Belair Stable, *146*
Belle Grove, *180*
Beltsville Agricultural Research Center, *144–145*
Berkeley Plantation, *218, 274*
Berlin, MD, *459–460*
Beth Ahabah Museum and Archives, *210*
Bethesda, MD, *129–135*
Bicycling
Annapolis and Southern Maryland, 411
Baltimore, 350
Central and Western Virginia, 173–174, 191, 200
Frederick and Western Maryland, 361, 390
Maryland's Eastern Shore, 446, 449, 456, 459, 465
Northern Virginia, 96
Washington, D.C., 72–73
Williamsburg and Hampton Roads, 255
Birchmere, The (music club), *70*
Black Cat (music club), *70–71*
Black History Museum & Cultural Center of Virginia, *212*
Blacksburg, VA, *197–200*
Blackwater National Wildlife Refuge, *456*
Blue Duck Tavern ✕ , *63*
Blue Ridge Mountains. ⇨ *See* Central and Western Virginia
Blue Ridge Music Center, *201*
Blue Ridge Parkway, *196–197*
Blue Ridge Parkway Visitors Center, *196*
Boat and ferry travel, *471–472*

Boat races, *14, 412*
Boat tours, *17*
Annapolis and Southern Maryland, 402
Baltimore, 310
D.C.'s Maryland Suburbs, 151
Maryland's Eastern Shore, 435, 446, 447, 449, 458, 459
Richmond, Fredericksburg, and the Northern Neck, 216, 242
Williamsburg and Hampton Roads, 256
Boating. ⇨ *See also* Canoeing; Kayaking; Sailing
Frederick and Western Maryland, 361, 386, 390
Maryland's Eastern Shore, 435, 446, 449
Northern Virginia, 95
Washington, D.C., 73–74
Bodo's Bagels ✕ , *161*
Bolton Hill (Baltimore), *334*
Booker T. Washington National Monument, *194*
Booking the trip, *474*
Books and bookstores
Baltimore, 353–354
Central and Western Virginia, 166
Washington, D.C., 76
Boonsborough Museum of History, *381*
Booth, John Wilkes, *50, 149, 423–424*
Bowie, MD, *146–147*
Bowling, *351*
Boyhood Home of Robert E. Lee, *87*
Bridges
Central and Western Virginia, 188
Frederick and Western Maryland, 377, 387
Northern Virginia, 117
Broadway Market, *324*
Brome-Howard Inn ⊠ , *422–423*
Brooks Tavern ✕ , *438*
Brookside Gardens, *140*
Broomes Island, MD, *416*
Brunswick Railroad Museum, *22, 373*
Brush-Everard House, *261*
Bruton Parish Church, *257*
Bull Run (Manassas National Battlefield Park), *16, 113*
Bureau of Engraving and Printing, *34*
Burley Tobacco Festival, *200*

Bus travel, 472
Annapolis and Southern Maryland, 396
Baltimore, 307–308
D.C.'s Maryland Suburbs, 126
Washington, D.C., 26
Busch Gardens (amusement park), 269–270
Business hours, 478

C

C&O Canal, 52, 137, 384
C&O Canal National Historic Park, 137, 384
C&O Heritage Center, 192
C&O Restaurant ✕, 163
Cabin John Regional Park, 134
Calvert County, MD, 394, 412–419
Camberley's Martha Washington Hotel & Spa ☰, 200, 202
Cambridge, MD, 453–456
Camping, 474, 476
Frederick and Western Maryland, 386
Maryland's Eastern Shore, 442
Richmond, Fredericksburg, and the Northern Neck, 239–240
Canal Walk, 216
Canals
D.C.'s Maryland Suburbs, 137, 384
Frederick and Western Maryland, 384
Richmond, Fredericksburg, and the Northern Neck, 216
Washington, D.C., 52
Canoeing
Central and Western Virginia, 166, 176
Frederick and Western Maryland, 386
Maryland's Eastern Shore, 441, 455, 458, 459
Canton (Baltimore), 340, 346–346
Cape Charles, VA, 301–302
Capitol, The (Colonial Williamsburg), 257
Capitol, The (Washington, D.C.), 44
Capitol Hill, 44–45, 48, 55–56, 65, 75, 76
Capitol Visitor Center, 44
Captain's Row, 89
Car racing, 224
Car travel, 472–473
Annapolis and Southern Maryland, 396, 399

Baltimore, 308
Central and Western Virginia, 156–157
D.C.'s Maryland Suburbs, 126
Frederick and Western Maryland, 364
Maryland's Eastern Shore, 429
Northern Virginia, 82–83
Richmond, Fredericksburg, and the Northern Neck, 206
Washington, D.C., 26
Williamsburg and Hampton Roads, 248, 255
Carlos Brazilian International Cuisine ✕, 195
Carlyle House, 87
Carmel Cove Inn ☰, 392
Carousels, 136
Carroll County Farm Museum, 22
Carroll Mansion, 322
Carroll-Barrister House, 404
Carter Family Fold, 201
Carter's Mountain Orchard, 166
Carytown Watermelon Festival, 206
Casselman River Bridge, 387
Catoctin Mountain Park, 375–376
Catoctin Wildlife Preserve & Zoo, 376
Cavalier Hotels ☰, 294–295
Cecil County, MD, 427, 441–443
Cedar Creek and Belle Grove National Park, 177
Celtic Festival and Highland Gathering of Southern Maryland, 395
Cemeteries
Arlington National Cemetery, 81, 98–99, 101
Baltimore, 326
Frederick and Western Maryland, 368
Richmond, Fredericksburg, and the Northern Neck, 218, 226, 233, 234, 236
Center in the Square, 193
Central and Western Virginia, 8, 153–202
Charlottesville and the Blue Ridge, 154, 158, 160–161, 163–168, 170–176
children's activities, 161, 185, 188, 192, 193, 194
discounts and deals, 157, 192
essential information, 157

festivals and seasonal events, 155, 166, 181, 182, 200, 201
guided tours, 155, 161, 175, 185, 187
lodging, 157, 163–165, 168, 170–171, 173, 175–176, 179–180, 181, 183, 186, 188–189, 190–191, 195–196, 197, 199, 200, 202
nightlife and the arts, 166, 182, 186, 191, 196, 202
price categories, 157
restaurants, 157, 161, 163, 173, 179, 183, 186, 188, 190, 195, 199
Shenandoah Valley, 154, 176–192
shopping, 166–167, 181
Southwest Virginia, 154–155, 192–202
sports and outdoor activities, 166, 173–174, 175, 176, 191, 196, 200, 202
transportation, 156–157
when to go, 155
Central Michel Richard ✕, 60–61
Centre Hill Museum, 226
Chain Bridge, 117
Channel Bass Inn ☰, 299
Chantilly, VA, 112
Charles City County, VA, 274–276
Charles County, MD, 395, 423–424
Charles Village (Baltimore), 305, 316–318, 334
Charleston ✕, 335–336
Charlottesville and the Blue Ridge, VA, 154, 158, 160–161, 163–168, 170–176
Château Morrisette Winery, 169
Chatham Manor, 234
Chesapeake & Ohio (C&O) Canal, 52, 137, 384
Chesapeake Bay Environmental Center, 434
Chesapeake Bay Maritime Museum, 447
Chesapeake Bay Railway Museum, 414
Chesapeake Beach, MD, 413–415
Chesapeake Beach Railway Museum, 414
Chesapeake Beach Resort & Spa, The ☰, 414–415
Chesapeake Beach Water Park, 414

Chesapeake City, MD, *441–442*
Chestertown, MD, *436–439*
Chestertown Tea Party,
 427–428
Children's activities, *22*
Annapolis and Southern Mary-
 land, 401, 404, 406, 408,
 414, 415, 417, 418, 422
Baltimore, 318–319, 320–321,
 323, 325–326, 327–328, 351
Central and Western Virginia,
 161, 185, 188, 192, 193, 194
D.C.'s Maryland Suburbs, 134,
 136, 140, 142, 147, 148,
 150, 152
Frederick and Western Mary-
 land, 368, 376, 378–379,
 385, 388–389, 390
Maryland's Eastern Shore, 435,
 437, 443, 447, 461–462,
 463, 464
Northern Virginia, 87–88,
 89, 90, 91, 93, 94, 104,
 107–108, 109, 110–111,
 113, 116
Richmond, Fredericksburg, and
 the Northern Neck, 210–211,
 214–215, 219, 220, 221, 236
Washington, D.C., 30–31,
 40–41, 44, 56, 57, 62, 63,
 64, 67, 68–69
Williamsburg and Hampton
 Roads, 252, 253, 255, 264,
 265, 269, 270, 272–273,
 279–280, 283–284, 285,
 286–287, 290, 293, 300
Children's Museum of Virginia,
 22, 210–211, 290
Chimborazo Medical Museum,
 216–217
Chinatown, *56–57, 60*
Chincoteague, VA, *297–300*
Chincoteague National Wildlife
 Refuge, *297–298*
Christ Church (Alexandria,
 VA), *87*
Christ Church (Port Republic,
 MD), *415*
Christmas on the Potomac, *22*
Chrysalis Vineyard, *118*
Chrysler Museum of Art,
 285–286
Churches
Annapolis and Southern Mary-
 land, 404, 405, 415, 421
Baltimore, 315, 317
Central and Western Virginia,
 168, 188
D.C.'s Maryland Suburbs, 138

Frederick and Western Mary-
 land, 384
Maryland's Eastern Shore, 454
Northern Virginia, 87
Richmond, Fredericksburg, and
 the Northern Neck, 215, 217,
 226, 243–244
Washington, D.C., 54–55
Williamsburg and Hampton
 Roads, 257, 272, 283, 287
Citie of Henricus, *212*
Citronelle ✕, *63*
City Center (Baltimore),
 341–343
City Park (Hagerstown), *379*
City Point (Hopewell), *276–277*
Civil War history
Baltimore, 319, 322
Central and Western Virginia,
 156, 167, 172–173, 177,
 178–179, 187
Frederick and Western
 Maryland, 361, 362, 367,
 373–375, 381
itinerary, 20–21
Northern Virginia, 87, 89, 98,
 102, 113, 119, 121
Richmond, Fredericksburg, and
 the Northern Neck, 211, 212,
 214–215, 226–227, 229, 233,
 234–235
Williamsburg and Hampton
 Roads, 272, 276–277, 279,
 280, 285
Clara Barton National Historic
 Site, *135–136*
Clay, Henry, *220*
Clifton Inn ▦, *164*
Clifton Forge, *192*
Climate, *10*
Clinton, MD, *148–149*
College Park, MD, *141–142,*
 144–145
College Park Aviation Museum,
 142
Colleges and universities
Hampton University, 283
Johns Hopkins University, 317
St. John's College, 403–404
United States Naval Academy,
 404
University of Maryland at Col-
 lege Park, 142
University of Virginia, 161
Virginia Military Institute, 187
Virginia Tech, 198
Washington College, 437
Washington and Lee University,
 187

Colonial Houses ▦, *266–267*
Colonial National Historical
 Park, *271*
Colonial Parkway, *272*
Colonial taverns, *265–266*
Colonial Williamsburg, *12–13,*
 255–258, 260–270
Colvin Run Mill Historic Site,
 116
Combsberry ▦, *452*
Comedy clubs, *349*
Commissioning Week, *395–396*
Communications, *477*
Community Bridge Mural, *368*
Concierges, *476*
Concord Point Lighthouse, *356*
Confederate Cemetery, *233*
Confederate War Memorial
 Chapel, *217*
Contemporary Museum, *311*
Corcoran Gallery of Art, *42–43*
Courthouse (Colonial Williams-
 burg), *261*
Cousteau Society, *283*
Covered bridges, *377*
Crabtree Falls, *197*
Cray House, *431*
Credit cards, *6, 478–479*
Crisfield, MD, *466–467*
Crooked Road: Virginia's Music
 Heritage Trail, *201*
Cross Island Trail, *434*
Crozet Pizza ✕, *163*
Cumberland, MD, *383–387*
Cunningham Falls State Park,
 376
Currency, *478–479*
Customs, *475*

D

D.C. United (soccer team), *74*
D.C.'s Maryland Suburbs, *8,*
 123–152
children's activities, 134, 136,
 140, 142, 147, 148, 150, 152
discounts and deals, 128
essential information, 128, 138,
 139, 145, 147
exploring, 130–131, 137, 138,
 139–140, 145, 146–147,
 148–149, 150
guided tours, 130–131, 135–
 136, 142, 144, 145, 147, 149
lodging, 128, 132–133, 141,
 142, 144, 147, 152
Montgomery County, 124,
 129–140
nightlife and the arts, 133,
 144, 152

price categories, 128
Prince George County, 124,
141–152
restaurants, 128, 131–132, 136,
137, 139, 140–141, 142,
147, 151
shopping, 134–135, 138–139
sports and outdoor activities,
134, 146
transportation, 125–128
when to go, 125
Daniel Harrison House, The,
184
Davidge Hall, *326*
Day Basket Factory, *442*
Dayton, VA, *184*
Decatur House, *43*
Deep Creek Lake, MD,
388–391
Deep Creek Lake State Park,
388–389
Defenders' Day, *306*
Delaplaine Visual Arts Educa-
tion Center, *368*
Delmarva Discovery Center,
458
Dentzel carousel, *136*
DeWitt Wallace Decorative Arts
Museum, *257, 260*
Dining. ⇨ *See* Restaurants
Discounts and deals
Baltimore, 310
Central and Western Virginia,
157, 192
D.C.'s Maryland Suburbs, 128
Northern Virginia, 84
Washington, D.C., 29
Williamsburg and Hampton
Roads, 249
Discovery Station and Hag-
erstown Aviation Museum,
378–379
Dixon's Furniture Auction, *437*
Dr. Samuel A. Mudd House,
423–424
Dr. Samuel D. Harris National
Museum of Dentistry, *326*
Dorchester County, MD, *427,*
453–456
Douthat State Park, *191*
Downrigging Weekend, *428*
Downtown (Fredericksburg,
VA), *230–234*
Downtown (Richmond, VA),
212, 214–218
Downtown (Washington, D.C.),
48–50, 60–62, 66–67, 66–67
Downtown Mall, The, *167*

Drug Enforcement Administra-
tion Museum, *101*
Druid Hill Park, *327–328*
Duckpin bowling, *351*
Duke of Gloucester Street
(Colonial Williamsburg), *261*
Dumbarton House, *52*
Dumbarton Oaks, *52–53*
Dumser's Dairyland, *461*
Dupont Circle, *53–55, 62,*
67–68, 75, 76

E

East New Market, MD, *456*
Eastern Market, *75, 76*
Eastern Neck National Wildlife
Refuge, *440*
Easton, MD, *444–446*
Eastport Yacht Club Lights
Parade, *396*
Edgar Allan Poe Museum, *212,*
214
Edith J. Carrier Arboretum and
Botanical Gardens, *182*
1848 Island Manor House, The
☒ , *299*
Electricity, *475*
Elizabeth Myers Mitchell Art
Gallery, *403–404*
Elk Forge B&B Inn and Retreat
☒ , *443*
Elk Neck State Park, *442*
Ellicott City, MD, *358*
Ellicott City B&O Railroad Sta-
tion Museum, *358*
Embassy Suites ☒ , *132–133*
Emmanuel Episcopal Church
and Parish Hall, *384*
Emmitsburg, MD, *377–378*
Endview Plantation, *279*
Enoch Pratt Free Library, *315*
Evergreen House, *316–317*
Exchange Hotel Civil War
Museum, *167*

F

Fager's Island ✕ , *462*
Fairfax County, VA, *81,*
111–117
Federal Hill (Baltimore),
336–337
Federal Hill Park, *319*
Fells Point (Baltimore), *305,*
323–324, 338–339, 346
Fells Point Maritime Museum,
324
Fell's Point Visitor Center, *324*
Ferry Farm, *236*
Ferry travel, *251*

Festivals and seasonal events
Annapolis and Southern Mary-
land, 395–396
Baltimore, 305, 306
Central and Western Virginia,
155, 166, 181, 182, 200, 201
Frederick and Western Mary-
land, 362
free events, 286
Maryland's Eastern Shore,
427–428
Richmond, Fredericksburg and
the Northern Neck, 206
Washington, D.C., 29
Williamsburg and Hampton
Roads, 247–248, 286
Film. ⇨ *See* Movies and film
Firestone's ✕ , *369*
First Unitarian Church, *315*
Fishing
Annapolis and Southern Mary-
land, 411
D.C.'s Maryland Suburbs, 146,
176
Frederick and Western Mary-
land, 386, 387
Maryland's Eastern Shore, 465
Fishing Bay Wildlife Manage-
ment Area, *455*
5&10 Antique Market, *443*
Five Gables Inn & Spa ☒ , *448*
Flag Ponds Nature Park, *417*
Floyd Country Store, *201*
Foggy Bottom, *52–53, 63–64,*
68–69, 77–78
Football
Annapolis and Southern Mary-
land, 412
Baltimore, 351
Washington, D.C, 74–75
Ford's Theatre, *50*
Forests. ⇨ *See* Parks and for-
ests, national and state
Fort Frederick State Park,
382–383
Fort Harrison, *184*
Fort McHenry, *16, 319*
Fort Monroe, *285*
Fort Washington Park, MD, *149*
Four Seasons Hotel ☒ , *68–69*
Fox hunting, *170*
Franklin Delano Roosevelt
Memorial, *36, 38*
Frederick and Western Mary-
land, *8, 359–392*
children's activities, 368, 376,
378–379, 385, 388–389, 390
essential information, 365,
367, 384

festivals and seasonal events, 362

Frederick, 362, 365, 367–373

guided tours, 365, 375, 383–384, 386–387

Hagerstown, 362, 378–380

lodging, 364, 370–371, 380, 382, 386, 389–390, 392

nightlife and the arts, 371–372, 380

price categories, 364

restaurants, 364, 369–370, 376, 379, 381–382, 385–386, 389, 391–392

shopping, 372, 388, 392

side trips from Frederick, 373–378

sports and outdoor activities, 361, 372, 375, 386–387, 390–391, 392

transportation, 364, 375, 377, 387, 381, 383, 387, 391

visitor information, 367

Western Maryland, 362, 378–392

when to go, 362

Frederick Festival of the Arts, 362

Frederick Visitor's Center, 367

Fredericksburg, VA. ⇨ *See* Richmond, Fredericksburg and the Northern Neck

Fredericksburg Area Museum and Cultural Center, 233

Fredericksburg/Spotsylvania National Military Park, 156, 235

Fredericksburg Visitor Center, 230–231

Free events, 286

Freer Gallery of Art, 34

Friendship Fire House, 90

Fritchie, Barbara, 367

Frontier Culture Museum, 185

G

Gadsby's Tavern Museum, 87–88

Garden Festival of Lights, 206

Gardens

Annapolis and Southern Maryland, 403, 405, 418

Baltimore, 317–318, 356

Central and Western Virginia, 171–172, 182

D.C.'s Maryland Suburbs, 140

Richmond, Fredericksburg, and the Northern Neck, 206, 211

Washington, D.C., 48, 52–53

Gari Melchers Home and Studio, 231–232

Garrett-Jacobs Mansion, 315

Geddes-Piper House, 437

Gentry Row, 89

George C. Marshall Museum, 187

George Washington Birthplace National Monument, 239

George Washington Masonic National Memorial, 88

George Washington and Jefferson National Forests, 191

George Washington's Birthday, 82

George Washington's Ferry Farm, 236

George Washington's Gristmill, 108

George Washington's Headquarters (Cumberland, MD), 384

George Washington's Office Museum, 179

George Wythe House, 260

Georgetown, 52–53, 63–64, 68–69, 75, 77–78

Geppi's Entertainment Museum, 319

Glen Echo, MD, 135–136

Glen Echo Park, 136

Glover Park, 64

Godiah Spray Tobacco Plantation, 422

Golf

Baltimore, 350

Central and Western Virginia, 191

Maryland's Eastern Shore, 436, 446, 465

Richmond, Fredericksburg, and the Northern Neck, 225

Williamsburg and Hampton Roads, 296, 302

Gordon-Roberts House, 384–385

Governor's Palace, 260

Grace Church, 272

Grand Illuminations (festival), 247

Grant, General Ulysses, 276–277

Grantsville, MD, 387–388

Grasonville, 434–435

Grayson Highlands State Park, 202

Great Blacks in Wax Museum, 315–316

Great Dismal Swamp National Wildlife Refuge, 290

Great Falls Park, 116–117

Great Falls Tavern, 137

Green Ridge State Forest, 383

Greenbelt, MD, 144–145

Guided tours

Annapolis and Southern Maryland, 399–400, 405

Baltimore, 309–310

Central and Western Virginia, 155, 161, 175, 185, 187

D.C.'s Maryland Suburbs, 130–131, 135–136, 142, 144, 145, 147, 149

Frederick and Western Maryland, 365, 375, 383–384, 386–387

Maryland's Eastern Shore, 437, 444, 452, 458, 459

Northern Virginia, 86, 108, 109, 117

Richmond, Fredericksburg and the Northern Neck, 209, 211, 215, 217, 219, 227, 230, 232, 241

Washington, D.C., 27–28

Williamsburg and Hampton Roads, 253, 255–256, 292, 296, 301, 302

Gunston Hall, 81, 106, 110–111

Gunston Hall Plantation, 110–111

H

H.M. Krentz (skipjack), 449

Hager House and Museum, 379

Hagerstown, MD, 362, 378–380

Hagerstown Roundhouse Museum, 379

Haley, Alex, 405

Hammond-Harwood House, 402

Hampden (Baltimore), 335

Hampton, VA, 282–284

Hampton History Museum, 283

Hampton Roads. ⇨ *See* Williamsburg and Hampton Roads

Hampton University, 283

Hampton University Museum, 283

Hanover Tomato Festival, 206

Harborplace and the Gallery, 319–320

Hardesty-Higgins House, 182

Harpers Ferry, MD, *375*
Harpers Ferry National Histori-
  cal Park, *374–375*
Harrisonburg, VA, *182–183*
Harrisonburg-Rockingham His-
  torical Society, *184*
Havre de Grace, MD, *355–357*
Havre de Grace Decoy
  Museum, *356*
Hawthorn Hotel & Suites at The
  Governor Dinwiddie 🔳, *291*
Health and fitness clubs, *350*
Heart of the Civil War Heritage
  Area Exhibit and Visitor
  Center, *381*
Helmand, The ✕, *329*
Hemphill Fine Arts, *76*
Henry, Patrick, *173, 219*
Hermitage Foundation
  Museum, *287*
Hiking
*Central and Western Virginia,
  176, 191, 196, 200, 202*
D.C.'s Maryland Suburbs, 134
*Frederick and Western Mary-
  land, 372*
Maryland's Eastern Shore, 434
Northern Virginia, 96
Hirshhorn Museum and Sculp-
  ture Garden, *34, 36*
Historic Alexandria Candlelight
  Tour, *82*
Historic Annapolis Antiques
  Show, *395*
Historic Christ Church,
  243–244
Historic Inns of Annapolis 🔳,
  409
Historic Jamestowne, *252–253*
Historic London Town and Gar-
  dens, *403*
Historic St. Mary's City, *422*
Historic Ships in Baltimore,
  318
Historic Smithfield Plantation,
  198
Historic Triangle, *246, 250–
  253, 255–257, 260–277*
Historical Society of Talbot
  County, *444*
HistoryQuest, *405*
Hockey, *74*
Holidays, *475*
Holly's Restaurant ✕, *435*
Hollywood Cemetery, *218*
Homeplace, The ✕, *195*
Homestead, The 🔳, *190*
Homewood House Museum, *317*
Hooper Strait Lighthouse, *447*

Hope and Glory Inn, The 🔳,
  244
Hopewell, VA, *276–277*
Horse racing, *146, 351*
Horseback riding, *176*
Hostels, *476*
Hotel George 🔳, *65*
Hotel Rouge 🔳, *67*
Hotels, *6, 11, 476–477*
*Annapolis and Southern Mary-
  land, 396–397, 408–410,
  414–415, 418–419, 422–423*
Baltimore, 340–347, 357
*Central and Western Virginia,
  157, 163–165, 168, 170–171,
  173, 175–176, 179–180, 181,
  183, 186, 188–189, 190–191,
  195–196, 197, 199, 200, 202*
*D.C.'s Maryland Suburbs, 128,
  132–133, 141, 142, 144,
  147, 152*
*Frederick and Western Mary-
  land, 364, 370–371, 380,
  382, 386, 389–390, 392*
*Maryland's Eastern Shore, 429,
  431, 438–439, 440, 442,
  443, 445–446, 448–449, 450,
  452–453, 454–455, 458,
  459–460, 463–464, 468*
meal plans, 6
*Northern Virginia, 85, 93–95,
  104–105, 113–114, 115,
  118–119, 121*
*price categories, 65, 85, 128,
  158, 208, 250, 340, 364,
  397, 429*
*Richmond, Fredericksburg and
  the Northern Neck, 208,
  222–223, 228, 237–238,
  239–240, 241, 243, 244*
Washington, D.C., 65–69
*Williamsburg and Hampton
  Roads, 249–250, 266–269,
  273–274, 276, 281–282, 284,
  288–289, 291, 294–295,
  299–300–301*
House rentals, *390, 474*
Hugh Mercer Apothecary Shop,
  232
Hunting, *146, 170*

I

Ice skating, *74*
Ingleside Vineyards, *241*
Inn at Gristmill Square 🔳,*191*
Inn at Little Washington, The
  🔳, *170–171*
Inn at Perry Cabin 🔳,
  448–449

Inn at Vaucluse Springs, The
  🔳, *180–181*
Inner Harbor/Downtown (Bal-
  timore), *13, 305, 318–323,
  335–336, 343–346*
InterContinental Harbor Court
  🔳, *345*
International Spy Museum,
  48–49
International travelers, tips
  for, *475*
Internet, *477*
Irish Inn at Glen Echo ✕, *136*
Irvington, VA, *243–244*
Isabella's ✕, *369*
Itineraries, *18–21*
Iwo Jima Memorial (United
  States Marine Corps War
  Memorial), *102–103*

J

J. Millard Tawes Museum &
  Visitor's Center, *467*
Jackson, Stonewall, *178–179,
  187*
James Anderson's Blacksmith
  Shop, *262*
James Madison Museum,
  167–168
James Monroe Museum and
  Memorial Library, *233–234*
Jamestown, VA, *251–254*
Jamestown Settlement, *253*
Jefferson, Thomas, *36, 38, 40,
  161, 162, 172, 188, 191*
Jefferson Hotel 🔳, *223*
Jefferson Memorial, *36, 38, 40*
Jefferson National Forest, *191*
Jefferson Patterson Park and
  Museum, *416*
Jefferson Pools, *191*
Jefferson Vineyards, *169*
Jewish Museum of Maryland,
  322
John F. Kennedy Center for the
  Performing Arts, *71*
John Marshall House, *214*
Johns Hopkins University, *317*
Joint Services Open House &
  Air Show, *125*
Joshua Wilton House 🔳, *183*

K

Kayaking
*Central and Western Virginia,
  166, 176*
*Frederick and Western Mary-
  land, 386, 390*

Maryland's Eastern Shore, 441, 455, 456

Williamsburg and Hampton Roads, 296, 302

Kenmore, *232*

Kennedy graves (Arlington National Cemetery), *99*

Kensington, MD, *137–139*

Kent County, MD, *427, 436–441*

Keswick Hall at Monticello ▦ , *164*

Kid's Closet (shop), *76*

King Jr., Martin Luther, *38, 40*

Kingsmill Resort and Spa ▦ , *267*

Kite flying, *428, 466*

Kluge Estate, *169*

Komi ✕ , *62*

Korean War Veterans Memorial, *38*

Kramerbooks & Afterwords (shop), *76*

Kunta Kinte-Alex Haley Memorial, *405*

L

La Grange Plantation, *454*

Lacrosse, *317, 351–352*

Lacrosse Museum and National Hall of Fame, *317*

Ladew Topiary Gardens, *356*

Lafayette, Marquis de, statue of, *43*

Lafayette Square, *43*

Largo, MD, *147–148*

L'Auberge Chez François ✕ , *117*

L'Auberge Provencale ✕▦ , *179–180*

Laurel, MD, *145–146*

Laurel Park, *146*

LaVale Toll Gate House, *387*

Le Yaca ✕ , *264*

Lee, Robert E., *87, 88, 98, 214, 225, 229, 235, 240–241, 285*

Lee Chapel and Museum (Washington and Lee University), *188*

Lee Hall, *279*

Lee-Fendall House, *88*

Leesburg, VA, *119, 121–122*

Legacy Museum of African-American History, *172*

Lemaire ✕ , *221–222*

L'Enfant, Pierre-Charles, *47*

Lewis Ginter Botanical Garden, *211*

Lexington, VA, *186–189*

Lexington Park, MD, *420*

Libraries

Baltimore, 315

Central and Western Virginia, 185–186

Maryland's Eastern Shore, 437

Richmond, Fredericksburg, and the Northern Neck, 217, 233–234, 243

Washington, D.C., 45, 49

Library of Congress, *45*

Library of Virginia, *217*

Lighthouse Club Hotel ▦ , *464*

Lighthouses

Annapolis and Southern Maryland, 422

Baltimore, 318, 356

Maryland's Eastern Shore, 442, 447

Williamsburg and Hampton Roads, 292

Lincoln, Abraham, *38, 50, 54, 423–424*

Lincoln Memorial, *38*

Little Italy (Baltimore), *337–338*

Lloyd House, *90*

Lodging, *474, 476–477.* ⇨ *See also* Hotels

Long, Robert, *324*

Loudoun County, VA, *81, 117–119, 121–122*

Lovely Lane Methodist Church, *317*

Lower Eastern Shore, MD, *427, 456–468*

Loy's Station Covered Bridge, *377*

Luray Caverns, *175*

Lusby, MD, *417*

Lyceum, *88*

Lynchburg, VA, *171–174*

M

M&T Bank Stadium, *325*

Mabry Mill, *197*

MacArthur, General Douglas, *286*

MacArthur Memorial, *286*

Madison, James, *167–168*

Magazine, *262*

Maggie L. Walker National Historic Site, *217*

Mail and shipping, *475*

Mall, The, *30–31, 34, 36, 75*

Manassas, VA, *113–114*

Manassas National Battlefield Park (Bull Run), *16, 113*

Mariners' Museum, *279–280*

Market Square (Colonial Williamsburg), *262*

Market Square (Roanoke, VA), *193*

Marshall, George C., *187*

Marshall, John, *214*

Marshall, Thurgood, *405–406*

Martin Luther King Jr. National Monument, *38, 40*

Mary Ball Washington Museum and Library, *243*

Mary Washington Grave and Monument, *234*

Mary Washington House, *232–233*

Maryland Art Place, *323*

Maryland Historical Society, *314*

Maryland Preakness Celebration, *306*

Maryland Science Center, *320*

Maryland State Fair, *306*

Maryland State House, *403*

Maryland Zoo in Baltimore, *327–328*

Maryland's Eastern Shore, *8, 425–468*

beaches, 434, 437, 441, 465, 466

camping, 442

Cecil County, 427, 441–443

children's activities, 435, 437, 443, 447, 461–462, 463, 464

Dorchester County, 453–456

essential information, 436, 437, 444, 453, 461, 468

exploring Eastern Shore, 430

festivals and seasonal events, 427–428

guided tours, 437, 444, 452, 458, 459

Kent County, 427, 436–441

lodging, 429, 431, 438–439, 440, 442, 443, 445–446, 448–449, 450, 452–453, 454–455, 458, 459–460, 463–464, 468

Lower Eastern Shore, 427, 456–468

nightlife and the arts, 439, 446, 464–465

price categories, 429

Queen Anne's County, 427, 430–431, 434–436

restaurants, 428, 429, 431, 434–435, 438, 440, 441–442, 443, 444–445, 447–448, 452, 454, 457, 459, 462–463 shopping, *434, 436, 465–466, 467*

sports and outdoor activities, *428, 434, 435, 436, 441, 446, 449, 450, 455–456, 458, 465*

Talbot County, *427, 443–453*

transportation, *428–29, 440, 450, 452, 460*

when to go, *427–428*

Maymont, *219*

Maymont Park, *22*

McDowell Hall (St. John's College), *403*

McGuffey Art Center, *160*

Meadow Farm, *211*

Meal plans, *6*

Melchers, Gari, *231–232*

Meredith House, *454*

Middleburg, VA, *117–119*

Middletown, MD, *373*

Middletown, VA, *180–181*

Military Through the Ages (battle reenactments), *247*

Mill Mountain Star, *193*

Mill Mountain Zoo, *193*

Mills

Central and Western Virginia, *197*

Northern Virginia, *107, 116*

Money matters, *478–479*

Monocacy National Battlefield, *373–374*

Monroe, James, *160, 233–234*

Montgomery County, MD, *124, 129–140*

Monticello, *161*

Montpelier, *168*

Montpelier Mansion, *145*

Monuments, statues, and memorials

Annapolis and Southern Maryland, *404, 405–406*

Baltimore, *314*

Central and Western Virginia, *173, 194*

D.C.'s Maryland Suburbs, *151*

Frederick and Western Maryland, *377–378*

Northern Virginia, *87*

Richmond, Fredericksburg, and the Northern Neck, *217, 218, 235, 239*

Washington, D.C., *36, 38–41*

Williamsburg and Hampton Roads, *286*

Moore House, *272*

Morrison House ⊡, *94–95*

Morven Park, *119, 121*

Moses Myers House, *287*

Mount Clare Museum House, *326–327*

Mount Olivet Cemetery, *368*

Mount Rogers Recreation Area, *202*

Mount Vernon (Baltimore), *305, 311, 314–316, 328–329, 332–333, 341*

Mount Vernon, VA, *80–81, 106–108*

Mount Vernon Place (Baltimore), *314*

Mountain biking, *191, 200, 390*

Mountain music, *201*

Movies and film

Baltimore, *349*

Central and Western Virginia, *155, 166*

D.C.'s Maryland Suburbs, *139–140*

Mrs. Rowe's Restaurant ✕, *186*

Mudd, Dr. Samuel A., *423–424*

Museum and White House of the Confederacy, *214, 235*

Museum of the Confederacy, *156*

Museum of the Shenandoah Valley, *178*

Museums and art galleries, *22*

Annapolis and Southern Maryland, *401, 402, 403–404, 405, 414, 416, 420, 422, 423–424*

Baltimore, *22, 305, 311, 314, 315–316, 317, 318–319, 320–321, 322, 323, 324, 325, 326–327, 356, 357, 358*

Central and Western Virginia, *156, 160, 161, 167–168, 171–172, 173, 178–179, 182–183, 184, 185–186, 187, 188, 192, 193–194, 198, 201*

D.C.'s Maryland Suburbs, *133, 140, 142, 145, 149, 150–151*

Frederick and Western Maryland, *367–368, 369, 378–379, 381, 384–385*

Maryland's Eastern Shore, *434, 437, 440, 443, 444, 447, 452, 454, 456, 457, 461, 467*

Northern Virginia, *87–88, 89, 91, 101, 110, 111, 112, 117, 119, 120*

Richmond, Fredericksburg, and the Northern Neck, *210–211, 212, 214, 215–216, 217, 218, 219, 226, 227,*
231–232, 233–234, 235, 242, 243

Washington, D.C., *30–31, 34, 36, 43–44, 48–50, 52–53, 54, 76*

Williamsburg and Hampton Roads, *257, 260, 261, 272, 275, 276–277, 279–280, 283–284, 285–286, 287, 289, 290–291, 293, 299*

Music, *15*

Annapolis and Southern Maryland, *410–411*

Baltimore, *348–349*

Central and Western Virginia, *155, 182, 191*

D.C.'s Maryland Suburbs, *133, 136, 152*

Frederick and Western Maryland, *362, 372*

Maryland's Eastern Shore, *439, 464–465*

mountain music, *201*

Northern Virginia, *95, 105*

Richmond, Fredericksburg, and the Northern Neck, *224*

Washington, D.C., *70–71*

Williamsburg and Hampton Roads, *269, 298*

Myers, Moses, *287*

N

Narrows, The ✕, *435*

Nathan of Dorchester (skipjack), *456*

National Air and Space Museum, *30–31*

National Air and Space Museum, Steven F. Udvar-Hazy Center, *112*

National Aquarium in Baltimore, *320*

National Archives, *49*

National Building Museum, *50*

National Capital Trolley Museum, *140*

National Cemetery, *236*

National Colonial Farm, *150*

National D-Day Memorial, *194*

National Gallery of Art, East Building, *31*

National Gallery of Art, West Building, *31*

National Harbor, *150–151*

National Hard Crab Derby, *428*

National Institutes of Health (NIH), *130–131*

National Museum of American History, *31, 34*
National Museum of Civil War Medicine, *367*
National Museum of Health and Medicine, *140*
National Museum of Natural History, *31*
National Museum of the American Indian, *36*
National Museum of the Civil War Soldier, *226–227, 235*
National Museum of the Marine Corps, *111*
National Portrait Gallery, *49*
National Shrine Grotto of Lourdes, *377*
National Shrine of St. Elizabeth Ann Seton, *377–378*
National Wildlife Refuges, *302*
National World War II Memorial, *40*
National Zoo, *53–54*
Natural Bridge of Virginia, *188*
Nauticus, *286*
Naval Air Station, Oceana, *292*
Neild Museum, *454*
Nelson House, *272*
Netherlands Carillon (Arlington National Cemetery), *101*
New Germany State Park, *387*
New Market, VA, *181–182*
New Market Battlefield Historical Park, *156, 177, 181–182*
New River Valley, VA, *197–200*
New Year's Eve, *306*
Newport News, VA, *278–282*
Newseum, *49–50*
Nightlife and the arts
Annapolis and Southern Maryland, *410–411, 417*
Baltimore, *347–350*
Central and Western Virginia, *166, 182, 186, 191, 196, 202*
D.C.'s Maryland Suburbs, *133, 144, 152*
Frederick and Western Maryland, *371–372, 380*
Maryland's Eastern Shore, *439, 446, 464–465*
Northern Virginia, *95, 105*
Richmond Fredericksburg, and the Northern Neck, *205, 223–224*
Washington, D.C., *70–72*
Williamsburg and Hampton Roads, *269, 289, 296*

Nine Front Street (Baltimore), *322–323*
No Frill Bar and Grill ✕, *288*
Nora ✕, *62*
Norfolk, *285–289*
Norfolk Naval Station, *286–287*
North Beach, MD, *412–413*
North East, MD, *442–443*
Northern Neck, VA. ⇨ See Richmond, Fredericksburg and the Northern Neck
Northern Suburbs (Baltimore), *347*
Northern Virginia, *8, 79–122*
Alexandria, *80, 85–87*
Arlington, *80, 97–99, 101–106*
children's activities, *87–88, 89, 90, 91, 93, 94, 104, 107–108, 109, 110–111, 113, 116*
discounts and deals, *84*
essential information, *83–84, 97–98, 107, 114*
exploring, *87–91, 98–99, 101–103, 107–108,109, 110–111, 112, 113, 118, 119, 121*
Fairfax County, *81, 111–117*
guided tours, *86, 108, 109, 117*
lodging, *85, 93–95, 104–105, 113–114, 115, 118–119, 121*
Loudoun County, *81, 117–119, 121–122*
Mount Vernon, Woodlawn, and Gunston Hall, *81, 106–111*
nightlife and the arts, *95, 105*
price categories, *84–85*
restaurants, *84–85, 89, 91–93, 103–104, 114, 121*
shopping, *96–97, 106, 111, 115*
sports and outdoor activities, *95–96, 106*
transportation, *82–83, 97, 106*
when to go, *81–82*
Northwest D.C., *53–55*

O

O. Winston Link Museum, *193*
Oakland, MD, *391–392*
Oatlands, *119*
Ocean City, MD, *460–466*
Ocean City Life Saving Station Museum, *461*
October Homes Tour and Crafts Exhibit, *155*
Old Angler's Inn ✕, *136*
Old Blandford Church, *226*
Old Cape Henry Lighthouse, *292*

Old Coast Guard Station, *293*
Old Fiddlers Convention, *201*
Old Hickory Steakhouse ✕, *151*
Old Presbyterian Meeting House, *90–91*
Old Stone House, *53*
Old Town Alexandria, *86*
Old Trinity Church, *454*
Omni Newport News Hotel ⬚, *281–282*
Omni Shoreham Hotel ⬚, *69*
Onancock, VA, *300–301*
Orange County, VA, *167–168*
Oriole Park at Camden Yards, *325–326*
Oxford, MD, *450, 452–453*
Oxford Museum, *452*
Oxford-Bellevue Ferry, *450, 452*
Oxon Cove Park, *148*
Oyster and Maritime Museum, *299*

P

P. Buckley Moss Museum, *185*
Paca, William, *405*
Packing for the trip, *479*
Palace Green, *262*
Pamplin Historical Park, *156, 226–227, 235*
Paramount's Kings Dominion (amusement park), *220*
Parks and forests, national and state, *12*
Annapolis and Southern Maryland, *416, 417, 420–421, 422*
Central and Western Virginia, *156, 174–176, 177, 181–182, 191, 202*
D.C.'s Maryland Suburbs, *134, 136, 137, 148, 149, 150*
Frederick and Western Maryland, *368, 374–376, 382–383, 384, 387, 388–389, 391*
Maryland's Eastern Shore, *442*
Northern Virginia, *113, 115–116, 117, 119, 121*
Richmond, Fredericksburg, and the Northern Neck, *214–215, 218–219, 226–227, 235, 239–240*
Williamsburg and Hampton Roads, *271*
Patriot, The (yacht), *447*
Patriot Plaza (outlet shop), *271*
Patuxent National Wildlife Visitor Center, *145–146*

Patuxent Research Refuge, *146*
Pazo ✕ , *339*
Peaks of Otter Recreation
    Area, *197*
Penn Quarter, *48*
Pentagon, *101–102*
Petersburg, VA, *225–228*
Petersburg National Battlefield,
    156, 227, 235
Petersburg Visitors Center, *227*
Peyton Randolph House, *260*
Phillips Collection, *54*
Phoenix Shot Tower, *323*
Pickersgill, Mary, *323*
Piedmont Vineyards and Win-
    ery, *118*
Pier 4 Building, *323*
Piney Point Lighthouse,
    Museum & Historic Park, *422*
Piscataway Park, *150*
Plane travel. ➪ *See* Air travel
Plantations
Annapolis and Southern Mary-
    land, 422, 424
Central and Western Virginia,
    161, 198
Gunston Hall, 81, 106,
    110–111
Maryland's Eastern Shore, 454
Monticello, 161
Mount Vernon, VA, 81, 106,
    107–108
Northern Virginia, 81, 106,
    110–111
Oatlands, 119
Pamplin Historical Park, 226
Richmond, Fredericksburg and
    the Northern Neck, 218, 219,
    240–241
Williamsburg and Hampton
    Roads, 247, 274–275, 277,
    279
Woodlawn, 109
Poe, Edgar Allan, *212, 214,*
    285, 327
Poe House, *327*
Point Lookout State Park,
    420–421
Point of Honor, *172*
Pope-Leighey House, *109*
Poplar Forest, *172*
Port Discovery–The Baltimore
    Children's Museum, *22,*
    320–321
Port Republic, MD, *415–416*
Port Republic School No. 7,
    416
Port Tobacco, MD, *424*
Portsmouth, VA, *290–291*

Portsmouth Naval Shipyard
    Museum, *290–291*
Potomac, MD, *136–137*
Potomac Point Winery, *233*
Potomac Riverboat Company,
    151
Power Plant, The, *323*
President Lincoln's Cottage, *54*
Price categories
Annapolis and Southern Mary-
    land, 397
Baltimore, 328, 340
Central and Western Virginia,
    158
D.C.'s Maryland Suburbs, 128
dining, 55, 85, 128, 158, 208,
    250, 328, 364, 397, 429
Frederick and Western Mary-
    land, 364
lodging, 65, 85, 128, 158, 208,
    250, 340, 364, 397, 429
Maryland's Eastern Shore, 429
Northern Virginia, 85
Richmond, Fredericksburg, and
    the Northern Neck, 208
Washington, D.C., 55, 65
Williamsburg and Hampton
    Roads, 250
Prime Outlets at Williamsburg,
    271
Prime Rib, The ✕ , *332*
Prince George's County, MD,
    124, 141–152
Pry House Field Hospital
    Museum, *381*
Public Hospital, *262*

Q

Queen Anne's County, MD,
    427, 430–431, 434–436
Queenstown, MD, *435–436*

R

Rafting, whitewater
Frederick and Western Mary-
    land, 375, 387
Richmond, Fredericksburg and
    the Northern Neck, 225
Raleigh Tavern, *260*
Ralph Stanley Museum and
    Traditional Mountain Music
    Center, *201*
Rams Head Tavern ✕ , *408*
Ramsay House, *88*
Randolph, Peyton, *260*
Rappahannock River Cruises,
    242
Rasika ✕ , *60*

Rebecca T. Ruark (skipjack),
    450
Red Hill-Patrick Henry National
    Memorial, *173*
Reedville, VA, *242–243*
Reedville Fishermen's Museum,
    242
Regency Room ✕ , *264*
Reginald F. Lewis Museum of
    African American History &
    Culture, *321*
Renwick Gallery, *43–44*
Restaurants, *6, 11, 477–478*
Annapolis and Southern Mary-
    land, 396, 401–402, 403,
    406–408, 413, 414, 416, 418
Baltimore, 315, 323, 324, 327,
    328–329, 332–340, 357
Central and Western Virginia,
    157, 161, 163, 173, 179,
    183, 186, 188, 190, 195, 199
D.C.'s Maryland Suburbs, 128,
    131–132, 136, 137, 139,
    140–141, 142, 147, 151
Frederick and Western Mary-
    land, 364, 369–370, 376,
    379, 381–382, 385–386, 389,
    391–392
Maryland's Eastern Shore, 428,
    429, 431, 434–435, 438,
    440, 441–442, 443, 444–445,
    447–448, 452, 454, 457,
    459, 462–463
Northern Virginia, 84–85, 89,
    91–93, 103–104, 114, 121
price categories, 55, 85, 128,
    158, 208, 250, 328, 364,
    397, 429
Richmond, Fredericksburg,
    and the Northern Neck, 208,
    220–222, 227–228, 231, 232,
    236–237, 244
Washington, D.C., 43, 45, 48,
    55–57, 60–65
Williamsburg and Hampton
    Roads, 249, 263–266, 273,
    275–276, 277, 280–281, 284,
    287–288, 293–294, 298–299,
    300
Rex Theatre, *201*
Richard Johnston Inn 🖫 , *238*
Richmond, Fredericksburg,
    and the Northern Neck, *8,*
    203–244
camping, 239–240
children's activities, 210–211,
    214–215, 219, 220, 221, 236
essential information, 209–210,
    230

festivals and seasonal events,
206
Fredericksburg, 205, 228–238
guided tours, 209, 211, 215,
217, 219, 227, 230, 232, 241
lodging, 208, 222–223, 228,
237–238, 239–240, 241,
243, 244
nightlife and the arts, 205,
223–224
Northern Neck, 205, 238–244
Petersburg, 204–205, 225–228
price categories, 208
restaurants, 208, 220–222,
227–228, 231, 232, 236–237,
244
Richmond, 204, 209–212,
214–225, 220–222
shopping, 225
sports and outdoor activities,
224–225
transportation, 206–208, 226,
230
visitor information, 208
when to go, 206
Richmond Canal Cruises, 216
Richmond Folk Festival, 206
Richmond National Battlefield
Park Visitor Center, 156,
214–215, 235
Richmond Slave Trail, 215
Rising Sun Tavern, 233
Riverwalk Landing, 271–272
Roanoke, VA, 192–196
Roanoke Star, 193
Robert Long House Museum,
324
Robertson's Windmill, 262
Rock climbing, 387
Rock Hall, MD, 439–441
Roddy Road Covered Bridge,
377
Rodgers House, 356
Roger Brooke Taney House,
367–368
Roland Park (Baltimore), 347
Roosevelt, Franklin Delano,
36, 38
Rose Hill Manor Park/The Chil-
dren's and Farm Museum,
368
Rotunda, The, 44
Round House Theatre, 133
Running, jogging and walking
Baltimore, 351
Washington, D.C., 75
Williamsburg and Hampton
Roads, 270
Ruth, Babe, 325

S
Sailing, 14, 73–74, 402,
411–412, 428
Sailor's Creek Battlefield State
Historical Park, 177
St. Anne's Church, 405
St. Ignatius Church, 421
St. John's Church, 283
St. John's College, 403–404
St. John's Episcopal Church,
215
St. Mary's City, MD, 421–423
St. Mary's County, MD, 394–
395, 419–423
St. Michaels, MD, 446–449
St. Paul's Church, 287
St. Regis Washington, DC 🏨,
66–67
St. Thomas's Episcopal Church,
168
Salisbury, MD, 457–458
Savage River Lodge ✕🏨, 386
Schifferstadt Architectural
Museum, 368–369
Science Museum of Virginia,
211
Scossa ✕, 445
Section 7A (Arlington National
Cemetery), 99
Section 27 (Arlington National
Cemetery), 102
Segway tours, 387
Sessions House, 272
Shakespeare Theatre, 86
Sharpsburg, MD, 380–382
Shenandoah Valley Apple Blos-
som Festival, 181
Shenandoah Valley Battlefields
Foundation, 177
Shenandoah National Park,
12, 174–176
Shenandoah Valley, VA, 154,
176–192
Shenandoah Valley Music Fes-
tival, 182
Sherwood Forest Plantation,
274–275
Sherwood Gardens, 317–318
Shirley Plantation, 219, 275
Shopping
Baltimore, 352–355
Central and Western Virginia,
166–167, 181
D.C.'s Maryland Suburbs,
134–135, 138–139
Frederick and Western Mary-
land, 372, 388, 392
Maryland's Eastern Shore, 434,
436, 465–466, 467

Northern Virginia, 96–97, 106,
111, 115
Richmond, Fredericksburg, and
the Northern Neck, 225
Washington, D.C., 75–78
Williamsburg and Hampton
Roads, 270, 271, 289
Siege Museum, 227
Silver Spring, MD, 139–141
SILVERDOCS, 125
Six Flags America (amusement
park), 147
Skiing, 174, 390–391
Skipjacks, 450, 451
Skyline Drive, 175
Smith, Captain John, 229, 254
Smith Island, MD, 467–468
Smith Island and Chesapeake
Bay Cruises, 242
Smith Island Crabmeat Co-op,
468
Smith Island Sweet Shoppe, 467
Smithsonian American Art
Museum, 50
Snow Hill, MD, 458
Snowboarding, 174, 390
Soccer, 74
Solomons, MD, 417–419
Somerwell House, 272
Sotterley, 420
South Mountain Creamery, 22
Southern Maryland. ⇨ See
Annapolis and Southern
Maryland
Southwest Virginia, 154–155,
192–202
Spencer, Anne, 171–172
Sports and outdoor activities
Annapolis and Southern Mary-
land, 402, 411–412
Baltimore, 350–352
Central and Western Virginia,
166, 173–174, 175, 176,
191, 196, 200, 202
D.C.'s Maryland Suburbs, 134,
146
Frederick and Western
Maryland, 361, 372, 375,
386–387, 390–391, 392
Maryland's Eastern Shore, 428,
434, 435, 436, 441, 446,
449, 450, 455–456, 458, 465
Northern Virginia, 95–96, 106
Richmond, Fredericksburg, and
the Northern Neck, 224–225
Washington, D.C., 72–75
Williamsburg and Hamp-
ton Roads, 269–270, 296,
297–298, 301, 302

Spruce Forest Artisan Village and Penn Alps, *388*
Stabler-Leadbeater Apothecary, *91*
Stanley, Ralph, *201*
Stanley's Seafood House ✕, *416*
Star Hill Brewery, *165–166*
Star-Spangled Banner House, *323*
State Arboretum of Virginia, *178*
State House of 1676, *422*
Statuary Hall, *44*
Staunton, VA, *184–186*
Staunton Grocery ✕, *186*
Steppingstone Museum, *356*
Stevensville, MD, *430–431, 434*
Stevensville Train Depot, *431*
Stone, Thomas, *424*
Stonewall Jackson House, *187*
Stonewall Jackson's Headquarters Museum, *178–179*
Strasburg Antique Emporium, *181*
Stratford Hall Plantation, *240–241*
Subway travel
Baltimore, 308
D.C.'s Maryland Suburbs, 126–127
Northern Virginia, 83
Washington, D.C., 27
Sully, *112*
Sultana (schooner), *437*
Sunfest Kite Festival, *428*
Supreme Court Building, *44–45*
Surratt House Museum, *149*
Susquehanna Museum, *357*
Swallow Falls State Park, *391*
Swan Tavern, *272*
Swedenburg Estate Vineyard, *118*
Symbols, *6*

T

Talbot County, MD, *427, 443–453*
Talbot County Courthouse, *444*
Taney, Roger Brooke, *367–368*
Tangier Island, VA, *301*
Tangier Island & Chesapeake Cruises, *242–243*
Taste of Bethesda, *125*
Taubman Museum of Art, *193–194*
Taxes, *480*

Taxis
Baltimore, 308–309
Central and Western Virginia, 157
D.C.'s Maryland Suburbs, 125–126, 127–128
Northern Virginia, 83
Richmond, 209
Washington, D.C., 27
Williamsburg and Hampton Roads, 248
Teaism ✕, *61*
Tecumseh Statue (United States Naval Academy), *404*
Temple of the Church of Jesus Christ of Latter-day Saints, *138*
Tennis, *351*
Terrapin Nature Area, *434*
Theater and performing arts
Annapolis and Southern Maryland, 411
Baltimore, 349–350
Central and Western Virginia, 182, 186, 201, 202
D.C.'s Maryland Suburbs, 133, 139–140
Frederick and Western Maryland, 372, 380
Maryland's Eastern Shore, 446
Northern Virginia, 115–116
Richmond, Fredericksburg, and the Northern Neck, 220, 223, 224
Washington, D.C., 71–72
Williamsburg and Hampton Roads, 269
Theodore Roosevelt Island, *102*
Thomas Jefferson Building, *45*
Thomas Stone National Historic Site, *424*
Thrasher Carriage Collection Museum, *385*
Thurgood Marshall Memorial, *405–406*
Tilghman Island, MD, *449–450*
Time, *480*
Timing the visit, *10*
Tipping, *479*
Tollhouses, *387*
Tomb of the Unknowns (Arlington National Cemetery), *99, 101*
Torpedo Factory Art Center, *89*
Tours. ⇨ *See* Guided tours
Train travel, *473*
Baltimore, 309
Central and Western Virginia, 157
D.C.'s Maryland Suburbs, 128

Frederick and Western Maryland, *364, 385*
Northern Virginia, *83*
Richmond, Fredericksburg, and the Northern Neck, *210*
Washington, D.C., *27*
Williamsburg and Hampton Roads, *248–249*
Transportation, *11, 470–473*
Annapolis and Southern Maryland, 396, 399
Baltimore, 306–309
Central and Western Virginia, 156–157
D.C.'s Maryland Suburbs, 125–128
Frederick and Western Maryland, 364, 375, 377, 387, 381, 383, 387, 391
Maryland's Eastern Shore, 428–29, 440, 450, 452, 460
Northern Virginia, 82–83, 97, 106
Richmond, Fredericksburg, and the Northern Neck, 206–208, 226, 230
Washington, D.C., 25–27
Williamsburg and Hampton Roads, 248–249, 251, 255, 271, 276, 279, 282, 291
Travel tips
air travel, 470–471
boat and ferry travel, 471–472
booking, 474
bus travel, 472
business hours, 478
car travel, 472–473
concierges, 476
credit cards, 6, 478
customs, 475
electricity, 475
holidays, 475
for international travelers, 475
internet, 477
lodging, 474, 476–477
mail and shipping, 475
meal plans, 6
money matters, 478–479
packing, 479
restaurants, 477
taxes, 480
time, 480
tipping, 479
train travel, 473
visitor information, 480
weather, 10
Tremont Plaza Hotel ▦ , *343*
Trimper's Amusement Park, *461–462*
Trolley travel, *413, 414*

Tuckahoe, Plantation, *219*
Turkey Point Lighthouse, *442*
Tyler, John, *274–275*
Tysons Corner, VA, *114–115*

U

U Street (Washington, D.C.),
64–65, 75, 78
U.S. Army Transportation
Museum, *280*
U.S. Naval Academy Museum
& Gallery of Ships, *404*
Union Station, *48*
United States Sailboat and
Powerboat Shows, *396*
United States Botanic Garden,
48
United States Holocaust Memo-
rial Museum, *34*
United States Marine Corps
War Memorial (Iwo Jima),
102–103
United States Naval Academy,
404
University of Mary Washington
Galleries, *234*
University of Maryland at Col-
lege Park, *142*
University of Virginia, *161*
University of Virginia Art
Museum, *161*
Upper Bay Museum, *443*
Upper Northwest (Washington,
D.C.), *69*
USNA Armel-Lefwich Visitor
Center, *404*
USS Constellation, *321*

V

Valentine Richmond History
Center, *215–216*
Vietnam Veterans Memo-
rial, *40*
Viewtrail 100, *459*
Virginia Air and Space Center,
283–284
Virginia Annual Garden Week,
206
Virginia Aquarium and Marine
Science Center, *293*
Virginia Aviation Museum, *217*
Virginia Beach, VA, *12,
291–296*
Virginia Center for Architec-
ture, *217*
Virginia Civil War Trails, *156,
235*
Virginia Creeper Trail, *202*

Virginia Discovery Museum,
161
Virginia Festival of the Book,
166
Virginia Film Festival, *155, 166*
Virginia Gold Cup, *82*
Virginia Highlands Festival,
155, 200
Virginia Historical Society
Museum of Virginia History,
211
Virginia Holocaust Museum,
217–218
Virginia Living Museum, *280*
Virginia Military Institute, *187*
Virginia Military Institute
Museum, *187*
Virginia Museum of Fine Arts,
216
Virginia Museum of Natural
History, *198*
Virginia Museum of Transpor-
tation, *194*
Virginia Quilt Museum,
182–183
Virginia State Capitol, *216*
Virginia State Fair, *206*
Virginia Tech, *198*
Virginia War Memorial, *218*
Virginia War Museum, *280*
Virginia Zoological Park, *22*
Virginia's Annual Garden
Walk, *206*
Virginia's Eastern Shore, *247,
296–302*
Visitor Center (Baltimore), *321*
Visitor Center (Colonial Wil-
liamsburg), *260–261*
Visitor information, *480*

W

Waldorf, MD, *423–424*
Walker, Maggie L., *217*
Wallops Island, VA, *300*
Walters Art Museum, *314*
Ward Museum of Waterfowl
Art, *457*
Warsaw, VA, *241–242*
Washington, Booker T., *194*
Washington Capitals (hockey
team), *74*
Washington College, *437*
Washington County Museum of
Fine Arts, *379*
Washington, D.C., *8, 13, 23–78*
*Capitol Hill, 44–45, 48, 55–56,
65, 75, 76*

*children's activities, 30–31,
40–41, 44, 56, 57, 62, 63,
64, 67, 68–69*
Chinatown, 56–57, 60
discounts and deals, 29
*Downtown, 48–50, 60–62,
66–67, 66–67*
*Dupont Circle and Northwest
D.C., 53–55, 62, 67–68,
75, 76*
Eastern Market, 75, 76
essential information, 28
*exploring Washington, D.C.,
29–30*
*Georgetown and Foggy Bot-
tom, 52–53, 63–64, 68–69,
75, 77–78*
Glover Park, 64
guided tours, 27–28
lodging, 65–69
Mall, 30–31, 34, 36, 75
Monuments, 36, 38–41
nightlife and the arts, 70–72
price categories, 55, 65
*restaurants, 43, 45, 48, 55–57,
60–65*
shopping, 75–78
*sports and outdoor activities,
72–75*
transportation, 25–27
U Street, 64–65, 75, 78
when to go, 25
White House area, 41–44
*Woodley Park and Upper
Northwest, 69*
Washington, George, *16,
40–41, 82, 88, 98, 108, 149,
179, 188, 228, 229, 232–
233, 236, 239, 314, 384*
Washington, Mary Ball,
232–233, 234, 243
Washington, VA, *170–171*
Washington and Lee University,
187–188
Washington Monument (Baltimore), *314*
Washington Monument (Washington, D.C.), *40–41*
Washington National Cathe-
dral, *54–55*
Washington Street Historic Dis-
trict (Cumberland, MD), *384*
Water Country USA (amuse-
ment park), *270*
Water sports, *296, 361, 390*
Waterfalls
*Central and Western Virginia,
197*

Frederick and Western Maryland, 376, 391
Northern Virginia, 116–117
Waterford, VA, 121–122
Waterford Foundation, 122
Waterman's Beachwood Grill ✕, 294
Waterman's Museum (Rock Hall), 440
Watermen's Museum (Yorktown), 272
Waterwheel Restaurant ✕, 190
Weather, 10
West Baltimore, 324–327
Western Maryland. ⇨ *See* Frederick and Western Maryland
Western Maryland Scenic Railroad, 385
Western Virginia. ⇨ *See* Central and Western Virginia
Westminster Cemetery and Catacombs, 326
Weston Manor, 277
Westover, 275
Wetherburn's Tavern, 262
When to go, 10
White House, 41–42
White House area, 41–44
White House Visitor Center, 41–42
White Swan Tavern 🛏, 439
Wickham House, 215–216
Wilderness Road Regional Museum, 198
Wildlife refuges
Annapolis and Southern Maryland, 415
D.C.'s Maryland Suburbs, 130, 145–146
Frederick and Western Maryland, 376
Maryland's Eastern Shore, 440, 456
Northern Virginia, 102
Williamsburg and Hampton Roads, 290, 297–298, 302
William Paca House and Garden, 405

Williamsburg and Hampton Roads, 8, 245–302
beaches, 12, 291–296
children's activities, 252, 253, 255, 264, 265, 269, 270, 272–273, 279–280, 283–284, 285, 286–287, 290, 293, 300
discounts and deals, 249
essential information, 249, 256, 271, 279
exploring Williamsburg and Hampton Roads, 250
festivals and seasonal events, 247–248, 286
free events, 286
guided tours, 253, 255–256, 292, 296, 301, 302
Hampton Roads area, 246–247, 277–296
Historic Triangle, 246, 250–253, 255–257, 260–277
lodging, 249–250, 266–269, 273–274, 276, 281–282, 284, 288–289, 291, 294–295, 299–300–301
nightlife and the arts, 269, 289, 296
price categories, 250
restaurants, 249, 263–266, 273, 275–276, 277, 280–281, 284, 287–288, 293–294, 298–299, 300
shopping, 270, 271, 289
sports and outdoor activities, 269–270, 296, 297–298, 301, 302
transportation, 248–249, 251, 255, 271, 276, 279, 282, 291
Virginia's Eastern Shore, 247, 296–302
when to go, 247
Williamsburg Inn 🛏, 268
Williamsburg Outlet Mall, 271
Williamsburg Pottery Factory (outlet shop), 271
Williamsburg Winery, 263
Wilson, Woodrow, 185–186
Wilton, 219
Winchester, VA, 177–180
Windmills, 262

Wine, beer, and spirits, 477–488
Wineries, 15, 120
Central and Western Virginia, 155, 169
Northern Virginia, 118
Richmond, Fredericksburg, and the Northern Neck, 233, 241
Williamsburg and Hampton Roads, 263
Wisp Resort, 389, 390–391
Wolf Trap, VA, 115–116
Wolf Trap National Park for the Performing Arts, 115–116
Woman's Industrial Exchange, 316
Women in Military Service for America Memoria, 103
Woodberry Kitchen ✕, 335
Woodlawn, 81, 105, 109–110
Woodley Park, 69
Woodrow Wilson Presidential Library and Museum, 185–186
Woolly Mammoth (theater), 72
World Trade Center, 322
Wren Building, 263
Wyndham Virginia Beach Oceanfront 🛏, 295
Wythe, George, 260

Y

Yorktown, VA, 270–274
Yorktown Battlefield, 16, 272–273
Yorktown Day, 247–248
Yorktown Victory Center, 273

Z

Zaytinya ✕, 60, 61–62
Zoos
Baltimore, 327–328
Central and Western Virginia, 193
Frederick and Western Maryland, 376
Washington, D.C., 53–54

PHOTO CREDITS

ABOUT OUR WRITERS

Nina Callaway is a Virginia-raised freelance writer who writes about food, travel, and community. Based in Brooklyn, she is the editor for weddings.about.com and the founder of Pieathon, a 24-hour bake-a-thon that raises money for cancer patients. For this edition she updated Virginia's Eastern Shore.

Born and raised in Virginia, **Mike Lillis** now lives in Washington, D.C., where he covers politics for the *The Hill*. Most weekends, though, find him back in Virginia, paddling canoes on streams toward no place in particular. For this edition, he updated the Travel Smart chapter.

Amy McKeever spent most of her childhood in Northern Virginia, when she wasn't traveling Europe as a Foreign Service brat. She has worked for *National Geographic Traveler*, AOL Travel, and LivingSocial. She is now a freelance travel and food writer based in D.C.—where you can often find her interviewing local chefs for City's Best. For this edition, she updated the Northern Virginia and D.C.'s Maryland Suburbs chapters.

Donna M. Owens is an award-winning freelance journalist who happily juggles roles as a multimedia reporter, producer, and editor. She's reported for outlets that include NPR, the *Chicago Tribune; Baltimore Sun; O, the Oprah Magazine; Essence;* and AOL. Owens has covered politics and other beats for Maryland newspapers, and held staff positions as a producer and investigative reporter for CBS and NBC stations nationwide. A frequent globetrotter, she's based in Baltimore. Owens penned the Frederick and Western Maryland chapters, and Experience Virginia and Maryland.

Alice Leccese Powers edits literary anthologies for Random House and writes guidebooks and innumerable articles for national magazines and newspapers. She also teaches writing at the Corcoran College of Art + Design. Powers has masters degrees from the University of North Carolina at Chapel Hill and the Slade School of Fine Art in London. She lives in Washington, D.C., and updated the Maryland's Eastern Shore and Annapolis and Southern Maryland chapters and our Williamsburg coverage.

Evan Serpick, who edited and updated the Baltimore chapter, is a native Baltimorean and senior editor at *Baltimore* magazine. Although he moved to New York to work as a writer and editor at *Entertainment Weekly* and *Rolling Stone,* he was lured back to Charm City by the smell of Old Bay and Berger cookies. His work has also appeared in *The New York Times, USA Today,* and *Spin.*

When not working her "day job," **Ramona Settle** loves to travel, including being a tourist in her own state of Virginia. Other times she is in quest of the best beaches in the world and updates *Fodor's Caribbean Turks and Caicos* and the San Salvador chapter of *Fodor's Bahamas.* She also wrote *Fodor's In Focus: Turks and Caicos.* She has written articles for T&C magazines *Times of the Islands* and *Where When How,* and has had pictures published in numerous Fodor's publications, *Caribbean Travel & Life* magazine, and *Islands* magazine. She also sells pictures at www.alamy.com.

Ginger Warder grew up in Virginia horse country, and when she wasn't riding, she was on a boat or skiing behind one in the Potomac River. Her "I'll try anything once" philosophy has taken her from Japan to the rain forests, and, most recently, on an exploration of the small towns, stunning mountains, and historic sites of her native state. An active member of the Society of American Travel Writers, she updated Richmond, Fredericksburg and the Northern Neck, and Central and Western Virginia.